New World Archaeology and Culture History

New World Archaeology and Culture History

COLLECTED ESSAYS AND ARTICLES

Gordon Randolph Willey

UNIVERSITY OF NEW MEXICO PRESS

ALBUQUERQUE

Library of Congress Cataloging-in-Publication Data

Willey, Gordon Randolph, 1913–
New world archaeology and culture history :
collected essays and articles / Gordon Randolph Willey.
p. cm.
Includes bibliographical references.
1. Indians—Antiquities. 2. America—Antiquities.
3. Archaeology—Philosophy. I. Title.
E58.W55 1990
970.01—dc20 89-70421
CIP
ISBN 0-8263-1184-9

To My Students

Contents

II. Patterns in the Data

III. *A Priori* Hypotheses

IV. Settlement Patterns

V. Method and Theory

VI. The Recovery of Ideology

Preface and Acknowledgments

Retrospection, I suppose, inevitably comes with age, and I have indulged myself in it here. After 50 years in the profession of archaeology, I have looked back over some of my writings during that long period. I have tried to remember the intellectual and academic contexts in which the articles were written, to recall my own attitudes in those times, and to appraise these pieces now in the light of advances in archaeological knowledge and changes in the procedures of the discipline. The 30 essays or articles that compose the main body of this book were written between 1945 and 1986. All deal with Americanist subjects. While they are grounded in the date of archaeology, many of them are concerned with synthesis, ranging from hemisphere-wide, culture-historical perspectives to those of more restricted geographical scope. Others treat of various matters, both substantive and theoretical, but all are to some degree of a generalizing nature. None of the articles included here is a descriptive account of sites or materials or a preliminary field report. I suppose I could say that these writings represent my attempts to understand and elucidate a portion of that Precolumbian past with which I was concerned during my career.

I have arranged the essays and articles under a series of thematic headings and subheadings. I do not want to be too arbitrary about this classification; instead, the groupings are intended to serve as a guide to readers. The commentaries that open these different sections explain how I view the themes and the papers so grouped. The commentaries represent my present views about what I wrote in the past. While it is up to the reader to decide, I think that this provides some historical perspective on the development of Americanist archaeology, as seen through the eyes of only one of its practitioners.

Although they are cited individually with each essay or article in the volume, I should like to offer my collective thanks here to all of the publishers and editors who have given me the permissions to reproduce my works in this volume. My wife, Katharine, has read over and advised upon the several sections of commentary that I have provided for this book, and I thank her for her patience and help. At the University of New Mexico Press, I am grateful to Elizabeth Hadas, Director, and Claire Sanderson, Editor, for the attention they have given to this project, and I also wish to express my gratitude to Lys Ann Shore, who did much of the copy-editing of this long manuscript, and to Cynthia Welch, who designed the book.

G.R.W.
Cambridge, Massachusetts
15 June 1989

I

Culture Historical and Developmental Syntheses

What I am calling *culture historical and developmental syntheses* composes a very large part of my writings over the past 40 years. I so classify 13 of the 30 essays or articles in this volume. Most of these syntheses range widely in space and time—the high cultures of Mesoamerica and Peru, the entire continent of South America, or all of the New World—but others are of more limited geographical and cultural scope. By *cultural historical*, I mean descriptive definitions and culture unit classifications of the basic data of archaeology and the space-time placements of these data; by *developmental*, I refer to the growth and development of cultures and societies—the ways in which they can be observed to have changed through time. The processes of these changes are sometimes implied or speculated upon in my presentations. I was concerned with both diffusion and evolution, though I made no systematic attempts to explicate the many ways in which such processes may have operated, and when I did so this was largely in passing and speculatively. My primary intent, as I look back on it, was to lay out the accumulating data of Americanist prehistory, to summarize and synthesize them both for myself as well as for my readers.

A

Mesoamerica and Peru

I am inclined to think that one either basically approves or disapproves of comparative analyses of the developmental trajectories of civilizations. I have always counted myself as one of the "approvers"; and, as the first essay of this group indicates, I seem to have been of this turn of mind early in my career. I should warn, however, that "Growth Trends in New World Cultures" is by no means a good example of the comparative genre. It suffers from the enthusiasms of youth. Some of my figures of speech are less than felicitous (see, for example, my extraordinary peroration in the final paragraph), and many of my working assumptions are naive. It was written in early 1947, just after I had returned from my Viru Valley work in Peru. I was much under Julian Steward's influence at the time. Later, Steward (1949a) was to publish an essay on the developmental parallels theme, and in this now famous paper he addressed the subject from a worldwide perspective and with considerably more polish and sophistication than I brought to mine. I should add that, though Steward and I had discussed the general idea of similarities in the growth of civilizations on many occasions, our papers were prepared separately. He did not see a copy of mine before his appeared, and I did not read his until after I had submitted mine for publication.

As I read over the essay now, I am immediately struck by the way in which I conceived of the Formative. I thought of it as a stage of simple village agricultural beginnings, despite the fact that there was little archaeological evidence at that time to support such an interpretation. For the most part, my Formative stage was composed of what we would now consider Late Preclassic or Late Formative cultures—societies for which the archaeological evidence, even then, implied an order of nonegalitarian complexity for which the word *simple* was inappropriate. I will make no attempt here to make thoroughgoing corrections. Obvious examples, if I were to do so, would be to push my chronological assignment of the Olmec cultures back in time (see Coe and Diehl 1980, for an update) or to add the entire Peruvian Preceramic and Initial Ceramic periods to the chronological charts (see Donnan 1985). My 1947 description of Classic Maya society is amusing:

> Luxuriously supported by their subjects on their many jungle farms, freed from the pressure of devising social and political controls for large groups of people living in urban-type contact, the Maya priest-leaders in peaceful and sanctified isolation devoted their full energies to the generation and codification of ritualized learning.

"Peaceful and sanctified isolation" is hardly the way most modern Mayanists would describe ancient Maya life, especially since recent hieroglyphic translations (Houston and Mathews 1985, Johnston 1985) reveal the old Maya as every bit as quarrelsome and conquest-motivated as, say, their Peruvian Moche contemporaries.

In "The Interrelated Rise of Middle and South American Civilizations," I shifted the emphasis from developmental parallelisms to diffusional relationships. My basic conclusions about such diffusions between the two areas were then positive, and they still are. Mesoamerica and Peru are related through a number of historically linked traits. Maize is one of these. Its north-to-south diffusion is still accepted, but we know now that this first occurred at a much earlier time than formerly believed and that the situation is complicated by the development of many new strains of maize in Lower Central and South America and the "back-diffusion" of these to Mesoamerica. In 1955 I argued for Formative ceramic connections between Mesoamerica and Peru, but we know now that many of the shared ceramic traits of the two areas may have been earlier in the Intermediate Area of Ecuador and Colombia and to have spread from there both north and south (Bray 1984; Hoopes 1985). Indeed, the Intermediate Area and the adjacent portions of the South American tropical forests played a very important part in Nuclear American agricultural and ceramic diffusions (Lathrap 1975).

The diffusion of the platform mound idea, in either direction, seems less likely to me now than it did in 1955. At that time, I suggested a north-to-south spread of the idea, but big platform mounds are currently dated much earlier in Peru (Donnan 1985) than in Mesoamerica. The trait is certainly one that could have arisen separately in the two areas, in response to social growth and political complexity.

I would now definitely favor the movement of the figurine-mold from Mesoamerica to South America, especially to coastal Ecuador (Evans and Meggers 1966).

As for metallurgy, the case is more secure than ever that Ecuadorian and north Peruvian techniques were carried by sea from South America to the west coast of Mexico at *ca.* A.D. 800–900.

The third essay of the group, "The Prehistoric Civilizations of Nuclear America," is a better synthesis than either of the two previous essays, combining as it does both evolutionary and diffusionistic perspectives. Kroeber's concept of "Nuclear America" (Kroeber 1948a) and his analogy with the Old World "Oikoumene," or "the civilized world" (1952), helped me put the Mesoamerican-Peruvian axis in perspective. Going back to Spinden (1917, 1928) and his concept of the American "Archaic" (now to be read as "Formative"), I could say with some justification that "Formative cultures are . . . the foundation layer of the New World 'Oikoumene'." Although we had more radiocarbon dates by 1960, I still thought that Olmec great monumental art was of Classic date—in spite of Olmec-like ceramics, which were then known from Tlatilco in the Valley of Mexico (Porter Weaver, 1953). Under the subhead "Chronological Correlation of Middle American and Peruvian Sequences" I took a brief glance at Ecuador, Colombia, and Lower Central America ("the Intermediate Area"), but it is obvious from what I said that there was very little archaeological sequence information then for these regions.

The final section of the paper considers both developmental parallelism and diffusional interconnectedness under the subhead of "Configurational Correlation of Middle American and Peruvian Sequences." If I were to rewrite this, I would have to modify the description of the Formative, for both Mesoamerica and Peru, to indicate a sociopolitical complexity for the millennia antecedent to the Christian era that was largely unknown then, though this had been adumbrated by Wauchope's (1950b) concepts of an earlier "Village" versus a later "Urban Formative." I finished by saying that the synchrony between the Mesoamerican and Peruvian culture stages did, indeed, indicate that diffusion between the two areas had played an important role in what happened. At the same time, I emphasized that other forces had something to do with the stage parallelisms in development. I did not try to name these other forces. As I face this big question today, I would say that they involve population growth, population concentration, and resource utilization—and yet I realize that people can respond to these pressures in very different ways. One thinks of the markets and the merchandising of the Aztecs in contrast to the vast redistributive system and warehousing of goods favored by the Inca.

1

Growth Trends in New World Cultures

(From *For the Dean, Essays in Honor of Byron Cummings*, E. K. Reed and D. S. King, eds., pp. 223–248, Hohokam Museums Association and the Southwestern Monuments Association, Tucson and Santa Fe, 1950. Reprinted by permission of the Arizona Historical Society and the Southwest Parks and Monuments Association.)

Introductory Statement

Distinctive cultural patterns of the New World have been characterized by anthropologists in a number of different ways, and the functionings of these patterns as they affect the lives of the individuals within their matrices have been compared in considerable detail. On the other hand, the long growth and development behind these patterns has received somewhat less attention from this comparative point of view. Archaeologists, by necessity, have devoted their efforts during the past 50 years to the piecing together of the specific prehistories which lie beneath the modern societies or their documented records. Perhaps only now archaeological data are attaining a richness and completeness necessary for the study of the formation of cultural patterns through the centuries of the native American past. This paper is an attempt to consider, briefly and in a trial way, the trends of culture growth and development as these are exemplified in certain New World prehistoric culture sequences. What are the parallels and divergences in these configurations of cultural direction through time? And to what extent can we reconstruct the determinative factors which are responsible for these vertical patternings?

The two great areas of aboriginal horticultural society, Middle America and the Peruvian Andes, have been selected for these comparisons. Not only are the available data more fully presented, especially at the documentary level, but the life basis for both areas, the cultivation of native food plants (in many instances the same plants), has remained the same for at least 1,500 years of the precolumbian past. Within each area two specific regional sequences were chosen. For Middle America these are the Mayan and the Mexican, and for Peru the North Coast and the South Coast.

The Maya Sequence

In its major outlines the Mayan archaeological sequence applies throughout the lowland jungle country of the Peten and Yucatan and in the Guatemalan highlands. The

Goodman-Thompson correlation dating places the beginnings of the sequence somewhere in the first century A.D. (see Figure 1.1). As the earliest periods represent well-developed farming communities with respectable technological accomplishments it is reasonable to suppose that an interval of several centuries of horticultural experimentation and practice in the sedentary arts preceded such complexes as the Mamom, Chicanel, and Miraflores. These periods have been grouped together by Thompson (1943, pp. 106–134; 1945, pp. 2–24) into what he has called the Formative Period of Maya prehistory, with the implication that such a Formative Period extends back for an unknown earlier time span. Ceramic skills in the Maya Formative were well advanced. The pottery runs to monochromes with incised decoration although simple positive and negative painting also occur. Villages were small to middling in size, and represent, presumably, autonomous political units. Dwellings were constructed of perishable materials. There is no inferential evidence for marked status differentiation or social classes. Judging from appearance most artifacts were for household use and their manufacture was probably the work of each family rather than restricted to specialized artisans. The beginnings of organized religion and religious control are exemplified in the building of small mounds. Art existed chiefly as embellishment for utility artifacts although there are exceptions to this, such as the famous "cat faces" on the temple "E-VII-sub" at Uaxactun. Intellectual achievement, as differentiated from technological knowledge, was presumably under way; astronomical, astrological, and historical lore contingent upon the Mayan calendar must have been available during this time.

In the succeeding Initial Series Period of Maya development (300 to 1000 A.D.), technology, architecture, art, and religion reached their apogee. Population was undoubtedly much greater at this time than in the Formative Period. These same centuries saw a similar regional classicism in other parts of Middle America. Monte Alban, Teotihuacan, and La Venta are examples of contemporaneous intensely localized florescences. Among the Maya the elaborate temple center exercised nuclear sociopolitical and religious jurisdiction over the scattered and outlying populations from which their support was derived. Quite possibly some of these centers established hegemony over others in religious and intellectual prestige. There is a strong religious overtone to Maya society of this period, with marked class and rank distinctions. Widespread trade with other regions was carried on, particularly in ritual objects. In manufactures a distinction arose between ritualistic and mundane products. Art was both representational and discrete with religious subjects predominating. In the calendar and history this appears to have been the high point of intellectual activity.

In the Mexican Periods of the Maya region, beginning at about 1000 A.D. and continuing to the Spanish Conquest, Maya ceramic and sculptural arts underwent a decline; architecture maintained, perhaps, for the first part of this period a high quality and then lapsed; minor technological gains were registered in the advent of metal ornaments and metallurgical techniques. Populations were probably as large, if not larger, than in the Initial Series Period, and there was a trend toward their concentration in fortified, permanently inhabited towns. Strong militaristic tendencies appeared with the invading Mexicans, and militaristic ruling-group and serf class distinctions were established. Larger political groupings, "empires" or confederacies, came into being under the leadership of the fortified towns. Intellectual achievement appears to decline, with the "long count" dating and the mental abstractions which it involved being lost. Trade was more widespread than ever before. Toward the end of this period there was a partial resurgence of the old Maya ideas and values, particularly those centering on religion, yet this aborted renaissance was followed by a very abrupt decline and desertion of the towns in the closing 80 years prior to 1540.

Compare with:
Strong, 1943, chronology chart
Thompson, 1943, p. 106 ff.
1945, p. 2 ff.
Vaillant, 1935, see Table III
The Maya and Their Neighbors, 1940, Tables X and XI (see Hay and others, eds., 1940).

Estimated Dates (A.D.)	Culture Periods	Stage Characterization	Cultural Synopsis
1540 1400 1300 1200 1100 1000	Mayan Disintegration Mexican Absorption Mexican Contact	Political Expansion and Conquest	General decline in ceramic and sculptural arts, although metal and metallurgical techniques appear (used for ornaments only). There is a trend toward concentration of populations in fortified, permanently lived-in towns. Strong militaristic tendencies appear with invading Mexicans. Militaristic ruling group–serf class distinctions. Larger political groupings, "empires" or confederacies come into being. Religion subordinated to the war-state. New deities appear. Intellectual achievements remain static or decline. Long-count dating system disappears. Trade widespread and more active than before. Toward the end of this period there is a partial resurgence of old Maya ideas and values, particularly religion, but there is a relatively abrupt decline and desertion of the towns in the closing 80 years.
900 800 700 600 500 400 300	Tepeu Tzakol Esperanza	Regional Classic	Technology increases rapidly to a climax in this period. There is evidence of specialized handicraft work in ceramics, stone-carving, and architecture. Rise of politico-religious temple centers, each supported by its outlying population. Evidence of class and rank. Population steadily increases. Each temple center maintained nuclear sociopolitical and religious control over outlying inhabitants with, possibly, some centers establishing hegemony over others in religious and intellectual prestige. There are strong religious overtones to the society with theocratic leadership. Art both representational and discrete and highly conventionalized. Aesthetic climax in ceramics, minor artifacts, sculpture, and architecture. There is a marked difference between ritualistic and mundane goods. Great strides in intellectual achievement as seen in astronomy and history. A period of religious, artistic, and intellectual, but not political, coherence.
200 100 0	Chicanel Miraflores Mamon	Formative	Establishment of competent techniques in ceramics (monochrome incised styles, hand-made figurines, simple positive-negative painting), household goods, and New World agriculture. Moderate-sized villages, presumably autonomous. Beginnings of organized religion and religious control exemplified in small mound centers. No evidence of marked differences in class or rank. Art exists chiefly as an adjunct to utility artifacts. Intellectual achievements presumably well under way as astronomical, astrological, and historical lore contingent upon the calendar and a time-counting system must have been in formation in this period.

Figure 1.1. The Maya.

THE MEXICAN SEQUENCE

The cultural sequence in the temperate and fertile Valley of Mexico (see Figure 1.2) opens on a subsistence, technological, and sociological level quite comparable to the Maya Formative (Vaillant, 1941). The Mexican "Middle Cultures" begin with El Arbolillo and Zacatenco in probably the first century A.D. and extend through Copilco, Gualupita, Ticoman, and Cuicuilco up to an estimated date of about 500 A.D. Pottery of

Compare with:
Strong, 1943, chronology chart
Vaillant, 1941, chart, p. 26
The Maya and Their Neighbors, 1940, Table XI (see Hay and others, eds., 1940).

Estimated Dates (A.D.)	Culture Periods	Stage Characterization	Cultural Synopsis
1540 1400 1300 1200 1100 1000	Aztec Period "Chichimec" Period	Political Expansion and Conquest	Technology maintains itself and metallurgical skills are added. Greater uniformity in ceramic production with use for figurines continuing. In general, technological and artistic production appears to have been greater than ever before if somewhat lavish. Early periods show chaotic political conditions with several tribal states fighting for control. Population pressure increasing with new semi-nomadic tribes entering valley. Tribute systems of conquest for profit and sacrifice predominates but with late trends toward incorporation of the conquered into an "empire". Social classes and status. Religious and political leadership still related but with trend toward continued differentiation. Great religious pyramids still constructed but usually placed within the community center which was a defensible city. Introduction of picture writing in Aztec Period. Calendrical system based on tonalamatl. Cultural and linguistic unification of valley proceeding rapidly.
900 800 700 600 500	Teotihuacan 4 Teotihuacan 3 Teotihuacan 2	Regional Classic	Excellence in cotton weaving, ceramics (4-color polychromes, negative painting, champlevé and intaglio ritualistic jars), and stone sculpture. Advent of mold in figurine art. Marked differentiation between household and ritualistic manufactures. Implications of class and rank. Definite warrior group. Differentiation between "priests" and "kings" or the religious and the secular beginning to emerge. Great religious center of Teotihuacan built. Huge and elaborate pyramids. Large communal residential sites are located a few miles distant from Teotihuacan. Aesthetic peak occurs with artistic conventionalization. In the late periods there is a shift to Azcapotzalco. It is probable that any intellectual attainments arrived at during the Formative Stage were increased and elaborated upon at this time.
400 300 200 100 0	Cuicuilco-Ticoman Gualupita Copilco Zacatenco-Early El Arbolillo	Formative	Establishment of competent techniques in horticulture and ceramics (essentially monochromes but with painted decoration appearing toward the close; incising common). Figurines are hand-made. Large villages with perishable dwellings, presumably socially and politically autonomous. Absence of social classes or specialized artisans implied. Evidences of trade in upper periods. Beginnings of organized religion and religious control exemplified by great Cuicuilco mound and by formalized representations of deities. Figurine cult art well controlled but simple. Little known of intellectual attainments but it is quite possible that some calendrical knowledge was in process of systematization.

Figure 1.2. The Valley of Mexico.

these periods, although differing in many features of style from that of Mamom or Chicanel, was predominantly monochrome and incised. Solid, hand-made figurines were produced in abundance. Villages were quite large, and dwellings were made of perishable materials. An absence of social classes and specialized artisans is implied in the lack of prominent politico-religious buildings, elaborate tombs, and excellence in manufactures. The beginnings of organized religion and a priesthood are, however, presaged by the great mount of Cuicuilco and the sculptured idols or deities made toward the close of the

"Middle Cultures." It is difficult to make any inferences about intellectual attainments, but it is quite possible that rudimentary calendrical knowledge was in process of systematization.

The Mexican "Middle Cultures," or Mexican Formative, closes with the rise of the great site of Teotihuacan and the Classical Toltec culture.[1] For 500 years this brilliant regional development held sway in the Valley of Mexico. Excellence was attained in polychrome, negative painted, champlevé, and intaglio ceramics; figurines were manufactured with the use of the mold; fine cotton weaving was known; and stone sculpture flourished. The differentiation between household and ritualistic manufactures was marked. Implications of class and rank are strong. A warrior group arose, and there is evidence for an emerging distinction between the priesthood and secular authority. A mammoth religious center was built with huge and elaborate pyramids. Residential dwellings were constructed of imperishable materials, and a big urban town was located a few miles distant from the sacred precincts of Teotihuacan. There is an artistic climax during the occupation of Teotihuacan, but a decline sets in later in the period when there is a shift to another religious center at Azcapotzalco. It is probable that any intellectual attainments arrived at during the "Middle Cultures" were increased and elaborated upon by the Classic Toltecs.

The final 500 years of the Mexican sequence saw the interim "Chichimec" Period of warring tribes, the culminant rise of the Tenochtitlan group, and the spread of Aztec culture. Technologically, this "New Toltec" and Aztec Period maintains the level reached under the Classical Toltecs and, in addition, metallurgy is acquired. In general, there is a greater uniformity in ceramic production, and the use of the mold for figurines continues. Quantitatively, production seems to increase even though quality of individual pieces may be somewhat inferior to the preceding period. Between 1100 and 1300 A.D. population pressure was increasing; new semi-nomadic tribes were making their way into the valley; and political conditions were chaotic with several tribes fighting for control. Tribute systems of conquest for profit and sacrificial captives were the rule, but with a late trend toward the incorporation of the conquered into an "empire" unit. Social classes and individual status differences were marked. Religious and political leadership remained related but the drift toward a cleavage noted in the Classical Toltec Period was even stronger. Religious pyramids were still constructed, but these were usually placed within the community center which was a defensible city. Picture writing was introduced in the Aztec Period, as well as a calendric system based on the tonalamatl. Throughout the entire period the cultural and linguistic unification of the valley was proceeding rapidly.

THE PERUVIAN NORTH COAST SEQUENCE

In the rich Chicama, Santa Catalina (Moche), and Viru Valleys of the Peruvian North Coastal desert the introduction and development of fundamental horticultural, ceramic, stone-carving, and architectural techniques are dimly seen arising above an earlier preceramic base in the first century A.D.[2] (see Figure 1.3). By the time the Chavín Periods[3] are well advanced, Peruvian coastal culture presents a developed horticultural economy, good incised and simple painted pottery, and rather elaborate stone and plastic sculpture. Even metallurgy is seen in its beginning stages. As such, the Cupisnique Period is comparable to, or in advance of, the similar Formative Stage cultures of Middle America.[4] Communities at this time were small to moderate-sized, and temples were constructed at Guanape (very simple) and in the Nepeña Valley (quite ornate). It is probable that irrigation had its beginnings in the Chavín Periods; certainly a little later, in Salinar

Compare with:
Bennett, 1946a, p. 80
Kroeber, 1944, Figure 6
Rowe, 1945, pp. 265–284
Strong, 1943, chronology chart
The Maya and Their Neighbors, 1940, Table XI (see Hay and others, eds., 1940).

Estimated Dates (A.D.)	Culture Periods	Stage Characterization	Cultural Synopsis
1540 1400 1300 1200 1100 1000	Inca Conquest Chimu Black-White-Red Period Coast Tiahuanaco	Political Expansion and Conquest	Technological improvements seen only in appearance of bronze. A general aesthetic decline in ceramics and arts but a production increase. Rise of great urban communities or true cities, such as Chanchan. Religious structures smaller and within urban site. Pan-Peruvian political and cultural conquests, probably beginning with Coast Tiahuanaco. Empire building and incorporation techniques. Well-developed roads and communication. Architectural energies directed toward urban centers, great fortresses, public works. Standing armies. Class and wealth distinctions. Religion subordinate to temporal power. Little abstract intellectual achievement. Quipu mnemonic system, verbal history and lore.
900 800 700 600 500	Mochica Mochica-Negative	Regional Classic	Brilliance in ceramics, metallurgy, carving in wood, stone, and shell. Remarkable architectural accomplishments and great irrigation and road-building projects. Excellent evidence for a well-controlled social and political order with class and status concepts highly developed. Huge politico-religious centers such as Moche. Residential communities probably still of moderate size and scattered in distribution. Warfare developed and beginnings of "empire" amalgamations seen in Mochica conquests to south. Art shift to profane completed with actual portraiture in ceramics. Religious and mythological subjects in minority. Peak of realistic sculptural art. Two and three color painting in pottery. Intellectual activity seen in ideographic system of writing.
400 300 200 100 0	Salinar Cupisnique Basic Chavín (Guanape) Pre-ceramic levels	Formative	The beginnings and development of fundamental agricultural, ceramic, stone-carving, and architectural techniques. Ceramics begin extremely simple and increase in form and decorative complexity. Monochromes predominate. Incision-punctation techniques more common that use of color. Ornate religious art expression in some Cupisnique pottery. Also crude beginnings of life form sculpturing in both Cupisnique and Salinar. Small to moderate-sized communities. Probable beginnings of irrigation. Little evidence for strong class distinctions or political prestige but beginnings of religious dominance and theocratic control. Art is discrete, conventional, and probably high in religious symbolism (Cupisnique). Intellectual achievement unknown.

Figure 1.3. The North Coast of Peru.

times, it was quite well established. There is only slight evidence for class distinction and political prestige, but some type of theocratic control is inferable. Cupisnique art is discrete, conventional, and probably highly symbolical in religious content. There is little evidence for a dichotomy of ritual and profane goods for Basic Chavín but ornate sculptured burial pottery was made in the Cupisnique Period. With the transition to Salinar, at the close of the Formative, there is a shift in artistic canons to rather crudely conceived and executed realism, and there is much less concern with religious or mythical representations. There is no evidence for intellectual activity aside from technological knowledge.

In the Mochica Period (500–1000 A.D.)[5] there is a brilliant rise in technology and art. This regional florescence is paralleled elsewhere in Peru at the same time, with Early Nazca, Classic Recuay, Early Lima, and Classic Tiahuanaco providing such examples. Ceramic art is varied and masterfully executed; the use of the mold in the manufacture of both vessels and figurines is the rule rather than the exception; carving in wood, stone, and shell is extremely competent; and such metallurgical techniques as welding, casting, and gilding were known. Architectural accomplishments were outstanding and chiefly in the field of large adobe pyramids, public buildings, and "castillos" or fortresses. Irrigation and road-building projects were undertaken. Huge politico-religious centers were constructed and residential sites became larger than in the Formative Stage. There is ample evidence for a well-controlled social and political order with class and status concepts highly developed. Considerable emphasis and prestige were accorded to warfare, and the beginnings of empire are seen in the Mochica conquests to the south. Secular authority would seem to command more attention in most aspects of the culture than ecclesiastical sanctions. There was considerable increase in populations over the Formative Stage. Inter-valley and coastal-highland trade flourished. The art shift from the strictly esoteric, probably religious, motives of the Cupisnique style to profane subjects, begun in the Salinar Period, is completed in Mochica. Although religious, mythological, and fantasy subjects are still represented they are in the minority. In both painting and ceramic sculpture there is realism of high quality, even portraiture. Intellectual activity is represented by what appears to be a form of ideographic writing (Larco Hoyle, 1946, p. 175).

The Middle and Late Peruvian Periods on the North Coast are represented in succession by Coast Tiahuanaco and its derivative, Chimu, and Inca. The inception of the Coast Tiahuanaco invasion is placed at about 1000 A.D. and the beginnings of the Chimu state at about 1300 A.D. The Inca reached the North Coast relatively late in the fifteenth century. The outstanding technological gain during these periods was the appearance of bronze, a metal used for ornaments and for tools and weapons. Although there was an aesthetic decline in ceramics and the arts, there was a production increase suggesting primitive "mass production" methods. Beginning with Coast Tiahuanaco there was a trend toward population concentration in what became urban centers, and architectural energy was directed toward their construction. Chanchan, near Trujillo, the great Chimu center, is such a city. Public works, such as roads, irrigation systems, and great walls, are very common. Pan-Peruvian political and cultural conquests probably began with Coast Tiahuanaco and certainly continued with Chimu and Inca. Definite empire building with tight incorporation of conquered territories and populations is the result. Inter-valley road communications were perfected, and trade and wide contacts were further stimulated. The building of fortresses continued and some of these are examples of military genius. Standing armies were organized and maintained by rulers. Class and wealth distinctions were very obvious. Religion was definitely subordinate to temporal power. Temples and pyramids were still constructed but these were placed within the urban centers. There seems to have been little in the way of abstract intellectual achievement. The quipu mnemonic system was spread by the Inca conquest.

The Peruvian South Coast Sequence

The South Coast region is known from the valleys of Chincha, Pisco, Ica, and Nazca. The agricultural potential was much less for these valleys than for those of the North Coast, and the general conditions for life more difficult. The earliest archaeological period for the region is the Paracas Cavernas (see Figure 1.4), a culture which has certain

Compare with:
Bennett, 1946a, p. 80
Kroeber, 1944, Figure 6
Rowe, 1945, pp. 265–284
Strong, 1943, chronology chart
The Maya and Their Neighbors, 1940, Table XI (see Hay and others, eds., 1940).

Estimated Dates (A.D.)	Culture Periods	Stage Characterization	Cultural Synopsis
1540 1400 1300 1200 1100 1000	Inca Conquest Late Inca Middle Inca	Political Expansion and Conquest	Technological improvements only in advent of metallurgy. Is possible that organized irrigation was best developed at this time. Some large adobe or stone buildings which appear as politico-religious centers, not urban communities. Living sites probably small or moderate in size and scattered. Increased emphasis on sociopolitical organization implied in earlier periods and known from Inca Period. Art becomes rigidly geometric and repetitive. Intellectual achievement other than that known to Inca unknown.
900 800 700 600 500	Pacheco Epigonal Nazca B Paracas Necropolis Nazca A	Regional Classic	Technological excellence in weaving and textiles that surpasses any in the Andean area. Ceramics decorated in beautiful polychromes. Goldwork appears but true metallurgy still lacking. Adobes used in buiding but no known examples of Nazca politico-religious building or large residential sites. Great emphasis on burial elaboration suggests organized religious cults and some degree of status and rank differentiation. Warfare of a sort indicated by trophy-head representations on pottery and textiles. Art has representations of life motives but these are quite stylized and in some cases discrete. Religious symbolism would seem to be expressed in many instances. Intellectual achievement unknown.
400 300 200 100 0	Paracas Cavernas	Formative	Agricultural-ceramic first culture of the south known at present time. It is quite possible that earlier ceramic horizons underlie Cavernas. Pottery combines poorly applied polychrome painting and incision as decoration. Little is known of sites, but there are no evidences of large mounds or habitation groups. Most likely social and political organization revolved around small independent villages. Religious motives suggested in ceramic art (feline concept).

Figure 1.4. The South Coast of Peru.

stylistic correlates with the Salinar of the North and is equivalently dated at about 400 A.D. It is possible that still earlier horticultural-ceramic periods for the south, probably of a Basic Chavín type, will eventually be disclosed. Pottery of Paracas Cavernas combines poorly applied polychrome pigments and incision as decorative techniques. There is also simple negative painting. Little is known of Cavernas sites, but it is certain that no large mounds or big habitation clusters were constructed. Most likely social and political life revolved around small independent villages. Religious motives are suggested in ceramic art.

The South Coast flowered in a unique regional classicism following the Paracas Cavernas Period. This was the Nazca Period dating at about 500 to 1000 A.D. There is a technological excellence in weaving and textiles for this period that outstrips anything in the Andean area. Ceramics are finely made and beautifully painted in polychrome. The mold was not used. Simple hammered goldwork appears, but metallurgical techniques were unknown. Very little is known of Nazca architecture, but apparently no large politico-religious or residential sites were constructed. The emphasis on burial elaboration suggests organized religious cults and some degree of status and rank differentiation. Warfare is indicated by trophy-head representations on pottery and textiles. Population undoubtedly increased over the Formative Stage. Pottery and textile art has naturalistic representations of life motives but these are quite stylized, in some cases bordering on the discrete. Religious symbolism would seem to be expressed in many instances. Intellectual achievement is unknown.

Pacheco Epigonal marks the Coast Tiahuanaco invasion of the Nazca region. Subsequently, a local style, divided into a Middle and Late Ica prevailed with the Inca conquest following sometime in the mid-fifteenth century. Technological improvements are noted only in the advent of copper, silver, and bronze. It is possible that organized irrigation was best developed in the South at this time although this is uncertain. There appear for the first time a number of large stone or adobe buildings which seem to have been politico-religious centers rather than urban cities. Living sites probably continued small or moderate in size and remained scattered. Art, as expressed in ceramics and textiles, became rigidly geometric and repetitive. Intellectual achievement, other than that common to the Inca Empire, is unknown.

A Comparative Interpretation

The four synopsized culture sequences have been divided into three horizontal categories of characterization: Formative, Regional Classic, and Political Expansion and Conquest. That these characterizations may take on somewhat different meanings in each culture growth is also obvious, but, in general, the gross configuration holds. We can see for each sequence an opening stage in which a sedentary horticultural way of life was being adapted to a particular natural environment. This was succeeded by a second stage of technological and artistic richness, one in which the maturing regional culture strove to fulfill its boundaries and exhaust its potentialities. Finally, a third stage is characterized by mounting conflict among the formerly localized but now expanding culture growths; and this is accompanied by a greater emphasis on enlarged sociopolitical forms.

Of these three stages, there is a striking similarity in both cultural direction and cultural content among all sequences for the Formative level. It is a time of technological progress, and there is another strong bond of likeness in that the village community was the basis of the social and political order. This is to a great extent inferential, yet it is clear that there were virtually no great central sites of authority in any of the four regions during their Formative stages. Sites were simple habitation places. Some of these are fairly extensive, as in the Valley of Mexico and the North Coast of Peru, but most of them indicate only small communities. In the Maya zone, Mexico, and North Peru the appearance of ceremonial mounds and temple centers, especially toward the close of the Formative, implies a directional trend toward theocratic control over the scattered village farmers. On this early level it is impossible to say that any one region appears to be placing a greater emphasis upon religion or religious authority. The Nepeña temples, "E-VII-sub," and Cuicuilco are about on a par in the impressiveness with which they would be viewed from their cultural backgrounds. Only Paracas Cavernas, in South Peru, is lacking in specialized religious sites. The art of the Formative Stage shows greater divergence than the technological, sociopolitical, or religious trends. Peruvian Formative art seems concerned with religious themes; Middle American art, not particularly so. In abstract intellectual achievement the probabilities are that Middle America, particularly the Maya region, was already far ahead of Peru even on this Formative level. In the matter of cultural content as apart from cultural direction, the Formative level also shows decided uniformity. This is true even between the Middle American sequences and those of Peru. On the whole, the Andean and the Central American–Mexican cultures seem to have developed quite independently of each other, but on this early pre-specialized horizon there are a number of specific resemblances, such as in certain basic food plants, a predominance of monochrome and incised pottery, negative painting, and stone carving techniques, which are lost or obscured by an overlay of intricate cultural complexity as we go up in the time scale.

The determinative factors operating for a similarity of both cultural patterning and content on the Formative level would seem to be of two kinds. First, the content parallelism noted for all four sequences can, I think, be attributed in large part to common historical origins. Second, the relatively unspecialized nature of New World horticultural societies at this stage of their development and adaptation to their particular settings makes for some uniformity of cultural direction. At the same time it is quite likely that important potential differences in trends, latent within the cultures, are now just beginning to emerge. At this subsistence level the natural resources of the Valley of Mexico and the North Peruvian Coastal valleys were more favorable than those in the Maya region or on the Peruvian South Coast. This seems to have been the basis for the much larger population concentrations in the two former regions and all that this eventually entailed in the succeeding stages.

It is with the Regional Classic Stage of development that divergent tendencies begin to give special directional character to the different culture growths. In this second stage all four regions enjoy a technological and artistic flowering, but with differing connotations as to cultural significance. With the Maya, both art and technology are devoted to the glorification of a priestly hierarchy whose position within the society is further reinforced by its control of highly esoteric and ritualized knowledge. Mochica art and technology appear to have had a broader basis of vulgar appeal and common utilization among the total population. The Classical Toltecs fall somewhere between these two. Art must have had strong religious motivations in Nazca culture, but unlike Maya or Toltec one has the feeling that popular folk incentives, rather than "high church directives, lie behind it. But it is in the spheres of social, political, and religious organization that the fundamentally different channeling of cultural forces now impresses us. Maya society is priest-controlled and built around the imposing dignity of the theocratic temple center. In North Coast Peru and the Valley of Mexico great religious sites were constructed; but large residential communities were also in process of formation. The power and pomp of warfare, the warrior, and the secular arm are as much in evidence as religious symbolism. In Peru, the Mochica, in their closing periods, were no longer a tribal state but an inter-valley empire. Nazca, forming still another pattern, had neither the all-powerful temple cult nor the war-state but probably retained the simple autonomous village system. There is less evidence for actual and significant cultural contact among the various regions during the Regional Classic Stage than either before or after. As the regional cultures grew and specialized, each developed distinctive content within the limits of the basic inventions that were made common knowledge during the Formative Stage. In spite of the fact that trade was active and widespread in the Regional Classic, it accounted for the inter-regional exchange of only a limited amount of material goods and, apparently, ideas. To judge from the archaeological evidence trade at this time was mainly in ritualistic, unusual, or costly items, not in the everyday possessions of the people.

Apparently evolving out of a related basic culture the four unique growths of the Maya, Teotihuacan, Mochica, and Nazca attained a regional classicism essentially as a response to the interaction of their horticultural technology with their respective environments.

Vaillant (1940, pp. 295–305) has pointed out that in adapting intensive horticulture to the Guatemalan and Yucatecan jungles the Maya were led to pattern their community life in small scattered or mobile villages. Tribal solidarity was maintained by the focal point of the temple center rendezvous. In this way, the concept of the ceremonial mound or sacred shrine, a Formative Stage component of at least three of the four culture sequences considered, became extremely important in Maya life in its period of Regional Classic crystallization. The social limitations which this imparted restricted also the political form of the culture, and the original religious sponsorship of the shrine centers quite easily took over leadership in a self-perpetuating system of theocratic control. Under such an arrangement an amazing degree of abstract intellectual activity was possible in the great temple capitals. Luxuriously supported by their subjects on the many jungle farms, freed from the pressure of devising social and political controls for large groups of people living in urban-type contact, the Maya priest-leaders in peaceful and sanctified isolation devoted their full energies to the generation and codification of ritualized learning. Maya art reflects such an existence. For almost 700 years the growth of Maya culture was held in such a mold.

The Mochica pattern is in greatest contrast to this. With irrigation techniques, which appeared in the Formative Stage, the valleys of the North Coast of Peru had a great potential for stable horticulture. In actual acreage suitable for cultivation these valleys are relatively small, compact units, and their water supply, coming down from the Andes in narrow gorges, is easily controlled at a few key points. For maximum utilization of a valley with canal distributary and related techniques a single or master irrigation system for each valley was mandatory. With the mounting population pressures of the late Formative and early Regional Classic stages, deriving out of the increased food supply concomitant with full exploitation of the agricultural potentialities of the valleys, the inhabitants were forced into concentrated, face-to-face living conditions. Unlike the Maya, the Mochica leaders were forced to turn their efforts to the problem of the social organization and control of the large masses of people who were actually clustered within sight of the temple pyramids and upon whose close social control the maintenance of the complicated and highly centralized life-giving irrigation systems was dependent. In consequence, secular authority soon overtook religious authority. Possibly the two were combined, and no doubt religious sanctions were always used to support temporal mandates; but the practical manipulations of force politics must have begun to outweigh religious prestige gained from the control and mastery of ritual. A combination of population pressures within the North Coast valleys and firm political control of these increasing numbers of people opened the way for inter-valley war and conquest, a major feature in the Mochica way of life. This, again, further elevated force over religious prestige. By the close of the Mochica Period the orientation of North Coast culture was unmistakable. Both the popular quality and the representational themes of Mochica art are reflections of these trends.

Mexican culture follows a course intermediate between these two during the Regional Classic Stage. Although their art and technology are closer to those of the Maya, undoubtedly for historical reasons, the formation of the Teotihuacan or Classical Toltec religious and sociopolitical institutions derives out of an environmental situation more comparable to North Peru. The rich Valley of Mexico made large, permanent horticultural communities possible as early as the Formative Stage. But because of the much greater size of the valley, congestion of population was seemingly not as great during the Regional Classic as it was in the narrow North Peruvian valleys. Large habitation communities and sacred temple centers are both developed, and religious prestige and secular authority are both strong. There is, though, a differentiation between the two. Presumably, as the population increased in late Classical Toltec times warfare and conflict became more common and with this there was probably a rise in political and military authority.

On the South Coast of Peru the relatively poorer and drier valleys, although geographically and geologically similar to those of the North, clearly limited community size and total population. Unlike the Mochica the pressure for social planning was not great; and unlike the Maya wealth and population were not sufficient to sustain large scale religious centers. An adjustment to allow ample leisure for the production of fine art and craft goods seems to have been won by the beginning of the Regional Classic Stage. After this, a balance was maintained in South Coast culture, without marked social, political, or religious change, until the Tiahuanaco Period.

In the last stage, that of Political Expansion and Conquest, two of the culture growths under consideration develop the conquest-state configuration through a combination of internal direction and outside pressures, whereas the other two were modified by conquest patterns enforced solely from without. In North Peru we have seen that the trends toward military power were formulated in the Regional Classic Stage with the rise of the Mochica. Then, during the Coast Tiahuanaco Period there is a blanking out of Mochica culture. That a growing war-state, such as the Mochica were fast becoming, could be so completely submerged in its nationalistic symbols is a strong argument for representing the Tiahuanaco wave as a military conquest. In any event, from this point forward all the tendencies of Peruvian North Coast culture are toward a heightening of political imperialism. Planned communities, public works, evidences of military activity, and an increasing homogeneity in material culture continue on to a climax in the Chimu Period; and both archaeology and legendary history attest to the extensive sovereignty and power of the Chimu government until it was incorporated into the Inca Empire. Of the other regional sequences the closest parallel to North Peru in the stage of Political Expansion and Conquest is the Valley of Mexico. In the Toltec Period organized war for conquest seems to have been only little developed; but the succeeding "Chichimec" Period was one of fierce, though petty, military rivalry for power. Aztec dominance probably represents only the beginning of coordinated government based on force rather than a refined culmination of the system produced after centuries of experimentation as was the case for the Chimu and Inca. Many of the same trends are present, though, including the subordination of religion to the war cult and a leveling uniformity in artistic and technological production. In the other regional growths, the Maya and South Peru, the expansive military power of alien peoples struck cultures rigidly set in their Regional Classic molds. For both, the old cultural directives were radically changed and the old symbols perished. South Peru appears to have "come back," during the Ica Periods, after the Coast Tiahuanaco invasion and before being swallowed up by the Inca. Maya culture, on the other hand, after an attempt at re-establishment, falls to pieces trying to adjust to the war-state ideology. Both regions, as with the Valley of Mexico and North Peru, undergo a technological and artistic unification and leveling. The culture content of the Political Expansion and Conquest Stage attains, between those regions within the same major culture area, a similarity as great, but of a different order, as that of the Formative Stage. Similarity appears as specific likeness of style obviously imposed as a process or byproduct of the social and political amalgamative tendencies, not as in the Formative, because of linkages of origin of the basic technologies. Thus, between Middle America and Peru, where there was as yet no inter-activity of the growing political empires, there is very little common cultural content on this final level.

The direction and shaping of the four culture growths during the Regional Classic Stage became a crucial factor in determining the outcome of events on the subsequent level of Political Expansion and Conquest. By the end of the Regional Classic, the North Coast of Peru and the Valley of Mexico seem to have developed military traditions of sufficient strength to sustain war-states, either internally or as the result of outside conquest. As Bennett (1945, pp. 95–99) has remarked concerning the Mochica, the sociopolitical essence of their culture, as expressed in such institutions as corvée labor and organized military conquest, was not destroyed by the Coast Tiahuanaco expansion but reasserted itself in the Chimu Period. In like manner, the Inca conquest would appear to have had very slight effect on the general cultural orientation of the North Coast as its objectives and methods were assuredly those which had long been in operation in the region.[6] In the Valley of Mexico the period of the petty war-states following the Classical Toltecs was probably more destructive of the old patterns formed in the Regional Classic Stage than the Tiahuanco dominance was in North Peru; yet a modified Mexican culture continued on into the Tenochtitlan state which was fast adapting to war institutions and conquest patterns.

The Maya, without a Regional Classic orientation toward war and conquest, were unable to make a successful adaptation to it on their home ground. Mexican conquerors succeeded temporarily in fusing their type of military authority to Mayan traditions, but eventually this proved unsuccessful and a rather complete breakdown of higher social, political, and religious forms ensued. The peculiar and precarious balance by which the Old Mayan theocratic society had been maintained upon a base of jungle horticulture not only was destroyed by the Mexican institutions, but these institutions of the invaders apparently could not be supported in the new environment. Nazca culture seems to have been completely eclipsed by the Tiahuanaco deluge, and, subsequently, there is evidence of more complicated social and political systems in the Peruvian South Coast valleys. There is, however, no breakdown comparable to that of the last Precolumbian century in the Maya region. Late Period cultures in the South Coast valleys, though never rivaling those of the North Coast in power or spread, seem to have flourished in a modest fashion. Perhaps the less rigidly specialized character of the old South Coast Regional Classic culture allowed for a greater flexibility in the face of the sudden changes brought in during the stage of Political Expansion and Conquest; and, although never excelling in the institutions of empire, culture growth continued.

To conclude, we have noted that in four distinctive natural regions, two in each of the major culture areas of the New World, a surplus economy of a horticultural type was established upon a similar technological plane. This is the Formative Stage. Following this, the interaction of this subsistence technology with four differing natural environments produced four separate types of cultural growths or patternings. This has been designated as the Regional Classic Stage. In a third stage, one of Political Expansion and Conquest, various historical factors come to impinge upon these four culture growths, bringing about alterations. It is probable, I suppose, that if there had been no outside conquest of the Maya region, or the Nazca region, these self-contained, rather static cultural forms would have continued relatively undisturbed for several centuries more. But cultures do not exist in a vacuum, and change from within or without proceeds. What is particularly interesting and important is that the molding and channeling forces of the Regional Classic Stage, those forces growing out of the interaction of technology and environment, give terrific impetus to the culture; and this impetus, mounting snowball fashion, carries the society along in its momentum. Sooner or later historical forces concur to smash or disarrange these dynamic patterns. The result—cultural death, deflection, or a new integration—depends to a great extent on the rigidity and velocity with which the original culture growth has been molded and propelled toward its fate.

Notes

[1]The use of the term *classical Toltec* in this paper refers throughout to the culture of periods Teotihuacan 2–4, *not* to the Toltecs or New Toltecs as associated with the site of Tula, Hidalgo.

[2]The estimated dating used here is slightly earlier than that usually given (see Bennett, 1946a, p. 80). It is my opinion that what connective evidence exists between Peru and the more securely dated Middle American sequences argues for an equation of the Chavín horizon with the Formative Maya levels.

[3]Bennett (1946a, pp. 81–92) uses the name "Chavín Periods" to designate a series of cultures, both coastal and highland, which are demonstrably early and are linked by the Chavín feline art motif and an incised ceramic style. Cupisnique and the presumably earlier and simpler "Basic Chavín" cultures of the coast fall within this horizon. Salinar, in my opinion, does not.

[4]Recently both R. Larco Hoyle and W. D. Strong (see Willey, 1946b, *American Antiquity*, vol. 12, no. 2, pp. 132–134, for a report of the *Chiclín Conference on Peruvian Archaeology*) have used the name "Formative" as one term to describe the simpler cultures which precede the outstanding regional growths such as Mochica. (See also, Strong, 1947, "Finding the Tomb of a Warrior God," *National Geographic Magazine*, vol. XCI, no. 4, p. 464.) Steward (1948b, 1949b) has also used the term in summary articles included in both the 4th and 5th volumes of the *Handbook of South American Indians*, Bulletin 143, Bureau of American Ethnology, Smithsonian Institution. Although their uses of the term vary, and do not completely coincide with the way I have employed the concept here, it should be noted that in the main they refer to cultures which resemble in content and organization the cultures called "Formative" by Thompson in the Maya region (Thompson, 1943, pp. 106–134).

[5]I include here, along with Mochica, the Negative or Gallinazo culture, best known from the Virú Valley. Although pre-Mochica in the Virú Valley, the Negative or Gallinazo culture represents the technical and artistic maximum of the local cultural development in Virú. It probably developed coevally with Mochica, being overrun by the Mochicans toward the end of the Regional Classic Stage.

[6]Benedict (1943, pp. 207–212) has pointed out that the deeply implanted traditions of corvée labor and empire techniques made easy the still later conquests by the Europeans who helped continue these same trends.

2

The Interrelated Rise of the Native Cultures of Middle and South America

(From *New Interpretations of Aboriginal American Culture History*, 75th Anniversary Volume of the Anthropological Society of Washington, pp. 28–45, Washington, D.C., 1955.)

Introduction

The peaks of native American civilization were attained in the Middle American regions of Mexico and Guatemala and in Peru[1] in the two millennia preceding the Spanish conquests of the sixteenth century. These two summits of New World cultural achievement are widely separated from each other by the intervening areas of lower Central America, Colombia, and Ecuador. What is the significance of this geographical separation? To what degree does it reflect a cleavage in the common histories of Peruvian and Middle American cultures? To what extent may the similarities that exist be derived from historical interconnections? Or may these similarities be attributed to factors of independent growth? These questions have long been a matter of interest and speculation.

The considerable literature centering upon these themes is too much to summarize within the scope of this paper; however, certain writings seem particularly important because they show the development of a very definite body of theory concerned with this problem. As early as 1917, H. J. Spinden conceived of a fundamental underlying cultural substratum for all New World high cultures, which he called "Archaic." This was a sort of American "neolithic" diffusion representing the spread of a sedentary-agricultural way of life from Middle America to the north and to the south. In spite of specific defects, this hypothesis in its broader aspects is still an operational theory in American archaeology. A. L. Kroeber (1930b) developed a similar line of reasoning when he visualized the Mexican and Peruvian culture climaxes as rising from the same historically interrelated platform of technology and basic cultural content. The same food plants, the same kinds of ceramic, textile, metallurgical, and architectural achievements appeared to him as indisputable linkages. He saw Middle America and Peru as alike in that both drew upon this common background to give "finer form" or "more intensive organization or expression" (op. cit., p. 21) to the materials of their mutual American heritage.

In the two decades since Kroeber's synthesis, archaeological research in both the Andean and Middle American areas has moved ahead rapidly, particularly with regard to the definition of culture sequences and the integration of these into relative chronologies of area-wide scope (Kroeber, 1948b). W. D. Strong (1943) has shown how Middle to South American comparisons take on sharpness of definition when these comparisons can be made with proper regard for their chronological order. Julian H. Steward (1949b) has utilized the same sequence data described by Strong for correlating the two areas period for period from a different point of view. Steward's interest has been functional development. He tends to take diffusion between the two Americas for granted and concentrates on the question: What does diffusion amount to as an explanation of culture growth and process? Rather than comparing specific content, Steward turns to overall cultural configurations in the major periods within each area. It is here that he notes a series of strong similarities in the rise and development of sociopolitical, religious, and military institutions.

In the present discussion, I am interested in reviewing the case for *Diffusion* between the centers of American high culture but I do not mean to minimize developmental analyses. Diffusion and independent invention are, after all, polar abstractions concerning complex human events, and the two processes work in concert. Nevertheless, the tracing out of diffusion remains a respectable anthropological problem. It is not the whole story but it is an important part of the story. Let us turn, then, to the evidence for culture contact between Middle and South America and observe the patterning of this evidence in space and in time.

In doing so, it might be well to pause to review the nature of the evidence we are to consider. In a brief paper, it is impossible to cover all of the data that have been brought forward by many scholars on this complex subject of inter-American cultural connections. In this treatment, some categories of evidence such as linguistic and physical anthropometric details will be ignored. From ethnographical records, there are a number of traits which almost certainly have a common history and which link Middle and South America. The arrow sacrifice of captives is an example often cited. The rubber ball game, which is known in lowland South America and throughout Middle America, is another. There is little doubt but what these features or ideas have been transmitted intercontinentally but it is extremely difficult, if not impossible, to pin down their occurrences in the contexts of archaeological sequences. Either no traces are left in the archaeological records or the traits are of such a nature that they might well be passed from one region to another without leaving any clues that could be appraised chronologically from archaeological evidence. For the present study, then, we are restricting the evidence to a certain limited number of traits or elements which are verifiable by archaeological means and which also may be treated with reference to cultural chronologies over a wide geographic range.

Early Lithic Stage

Cultural interconnections between North and South America undoubtedly began at a remote period, well before the rise of Spinden's "Archaic" or "American neolithic" stage. Middle and South American pressure-flaked points found under conditions of geological antiquity resemble certain less specialized North American point types. Wormington (1953) has noted a projectile point found in the upper Becerra formation of the Valley of Mexico as being reminiscent of the North American Scottsbluff type and another from the earliest cultural level of the Straits of Magellan as resembling the Plainview type. For the most part, Scottsbluff and Plainview points are dated somewhat later than the Clovis

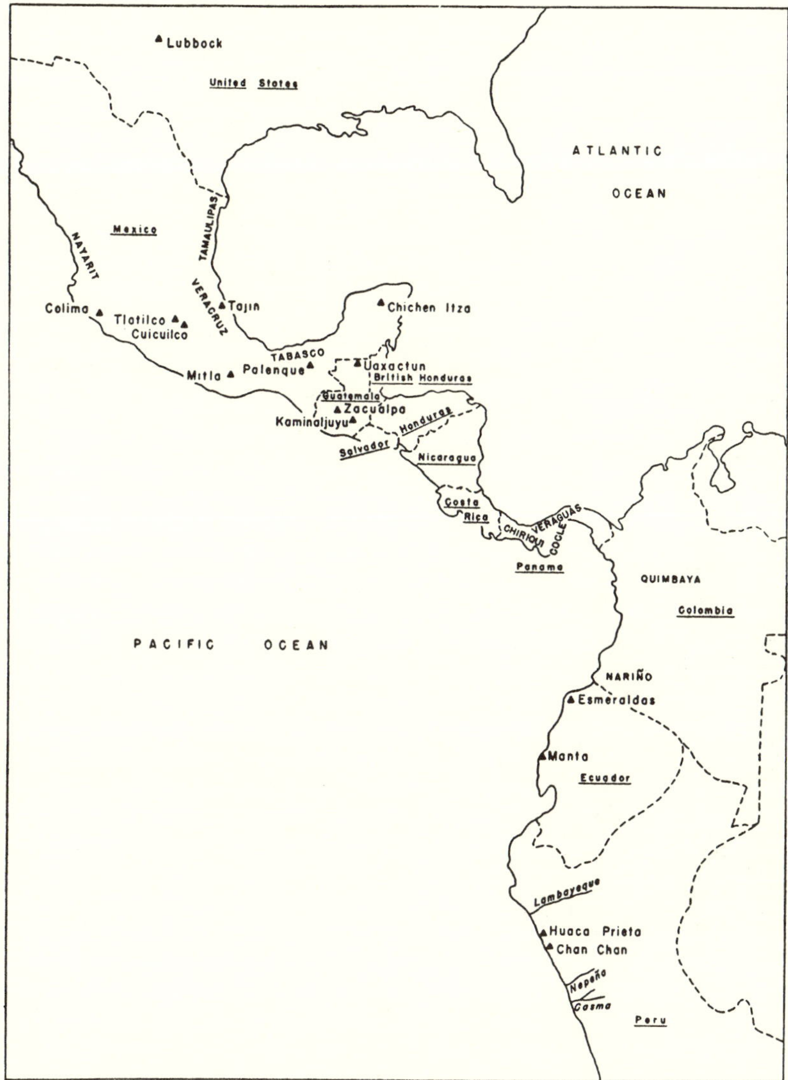

Figure 2.1. Sites and Cultures in Middle and South America.

and Folsom types in North America. There is a radiocarbon date from a Folsom site near Lubbock, Texas (Figure 2.1) which is 7932 B.C.±350 years.[2] The radiocarbon reading from the earliest Straits of Magellan level is a little over 1000 years later, with the exact date recorded as 6638 B.C.±450 years.

The data are still too few and radiocarbon dating is still too experimental to treat this subject any more definitely. However, if pressure-flaking in the New World is accepted as a diffused technique from the Old World, then the distribution of pressure-flaked tools in the Americas must have some historical connective significance within this hemisphere.

Presumably, movement of both peoples and cultures in the early periods of the settlement of America was from north to south. The information available thus indicates intercontinental ties and even suggests a rough dating of events.

The Archaic Stage

In the long interval that appears to exist between the Early Lithic complexes antedating 5000 B.C. and the beginnings of maize agriculture, the cross-ties between the American continents remain of a general nature. If one assumes that such a technique as pressure-flaking of chipped stone was diffused from north to south during or at the close of the Mankato Substage of the Wisconsin glaciation, then it is difficult to deny that other industrial techniques were similarly diffused at a later time. The grinding and polishing of stone and the manufacture of polished stone objects of both utilitarian and nonutilitarian forms date from this interval in both the eastern United States Archaic[3] cultures and in similar Archaic-like contexts in California. Radiocarbon dates for these Archaic ground stone assemblages fall between 2000 and 4000 B.C. Ground stone materials occur in South America along the Brazilian and Chilean shores in shell refuse mounds which are either preceramic or nonceramic. Although the specific forms vary in all these widely separated areas, it is worthy of note that there is at least one type which is common to all. The plummet of the eastern North American Archaic, the "charmstone" of the early California horizon, the Brazilian "fusos" of the sambaquis, and the Chilean fish-line sinker are essentially the same form, an elongated, pointed stone, grooved or perforated for suspension. Not all of the cultures in this post-Early Lithic, preagricultural era, however, are associated with the making of ground and polished stone implements. The Mexican Chalco complex, which appears to fill this time gap in the Valley of Mexico, lacks such technologies and is known by its chipped stone work and rather crude grinding implements. Similarly, the earlier stages of the Arizona Cochise Culture, to which the Chalco has been compared, do not have the polished stone objects.

To sum up thus far, there is evidence for the continued exchange of stone technology between North and South America in the time interval which can be described as following the Mankato Substage of the Wisconsin glaciation (about 11,000 years ago) and extending up to perhaps 2500 B.C. Inadequate archaeological sequences in South America and the absence of radiocarbon dating make it impossible to determine the exact direction and time of these influences although probabilities favor a north-to-south drift. Also, there is no really solid clue as to whether these were migrations of people or diffusions of ideas. Even at this early date, there seems to have been considerable cultural diversity from area to area.

The diffusion of maize agriculture appears to have begun sometime toward the close of the era to which we have just referred. Radiocarbon dates show an early form of maize with definite pod-like characteristics appearing in the North American Southwest as early as 2500 B.C.[4] A different, but equally primitive, strain of corn has been assigned a comparable radiocarbon date in the La Perra Culture of Tamaulipas, Mexico (MacNeish, 1950, pp. 92–93). In both of these contexts, pottery is lacking and the total cultural content is such as to suggest a way of life not differing greatly from the early American hunters and gatherers. By 1359 B.C. ±250 years, according to the radiocarbon "clock," a fully developed sedentary-agricultural, pottery-making culture was under way in the Valley of Mexico. The Middle and North American data thus show primitive strains of maize at amazingly early dates and the establishment of an American Formative Period or "neolithic" in central Mexico by the middle of the second millennium B.C.

What does the South American evidence show? Bird's (1948) excavations at Huaca

Prieta on the Peruvian Coast disclose a long period of nonmaize, simple agriculture beginning over 2000 years B.C. Maize was introduced into this setting around 700 B.C. This first Peruvian appearance of maize coincides with the arrival of Chavín-style pottery and marks, in effect, the beginnings of a fully developed Formative stage. These datings argue for a Middle American domestication of maize over a long time period, the rise of Formative stage cultures in Middle America, and a somewhat later diffusion of maize and Formative level culture to Peru. Obviously, the case is not closed but a South American origin for domesticated *Zea mays* seems much less likely than it did a few years back. At the present writing, it appears that one of the most important items in the rise of New World civilizations was diffused from north to south in the first millennium B.C.

The Formative and Classic Stages

When we arrive at the level of Formative culture, the criteria for detection of interarea diffusions become considerably more complex. For the Early Lithic and Archaic stages, we are utilizing stone technologies or an invention like the domestication of maize to establish common cultural bonds. But in the various Formative phases of Middle and South America there are traits whose peculiarities of form appear to afford clues to historic linkages of a more limited and intimate sort within these wider bonds. In the following discussion, I will treat several cultural elements, or complexes of elements, selected for their definitive characteristics and for their demonstrable chronological contexts. For the most part, these selected elements will be presented in what appears to be their chronological order, from earliest to latest. As will be apparent, most of these elements are not indisputable proof of cultural contact in the same way that an actual trade object or a specific style embodies such proof. On the other hand, they have a greater specific value than a fundamental invention such as pottery-making or agriculture. They are criteria of an intermediate grade of definitiveness. Their value appears to vary with the dimensions of their space-time contexts. There is no set rule we can follow. Each instance must be examined and judged on its own merits; however, it is with these data that we must test the case for inter-American culture contacts.

Rocker-Stamped Decoration of Pottery

Rocker-stamping of pottery is a decorative technique employed on the soft, unfired surface of the vessel. It is effected with a plain or notched-edged implement manipulated in a rocker or roulette fashion. It is found in many places in the New World and also appears in Old World prehistoric contexts. Griffin and Krieger (1947) have discussed the Middle American occurrences of rocker-stamped pottery, particularly with comparative reference to the eastern United States. Strong (1943) has pointed to Peruvian similarities. More recently, Porter Weaver (1953) has reviewed the problem in the Americas suggesting that it is a diffused phenomenon. It is, of course, questionable as to just how reliable this technique may be as a historical connective. Was it invented once or many times? I am inclined to believe that rocker-stamped pottery in the New World has a common history. Beyond that, I think it an even chance that the American and the Asiatic occurrences are also remotely related. In the New World, the most interesting fact concerning this decorative technique on pottery is that it is almost uniformly early. It appears in the Formative Stage periods of Middle America and Peru and has a respectable antiquity in the eastern United States, giving an excellent illustration of chronological context strengthening the diffusional hypothesis.

By using the ceramic decorative technique of rocker-stamping as a tracer, we arrive at the following construct for Middle America and Andean South America. First, the technique appears on the Mexican scene between 1000 and 500 B.C. It is associated with Upper Formative cultures in central Mexico, Veracruz, and in the Atlantic drainages of Honduras. It occurs in north lowland Colombia where it is early in a relative sense (Reichel-Dolmatoff, 1954). In north Peru, it is associated with the appearance of maize and the first "full blown" Formative type cultures (Chavín and Cupisnique) at around 700 B.C. Comparative dates at the Mexican and Peruvian ends of the chart are approximately the same and give no good clue to the direction of diffusion. However, the cultural milieu into which rocker-stamping first appears in Middle America is considerably richer and deeper than that for Peru where the technique is known only from Chavín horizon. Such a consideration favors a north-south movement of the technique. Further, we know that rocker-stamping is an ancient pottery technique in Asia, placed by some authorities at 2000 B.C. in Mongolia-Manchuria (Liang, 1930). In Ohio and Illinois, rocker-stamped pottery reaches its climax in the Middle Hopewellian period at around 300 to 0 B.C. according to recent radiocarbon dates, but it has a long previous history in those regions according to some authorities (Griffin, ed., 1952) which may well carry the technique back to dates equivalent with or earlier than those of Middle and South America. In the light of these facts, it is by no means an unfounded speculation that rocker-stamping as a pottery technique entered the eastern United States from Asia, was diffused southward to the lowlands of eastern Mexico, and continued in that general direction through Honduras, Colombia, and Ecuador into Peru.

It should be pointed out that this technique fits into a remarkably similar context in both Mexico and Peru. Traits common to Tlatilco in Mexico and Coastal Chavín in Peru include such elements as incised color zones in pottery decoration, stirrup-spouted vessels, pottery stamps, whistling jars, a jaguar motif, and a curious concept of dualism as artistic representations. Some of these traits, but not all of them, are associated with the other Middle American occurrences of rocker-stamped pottery. Many are features which continue until much later times in both areas. The stirrup-spouted jar trait continues in post-Chavín periods in north Peru to become one of the most common pottery forms; in Middle America it is always a minor element. Conversely, pottery stamps disappear in the later Peruvian periods but remain a common Middle American artifact. In connection with this, we observe that in some of the interlying regions, such as Colombia, both stirrup-spouted jars and pottery stamps are significant elements in most archaeological complexes.

Platform Mounds

In the Valley of Mexico, platform mounds date from the late Upper Formative Stage phases, such as Cuicuilco. In the Maya lowlands, a small platform like A-I at Uaxactun also appears in the Upper Formative. The stepped pyramid (E-VII-sub) at Uaxactun is either late Formative or belongs to the succeeding Early Classic phase. In Yucatan, mound building appears in the latter part of the Formative (Brainerd, 1951a, p. 76). In the lowlands of the Gulf Coast of Mexico, platform or substructure mounds are found in the Veracruz-Tabasco region, and in every instance the relative sequence position is the Upper Formative Period or later. In Honduras, large platform mounds were constructed in association with a complex which, from all indications, belongs on this same general time level. Only in the Guatemala highlands is there any substantial evidence indicating an earlier position for the flat-topped pyramid or platform mound. There, puddled adobe mounds came into the sequence during the Arevalo phase (personal communication, A.

V. Kidder and E. M. Shook) which is, unfortunately, not satisfactorily cross-dated to other Middle American sequences. However, there is at least the possibility that it may be Lower rather than Upper Formative.

In Peru, the earliest platform mounds are Chavín horizon structures in Cupisnique, Nepeña, and Casma Valleys. Their appearance on the north coast of Peru coincides with the introduction of rocker-stamped pottery and maize agriculture, and marks the beginning of the Peruvian Formative Stage. Radiocarbon dating places this period in Peru approximately contemporary with the earliest platform mounds in the Middle American Upper Formative period.[5]

This chronological coincidence would appear to signify another interrelationship between Peru and Middle America on about the same time level as that of the presumed diffusion of rocker-stamped pottery. The counter-possibility of the independent development of large ceremonial structures in Peru and in Middle America deserves more consideration here, however, than in the case of rocker-stamping. Mound building is directly tied to population concentration and organization; the rocker-stamped marking of pottery is not. In examining the independent developmental hypothesis, it may be significant to observe that whereas platform mounds do not occur in Middle America until well after the start of Formative sedentary-agricultural life, they are part of the Peruvian Formative at its inception. Of course, if the phenomena are independent of each other, this could have resulted from an acceleration of population growth on the Peruvian coast; however, it also suggests the other interpretation—that the platform mound was diffused to Peru from Middle America where it is underlain by a longer Formative heritage.

The distribution of the platform mound in the intervening areas of lower Central America, Colombia, and Ecuador throws little light on the problems of diffusion. In general, substructure mounds decrease in size and numbers through Nicaragua, Costa Rica, and Panama. Relative dates are as yet unavailable from these regions, so there is no proof that mounds were built on a time level corresponding to the Formative of either Middle America or Peru. In Colombia, there is little clear evidence of large mounds although small tumuli are reported from various sections of the country. In some instances these tumuli may be substructures, but in others, they seem to have served only as burial places. Temple or palace platform mounds are common in Ecuador, particularly along the coast and slightly inland from the coast. The Ecuadorian chronologies are sketchy, at best, and cannot be securely tied to the north Peruvian sequences; however, there is a fair possibility that the platform-mound trait on the Ecuadorian coast may be as early as the Peruvian Formative period. In reviewing the distributional evidence, the weakest link is seen in Colombia. This Colombian link, or lack of a link, is an argument against the diffusion of the platform mound idea; however, it is quite possible that the Colombia area was bypassed in such a diffusion. As will be noted further along, there are a number of other curious similarities between Peru and Middle America and between Ecuador and Middle America that are not registered in Colombia.

RESIST-DYE PAINTING OF POTTERY

This pottery technique has sometimes been referred to as negative-painting or lost-color painting, but the term *resist-dye* probably approximates the actual techniques used most closely. Pottery decorated by this technique was apparently treated in somewhat the same manner as batik-processed textiles. Certain design areas were blocked out by a wax, gum or other resist material and the vessel was then immersed in, or covered with, the over-coat dye or paint. Upon firing or cleaning of the surface, the design then stood out in the lighter under-color of the original slip or surface color while the background to these designs was blocked out in the darker (usually blackish) dye. As can be seen, the process possesses a certain complexity that makes it suitable as a tracer in diffusion studies.

In Middle America, resist-dye pottery has a late or Upper Formative occurrence in the central Mexican regions and in Maya lowlands. In Guatemala, Salvador, and Honduras, a ware known as Usulutan appears to have been decorated by a resist technique. There is some dispute about the Usulutan technique but its appearance impresses me as a resist or negative ware, not unlike the various resist-dye pottery styles of Peru, Ecuador, Colombia, and Central America. There are several instances of both Usulutan and other resist-dye potteries continuing after the late Formative level into Classic times; but only in highland Guatemala does there seem to be an earlier beginning. In brief, resist-dye painted pottery in Middle America is mainly a feature of the Upper Formative and occurs contemporaneously with, or slightly later than, rocker-stamped pottery.

In Peru, resist-dye pottery, more commonly known in this area as negative-painted pottery, is best known from the north highlands and the north coast. The overall time position of the technique is best summarized by saying that it has its Peruvian inception immediately following the Chavín horizon, and perhaps, overlapping slightly with that horizon. Using the Coast Chavín radiocarbon date of about 700 B.C. as a basic line, the beginnings of Peruvian resist-dye painting on pottery lie somewhere in the three or four centuries following this date. This is approximately the same temporal position as in Middle America, with the possible exception of the early Usulutan occurrences at the site of Kaminaljuyu, Guatemala.

There is little upon which to base a guess as to the direction of the diffusion of the resist-dye technique. As far as abundance and elaboration of resist-dye wares are concerned, north Peru and Ecuador are undoubtedly a center. Resist-dye painted pottery enjoys a vogue northward through the Nariño and Quimbaya regions of Colombia and is a major element in the Chiriquí pottery of Panama and Costa Rica. Presumably, the latter styles are relatively late chronologically but little is known as yet of earlier archaeological periods in these regions. For the present, the case for a diffusion of the resist-dye painting technique on pottery between Middle America and Peru is based upon mutually early and approximately contemporaneous occurrences in each area. The diversity of distribution of the technique suggests a South American hearth, but this gives no real assurance of chronological priority.

Mold-Made Figurines

Mold-made figurines first appear in the central Mexican sequence in Early Classic times. They are preceded in that region by a long and continuous Formative tradition of hand-made figurines. In the Maya area, the earliest mold-made figurines have been placed at somewhere between 500 and 800 A.D. (Butler, 1935). The inferred diffusion is from central Mexico southward inasmuch as the tradition of figurine-making was missing from the Maya lowlands following the Early Formative level. The obvious implication is that figurines were reintroduced, along with the technology of the mold, from Classic Teotihuacan or closely related cultures of central Mexico. This general dating of mold-made figurines in the Classic Period is consistent for the rest of Middle America.

In Peru, the mold was used for figurines for the first time in the Mochica Culture of the north coast of Peru. It is possible that molds were used earlier for the manufacture of some pottery vessels, but there is no evidence as yet for an earlier application of the figurine mold. There is some indication that the Mochica Culture lasted over a considerable span of centuries and it is not as yet possible to place the mold-made figurine trait within this span. In the central and southern highlands of Peru, the mold and mold-made figurines are less common than on the north coast, and there is every indication they are also later than in the north.

A comparison of radiocarbon dates in Middle America and Peru suggests that the invention of the figurine mold was older in Peru than in Middle America. As opposed to this, the deep tradition of hand-made figurine manufacture in Middle America, which antedates the use of the mold, is an argument for a Middle American origin of this trait. A crucial datum in this matter is the presence of a highly developed, mold-made figurine industry on the north coast of Ecuador. This industry centers around Esmeraldas, but related figurine types are found farther south as well. The Esmeraldas style of figurines and figurine plaques (D'Harcourt, 1947) shows similarities to Mochica figurines and to Mochica relief-modeled erotica on pottery. At the same time, other Esmeraldas types resemble Middle American mold-made figurines, especially those from the Veracruz lowlands (Bushnell, 1951) and the Colima-Nayarit styles of the Mexican west coast (Lehmann, 1951). From this, it seems at least a likely possibility that sea-faring Ecuadorean coastal cultures may have served as intermediaries in transmitting certain figurine concepts and the ceramic mold technology between the Mexicans and the Peruvians. Chronological studies on the development of figurines in the Esmeraldas region are needed to check such a hypothesis.

THE TALL TRIPOD POTTERY VESSEL

Up to now, the traits discussed in this Middle American–Peruvian comparison have appeared to assemble on chronological horizon lines. The radiocarbon dates have indicated that certain elements made their initial appearance in Middle America at about the same time that they are first noted in Peru. Undoubtedly, this is an oversimplified appraisal, and we are not trying to skip over contradictory data. The rather early radiocarbon date for Mochica Culture in Peru (Strong and Evans, 1952, footnote p. 226) and possibly for the figurine mold is one such exception which does not fit the horizon picture. Nevertheless, rocker-stamping, resist-dye painting, and mold-made figurines succeed one another in reasonable chronological regularity in both Middle America and Peru. There are, however, certain elements which violate even the broadest time horizons but which, in spite of this, offer clues to cultural connections. One of these is the tall, solid, tripod support to a pottery vessel.

There are a variety of vessel supports in Middle American archaeology. The earliest form seems to be a small, hollow tripod foot which appears in the Lower Formative of the Valley of Mexico. Podal supports are more common in the Upper Formative and include a variety of hollow forms as well as small, solid, nubbin feet. What appears to be a late Upper Formative or Proto-Classic horizon marker in parts of Middle America is the large mammiform support (Wauchope, 1950b). Tall, solid, tripod supports are less common in Middle America than some of these other forms, but they appear at the beginning of the Upper Formative. Similar tall, solid, tripod supports are reported in highland Guatemala but here they come into the sequence in the Early Formative. The trait thus has considerable antiquity in Middle American cultures.

The Peruvian pottery tripod is almost exclusively a Postclassic feature, occurring with and after the Tiahuanaco horizon. Certainly, this is true of the tall, solid-legged variety, which most closely resembles the Mexican and Guatemalan form (King, 1948). All estimated dating would indicate that the tall tripod element does not occur in Peru until almost 1000 A.D., perhaps 1500 to 2000 years after its Middle American appearance. Such a tremendous slope leaves little doubt as to the direction from which the tall tripod idea was spread to Peru. There is, of course, no definite proof that the invention is a Middle American one. The tall tripod is a pottery trait of the Colombian-Ecuadorian regions and although an antiquity for the tripod in these regions comparable to that of Guatemala or Mexico cannot be demonstrated as yet, it is quite possible that tripod supports were an important part of Ecuadorean ceramics well before the Tiahuanaco horizon in Peru. It would seem that either the tall tripod idea was diffused south from Middle America into Colombia and Ecuador, where it was retained for a considerable time before being transmitted to Peru, or the tall tripod had its origins in Colombia-Ecuador and diffused in both directions, reaching Middle America far earlier than Peru.

Metallurgy

Metallurgy, like the tall tripod, describes a "sloping horizon" in its Middle American–Peruvian space-time distribution. It differs from the tripods in that it slopes the other way. American metallurgical techniques were first developed in South America, some of them possibly in Peru. The earliest annealing and soldering, in addition to cold hammering and repoussé designing, belong to the Coast Chavín horizon and come from the Chongoyape graves in the Lambayeque Valley of the north Peruvian coast. Gold was the primary metal used, with small bits of silver in association. It is possible that this represents technical influences diffused into Peru from Ecuador or from Colombia via Ecuador. There is, however, no proof of this diffusion, and Lothrop (1951b, pp. 223) feels that this earliest Peruvian metallurgy was a local development.

There was little advance in Peruvian metals following the Chavín horizon until Gallinazo times, which mark the close of the Formative and the beginning of north coast Classic culture. Copper was introduced in the Gallinazo period and the techniques of casting, gilding, and overlaying were added to those already known. In the subsequent Mochica period, alloying and casting were widely employed, *tumbaga* (an alloy of gold and copper) was known, and metal (copper) was used for the first time on the north coast for weapons and tools. Lothrop (1951b) believes that *tumbaga, cire perdue* (lost wax) casting, and *mise-en-couleur* gilding moved into Peru on this level from centers in Colombia such as the Quimbaya region. This is certainly a possibility but, again, lack of Ecuadorian-Colombian sequence data makes a diffusion from Peru northward an equally good possibility. The central and southern regions of Peru seem to have been remote from this northern orbit of the development of metals, and the early south coast and south highland centers show little in the way of metallurgical skill. During Classic Tiahuanaco times, however, the south highlands appear to have become an important secondary metallurgical center where bronze was developed. In the subsequent Tiahuanaco horizon, and in the late kingdoms and the Inca empire, bronze tools, weapons, and other artifacts were widely diffused throughout Peru. Bronze reached Ecuador on the Inca horizon.

With regard to Ecuador, it is certain that metals and metallurgical techniques, including the use of copper tools and axes, were known on a time level equivalent to that of Peruvian Mochica. Whether these crafts antedate their appearance in Peru or are a result of Peruvian stimulus, is still an open question.

There is every indication that cast gold and *tumbaga* and gilded metal objects were a relatively late introduction in such cultures as Veraguas and Coclé in Panama. Northward, metals were unknown in the Maya area until very late Classic times (about 900 to 1000

A.D.) and then they appear as foreign manufactures. The Middle American center for metal work was along the Mexican southwest coast in late Post-Classic times. Some of the objects found here are strikingly like those of Ecuador and Peru, particularly the axes and the copper ax form used as a medium of exchange. These similarities point to direct Ecuadorian-Mexican contact by sea as they are not shared by the intermediate Colombian and lower Central American regions.

Miscellaneous Late Traits

The northward diffusion of metallurgy into Middle America at what was almost certainly a late period brings to mind a number of other late examples, which indicate that a vigorous coast-wise trade was in operation. I believe it likely that the Ecuadorian coastal trading cities of late prehistoric times, such as the center of Manta, were the principal agents by which this commerce was carried out. The Manteño were skilled navigators and occupied a favorable geographic position to have served as middle men between the Aztec, Mixtec, and Guatemalan tribes in the north and the Chimu kingdom of Peru. In addition to copper axes and metallurgy, occasional objects have been found which show definite linkages in one direction or the other. A pottery seal picked up on the Ecuadorean coast bears a design incorporating a speech-scroll feature and, although made locally and in a local style, the speech-scroll element is a highly specific Mexican feature (Brainerd, 1953). On the Pacific Coast of Guatemala, a pottery vessel of the Peruvian Coast Tiahuanaco kero-form, bearing a painted Nazca-style fish design, is an element from the other direction (Dieseldorf, 1933, pl. 53, fig. 141). Also, there are the Chimu-like vessels which Lothrop has reported from Zacualpa, Guatemala (1936, fig. 92) and from Panama (1942, fig. 440). These are either actual trade pieces or local imitations. Then there are the rather startling design similarities between the stone wall mosaics of Mitla in Oaxaca, Mexico, and the arabesques of Peruvian north coastal cities like Chan Chan. All of these features are isolated in themselves, clearly not a part of any cultural complex which has been transferred *in toto*; but such indeed is expectable if they were transmitted and reproduced through the random impressions of traders and voyagers.

Conclusions

What can we conclude concerning the case for culture contact between prehistoric Middle America and South America? Let us summarize the evidence in a series of major time bands. First, the earliest human occupations of South America equate chronologically, and to some extent typologically, with the North American lithic complexes which follow the Folsom horizon and appear to date between 7500 and 5000 B.C. The mutual traits are few, but hunting cultures in both continents share flint-chipping technologies and certain projectile point forms. In spite of the lack of complex evidence, a relationship between these cultures of the Early Lithic Stage is indicated since from where else could ideas of stone work have entered South America except from North America?

The second time band, extending perhaps from 5000 to 2500 B.C. and here called the Archaic Stage, is characterized by the rather general traits of stone grinding, carving, and polishing. Occasional forms from South and North America are similar but these are not the crux of the argument. Again, from where else could these technologies in South America have been diffused except from North America? It is somewhere near the upper range of this second time band that domesticated maize is found in northeastern Middle America and in the southwestern United States. No maize with radiocarbon dates anywhere near this early has been discovered in the southern continent.

The third time band may be approximated as from 2500 B.C. to the beginning of the Christian era. This corresponds to the Formative Stage cultures characterized by the establishment of sedentary, agricultural village life in both Middle America and Peru. The earliest actual dates are in Mexico where the bottom of the Formative column of cultural phases is placed at 1350 B.C. Middle American culture at this time was well advanced in the ceramic arts. The evidences for specific lines of diffusion between Middle America and Peru within this time band assemble on a chronological level of about 800 to 400 B.C. They include the technique of rocker-stamped decoration on pottery, the construction of platform mounds, and the technique of resist-dye painting of pottery. The last of these traits may be slightly later than the other two. One of the most interesting facts emerging from these correlations is that rocker-stamped pottery and the platform mound seem to appear in Peru simultaneously, and that their appearance is also synchronized with the earliest finds of domesticated maize. The Peruvian cultures antedating these appearances or arrivals were definitely of a sub-Formative type. These circumstances suggest a significant diffusion of "neolithic" traits from Middle to South America at a time corresponding to the beginning of the Middle American Upper Formative cultures. Although this does not correspond in all specifics to the various theories of Uhle, Jijón y Caamaño, and Spinden as regards the fundamental agricultural pottery-making diffusions from Middle to South America, it tends to confirm the general structure of their hypotheses. Resist-dye painting may be a reverse diffusion from Peru back to Middle America, although we cannot be sure of this. The respective dates for the inception of the trait in the two areas are about the same.

A fourth time band lies somewhere between 1 A.D. and 1000 A.D. and corresponds roughly to the periods of the Classic cultures in both Peru and Middle America. I have selected the mold-made figurine as the key element of this time band. The principle is a technological one, and the figurines themselves show no close stylistic correspondence although certain Ecuadorean specimens are reminiscent of both Mexican and Peruvian designs. The historical connective value of the trait is assumed to lie in the technological process itself, the use of the mold to produce the pottery image. The direction of diffusion is questionable. Mochica radiocarbon dates from Peru are earlier than the dates imputed to Teotihuacan III in Mexico but the long tradition of figure-making in Middle America, antecedent to the appearance of the mold, tends to favor a Middle American origin.

A fifth time band runs from 1000 A.D. to the Spanish conquests of the early sixteenth century. We have noted a number of miscellaneous items here such as the pottery seal with the speech scroll design from the Ecuadorean coast and the Peruvian-like pottery specimens from Guatemala. Intersecting into this fifth time band are the traits of tall tripod vessels and of metallurgy. Both have a diagonal or "sloping" horizon conformation on the time chart. The tall tripod is definitely early (appearing in the Formative) in Middle America and the late (Post-Classic) in Peru; and metallurgy, which has a Formative stage occurrence in Peru, does not reach Middle America until about 1000 A.D. or later. In connection with this latter trait complex, it has been noted that the center for Mexican metalcraft is the southwest coast of Mexico, a region which shows other evidences of contact with the Ecuadorean and Peruvian coasts. Sea trade between Ecuador and Mexico seems the most likely explanation of these particular phenomena.

This discussion has been directed toward establishing a case for culture contact between Middle America and Peru during the prehistoric past. I have dealt with a selected number of traits and have tried to show how these traits may be organized in space and in time so that the historical possibilities of diffusion may be demonstrated. To my mind, there seems little doubt that various contacts took place, some indirectly and others, perhaps, more directly. Accepting the currently available radiocarbon dates, a definite case may be made for the priority of American Formative type cultures in Middle America and their subsequent influencing of Peru. As stated at the outset, I have made no attempt to interpret the cultural and developmental significance of the traits discussed or, with the exception of casual references, to draw inferences as to the means or processes by which such ancient contacts and diffusions were accomplished. Almost certainly, contact of one sort or another was maintained from remote Early Lithic times down to the end of an autonomous native America. What it meant in the various American areas and how it played a part in cultural acceleration and change is an infinitely more complex story than the one I have sketchily outlined here.

Notes

[1]For the purposes of this paper, these areas are defined as the southern one-half to one-third of Mexico, all of Guatemala and British Honduras, parts of Salvador, Honduras, and perhaps Nicaragua and Costa Rica, or the "Mesoamerican" area as defined by Kirchoff (1943), the Peruvian coast and highlands and the adjacent Bolivian altiplano, or essentially the area defined by Bennett (1946a) as the "Central Andes."

[2]All radiocarbon dates are from Johnson, 1951.

[3]It should be noted that the term *Archaic* as used in the eastern United States and in California pertains to cultures of a nonagricultural type. Spinden's use of *Archaic* is quite different, referring to the sedentary agricultural way of life designated here as *Formative*.

[4]There is considerable confusion about these early Bat Cave dates. In the early reports (Mangelsdorf and Smith, 1949), Antevs' geological estimate of 2500 B.C. was accepted as conservative. A later account (C. E. Smith, 1950) shifted this to 2000 B.C. Radiocarbon dates alluded to in this same article were somewhat later, 1162 B.C. to 662 B.C. However, charcoal from the 6-foot stratum of the cave, found associated with the earliest corn, has a radiocarbon date of 3980 B.C.$\pm$310 years. In view of all these data, a medium figure of 2500 B.C. seems reasonable pending further radiocarbon runs.

[5]This correlation is essentially the same as that presented by Wauchope (1954) in his "Scheme A."

3

The Prehistoric Civilizations of Nuclear America

(From *American Anthropologist*, vol. 57, pp. 571–593, 1955. Reprinted by permission of the American Anthropological Association. Not for sale or further reproduction.)

Introduction

The native agricultural civilizations of the New World had their beginnings and their highest development in those areas that have been subsumed under the term *Nuclear America* (Kroeber 1948a:779). The designation has both a geographical and a cultural connotation. The areas involved embrace central and southern Mexico, Central America, the north Andes, and Peru. This is the axis of aboriginal high culture in the Americas and, as such, the major center of prehistoric diffusion for the western hemisphere. To the best of our knowledge, it stands clearly apart and essentially independent from the comparable culture core of the Old World.

Kroeber (1948a:784–85; 1952:377–95) has suggested the analogy between the American civilizational nucleus of Mexico-Peru and the "Oikoumene" of the Old World. Readapting the old Greek concept of the "inhabited" or civilized world (Kroeber 1952:379 and 392), he has defined the Oikoumene for purposes of culture-historical analysis as "the millennially interrelated higher civilizations in the connected mainland masses of the Eastern hemisphere," and as "a great web of culture growth, areally extensive and rich in content." It is, in effect, a vast diffusion sphere (see Hawkes 1954) interlinked across continents by common cultural content. The comparison with Nuclear America seems particularly apt. In both cases the great historic nexuses have considerable time depth at their centers, and in both they have influenced those cultures marginal to them at relatively later points on the time scale. Further, as Kroeber (1952:383–84) has also pointed out, the essential and underlying bonds in each are those of content as distinguished from style or value. Within each, diverse civilizations (or styles) have sprung up as unique reworkings of a common cultural content held within the "Oikoumene." The differences in configuration between the Oikoumene of the Old World and what might be considered the New World "Oikoumene" appear to be functions of time. The much greater age of civilization in the eastern hemisphere seems to have allowed for a more complete dispersal of cultural content throughout the Old World Oikoumene. As Kroeber (1952:392) has stated: "inventions or new cultural materials have tended to be transmitted, sooner or later, from end to end." Within the Americas these processes of dissemination were well under way, spreading fanwise from the Middle American and Peruvian nuclei, but they were terminated by the European conquests before much of the content of the New World "Oikoumene" had reached its outermost marches in the northern and southern continents. Similarly, certain styles, specific civilizations, and their value systems spread throughout large parts of the Old World Oikoumene—their propagation and acceptance undoubtedly facilitated by the ancient base of mutually held cultural content upon which they rode; and these knit together more tightly the grand diffusion sphere of Eurasia-Africa. In America these epiphenomena of the "Oekoumenical" base were in their infancy, yet the Inca style and civilization and its diffusion throughout much of Andean South America may be prototypical of events which, with opportunity, might have transpired on a wider scale.

This analogy between the Oikoumene of the ancient world and Nuclear America provides a basis of understanding for the following discussions of New World prehistory. We are considering the cultures of Mexico-Peru (and intervening areas) as a great historical unit or diffusion sphere which, in spite of important regional stylistic differences, possesses a certain common culture content. In the succeeding pages I propose to examine this content, to offer hypotheses as to its origins and dissemination, and to further treat the similarities and differences of the course of civilization in the two principal subcenters of Nuclear America—Middle America and Peru. Before setting out on this task it seems advisable to review, briefly, a concept which is closely related to the Oikoumene analogy and which is fundamental to all our ensuing discussions. This is the idea of an "Archaic" or "Formative" type of culture (or cultures) as underlying, and basic to, the later American high civilizations.

The theory of an "Archaic" cultural substratum, characterized by sedentary village life, agriculture, pottery making, and other "neolithic" arts, as being basic to the later New World civilizations was first advanced by Spinden (1917, 1928). He concluded that these ideas of the old substratum were diffused north and south from Middle America to provide the basis for much of aboriginal culture in the New World. At the time Spinden proposed this, many of the earlier culture phases of Middle American and Peruvian prehistory, which have since been revealed, were unknown; hence he lacked data to support his hypothesis. Certain particulars of the scheme—such as the specific center of "Archaic" origins being attributed to the Valley of Mexico and the selection of pottery figurine types as inevitable hallmarks of an American "Archaic"—remain unproved or highly unlikely (see Kidder 1936). Nevertheless, the central theoretical theme stands. Continued archaeological research has shown that the Middle American and Peruvian civilizations are preceded by less complex cultures of a village agricultural type, that these earlier cultures have a generally similar content, and that significant portions of this content were diffused widely beyond the geographical boundaries of the later civilizations. Recent recognition of New World "Formative" cultures is based upon these stratigraphic facts and their interpretation. The "Formative" concept, as it has been used in Peru (Larco Hoyle 1948; Strong 1948a; Willey 1948), Middle America (Armillas 1948; Caso 1953), and for inter-areal comparisons (Steward 1948a, 1949a; Willey 1950; Strong 1951), is a reformulation of the Spinden "Archaic" hypothesis. The Formative cultures are, in the sense of our foregoing analogy, the foundation layer of the New World "Oikoumene."

THE RISE OF THE AMERICAN CIVILIZATIONS: A SYNOPSIS

MIDDLE AMERICA

The prehistory of Middle America (central and southern Mexico and the Mayan regions of upper Central America—see Kirchhoff [1943] for a geographical definition of "Mesoamerica") is usually generalized under three main chronological subdivisions for which various terms have been used. Alternatives are included in parentheses:

1. Formative (Archaic, Developmental, Preclassic)
2. Classic (Florescent)
3. Postclassic (Militaristic, Expansionistic, Historic).

All these subdivisions refer to agricultural-sedentary patterns. Cultural remains preceding the Formative have been found, and some of these appear to be of remote age and to represent early hunting groups (De Terra 1949; Aveleyra and Maldonado-Koerdell 1953). Others, such as the Tamaulipas cave finds on the northeastern periphery of the Middle American area, are somewhat later, dating at about 2500 B.C. (MacNeish 1950; Libby 1952a, no. 687–2494±280 B.C.[1]). The Tamaulipas caves reveal a primitive type of maize but no pottery, and the total artifact assemblages indicate hunting and collecting economies in spite of the presence of maize.

The earliest Formative culture phases, according to radiocarbon dating, are in the Valley of Mexico. Here, the Early Zacatenco level dates from the middle of the second millennium B.C. (Arnold and Libby 1951, no. 196—1360±250 B.C.). Early Zacatenco (Vaillant 1930) is represented by a large village site of deep living refuse. Corn-grinding metate and mano implements are numerous; the ceramic art is revealed in competently made incised and simply painted vessels; and handmade figurines of human form are abundant. A number of successive culture phases of the Formative follow the Early Zacatenco (Vaillant 1941; Porter Weaver 1953). There is substantial cultural continuity from one phase to the next, but the sequence also registers strong outside influences at various times. Toward the close of the Formative stage flat-topped or platform mounds appear, and these constructions seem to mark ceremonial sites. These are the first evidences in the Valley of Mexico of large-scale architectural works.

Elsewhere in Middle America the Formative pattern is repeated (Wauchope 1950b, MacNeish 1954). This is not to say that culture is uniform throughout the area on the early time levels. There are some close cross-ties, such as the ones between the Formative phases of the Valley of Mexico and Michoacan (Noguera 1939) or between the earliest periods of the Huasteca and Peten Maya chronologies (Ekholm 1944; MacNeish 1954); but there are few widespread stylistic linkages at this time. The widely held similarities tend to be of a general technical sort—the predominance of plain and incised wares, handmade figurines, and the absence of well-developed architectural features—indicating a gradual diffusion of certain technologies rather than rapid dissemination of more specialized traits. Apparently, the mound building–ceremonial center complex is a late Formative concept, belonging to such phases as the Peten Chicanel (but not the earlier Mamom), the Cuicuilco (but not Early Zacatenco or other pre-Cuicuilco manifestations), and the Monte Alban I (see Wauchope 1950b; MacNeish 1954). Yet it should be pointed out that the case for a "village farmer" preceding a "village farmer plus ceremonial center" complex is not a clear-cut one. In the long Formative sequence in the Guatemalan highlands at Kaminaljuyu (Shook 1951; Shook and Kidder 1952) platform mounds are placed in the next-to-earliest Arevalo phase and may even be part of the still earlier Las

Charcas phase. In Yucatan there is also evidence that mounds belong to the earlier part of the Formative (Brainerd 1951a). The difficulties in resolving this problem are those of cross-dating. For example, we cannot be certain just where the Guatemalan highland Arevalo phase equates with the Peten or Valley of Mexico Formative chronologies. Until this is established, the earliest appearances of a trait like temple mound construction and its diffusion cannot be pinned down and plotted.

In brief, the Formative cultures of Middle America come upon the scene as fully integrated sedentary agricultural, pottery making complexes. Formative pottery, though usually not elaborately decorated, was by no means crude or experimental. The total impression is that the Formative cultures have behind them a considerable period of growth and development. Evidences of this have not yet been found. The Tamaulipas cave cultures, such as the La Perra phase, may show the ancient beginnings of agriculture; but the intermediate periods, if such do exist, are still lacking. In the latter part of the Formative, ceremonial center construction began, and many of the mounds built at this time are of impressive size. Radiocarbon dates from the late Formative cluster between about 600 B.C. and 200 B.C. (Arnold and Libby 1951, no. 202—615±200 B.C.; no. 200—472±250 B.C.; no. 424—650±170 B.C.; no. 425—273±145 B.C.), suggesting a closing date for the Formative cultures at just before the beginning of the Christian Era.

The beginnings of Middle American Classic cultures coincide with the first Initial Series stelae of the Maya calendar in the Peten, with the Teotihuacan II (or Miccaotli) phase (Armillas 1950) of the Valley of Mexico, with Monte Alban IIIa in Oaxaca, and the Aurora-Esperanza phases of Kaminaljuyu. It is believed that these events are more or less contemporaneous. It is possible that the opening of the Teotihuacan II phase antedates the earliest Uaxactun stela by three hundred to four hundred years; however, if the 12.9.0.0.0 (Spinden) correlation of the Maya long count is followed rather than the 11.16.0.0.0 correlation (Goodman-Thompson), lowland Maya early Classic (Tzakol phase) beginnings would be about coeval with the advent of Teotihuacan II. The demographic trends between Middle American Formative and Classic are not clear. In some localities, such as the Valley of Mexico, the settlement indications imply population increase and population concentration (Armillas 1950); in others, as is the case in the Guatemalan highlands, overall population size appears to be as great in the Formative phases as in the Classic, and concentration of population seems to be even greater in the earlier periods (Shook and Proskouriakoff 1956). A number of Classic trends are, however, definite and distinguish the stage quantitatively and qualitatively from the Formative. Ceremonial architecture is more elaborate, architectural devices such as apron moldings and plinths are widely used, and the ceremonial units themselves—the mounds, plazas, temples, and palaces—are more numerous and more carefully planned than in the late Formative. There is a general tendency toward the production of more finely decorated pottery with the use of polychrome painting and ornate modeling. Similarly, other craft products enjoy an aesthetic refinement.

There is observable continuity of early Classic out of late Formative cultures in most regions. In the Valley of Mexico the strong figurine tradition of the Formative is maintained in the Classic phases, but with the technical innovation of the mold. At Monte Alban the Classic anthropomorphic modeled urns have Formative prototypes in the same site zone, and the development of the Classic Zapotecan glyphs can be traced back to the Preclassic inscriptions (Caso 1938). In the lowland Maya regions there are a number of carry-overs in ceramic shapes and technical features from the late Formative Chicanel phase into early Classic Tzakol, but a host of new Maya traits—the stelae, sculpture, the corbeled vault, writing, and the calendar—appear with dramatic suddenness. Thus, in addition to local growth, the early Classic was a period of new ideas. Some of these ideas, like the basal-flanged bowl of Maya or the tripod fresco jar of Teotihuacan II–III, can be traced approximately as to original source and distribution; others are more difficult to plot as to origins and routes of dispersal. To generalize, the trait diffusions of the Classic, particularly the early Classic, must have resulted from rapid processes of dissemination of ideas and products (trade), whereas the Formative diffusions seem to have been much more gradual.

The end of Classic Teotihuacan is marked by the catastrophic destruction of that great site and by the appearances of new styles and, perhaps, peoples. In the south, the Maya Classic centers of the Peten, the Usumacinta, and the Motagua-Chamelecon were all abandoned shortly after the beginning of the tenth cycle of the long count. How closely coordinate in time these events were is debatable. If Teotihuacan was destroyed by A.D. 700, the collapse of the "Old Empire" Maya centers would be approximately coeval if the terminal date for the Maya lowland Classic is interpreted in the 12.9.0.0.0 correlation. Recent radiocarbon dates from the late Classic period at Tikal support this correlation (Kulp, et al. 1951, no. 113—A.D. 481±120; Libby 1954, no. 948—A.D. 468±120; Libby 1954, no. 949—A.D. 432±170). On the other hand, the 11.16.0.0.0 correlation places the end of Maya lowland Classic at about A.D. 900. In general, the archaeological sequences of Middle America as a whole seem to accord more closely with the 11.16.0.0.0 correlation than with the 12.9.0.0.0.

Causes of the decline and fall of the Middle American Classic cultures have been the subject of a good deal of speculation. In the Valley of Mexico there seems little doubt but what the immediate cause was military disaster, probably resulting from the pressure of new population groups entering the orbit of Mexican high civilization from the northern frontiers. Such happenings may also have had indirect effects upon the southern centers; the Tula-Toltec influences into Yucatan after the close of the Maya Classic certainly suggest this. There are, in addition, other possibilities as to causes which may have contributed to the Maya Classic decline (see Ricketson and Ricketson 1937; Thompson 1954; Meggers 1954).

The Postclassic stage of Middle American prehistory, which dates in the last eight hundred to five hundred years preceding the Spanish conquest, has been characterized as militaristic, expansionistic, secularized, and urbanized. There are evidences for these trends, but they are not manifested in all Middle American regions. An increase in warfare is reflected in the appearance of fortifications and fortified sites in many regions. This trend is paralleled by what were probably larger political domains than existed earlier, the Aztec state of the late Postclassic being the outstanding example. There is also considerable evidence of "expansionism" in the archaeological and legendary-historical records. Toltec-style Chichen Itza in the heart of Yucatan, in the early Postclassic, and Nahua towns deep into Central America, in the late Postclassic, are examples. Secularism must be judged relatively. Religion seems always to have been a powerful force in Middle American civilizations. There is, it is true, something of a decline in the size, amount, and fineness of religious architecture in the Postclassic as opposed to the Classic. There are, however, exceptions to this; and, also, it must be questioned just how sure and sensitive a guide architecture is for the interpretation of cultural values. Urbanism, in the sense of population size and density, is easier to measure than the attribute of secularism, at least from the archaeological standpoint; but, unfortunately, there has been little field research along these lines. In the Valley of Mexico there are some indications that Teotihuacan had, in effect, become an urban zone, in addition to the ceremonial precincts, before the close of the Classic stage. Certainly Postclassic Tenochtitlan, with its estimated 60,000 inhabitants appears to have had urban qualifications. In Yucatan, Mayapan (Ruppert; and Smith 1952), with its some four thousand houses within the enclosure wall suggests the urban trend, but we know too little of the preceding Classic Maya settlement patterns to be able to judge its full significance. In highland Guatemala the Postclassic sites, although frequently fortified, are not especially large.

There are a number of horizonal traits which characterize the Middle American Postclassic, such as the widespread appearances of Plumbate and Fine Orange wares in the early part of the stage and the popularity of Mixteca-Puebla polychrome pottery and related styles in the later periods. Metals come into use in the Postclassic, particularly in southwestern Mexico, and there is some evidence to suggest that irrigation now became important in western Mexico and in the Valley of Mexico (Angel Palerm, personal communication, 1954).

Finally, and somewhat impressionistically, most Middle American prehistorians agree that there is a tendency for aesthetic decline in the Postclassic. This is difficult to measure, and it may be that, rather than decline, a plateau of achievement was attained in the Classic which was not, subsequently, surpassed in the Postclassic cultures. In some places, as in the Mayan regions, this putative decline does seem to have been accompanied by a lessening of intellectual and scientific accomplishments, as revealed in the calendar, astronomy, and writing.

PERU

The natural environment of the Peruvian area, by contrast with the varied regional settings which compose Middle America, has an impressive uniformity. There are essentially two types of country for human occupation: the small oases valleys of the desert coast and the highland basins. These two types are in juxtaposition to one another. Many of the coastal streams head up into the highlands in such a way as to offer reasonably easy means of contact between sierra and coast. The archaeology of Peru, or Peru-Bolivia, seems to reflect this environmental homogeneity. Regional styles develop, but they are, again and again, interpenetrated by styles which have an areawide or broad horizonal significance (Kroeber 1944; Willey 1945). This complex interlacing of small regional cultures, over long periods of time, has given rise to the "cotradition" or culture-area-in-time-depth concept (Bennett 1948). Regional independence should not be minimized, but it is important to note that Peruvian prehistoric cultures, *in toto*, form a somewhat tighter diffusion sphere than do those of Middle America.

Peruvian archaeology has been divided into major chronological segments in much the same fashion as Middle America. These divisions have varied in name, number, and, to some extent, in attributed content, but in essentials they are similar. All classifiers agree upon a Formative (Evolutive, Cultist-Experimenter) stage or epoch as marking the beginnings of maize agriculture and developed pottery (see Larco Hoyle 1948; Strong 1948a, 1951; Willey 1948, 1950; Bennet and Bird 1949). This is followed by a Classic (Regional Classic, Florescent, Mastercraftsman) stage of artistic climax and architectural achievement. The final stage, or stages, which we will refer to here as Postclassic, have been designated variously at Fusional-Imperialist, City Builder–Imperialist, Expansionist, and Militarist.

As with Middle America, this classification refers to the fully agricultural patterns. The projectile points and other flint tools of early hunting groups have been found in both Peruvian highlands and coast (Bennett and Bird 1949), but these remains appear to long antedate the Peruvian Formative. On the north Peruvian coast, immediately precedent to the Formative phases of that region, there is evidence of a long occupation of agricultural-collecting peoples which ranges from about 2500 B.C. (Libby 1951, no. 598—2348±230 B.C.) up to the advent of the Formative Cupisnique and Middle Guañape phases at approximately 1000 B.C. (Libby 1952b, no. 75—715±200 B.C.; Kulp, et al. 1952, no. 122A—1199±90 B.C.). This agricultural-collecting period is without maize and lacks pottery except for its final three or four centuries when a plain ware of simple vessel forms makes its appearance. There is, however, a continuity, or near-continuity, of occupation and culture between the premaize period and the subsequent Cupisnique phase of the early Formative.

The early Formative cultures of the Peruvian coast have as their basis the small agricultural village. It is doubtful if the canal irrigation, which was to make possible the dense populations of the later periods, had yet appeared. Sites are relatively few in number. Platform mounds, which almost certainly represent religious, or politicoreligious, centers, were constructed. Cerro Blanco and Pungurí in the Nepeña Valley are the best-known coastal examples (Tello 1943), and others have been reported from the Chicama Valley (Larco Hoyle 1941). These early-period phases of Peru are linked by a developed and sophisticated art style, the Chavín. The Chavín style, with its specialized feline-condor iconography, covered all north and central Peru on this early horizon, varying in its expression from the monumental stone carving of highland Chavín de Huantar to the incised pottery decoration of the coastal valleys.

Most of our knowledge of the development of the Peruvian Formative cultures comes from the north coast, so it is from this region that the trends or changes which are here briefly reviewed have been observed. Between early and late Formative there was a great population upswing, and this increase in numbers of people in each valley almost certainly is related to the appearance of canal irrigation (Willey 1953a). Village communities remained small, but there are numerous evidences of multivillage activity in addition to the canal systems. Large hilltop fortifications and platform mounds are the principal examples. At the very close of the late Formative, or the beginning of the Classic phases (depending upon where the classifier draws the line), canal systems are so complex that it is obvious that there were sociopolitical means of close cooperation within each coastal valley. The degree of centralization and authoritarianism can only be speculated upon, however. In general, the late Formative was a time of technical advance or experimentation. Metallurgical techniques, as applied to ornaments, were diffused. Ceramics lacked the distinctive Chavín-style incised decorations, and a variety of simple painting techniques (white-on-red, two-color negative) were substituted; but new firing methods, vessel forms, and life modeling came to the fore.

Regionalism and regional traditions in prehistoric Peru must not be lost sight of in the above generalizations, which, as stated, apply to the north coast. It is probable that population increase characterized most of Peru during the Formative, but this is not certainly known. Some strong regional tendencies are, undoubtedly, tied to environmental differences between coast and highland. Adobe architecture as opposed to stone, or the emphasis upon canal irrigation versus terracing, is self-evident. Other regional differences cannot be explained so readily. On the south coast and in the south highlands Formative pottery is often multicolored, whereas in the north painting always took a secondary role to incising and modeling. It is noteworthy, too, that Chavín stylistic influence was never strong in the south and that the art of the south, while showing some element similarities to the central and northern Peruvian regions, followed traditions of its own.

Peruvian Classic cultures, such as Mochica, Early Lima (or Maranga), Nazca, Classic

Tiahuanaco, and Recuay, apparently date from about the beginning of the Christian Era. This is in accordance with radiocarbon datings (Libby 1951, no. 619—A.D. 112±190—Mochica; Arnold and Libby 1951, no. 460, no. 521—38±200 B.C. and A.D. 272±200—Nazca; Libby 1952a, no. 658—A.D. 636±250—Nazca). Guess estimates (see Bennett and Bird 1949; Strong and Evans 1952; Willey 1953a) have been somewhat later. Judging from the settlement studies in a single north coast valley (Willey 1953a), there was little population increase between late Formative and early Classic. However, larger site concentrations are reported, as well as more impressive mound and ceremonial constructions. This increase in site size, particularly of ceremonial or politicoreligious centers, seems to hold for the north and central coasts (Stumer 1954) and, probably, for the south coast (Strong 1954). In the highlands this trend is not definite. Classic Tiahuanaco and Pucara of the south highlands, both large and elaborate architectural complexes, would seem to be consistent with it; but Chavín de Huantar, the Formative stage center, is probably larger than later shrines or centers in the north highlands. On the north coast the fortified strong points of the late Formative developed into specialized military centers, and Mochica representative art is a testimonial to warfare. Large buildings with big rooms and corridors are also constructed in conjunction with great platform mound sites. Presumably these had palace or administrative functions.

The art of the Peruvian Classic is regionally specialized and technically and aesthetically climactic. Old regional continuities can be detected in all the great styles. Mochica sculptured and moldmade pottery derives from the sculptural and modeling tendencies of the earlier north-coast Cupisnique, Salinar, and Gallinazo phases. In the same manner the polychrome features of the south-coast Paracas phase are retained and elaborated in the subsequent Nazca styles. Trade and exchange among regional centers appears to have been going on at this time, particularly between coast and highland but these contacts do not seem to have been sufficient to have deflected or modified well-organized regional styles.

The Tiahuanaco horizon style has been used by archaeologists to mark the termination of the Classic cultures. However this style and its near pan-Peruvian diffusion are interpreted, there can be no doubt that it was concomitant with significant social and political changes (Willey 1948, 1951b). New settlement and architectural types appear on the central and north coasts at this time. These new types and changes include the planned rectangular inclosure site; a multiroomed dwelling unit of symmetrical plan ranging from small to great size; large, apparently empty, garrison-like inclosures; the widespread use of massive tapia, rather than small brick, adobe; and a definite decline in platform mound construction. Stylistic changes vary in kind and intensity during the Tiahuanaco horizon. On the south coast the changes are definite, but there is a tendency for a blending of old Nazca vessel shapes, designs, and colors with the Tiahuanaco iconography. On the central coast the Tiahuanaco artistic impact is somewhat starker, while north coast Mochica styles are virtually obliterated by the new influences. The origins of the Tiahuanaco influences are still a puzzle. Wari, a great ceremonial and dwelling site in the central highlands, may be the most important source of the art style and, perhaps, some of the forces behind the diffusion of the style (Bennett 1953). The actual iconography of the pottery paintings and textiles which are found so widespread over coast and highland may have an earlier and Classic-level origin at the Tiahuanaco site proper in highland Bolivia. Rowe (1945), by historical reckoning, has placed the onslaught of the Tiahuanaco stylistic wave at A.D. 1000. If this is correct, and if radiocarbon dates are also correct, the Classic civilizations of Peru had a time range of a millennium or more.

The latter part of the Peruvian Postclassic stage is the period of the large local kingdoms of the coast, such as the Chimu and the Chincha, and of the various states of the highlands which were, subsequently, overrun by the Inca empire. On the coast the late Postclassic sites—Chan Chan, Pacatnamu, and Cajamarquilla, to name a few—represent the largest population concentrations of Peruvian, and perhaps New World, prehistory. The planned rectangular inclosure community, noted in early Postclassic times, is the dominant architectural motif of these late coastal cities. Some of these aggregates and complexes of inclosures with their numerous rooms and courtyards also contained units which appear to be palaces or temples. These have been referred to as "urban elite" centers; other massed clusters of houses and rooms without the more elaborate specialized buildings are designated as "urban lay" centers (Schaedel 1951). The various late Postclassic states are characterized by distinct new styles, but styles of a quality inferior to those of the Classic cultures. The Chimu pottery and metalwork show an interesting blend of old Classic Mochica concepts, Tiahuanacoid infusions, and other less readily identifiable elements. Similar fusions of local and Tiahuanacoid traditions are seen elsewhere. Throughout Peru, at this time, metalcraft was widely known. Ornaments of gold, copper, silver, and alloys were manufactured and widely traded, and in some regions weapons and tools were made of copper or bronze.

The Inca expansion from a small national hearth around Cuzco, in the south highlands, to a domain reaching over the entire Peruvian area and far beyond was a series of events that can be telescoped into the last century before the arrival of the Spanish in 1532. In general technology and culture the Inca participated in the common Peruvian cotradition. Their empire thus appears to be an achievement of social and political organization. That there was precedent or tradition for empire building in pre-Incaic Peru is probable in the light of such a phenomenon as the Tiahuanaco stylistic diffusion.

Chronological Correlation of Middle American and Peruvian Sequences

The above synopses are attempts to present the salient facts—plus some integrative interpretation—of the prehistory of native Middle America and Peru. These are the peaks of New World civilization, the high contours, so to speak, of the American "Oikoumene." What is their interrelationship? What archaeological traces of historical contact can be identified between these two centers? That some relationship existed is evident. Maize and a variety of other cultivated plants are shared by the two areas. So are numerous culture elements. To deal with these problems most effectively it is necessary to turn to chronologies—absolute and relative—and to see if we can coordinate in time, in any manner whatsoever, the sequences of events in prehistoric Peru and Middle America.

The greatest difficulty in effecting chronological correlations between Middle America and Peru is the lack of adequate archaeological sequence data in the intervening regions of lower Central America, Colombia, and Ecuador. Middle American relative chronologies have been pushed southward only to the Ulua-Comayagua drainages in Honduras, and reliable Peruvian archaeological sequences have been established only as far north as the Chicama Valley and the Callejon de Huaylas. For the vast area between, there is a substantial amount of survey information, but, except for an occasional, isolated stratigraphic datum, there is little in the way of time ordering of prehistoric cultures. A long sequence in northeastern Colombia (Reichel-Dolmatoff 1954) which as yet has only local significance, the beginnings of chronology in Panama (Willey and McGimsey 1954), and some partly established, partly inferential, chronological arrangements in Ecuador

(Jijón y Caamaño 1927, 1930; Collier and Murra 1943; Bennett 1946b; Bushnell 1951) are among these few exceptions. It is, of course, possible to trace various traits through these intervening areas, between Middle America and Peru, without reference to the time factor; but in the absence of relative chronological alignments such trait distributions are not convincing as proof of historical interrelationships. In attempting cultural and chronological correlations between Peru and Middle America we must, then, rely chiefly upon sequences within these two areas and upon means of supplying absolute dates for these sequences. Where possible we shall utilize such chronological information as is available from the intervening regions.

In a recent paper (Willey 1955a) I have reviewed the subject of Middle American–Peruvian interrelationships from an archaeological point of view, discussing certain conditions and limiting circumstances which surround the problem. In the first place, the nature of the evidence linking the two major American civilizational areas is that of culture content, not style. Second, certain myths and nonmaterial traits recorded from the ethnohistoric periods, while strong arguments for ancient contacts, are not, in most cases, identifiable in the archaeological and relative chronological records. Third, the data of physical anthropology are not yet complete enough, or are not sufficiently specific, to be of much help on this problem. A possible exception is the cultural-physical trait of cranial deformation. The case for contact, then, is essentially an archaeological one.

Prior to about 1000 B.C. there are no good evidences of diffusion between the Middle American and Peruvian centers of Nuclear America. That New World migrations and diffusions of a general north-to-south direction took place long before this date is attested by the presence of people in the Valley of Mexico and at the Straits of Magellan as early as 9000 and 6000 B.C. (Libby 1952b, nos. 204, 485). A few thousand years later it is likely that techniques of grinding and polishing stone and certain stone forms, such as the California "charmstone," were diffused from North to South America. But such contacts antedate the rise of American maize agriculture and have no immediate bearing upon the growth and historical interrelatedness of the New World "Oikoumene." Maize agriculture, it will be remembered, is at least as early as 2500 B.C. in northeastern Mexico, and a similar primitive strain of corn was present in preceramic cultures in New Mexico as early or earlier (Libby 1952a, various dates on Bat Cave, New Mexico). A local agricultural complex of the Peruvian coast is approximately contemporaneous with these dates, but this complex is without maize. The first substantial evidence of interrelationship between Middle America and Peru comes several hundred years later with the appearance of more fully developed maize and the Cupisnique culture of north Peru. The most reliable radiocarbon dating association with Cupisnique culture is the mean date of 715 B.C. (Libby 1952b, no. 75).

Historical connections between Middle American cultures of about 700 B.C. and Peruvian Cupisnique are suggested by much more than the common possession of developed maize. As Porter Weaver (1953) has shown, there are a number of fairly complex items which are shared by Cupisnique and the Valley of Mexico Tlatilco phase. Tlatilco appears to date somewhere in the middle Formative sequence of Mexico. Such a placement would be approximately midway between the Early Zacatenco and Cuicuilco phases whose previously cited dates are 1350 and 400 B.C., respectively. Such a time position is reasonably consistent with the Cupisnique radiocarbon dates, and this chronological alignment enhances the possibilities of Middle American–Peruvian diffusions of Tlatilco-Cupisnique culture elements (see Wauchope 1954, "Scheme A" for a similar alignment). One of the trait elements which Cupisnique and Tlatilco share is rocker-stamped pottery. In general, rocker-stamped ware has a consistent middle to late Formative time position wherever it is found in Middle America. Between Honduras and Peru the rocker-stamped technique has been found in only one locality. This is on the lower Magdalena River in northern Colombia where Reichel-Dolmatoff (1954) places it at the bottom of a sequence of polychrome wares and postulates a respectable antiquity for it. In Peru, rocker-stamped pottery is known only from Cupisnique and other Chavín horizon phases. Traits besides the one of rocker-stamped decoration of pottery which link Tlatilco and Cupisnique include stirrup-spouted vessels, combined incised and painted pottery, predominance of polished black-brown wares, whistling jars, the jaguar motif, and pottery stamps. All these traits are found in one or another region of the interlying Ecuadorian–Colombian–Central American areas, but they are not found as a complex nor can their earliest occurrences be defined as to sequence position.

Another important trait which is first known from Peru on the Chavín horizon is the platform mound used as a base for presumed religious or politicoreligious buildings. In coastal Peru these are constructed largely of adobe; in Middle America they consist, variously, of adobe, rubble, and stone masonry. In Middle America, as we have noted before, the platform mound is a late Formative trait in most regions although it appears to be somewhat earlier in the Guatemalan highlands (Libby 1954, no. 886—1017±240 B.C.—Majadas phase[2]). Thus, although platform mounds are not associated with the Tlatilco phase in the Valley of Mexico middle Formative, they are widespread throughout Middle America at a slightly later time and, in Guatemala, seem to be as early as, or earlier than, Tlatilco. It is suggested that the idea of the platform mound diffused from Middle America to Peru between 1000 and 500 B.C. and that it was a part of the same general diffusion that introduced developed maize and rocker-stamped pottery. This is, in effect, a restatement of Spinden's "Archaic" hypothesis. At the present time it cannot be proved, but the typological, stratigraphic, and radiocarbon dating evidences so far assembled favor the interpretation. Temple or platform mounds are found in Nicaragua and Costa Rica (Strong 1948b), and a few small ones have been reported from Panama (Stirling 1949). Large mounds are known from parts of the Ecuadorian coast, but in Colombia mound building seems to have been restricted mainly to burial tumuli (Bennett 1946c; Hernandez de Alba 1946). Nowhere in these geographically intervening areas can the earliest appearances of platform mounds be dated securely or with reference to Middle American sequences. The distributional data, thus, do little to support the hypothesis of the diffusion of the platform mound from Middle America to Peru, but, at the same time, they do not rule it out.

Historical contact between Middle America and Peru seems to have continued, following these earliest evidences for diffusion. Resist-dye painting of pottery, which in Peru is just post-Chavín horizon, has its first Valley of Mexico occurrences as a minority type in Tlatilco and as a more important type in the late Formative Ticoman phase (Vaillant 1931). This is, for the most part, the chronological position of negative painted ware in other Middle American regions. An exception is Usulutan ware which, in the Guatemalan highlands, is as early as the Las Charcas phase. There is, however, some doubt whether Usulutan is a resist-dye technique. Considering the popularity of negative painted ware in intervening Ecuador, Colombia, and much of lower Central America, it is reasonable to suspect that it diffused between Peru and Middle America. Inasmuch as chronological priority cannot be established for either the Middle American or the Peruvian negative painting occurrences, the point of origin of the technique is obscure. Its greatest frequency would appear to be in the north Peruvian and Ecuadorian highlands.

Another technical trait, the figurine mold, has a later inception than negative painting or any of the traits yet discussed. It first occurs in the Valley of Mexico in the early Classic

Teotihuacan III (Xolalpan) phase (Armillas 1950), where moldmade figurines are common. In the Maya region the date for the figurine mold seems to be a few centuries later, coincident with the late Classic Tepeu phase. In Peru, the first moldmade figurines date from the Mochica culture of the north coast. The Teotihuacan III (or Xolalpan) phase of the Valley of Mexico, as placed on the early Classic horizon, would date from about A.D. 300–600 if we follow the 11.16.0.0.0 correlation as it applies to the cross-datable Tzakol phase of lowland Maya. Following the 12.9.0.0.0 correlation, these dates for Teotihuacan III might be pushed back to about A.D. 0–300. Radiocarbon is of little or no help in dating Teotihuacan III.[3] In Peru, the Mochica date which seems most consistent with other dates and with the stratigraphic record is A.D. 112±190 (Libby 1951, no. 619). From this, about all we can conclude is that the use of the mold appeared in the early centuries of the Christian Era in the Valley of Mexico and in north Peru. No continuity of distribution by land from Mexico to Peru can be demonstrated, but the argument for diffusion is strengthened by the occurrences of moldmade figurines on the north and central coasts of Ecuador. In the Guayas region of Ecuador, moldmade figurines first date from the middle periods of the prehistoric sequences (Bushnell 1951)—a position which can be reconciled, in a general way, with their Classic-stage chronological appearance in Peru and Mexico. Added to this, there are a number of rather specific resemblances between figurines of various Mexican regions and those of the Ecuadorian coast (Lehmann 1948, 1951). There is in all this a strong suggestion of contacts by sea between Middle America and Ecuador-Peru which were responsible for the diffusion of the figurine mold as early as the first centuries of the first millennium A.D. The center of origin of the figurine mold in the Americas is uncertain, but the ancient and well-established tradition of handmade figurines in the Formative phases of Mexico offers a logical situation for the development of the mold device.

Metallurgy—in the sense of technical processes such as casting, gilding, annealing, soldering, and alloying—appears to have its earliest American centers in Peru. On the north coast metalwork goes back to the Chavín horizon (Lothrop 1941), and by the Gallinazo phases of the late Formative–early Classic it was well developed. Gold and copper and alloys of these were the principal metals of the Formative and Classic; silver and bronze came into common use in the Postclassic. Both ornaments and utilitarian artifacts were fashioned. The age of metallurgy in Ecuador and Colombia is unknown, but it seems likely that the Guangala-phase occurrences of copper tools and ornaments (Bushnell 1951) are contemporaneous with the Peru Classic periods. Colombian metallurgical centers, such as the Quimbaya, may have arisen as the result of Ecuadorian and Peruvian stimuli. Certainly the Panamanian, Costa Rican, and Nicaraguan prehistoric metalcraft is closely allied to Colombia both in technology and in style, and all these lower Central American metallurgical developments appear to be relatively late (within the last five hundred years preceding the Spanish conquests). Although some metal trade objects undoubtedly reached Middle America from lower Central America, it is likely that the most important Mexican metallurgical centers resulted from direct sea trade with Peru or Ecuador. The abundance and variety of metals in southwest and west Mexico substantiate this. Middle American metals are generally thought of as being entirely Postclassic, but occasional copper and gold finds come from contexts which are Classic and, perhaps, even earlier (Sorenson 1954). Continued research in west Mexico may reveal a deeper tradition of metallurgy than has heretofore been admitted for Middle America.

There are other traits which strongly indicate the possibility of at least an occasional coastwise sea trade between Middle America and Peru-Ecuador on a relatively late time horizon (see Kidder 1940). Pottery, reminiscent of Postclassic Peru in shape and design, has been found in Pacific Guatemala (Dieseldorf 1933, pl. 53, fig. 141). A pottery seal from the Ecuadorian coast has a design which incorporates the Middle American concept of the speech scroll (Brainerd 1953). These and other items suggest a pattern of random acceptance, and rejection, in the diffusion between the two areas—a pattern consistent with intermittent and casual contacts.

In summation, the archaeological records in the Middle American and Peruvian centers support the hypothesis of an early and significant contact between the two areas. Maize agriculture, temple platform mounds, and several ceramic traits may have been diffused at a time between 1000 and 500 B.C. As there is a still earlier record of agricultural-sedentary, pottery-making civilization in Middle America, it is further suggested that this primary diffusion moved from Middle America to Peru. For later times, these evidences of contact continue to appear in both the Middle American and Peruvian sequences. The direction of diffusion can only be postulated, but there is a suggestion that it was, first, from north to south and, later, from south to north.

So far this discussion has not taken into account the question of contacts between Old and New World. Nuclear America has been treated as an entity, separate in its history, from the Old World Oikoumene. This may have been the case, but we are, as yet, unable to rule out all possibilities of trans-Pacific diffusion. There are a number of writings on this theme, and they cannot be dealt with, or even summarized, here. I am unconvinced of the linkages of style, in art and architecture, which have been advanced (Heine-Geldern and Ekholm 1951; Ekholm 1953). On the other hand, certain technical inventions, modes, or complex features do argue for Precolumbian contact. Some of these traits, like the well-known patolli game, may be of trans-Pacific derivation, or, possibly, the results of ancient migrations and diffusions across the Bering Straits and down through the Americas. One such trait is the rocker-stamped technique of pottery decoration which we have pointed to as a Middle American–Peruvian connective. Rocker-stamped ware dates back to 2000 B.C. in Mongolia-Manchuria (Liang 1930). I am inclined to believe that it has a common worldwide history. The rocker-stamped technique may have been diffused into the New World from across the Pacific. From an original American focus in Middle America it may have spread to Peru (as we have argued), and it may also have spread into the Mississippi and Ohio valleys. We should not, however, overlook the other possibility—that the diffusion of the trait was from north Asia into North America and, thence, from Mississippian and Ohio centers into the pottery complexes of Middle America. Radiocarbon dates on the rocker-stamped technique in the Ohio-Illinois regions range from about 300 B.C. to A.D. 200, seemingly a bit too late to have antedated the Middle American occurrences; but the data and radiocarbon dates are still few, and the question must be kept open.

It is, then, possible that technical and other traits and elements of the New World civilizations are Old World inventions and that they have, by one route or another, moved into Middle America or Peru. I do not feel, however, that these possibilities invalidate the arguments for diffusion within the Nuclear American orbit. It is a possibility, but in my opinion a very remote one, that trans-Pacific diffusions introduced the same trait onto the shores of both Middle America and Peru, thereby complicating the timing and tracing of diffusion between these two areas.

Configurational Correlation of Middle American and Peruvian Sequences

In the preceding section an attempt was made to align Peruvian and Middle American archaeological sequences with absolute time and, thereby, with each other. In so doing, certain culture elements in the two sequences have been brought into approximate chronological juxtaposition, and this has served to suggest diffusion and a degree of historical unity between the two areas. It is not, however, these occasional similarities of element content (of which there are many more than the few just described) which provide the most spectacular resemblances between the high civilizations of Precolumbian Middle America and Peru but the striking likenesses in total cultural configuration.

These configurational parallels in the rise of Middle American and Peruvian civilizations are evident in the synopses which have been presented in this paper. They may be summarized here.

On the Formative stage, Middle America and Peru are similar in that the agricultural village is the basic community. Significant cultural content, as well as treatment of content, is shared by the two areas. Arts and crafts show competence but lack the aesthetic brilliance of the later Classic stages. Special structures, probably of a religious nature, were built on flat-topped pyramidal mounds. Throughout, the Formative population seems to have increased. Differences are seen in the presence of a "Village Formative," or early Formative, period in Middle America, where religious or central structures are lacking (Wauchope 1950b; MacNeish 1954), and in the absence of a comparable "Village Formative" in Peru.[4] The Peruvian Formative, at least on the north coast, begins with temple mound structures. In other words, the Peruvian Formative has a closer configurational resemblance to Middle American late Formative. There is also, in the beginning of the Peruvian Formative, the Chavín art style and its remarkable distribution. A partial parallel to this is the Middle American, late-Formative Olmec style, although the intensity and wide geographical spread of Olmec is not as great as that of Chavín. Military architecture characterizes the Peruvian Formative in Post-Chavín times; it was unknown in the Middle American Formative.

Classic-stage configurations in Middle America resemble those of Peru in the achievement of a climax in pyramid mound and temple construction. In both areas this was foreshadowed in the Formative. During the Classic there was a mutual trend in the construction of what appear to be "palaces" (elaborate multiroomed buildings) in connection with ceremonial centers. Arts and crafts were brought to a peak of refinement and elaboration. Regionalism in style was marked—more so than in the preceding Formative or the succeeding Postclassic. Differences at this time are striking. Although we are speaking mainly of configuration, there are sharp distinctions in cultural content and in emphasis of content that deserve to be mentioned. Metallurgy and the working of gold, copper, and alloys was common to most of Peru but rare or absent in Middle America. The precious material of the latter area was jade rather than gold. Irrigation and terracing begun in the Peruvian Formative was perfected in the Classic. The evidence for Classic-period appearances of these traits in Middle America is uncertain. Writing and the calendar were carried to great heights in some parts of Middle America on the Classic level and were possessed in all parts. Comparable developments are lacking in Peru. Organized warfare and conquest states are very much a part of the Peruvian Classic, at least as far as the north coast is concerned. Although organized fighting and conflict were not completely absent from Middle America at this time, there is much less evidence for them in the archaeological record than there is in the central Andes.

Middle American–Peruvian resemblances on the Postclassic stage include the phenomenon of cultural fusion over multiple regions and the apparent large-scale movements of peoples. Probably related to this is the tendency for increased military activities and empire building. In Peru there were Classic forerunners of these trends, but in Middle America the change seems to have been a sharper one. In certain regions of both areas there are evidences of urban concentrations of populations during the Postclassic.

In Peru this trend can be traced from the Classic; in Middle America there are some evidences of earlier urbanism but the record for the Postclassic is more convincing. In both areas there are indications of the growing power of secular authority in the Postclassic. There are significant differences between the Peruvian and Middle American civilizations on this late stage, and knowledge of some of these comes from ethnohistoric accounts in addition to the archaeological record. Although the two areas share the pattern of cultural fusion of their component regions at this time, it is interesting that horizon style phenomena are Peruvian but not Middle American. In the latter area certain traits like Fine Orange ware or the basal-flanged bowl are widely distributed at specific periods; but Middle American styles, in the sense of a complex iconography, do not have the same far-flung distributions and pervasive qualities that characterize Peruvian Chavín, Tiahuanaco, or Inca. In Peru the Inca state was all-powerful and extended well into the adjoining northern and southern Andes. Effective systems of political and social incorporation had been developed. In Mexico, the Aztec domain was much smaller and less systematically administered. Under the Inca the Peruvian became a government worker or bureaucrat whose duty it was to produce and to distribute the productions; in Middle America strong and independent artisan and merchant classes were important parts of the Aztec nation.

The meaning of these configurational parallels between the Peruvian and the Mexican–Central American cultures has been the source of speculation as to causality (Kroeber 1948a, b; Steward 1948a; Strong 1951; Adams 1956). The differences and divergences have also given rise to speculation (Willey 1950). I do not believe that we can arrive at satisfactory solutions to the problems posed at the present state of Americanist knowledge. We have reviewed the case, or part of the case, for element diffusion between Middle America and Peru, and it is a relatively strong one. The nature of the evidence implies both gradual indirect (Strong 1951) and rapid direct (Lehmann 1951) transferences. In following out the arguments for diffusions it was noted that the major chronological divisions of Middle American and Peruvian archaeology have a rough time coincidence. That is, assuming the correctness of a majority of the radiocarbon dates, the Formative stage in the two areas is largely restricted to the millennium preceding the Christian Era, while the Classic stage appears to begin early in the first millennium A.D. and is estimated to continue until approximately A.D. 1000. Postclassic cultures are, then, confined to the last five hundred years preceding the arrival of the Europeans. Thus, the two configurations of culture growth are not only similar but *synchronous*. This synchroneity—of over two thousand years' duration—is a powerful argument for historical interrelatedness. Yet, in spite of this evidence and the acceptance of the historical relationship between these two areas of Nuclear America, the story is obviously not one of diffusion alone. Styles and other complex patterns of Middle America and Peru are quite distinct, and this suggests a considerable independence in cultural creativeness.

Summary

The New World has an orbit of prehistoric and native agriculture which covers perhaps two thirds of the South American continent and nearly half of North America. The generative center for this diffusion sphere lies in the central areas of Middle America, Peru, and the lands which lie between them. This center is Nuclear America—a sort of American "Oikoumene" comparable to the heartland of civilization of the Old World. The available data of archaeology indicate that sedentary village life, based upon this agriculture, was fully developed by 1500 B.C. and that the actual domestication of the maize plant was at least one thousand years earlier. The evidence also indicates that this kind of culture was widely diffused at a relatively early date. In Middle America and in Peru these sedentary agricultural beginnings of the later American civilizations have been designated as the Formative. Radiocarbon dates suggest that the Middle American Formative cultures had an earlier inception than those of Peru, and a case can be argued for the diffusion of significant Formative elements from Middle America to Peru at a time between 1000 and 500 B.C. The close of the Formative stages and the opening of the Classic stages appear to be roughly synchronous in both major areas—a date of approximately A.D. 1. Throughout the Classic and Postclassic stages there was continued diffusion, direct and indirect, between Peru and Middle America. Traces of some of these Middle American–Peruvian contacts are seen in the intervening regions of lower Central America, Colombia, and Ecuador, but lack of sufficient archaeological sequence information from this geographical intermediate area makes synchronization difficult.

It should be emphasized that the evidences of diffusion between Middle America and Peru are those of culture elements and culture content. In style and patterning the arts and institutions of the two areas are quite distinct. This distinctiveness is more pronounced in the Classic and Postclassic cultures than in those of the Formative. There is little question but what styles and patterns resulted from local creativeness and inventiveness in each area and within smaller local regions of each area.

On a grander scale than either cultural content or cultural patterning are the similarities in overall configurations of culture growth in Middle America and Peru. We do not yet know how to account for these parallels—of trends and emphasis—through time. Perhaps they were conditioned, directed, and given momentum by the intermittent but continued diffusions between the two areas. Perhaps they were largely the result of similar human and social responses to similar situations. And in attempting to appraise the parallels we should not overlook the divergences in cultural configuration. They are of equal interest in the prehistory of Nuclear America and of equal importance in the study of this prehistory for the elucidation of cultural process.

Notes

[1]It should be cautioned that not all radiocarbon dates from Middle America are consistent with each other or with archaeological stratigraphy. About 80 percent of the published dates can be so reconciled or harmonized. These dates have a general tendency to lower the beginning and ending of the Classic-stage phases from previous estimates (A.D. 300–900), which are in cross-dating accord with the 11.16.0.0.0 (Goodman-Thompson) Maya calendrical correlation, to dates (A.D. 0–600) which are closer to the 12.9.0.0.0 (Spinden) correlation.

Archaeologists cannot accept, uncritically, the radiocarbon datings that have, thus far, been provided. At the same time they cannot ignore this important new line of evidence.

[2]The Majadas phase follows the Arevalo phase in which platform mounds are also known.

[3]An averaged date for the immediately preceding Teotihuacan II period is 294±180 B.C. (Arnold and Libby 1951, no. 422). This seems too early, although it can be reconciled with the Cuicuilco dates. A Teotihuacan III reading of 1474±230 B.C. is obviously in error.

[4]An early "Village Formative," as opposed to a later "Temple Formative," seems to hold for most Middle American regions. In Peru the earliest Formative phases of the north coast and north highlands have temple mounds, but in other Peruvian regions the temple or platform mound feature seems to be lacking at this time (Willey and Corbett 1954).

B

THE INTERMEDIATE AREA

The *Intermediate Area* is that territory lying between the southern frontier of the Maya and northern Peru. It is today composed of the countries of Lower Central America, much of Colombia, and Andean and coastal Ecuador. In Precolumbian times it was the land lying between the "high civilizations" of Mesoamerica and those of Peru. The concept of such an Intermediate Area has meaning in the context of Kroeber's (1930b) observation of almost 60 years ago, when he said that all of "Nuclear America"—that portion of the New World extending from Mexico to and including Peru—shared a common cultural content in Precolumbian times. If Kroeber was correct in this assumption—and I have always been inclined to think that he was—then such a commonly held cultural base must have been achieved through mutual borrowing, and the Intermediate Area must have had an important role in such diffusions between Mesoamerica and Peru.

I had touched upon the role of the Intermediate Area in "The Interrelated Rise of the Native Cultures of Middle and South America" (Willey, 1955a); but I wanted to address the subject more directly and did so in the first of the three essays in this section, "The Intermediate Area of Nuclear America: Its Prehistoric Relationships to Middle America and Peru". In 1958, when I wrote it, the great time depth and early complexity of the Intermediate Area cultures were still unknown. I did not realize that agriculture, including maize agriculture, was as early as it was in Ecuador. I speculated that the beginnings of ceramics had diffused southward from Mesoamerica, through the Intermediate Area, into Peru—a speculation that was well off the mark—though I did give myself an escape hatch by saying that "it is possible, of course, that there was a ceramic development in the Intermediate Area antedating that of Middle America and that many of the Formative traits came from here [meaning the Intermediate Area]." As of now, available radiocarbon dates leave little doubt that the earliest securely dated pottery in the Americas is, indeed, in the Intermediate Area, and specifically in Colombia and Ecuador. These and other radiocarbon dates do imply a spread of the pottery-making idea both north and south from the Intermediate Area into Mesoamerica and Peru, respectively. These diffusions took place between 4000 and 2000 B.C.

The extent to which the Intermediate Area may have been precocious in traits other than ceramics remains an open question. Complex society, as attested archaeologically by the construction of special ceremonial or elite centers, appears in Ecuador by *ca.* 2000 B.C. This is earlier than signs of such activity in Mesoamerica and about as early as large mound centers in Peru.

The second paper in this section, "The Mesoamericanization of the Salvadoran-Honduran Periphery: A Symposium Commentary," was written as a summary and commentary for a symposium at the 38th International Congress of Americanists (Stuttgart-Munich, 1968) on the theme of Mesoamerican influences into El Salvador and Honduras. In the symposium, John M. Longyear (1969), in discussing the possibility of Olmec influences in Honduras, had argued that certain ceramics, often found in Olmec sites in Mesoamerica proper, did not in themselves indicate Olmec influence in this southern periphery. Agreeing with him, I stated that it would be more appropriate to consider such pottery as part of a widespread and early "Southern Mesoamerican pottery tradition," which was frequently associated with Olmec art but not inevitably so. He and I differed about the date of the Playa de los Muertos complex. He thought it to be Late Preclassic; I wanted to call it Middle Preclassic. Recent stratigraphic studies at the site would seem to split the difference between us on this issue; they place the earliest phase there, the Zanjos, at 600–400 B.C. (Kennedy 1986). While this span of time is generally considered as Middle Preclassic, it is late Middle Preclassic, or post-Olmec, as Longyear was claiming. One important point that Longyear made was that it was a mistake to think of western Honduras as "peripheral" to Mesoamerica on a Formative or Preclassic time level. I agreed then, and I do so more than ever now. Continued studies in the region—and there have been a good many since 1968—make it clear that the Ulua-Yojoa region of Honduras developed complex societies quite independently from what was going on in the Maya Lowlands or elsewhere in Mesoamerica proper at that time (see Kennedy 1986; Baudez 1986; Sharer 1986).

The papers by Stone (1969), Thompson (1968 Ms.), Borhegyi (1969), and Rands (1969) of the Stuttgart-Munich symposium all discussed Mesoamerican influences into El Salvador–Honduras on Classic or Postclassic time levels. That the principal currents of influence were running from Mesoamerica south and east at these times seemed evident and still does.

The third paper in this group, "Some Thoughts on the Chronological-Developmental Configuration of Lower Central American Cultures," was written in 1981–82 and is concerned with the developmental profile of this part of the Intermediate Area rather than with problems of diffusion. I reviewed how Lower Central America (Panama, Costa Rica, Nicaragua, eastern Honduras, and eastern Salvador) resembled, or failed to resemble, the developmental picture in Mesoamerica, and asked what kind of a chronological-developmental scheme we could apply to the area. I suggested that the agricultural and pottery-making cultures of the area had passed through an "Early Formative" stage characterized by village societies of an egalitarian kind. This had been followed by a "Late Formative" stage featuring the rise of chiefly centers or towns and a complex society. Such Late Formative developments appeared as early as 300 B.C. to A.D. 300—not much later than in Mesoamerica. After that, however, Lower Central America did not follow a Mesoamerican pattern of development. Certainly, it was difficult to detect any broad trends in sociopolitical change.

Shortly after writing the essay, I participated in a School of American Research at Santa Fe seminar on Lower Central American archaeology (Lange and Stone, eds., 1984). This same question of a developmental profile for the area was raised there. The seminar group agreed upon six major "periods," which may also be considered as stages rather than strictly time-delimited periods (see Willey 1984). They are, from earliest to latest:

Period I (?–8000 B.C.). Paleo-Indian or Early Lithic.

Period II (8000–4000 B.C.). Archaic.

Period III (4000–1000 B.C.). Transitional period between hunting-foraging and farming, with the appearance of both manioc and maize and the earliest appearances of pottery.

Periov IV (1000 B.C.–A.D. 500). Period of established sedentary farming life and the subsequent developments of chiefdoms. (As such it would correspond to what I was considering as the latter part of the Early Formative stage plus the Late Formative.)

Period V (A.D. 500–1000). Difficult to characterize other than by such first-trait occurrences as the appearance of metals and, in general, more rapid changes in pottery styles and more regional differentiation among them than in previous periods.

Period VI (A.D. 1000–1500). Also difficult to characterize. Even greater regional distinctiveness in ceramic styles than previously and the indications (such as fortified sites) of increased competition among groups. (It can be seen that for Periods V and VI the seminar was no more successful than I was in breaking down a late "Regional Developmental" stage.)

Attempts to provide major "periods" or "stages" for the other parts of the Intermediate Area (Colombia and Ecuador) also reveal that the developmental configurations for these regions were clearly not the same as those for either Mesoamerica or Peru.

4

The Intermediate Area of Nuclear America: Its Prehistoric Relationships to Middle America and Peru

(From *33rd International Congress of Americanists, San Jose, Costa Rica,* Vol. 1, pp. 184–191, 1959.)

Introduction

The designation *Intermediate Area* refers to the lands between western Honduras and northern Peru, in effect Lower Central America and the North Andes. A concern about the cultural relationships of this Intermediate Area of Nuclear America with areas to the north and to the south is another way of posing the problem of Middle American–Peruvian relationships. By turning the question around in this way I do not mean to imply that Lower Central America and the North Andes are significant only as a conduit through which influences or peoples passed between the two areas of the American high civilizations; but by the logic of geography these interlying lands were a vital part of the affairs of all of Nuclear America, and it is evident that we will not understand properly what went on in any one part of the heartland of agricultural native America until we can view this part with relation to the whole.

In 1928, at a Congress of Americanists meeting, A. L. Kroeber summarized the basic unity of Mexican and Peruvian Indian cultures by pointing to their common sharing of domesticated food plants, farming practices, textiles, ceramics, metallurgy, clothing types, architecture, political forms, and certain iconographic symbols, such as the interlocking fish and double-headed serpent motifs (Kroeber, 1930b, pp. 20–21). Although limiting himself to Peruvian-Mesoamerican comparisons, Kroeber (*ibid.*) embraced the Intermediate Area in the following generalization:

> In fact the general cultural relation may be described as of this order: Mexico and Peru, where they are alike, differ from the intervening regions not in possessing culture material that is lacking there, but in having carried the degree of its development farther. . . . This means in short that, from Mexico to Peru, culture had attained to the continuous level of a plateau so far as its ingredients were concerned, and that the cultural peaks of Mexico in one hemisphere, and Peru in the other, represented not so much additional cultural material shared by the two, as a finer form or more intensive organization or expression of the common . . . material.

This concept of Kroeber's presupposed the early diffusions of the fundamental Nuclear American traits, from whatever points of origin, over the entire vast territory extending from central Mexico to southern Peru. In 1949, at another Congress meeting, W. D. Strong (1951) outlined archaeological sequences of events and traits in Peru and Mesoamerica showing their similarity and, more significantly, their approximate synchroneity. Kroeber's hypothesis was, thus in part substantiated, particularly so in that many of the firmest resemblances were found to be on an early or Formative horizon. Since then, additional archaeological digging and analyses, together with radiocarbon dating, in both Middle America and Peru have further confirmed the soundness of the Formative period linkage between these two areas (Porter/Weaver 1953; Wauchope, 1954; Willey, 1955 a, b).

At this Congress, and in previous writings (Willey and McGimsey, 1954; Reichel-Dolmatoff, 1954, 1957; Estrada, 1956; Evans and Meggers, 1957), you have been made aware of the most recent important developments on this problem of Nuclear American interrelationships: namely, the discovery of archaeological complexes in the intervening or Intermediate Area which relate to the cultures of the Middle American and Peruvian Formative periods. In this short paper I want to review briefly these findings and comparisons and to comment upon what seems to me to be a striking difference in the quality of Intermediate Area culture development in contrast to either Middle America or Peru.

Cultural Relationships of the Intermediate Area

The earliest pottery cultures in the Intermediate Area have been reported from three places: Monagrillo, in Panama; Barlovento, in Colombia; and Valdivia, in Ecuador. All three sites are coastline shell midden stations, and all feature grey-black, unslipped ceramics of simple forms decorated with incisions, punctations, or other modes of plastic surface modification. These pottery complexes are not the same, but they share a similarity over and above that of their general simplicity. The subsistence mode of these old coastal societies is not known definitely; but from the ecological settings, the tool and artifact inventories, and the contrast of these with later cultures in all three regions, it is likely that fishing and collecting outweighed farming. Comparisons to the south indicate Valdivia relationships to the earliest Peruvian pottery phases of the north coast, the Preformative Early Guañape (Strong and Evans, 1952, pp. 206–207) and the pre-Chavínoid levels of Huaca Prieta (Bird, 1948). The time horizon, estimated from Peruvian sequences and radiocarbon dates (Bird, 1951; Kulp, Feely, and Tryon, 1952) is a few centuries prior to 1000 B.C. This coincides reasonably with as yet unreleased dates for the Valdivia phase (C. Evans and B. J. Meggers, personal communication, 1957). Comparisons of these early cultures toward the north are less rewarding. Comparable Preformative assemblages have not yet been found in Middle America. The shell mounds of the south Mexican Pacific coast at Islona de Chantuto (Drucker, 1948) may be a parallel, but evidence from this region is still insufficient. As the Middle American radiocarbon dates for developed, fully agricultural Formative phases extended back earlier than 1000 B.C., it may be that undiscovered Mexican or Guatemalan incipient farming cultures are yet to be revealed; or it may be that the pottery of Monagrillo is a marginal and much reduced imitation of Middle American Formative period ceramics.

Pottery like that of the Middle American and Peruvian Formative period phases has been found in several localities in the Intermediate Area. In Ecuador some of the Valdivia pottery resembles that of Peruvian coastal Chavín. Rocker-stamped sherds and occasional stirrup-mouthed jar fragments are items in point. The succeeding Ecuadorean Chorrera phase of the coast and Guayas Basin continues these Peruvian Formative similarities with spout-and-bridge modeled figure jars and outline-incising of painted designs as well as rocker-stamping. In the phase after the Chorrera, the Guangala, white-on-red, and negative-painted (resist-painted) wares are common (Bushnell, 1951). Thus, the Peruvian north coastal sequence of Chavinoid-Salinar-Gallinazo decorative techniques is paralleled in Ecuador. It is significant, too, that many of the site locations of Chorrera and Guangala suggest an agricultural setting as do their Peruvian counterparts.

The Momíl site, in northern Colombia, near the mouth of the Sinú River, seems to fit on this same horizon. Momíl I phase pottery is monochrome with incised and dentate stamped decoration. Simple bowl and jar forms and flat griddles belong on this level, and solid, handmade pottery figurines are present. In the succeeding Momíl II phase there are rocker-stamped pottery and both positive and negative bichrome and polychrome painted decoration along with tall tripods, hollow mammiform vessel supports, and basal-flanged bowls. Cylinder seals and hollow figurines are also associated. The stone metate and mano appear, and Reichel-Dolmatoff (G. and A. Reichel-Dolmatoff, 1956, pp. 270–72) has suggested that maize may have been introduced at this time, with manioc as the food staple during the preceding Momíl I phase. The Reichel-Dolmatoffs have drawn detailed comparisons between their Momíl material and the north Peruvian Cupisnique-Salinar-Gallinazo sequence, on the one hand, and with various Middle American Formative period cultures, on the other. The linkages are substantial in both directions.

Most of these ceramic traits referred to in making these general Formative period comparisons occur in Middle America toward the end of the Early, or Village, Formative and at the beginning of the Late, or Urban, Formative period (Wauchope, 1950b; Willey, 1955a, b). The bottom dating would be in the neighborhood of 1000 to 800 B.C. while the upper ranges go to the beginning of the Christian Era. These dates correspond to the inception of Peruvian coastal Chavín pottery and the subsequent Salinar and Gallinazo phases; and, presumably, the Colombian and Ecuadorean occurrences of the traits date from about the same time.

It is suggested, then, that during the first millennium B.C. a series of diffusions took place throughout Nuclear America carrying along the ceramic decorative techniques of rocker-stamping, incised outlining of painted zones, and negative or resist-painting. Along with these came stirrup-mouthed jars, spouted vessels, tall tripods, mammiform supports, basal-flanged bowls, pottery seals, and handmade pottery figurines. It is obvious that this was not the rapid spread of a single complex; the distributions of the traits vary both in space and in time, and there are notable differences in the receptions accorded the several traits. For example, pottery figurines and clay seals have been found in small numbers on the Chavín horizon in Peru (Strong, 1925; Larco Hoyle, 1946), but neither enjoyed a vogue in the area as they did in Middle America, Ecuador, and Colombia. On the other hand, stirrup-mouthed jars remained a minor element in Middle American pottery-making, but became the hallmark of Peruvian north coast cultures of virtually all periods. In spite of temporal and spatial variations, this dissemination of traits is confined essentially to the first millennium B.C. and to the Formative periods of Middle America and Peru.

We cannot, as yet, be certain of the origins of these several Nuclear American pottery traits, nor can we plot the paths of their movement. I offer, however, the speculation that most of them spread from Middle America southward through Central America, Colombia, Ecuador, and Peru. This hypothesis is based upon the greater antiquity of Formative-type cultures in Middle America than in Peru. Sedentary, agriculture-based village life and well-developed ceramics have been dated back to 1500 B.C. in Middle America (see dates on Early Zacatenco and Las Charcas, Libby, 1955, C-196, C-885), and cultivated maize is considerably earlier than this (MacNeish, 1958). It is possible, of course, that there was a ceramic development in the Intermediate Area antedating that of Middle America and that the spread of many of the Formative pottery traits came from here. This development might have been allied with an early nonmaize agriculture. We know that plant domestication had been going on in Peru for several centuries prior to the introduction of maize (Bird, 1948); Reichel-Dolmatoff interprets the oldest Momíl levels as being representative of a manioc agriculture; and Rouse (personal communication, 1958) has reasoned that premaize, root-crop cultures, with pottery, once centered in northern South America.

Whatever the point, or points, of origin for these Formative pottery traits, the most curious gap in the overall Nuclear American distribution is Lower Central America. Except for Monagrillo, which has a Preformative or sub-Formative appearance, there is no archaeological complex between Salvador-Honduras and northern Colombia which has the typological or chronological attributes of the Formative period. I am inclined to think that the evidences must be here although they have not yet been isolated. Doris Stone (1948) has noted that there are many pottery elements in Lower Central America which, although on a demonstrably later time level are strongly reminiscent of Middle American Formative types. S. K. Lothrop has called my attention to a Costa Rican–Panamanian pottery style named by Holmes (1888, pp. 87–90; see also MacCurdy, 1911, pp. 96–100) "scarified ware." This "scarified ware," in its vessel forms and alternating use of scratched and red-zoned decoration resembles early Middle American and Peruvian ceramics. Interestingly, a Panamanian grave containing "scarified ware" has also yielded a radiocarbon date of about 200 B.C. (personal communication. S. K. Lothrop, 1958). Perhaps this is a clue to the older horizons in Lower Central America.

Although the basic diffusions resulting in the entity which we call Nuclear America took place in the first millennium B.C., there are other linkages of traits which must date from a later time. A thorough listing and examination of these is beyond the scope of this brief statement, but among the better known are the use of the mold in figurine manufacture and metallurgical techniques. Mold-made figurines seem to be earliest in Middle America in the Teotihuacan Classic period civilization (Armillas, 1950). They are somewhat later than this in the Maya Lowlands (Butler, 1935). In Ecuador they occur in the Guangala phase, and in north Peru they date with the Classic period Mochica. I think the probabilities favor their Middle American origin and southward diffusion. This view is strengthened somewhat by certain stylistic resemblances between Ecuadorean coastal figurines and those of Middle America (Bushnell, 1951; Lehmann, 1951). Metalworking, including the technique of casting, is almost certainly older in South America than in Middle America. Cast and gilded copper and gold ornaments are known in Gallinazo times in north Peru (Willey, 1955a). In Ecuador copper celts are present as early as the Guangala phase (Bushnell, 1951). Farther north, in northwestern Colombia, there are occasional pieces of hammered gold in the Tierra Alta phase, which is probably contemporaneous with Guangala; but it was not until the late Precolumbian Betancí phase that cast gold ornaments were manufactured (G. and A. Reichel-Dolmatoff, 1958). The rich metallurgy of Panama and Costa Rica is not yet satisfactorily dated, but in Middle America metals do not occur until the Late Classic or Postclassic horizons.

The Cultural Significance of the Formative "Great Styles"

In concluding, let me turn again to the Formative level as it has been revealed in Middle America, the Intermediate Area, and Peru. One very striking pattern emerges. In Middle America, at the close of the Early Formative period we have the first signs of great art: the Olmec style. That the Olmec style belongs on this early horizon is now certain. The several radiocarbon dates from La Venta, clustering from 800 to 400 B.C., support this (Drucker, Heizer, and Squier, 1957) as does the placement of the Olmec-impregnated Tlatilco phase in the Valley of Mexico sequence (Porter Weaver, 1953). Contributing also to this Formative dating of Olmec art are the carved bones from Chiapa de Corzo (Agrinier, 1960) and the altar fragments from the Miraflores phase of Kaminaljuyu (personal communication, E. M. Shook and S. B. Miles, 1958). Along with Olmec, and Olmec-related, sculptures are ceremonial centers with large mounds, elaborately furnished burials, and the beginnings of writing and calendrics. The subsequent Classic civilizations of Middle America—Lowland and Highland Maya, Monte Alban, Tajín, Teotihuacan—all draw upon this Formative period art and intellectual achievement. It is as though from Late Formative times forward Middle American societies were participating not only in common technical traditions but in an ideational heritage. In turning to Peru we see an analogy in the great art style of Chavín which, at a time contemporaneous with that of the Olmec horizon, dominated the northern and central parts of the country and also influenced the south. As in the Middle American parallel, a residue of Chavín art is retained in the later Peruvian Classic civilizations of Mochica, Nazca, Recuay, Pucara, and Tiahuanaco. Again, the picture is that of Formative period populations sharing in a widespread idea system and transmitting at least a part of this system to later generations and cultures.

Formative period culture of the Intermediate Area does not adhere to this pattern. There is, as far as we can see, no great style in Lower Central America, Colombia, or Ecuador which will compare with that of the Olmec or the Chavín. It has been suggested (Drucker, 1952, p. 231; see also Wauchope, 1954) that Olmec and Chavín, with their mutual emphasis upon jaguar symbolism, may be related. There are, perhaps, hints of this connection in the intervening area. The San Agustaín sculpture of southern Colombia comes first to mind, with its jaguarized men or demon figures. San Agustín may be relatively early, possibly contemporaneous with the more definitively placed Colombian Momíl culture, although this is uncertain. But compared to either Middle American Olmec or Peruvian Chavín its area of geographical distribution is tiny, and its intrinsic qualities are inferior. Kroeber (1951, p. 214) has described San Agustín as "crude in conception and execution. Everything wavers in this art. . . . The figures are if anything even less extricated from the block than in Highland Peruvian sculpture. At any rate they seem less channeled into a coherent style." I think that these same statements could be made about Manabí art or the stone sculptures of Nicaragua and Costa Rica. If, in the Formative period, certain religious and mythological ideas were gradually transmitted from Middle America to Peru, along with maize agriculture and the ceramic traits I have considered, they did not have the same reception or the same dynamic effect in the Intermediate Area as they did in the two areas of the native American high cultures.

As to why it was that southern Middle America and northern Peru developed, at an early time, these universal idea systems or moral orders—symbolized by great, coherent styles—and the territories in between lagged behind, we can only wonder. Almost certainly, though, the presence of these systems, on a Formative level, presages the subsequent rise of Middle American and Peruvian urban civilizations.

5

The Mesoamericanization of the Salvadoran-Honduran Periphery: A Symposium Commentary

(From *38th International Congress of Americanists, Stuttgart-Munich*, Vol. 1, pp. 536–542, 1969.)

The announced theme of this symposium, to which my comments are addressed, was that of the "Mexicanization" of the Honduran-Salvadoran periphery of Mesoamerica. In effect, the questions posed by Dr. Stone could be phrased as follows. To what degree was this Honduran-Salvadoran territory a part of the culture-area-with-time-depth that we call Mesoamerica? And when and how did the processes of "Mesoamericanization" take place?

The Stone (1969) paper is addressed to these questions and so is the essay by Longyear (1969). There was also a third paper in the original symposium collection, one by J. E. S. Thompson (1968 Ms.), which was concerned with Mesoamerican penetrations into western Honduras and Salvador. Unfortunately, Thompson was unable to appear at the symposium session to read his paper, and it is not published here with the others; however, I was privileged to read it, and, with his permission, have made here a few comments upon it that are of a nature that can be understood by the general reader of Mesoamericana even though Thompson's text is not reproduced. Two other papers which were delivered at the symposium session, and which are published in its proceedings, those by Borhegyi (1969) and Rands (1969), are not directed primarily to the symposium theme. What comments I make upon them here are very tangential and have been developed out of the symposium discussion which followed their presentation rather than from the papers themselves.

I shall deal with the Longyear paper first at greatest length. He deals with the earliest time level of any of the papers in the group—that of the Middle Preclassic Period and the Olmec horizon—and my own interests lie closest to his particular topic. Longyear begins by synthesizing an Olmecoid or La Venta–Tlatilco ceramic complex. Such a complex consists of the pottery types that are associated with Olmec monumental stylistic manifestations in the Veracruz-Tabasco lowlands or that are found with Olmec figurines at

Tlatilco. These pottery types are not in themselves marked by Olmec art, a point which Longyear is at pains to make clear, but are considered as Olmecoid only in the sense of their context. Longyear then compares this La Venta–Tlatilco complex with the Playa de los Muertos pottery of Honduras. There are some trait-for-trait matchings, but these are insufficient to justify the inclusion of Playa de los Muertos into any sort of a greater Olmecoid ceramic complex. Also, the traits which La Venta–Tlatilco and Playa de los Muertos hold in common are those which are rather widely shared by other Mesoamerican Early and Middle Preclassic complexes.

I would agree with all of this and only begin to argue at that point where Longyear attempts to "rule out" Playa de los Muertos on the grounds that it is Late Preclassic rather than Middle Preclassic. To the contrary, I would suggest that Playa de los Muertos is of the Middle Preclassic Period and that it is a part of a very early and widespread pottery tradition. Let us, in developing this discussion, call this larger entity the "Southern Mesoamerican pottery tradition." It is the old tradition that featured such things as flat-bottomed bowls, tall-necked bottles, tecomates, incised zoned red bands, and rocker-stamping. It had its origins in the Early Preclassic, as witnessed at Ocos (Coe, 1961b) or in the early levels of the San Lorenzo site (M. D. Coe, personal communication, 1967). We do not know just where this "Southern Mesoamerican pottery tradition" originated. It appears to be the first well-developed ceramic tradition of the Mesoamerican area although it is preceded by the crude Purron (MacNeish, 1962) and Pox (Brush, 1965) potteries of southern Mexico and may be derived from them. It may also have more remote points of origin in northwestern South America (see, for example, Ford's arguments, 1966). These questions, however, take us beyond the scope of our present theme. For the moment, what is probably more important is that this "Southern Mesoamerican pottery tradition" is, indeed, "southern" in its distribution in the Mesoamerican area and that it is at least a possibility that its origins will prove to lie in a region that we consider to be south of Mesoamerica proper. If so, then the Playa de los Muertos occurrence of the tradition would not be peripheral to the Mesoamerican area at this early time level.

The "Southern Mesoamerican pottery tradition" was succeeded in southern Mesoamerica by what Longyear has called the "Southeastern Usulutan Complex" (or tradition). This "Southeastern Usulutan tradition" appears to have had its center somewhere in the Guatemalan-Salvadoran highlands. It begins in the Middle Preclassic Period although its great horizonal spread, as Longyear indicates, was in the Late Preclassic. Its action is, thus, comparable to, but a step later than, the "Southern Mesoamerican pottery tradition," which, as we have seen, began in the Early Preclassic but enjoyed its widest geographical distribution in the Middle Preclassic. That a few "Southeastern Usulutan tradition" traits, such as the tall-spouted jar form, should be a part of the Playa de los Muertos complex is not too surprising as such traits, along with Usulutan decorated wares, date back as early as the Middle Preclassic Las Charcas phase at Kaminaljuyu (Shook, 1951). But the main impact of the "Southeastern Usulutan pottery tradition" was in the Late Preclassic Period; and in Honduras it is the Ulua Bichrome complex which is on this time level and has these relationships while Playa de los Muertos displays a "Southern Mesoamerican tradition" linkage on the earlier Middle Preclassic level (see Strong, 1948c). This sequence of pottery events in Honduras is now further supported by the recent work of Baudez and Becquelin (1973) in which their Jaral complex appears to relate to the "Southern Mesoamerican pottery tradition" while their Eden complex, which follows in their chronological series, is linked to the "Southeastern Usulutan tradition."

To return to the Olmec style and to the La Venta–Tlatilco ceramic complex, I would see them, in the light of this "Southern Mesoamerican pottery tradition" concept, as follows. The La Venta–Tlatilco complex is a regional manifestation of the more inclusive "Southern Mesoamerican pottery tradition." Playa de los Muertos–Jaral is another. Ocos (Coe, 1961b) and Early Ajalpan (MacNeish, 1962) would be still other examples. In some localities this "Southern Mesoamerican pottery tradition" of flat-bottomed vessels, tecomates, and zoned-red and rocker-stamped decoration became associated with the Olmec monumental art style, in greater or lesser degrees; in other localities it did not. With Longyear, I would consider that the style spread, from its southern Veracruz-Tabasco hearth, in various directions. One such direction was to what was now becoming the southern periphery of an emerging Mesoamerican culture area. For example, we see it in the stone sculptures at Chalchuapa, in Salvador (Boggs, 1950), where, as Longyear suggests, it was probably carried by militaristic or trading expeditions in a true and conscious "Mesoamericanization" of the southern periphery. But this was an event distinct from, and somewhat later than, the quite different diffusional spread of the "Southern Mesoamerican pottery tradition."

Doris Stone's paper treats of a substantially later time level, examining the evidence for the spread of those forces that arose in the Mexican highlands in the Classic and Postclassic Periods and that from there pressed southward to Honduras and Salvador and even beyond. She sees three successive waves of influence—probably carried by actual migrations—into the Sula Plain of northwestern Honduras. From the archaeological evidence, the first of these "invasions" is registered in such items as the Teotihuacan III-type candeleros, slab-footed cylinder tripods, and certain incense burners, all of which are found at the Ulua Valley Travesia–Santa Ana site. This is, of course, the southern peripheral, tail-end occurrence of Early Classic Period Teotihuacan traits that also show up, in varying degrees of intensity, in the Guatemalan highland and Peten–British Honduras sites. The extent to which this was an invasion has been debated. The late A. V. Kidder (Kidder, Jennings, and Shook, 1946) thought that the Teotihuacanos had established a base at Kaminaljuyu in the Guatemalan highlands and supported this hypothesis with architectural as well as ceramic evidence. At Tikal, in the northwest Peten, the Teotihuacan influence is not quite so strong; yet here it enters into monumental art as well as ceramics, and I think it reasonable to assume that the lowland Classic Maya were more than casually affected by Teotihuacan trade (W. R. Coe, 1965). Perhaps the same can be said of the Honduran periphery. In this connection, it is interesting that Stone assumes the Teotihuacan influence to have been brought by a "Nahuat-Pipil" group. This is offered without qualification or discussion, and, of course, it is in line with some of the present thinking about the ethnic and linguistic identity of the builders of Teotihuacan. I suppose that a Nahua identification is the best guess; I personally would favor it; however, there are other opinions, and it might be best to label any Teotihuacan-Nahua linkage as speculative—especially when Nahua linguistic influences into a region as distant as the Honduran periphery are, indirectly, a part of this whole reconstruction.

Stone's second "invasion" is placed at A.D. 700–900, or in the Late Classic Period. She postulates a Tabasco-Usumacinta-Peten route for this, leading into northwestern Honduras. A number of traits are listed, among them, Tlaloc effigy vessels, owl effigy figurine-whistles, and feathered serpent motifs. A similar route is also proposed for a third "invasion." This one is Early Postclassic and Toltec and relates to Plumbate pottery and copperwork. In general, I agree; I do not think that a Nahua or Nahua-inspired movement through the southern Mesoamerican lowlands in the Late Classic and Postclassic can be seriously disputed; there is too much evidence for it. Recently, I have been arguing the case for such an intrusion into the Usumacinta-Pasion drainage as supported by Fine Orange pottery and the stelae art of Seibal (Sabloff and Willey, 1967). This particular intrusion would have been on a Tepeu 3 or ninth-century time level, and I am inclined to see it as the beginning of a Toltec or Toltec-inspired expansion. Such expansionism then continued, more or less intermittently, for the next several centuries. Just how all this might be integrated into Stone's scheme of a "second invasion" and a "third invasion" is uncertain, although most likely it is a part of her "second." Obviously, more study and firm evidence are needed in any attempts to "phase" or "time" these waves of "influence" or "invasion." Further, we must have detailed examinations of the actions and effects of alien traits or Toltec traits into the Mayan and Honduran settings as a prerequisite to a functional understanding of the events that took place.

Thompson (1968 Ms.)—in the paper which I have mentioned but which is not published with the symposium group—was concerned with Pipil incursions in Honduras and Salvador, as well as Mayan expansions in that direction. He offers impressive documentation for the Late Postclassic–ethnohistoric horizon, and on this time level there does not seem to be much doubt that the Maya frontier conformed pretty closely to the present-day eastern and southern boundary of the Republic of Guatemala. For an earlier time period—the Classic—Thompson rejects Lothrop's (1939) Ulua-Yojoa-Lempa line as being too far east and south for a Maya frontier. Thompson accepts such sites as La Union, 35 kilometers southeast of Copan, as Maya but goes no farther. This is a conservative archaeological inference, based on major architectural features such as Maya-style ball courts and vaulted buildings; however, I still think it is a working alternative hypothesis to consider the Ulua-Yojoa Mayoid polychrome wares as truly Maya-made and to hold to Lothrop's frontier for the Late Classic Period. Thompson's argument is so firmly buttressed on the Late Postclassic–ethnohistoric time level that, I think, it overconditions his opinions against earlier Classic Maya territorial expansion to the south. Thompson would bring the Pipil into the Guatemalan-Salvadoran boundary region as early as the Early Classic and, in so doing, suggest a linkage to the Cotzumalhuapa sculptural style. I assume that in this interpretation he is following the recent conclusions of Parsons (1966), on Bilbao, where the Cotzumalhuapa style, and inferentially a Nahua-Pipil presence, is estimated to date to the Early Classic, rather than Thompson's (1948) own previous dating of the Cotzumalhuapa style as Late Classic. All of which, of course, brings us around, again, to Teotihuacan, its ethnic identity, and to Teotihuacan influences in Cotzumalhuapa.

Rands, in his paper, is concerned with Copan, and only in this literal geographic sense does what he has to say fall within the scope of Honduras. I am sure he would agree that Copan art is not in any way, related to Lower Central American sculptural styles, but is, instead, a part of the Maya Lowland tradition and belongs to Mesoamerica proper rather than to a Honduran-Salvadoran perphery of Mesoamerica. In the symposium discussions I put the question as to whether or not he felt that the "non-Maya" elements which he sees in Copan art are in any way related to Lower Central American sculptural styles, such as those best known from Nicaragua and Costa Rica (see Richardson, 1940). His answer was definitely negative although he agreed that it is possible that Guatemalan highland and Pacific coastal Preclassic monumental stone sculpture (see Miles, 1965) might have contributed something to both Copan and Lower Central American styles. This is an idea that needs further exploration. Are the peg-based full-round carved figures that are found in the Guatemalan highlands and attributed to the Preclassic Period related to similar forms found farther south? And does this not suggest an early and close relationship between southern Mesoamerica and Lower Central America?[1]

Borhegyi's paper is devoted to the ball-game in Mesoamerica. In response to my questions about the evidence for the game in Honduras-Salvador he noted that the earliest ball-courts in these regions dated back only to a Late Classic level. This, of course, suggests that the typical Mesoamerican ball-court was one more element brought to the Honduran-Salvadoran "outlanders" by Mayas or Nahuas, presumably after A.D. 700. Yet Borhegyi has also shown us that the ball-game, as attested to by other kinds of archaeological evidence than the ball-courts, has a substantial antiquity in Mesoamerica, going back to the Middle Preclassic in some regions. Figurines depicting ball-players and stone paraphernalia (or stone replicas of paraphernalia?) used in the game date this early. Archaeologists should be alert to such possible clues to the game in Preclassic era contexts in Honduras and Salvador. The presence of the game in these regions at that early time would be another indication of an early close relationship between southern Mesoamerica and Lower Central America to the kind speculated upon in the comments on stone sculpture.

To recapitulate, I do not think we can as yet discuss with any definitiveness a southern boundary to the Mesoamerican culture area on the time level of the Preclassic. Certainly for the Early Preclassic, the period in which our "Southern Mesoamerican pottery tradition" was being generated, we do not have sufficient information to speak of "centers of origin" nor of "peripheries." Indeed, it may be that at this time the southern portion of what was to become the Mesoamerican culture area was more closely affiliated with Honduras and Salvador, and even regions still farther to the south, than it was to central or western Mexico. With the Middle Preclassic, and the rise of the Olmec style and the first great Mesoamerican ceremonial centers, there are some indications that western Honduras and Salvador were becoming "marginal" to the developments taking place to the north; yet even at this time, and on into the Late Preclassic, there are hints of affiliations in important ceremonial aspects of culture between Honduras-Salvador and Guatemala–southern Mexico. In the Classic Period, Maya civilization formed a southern frontier to a Mesoamerican culture area, and Honduras and Salvador followed a somewhat more separate course of development. Mesoamerican elements were diffused or carried south across this frontier, first under the expansive power of the Teotihuacan civilization and later from Classic Maya sources. In the terminal Late Classic and Early Postclassic the "Mesoamericanization" of the southern periphery continued, probably as a part of the general diaspora of Toltec and Toltec-influenced peoples. This process of "Mesoamericanization" was still going on at the time of the European entry into the Americas.

Notes

[1]An observation and an idea suggested by Tatiana Proskouriakoff (personal communication 1962) some time ago.

6

Some Thoughts on the Chronological-Developmental Configuration of Lower Central American Cultures

(From *Gedenkschrift Walter Lehmann, Indiana* No. 7, pp. 177–182, Reprinted by permission of Ibero-Amerikanisches Institut, West Berlin, 1982, and Gebrn. Mann Verlag, West Berlin)

While there have been some general summary treatments of Lower Central American archaeology in recent years (Baudez 1970; Willey 1971b, Chapter 5; Stone 1972), no very satisfactory chronological-developmental scheme has yet been devised to synthesize the area, nor has this question been explored in any depth. An in-depth exploration of the matter is beyond the scope of this brief paper, but I would like to open up the problem on a more self-conscious or explicit level than has been the case up to now.

The very fact that there is no precise and agreed-upon definition of a "Lower Central American culture area" is, in itself, an expression of our uncertainty about synthesis. For working purposes, however, we can take the modern republics of Panama, Costa Rica, Nicaragua, and most of Honduras and Salvador as composing such an area. The southern boundary, at present, must stand as a very arbitrary one; there is little known archaeologically of the Panama-Colombian border country. The northern boundary has received more attention and debate. How does one distinguish between Mesoamerica and Lower Central America? How fast or how fluid was any such line in times past? But, again for our purposes, I think that we can say that the minimum southern border of Mesoamerica would include only far western Honduras and western Salvador, leaving the rest of those countries in Lower Central America.

Let me make one more preface to my remarks. A chronological-developmental scheme is an evolutionary or stage device. It is not a chronological framework based purely on absolute dates. It employs chronology, but chronology is linked to culture content and configuration. The early synthesizing schemes for Mesoamerica were such. They have since become more strictly chronological in their implications, and a recent new scheme attempts to do away with the developmental factor altogether (Price 1976). I think that all archaeologists recognize the difference between the two concepts. Chronology is, obviously, a *sine qua non* of archaeology. Developmental concepts are less basic, and some object to them because they introduce a theoretical element into data handling; however, we are trying to understand, as well as to order, the data, and if we are aware of what we are doing I see no danger in them.

For Lower Central America there have been some tentative beginnings for an area-wide chronology. Perhaps the most thorough-going is Haberland's (1978) recent summarizing statement. In it he was forced, largely, to rely upon radiocarbon dates for the equations of regional columns of culture phases. To a more limited extent he used trait content, such as the appearance of Zoned-Bichrome ceramic decoration, for the construction of some horizons. In gross perspective, of course, he could arrange a developmental sequence beginning with a few Early Lithic or Paleo-Indian type remains. These were followed with a stage of Archaic-type cultures, without ceramics and essentially nonhorticultural. Finally, there is a pottery-making, presumably agricultural stage. Can we generalize in any useful way beyond this on the basis of our present data?

To begin, I think we can admit at the outset that there is little hope of extending Mesoamerican developmental constructs into lower Central America insofar as these would apply to divisions of the pottery-making, farming stage. Lower Central America just does not have the same configurations of demographic, settlement, and sociopolitical development through time that characterize Mesoamerica. Or, at least, it is very difficult to detect them in the archaeological records. But let us review the situation and attempt some comparisons.

To borrow terms, at least tentatively, from Mesoamerica, an Early Formative or an Early Preclassic stage might be projected for Lower Central America. This would be a stage transitional from the hunting and collecting economies of both upland and littorine zones into economically successful farming. Olga Linares and her colleagues (Linares 1976, 1977a; Linares and Ranere 1971) now feel that the Panamanian shell midden Monagrillo culture was, to a degree, horticultural; and, to judge from what was going on elsewhere at this time—as in northwestern South America (Lathrap, Marcos, and Zeidler 1977)—it is reasonable to surmise that both maize and manioc may have been raised in a Lower Central American Early Formative Period as early as 2500–2000 B.C. Unfortunately, Central American archaeologists have not found much to fill out such an Early Formative Period, although Sarigua in Panama (Willey and McGinsey 1954) and Dinarte in Nicaragua (Haberland 1966) may belong in its later time reaches. Such a Lower Central American stage would resemble the pre-Olmec, Early Preclassic or Early Formative in Mesoamerica (Lowe 1978) in being a level of simple village agriculture, early ceramics, and, apparently, of egalitarian society.

A Late Formative stage would find us on somewhat firmer ground in Lower Central America. This would be the Zoned-Bichrome ware horizon of Baudez and Coe (1962) and the Scarified ware horizon of Haberland (1962). The time span here is usually set at about 300 B.C. to A.D. 300, and, as such, is more or less the chronological equivalent of Mesoamerican Late Preclassic and Protoclassic cultures; however, the actual ceramic similarities between the Lower Central American Zoned-Bichrome wares and Mesoamerican pottery are with much earlier Mesoamerican horizons, suggesting a lag phenomenon from an era of Mesoamerican Middle Preclassic contacts (*ca.* 1000–300 B.C.) that had then ceased to continue. Lange (1976) tells us this Lower Central American Late Formative stage was one of successful inland agriculture in Costa Rica, and I think this was probably also true for the various "scarified ware" cultures of far southern Costa Rica and adjacent Panama. From a developmental standpoint, the lower Central American cultures of 300 B.C. to A.D. 300 are strikingly different from those of southern Mesoamerica on this same time level. Indeed, in southern Mesoamerica, Olmec developments of *ca.* 1200 B.C. and later mark the beginnings of complex nonegalitarian societies. Such societies featured central site establishments of large mound structures and monumental art, clearly indicative of a high chiefdom level of organization. For the most part, the Lower Central American archaeological cultures never matched this kind of politico-religious or ceremonial center development, either in a Late Formative stage or later; however, it is pertinent to point to the site of Barriles in far western Panama. It is on the Scarified ware horizon.

> Barriles was a ceremonial center of some importance, as is indicated by a number of sculptures, which are among the largest in Lower Central America. They include lifesize statues of chiefs or warriors usually represented as holding an ax in one hand and a trophy head in the other. Such dignitaries are often shown as being carried 'piggyback' style on the shoulders of other men. Besides the statues, there are huge, obviously ceremonial stone metates or tables several feet high and several feet in length. Assuming the Barriles sculptures to be dated by the associated pottery, we have here an earlier—and more elaborate—aspect of the style of sculpture that has always been associated with the (later) Chriquí phase (Willey 1971b:335).

From this, including the master-and-servant representations in the sculptures, it would appear that a nonegalitarian kind of social order had appeared at some places in Lower Central America in what we are calling its Late Formative stage.

What kind of stage formulations can we project after this? I will suggest a Regional Developmental stage as extending from A.D. 300 to the Spanish Conquest. This terminology derives from usages in northwestern South America. In Ecuador, Meggers (1966) has defined a Regional Developmental Period as running from 500 B.C. to A.D. 500 and as being characterized by a regionalization in ceramic styles after a Late Formative relative uniformity. The Lower Central American Regional Developmental stage would be substantially later than this in actual time, but one could argue, although not altogether convincingly, for ceramic stylistic regionalism, in contrast to uniformity, for this time. For Ecuador Meggers then defined A.D. 500 to 1500 as a period of Integration, of geographically more extensive ceramic stylistic units and geographically larger polities. This distinction between Regional Developmentalism and Integration does not emerge in the Lower Central American data. In fact, it is difficult to split up the Lower Central American Regional Developmental stage in any way other than one of arbitrary ceramic periods—periods which are difficult to project over the entire area. Baudez and Coe (1962) suggest an Early, Middle, and Late Polychrome pottery breakdown for the stage, but this has meaning mainly for the Nicoya Region of northwest Costa Rica. There are suggested differences here, other than those of ceramic style. According to Lange (1978), in the Middle and Late Polychrome Periods, or after A.D. 800, there was a shift from inland back to coastal locations and from farming to a greater dependence on sea foods. The movement may have been occasioned by a climatic shift; or, perhaps, it might have been an attempt to accommodate a population growth which was becoming increasingly too large for the agricultural potential of the lands settled in the Late Formative Zoned-Bichrome Period. To put it another way, was there an inland depopulation at this time, or were both interior and coastal zones carrying their maximum populations as these could be sustained, respectively, by agricultural and marine produce? These questions, however, pertain largely to Pacific and inland Costa Rica, and they may have little meaning for other regions of Lower Central America.

To sum up the stage picture for Lower Central America, I would see, after the initial

Paleo-Indian and Archaic stages, an Early Formative, comparable in its characteristics and implied life styles to that of the Early Formative or Early (pre-Olmec) Preclassic of Mesoamerica. The Lower Central American Late Formative stage sees a step up from egalitarian village farming societies to those which have chiefly centers and a non-egalitarian order. These may have not appeared everywhere, but they were present in parts of the area. In a general developmental way what was happening was comparable to the Middle (Olmec and after) Preclassic and Late Preclassic stages of Mesoamerica, although it is obvious from the nature of the Lower Central American achievements that the societies of the latter area were not developing with the same vigor or rhythms as those of Mesoamerica. The Classic rise of the state and the Postclassic attempts at imperial formations, as these came about in Mesoamerica, were never approached in Lower Central America. Indeeed, a Regional Developmental stage, if this term is taken to mean a significant structural change of society and the sociopolitical order, is difficult to define in Lower Central America. It can be defined, and subdivided for archaeological purposes of chronology, on the base of ceramic stylistic changes—but, probably, little else. This, of course, is a question for future research. At present, it looks as though the cultures of Lower Central America achieved the lower rungs of chiefdom development, stabilized there, and underwent no further major structural changes. Was this because subsistence potential and demographic limitations in Lower Central America precluded the societal sizes and population concentrations that are the requisites for the creation, or the easy reception and assimilation, of the high chiefdom or incipient state-type organization that characterized the Mesoamerican Olmec cultures?

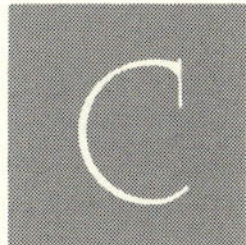

The Maya

The following paper is a straightforward summary synthesis of the archaeology of the Maya Lowlands. I wrote it in the spring of 1981 and published it the following year. It was not reprinted in my collection, *Essays in Maya Archaeology* (Willey 1987). I told the Maya story chronologically: (1) beginnings; (2) the rise of complex society; (3) the Classic civilization; and (4) the Postclassic period. What new data have accrued in the past six years to modify the story?

To begin, the early ceramic occupation of the Swasey phase in northern Belize does not appear to have been as early as 2000 B.C. Norman Hammond (personal communication 1988), who did the original work on Swasey, now feels that the radiocarbon dates are too old, and he is willing to accept an initial date of *ca.* 1000 B.C. This brings Swasey in line with other early Middle Preclassic Period pottery in the Maya Lowlands. Moving up a few centuries in time, we can note that as evidence accumulates it seems more than ever certain that complex society came into being in the Maya Lowlands in the latter half (600–300 B.C.) of the Middle Preclassic Period. Maya civilization unfolded in the Late Preclassic Period (*ca.* 300 B.C.–A.D. 250), though we still remain somewhat in the dark as to the events and processes of this unfolding. Maya Highland and Pacific Coast cultures were in some way involved, but just how and where remain to be determined.

On the Classic Period level, the most exciting new front in Maya research has come about with the reading of the hieroglyphic stelae texts. What did the ancient Maya say about themselves and their political and dynastic struggles? And how does this contemporary written history compare with the arrangements of sites found on the landscape and the "central place" theoretical implications that might be read into these arrangements? The potential here is enormous (see Culbert 1988).

Postclassic Period information has steadily increased over recent years, and this has brought new interpretations of the data (Sabloff and Andrews, eds., 1985; Chase and

Rice, eds., 1985). The role of the "Toltecs" or "Mexicans" in northern Yucatan is still something of a mystery. We know that the "Classic collapse" was certainly different in the north than in the south. Among other things, it occurred somewhat later and probably was marked by the fall of Chichen Itza at *ca.* A.D. 1250. But the reasons for the "collapse" in the north remain as mysterious as they do in the south.

7

Maya Archaeology

(From *Science*, Vol. 215, pp. 260–267, 1982. Reprinted by permission of *Science* and the AAAS.

Archaeological research into the civilization of the ancient Maya has been going on for more than a century. What do we now know about these former inhabitants of souther Mexico and Central America, their origins, their way of life, and the development of their institutions? A review of the status of the field—its solid background findings, its more important recent discoveries, and its intriguing new interpretations—seems in order.[1]

The focus of this article is on what archaeologists have traditionally referred to as Classic Maya civilization, which is represented by those ruined cities, monuments, and other remains that are found in the low-lying tropical terrain of southern Mexico and adjacent Central America (Figures 7.1 and 7.2). It is here that the famed Precolumbian stone temples and palaces, monumental sculptures, and mysterious hieroglyphic inscriptions were explored and brought to the attention of an extensive American and European reading public by John Lloyd Stephens and Frederick Catherwood in the 1840s. The ancient Maya who built these lowland cities did not exist in complete isolation. To the south were other peoples, also of Mayan speech, who occupied the region generally referred to as the Maya highlands and who had a well-developed civilization comparable in antiquity to that of the lowland region; the Maya of both regions were also related culturally, in greater or lesser degrees, to other peoples and civilizations of the larger Precolumbian world, which is referred to as Mesoamerica. Thus, any attempt to understand the lowland Maya past demands some attention to this larger cultural setting and context.[2]

Maya archaeology, like any other branch of the discipline, is dependent primarily on material remains; on sites, monuments, and artifacts; and on settlement pattern dispositions and the ecological interface between people and the natural environment; at the same time a traditional direction of Maya studies, that dealing with hieroglyphic inscrip-

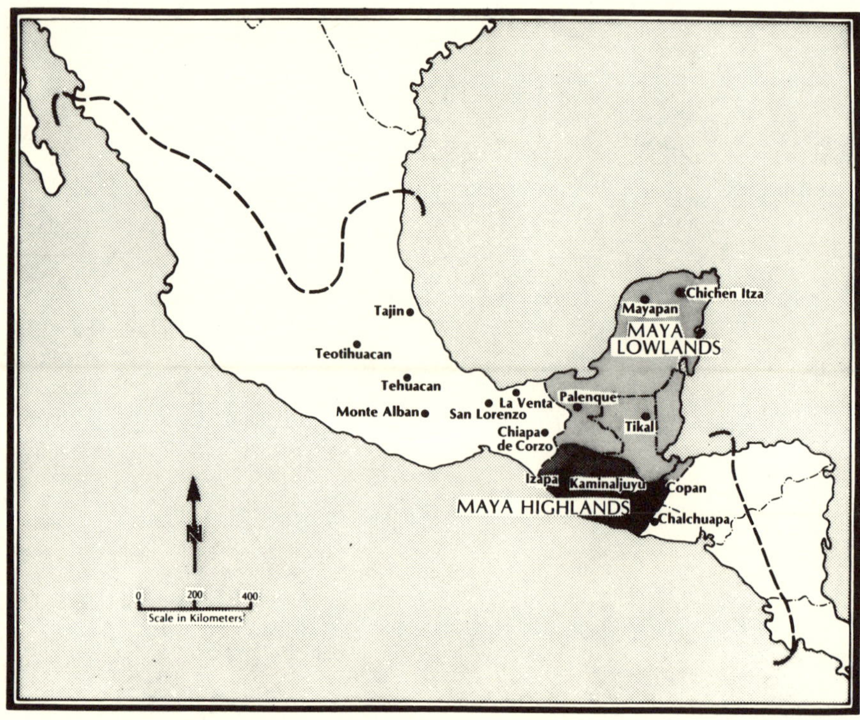

Figure 7.1. Mesoamerica and the Maya lowland and highland regions with important archaeological sites indicated.

tions and their decipherment, has continued to be vigorously pursued.[3] Thus, unlike any other branch of American prehistory, Maya archaeology is "text aided." For example, specific individuals and events can be identified from contemporary written texts as far back as the fourth and fifth centuries A.D., or a thousand years before Columbus made his New World landfalls. Maya archaeological studies are further enriched by an ethnohistorical literature dating to the time of the Spanish Conquest,[4] and interpretation of the Maya past is, in addition, expedited by modern ethnological studies among the living Maya descendants.[5] Finally, students of modern and historically known Mayan languages have made significant contributions to the archaeologist's understanding of the Maya past through their reconstructions of migrations of peoples and the content and nature of the cultures and societies involved.[6]

Beginnings

Until recently the archaeological record in the Maya lowlands began with evidences of pottery-making village farmers.[7] Other regions of Mesoamerica were known to have sites and remains of preceramic hunters and food collectors, but these had not been disclosed in the tropical lowlands. Now, however, evidence has been brought forward from Belize that indicates the presence of such preagricultural populations, perhaps as early as 9000 B.C.[8] The stone artifacts found in these Belizean sites imply a development generally

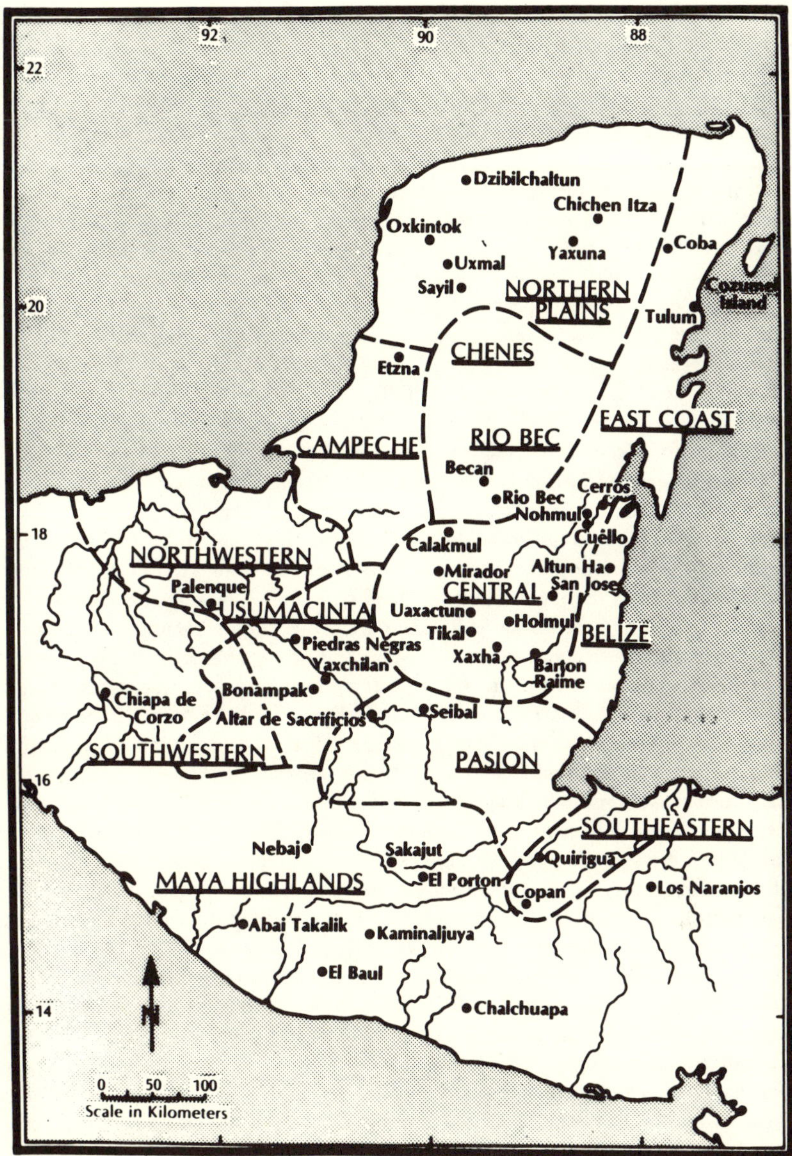

Figure 7.2. The major Maya regions, subregional or zonal divisions of the lowlands, and important archaeological sites.

consistent with that known in other parts of Mesoamerica and the New World: an early shift from Pleistocene hunting to hunting, fishing, and gathering followed by a steadily increasing sedentariness and a selection of living sites suitable for plant cultivation. Apparently the lithic implements of the latest preceramic Belizean complexes are similar or identical to those of the earliest pottery and farming sites of the same region, suggesting a degree of cultural and, perhaps, population continuity.

The earliest Belizean pottery phase, designated as the Swasey and discovered at the site of Cuello, is dated by radiocarbon to a time range of 2000 to 1000 B.C., which is the full span of what archaeologists call the Early Preclassic or Early Formative period.[9] This early Swasey pottery from Belize raises some interesting questions about its relation to other early pottery complexes in Mesoamerica and to other early pottery styles in the Americas at large. In Mesoamerica only the Purron [10] ceramics of the Tehuacan Valley and the Pox[11] pottery of the Guerrero coast are earlier (~2400 B.C.), but neither of these styles closely resembles Swasey. The same is true of the earliest known New World pottery complexes, those of northern Colombia and coastal Ecuador, which date back to about 3000 B.C..[12] Provisionally, at least, the Swasey pottery would seem to pertain to a southern Mesoamerican ceramic tradition, also represented by the early pottery groups of the Chiapas Pacific Coast[13], the Veracruz-Tabasco Gulf Coast[14], and, perhaps, the Valley of Oaxaca[15], all of which date in the range 1600 to 1400 B.C. This tradition continues in these regions for several centuries as it does in the Maya lowlands.

This preoccupation with early pottery and the relationships among its several styles is explained by the archaeologist's concern with origins. When did the earliest Mayan-speaking peoples come to the lowlands and where did they come from? A few years back two explanations of the origins of these people were posited: one, a movement of pottery-making farmers from the Guatemalan highland region into lowlands, or, alternatively, a movement of similar ceramic-agriculturalists from the Olmec Veracruz-Tabasco Gulf Coast eastward into what was to become Maya country. Historical linguists seemed to favor the first possibility. In their view a proto-Mayan language, from which all later known Mayan languages were derived, had its formation in the Guatemalan highlands at about 2200 B.C. From this region Mayan speakers began to descend into the lowlands at some time between 1400 and 1000 B.C. [6,16] But the recent evidence from Belize of preceramic occupations in the lowlands, as well as that of the early Swasey pottery, throw some doubts on this reconstruction. If there was a preceramic-to-ceramic cultural continuity in Belize, might there not also have been some population continuity and linguistic continuity? In any event, pursued this far the question of Maya lowland origins dissolves into tenuousness and speculation. In brief, the "beginnings" in any archaeological reconstruction are those of the sites, ceramics, and artifacts of the Early Preclassic (2000 to 1000 B.C.) and Middle Preclassic (1000 to 400 B.C.) occupation of the lowlands.

The villages of the Swasey,[9], Xe,[17], Mamom,[18] and related early Maya lowland settlements represent small communities of 200 to 300 persons at most. They were sustained by maize farming; manioc may have been grown; and hunting, fishing, and forest plant collecting were important subsistence adjuncts. The competently made pottery of these villagers can be divided into rough-surfaced storage and cooking vessels and more carefully finished and polished wares with simple incision and two-color decoration. There are few, if any, pieces that could be designated as luxury wares. Small human figurines of clay are of the handmade styles similar to those manufactured elsewhere in Mesoamerica at this same time. The presence of obsidian cores and bladelets (small prismatic flint or obsidian blades) in some sites reveals trade contacts with the Guatemalan highlands to the south. As early as the Swasey phase the villagers were constructing houses of wood and thatch with lime-plaster floors. These buildings were placed on low earth mounds or earth-rock platforms, and there was a tradition of constructing one platform over another so that in time some platforms took on the aspect of a most important, central, or public building. At the Cuello site[19] and at Altar de

Sacrificios[17] in the Petén of Guatemala these more imposing platforms, especially toward the end of the Middle Preclassic, were associated with more finely furnished burials that are indicative of the higher status of the persons interred. There can be little dispute about the rise of ceremonialism and sociopolitical authority in this gradual lowland Maya cultural development of the Middle Preclassic, and it can be easily argued that this development flows on into the architecturally imposing precincts of the subsequent Classic Maya civilization. At some point in this Middle Preclassic evolution Maya society changed from an essentially egalitarian to a more complex, nonegalitarian order.

The Rise of Complex Society

In examining the rise of nonegalitarian or complex society in the Maya lowlands it is well to view this in the perspective of what was happening in other parts of Mesoamerica. Large platform constructions, presumably of a public or politicoreligious nature, appeared in the Olmec region of the Gulf Coast by 1250 to 1150 B.C.[20] These constructions were also associated with a monumental art style, that of the well-known Olmec stone sculptures. Such archaeological manifestations strongly imply a ranked society with authority vested in permanent leaders. In the Valley of Oaxaca sizable platform constructions and a settlement hierarchy of principal centers and satellite communities also suggest an increasing complexity in the social order at about the same time;[21] there is some evidence of similar developments from Pacific Guatemala–Chiapas and adjoining highland regions by the beginning of the Middle Preclassic.[22] Thus, the lowland Maya may have been influenced by neighbors who were somewhat more advanced socially and politically. With known trading contacts with these neighbors, some ideological borrowing on the part of the lowland Maya would not be surprising. At the same time, *in situ* processes of social and cultural growth were at work in the Maya lowlands, and the rise of complex society cannot be explained as the result of diffusion alone. The entire Preclassic was a time of population growth, and the social and economic conditions of the lowlands were such as to ready them for the acceptance of the social inventions that constitute a complex sociopolitical structure.

An examination of the archaeological records at a number of lowland Maya sites, such as Altar de Sacrificios,[17] Uaxactun,[18,23] and Tikal,[24] reveals a similar story of the development of sociopolitical complexity. At Altar de Sacrificios the earliest central residential patio group from the beginning of the Middle Preclassic was a simple arrangement of small houses. By the end of that period, several hundred years later, this same residential complex had been greatly enlarged, and the largest mound was some 4 meters high. In the succeeding Late Preclassic and Protoclassic periods, or from about 400 B.C. to A.D. 250, this group included a pyramid mound that was stone-faced, terraced, and had an impressive stairway. The height of this temple pyramid was 13 m, and its terraces were adorned with stucco reliefs and carved stone censer-altars (stone altars with basins in which a substance, probably copal gum, had been burned as incense). Uaxactun shows a similar Late Preclassic–Protoclassic architectural florescence; and at Tikal, destined to be the greatest lowland Classic center, earlier and simpler Middle Preclassic occupation levels are succeeded by corbeled vault tomb construction, great pyramids and platforms, elaborate mortuary furnishings, and eventually hieroglyphic texts.

We know that these were not separate, isolated evolutions. For example, large-scale settlement pattern studies[25] show other major or primary centers, somewhat smaller secondary centers, and centers of tertiary size. Clustered around these centers, and also found throughout the landscape between centers, are numerous residential mounds or house mounds. In effect, there was a vast system that was interlinked in many ways. Political control radiating out of the major centers was undoubtedly one linking mechanism, although it is unlikely that there was ever a single territorial state in the Maya lowlands, at least in late Preclassic times. The centers and their satellites were also linked by trade in commodities such as food products, raw materials, and manufactured goods. Craft specialization appeared as early as the Late Preclassic. For instance, at Colha,[26] in northern Belize, there are huge deposits of chert wastage from workshops where thousands of bifaces and other tools and weapons were manufactured and then transported to a series of other centers, all several kilometers from Colha. Trade over even greater distances is also reflected in the increase in foreign and exotic items in lowland Maya, Late Preclassic elite graves. Foreign imports such as obsidian were found in earlier Preclassic lowland sites, but now the volume of such trade must have been much greater. Marine shells from both the Caribbean and Pacific coasts were a frequent item of trade. Highland jade, pyrites, and other stones or minerals were also imported, both in their raw states and as manufactured pieces. What the lowland Maya exchanged in return is still the subject of speculation, although it has been suggested that such things as jaguar pelts, tropical bird feathers, oils, spices, cacao, and drugs—all of which are foreign to highland environments—might have been the exports that served as an important source of wealth to the rising cities of the lowland Late Preclassic.[27]

As already mentioned, ideas as well as goods were disseminated through trading contacts, and this suggests further consideration of the origins of some of the more specific elements of lowland Maya elite, hierarchical, and ideological culture. The regions of Pacific Guatemala–Chiapas and the bordering highlands appear to have been somewhat in advance of the lowland Maya in the development of complex society. This is true, for example, of the sites of Izapa,[28] Abaj Takalik,[29] and Kaminaljuyu.[30] Artistic and iconographic analyses of the monumental sculptures from these centers suggest that they have earlier derivations in Olmec art and that, in turn, they bear certain resemblances to Late Preclassic, Protoclassic, and Early Classic sculptures of the Maya lowlands. The evolution of monumental art in Preclassic southern Mesoamerica is a complex question, and there are differences among authorities on its interpretation;[29,31] however, all agree that early major art of the Maya lowlands has its prototypes in these Pacific and highland regions.

Hieroglyphic writing is associated with some of the Abaj Takalik and Kaminaljuyu monuments, and these hieroglyphs are clearly related to those that developed so elaborately in the later lowland Maya Classic civilization. Again, the question of origins arises: Was Classic Maya elite or aristocratic culture, as exemplified in its great arts and hieroglyphic system, imported to the lowlands from the highland and Pacific Coast regions? But this question seems to be much too simplified, because there can be no simple answer.[32] A mass transference of a Pacific-highland elite culture, presumably by a migration of peoples, seems unlikely, even though there is evidence of some migration.[33] The many individual evolutions of sites in the Maya lowlands from the Late Preclassic to the Classic tend to preclude this. Furthermore, Pacific-highland Preclassic art and hieroglyphs undergo radical transformations and reworkings in the lowlands almost from their introduction. A borrowing of ideas—and especially ideas that could be integrated into the growing political, social, and commercial world of the Maya lowland cultures, which were evolving on a course somewhat similar to those of their neighbors—was the essential process by which the foundations of Maya Classic civilization were laid down. Studies of Maya civilization have shown that there is no single-source origin for any of its complex institutions. They were synthesized, instead, from many diverse sources, both foreign and local.

THE CLASSIC CIVILIZATION

The Classic Period of lowland Maya civilization is dated from A.D. 250. This is an arbitrary date, set at a few years before the dates of the earliest known Maya initial series stelae. At one time it was thought that these early initial series or long count[34] dates of the Maya calendar were synchronous with the first large temple and palace constructions, the first use of the corbeled vault, most Maya sculpture, hieroglyphic texts, and polychrome pottery, all of which appeared at about the same time. Now it is clear that these hallmarks of Maya Classic civilization were being developed and assembled throughout the Late Preclassic and Protoclassic. Thus, the A.D. 250 date signifies the full crystalization of Maya civilization. The Classic Period has been subdivided into an Early Classic (A.D. 250 to 550) first florescence, a brief interim known as the hiatus (A.D. 550 to 600), a Late Classic (A.D. 600 to 800) second florescence, and a Terminal Classic (A.D. 800 to 1000) dissolution. Some of this chronology, which will be referred to as the Classic Maya cultural system, is presented through a set of subsystems or themes: subsistence, settlement patterns, sociopolitical organization, trade, warfare, and ideology. I will show how these subsystems interlock in an attempt to reproduce a holistic view of Classic Maya civilization.[35]

Maize farming was the basis of Early Preclassic village life in the Maya lowlands, and it continued to be throughout Maya history. A long-fallow swidden method of clearing and planting was observed by the Spaniards in the sixteenth century, and it is probable that this method was very ancient in these tropical lowlands; however, more intensive farming methods were also used and, apparently, on a very large scale.[36] Extensive terracing or "silt trapping" has been reported in the Rio Bec region,[37] and artificially raised fields were constructed in swampy regions, or along sluggish stream beds.[37] These raised fields, which are comparable to the *chinampas* or floating gardens of the Valley of Mexico and similar constructions in other parts of the Americas, are constructed to provide both drainage and irrigation, and their agricultural productiveness far exceeds that of comparable acreages cultivated under a swidden system. Construction of the raised field system is far more costly in labor input than swidden farming, and this and its productiveness imply an association with large concentrated populations. Present evidence suggests that the raised field technology first came into use in the Maya lowlands in the Preclassic and was at its height in the Late Classic, which was also the time of population maximum for the area as a whole. Throughout the Precolumbian Maya past there are also indications that their outfield farming, whether swidden, raised field, or terraced, was supplemented with infield or kitchen-garden cropping of foods such as breadnuts, avocados, palm-nuts, probably manioc, and various fruits.[38] Site debris indicates that hunting of animals, such as deer and peccary, and fishing supplemented the agricultural diet.[39] In fact, by the Late Classic the Maya appear to have been using every available subsistence resource, suggesting population pressure on resources.

Maya settlement pattern studies are closely linked with those of subsistence. Indeed, it was the great numbers of residential mounds, which implied that populations were too large to be supported by long-fallow swidden farming, that made archaeologists search for evidences of more intensive cultivation methods and led eventually to the discoveries of the raised field and terrace systems. Maya ordinary residences are seen archaeologically as small earth and stone mounds, 1 to 2 m high on the average. These are the ubiquitous house mounds referred to in the archaeological literature. They once supported pole and thatch houses similar to those built today by the modern Maya. A standard residential pattern is a grouping of two, three, four, or sometimes more mounds built around a small open patio; these patio groups probably housed extended family units.[40] The patio group residential pattern dates back to the Early Preclassic and has continued throughout Maya history. As noted, house mounds are found both near to and between the temple-palace centers.

One of the major recent debates in Maya archaeology concerns the nature of lowland Maya urbanism.[41] Were the great centers true cities with concentrated populations and functions usually associated with an urban setting? Or were they politicoreligious precincts, occupied permanently only by an elite governing class and visited but occasionally by the supporting mass of an outlying peasantry? The question has not been answered to the satisfaction of all Maya archaeologists, at least in an either-or-fashion; however, residential surveys in and around some principal centers indicate significant population concentrations that certainly approach or attain an urban mode.[42] Thus, at Tikal it is estimated that 50,000 to 70,000 persons lived within a radius of 6 kilometers of the main center, or within an area of about 120 km^2.[40,43] Although this is a more dispersed settlement than that of the estimated 100,000 or 200,000 people who lived within the 20 km^2 zone of the contemporaneous Precolumbian Mexican highland city of Teotihuacan,[44] it would qualify as urban by most standards. Moreover, the urban designation for Tikal seems appropriate in view of the functions of manufacturing and trade that were carried out in this center in addition to those of administration and religion.[45]

What were the relationships among the Maya lowland centers or cities and what was the political structure of ancient Maya society? In the northeastern Petén, for example, Tikal, although the largest city, was not the only one. Uaxactun, 18 km to the north and smaller than Tikal, was still an impressive center with a sizable circumambient residential population. At short distances from both cities were others of a smaller urban order. The impression is that of a hierarchically organized settlement and political order, with great capitals, subcapitals, and so on down the line. As mentioned, this kind of a macrosettlement pattern was already evident in the Late Preclassic, with the rise of complex society, and in the Classic Period, as the population grew and spread throughout the lowlands, it became even more pronounced.

Archaeologists have been trying to plot out ancient domains or politics in these larger patterns through the application of central-place theory and polygonal representations of settlement hierarchies.[46] This work has been supplemented by comparisons of site sizes and by hieroglyphic research whereby emblem glyphs or badges of the various major cities have been used to trace out inferred political allegiances among presumed secondary or tributary centers.[47] One possible sociopolitical model is that of a feudal type of organization, where the largest centers may have been the seats of kings, secondary and tertiary ones the domains of lesser nobles, and the whole supported by an agrarian peasantry.[48] Advances in hieroglyphic research, such as the identification of emblem glyphs, offer substantiations of such a system; texts have been deciphered that describe wars, alliances, intermarriages, and king lists that are reminiscent of the relationships among the royal houses and nobles of medieval Europe.[49] Trade and manufacturing also had roles in the Maya system.[50] The population of Tikal and other urban-like concentrations suggests the rise of a middle class of artisans, traders, and minor bureaucrats. It is not known, however, whether trade was of an open market type or was of a redistributive nature.

Foreign or external influences[32] continued to affect Maya lowland society during the

Classic. Some of the most interesting evidence for this comes from hieroglyphic texts and associated art at Tikal. One fourth-century A.D. text describes a "foreigner," one "Curl Snout," whose accouterments and attendants suggest a close relation with the central Mexican city of Teotihuacan and who married into the local royal family and founded a new lineage.[51] This bit of historical information fits nicely with Teotihuacan influences, as represented in imported pottery styles and the appearance of central Mexican obsidian throughout the Maya lowlands in the Early Classic. Taken together, such evidences begin to outline some of the processes involved in lowland Maya state development.

During the Early Classic it seems probable (at least from evidence of stylistic similarities and hieroglyphic texts) that Tikal maintained a leadership, a hegemony over much of the Maya lowlands, or at least the southern portions, founding dynasties at Quirigua and Copan[52] and marrying its royal daughters to the rulers of other cities.[47] The latter part of the sixth century was the time of the hiatus, a curious slackening of elite activities in most southern Maya lowland cities.[53] Few dates were inscribed on the stelae, few rulers were commemorated, and there was little temple and palace construction. Then shortly after A.D. 600 there was a resurgence of stelae dedication, of building, and of the founding of new cities and the renovating of old ones. Tikal revived, as did many other cities, including Copán, Quirigua, Palenque, and Piedras Negras. It is difficult to say what city had preeminence in the Late Classic. Quite probably it was a time of intense intercity competition, but it also marked an apogee in the Maya achievement.

In attempting to understand Maya civilization we may view it as an integrated system.[35] Agriculture and land use clearly link to demography. Insights into both are provided from settlement pattern information; settlement data, in turn, throw some light on Maya political and social structures, which are further elaborated by interpretations of hieroglyphic texts[51,54] and of art and iconography.[55] The texts and art open up a small window on the ideological world of the Maya. The Classic period spans more than seven centuries, and the conditions and institutions archaeologists are trying to understand were undoubtedly changing ones. Research advances of the future will be addressed to these changes in Maya culture and the processes that brought them about.

The most dramatic change, or set of changes, resulting in the disintegration of classic Maya civilization, began in the ninth century A.D. and continued for 200 years or over the period called the Terminal Classic. The cause of this dissolution or collapse has been the topic of much speculation; natural disasters, disease, crop failures, overpopulation, peasant revolt, foreign wars, and trade failures have been proposed, but no single explanation seems satisfactory.[56] The facts of the collapse can be set down quite simply. Evidences of the decline appear first in the southern lowlands at the close of the eighth century and accelerate rapidly through the ninth century. They are manifest in the cessation of the recording of commemorative dates and stelae dedications and in the slowdown or stoppage of center constructions. Indeed, the phenomena of the collapse are reminiscent of those of the hiatus, but this time there was no recovery. This withering of the elite aspects of the culture was accompanied by the marked depopulation of the once great cities and of much of the surrounding countryside. The processes of disintegration, whatever they may have been, appear to have drifted gradually north, through central Yucatan and eventually into the northern part of that peninsula.

Although there is little consensus about the cause or causes of the Maya collapse, there is one thing about which there is general agreement. This is that the Terminal Classic was a time of radical political and social change throughout much of civilized Mesoamerica. Old Classic period centers of power, in Oaxaca, in central Mexico, and elsewhere, were overthrown and abandoned. New political formations—some of them, like that of the Toltecs, of imperial dimensions—were in the making. Military competition increased. Old trading routes and alliances were rearranged. And whatever the specific causes and events, as these may have occurred from place to place, it seems certain that the Classic Maya civilization of the lowlands was affected by this general unrest.

The Postclassic Period

At about A.D. 1000 a group that is often identified as Toltec settled at and rebuilt an earlier Classic Maya center in northern Yucatan and renamed it Chichen Itza.[57] The Toltec identification may not be strictly correct; these invaders may have been peoples of Maya speech, the Putun Maya, who had lived along the extreme western margins of Classic Maya civilization in the Gulf Coast country of Tabasco.[58] The Putun Maya, who came under Toltec and central Mexican influences earlier than the lowland Maya, were acculturated to Toltec ways and ideologies by the end of the eighth century. From later ethnohistoric accounts these Putun Maya were known as warriors and riverine and coastal canoe traders, and it is possible that their military and commercial incursions were instrumental in setting the Maya decline in motion some 200 years before they actually implanted a city at Chichen Itza.

The establishment of Toltec or Putun Chichen Itza marks the beginning of the Postclassic period in the Maya lowlands. Except for this one great site, the early part of the period is poorly known. In the north some towns and cities of the Terminal Classic continued to be occupied, but populations were reduced, and there was little notable construction. The entire south appears to have been virtually abandoned. Only in the east, in northern Belize, are there former Classic sites that show substantial activity.[59] This locality is the part of the Maya lowlands that was most remote from the Putun homeland.

Chichen Itza's great days were over by the beginning of the thirteenth century. In the Late Postclassic, the period that is sometimes referred to as that of Maya resurgence, the leading city was the walled center of Mayapan in northern Yucatan.[60] The principal religious pyramid of Mayapan appears as a poor and reduced replica of the great Castillo at Chichen Itza; otherwise, the center retains little of the Toltec or Putun tradition. The urban zone within the walls, which measures 2 by 3 km, is estimated to have contained about 12,000 persons, a fraction of the population of the great Classic period cities. It gives the impression of a relatively close-packed arrangement of the standard Maya patio-group residences, as though these had been gathered up and confined within the perimeter of the city's defense wall.

Some archaeologists suggest that the Late Postclassic was an era of active long-distance trade along the coast and that the Maya of Yucatan played an important part in that trade.[61] Archaeological evidences from coastal Tulum and from the island of Cozumel, both Late Postclassic centers, support this, as do sixteenth-century Spanish accounts. It has also been argued that to conceive of a Classic period collapse and a reduced Postclassic civilization is a mistake.[62] As an alternative the concept of an "upward collapse" has been offered; the explanation of the archaeological record is a progressive evolution marked by radical sociopolitical changes, including the abandonment of the values of the Classic period aristocratic elite in favor of an order that laid more stress on extended commerce, the mass distribution of goods, and a greater participation in many spheres of life by larger numbers of people.

Although it is true that there was cultural activity in the northern lowlands during the Postclassic, and especially trading activity in the Late Postclassic, I do not feel that a full review of the archaeological evidence gives much support to this fulsome picture of the last Precolumbian centuries of lowland Maya life. Whatever the nature of activities—at least insofar as these can be measured in material archaeological remains—the present data indicate a definite lack of Late Postclassic population numbers comparable to those of Classic times. If there was, indeed, a greater participation in many spheres of life by larger numbers of people, there were not as many people around to observe this or to have the opportunity to partake in the participation. If a wider view is taken and the field of action expanded beyond the lowland Maya area to Mesoamerica as a whole, there is, perhaps, something to the concept of an upward collapse. Certainly the Postclassic, as has been observed, marked the rise of new state and imperial politics. These, however, radiated out of central Mexico, that ancient locus of early Mesoamerican urbanism and state formation dominated successively by Teotihuacan, the Toltecs, and the Aztecs. This was the region that was in the vanguard of Mesoamerican social, political, and commercial evolution. The lowland Maya were caught up in the processes of this evolution, at a geographic remove and always in a somewhat delayed way; and the trials of their Classic dissolution and their not altogether successful attempts at a Postclassic reintegration reflect their difficulties in attempting to adapt to these processes.

References and Notes

[1]For general background, see J. E. S. Thompson [*The Rise and Fall of Maya Civilization* (Univ. of Oklahoma Press, Norman, ed. 2, 1966)] and M. D. Coe [in *The Maya*, G. Daniel, Ed. (Ancient Peoples and Places Series, Thames & Hudson, New York, 1966)].

[2]For general references, see M. Porter Weaver [*The Axtecs, Maya, and Their Predecessors* (Seminar Press, New York, 1972)] and R. E. W. Adams [*Prehistoric Mesoamerica* (Little, Brown, Boston, 1977)].

[3]D. H. Kelley, *Deciphering the Maya Script* (Univ. of Texas Press, Austin, 1976).

[4]For example, "Landa's relacion de las cosas de Yucatan," a translation of a 16th-century document by A. M. Tozzer [*Pap. Peabody Mus. Archaeol. Ethnol. Harv. Univ.* 18, (1941)], entire volume.

[5]A. Villa Rojas, in *Handbook of Middle American Indians*, R. Wauchope and E. Z. Vogt, Eds. (Univ. of Texas Press, Austin, 1969), vol. 7, pp. 244–275; E. Z. Vogt, *Zinacantan* (Harvard Univ. Press, Cambridge, Mass., 1969).

[6]T. Kaufman, *World Archaeol.* 8, 101 (1976).

[7]G. R. Willey, in *The Origins of Maya Civilization*, R. E. W. Adams, Ed. (Univ. of New Mexico Press, Albuquerque, 1977a), pp. 383–423.

[8]R. S. MacNeish *et al.*, *First Annual Report of the Belize Archaeological Reconnaissance* (Peabody Foundation, Andover, Mass., 1980).

[9]N. Hammond *et al.*, *Am. Antiq.* 44, 92 (1979).

[10]R. S. MacNeish, F. A. Peterson, K. V. Flannery, in *The Prehistory of the Tehucan Valley*, F. Johnson, Ed. (Univ. of Texas Press, Austin, 1970).

[11]C. F. Brush, *Science* 149, 194 (1965).

[12]G. Reichel-Dolmatoff, "Excavaciones arqueologicas en Puerto Hormiga, Departamento de Bolivar, Colombia" (Publicación Antropologia 2, Universidad de Los Andes, Bogotá, 1965); D.

[13]D. W. Lathrap, *Ancient Ecuador* (Field Museum of Natural History, Chicago, 1975).

[14]G. W. Lowe, "The Early Preclassic Barra phase of Alta Mira, Chiapas" (Paper 38, New World Archaeological Foundation, Brigham Young University, Provo, Utah, 1975).

[15]M. D. Coe, in *Dumbarton Oaks Conference on the Olmec*, E. Benson, Ed. (Dumbarton Oaks, Washington, D.C., 1968), pp. 41–78.

[16]K. V. Flannery in *ibid.*, pp. 79–118.

[17]T. Kaufman, personal communication; E. Z. Vogt, in *Desarrollo Cultural de Los Mayas*, E. Z. Vogt and A. Ruz, Eds. (Universidad Nacional de Mexico, Mexico, D. F. 1971a, b), pp. 9–48 and 409–447. It has also been proposed that the earliest ceramics of Belize could be pre-Maya or non-Maya [G. W. Lowe, in *Chronologies in New World Archaeology*, R. E. Taylor and C. W. Meighan, Eds. (Seminar Press, New York, 1978), pp. 331–394.

[17]G. R. Willey, *Pap. Peabody Mus. Archaeol. Ethnol. Harv. Univ.* 64, No. 3 (1973b).

[18]O. G. Ricketson, Jr., and E. B. Ricketson, *Carnegie Inst. Washington Publ. 477* (1937).

[19]N. Hammond, *Antiquity* 54, 176 (1980).

[20]M. D. Coe and R. A. Diehl, *In the Land of the Olmec* (Univ. of Texas Press, Austin, 1980).

[21]K. V. Flannery and J. Marcus, in *Cultural Continuity and Change*, C. Cleland, Ed. (Academic Press, New York, 1976a), pp. 205–221.

[22]M. D. Coe and K. V. Flannery, *Smithson. Contrib. Anthropol. No. 3* (1967).

[23]A. L. Smith, *Carnegie Inst. Washington Publ. 588* (1950).

[24]W. R. Coe, *Expedition*, No. 8 (1965).

[25]W. Ashmore, Ed., *Lowland Maya Settlement Patterns* (Univ. of New Mexico Press, Albuquerque, 1981).

[26]Hestor and Shafer (1984).

[27]B. Voorhies (1982).

[28]V. G. Norman, "Izapa sculpture" (Paper 33, New World Archaeological Foundation, Provo, Utah, 1976).

[29]J. A. Graham, *Actes 42nd Congr. Int. Americanistes* 8, 180 (1979).

[30]S. W. Miles, in *Handbook of Middle American Indians*, R. Wauchope and G. R. Willey, Eds. (Univ. of Texas Press, Austin, 1965), vol. 2, pp. 237–275.

[31]J. Quirarte, *Actes 42nd Congr. Int. Americanistes* 8, 189 (1979).

[32]G. R. Willey, in *Social Process in Maya Prehistory*, N. Hammond, Ed. (Academic Press, New York, 1977b), pp. 58–81.

[33]P. D. Sheets [in *Volcanic Activity and Human Ecology*, P. D. Sheets and D. K. Brayson, Eds. (Academic Press, New York, 1979), pp. 525–564] proposed that the eruption of Ilopango in El Salvador led to migrations from that region to Maya lowlands at about A.D. 200 and that this migration sparked Maya Classic cultural development.

[34]Initial series or long count dates of the Maya refer to a time counting system of days computed in units (days) of descending magnitude of 144,000, 7,200, 360, 20, and 1. This system was reckoned from a mythical starting point in 3114 B.C. Dates associated with the Maya Classic period pertain to the eighth, ninth, and tenth great cycles or *baktuns* (144,000 days). Accessions of rulers to thrones, royal births, deaths, marriages, wars, conquests, and so on, were dated and commemorated in this time counting system. The dates referred to in this article follow a long count-Julian calendrical correlation known as the 11.16.0.0.0.

[35]G. R. Willey, *Man* 15, 249 (1980a).

[36]P. D. Harrison and B. L. Turner II, Eds., *Pre-Hispanic Maya Agriculture* (Univ. of New Mexico Press, Albuquerque, 1978).

[37]B. L. Turner, in (*36*), pp. 163–184.

[38]R. Netting, in *The Origins of Maya Civilization*, R. E. W. Adams, Ed. (Univ. of New Mexico Press, Albuquerque, 1977), pp. 299–334.

[39]F. M. Wiseman, in (*36*), pp. 63–116; F. W. Lange, *Am. Anthropol.* 73, 619, (1971); M. Pohl (1976).

[40]G. R. Willey, in (*25*), pp. 385–415.

[41]M. J. Becker, in *Maya Archaeology and Ethnohistory*, N. Hammond and G. R. Willey, Eds. (Univ. of Texas Press, Austin, 1979), pp. 3–20.

[42]G. R. Willey and D. B. Shimkin, in *The Classic Maya Collapse*, T. P. Culbert, Ed. (Univ. of New Mexico Press, Albuquerque, 1973), pp. 457–502.

[43]W. A. Haviland, *World Archaeol.* 2, 186 (1970). Not only have settlement studies and small residential mound counts been made in the immediate vicinity of Tikal, but these have been conducted around and between other major centers [D. S. Rice and D. E. Puleston, in (*25*), pp. 121–157].

[44]R. F. Millon, *The Teotihuacan Map* (Univ. of Texas Press, Austin, 1973), part I.

[45]M. J. Becker, *Am. Antiq.* 38, 396 (1973); *ibid.*, p. 222.

[46]J. Marcus, *Science*, 180, 911 (1973); N. Hammond, in *Mesoamerican Archaeology: New Approaches*, N. Hammond, Ed. (Duckworth, London, 1974), pp. 313–334.

[47]J. Marcus, *Emblem and State in the Classic Maya Lowlands* (Dumbarton Oaks, Washington, D.C., 1976).

[48]R. E. W. Adams and W. D. Smith, in (*25*), pp. 335–350; W. T. Sanders, in (*25*), pp. 351–370.

[49]The interpretation of the emblem glyphs was first made by H. Berlin [*J. Soc. Americanistes Paris* 47, 111 (1958)]. Historical information from glyphic texts has been interpreted by various scholars but T. Proskouriakoff [*Am. Antiq.* 25, 454 (1960); *Estud. Cultura Maya* 3, 149 (1963)]; *ibid.* 4, 177 (1964)] was one of the first. For references bearing on settlement arrangements and hierarchies and their relation to hieroglyphic texts, see J. P. Molloy and W. L. Rathje [in *Mesoamerican Archaeol-*

ogy: New Approaches, N. Hammond, Ed. (Duckworth, London, 1974), pp. 431–444] and J. Marcus (*47*).

[50] Christopher Jones, personal communication, 1979.

[51]C. Coggins, in *Maya Archaeology and Ethnohistory*, N. Hammond and G. R. Willey, Eds. (Univ. of Texas Press, Austin, 1979a, b), pp. 38–50.

[52]C. Jones and R. Sharer, *Expedition*, No. 23 (1980), p. 11.

[53]G. R. Willey, in *Mesoamerican Archaeology: New Approaches*, N. Hammond, Ed. (Duckworth, London, 1974a), pp. 417–430.

[54]C. Jones, *Am. Antiq.* 42, 28 (1977).

[55]D. E. Puleston [in *Social Process in Maya Prehistory*, N. Hammond, Ed. (Academic Press, New York, 1977), pp. 449–469] links Maya aquatic-agricultural ecology with artistic symbolism in a most convincing way.

[56]T. P. Culbert, Ed., *The Classic Maya Collapse* (Univ. of New Mexico Press, Albuquerque, 1973).

[57]A. M. Tozzer, *Mem. Peabody Mus. Archaeol. Ethnol. Harv. Univ.* 11 and 12 (1957).

[58]J. E. S. Thompson, *Maya History and Religion* (Univ. of Oklahoma Press, Norman, 1970).

[59]Examples are Lamanai, Colha, and Cerros (D. Pendergast, T. R. Hester, D. Freidel, personal communications).

[60]H. E. D. Pollock *et al.*, *Carnegia Inst. Washington Publ. 619* (1962).

[61]J. A. Sabloff and W. L. Rathje, *Sci. Am.* 223, 73 (October 1975).

[62]C. Erasmus, *Southwest. J. Anthropol.* 24, 170 (1968).

The West Indies

In the spring of 1978 a former student of mine, Ricardo Alegria, now a leading West Indian archaeologist and anthropologist, invited me to San Juan, Puerto Rico, and asked if I would be willing to give a public lecture on Taino art. I had long been interested in West Indian archaeology (Willey 1940; Alegria, Nicholson, and Willey 1956; Willey 1976b), though I didn't know much about it. I accepted Alegria's offer in the hope that I would learn something with the assignment.

I made two points in my essay. One is strictly culture-historical and diffusionist. It is an argument for a Mesoamerican involvement in the West Indian ball-game. The game was known ethnographically in Venezuela, and the idea of it may very well have been carried out to the Antilles from the South American mainland in quite early Precolumbian times. However, the peculiar coincidence of carved stone paraphernalia being associated with the ball-courts and the game in both the West Indies and in Mesoamerica—and nowhere else in the New World—seemed to me more than just a coincidence. In my essay, I attempted to explain this as resulting from a Mesoamerican–West Indian connection of a "stimulus" kind. While I do not feel that my case is a certainty, I believe that it deserves serious consideration.

The other fact that particularly interested me about the Taino was of a different nature. It was the peaceful coexistence of their several chiefdoms. While it is true that they fought with the raiding Caribs in late prehistoric times, their relations with each other seem to have been amazingly tranquil as they developed, side by side, frequently on the same islands. It struck me as unusual behavior for chiefly polities—as witnessed by the conditions of endemic warfare among such societies in places like the Amazon, Lower Central America, or the southeastern United States—and hence seemed worthy of comment.

8

Precolumbian Taino Art in Historical and Sociocultural Perspective

(From *La Antropologia Americanista en la Actualidad*, Vol. 1, pp. 113–128, Editores Mexicanos Unidos, Mexico, D.F. 1980. Reprinted by permission of Editores Mexicanos Unidos.)

Introduction

Taino art of the West Indies composes a strikingly distinct style, easily separable from any other in Precolumbian America. It is my intent to review this Taino style from three points of view. First, let us examine it within the framework of West Indian prehistory, its apparent antecedents, course of development, dates, and distributions. Second, what are its possible relationships to styles and cultures of the nearby mainlands of North, Central, and South America? And third, let us try to analyze the ways in which this Taino art articulated with its social and cultural setting.

The West Indian Archaeological Scene

West Indian archaeological cultures are well ordered by types, space, and time (Rouse, 1964; Rouse and Allaire, 1978). A Paleo-Indian ancestry from the mainland is uncertain; but Meso-Indian cultures in the islands date back to the third millennium B.C. (Willey, 1976b). These Meso-Indian cultures are defined by hunting, fishing, and collecting subsistence patterns and by the absence of ceramics. Although they have early beginnings, in some regions, such as western Cuba, they persisted up until the Spanish Conquest, so that they may be said to define a stage rather than a strict chronological period. Their mainland links are uncertain, with hints in lithic and shell technology that point in various directions: Caribbean South America, Florida, and Lower Central America. What is more directly pertinent to our concern with art, and with the evolution of an art style in a later period, is that there are some few evidences in the Meso-Indian cultures of such things as ornamented stone pestles and little carved amulets or ritual objects of wood, stone, and shell which seem to foreshadow later Antillean decorative art (e.g., Rouse, 1964, Fig. 8, D).

Meso-Indian cultures began to be replaced by those of the farming, pottery-making

Neo-Indian stage by about the beginning of the Christian era. This radical change in West Indian life-style seems to signal the appearance of a new people, generally thought to be groups of Arawakan speech who moved out into the islands, along a Trinidad and Lesser Antillean chain, from the South American mainland. It took a few centuries, or until about A.D. 800, for the agricultural pattern to extend through Puerto Rico and Hispaniola and eventually to reach Jamaica and eastern and central Cuba. In other words, this was not a lightning-like transformation, and, quite probably, population replacement was not total. The archaeological data suggest a gradual, acculturative spread of innovations, with earlier bases of the immigrants in Puerto Rico and Santo Domingo from which people, ideas, or both moved slowly west and north.

The early Neo-Indian pottery of the Lesser Antilles and Puerto Rico was a white-on-red and simple incised decorated ware which has been collectively referred to as the Saladoid series after its apparent region of origin on the South American mainland. This Saladoid pottery tradition obviously marks the introduction of a new art style into the West Indies. The style is known almost entirely from pottery decoration, mostly painted and incised but with some effigy adorno and figurine elements. More elaborate ritual art is lacking. A few curious cylindrical vessels, quite possible incense burners, might be a minor exception (Pons Alegria, 1976).

The Saladoid tradition was never carried much farther west than Puerto Rico. It was succeeded by the Ostiones pottery complex which spread into Santo Domingo, Haiti, and Jamaica. There is something of a question as to whether or not Ostiones is a direct and local development out of Saladoid (Rouse, 1964) or the result of a second migration of pottery-bearing peoples from Venezuela (R. E. Alegria, personal communication, 1978). The two potteries are quite different in many respects. The effigy modeling on vessels that appears in Ostiones is unlike that of the Saladoid complexes. Significantly, it looks more like the modeling of the later Taino pottery; however, it should be recognized that there are some Saladoid-Ostiones carryovers, such as the oval design element with the single bar-like enclosed line. This design motif also continues on into Taino pottery. Ostiones influence probably inspired the Meillac pottery style of Haiti, Jamaica, and Cuba. Interestingly, Meillac pottery decoration, which is largely incised, may hark back, in part, to ancient Meso-Indian design elements carved on shell or stone.

These various processes of cultural synthesis—migration, diffusion, and *in situ* development—set the scene for the final, climactic development of West Indian culture, and art, that is generally associated with the Taino of the late Precolumbian centuries. Quite possibly, this Taino florescence came about with the aid of a final additive influence from the South American Caribbean mainland, an influence apparently deriving from the Venezuelan Barrancoid pottery tradition. The process was probably diffusion rather than migration of peoples. For one thing, the primary and earliest locus of Taino cultural development was not in those islands closest to the South American mainland, but in western Puerto Rico and Santo Domingo. And the Barrancoid influence in Taino should not be overemphasized, for the Taino art style is by no means a duplicate of anything found on continental South America. The pottery tradition of the Taino culture is known as the Chicoid, after the Boca Chica phase of Santo Domingo. It had its rise there between A.D. 800 and 1000, and shortly thereafter it became a near pan-West Indian horizon, extending out from the nuclear Dominican–Puerto Rican zone as far west as Cuba and the southern Bahamas and eastward into the Virgin Islands. Chicoid pottery is readily recognizable by its generally curvilinear, bold, deep incised line decorations and by its modeled adornos of men or figures which may be anthropomorphs, bats, or monkeys. It is one expression, and an important expression, of Taino art.

The art style goes well beyond the pottery medium, however, in a way that none of the preceding West Indian styles did. The more spectacular expressions are in stone and wood carving, which compose the principal body of the art. These sculptures are well known and justly famous. A survey of them by Fewkes (1907), based largely upon Puerto Rican collections, provides an illustrated corpus and shows the range and variety of forms and materials. In spite of this variety, the sculptures are remarkably uniform from the standpoint of style. One has the impression that the native artist worked within very narrow canons. For the most part, there is a great sureness of line, both with incision and in deeper, more fully rounded cutting. Little seems experimental or unformulated. The deep-line designs are deployed in much the same way as on pottery except, generally, with greater expertness. Design motifs, however, tend to be more complex than those on the pottery vessels. They combine stylized life forms, probably anthropomorphic, and carefully balanced geometric arrangements. They are also considerably more ambitious than most of the pottery in the execution of rounded sculptures, depicting men, animal, and god forms. In general, motifs and life-form creations are relatively few in number although the ways in which carving has been adapted to individual pieces show great ingenuity and virtuosity.

None of the Taino sculptures is large. It is not a monumental style. The largest specimens—some wooden idols and a very few large, columnar-like stone carvings—never exceed four feet in height. These largest pieces are, for the most part, the least successful from an esthetic point of view, suggesting that the Taino artist was not as confident and adept working at this scale as on smaller pieces. Other stone sculptures and wood-carving—the finest pieces—rarely exceed two feet in height or diameter, and many are much smaller. Indeed, many artfully carved small sculptures of stone, wood, shell, or bone are no more than a few inches in height or length. Among the medium-sized pieces are very nicely shaped wooden stools. These are legged and often anthropomorphic, with an animal or human head in front. Some of these effigies have been inlaid with shell and, in one case, bits of gold. Low-relief carvings may adorn the seat area. Stone carvings include the well-known three-pointed stones which may vary from a few inches to a foot or two in length. Some are plain and beautifully smoothed and polished; others are carved with heads and partial bodies of men, animals, and deities. The most constant factor in the three-pointed stones is their shape. They are trianguloid in side view, with a humped back between the two lower points. Anthropomorphic faces or animal faces are sometimes carved on one or both points or on one side of the raised central point or hump. An even more impressive stone sculptural object is the "collar" or oval. These are a foot or more across and relatively delicate in that the stone of the oval or ring is proportionately quite thin with relation to the diameter of the hole. Many bear incised and deep grooved carvings of human, deity, and animal faces, together with esthetically pleasing little geometric panel designs. The body of the art also includes small idols and disk-like human faces. Some forms, too, appear to have been utility artifacts. Pestles are the most common among these, the handles of which have been carved with anthropomorphic or animal figures similar to those of the other sculptures.

A ceremonial or ritual purpose must have been associated with most of the sculptures. Thus, the stone "collars," along with some L-shaped stones, or "elbow stones," were very probably associated with a ball-game which was played in specially prepared plazas or courts and which was a central feature of Taino ceremonial life. The stone "collars" and "elbow stones" may only have been replicas of wooden game belts, or they may actually have been worn around the waists of the players (Ekholm, 1961). The three-pointed stones probably were god representations or symbols of magical or religious powers; and the stone, wooden, and other figures, collectively referred to as idols, presumably were just that, fetishes or portraits of gods. The faces of the beings carved on all of these forms—"collars," three-pointed stones, and idols—are remarkably similar. Generally anthropomorphic, they are depicted with bold, staring eyes, carved or drilled as circular pits. Mouths are frequently grimacing. The beings usually have a demonic aspect. It is presumed that these were *zemi* representations, the term used at the time of the Spanish Conquest by the Taino for their deities and spirits. The term *zemi*, however, was widely applied, not only to idols, the three-pointed stones, the faces on "collars," and so forth, but to many objects. Apparently, the Taino religious system was pervaded by animistic beliefs, and these beliefs were the inspiration for their art.

THE QUESTION OF EXTERNAL RELATIONSHIPS

To what extent did West Indian cultures, and especially Taino culture and Taino art, reflect influences from cultures and areas beyond the West Indies? We have mentioned that the original peopling of the islands, presumably in Meso-Indian times, may have involved movements from Venezuela (Rouse, 1964), Florida (Sears, 1977), and Lower Central America (Alegria, Nicholson, and Willey, 1956, Willey, 1976b); but certainly Taino art, in any recognizable form, was not present then. Neo-Indian arrivals came from the Venezuelan mainland almost certainly (Rouse, 1964), and it is probable that more than one wave of people, or at least diffused influence, can be referred back to that direction. Ostiones pottery and small artifacts do contain elements and traits that are to be found in much more elaborate form in classic Taino culture so, perhaps, we can say that Taino art was beginning to take shape in those centuries before A.D. 1000. In this connection the use of modeled pottery adornos has been mentioned, and to this we can add the first appearances of small, plain three-pointed stones and a simple plain "collar" of stone in Ostiones contexts. From this we might reason that from simple artistic traditions, originally brought from the South American mainland, Taino art, and Taino ideology, was beginning to take shape in the islands, especially in the Puerto Rican–Dominican zone. It is when we come to full-blown Taino art and ritualism that the question of external relationships becomes more interesting and difficult. Given the presence and great elaboration of the ball-game—as played with a rubber ball and on or in a stone-walled court—it is inevitable that we should look at Mesoamerica. What were the relationships of the Mesoamerican game with that of the West Indies?

A number of scholars have concerned themselves with this question over the past three quarters of a century. I cannot refer to all of them here; however, there is a recent work by a Puerto Rican anthropologist which draws much of this previous research together. I refer to Eugenio Fernandez Mendez and his book, *Art and Mythology of the Taino Indians of the Greater West Indies* (1972). This is a thorough piece of research in which the author courageously tackles Mesoamerican-Taino relationships on an ideological and artistic level, with special attention to *zemi* ritual and the ball-game. Fernandez Mendez draws upon early Antillean historical sources of the sixteenth century, Pane, Oviedo, and others and also upon early Mesoamerican source materials, including native documents and especially the *Popul Vuh*. With this ethnohistoric base line he attempts to relate myths and gods, as indicated in both sets of ethnohistoric materials, to Taino archaeology. The method is, in effect, the direct historical approach of Seler as used within a Mesoamerican context. When both Mesoamerica and the West Indies are studied in this fashion it is true that deity concepts of a generally similar sort can be identified in both areas. There is in each an "Old God" or "Old Fire God," a "Wind

God," "God of Water," of "Fertility," a "Death God," and the concepts of "Twin" or "Quadruple" deities. A difficulty, however, is in clearly identifying archaeological objects, in this case *zemi* carvings, in the Taino inventories, with such beings. Are frog representations to be surely identified with a rain god and, thereby, linked to a Mesoamerican Tlaloc or Chac? Is the figure of a humpbacked man or of a human with the arms held stiffly in front of the chest a specific enough entity to secure the identification of the Mesoamerican "Fire God" in a Taino pantheon? I am seriously doubtful.

Such concepts as deities of fire, wind, water, and so forth are, as Fernandez Mendez admits, as old in Mesoamerica as the Olmec or "Proto-Olmec" horizon. If we carry them back this far—to 1200 B.C. or before—might they not have an even greater antiquity? And with such an antiquity could they not have been a part of the mental and mythological imagery of a large part of the Americas, being brought to the West Indies, perhaps, in Meso-Indian times? In sum, my first objection is an archaeological one. The iconography of the Taino figures does not seem to me to be specific enough to pin down certain *zemis*, as found among the artifacts, with the religious concepts of the Indians described by Pane and others. This objection, of course, would also apply to J. T. Arrom's (1975) work, *Mitologia y Artes Prehispanicas de Las Antillas*. Undoubtedly, the Taino were representing the god concepts which Pane describes in their art, but what concepts apply to what forms seems to me to leave much for the imagination. My second objection, which applies to Fernandez Mendez's interpretation, is that the mythological links with Mesoamerica are of such a general nature that they could apply to a very widespread and ancient substratum of New World beliefs.

On the other hand, when it comes to certain aspects of the ball-game, I think Fernandez Mendez has a case. Originally, I argued that the Mesoamerican and Antillean games were related only by a very ancient diffusional spread (Willey, 1971b, pp. 392–93); but is it reasonable to suppose that the only two places in the New World where the game was associated with carved stone "belt" paraphernalia—the Mesoamerican stone "yokes" and the Antillean stone "collars"—had arrived at such a curious trait independently? Ekholm (1961) has said no to this question, and I am now inclined to agree with him and with Fernandez Mendez. But I also feel that the full story may be a rather complicated one. For one thing, we know that the ball-game has a somewhat greater antiquity in the Dominican–Puerto Rican nuclear zone than the post-A.D. 1000 horizon of classic Taino culture. Ball-courts occur with the previous Ostiones culture, dating back, perhaps, to A.D. 700 (Alegria, 1977). The same dating is also indicated for the associated stone sculptural tradition (Rouse, 1961; Veloz Maggiolo, 1970). Thus, we know that the ball-game complex was not a sudden introduction to the Antilles, brought there in fully developed Taino form, but something with a longer and more gradual history of West Indian development. There is also another consideration that is puzzling with relation to a swift Mesoamerican introduction of the ball-game to the Antilles. This is the fact that its earliest occurrences, as well as its later elaborations, are not in those islands closest to Mesoamerica, namely Cuba and Jamaica, but, as we have noted, in the Dominican–Puerto Rican zone. In view of all this, I would like to offer another scenario for the origins of the Antillean ball-game and the sculptural art that is associated with it.

My hypothetical reconstruction would go something like this. As the earliest pottery-making and farming Arawaks moved out into the West Indies along the Lesser Antillean chain, the first island of any size at which they arrived was Puerto Rico. It was here, and in adjacent Santo Domingo, that the first concentrated population buildups occurred. The smaller islands could not contain such large numbers of people; these larger ones could do so, and they did, as an agricultural economy was spread into their territories. These population buildups, under conditions of insular circumscription, led to the development of the first nonegalitarian societies, the first West Indian chiefdoms; and it was under the aegis of these chiefdoms that a ritual hierarchical art and the ball-game ceremonialism developed and flourished. I would further speculate that the ball-game idea was an ancient inheritance—that it had been brought out to the islands with the first farming settlers but that under the conditions of simple egalitarian tribal societies it was played under much simpler conditions. With chiefly power it became possible, in Ostiones times, and certainly by Taino times, to organize the corporate labor activities necessary to build the stone-walled courts or plazas, as well as to build temples and furnish them with the sophisticated stone sculptures that are the hallmark of classic Taino art. These activities, I would surmise, were not entirely *sui generis*, at least not in the particular forms that they assumed. The stone collars and elbow stones, and perhaps the very idea of playing the rubber-ball game in a stone-walled court, do suggest, very strongly, as Fernandez Mendez has argued, Mesoamerican inspiration. If so, would it not have been likely that those West Indian sailors who coasted Mesoamerica would have brought these ideas back to those West Indian polities which were socially and politically the most advanced and, thereby, the ones most able to put into practice, in the context of the old local ball-game tradition, these new and fascinating aspects of the game they had glimpsed on foreign shores? Or, conversely, would not Mesoamerican sailing traders have been more likely to establish their strongest commercial contacts with the advanced Puerto Rican and Dominican centers rather than with the less advanced groups of Cuba and Jamaica?

Such a reconstruction is consistent with my interpretation of the Taino mythology and iconography. Deities and concepts of the islands would be linked to Mesoamerica only on a very ancient level of shared myths and beliefs. Similarities in iconography between the two areas would be slight or nonexistent, as I believe that they are. This, of course, would fit the radically different stylistic qualities of Taino art from anything in Mesoamerica. In other words, style as a system, as a "language," did not diffuse from Mesoamerica to the West Indies. The similarities to the Mesoamerican ball-game—the concepts of the stone-walled court and, especially, the stone paraphernalia associated with the game—could represent Tainian borrowings from Mesoamerica. These were on a late level, and in this connection it is interesting to note that the ball-game court did not diffuse widely in Mesoamerica itself until after about A.D. 700 a time consistent with the first appearances of the court in the West Indies. But for the Taino these borrowings were highly selective. They were incorporated and assimilated into an already established ball-game institution; and this was accomplished without accepting anything of the Mesoamerican stylistic system nor, I would argue, any specific ideologies represented by such a stylistic system.

The Sociocultural Context of Taino Art

This matter of selective borrowing brings us to our third consideration, the sociocultural context of Taino art. What were the values of Taino society? And how did Taino art reflect these? How can this be compared with other native New World societies and cultures? The assumptions behind these questions are that art is, indeed, functional and that it has a structure that is compatible with its social and political setting. As J. L. Fischer (1961, p. 80) has stated, visual art is "the expression of some fantasied social situation which will bear a definite relation to the real and desired social situations of the artist and his society."

As ready examples of these assumptions, and of Fischer's remark, consider some of the well-known art styles of the great Precolumbian civilizations. The Moche culture of northern Peru dealt with such themes in an obvious representational way. Warriors are shown leading defeated and bleeding captives before dignitaries seated upon thrones. Social, political, and religious hierarchical situations abound in the art. Such painted pottery scenes often incorporate actual architectural features expressive of the power of the state, for example, platform pyramids surmounted by temples or palaces. In Maya vase painting and relief sculptures we have similar scenes of hierarchical power, pomp, and circumstance. Other Maya portraits are less directly representational and obviously embody elements and situations of a mythical nature and the afterlife, but even in these a Maya world view of a hierarchically arranged, very formal social order is evident. Such art styles and artistic traditions have a structure that clearly relates to a definite kind of social order, briefly, that of the state, with all of its formal institutions of power and its multiple levels of organization. Before leaving the subject of the art forms of the state, we should note, too, that monumentality in both architecture and representational art is characteristic. The very presence of such monuments, regardless of the characteristics of the art itself, is expressive of the authoritarian power of the state, its capacity to mobilize and direct the energies of thousands of persons.

We may begin our structural analysis of West Indian art by inquiring into the nature of the Taino social and political order. Fortunately, the early spanish accounts provide information on this score. When discovered by the Europeans, the islands were densely populated, and these populations were organized by sovereign chiefdoms. On Hispaniola, for example, there were six such paramount chiefs, each of whom controlled a specified territory. Subchiefs ruled under each paramount chief, and village headmen held authority below these (Rouse, 1948). In Puerto Rico the situation seems to have been similar although that smaller island may have had only two such top rulers (De Hostos, 1948; Fewkes, 1907). These rulers were complete despots in their own small realms. They were in charge of economic organization and military matters. They presided at feasts, dances, and religious rites. Theirs were the most powerful gods or *zemis*. The office is said to have been inherited matrilineally. A class system was obviously beginning to emerge in Taino society, with higher ranking clans and probably stratification within clan structure. In brief, Taino society of the beginning of the sixteenth century fits the classic chiefdom pattern as has been defined by Service (1962), Fried (1967), Peebles and Kus (1977), and others. Its complexity of organization, despotic rulers, and social ranking clearly differentiate it from a simple egalitarian society. On the other hand, it had not yet reached the level of the state, after the manner of the Mesoamerican or Peruvian polities, with their various institutions of multiple level hierarchies, police power, and heterogeneity of urban life.

Taino archaeological remains are consistent with this ethnographic description and developmental classification (cf. Rouse, 1952). Settlement patterns indicate distinctions between ordinary villages and ceremonial centers or politico-religious "capitals." Public or corporate labor works are present in the form of the plazas or ball-courts although these are relatively modest structures in comparison to the great platforms and buildings of Peru or Mexico. There was a definite production of luxury goods—idols, elaborate threepointed stones, carved stone collars, wooden stools set with gold inlays—and we know from ethnohistoric accounts that such goods were in the possession, or at the disposition, of the ruling aristocracy.

With these ethnographic and archaeologic data in mind, how did Taino art articulate with Taino society and its political order? Is there a compatability? In considering these questions let us look at the West Indian artistic products in three ways. The first of these would be from the point of view of technology and production. Looked at in this way, I think we might agree that the pottery and many of the smaller stone carvings could have been made as the routine manufactures of the ordinary household. In contrast, the stone carvings, and especially the larger and more elaborate ones, bespeak at least part-time craft specialization. They are extraordinarily sure and skilled, implying community traditions in the craft, with frequent exchange of information among craftsmen. Moreover, many of the pieces represent a good many hours of labor. Such considerations, together with our additional archaeological knowledge of the culture, can be coordinated with a chiefly society.

Second, there is the formal nature of the art, what Fischer (1961) has called its "latent content." In a study of art in its social matrices, Fischer has analyzed the art style of 30 relatively homogeneous cultures from various parts of the world, including the Americas. All of the societies in his sample would be rated as either egalitarian tribes or nonegalitarian chiefdoms. He examined four formal variables: (1) degree of complexity of design; (2) degree of crowding in the design area; (3) symmetry versus asymmetry in the designs; and (4) the presence or absence of enclosed figures. From these examinations he arrived at significant correlations between "latent content" or formal structure of art and sociopolitical type. The pictorial art of societies at the chiefly end of the scale tended to be more complex, to avoid unfilled spaces, to be asymmetrical rather than symmetrical, and to employ more enclosed figures. I think that Taino art, insofar as we are treating with flat surface decoration, conforms fairly well toward the chiefdom configuration. Recall the rather intricate complexity of design layout in Boca Chica or Capá incised pottery, or the small but involved design panels on some of the stone "collars." On crowding of the design area or the avoidance of empty spaces, I should rate Taino art as somewhere in the middle of the spectrum considered by Fischer. As to symmetry versus asymmetry, Taino art is definitely on the symmetrical side. There is a careful and harmonious balance to the incised or carved motifs on the pottery or on the backs of the three-pointed stones. In this Taino art does not conform to the Fischer expectation; however, for the last characteristic, the use of enclosed designs, Taino artistic canons fulfill the chiefly prediction in striking manner. Think of the cartouche-like confinement of design in the panel arrangements on the collars or on the pottery. Assuming that these "latent content" correlations have some validity, they tell us that Taino art was the product of a society that was reasonably well advanced along the course to nonegalitarian authoritarianism.

Even more significant, to my mind, is the representational nature of Taino art. It has been emphasized that it has very few themes. Most of its representations are anthropomorphic, quite often demonic in appearance. Such beings are found on or integrated with many objects, both utilitarian and ritual. I have suggested that Taino religion was deeply animistic and was imbued with the concept that spirits, magic, and power were integral parts of many inanimate objects. Such a belief system is compatible with a much simpler society than that of the Taino; however, in their case there is every reason to believe that this animistic view of the world had evolved into something whereby the rulers had first call upon "*zemi* power." Theirs were the most powerful *zemis*, and, as such, their *zemis* were the ones most likely to be revered as gods by the society as a whole. Certainly, by the time of the Spanish Conquest something like a pantheon of *zemi* deities had emerged, with the chiefs serving as the official priests. To go back to our discussion of external influences, it has been claimed that this Taino pantheon owed something to Mesoamerican inspiration, but I am skeptical. Until we have stronger evidence, I would prefer to see it as a local evolution paced by population growth and sociopolitical changes on the larger islands.

One aspect of the representational side of Taino art is especially fascinating. This is the complete absence of themes of warfare; or if they are present they are so concealed by symbolism that I cannot recognize them. From the early Spanish accounts the Taino would appear to have been a relatively peaceful people, so much so in fact that they seem to have been a poor match for the marauding Caribs who were of a simpler sociopolitical order. Generally, on the New World scene—and this is also true of Old World areas as well—warfare is constant and attritive among coexistent and neighboring chiefdoms, especially those of high population density and tight territorial circumscription, as was the case in the late Precolumbian centuries in the West Indies. Indeed, R. L. Carneiro (1970) has seen this kind of warfare as one of the prime mechanisms in the rise of the state. One chiefdom comes to dominate the others and in extending and maintaining its control develops state institutions. Such a possibility never came to pass in the Precolumbian West Indies. Perhaps the numerous petty polities fought each other to a standstill, as often happens; but, as I say, this kind of competition does not appear to be registered in their art.

In this connection, Olga Linares (1977b) in a recent work on the Precolumbian chiefdoms of Central Panama—those associated with the Cocle and related cultures, some of which were approximate contemporaries of the Taino—has made out an ingenious and excellent case for the meaning in their pottery art, one which attests to a warlike message. While this art does not depict battle scenes between humans, its metaphorical "language" could very well carry such a story. Humans when depicted are accoutered with status symbols. The other themes of their art are all animals. Interestingly, the animals shown are dangerous, painful, or aggressive species—sharks, stingrays, crocodiles, felines, serpents, crabs, scorpions, raptorial birds, and even stinging insects—or "armored" forms such as turtles and armadillos. Many other animals in the Panamanian environmental setting, including those which were frequently eaten, are generally ignored in the art. This choice of subject matter, plus the context in which the art was viewed on important occasions—as massed grave goods of dead rulers—has led Linares to interpret these animal themes as signifying the highly competitive and aggressive nature of the societies involved. In her own words:

> The central Panamanian art style was centered on a rich symbolic system using animal motifs metaphorically to express the qualities of aggression and hostility that characterized the social and political life of this and later periods in the central provinces. . . . It seems to me that they were emphasizing certain values, most especially those that would be held by warriors (Linares, 1977b, p. 70).

For this Panamanian case it remains only to be added that the early sixteenth-century ethnographic accounts for the region thoroughly support the warlike and intensely competitive nature of these chiefdoms.

The contrast with the West Indian chiefdoms, and with West Indian art, is striking. Of course, one may counter by saying that the animal species represented in Panamanian art are largely lacking in the West Indian environment; hence, it should come as no surprise that they are lacking in the native art. This is an undeniable argument, up to a point; but there is certainly other symbolic subject matter that could be used to transmit values of warfare and aggression, and this does not seem to have been used in the Taino case. The Taino *zemi* representations could readily be interpreted as authoritative, even fear-inducing, but this is not quite the same thing as "warlike."

In overall New World perspective, the relative pacifism of the Taino, as indicated by ethnohistoric accounts, general archaeological remains, and their art, is rare in chiefdom-type societies. Not only those of Panama, but Costa Rican, Nicaraguan, Intermediate Area, and South American Caribbean area cultures of this level give substantial indication of warlike competitiveness, and the same may also be said about those of Amazonia and the southeastern United States (see, for examples, accounts in the *Handbook of South American Indians*, J. H. Steward, ed., Vols. 3–5, 1948–49, or G. R. Willey, 1966a, 1971b). Is it possible for populous, rival, small polities to live in close proximity to one another, utilizing essentially the same kinds of environment and resources with the same kinds of technologies, and still not be constantly engaged in combat? It flies in the face of Carneiro's hypothesis about the origins of the state. But perhaps this is the answer: the attainment of the state is foregone. Competition carried to the point of the extinction or complete subjugation of one's rivals is, in some way or another, declared out of bounds (Demarest, 1977 Ms.).

To conclude, I see the West Indian cultural achievement as one which attained a rather remarkable harmonious balance between people and nature and between peoples. Although these West Indian societies did not live in complete isolation from mainland neighbors, they had a degree of semi-isolation that allowed for a largely independent development. While Taino florescence may have owed some of its ultimate panache to Mesoamerican inspiration, the ideologies of the Mesoamerican states and empires were fundamentally alien to the balanced West Indian life style. The Taino chiefdoms had their origins and development in Puerto Rico and Santo Domingo, and it was in this island setting that they were able to achieve a *modus vivendi* that eluded most of their more powerful mainland contemporaries. In one sense, the evolution from chiefdom to state may be considered an "advance." The social organism grows in size and complexity as it attempts to deal with new horizons. In another sense, such growth produces a monster. The Taino, ultimately, were not spared much, but they were at least spared that.

SOUTH AMERICA: SPACE-TIME SYSTEMATICS

This rather extraordinary tour de force was an outgrowth of three of my graduate seminars at Harvard (those of 1952, 1954, and 1956), and it was done by way of preparation for my eventual textbook of American archaeology (Willey, 1966a, 1971b). In the course of the seminars it became obvious that relative chronologies were lacking or inadequate for much of the South American continent. In those years, only Peru and the West Indies had reasonably complete coverage. For other areas some attempts had been made at chronological synthesis for single sites and small regions, but such information needed to be appraised and drawn together. What I did was only the most rudimentary kind of "culture-historical synthesis," a space-time sorting. After it was published, some of my colleagues were quite indignant at the speculative nature of "Estimated Correlations and Dating of South and Central American Culture Sequences." I can only reply that the paper was written in the same spirit that has inspired a great many of my archaeological writings. This is that while we strive for a comprehension and an accuracy that will give permanence to our findings and conclusions, we also live with the realization that revision and reconsideration will inevitably overtake us all.

I will not attempt to review and correct all of my chronological charts or "lines" in this 1958 article. In the intervening 30 years there have been so many significant new chronological findings in virtually all parts of the continent as to make this impossible in a short commentary. Many newer data, at least up to 1970, have been incorporated in the area chronology charts in the South American volume of my textbook (Willey, 1971b), and there is a still later updating in my summary article (Willey, 1978b) in the volume *Chronologies in New World Archaeology*. Since that date, of course, new information has continued to pour in from many quarters, and the interested student must seek it in the primary field reports.

9

Estimated Correlations and Dating of South and Central American Culture Sequences

(From *American Antiquity*, Vol. 23, pp. 353–378, 1958. Reprinted by permission of the Society for American Archaeology.)

The correlation of culture sequences provides the basic framework of archaeology, the essential understructure of any interpretations which may follow. In the New World, prehistoric sequence correlations seldom are projected for territories of greater size than the conventional culture area. The southwestern United States, Peru, or, at the largest, eastern North America are classic examples. The reason for such a restriction seems to be that native American cultures but rarely outrun the boundaries of their natural environmental settings, and it is difficult to effect alignments of culture phases or units on an interareal basis. To be sure, diffusions of one kind or another have taken place across major area divisions, but these are complicated by factors of trait modification and time lag so that chronological organization is a most complex task. Nevertheless, long-distance sequence correlations are of such interest and importance in American studies that they must be attempted sooner or later. They are indispensable for the eventual solution of the main problems of migration, diffusion, and the movements of cultural influences and counter-influences of the Precolumbian past. Hence, as a beginning, I am presenting here a series of archaeological sequence correlations along lines which extend through most of the South American continent and into the West Indies and Central America (Figure 9.1).

The primary objective of these coordinated sequence charts is the placement of culture phases in time, with reference to each other and all with reference to B.C. or A.D. dates. This is, in effect, what Rouse (1955) has called "distributional correlation." It is not "genetic correlation" (Rouse 1955) or "synthesis" in the sense of an attempt to relate cultures as to their derivations and connections (Willey and Phillips 1958); nor is it a developmental scheme. Implications of genetic relationships and insights into developmental series may be derived from these correlations, but they are not the means of establishing them. In examining the charts it should be kept in mind that the horizontal

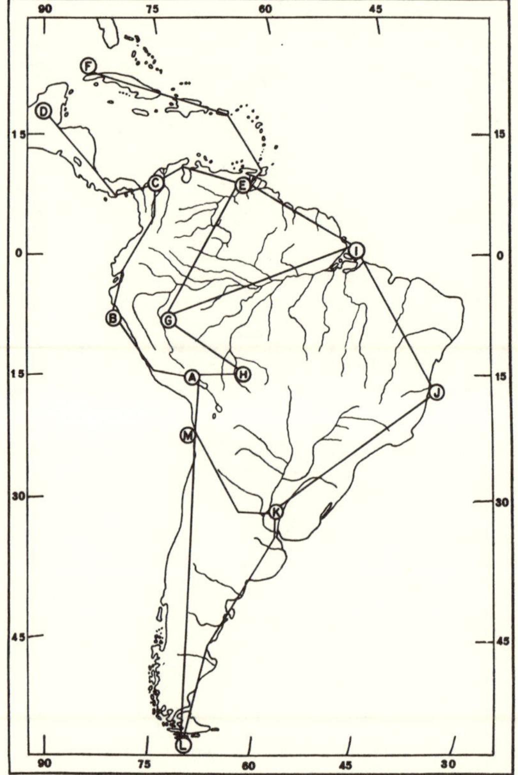

Figure 9.1. Lines of estimated sequence correlations in South and Central America. A-B, Peru-Bolivia; B-C, Peru-Ecuador-Colombia; C-D, Colombia-Central America; C-E, Northern Colombia-Northern Venezuela; E-F, Orinoco Delta-West Indies; E-G and G-H, Orinoco-Ucayali-Upper Madeira; E-I and I-G, Orinoco Delta-Amazon Delta-Ucayali; I-J and J-K, Amazon Delta-Eastern Brazil-Paraná River; K-L, Paraná River-Tierra del Fuego; L-M and M-A, Tierra del Fuego-Northern Chile-Bolivia; M-K, Northern Chile-Northwestern Argentina-Paraná River; A-H, Bolivia-Upper Madeira.

lines are put in only to facilitate the temporal correlations of archaeological cultures with each other and with the absolute dates. They do not mark off culture types or stages or serve to indicate specific breaks in local sequences. A minimum of specialized terminology and taxonomy is used. The concept of the *phase*, as the smallest meaningful culture unit with reference to the archaeological residue of a former society, is employed in the treatment of local and regional sequences (Phillips and Willey 1953: 620–3). Occasionally, the terms *horizon*, *horizon style*, and, to a lesser extent, *tradition*, come into the discussion in the attempt to correlate phases. Aside from these few devices there is no adherence to any classificatory scheme.

The methodology of correlation is varied. Radiocarbon dating provides most of the absolute dates, and it is obvious that without this aid even such a crude, initial effort as this would be next to impossible. I have not, however, placed sole and complete reliance upon the radiocarbon results but have considered and weighed the dates provided by this method in the context of all available dating evidence. In some areas it was possible to bring such diverse methods as glottochronology, native calendars, and geological estimates to bear upon correlations and to check radiocarbon readings. More frequently, I was forced to fall back upon interpretations of stratigraphies, seriations, and the cultural similarities between phases for relative dating and cross-dating. In instances of region-to-region correlations within major areas these more typically archaeological methods of sequence matching probably gave reasonably reliable results, but in the adjustments of sequences from area to area, cultural similarities are more generalized and attenuated and, consequently, more suspect as indicators of chronological equivalence. The text that accompanies the charts explains the methods and means employed in the various correlations, the bibliographic sources, and my opinions on the validity or dubiety of both the relative and absolute chronological placements. It is not, however, a detailed critique. Pages of argument and discussion could be written about most of these correlation charts. In fact, the purpose of presenting them at this time is as foci of discussion.

That this exercise is a trial and tentative one should not need saying. As we look back over the history of American archaeological errors that have attended enterprises of sequence correlating and "guess dating" of even much less ambitious scope, there can be no illusion about the permanence of these results. Admittedly, it is too early to bring off a secure chronological alignment of the data of South and Central American archaeology, but it is not too soon to take the first explanatory steps in this direction.

It should be mentioned that, for limitations of space, the various sequence charts do not comprehend all archaeological cultures that are described or named in the literature, nor do I present full bibliographies on any particular relative chronology or comparisons of chronologies; however, a sufficient number of cultures is taken into consideration in each locale or region so that the reader, with recourse to appropriate references, may appraise my opinions.

Finally, it should be explained that this has been, in large part, a cooperative study. The sequence charts are an outgrowth of my seminars in South American archaeology at Harvard during the years 1952–53, 1954–55, and 1956–57. The work of the graduate of students in these seminars, particularly the one of 1956–57, has been of great help. I wish to acknowledge, here, the seminar work of Donald W. Lathrap, Sophie D. Coe, John Ives, George Cowgill, Arthur Rohn, James Sackett, Alan Bryan, Roger Green, David Gradwohl, Donald Thompson, John Ladd, and Barbara Kerstein. In addition, colleagues, both in this country and in Latin America, have offered numerous suggestions and criticisms of an earlier draft of this paper or have provided me with information as yet unpublished. In this connection, I am in the debt of Clifford Evans and Betty J. Meggers, for information concerning Ecuadorean sequences and Amazonian archaeology, of Emilio Estrada, of Guayaquil, for data on Ecuador, of Gerardo Reichel-Dolmatoff for recent sequence information from northern Colombia, and of Irving Rouse and J. M. Cruxent for their advice and opinions upon Venezuela and the West Indies. With full credit to all of these individuals, I also absolve them of any responsibility for my less than conventional leaps through time and space.

PERU-BOLIVIA (LINE A–B)

The Peru-Bolivia chart (Figure 9.2) is an abbreviated version of various sequence presentations for that area or portions of it (Bennett and Bird 1949; Strong and Evans 1952; Rowe 1956; Strong 1957). The north coast column is based upon the Chicama, Moche, and Virú valleys; the central coast combines the Chancay, Ancon, and Chillon-

NORTH COAST CHICAMA —— VIRÚ	CENT. COAST	SOUTH COAST	TITICACA BASIN NORTH —— SOUTH	
				1500
Inca	Inca	Inca	Inca	
Chimu	Late Chancay	Late Ica	Colla Lupaca	
Black—White—Red Geom.	Late Ancon I	Middle Ica	Decadent Tiah.	1000
		Pacheco	↑	
Coast Tiahuanaco	Coast Tiah-Mid.Ancon	Huaca del Loro		
Mochica				500
Gallinazo 3	Maranga 3	Late Nazca (B)	(Derived Tiah.) ↑	
Mochica Gallinazo 2	Maranga 2	Early Nazca (A)	Pucara Tiahuanaco	A.D.
Gallinazo I	Maranga I	Proto-Nazca	Early Tiah.	B.C.
Salinar Puerto Moorin	Baños de Boza	Late Paracas		
			Chiripa	
Cupisnique Mid. Guañape	Early Ancon-Supe	Early Paracas	Qaluyu	1000
(Plain Pottery)	(Plain Pottery)			
Huaca Prieta Cerro Prieto	Chira-Villa	{Laguna de Otuma {Lomas		2000
		{Rio Ica (?) {San Nicolas		4000
				5000
San Pedro de Chicama			Ayampitín	6000
			Viscachaní	10,000

Figure 9.2. Peru-Bolivia (line A-B) sequence chart.

Rimac drainages; and the south coast centers upon Paracas-Ica-Nazca. North and central highland regions are omitted, but equations with sequences from those regions may be approximated easily. Similarly, although sequences are not presented in full detail on the accompanying chart the chronological positions of all phases and subphases not entered will be evident upon reference to the standard literature.

San Pedro de Chicama (Bird 1948) and Viscachani (Menghín 1953–54) are placed by sheer guess. The central Andean Hunancáyo cave lithic assemblages (Harry Tschopik 1946) might also be aligned on a comparable early level. Certain projectile points from the Viscachaní site zone resemble those of the Ayampitín phase of Córdoba, Argentina. Accordingly, a separation has been made in this column between a Viscachaní and an Ayampitín industry. There are possible old lithic industries on the Peruvian coast which may antedate the later incipient agricultural sites. San Nicolas (Strong 1954), south of Nazca, and the lower levels of a shell heap at the mouth of the Río Ica (Engel 1957) are examples.

The incipient agricultural, preceramic horizon along the coast is well established, but, so far, radiocarbon dates are all from the north. These dates are reasonably consistent, ranging from about 2500 to 1800 B.C. for the earliest agricultural levels. A plain pottery horizon marks the later centuries of this incipient agricultural era. It is attested to by the stratigraphy at Huaca Prieta (Bird 1948), the Early Guañape phase in Virú Valley (Strong and Evans 1952), the Early Ancon lower levels (Willey and Corbett 1954), and the excavations of Chira-Villa, near Lima (Engel 1957).

Cupisnique and Middle Guañape, both phases on the Chavín horizon, have dates of about 1200 to 700 B.C. Early Ancon-Supe relates closely to these. On the south coast, Early Paracas pottery has some design and element similarities in common with the Chavín horizon phases of the north and center, but is, otherwise, rather different. I have equated Early Paracas with Cupisnique on the chart, but do so with considerable hesitation. Negative painted pottery is an element in Early Paracas, and negative painted ware in the north is stratigraphically later than Cupisnique. Furthermore, although there are no available Early Paracas dates, the immediately subsequent Late Paracas phase has radiocarbon dates in the early centuries A.D. Thus, although I follow conventional alignments in the present chart, there is at least a reasonable possibility that the entire early ceramic sequence on the south coast may have its inception a few centuries later than the first appearance of pottery farther north.

In comparing the north and south coasts on the Mochica and Nazca level, some of the Mochica dates appear substantially earlier and produce the same failure of alignment observed for Cupisnique and Paracas. Other more recently rendered radiocarbon dates on Late Mochica are more in line with those of the Nazca culture. Like all charts this one gives an impression of greater certainty than actually exists. A single example of this of which Peruvian specialists will be aware is the Mochica-Gallinazo arrangement. It follows Strong and Evans (1952) and Willey (1953a) in seeing Mochica as a relatively late expansion into the Virú Valley. There is the other possibility that Gallinazo was a longer and more important period in the Chicama Valley than is shown and that the full run of the civilization was more or less contemporaneous in both Chicama and Virú.

The recent radiocarbon readings on, or very near to, the Tiahuanaco horizon on the south coast, are our first absolute dates for this important marker style. The dates, ranging from about A.D. 700 to 1000 average only slightly earlier than Rowe's (1945) reckonings. "Derived Tiahuanaco" on the chart is entered to indicate the estimated time point at which these "derived" influences began their spread from the Tiahuanaco cultural continuum down into the Bolivian lowlands (Bennett 1936; see also Figure 13).

RADIOCARBON DATES PERTINENT TO LINE A–B

For convenience, radiocarbon dates available and pertinent to the discussion of each chronological profile chart are tabulated following that particular chart discussion. Most dates have been rendered as B.C. or A.D. by the subtractions of, or from, the date A.D. 1950. Exceptions are those quoted from Strong (1957) or from Rouse (personal communication, 1957).

Huaca Prieta, beginning dates:
2348±230 B.C. (Libby 1955, C-598)
2307±250 B.C. (Libby 1955, C-313)
1910±100 B.C. (Broecker, Kulp, and Tucek 1956, L-116B)
1830±100 B.C. (Broecker, Kulp, and Tucek 1956, L-116A)
1700±400 B.C. (Kulp, Feely, and Tryon, 1951 L-116B)
Huaca Prieta, beginning plain pottery period date:
1016±300 B.C. (Libby 1955, C-321) (See also, Bird 1951.)
Early Guañape, plain pottery period dates (charcoal samples):
1850±150 B.C. (Kulp and others 1952, L-122C)
1150±200 B.C. (Kulp and others 1952, L-122F)
Cupisnique date:
715±200 B.C. (Libby 1955, C-75)
Middle Guañape date (charcoal sample):
1200±90 B.C. (Kulp and others 1952, L-122A)

Gallinazo (negative painted pottery at Huaca Prieta) date:
682±300 B.C. (Libby 1955, C-323)
Mochica (Moche and Virú Valleys) dates:
873±500 B.C. (Libby 1955, C-382)
A.D. 112±190 (Libby 1955, C-619)
A.D.656±80 (Strong 1957, L-335A)
A.D.656±80 (Strong 1957, L-335B)
Paracas Necropolis (probably Late Paracas phase) dates:
386±300 B.C. (Libby 1955, C-271)
240±350 B.C. (Libby 1955, C-271)
A.D. 100±250 (Kulp, Feely, and Tryon 1951, L-115)
A.D. 400±200 (Kulp, Feely, and Tryon 1951, L-115)
A.D. 200±90 (Broecker, Kulp, and Tucek 1956, L-115)
Late Paracas (Cahuachi, Nazca Valley) dates:
A.D. 110±80 (Broecker, Kulp, and Tucek 1956, L-268B)
A.D. 240±80 (Broecker, Kulp, and Tucek 1956, L-268A)
A.D. 116±100 (Strong 1957, L-335D)
A.D. 116±100 (Strong 1957, L-335C)
124±160 B.C. (Strong 1957, W-422)
Proto-Nazca (Cahuachi, Nazca Valley) dates:
A.D. 320± (Broecker, Kulp, and Tucek 1956, L-268D)
A.D. 490±80 (Broecker, Kulp, and Tucek 1956, L-268C)
Early Nazca (A) (Nazca Valley) dates:
527±200 B.C. (Libby 1955, C-521)
A.D. 269±250 (Libby 1955, C-521)
A.D. 271±200 (Libby 1955, C-658)
A.D. 636±250 (Libby 1955, C-460)
Middle Nazca (A) (Nazca Valley) dates:
A.D. 520±80 (Broecker, Kulp and Tucek 1956, L-268H)
A.D. 336±100 (Strong 1957, L-335G)
Late Nazca (B) (Chaviña and Nazca regions) dates:
A.D. 630±60 (Barendson, Deevey, and Gralenski 1957, Y-126)
A.D. 526±90 (Strong 1957, L-335E)
Huaca del Loro (Nazca Y to Taihuanacoid) (Nazca Valley) dates:
A.D. 750±80 (Broecker, Kulp, and Tucek 1956, L-268G)
A.D. 1050±70 (Broecker, Kulp, and Tucek 1956, L-268E)
A.D. 980±70 (Broecker, Kulp, and Tucek 1956, L-268F)
A.D. 756±90 (Strong 1957, L-335F)

PERU-ECUADOR-COLOMBIA (LINE B–C)

Line B–C chart (Figure 9.3) repeats the Peru north coast column and attempts to relate, in geographical order, regional sequences of the Ecuadorean coast and highlands, southern and central Colombia of the Cauca and Magdalena Valleys, and the lower Magdalena–Sinú River country of the Caribbean coast. The evidence linking north Peru with Ecuador is largely that of ceramic similarities seen in Cupisnique, on the one hand, and the Ecuadorean Chorrera phase on the other. The succeeding Guangala and Tejar phases of the Ecuadorean Guayas coast and basin likewise have a number of close ceramic parallels in the Peruvian Salinar and Gallinazo phases (Evans and Meggers 1957). It is also noteworthy that the earliest culture yet known from the Ecuadorean coast, the Valdivia, is associated with shell mound sites and has a pottery complex which shows some relationships to the Peruvian coastal mound shell phases of pre-Cupisnique times (Estrada 1956).

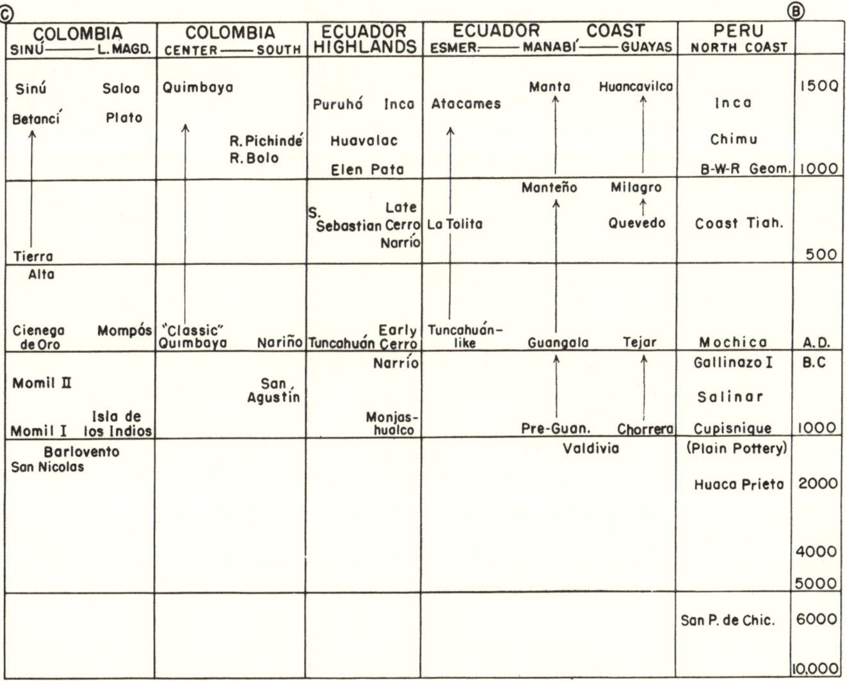

C
B
COLOMBIA
SINÚ——L. MAGD.
COLOMBIA
CENTER——SOUTH
ECUADOR
HIGHLANDS
ECUADOR COAST
ESMER.——MANABÍ——GUAYAS
PERU
NORTH COAST
Sinú
Saloa
Betancí
Plato
Quimbaya
R. Pichindé
R. Bolo
Puruhá
Inca
Huavalac
Elen Pata
Atacames
Manta
Huancavilca
Inca
Chimu
B-W-R Geom.
1500
1000
Manteño
Milagro
S. Sebastian Cerro
Late
Narrío
La Tolita
Quevedo
Coast Tiah.
Tierra
Alta
500
Cienega de Oro
Mompós
"Classic" Quimbaya
Nariño
Early
Tuncahuán Cerro
Tuncahuán-like
Guangala
Tejar
Mochica
A.D.
Narrío
Gallinazo I
B.C
Momil II
San Agustín
Salinar
Isla de
Momil I
los Indios
Monjas-hualco
Pre-Guan.
Chorrera
Cupisnique
1000
Barlovento
San Nicolas
Valdivia
(Plain Pottery)
Huaca Prieta
2000
4000
5000
San P. de Chic.
6000
10,000

Figure 9.3. Peru-Ecuador-Colombia (line B-C) sequence chart.

Within Ecuador it should be pointed out that Bushnell's (1951) Pre-Guangala phase is essentially the same as Chorrera (Estrada 1957a, b), and the Monhashuaico (Bennett 1946a), of the southern Ecuadorean highlands, is also a similar ceramic assemblage. The Valdivia, Chorrera, Guangala, and Manteño sequence of Guayas is duplicated in Manabí province (Estrada 1957b). The site of Cerro Jaboncillo (Saville 1907–10), famed for its U-shaped stone thrones, has pottery figurines relating it to Guangala. Whereas Manteño of the coast is a direct development out of Guangala, Quevedo and Milagro of the Guayas Basin are intrusives over Tejar and appear to be linked to the late burial mound cultures of Esmeraldas (Estrada 1957a). There is little sequence information from Esmeraldas as yet. Certain figurines (D'Harcourt 1947; Rowe 1949) and pottery resemble types at Cerro Jaboncillo and Guangala, and, presumably, such sites as La Tolita (Ferdon 1940–41) may date back as early as Guangala and Tuncahuán. La Tolita vessels and figurines have intriguing resemblances in both Middle American and Peruvian directions (Corbett 1953). Stratigraphic archaeology for this region is long overdue. Across the Colombian border, at Tumaco, Cubillos (1955) has made a start, and his 2-period sequence there probably parallels developments in Esmeraldas.

Jijón y Caamaño's (1927) Puruhá sequence is arranged in the Ecuadorean highland column, but, following Estrada (1957a) the dubious Proto-Panzaleo I and II phases have been eliminated. The remainder of Jijón's sequence is placed more or less as he has indicated (Jijón y Caamaño 1927, 1930, 1951), with the 3-color negative-painted style of Tuncahuán correlating with the 3-color negative of Guangala and, more remotely, with the Peruvian 3-color negative style of Recuay culture and Gallinazo. For a discussion of some of these problems and for a critical examination of Jijón's chronologies with reference to their own excavations in the Ecuadorean south highlands, see Collier and Murra (1943), Collier (1948), and Bennett (1946a). My equation of San Sebastian (Guano) and the Peruvian Tiahuanacoid horizon follows Jijón; Estrada (1957a) moves San Sebastian up to equate with Chimu; Kroeber (1944), on the other hand, sees Recuay-like elements in San Sebastian pottery.

In moving into southern and central Colombia there are very few clues to correlations with Ecuador. Typological resemblances in pottery and stone carving are the only possibilities so far, and none of these are definitive. The Nariño-Quimbaya negative-painted ware may have connections with Guangala and Tuncahuán through a Carchi negative-painted style in the north highlands of Ecuador (Bennett 1944b). San Agustín, with its stone statues, has been said to have resemblances to Peruvian Chavín. As yet, these seem to be extremely tenuous, and the placement of San Agustín as early as I have done is no more than a guess.

In northern Colombia, at the mouth of the Sinú River, the Momíl I and II phases (Reichel-Dolmatoff and Dussán de Reichel 1956; Reichel-Dolmatoff 1957) have ceramic decorative techniques, vessel forms, and other items which relate to Chorrera and Tejar and more widely to Middle American and Peruvian Formative cultures. They are dated as early as they are on this basis.

Colombia–Central America (Line C–D)

The Formative period similarities between Middle America and Peru, and the linkages of these with Momíl and Chorrera, suggest that important currents of diffusion were in existence in the first millennium B.C. This has been pointed out by several authors (Strong 1943; Porter Weaver 1953; Willey 1955a, b), and I have speculated that these currents were running from north to south (Willey 1955a, b). In view of this, the territory of lower Central America would appear to be a likely place in which to discover evidences of these early connections. To date, only the Monagrillo culture of Pacific Panama suggests such a possibility (Willey and McGimsey 1954). In most respects, however, the Monagrillo phase has an Archaic cast (Willey and Phillips 1958), and it is doubtful if it represents the village-based agriculture which is usually associated with the Formative period cultures of Middle and South America. It appears as a direct outgrowth of the preceramic Cerro Mangote phase (McGimsey 1956), being differentiated only by the addition of rather simple incised and punctated pottery. I see general resemblances between the Monagrillo pottery and that of the Ecuadorean Valdivia phase and the Colombian Barlovento phase (Reichel-Dolmatoff 1955). In the other direction there are slight similarities between Monagrillo and some of the incised pottery of the Guatemalan highland Formative period. The position of Monagrillo as just prior to 1000 B.C. (Figure 9.4) depends upon these rather slender threads; however, in view of the early Cerro Mangote radiocarbon date, and the cultural continuity btween Cerro Mangote and Monagrillo, the available radiocarbon reading on Monagrillo seems much too late.

My placement of Santa María (Willey and Stoddard 1954), in the Panamanian column, is based upon what we know of the stratigraphic position of that ceramic phase, upon my belief that it probably represents the earliest painted pottery horizon in Panama and may therefore correlate with the early painted pottery horizon of northern Colombia (Mompós, Loma, Horno, and so on, see Figures 4, 5), and upon a radiocarbon date in the neighborhood of A.D. 200 for painted pottery from Venado Beach, Canal Zone (S. K.

(D) (C)

MAYA LOWLANDS	HONDURAS	SALVADOR	COSTA RICA-NICARAGUA	PACIFIC PANAMA	COLOMBIA SINÚ —— L. MAGD.	
Mayapan Chichen	Naco North Coast		Chiriquí	Coclé	Sinú Saloa Betancí Plato	1500 1000
Itza Tepeu —— Puuc	Ulua Mayoid	Nicoya Copador	Nicoya		Tierra	500
Tzakol Matzanel		Esperanza-Tzakol		Santa Maria	Alta Cienega de Oro Mompós	A.D.
Chicanel	Ulua Bichrome — Yar. III P. de los Muertos — Yar. II Yarumela I	Cerro Zapote			Momil II Momil I Isla de los Indios	B.C. 1000
Mamom				Monagrillo ↑ Cerro Mangote	Barlovento San Nicolas	2000 4000 5000
						6000 10,000

Figure 9.4. Colombia-Central America (line C-D) sequence chart.

Lothrop, personal communication, 1957). The Venado Beach pottery is not Santa María but bears some resemblances to it.

In the Costa Rica–Nicaraguan column, Nicoya (Lothrop 1926; Strong 1948a) has certain resemblances in pottery vessel forms and design elements to the early Postclassic, or Plumbate horizon, pottery of Middle America. I have placed its beginnings as only slightly earlier than this.

Salvador-Honduras are conventional sequences (Longyear 1944; Strong 1948b; Canby 1951). Diagnostic Middle American Formative and Classic traits have not yet been found east and south of a Ulua River–central Salvadorean line. There are no real ties of any kind between western Salvador and Lower Central America when we drop below a Nicoya time level. In brief, Line C–D breaks in the middle in much the same way that Line B–C broke in southern and central Colombia.

RADIOCARBON DATES PERTINENT TO LINE C–D

The dates given below are, with 2 exceptions, Middle American. They have an important indirect bearing upon the "Maya Lowlands" column of Figure 4. Compare them with Peruvian dates, especially with reference to Formative phases of the first millennium B.C. (See Wauchope 1954 for comment in this connection.)

Valley of Mexico Formative dates:

1360±250 B.C. Zacatenco I (Libby 1955, C-196)

1457±250 B.C. Tlatilco site, probably Early Zacatenco associations (Libby 1955, C-199)

615±200 B.C. Loma del Tepalcate (Libby 1955, C-202)
472±250 B.C. Cuicuilco (Libby 1955, C-200)
484±500 B.C. Core of Pyramid of Sun, Teotihuacán (Libby 1955, C-203)

Oaxaca Formative and Classic dates:

650±170 B.C. Tilantongo, Monte Albán I level (Libby 1955, C-424)
273±145 B.C. Monte Albán II (Libby 1955, C-425)
A.D. 298±185 Monte Alban IIIA, Chachoapan (Libby 1955, C-426)

Guatemalan Lowland Classic dates:

A.D. 429±170 Tikal, Initial Series date 9.15.10.0.0. (Libby 1955, C-949)
A.D. 465±120 Tikal (same as above) (Libby 1955, C-948)
A.D. 480±120 Tikal (same as above) (Kulp, Feely, and Tryon 1951, L-113)

Guatemalan Highland Formative dates:

1550 ±800 B.C. Kaminaljuyú, Las Charcas phase (Libby 1955, C-885)
1192±240 B.C. Kaminaljuyú, Miraflores phase (Libby 1955, C-884)
1020±200 B.C. Kaminaljuyú, Majadas phase (Libby 1955, C-886)
120±300 B.C. Kaminaljuyú, Providencia phase (Libby 1955, C-879)
540±300 B.C. Kaminaljuyú, Miraflores phase (Libby 1955, C-887)

Panama dates:

4853±100 B.C. Cerro Mangote (C. R. McGimsey, personal communication, 1957; test by Yale Laboratory)
A.D. 1150±250 Monagrillo (Crane 1955, M-11)

Northern Colombia–Northern Venezuela (Line C–E)

Point C serves as the pivot, again, for the chart of Line C–E (Figure 5). The Sinú and Lower Magdalena River sequences of Caribbean Colombia are attached to the Río César, Sierra Nevada de Santa Marta, and Río Ranchería sequences (Reichel-Dolmatoff 1954, 1957; personal communication, 1957; see also Reichel-Dolmatoff and Dussán de Reichel 1951). The San Nicolas phase is preceramic and probably relates to El Heneal, Cabo Blanco, and Manicuare in Venezuela. Its position on the chart is based upon radiocarbon dates for El Heneal and Manicuare. Loma, Horno, Pueblo Bello, and La Paz are on the earliest painted pottery horizon. As noted, these relate to Mompós, in one direction, and to Tocuyano in the other. Both Tocuyano and Cerro Machado have radiocarbon dates in accordance with their chart positions. Higher up in the time scale there are close stylistic connections in pottery between Portacelli and Tierra de los Indios. These phases can be linked to the west and to the east, as indicated on the chart, and there are radiocarbon dates on eastern Venezuelan late cultures which confirm the general time position.

El Jobo (Cruxent and Rouse 1956), the presumed early lithic complex of western Venezuela, has typological affinities to the post-fluted-point horizon of western North America and to Ayampitín of Argentina (Rouse and Cruxent 1957). The guess-date of 6000 B.C. is in accord with both of these relationships.

The important column on the Lower Orinoco is well anchored in radiocarbon dating. Saladero and Barrancas (formerly Barrancas 1 and 2 phases) appear to be the earliest known manifestations of two quite different ceramic traditions or series. Saladero features white-on-red decoration while Barrancas is a broad-line incised and modeled style. Originally, Rouse (1953, see also bibliography to this title) placed Saladero as entirely earlier than Barrancas, but a large series of radiocarbon dates indicate their contemporaneity as shown on the chart. This is discussed in the monograph by Cruxent and Rouse

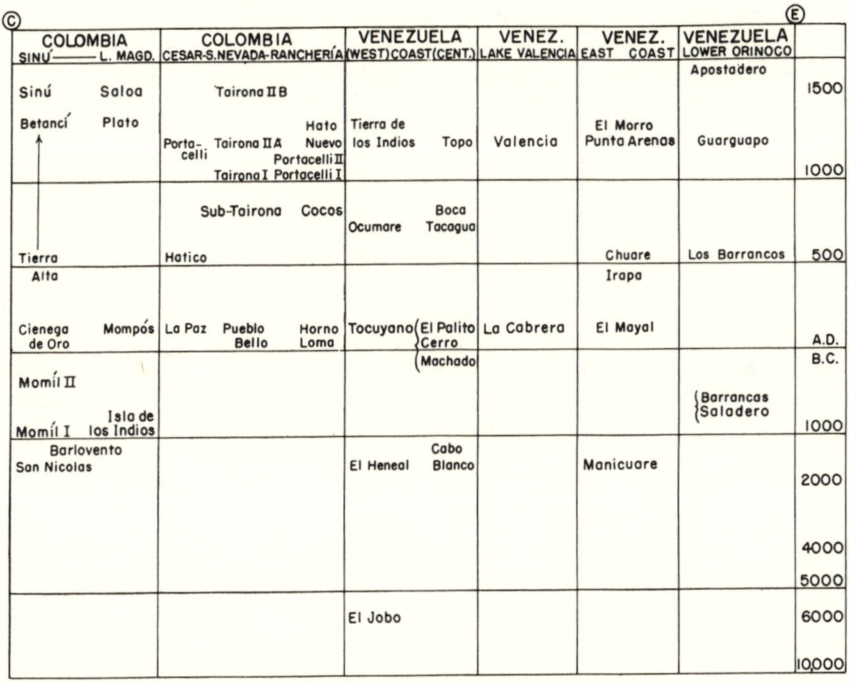

COLOMBIA SINÚ — L. MAGD.	COLOMBIA CESAR-S. NEVADA-RANCHERÍA	VENEZUELA (WEST) COAST (CENT.)	VENEZ. LAKE VALENCIA	VENEZ. EAST COAST	VENEZUELA LOWER ORINOCO	
					Apostadero	
Sinú · Saloa	Tairona IIB					1500
Betancí · Plato ↑	Portacelli · Tairona IIA · Hato Nuevo · Portacelli II	Tierra de los Indios · Topo	Valencia	El Morro · Punta Arenas	Guarguapo	
	Tairona I · Portacelli I					1000
	Sub-Tairona · Cocos	Ocumare · Boca Tacagua				
Tierra Alta	Hatico			Chuare	Los Barrancos	500
				Irapa		
Cienega de Oro · Mompós	La Paz · Pueblo Bello · Horno Loma	Tocuyano · {El Palito · Cerro Machado}	La Cabrera	El Mayal		A.D.
						B.C.
Momíl II						
Momíl I · Isla de los Indios					{Barrancas · Saladero}	1000
Barlovento · San Nicolas		El Heneal · Cabo Blanco		Manicuare		2000
						4000
						5000
		El Jobo				6000
						10,000

Figure 9.5. Northern Colombia-Northern Venezuela (line C-E) sequence chart.

on the archaeology of Venezuela (1958–59). Several radiocarbon dates, in addition to the ones listed in this present article, bolster the case for contemporaneity between Saladero and Barrancas (Rouse, personal communication, 1957). Both the white-on-red and the modeled-incised traditions seem to carry on for several hundreds of years following their first appearance. El Mayal, dated at about A.D. 200 by radiocarbon, is essentially Saladero-like in its pottery while Los Barrancos (formerly Barrancas 3) and Guarguapo (formerly Barrancas 4) phases are Barrancas-like. Radiocarbon dates on Irapa and Chuare give further substantiation to the chart.

Rapidly accumulating new information and the interpretations and codifications of it make it difficult for the nonspecialist in the Colombian and Venezuelan areas to relate these newer sequence formulations to existing literature (see Reichel-Dolmatoff 1954, 1957; Osgood and Howard 1943; Howard 1943; Kidder II 1944, 1948; Cruxent 1951; Rouse 1953). In an attempt to help in this regard I have indicated changes in the Lower Orinoco chronology in the preceding paragraph. Farther west, La Cabrera and Valencia may be readily identified (Kidder II 1944). Tierra de los Indios refers to material from near Quibor, in the State of Lara (Osgood and Howard 1943), and most of the painted pottery of tripod and pedestal-based forms now illustrated from northwestern Venezuela fits on this horizon. The earlier painted pottery of Tocuyano and related phases, which is probably ancestral to the later, will not be well illustrated until the Cruxent and Rouse (1958–59) monograph appears.

RADIOCARBON DATES PERTINENT TO LINE C–E

Manicuare and El Heneal dates:
1620±130 B.C. (Barendsen, Deevey, and Gralenski 1957, Y-295)
1100±80 B.C. (Barendsen, Deevey, and Gralenski 1957, Y-296g)
1444±120 B.C. (El Heneal; Rouse, personal communication, 1957; Yale Laboratory)

Saladero phase dates:
910±130 B.C., 930±130 B.C., and 570±140 B.C. (Preston, Person, and Deevey 1955, Y-42, 3 separate runs)
750±130 B.C. (Preston, Person, and Deevey 1955, Y-43)
620±130 B.C. (Preston, Person, and Deevey 1955, Y-44)

Barrancas (formerly Barrancas 1 and 2) phase dates:
4300±380 B.C. (Preston, Person, and Deevey 1955, Y-41)
950±150 B.C. (Barendsen, Deevey, and Gralenski 1957, Y-294)
900±120 B.C. (Preston, Person, and Deevey 1955, Y-40)

Cerro Machado and El Mayal phase dates:
A.D. 26±70 (Cerro Machado; Rouse, personal communication, 1957; Yale Laboratory)
A.D. 225±100 (Barendsen, Deevey, and Gralenski 1957, Y-297)

Tocuyano phase date:
230±300 B.C. (Crane 1955, M-257)

Irapa and Chuare phase dates:
A.D. 370±40 (Preston, Person, and Deevey 1955, Y-290, average of 3 separate runs on an Irapa specimen)
A.D. 595±80 (Barendsen, Deevey, and Gralenski 1957, Y-300)

Los Barrancos phase date:
A.D. 500 (approximate) (Rouse, personal communication, 1957; Yale Laboratory)

El Morro phase dates:
A.D. 1235±80 (Barendsen, Deevey, and Gralenski 1957, Y-298)
A.D. 1660±70 (Barendsen, Deevey, and Gralenski 1957, Y-299)

Orinoco Delta–West Indies (Line E–F)

The profile on Line E–F (Figure 9.6) is a synopsis of the detailed charts and statements that have been made by Rouse over the past years (Rouse, 1947, 1948, 1951a, 1951b, 1952, 1953, personal communication 1957). Only 2 West Indian radiocarbon dates are available, from the Ortoire phase of Trinidad. This preceramic complex dates at about 800 B.C., suggesting a somewhat more recent survival of an Archaic way of life there and in the other islands than on the mainland. Both radiocarbon datings from the mainland, and glotto-chronological evidence on the separation of mainland and island Arawak speech (Taylor and Rouse 1955) argue for the placement of the Cedros and Cuevas phases at about A.D. 200. This, presumably, was the first agricultural–pottery making culture to be carried into the islands, and the Arawaks are believed to have been associated with the event (Rouse 1957). There is little else to say about the chart (Figure 9.6). The West Indian area is one of the best organized, from the standpoint of relative and interrelated regional chronologies, of any in South America. The absolute dates given are, of course, much earlier than Rouse's old estimates. More radiocarbon dates from the various phases and islands will provide an interesting check on Rouse's hypothesis of the movements of cultures and peoples through the island chain.

RADIOCARBON DATES PERTINENT TO LINE E–F (See also those for line C–E)

Ortoire phase dates:
810±130 B.C. (Preston, Person, and Deevey 1955, Y-260-2)
800±130 B.C. (Preston, Person, and Deevey 1955, Y-260-1)

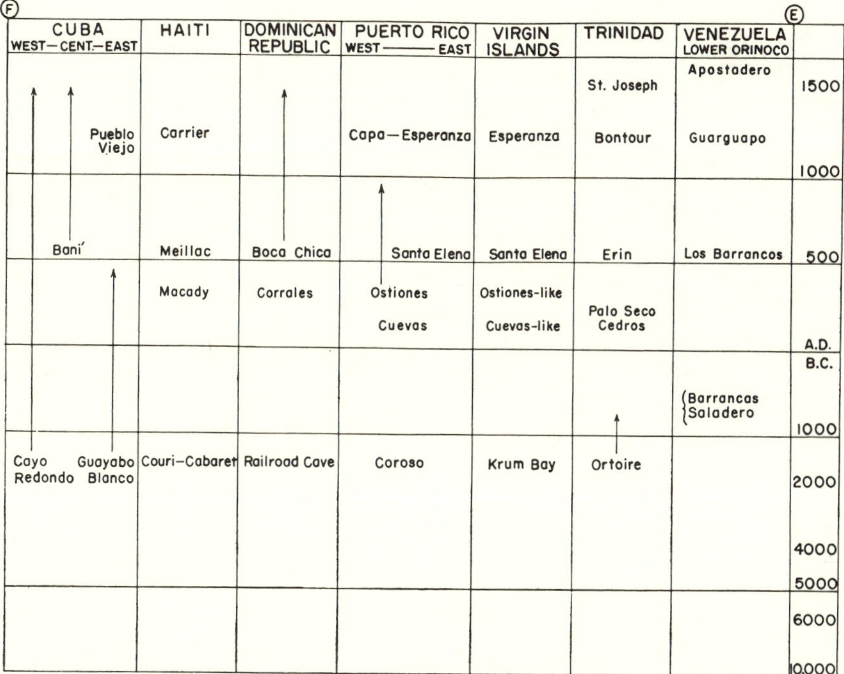

F
E
CUBA
WEST—CENT.—EAST
HAITI
DOMINICAN REPUBLIC
PUERTO RICO
WEST——EAST
VIRGIN ISLANDS
TRINIDAD
VENEZUELA
LOWER ORINOCO
Apostadero
St. Joseph
1500
Pueblo Viejo
Carrier
Capa—Esperanza
Esperanza
Bontour
Guarguapo
1000
Boní
Meillac
Boca Chica
Santa Elena
Santa Elena
Erin
Los Barrancos
500
Macady
Corrales
Ostiones
Ostiones-like
Cuevas
Cuevas-like
Palo Seco
Cedros
A.D.
B.C.
Barrancas
Saladero
1000
Cayo Redondo
Guayabo Blanco
Couri—Cabaret
Railroad Cave
Coroso
Krum Bay
Ortoire
2000
4000
5000
6000
10,000

Figure 9.6. Orinoco Delta-West Indies (line E-F) sequence chart.

Orinoco–Ucayali–Upper Madeira (Lines E–G and G–H)

The Lower, Middle, and Upper Orinoco columns (Figure 9.7) follow Rouse (1953; personal communication, 1957). Camoruco is Late Ronquín (Howard 1943). Ronquín (formerly Early Ronquín) is an interesting blend of Saladero and Barrancas traits.

The Ucayali sequence is based upon recent excavations of Lathrap (1958) at Yarinacocha in eastern Peru. Lathrap's earliest pottery, the Tutishcainyo, emphasizes incision, punctation, and zoned red painting. An incised jaguar on one sherd is somewhat similar to Chanapata and Pucara ceramic art in Peru, and Lathrap sees further resemblances between some of the Kotosh pottery, near Huánuco, Peru (Tello 1943) and Tutishcainyo. These similarities, plus certain vessel form features held in common between Momíl and Tutishcainyo, argue for a fairly early placement of the latter. Lathrap's Shakimu phase is characterized by polished, excised wares which he sees as distantly related to the excised types of the Napo, Miracanguera, and Marajoara (see Figures 9.8 and 9.9). Hupa-iya is a broad-line incised and modeled pottery style that has some resemblances to the Barrancas tradition. In Rouse's opinion it is most likely to follow after Los Barrancos (Barrancas 3). The sequence positions of excised and painted wares (Shakimu, Napo, Mircanguera, Marajoara) are placed to indicate a general west-to-east movement; the positions of the broad-line incised and modeled pottery complexes are arranged to suggest movement from the Lower Orinoco to the west.

(E) (G) (H)

VENEZUELA LOWER ORINOCO	VENEZUELA MIDDLE ORINOCO	VENEZUELA UPPER ORINOCO	UCAYALI	UPPER MADEIRA SANTA CRUZ—MOJOS	
Apostadero Guarguapo	Camoruco Arauquin	{Atabapo {La Ceiba	Shipibo	Rio Palacios Upper Velarde Hernmarck	1500 1000
Los Barrancos		Cotua	Hupa-iya	Lower Velarde	500
	Ronquín		Shakimu		A.D. B.C.
{Barrancos {Saladero			Tutishcainyo		1000
					2000 4000 5000
					6000 10,000

Figure 9.7. Orinoco-Ucayali-Upper Madeira (lines E-G and G-H) sequence chart.

(E) (I) (G)

VENEZUELA LOWER ORINOCO	BRIT. GUIANA	AMAZON DELTA BRAZ. GUIANA——ISLANDS	SANTARÉM-TO-IQUITOS	UCAYALI	
Apostadero Guarguapo	Mabaruma ↑ Koriabo	Aristé {Mazagão {Maracá Arũa	Tapajó Paura Santarém	Shipibo Cashibo	1500 1000
Los Barrancos	|	Marajoara	Konduri	Hupa-iya	500
	Palo Seco-like	Formiga Mangueiras	Miracanguéra Rio Napo	Shakimu	A.D. B.C.
{Barrancos {Saladero	Alaka	Ananatuba		Tutishcainyo	1000
					2000 4000 5000
					6000 10,000

Figure 9.8. Orinoco Delta-Amazon Delta-Ucayali (lines E-I and I-G) sequence chart.

(I) (J) (K)

AMAZON DELTA	BRAZIL NORTHEAST COAST	BRAZIL SOUTH COAST	BRAZIL MINAS GERAES	PARANÁ & URUGUAY RIVERS	
Mazagão Arũa				Chana'—Timbu', etc. Arroyo los Conchas	1500
	Burial Urns	Guaraní Pottery	Burial Urns	Malabrigo	
				Puerto de las Tunas	1000
Marajoara	Maranão Pile Villages			Brazo Largo	500
Formiga				Salto Grande (Pottery)	
Mangueiras	Sambaquís	(Pottery)	(Pottery)		A.D.
Ananatuba	(Pottery)	"Middle and Southern" Sambaquís			B.C.
					1000
		"Archaic" Sambaquís	Cerca Grande	Santa Lucia	2000
					4000
					5000
					6000
				Alto Paraná	10,000

Figure 9.9. Amazon Delta-Eastern Brazil-Paraná River (lines I-J and J-K) sequence chart.

Orinoco Delta–Amazon Delta–Ucayali (Lines E–I and I–G)

Going back to the Lower Orinoco datum Line E–I (Figure 9.8) is run through British Guiana down to the Amazon delta (Rouse 1953; Evans and Meggers 1950; Meggers and Evans 1955, 1957). The Alaka phase of northwestern British Guiana is preceramic, but Barrancas-like influence is seen in the Palo Seco-like and Mabaruma pottery. Barrancas influences are not reported further east or south toward the Amazon delta, and the only possible tie between the Orinoco sequences and the mouth of the Amazon may be in the fine-lined incised pottery that is typical of Camoruca (Late Ronquín) and Arauquín (Petrullo 1939) and the Mazagão phase of Brazilian Guiana. Aristé and Maracá are contemporary with Mazagão. The latter (Nordenskiöld 1930) is known for its elaborate human effigy funerary urns.

The remainder of the Amazonian delta sequence is assigned absolute datings by guess alone. Annanatuba and Mangueiras are represented by sites which indicate small hunting-fishing and marginal agricultural communities of an Archaic type, and the pottery is simple incised and brushed ware, not relating closely to any of the better known Venezuelan or Amazonian styles. I am assuming that the idea of pottery reached the Amazon delta from the west, and, considering the early date for ceramics at the Orinoco delta, the dates assigned to Ananatuba and Mangueiras appear to me to be conservative. These phases may possibly relate to an early diffusion of incised and surface-roughened pottery that goes back to the time of Monagrillo, Barlovento, Valdivia, and pre-Cupisnique.

Marajoara represents the intrusion of Formative type culture into the Amazon delta, and Marajoara ceramics have very specific resemblances in the Miracanguera and Río Napo burial urns (Howard 1947).* The remaining phases in the Santarém-to-Iquitos column are represented by ceramic collections from a great many sites between the mouth of the Tapajós and the city of Manaos. At Santarém, proper, Easby (1952) has pointed out 2 distinct styles: one, the ornate incised and modeled Santarém; the other, an incised and modeled style of much less elaboration and with some affinities to Hupa-iya of the Ucayali and, probably, Barrancas of the Lower Orinoco. Easby has called this second style "Unrelated Ware." Nordenskiöld (1930) mentions and illustrates it from the vicinity of Santarém, from the Río Trombetas, and elsewhere. Rydén (1937) quotes from Kurt Nimuendaju's manuscript, referring to this same "Unrelated Ware" at a number of locations between Santarém and Miracanguera. Nimuendaju's name for it was "Konduri" which I have used here. The assumption, expressed on the sequence chart (Figure 9.8) , is that Santarém style may be, in part, a development out of Konduri. At the same and other sites in this Middle Amazonian region is another type of pottery, the Paura, which is fine-lined incised and engraved with predominantly rectilinear design elements. Paura has some resemblances to Venezuelan Arauquin and Mazagão of Brazil.

The correlations along these lines, lacking supporting evidence of radiocarbon or other "extra-cultural" forms of dating, are highly speculative. We have seen the surprisingly long time span of certain pottery traditions, such as the Barrancas and Saladero in the region of the Lower Orinoco, the Venezuelan northeast coast, and the West Indies. Such spans, of 500 to 1000 years, may be represented in some of the similarities of pottery types noted along the Amazon. These lags or continuities would, obviously, render invalid many of the equations we have made here.

Amazon Delta–Eastern Brazil–Paraná River (Lines I–J and J–K)

This chart (Figure 9.9) is the least satisfactory of all. The Amazon delta column has a basis in the stratigraphy of Evans and Meggers (1950), but little in the way of related material has been disclosed in the archaeology of coastal Brazil. At the opposite end of the profile lines, a highly tentative sequence may be rationalized from the archaeological literature of the Paraná and Uruguay Rivers.

Along the coasts of Para and Maranão, south of the Amazon delta, there are pottery remains which are said to relate to the middle and later periods of the delta sequence. Lopes (1924, 1925, 1928, 1932) describes what appear to be the refuse remains of ancient pile-villages containing urns and painted pottery that he brackets with the Marajoara style. Farther south, in Bahia, red-and-black-on-white painted urns occur in shellmounds in what appear to be late, superficial contexts. These last are probably connected with late occupations, or uses, of the sambaquís still farther south. Krone (1914) and Pereira de Godoy (1952), among others, report painted pottery and burial urns from the state of Sáo Paulo. Some of these urns are of the corrugated surfaced type and are attributed to the protohistoric and historic Tupí-Guaraní.

The question of earlier pottery in the sambaquís is much less clear. I have indicated it as "sambaquís (pottery)" on the chart, suggesting an earlier occurrence in the north than in the south. Plain coarse ware is mentioned from sites in the State of Para (Ferreira Penna 1876) and either plain or simple incised and painted wares are described from the Minas Geraes caves (Walter 1948; Evans 1950; Hurt, ed. 1956). These plain or simple pottery

*Recent excavations of Evans and Meggers on the Río Napo, in Ecuador, reveal villages filled with pottery refuse of an early Marajoara type.

K — L

PARANÁ & URUGUAY RIVERS	PLATE DELTA	PAMPAS NORTH——SOUTH	PATAGONIA	TIERRA del FUEGO MAGELLANIC——BEAGLE	
Chaná Timbú, etc. Arroyo las Conchas	Guaraní Arroyo Malo	Querandí — Puelche	Tehuelche	Tehuelche (Pottery)	1500
Malabrigo	Arroyo Sarandí	Arroyo Frias — Hucal	Tehuelchense 3		
Puerto de las Tunas	El Cerrillo	Matanzas — Cem. de Los Indios	Tehuelchense 2 (Pottery)	Bird Per.5	1000
Brazo Largo	(Pottery?)	(Pottery?)			500
Salto Grande (Pottery)		{Litoral Garcia — Gama		Pit House	A.D.
				Culture	B.C.
					1000
Santa Lucia			Tehuelchense I	Shell Knife Culture	2000
				Bird Per.4	
		Lanceolate Points	Proto-Tehuelchense	Bird Per.3	4000
					5000
		Tandilense		Bird Per.2	6000
			Toldense I	Bird Per. I	
Alto Paraná			Solanense Oliviense		10,000

Figure 9.10. Paraná River-Tierra del Fuego (line K-L) sequence chart.

wares appear to have been introduced into Archaic-type sambaquí or cave cultures in eastern Brazil, and the guess-dates I have selected for the introductions are estimated with reference to the appearance of early pottery at the Amazon delta and diffusion from there southward. The Archaic-type cultures of the sambaquís are frequently referred to, although only sketchily described. The entries I have made on the chart follow Serrano (1946), although he has offered no stratigraphic proof for his sequence. In Minas Geraes, a Cerca Grande phase has been referred to (Hurt, ed., 1956) as the oldest occupation of the caves and may well be the culture of Lagoa Santa man. Time estimates on Cerca Grande are relatively modest.

The leap from the vague and highly tentative Brazilian sequences to the Paraná-Uruguay regional sequence is one of the most difficult of all. In brief, we are trying to correlate East Brazilian archaeology, where there are no reliable sequences, with the Paraná-Uruguay region in which sequences are also lacking. Menghín (1955–56) refers to a forthcoming work to be published in the *Boletín de la Junta de Estudios Historicos de Misiones* (Argentina). I have not seen this, but from his reference assume that it deals with sequences, preceramic and ceramic, of a part of this region. The reader is referred to Menghín (1957) who presents opinions on various south American sequences.

The reader may note that the treatment of the Paraná-Uruguay data (Figure 9.9), as well as that of the Argentine Pampas (Figure 9.10), is a departure from the strictly taxonomic approach which was tried several years ago (Howard and Willey 1948). In attempting to rationalize sequences for the Paraná-Uruguay and Pampas regions, I have followed the lead of Alan L. Bryan and Roger C. Green (personal communication, 1956).

They have seriated sites, or site collections as described and illustrated in the literature, upon the absence or presence of pottery and upon the complexity of pottery decoration and form. In general, pottery is more abundant and shows greater elaboration in the north along the Paraná. Hence, sites on the Paraná lacking pottery, or possessing only pottery of relatively simple types, are considered as earlier than those in which pottery is abundant and more developed. Pottery traits found farther south, in the Pampas or in Patagonia, are considered to occur on a later time level. This seriation may be considered as a suggestive guide for future research but is certainly nothing more than this.

Salto Grande (Serrano 1932) is on the middle Uruguay between Federación and Concordia. It is chosen as representative of a hypothetical plain, or very simple decorated, pottery phase. Brazo Largo (Gatto 1939), also in the Uruguay drainage, is a small station rich in bone tools and weapons, with some chipped and ground stone tools, and with considerable incised and punctate decorated pottery. It is the selected representative of what is considered the next link in the series. Puerto de las Tunas (Pennino and Sallazzo 1927), in south central Uruguay, shows a pottery complex somewhat similar to Brazo Largo but with the addition of the linear-punctate type of decoration. Malabrigo (Frenguelli and Aparicio 1923) is representative of the Paraná River style of pottery in its florescence. Linear-punctation, zoomorphic adornos, white slipping, red-line decoration, and fingernail impressions are all a part of the Malabrigo complex. The site is in the Paraná drainage in the Argentine province of Santa Fe. Arroyo de las Conchas (Serrano 1934), in Entre Rios, Argentina, shows a similar ceramic complex with the addition of 16th century European trade goods.

Although the above seriation is put forward as a chronological one, it will be noted that the presumed "earlier" sites all lie slightly to the east of the 2 later ones. A counter-interpretation might be offered which would explain the differences in artifact assemblages as functions of geographical space (and possibly environment?) rather than time.

On the preceramic levels there are a number of possibilities in the Paraná-Uruguay region. Serrano (1932) describes collections which were collected from riverbank washouts at Arroyo Santa Lucia, near Monte Caseros in the province of Corrientes, Argentina. These consist of pebble and core tools, flaked by percussion, and include cobble choppers, scrapers, and knives. In addition, stemmed projectile points were picked up, as were grooved bolas stones and a few other ground stone objects. A very few potsherds were found but not described. There is, at least, reasonable doubt that all of this stone material had ceramic associations. In general, the chipped and ground stone materials are similar to those found with pottery. Santa Lucia is entered on the chart as a putative preceramic, Archaic-type phase, representative of the hypothetical period in this region antecedent to the introduction of pottery. Postulated as still farther back in time is the Alto Paraná complex, formulated by Menghín (1955–56) and incorporating data of his own from sites in Misiones, Argentina, with earlier findings of Mayntzhusen (1928) from near Puerto Yaguarazapa in Paraguay. Percussion chipped hand axes, picks, and scrapers are the principal tools. They are reported as being found in red soils underlying the humus and without ceramic or ground stone tool associations. I make no attempt here to evaluate critically this or other chipped stone complexes for which considerable age is claimed. As described and illustrated the Alto Paraná material does not appear radically different from the Santa Lucia complex nor the stonework found with the pottery associations. This, in itself, is no strong argument against antiquity, however; a percussion flaking industry could well have had great age and long persistence in the region.

To shift, again, to the late ranges of the time chart, there is one evident tie between the Paraná and Eastern Brazil. This is seen in the large burial urns, corrugated or decorated with polychrome geometric bands. Ambrosetti (1895), Schmidt (1934), and others report these from burial fields in southeastern Paraguay where they are identified with the Guaraní Indians. These late urn burials are not accommodated in the Paraná-Uruguay column (Figure 9.9) but appear in Figure 9.10 as "Arroyo Malo" and "Guarani" in the Plate delta column.

PARANÁ RIVER–TIERRA DEL FUEGO (LINE K–L)

South from the Paraná River, through the Plate delta, the Pampas, Patagonia, and down to Tierra del Fuego, there are numerous similarities in both ceramics and stone implements. Accordingly, a series of correlations can be effected (Figure 9.10). The difficulty is that there is, with few exceptions, little stratigraphic proof of sequence or chronology at any one point.

In the Plate delta column, El Cerrillo, Arroyo Sarandí, and Arroyo Malo (Lothrop 1932) are given their chronological ordering on the basis of pottery decoration and elaboration. El Cerrillo has unslipped tan or brown ware decorated with incision and linear-punctation. Similarities to the incised and linear-punctated pottery of the Paraná River are obvious, although such ornamental features as the zoomorphic adornos are lacking. There is no painted treatment. Arroyo Sanardí continues with the Paraná River tradition of linear punctation but, in addition, has red banded and zoned red decorated pottery as well as red and white-slipped ware. Arroyo Malo, which is a European contact site, has Guaraní type urn burials, corrugated and fingernail-impressed ware, and polychrome decoration.

In the Pampas Menghín and Bórmida (1950) make claims for an early lithic industry from the Tandilia caves. Their estimates on this, taken from paleoclimatological dating, are around 7000 to 5000 B.C. This Tandilense complex is equated with Bird's Magellanic Period 2 (Bird 1938, 1946). Extrapolating from Bird's Magellanic Period 3, I have postulated a Pampean horizon upon the presence of long lanceolate projectile points in surface collections from the Buenos Aires coast (Holmes 1912; Outes 1909; Aparicio, 1932). The Literal (northern coastal) (Outes 1909), Garcia (northern inland) (Bonaparte and Pisano 1950) and Gama (southern) (Daguerre 1934) phases are formulated as relatively late, preceramic entities. They all have stemmed triangular points, similar to Bird's Magellanic Period 4. Bolas and other ground stone implements are common.

Río Matanzas (Villegas Basavilbaso 1937) is used as a phase name under which to subsume sites of the northern Pampas that are characterized by plain, incised, and linear-punctated pottery. The equation is made with El Cerrillo. Cementario de los Indios (Torres 1922), in the south Pampas, has incised and punctated pottery but no painting, and it is placed on the same date line. Paradero Arroyo Frias (Ameghino 1915) and Hucal (Outes 1904) show mixtures of linear-punctated and red painted pottery types.

The Patagonian column follows Menghín (1952), and the Tierra del Fuego column, both Magellanic and Beagle Channel, is after Bird (1938, 1946). Bird's Magellanic Period 1 is dated by radiocarbon at about 7000 B.C. The long, straight-stemmed projectile points of the Bird Period 1 relate to Menghín's Toldense 1 phase, near the Deseado River. Antecedent to Toldense 1 are Menghín's Solanense and Oliviense complexes. These last are from shell refuse deposits on old marine terraces in the region of Comodoro Rivadavia and the Bahia Solano. Datings are geological estimates. Solanense artifacts include points with rounded or rounded-asymmetric bases; Oliviense, which is placed at 9000 B.C. or earlier, is a flake and scraper assemblage. Proto-Tehuelchense seems to relate, on lanceolate projectiles forms, to both Bird's Period 3 and to Ayampitín (see Figure 9.11) of

NORTHERN CHILE ARICA —— PISAGUA	N. CHILE RIO LOA	N.WEST ARGENTINA NORTH-CENTER-SOUTH	SANTIAGO del ESTERO	CÓRDOBA HIGHLANDS	PARANÁ & URUGUAY RIVERS	
Caleta Vitor Arica II	Inca ↑	Inca Trans.-Humahuaca- Aimogasta	Inca-Derived Represas	Comechingón	Chaná—Timbú, etc. Arroyo las Conchas Malabrigo Puerto de las Tunas	1500 1000
Arica I	Atacameño	Middle-Calchaquí–Belén	Marías (Averías (L. Mauca	Ongamira I Ongamira II (Pottery)	Brazo Largo	500
Pichalo II Pichalo I		Candelaria-Barreales	Bislín	Ongamira III	Salto Grande (Pottery)	A.D.
Quiani 2 Pre-Cer. Per.						B.C. 1000
Quiani 1 Shell Fish-hook Per.				Ongamira IV	Santa Lucia	2000 4000 5000
				Ayampitín	Alto Paraná	6000 10,000

Figure 9.11. Northern Chile-Northwestern Argentina-Paraná River (line M-K) sequence chart.

the Córdoba highlands (Gonzalez 1952). The remainder of the Patagonian sequence parallels the flint forms of Bird's sequence, and in its pottery phases ties to the Pampas. Tehuelchense 1 and Bird's Period 4 are, presumably, coexistent. This is also the same general time span of the Litoral, Garcia, and Gama complexes which, perhaps, could be set back several centuries to correspond to the beginnings of Bird Period 4 and Tehuelchense 1. In the far south, pottery comes in only in historic times and is found on the mainland side of the Straits rather than on Tierra del Fuego proper.

Although not indicated on the chart, Vignati's (1927) Period A, at Río Chico in eastern Tierra del Fuego, has its most likely correlation at Bird's Period 2 level. Period C, Río Chico, most likely corresponds to Bird Period 3.

The 2-period Beagle Channel sequence (Bird 1938, 1946) is placed as it is in order to cross-date the earlier "Shell-Knife," or Alacaluf-type, culture to Bird's Period 4 with its large bolas stones and small hafted scrapers. As Bird (1946: 21) notes, this "Shell-Knife" culture "evolved with slight change into the modern *Alacaluf* in the territory between the Strait and the Gulf of Peñas." The second Beagle Channel period, the "Pit House" culture, is proto-Yahgan and Yahgan. Age estimates, based upon rising shore lines, set the beginnings of the period at no later than 1800 years ago.

RADIOCARBON DATES PERTINENT TO LINE K–L

Fuegian date:

6689±450 B.C. Palli Aike Cave, Bird's Period 1. (Libby 1955, C-485)

TIERRA DEL FUEGO–NORTHERN CHILE–BOLIVIA (LINES L–M AND M–A)

Nothing in northern Chile seems to correspond to the earlier lithic complexes of Tierra del Fuego (Figure 9.12). The preceramic complexes of the north Chilean coast have little specifically in common with the far south. The intercalation of Arica, Pisagua, and Taltal follows Bird (1943). The correlation of northern Chile with the Bolivian highlands, and the Peru-Bolivian sequences, rests on relatively little substantial evidence. I have set what appears to be the earliest Chilean pottery, Pichalo I, at the B.C.–A.D. line. If early Pichalo pottery has remote relationships with the pre-Chavín horizon plain pottery of the Peruvian coast, or with later Chavínoid materials, this placement assumes considerable time lag between Peru and Chile. The north Chilean preceramic phases are set to come up to the beginning of the Christian era, 1000 or more years later than the end of the preceramic in Peru. Perhaps this estimated lag is excessive. Higher up in the sequence, the Arica I position is assigned upon the basis of Tiahuanacoid sherds found in that context. My estimate for cross-dating is somewhere in the long interval between Classic Tiahuanaco and Decadent Tiahuanaco, or about where we have set the Tiahuanacoid horizon for most of Peru.

Around Coquimbo, the cultural phase that is referred to as Chilean Diaguita (Latcham 1928; Cornely 1951) has good Tiahuanacoid resemblances and, by all rights, should be somewhere within the time range of Derived Tiahuanaco. El Molle (Cornely 1940, 1953), another phase in the same region, has a predominantly plain ware tradition which, although not the same as Pichalo I or II, may have some remote relationships.

In the Central Valley of Chile there are suggestions of preceramic levels (Bird 1938, 1943). The Kofkeche period of Bullock (1955), featuring urns, generally plain but sometimes decorated with red and white painting, seems to precede the Araucanian period. Of the last there is little known archaeologically.

Throughout north and central Chile the Inca horizon sets a late prehistoric cross-dating line.

NORTHERN CHILE–NORTHWESTERN ARGENTINA–PARANÁ RIVER (LINE M–K)

In an attempt to relate the north Chilean cultures to their neighboring and somewhat similar cultural phases in the Argentine north, I have run a line from Arica across the Andes and down through northwestern Argentina to the Paraná sequence (Figure 9.11). Inland in northern Chile the oases of the Río Loa were occupied contemporaneously with the Arica I and II farmers of the coast (Latcham 1936, 1938; Rydén 1944; Bennett 1946d). There is no evidence of an earlier occupation. The Atacameño culture of these Río Loa oases shares many traits with the Middle and Late (Humahuaca) periods of an inferred sequence in the northern section of northwestern Argentina. An Inca overlay is present in both cases. A detailed sequence formulation and correlation of the north, central, south, and east sections of northwestern Argentina has already been advanced (Bennett, Bleiler, and Sommer 1948), and the general sequence which I offer in these columns is a summary of this. A revision and refinement of the sequence of the southern section is based upon recent studies by Rex Gonzalez (1955). Gonzalez's Aguada and Ciénega phases would be subsumed in my chart under Barreales. He has also subdivided what Bennett and associates (1948) have called Belén and Aimogasta. The early pottery

TITICACA BASIN NORTH—SOUTH (A)	NORTHERN CHILE ARICA—PISAGUA (M)	N. CHILE TALTAL—COQUIMBO	CENT. CHILE	TIERRA del FUEGO BEAGLE—MAGELLANIC (L)	
Inca Colla Lupaca Decadent Tiah.	Caleta Vitor Arica II	Inca	Inca	Bird Per. 5	1500 1000
	Arica I	Diaguita	Araucanian		500
(Derived Tiah.) Pucara Tiahuanaco	Pichalo II Pichalo I	El Molle	Kofkeche	Pit House	A.D.
Early Tiah. Chiripa Qaluyu	Quiani 2 Pre-Ceramic Per.			Culture	B.C. 1000
	Quiani I Shell Fish-hook Per.	Shell Fish-hook Per.	Pre-Ceramic	Shell Knife Culture Bird Per.4 Bird Per.3	2000 4000 5000
Ayampitín Viscachani				Bird Per.2 Bird Per.1	6000 10000

Figure 9.12. Tierra del Fuego-Northern Chile-Bolivia (lines L-M and M-A) sequence chart.

types, Candelaria, Barreales, and Bislín, are all essentially monochrome and feature incised decoration. I have equated these with the end of the plain pottery Pichalo phases of Chile.

The Córdoba–San Luis highlands, which form an intermediate zone between Andean cultures and those of the Paraná and Pampas, have a sequence beginning with Ayampitín. Ayampitín type projectile points have also been found in various regions of northwestern Argentina as well (Gonzalez 1955). The Córdoba sequence continues through the Ongamira IV and III phases, which are nonceramic and almost certainly hunting-gathering, into the pottery-bearing, small projectile point levels of Ongamira I and II (Menghín and Gonzalez (1954). These later phases are in many ways prototypical to Comechingón culture and are, possibly, agricultural. I have speculated that this ceramic introduction might have been from the northwest and have so placed Ongamira II as somewhat later than Bislín.

RADIOCARBON DATES PERTINENT TO LINE M–K

San Luis date:

6020±100 B.C. Ayampitín level at Intihuasi Cave (Barendsen, Deevey, and Gralenski 1957, Y-228)

Bolivia–Upper Madeira (Line A–H)

This profile (Figure 13) is a synopsis of the one offered by Bennett (1936) in which he attempted to correlate the Bolivian altiplano with his own Bolivian lowland excavations

TITICACA BASIN NORTH——SOUTH	U. MADEIRA ARANI	U. MADEIRA COCHABAMBA	U. MADEIRA MIZQUE	UPPER MADEIRA SANTA CRUZ—MOJOS	
			Incallacta		1500
Inca	Inca Ruin	Sipisipi			
Colla Lupaca	Arani III			Rio Palacios	
			Holquin		
				Upper Velarde	
Decadent Tiah.	Arani II	Tiquipaya		Hernmarck	1000
				Lower Velarde	500
			Perereta		
(Derived Tiah.)	Arani I	Cochabamba Tiah.			
Pucara Tiahuanaco					A.D.
Early Tiah.					B.C.
Chiripa					
Qaluyu					1000
					2000
					4000
					5000
					6000
Ayampitín					
Viscachaní					10,000

Figure 9.13. Bolivia-Upper Madeira (line A-H) sequence chart.

and with the earlier work of Nordenskiöld (1913, 1917). There is virtually no new information here. My chart omits several phases which Bennett enters, and it should be compared to his diagram (1936: 412) and to Howard's summary (1947: 74). The key correlation is the Derived Tiahuanaco–Arani I–Cochabamba Tiahuanaco line and the continuance of this horizon eastward to Lower Velarde.

OBSERVATIONS

This review reveals the difficulties in attempting correlations of archaeological culture sequences across major area lines in South and Central America. Many of these difficulties are simply due to the lack of "extra-cultural" dates, that is, radiocarbon, geological, or calendrical. Other complications derive from the lack of adequate local and regional sequences within single areas and of the synthesizing of these. Only in Peru-Bolivia and the West Indies are there sufficient numbers of well-tested regional sequences. In Venezuela, Colombia, Ecuador, the Amazon delta, parts of northwestern Argentina and north Chile, and Tierra del Fuego sequence work has been begun, and in some of these areas there is great promise for the future. For large parts of Brazil, southern South America, and lower Central America archaeological sequences are lacking or only partially outlined.

I would single out the recent field work in Ecuador, Colombia, Venezuela, and parts of the Amazon as producing the most exciting results of the last decade. Ties with Middle

America and Peru are seen in the North Andean sequences, and there are now opportunities to relate Andean cultures eastward along the Caribbean and down the Amazon. It seems fairly certain now that agricultural village life and pottery making was established in the eastern lowlands as early as the beginning of the first millennium B.C.

A number of interesting speculations come to mind in a review of these charts. First, evidence is slowly accumulating to support the view that agriculture-based societies from southern Middle America to Peru were linked very definitely by common participation in ceramic and other traditions as early as 1000 to 500 B.C. This evidence continues to suggest that the main currents of diffusion flowed from north to south. As a corollary of this there is also the suggestion of the diffusion of early pottery-making ideas antedating 1000 B.C. and, probably, antedating maize agriculture. Monagrillo, Barlovento, Valdivia, pre-Cupisnique, and, perhaps, Barrancas and Ananatuba-Mangueiras are the possible cultures involved. All appear to have had a fishing-gathering mode of subsistence, probably supplemented in some cases by farming. Rouse (personal communication, 1956), following Sauer's lead (1952) has postulated a possible premaize root-crop horticulture developing in lowland South America. It may be, that in some localities, manioc farming had its beginnings on this time level. Another observation is that early ceramic cultures were well established in the tropical Montaña of eastern Ecuador and Peru, that these cultures were related to those of the adjacent Andes, and that they were the sources for diffusions which spread from there to the east.

A summary of the problems and questions raised by this kind of rapid survey would run many times longer than all that I have said so far. I can only end on the hope that whoever undertakes the next such task of correlations will draw upon much new evidence from many places.

Author Notes

Author's Original Note: While this article was in press my attention was called to Hilbert's recent publication (1955) on the archaeology of the Santarém and Miracanguera region of the Amazon. I have not yet had access to this report.

Datings of the earlier Amazonian Delta phases shown in Figure 8 are somewhat earlier than those estimated by Meggers and Evans (personal communication, August, 1957).

For the Cochabamba column of Figure 13 Rydén (1952) has reported Classic Tiahuanaco graves at Tupuraya; he also postulates a Chullpa Pampa phase as being antecedent to Classic Tiahuanaco in the Cochabamba region. For more recent writings on Bolivian archaeology, which I have been able to consult only after this article went to press, see Ibarra Grasso (1956a, 1956b) and Ponce Sangines, ed. (1957).

F

The New World as a Whole

In 1958 I was invited to present a paper on the evolution of New World Precolumbian cultures at the Darwin Centennial conference to be held at the University of Chicago. I had just completed, with Philip Phillips, our book *Method and Theory in American Archaeology* (Willey and Phillips, 1958). Although the concept of cultural evolution was implicit in much that we had said, we had not addressed the idea directly. This invitation gave me the opportunity to do so. What did I think about it? How did it work? And to what degree did the concept explain the course of New World prehistory?

As I read back over my essay now, I am not sure that I answered these questions very clearly or effectively. I made a proper obeisance to the idea of evolution, but I was really writing about Americanist culture history. Reflecting on my current theoretical position about evolution, the best I can say is that I have an abiding belief that the spheres of subsistence, settlement, sociopolitical groupings and organization, and ideology are interlinked in very important ways in human culture and society, and that development in any one of these spheres will eventually effect changes in the others. This is both a systemic and an evolutionary view, but it is not necessarily a materialist evolutionary view. I am convinced that ideology—religion, world-view, or however one may wish to phrase it—had one of the determinative roles in the evolution of New World societies and cultures. Admittedly, the relationships between ideas and the material world are poorly understood, and their illumination remains an important task in archaeology and, indeed, in all historical studies.

The essay, "New World Prehistory" was written at the invitation of the journal *Science* in 1959, very soon after the Darwin Centennial piece. I enjoyed writing it more than I had the earlier paper. Rather than worrying about evolution, I looked upon it as a "straight telling" of culture history. Let me hasten to add that I am aware that there is no "straight telling" of any history—everyone who sets out on such a task in archaeology or any historical study is biased or has a point of view. I leave it to the reader to decide upon my bias in this article, evolutionary or nonevolutionary. I am not sure of this myself even today as I look back on it.

The eight problems or sets of questions with which I opened "New World Prehistory" are still good ones and worthy of continued investigation. For a quick update of 1960 opinions, let us take them up in the same order in which I originally listed them:

1. Today, the case looks much better for a "pre-big-game-hunter" population in the Americas than it did when this article was first published. Indeed, I am inclined to think that the case has been proven (see Adovasio *et al.* 1978; Dillehay *et al.* 1982); but, admittedly, we know very little about the life styles of very early Americans.
2. We still do not know if these "pre-big-game-hunter" Americans were the ones who invented the later big-game-hunting technology. My surmise would be that later immigrants from Asia had some input in the development of the New World Paleo-Indian industries.
3. Later Arctic and Boreal hunters and fishers of the New World almost certainly came into this hemisphere with what we think of in the Americas as Archaic stage cultural adaptations. Questions remain, though, as to how and in what ways Asiatic influences affected the development of Archaic stage cultures in areas farther to the south in the New World.
4. In 1960, it was known that the important seed plant maize was domesticated in southern Mexico at *ca.* 5000 B.C., though at that time it was of only marginal dietary importance. We now are aware that this primitive maize plant had an early dissemination from this hearth and was carried into South America, especially into the northern and central Andes and probably into the adjacent tropical forest regions. Recent datings of manioc cultivation place that cultigen at least as early as 2600 B.C. in these South American forest regions (Roosevelt 1980). On the bases of various lines of evidence, an earlier backward extension of this manioc date to 4000 B.C. seems reasonable.
5. We now know that pottery is at least as old as the fourth millennium B.C. in Ecuador (Bischof and Viteri 1972; Marcos 1980) and Colombia (Reichel-Dolmatoff 1980; Bray 1984), and perhaps in Panama (Cooke 1984). There are also indications of great age for pottery in the Amazon basin (Brochado and Lathrap 1980; Simoes 1971, 1978) and in eastern Brazil (Brochado 1980). Both Mesoamerican (MacNeish, Peterson, and Flannery 1970; Tolstoy 1978) and Peruvian (Conrad 1980) ceramics are substantially later than those of Colombia-Ecuador.
6. Sedentary life based upon farming may have first come into being in the Intermediate Area—that is, in Ecuador and portions of Caribbean Colombia—at *ca.* 3000–2500 B.C. It is possible that it is equally old in the Amazon basin. In both Caribbean Colombia and the Amazon, manioc was probably the principal cultivated plant at this early time. In the Ecuadorian highlands and coast the most important food plant was probably maize. Maize-farming-based villages were known from Mesoamerica *ca.* 2000–1500 B.C. In Peru they date from just after 2000 B.C. It should be noted, however, that by *ca.* 2500 B.C. the Peruvian coast had sedentary villages that appear to have been primarily dependent upon marine foods (Moseley 1975). Thus, there is no ready answer to the 1960 question about the origins and spread of sedentary life based upon farming, though we do know much more about the problem now than we did at that time.
7. We know more about sedentism, based upon subsistence other than agriculture, than we did in 1960, though we still have much to learn. Similarly, we still have much to learn about the way agriculture was diffused and accepted in regions of the Americas where it arrived in relatively late times.
8. It would now appear that New World "civilization"—if we define that term by the presence of great public works—first came into being in Peru, in the Initial Ceramic Period (*ca.* 1800–1000 B.C.). The dates for comparable phenomena in Mesoamerica are, perhaps, a little later (*ca.* 1200–600 B.C., the "Olmec horizon"). If we insist upon large

urban-zone settlements as the criterion for "civilization," the earliest dates remain at about the beginning of the Christian era, for either Mesoamerica or Peru (as the chart, Figure 1, in the article shows). There are as yet no fully satisfactory answers as to "how" the New World civilizations arose. But in addition to an adequate economic base and large population concentrations, it seems likely that one precondition for attaining the civilizational threshold must have been intensive intercommunication and interaction among the various regions that made up what we think of as a larger "culture area," or "archaeological culture area with time-depth." In both Mesoamerica and Peru this precondition of regional intercommunication and interaction within a larger area was met by at least the beginning of the first millennium B.C. Trade and commerce were certainly one aspect of this regional interaction, but the stimulation of ideas and the sharing of ideas was inevitably another.

"New World Archaeology in 1965" was a short paper presented at a meeting of the American Philosophical Society in that year, and it was an update of the 1960 New World culture history essay. In the short time allotted to me, I had to skate pretty rapidly over the New World scene, so I structured the talk along three very general themes: (1) early man in the Americas; (2) the rise of New World agriculture; and (3) the beginnings of complex society and civilization. Major changes over the 1960–65 period were few. A notable innovation, however, was the dating of big architecture in Peru to the second millennium B.C.

"New World Prehistory: 1974" was presented at the annual meeting of the Archaeological Institute of America in St. Louis, in December 1973. Subsequently, I revised it slightly for publication in the *American Journal of Archaeology*. In the intervening years between this paper and the one published in 1966, I had written my two-volume textbook, *An Introduction to American Archaeology* (Willey 1966a, 1971b)—a very detailed look at the prehistory of the entire New World. My organization of the 1974 article follows that of the American Philosophical Society paper. The article is, however, more discursive and theoretical than the earlier ones. My brief observations about art on the Paleolithic (Old World) and Paleo-Indian (New World) levels go off in a speculative direction. In speaking about agricultural beginnings I examine Lewis Binford's (1972a) hypothesis about "post-Pleistocene adaptations" and Kent Flannery's (1968b, 1972) ideas about "incipient agriculture." Looking at the growth of New World civilizations, as well as those of the Old World, I wonder about the apparent developmental or evolutionary process of culture growth through alternating periods of "horizonal unifications" of regional cultures and ones of regional separatism. Thinking about this issue now, it is my impression that we take the "unification" side of things for granted in cultural evolution. That is, the drawing together of peoples, products, and ideas is assumed to be a necessary process in the development of cultural complexity and elaboration. But what happens when "unification" breaks down in periods of regional separatism? Is such periodic "regionalism" to be thought of as "retrogressive," or is it necessary if new ideas are to be generated, free from the constraints of ideological "unifications" (empires, dominant world-views)?

10

Historical Patterns and Evolution in Native New World Cultures

(From *Evolution After Darwin*, Sol Tax, ed., Vol. 2, pp. 111–141, University of Chicago Press, 1960. Reprinted by permission of the University of Chicago Press.)

Culture is the means whereby man adapts himself to his natural and social environments and to his pre-existent cultural milieu. The history of this adaptation is the story of cultural evolution. Like biological evolution, the process of the evolution of culture are selective ones by which the species promotes it survival and fulfillment. The "species," in this case, is man and the social groups in which he lives. The courses which man, society, and culture follow in meeting the challenges of environmental opportunity and in seeking and achieving adaptations are not programmed by any laws of inevitability. "Evolution," as Dobzhansky has observed (1958, p. 1096), "is not striving to achieve some fore-ordained goal; it is not the unfolding of predetermined episodes and situations." Nor are these courses, as the same author makes clear, completely the result of pure chance.

Man adapts himself to his natural, social, and cultural settings. It is, however, in his relationship to the natural environment that his adaptive efficiency may be most easily adjudged. Depending upon a combination of the natural resources and the technical culture which he evolves to take advantage of them, he perishes or thrives as a hunter, collector, or farmer. There is abundant evidence from archaeology and history to see how man's technical culture, as directed toward the problems of subsistence, has evolved, more or less steadily, toward greater effectiveness.

The annals of human history also show that as man's technical heritage evolved, it did so concomitantly with significant changes in his social settings. These changes created environmental challenges of another order. The selective-adaptive equation of a better spear to kill more game became complicated by the factor of more people both to kill and to eat the game. Despite the fact that through the ages the spear has also been used by some to dissolve the demographic dilemma, the main trends of social inventiveness have been those which sought ways to accommodate man to man as well as man to nature. This accommodation is expressed in various forms of social and political organization; and, although it is more difficult to evaluate the adaptive efficiency of these social forms than it is to appraise the tool-making and food-producing aspects of culture, it is possible to trace a general evolution in their history of increasing size and complexity. Developing along with the technological order and the social order is the other aspect of man's culture which is concerned with the realm of ideas. Religion, art, science, world view—it has been summed up in essence by Redfield as the "moral order" (1953). The evolution of these institutions is not well understood; however, their growth appears, in some degree, to be related to both the technological order and the social order. Thus Kluckhohn (1960) states:

> The association of type of economy with a specific kind of social organization and of these and other aspects of culture with one sort of moral order as opposed to another is by no means altogether a random one. Hence one can anticipate that there will ordinarily be some determinable relationships between the size of social groups and characteristics of their value systems.

Perhaps an analogy with biological evolution may again be useful here. In this regard Dobzhansky (1958, p. 1097) has said:

> Genes determine the possibility of culture but not its content, just as they determine the possibility of human speech but not what is spoken. The cultural evolution of mankind is superimposed on its biological evolution; the causes of the former are non-biological without being contrary to biology, just as biological phenomena differ from those of inanimate nature but are not isolated from them.

In this same way it seems probable that the technological and social basis of a culture or civilization provides a platform for and sets limits to its artistic, religious, and philosophic forms, but the forms themselves and their content are the resultants of human genius and the events of particular culture histories.

In attempting to trace the courses and processes of the evolution of New World cultures, we will define, first, the major subsistence and settlement types that are found in prehistoric America. These will then be described and examined within the framework of what are called "basic New World life-patterns." These life-patterns are historical spheres or continuities of great geographic extent and long chronologic persistence. Each is characterized by an underlying natural environmental-subsistence ecology, as well as by particular societal or community types and by cultural institutions. The reconstructions of cultural ecology from natural environmental habitats and tool types, of social units from settlement patterns, and of cultural forms from whatever available clues are, of course, limited by the nature of archaeological data. The quantity and quality of archaeological inference will vary greatly as one moves from the relative security of subsistence and settlement interpretations to those involving the more abstract—and, at the same time, more uniquely and interestingly human—results of men's minds and hands. Inference and its reliability will also vary with the richness or poverty of the record and with the possibilities of injecting into it the reinforcements of ethnohistorical documentation. Nevertheless, any culture history of the native Americas which is to be more than a chronicle account of artifact types must reckon with such inferences.

The extent to which cultural institutions and forms are functionally and causally interrelated with each other and with subsistence and settlement (societal) types is, of course, a major nexus of the problem of human cultural evolution. We cannot pretend to offer many answers in this discussion, but if human beings living in social groups in the natural world are the creators and bearers of culture, it seems likely that such interrelationships exist.

NEW WORLD PATTERNS OF CULTURE

SUBSISTENCE TYPES

There are three principal subsistence types native to the New World: big-game hunting, gathering-collecting, and cultivation.

Big-game hunting refers to the stalking and killing of large mammals as a principal source of food and clothing. It was a mode of subsistence widespread in the Americas in Pleistocene times (antedating 7000 B.C.). In later eras it was also followed on a somewhat more restricted geographic scale. It is, obviously, conditioned strongly by natural environmental circumstances.

Gathering-collecting refers to all those means of procuring food from the natural setting except the hunting of big game or the cultivation and domestication of plants and animals. The nature of the foods may be small animals, fish, shellfish, roots, seeds, nuts, and berries. The occasional taking of large game is not precluded, although this is not a specialization. At one time or another gathering-collecting economies characterized most parts of aboriginal America. Although there are clues to their appearance as early as the Pleistocene, they are more typical of the recent geological era. *Gathering-collecting* may be subtyped into (*a*) *gathering*, where food resources were extremely meager, the techniques for obtaining them simple and unspecialized, and the efforts of the people involved devoted almost wholly to the food quest[1]; (*b*) *collecting*, where there are more ample resources and more effective techniques; and (*c*) *intensive collecting*, which is marked by abundant resources, specialized techniques, and the accumulation of food surpluses.

Cultivation of food plants is the only major type of food production in native America.[2] Its origins may begin as early as the close of the Pleistocene, but the pattern was one of only partial economic significance until the second millennium .B.C., when it became of primary importance in Nuclear America (Willey and Phillips, 1958, pp. 144–47). Maize was the most important stable crop, and at the time of the discovery of America by the Europeans it was found spread over the southern half of North America and the northern two-thirds of South America. Manioc, another staple, had a more limited distribution. From the points of view of techniques and productiveness, native American *cultivation* types may be considered as (*a*) *incipient*, where either food plants, farming techniques, or both are but partially developed, and the produce has only a minor role in the economy; (*b*) *established*, where the primary means of food-getting is farming; and (*c*) *intensive*, where, as a result of favorable soils, climatic conditions, a variety of nutritious plants, and the employment of techniques such as irrigation, terracing, "floating gardens," and fertilizers, a high productivity is assured.

SETTLEMENT PATTERNS

As they reflect the nature of the community, we have classified New World native settlements into five major types: *camps*, *semipermanent villages*, *permanent villages*, *towns-and-temples*, and *cities*.

The *camp* site is small in extent and marked by thin and scattered refuse. There are few or no clues to dwellings or other structures. When found as the only type of settlement for a society and culture, it is reflective of a small, nonsedentary community unit, probably a wandering band of fewer than one hundred individuals. Such bands roamed over territories of varying extent and followed a hunting or a gathering-collecting subsistence (Beardsley *et al.*, 1956, pp. 135–38.[3] On the American scene the camp is found in virtually all parts of both continents and at all time periods.

Semipermanent villages are those which give evidence of substantial occupation over an appreciable span of time. Traces of perishable dwellings may be found; accumulated refuse is often deep; and cemeteries may be in or near the site. They were the living places of communities which appear to have occupied such locations sporadically or to have shifted their site locus after every few years. Inhabitants must have numbered several hundred. The semipermanent village marks a shift from a wandering toward a sedentary life. In some American areas it is correlated with a change from food collecting to intensive collecting or to cultivation.[4]

The *permanent village* settlement is the locus of a community which has occupied the same spot steadily over a long period of time. It reflects this sedentism in permanence of architectural features as well as refuse concentration. Its occupants numbered from a few hundred to over a thousand. The social and political organization of these communities may have rested upon kinship, but there are instances from ethnohistory of chiefs and social class distinctions. In the New World the permanent village, in both archaeological and ethnohistoric times, is most often associated with established cultivation. The American data pertain to two subtypes of permanent villages. The first has a unitary or "undifferentiated" settlement plan. In this, the village is a compact unit of dwellings which may contain within itself a special temple or politicoreligious structure. The second—a dispersed or "differentiated" subtype—has a nucleus or politicoreligious center which is surrounded at varying distances by small hamlet or homestead satellites.[5]

The *town-and-temple* settlement pattern and community type is an enlargement and elaboration of the permanent village pattern. The total community is now likely to be a dispersed and differentiated one. The politicoreligious, or "ceremonial," center is the principal focus. It may, or may not, be within the confines of a compact town; but in either case it is usually surrounded by satellite villages and hamlets. The population of the total community probably ran to a few thousand. Their social and political organization was probably hierarchical, with governmental authority supplanting kinship. These towns were the centers of full-time artisans and the residences of rulers, and activities in connection with the temples were directed by an organized priesthood.[6] The town-and-temple settlement is associated with established or intensive cultivation and is best known from Middle America and Peru, although the type is also found in other parts of South and Central America, the West Indies, and in the southeastern and southwestern United States.

The *city*, as distinct from the town-and-temple, cannot be defined upon the basis of settlement features alone, although sheer size and population numbers are among the criteria. The native American city is known only from parts of Middle America and Peru. It was the nerve center of a civilization. It attracted to its precincts the artisans, artists, and specialists. Its temples housed pantheons of deities. It was a focus of trade, of the collection of taxes, and frequently of the military power of the state. It is characterized by monumental architecture, by great arts, and in some places, as in the territory of the lowland Maya, by evidences of true mathematical and astronomic sciences and writing. Its actual settlement pattern may be compact and truly urban, or it may be differentiated into a politicoreligious center surrounded at a distance by villages and hamlets. Its traditions may be relatively homogeneous, or it may have a more cosmopolitan cast. Among the native New World cities, some appear to have maintained a rather limited regional scope of power and influence, while others were undoubtedly the capitals of large empires.[7]

HISTORICAL OUTLINES OF BASIC NEW WORLD LIFE-PATTERNS

As noted in the introduction, the "basic New World life-patterns" are conceived of as historical entities of great geographic-chronologic scope, each distinguished by the persistences of certain subsistence and community types and cultural forms. The exact number of such life-patterns in the New World is, of course, debatable and somewhat arbitrary. A few major ones emerge from the welter of archaeological facts, and we shall discuss these and refer also to others with less ample data.

PLEISTOCENE GATHERERS (?)

There are suggestions, although the evidence is by no means conclusive, that the earliest inhabitants of the New World were peoples following a very simple gathering type of subsistence. At Tule springs, Nevada, there is an artifact assemblage of crude chipped scrapers and chopping tools found in association with extinct camel, bison, and horse bones and with a radiocarbon date of about 22000 B.C. (Harrington, 1955; Simpson, 1955; Wormington, 1957, pp. 197–98). The discoveries in Friesenhahn Cave, Texas, of scrapers and choppers date from well back into the Wisconsin glacial stage, if not earlier (Sellards, 1952; Krieger, 1953; Wormington, 1957, pp. 218–19). Somewhat later, but almost certainly of terminal Pleistocene age, are the rather nondescript scraper-chopper-like stone tools from the lowest levels of Fishbone Cave, Nevada (Orr, 1956; Wormington, 1957, pp. 192–93), and Danger Cave, Utah (Jennings, 1957).[8] None of these artifact groups clearly represents a big-game-hunting economy. Their extremely unspecialized nature is vaguely suggestive of Old World Lower Paleolithic cultures (Willey and Phillips, 1958, pp. 82–86). Their presence in the Americas may result from man's very early migrations to these continents, of which we have now only the most imperfect record. On the other hand, it is possible that these finds are merely partial or incomplete assemblages of the Pleistocene big-game-hunting pattern.

PLEISTOCENE BIG-GAME HUNTERS

The earliest life-pattern which can be clearly formulated for the New World is that of the Pleistocene big-game hunters (Willey and Phillips, 1958, pp. 85–103). Its origins are uncertain. In the pursuit of large Ice Age mammals and in the employment of pressure-flaked projectile points it has general Old World Upper Paleolithic parallels, but the forms of the American points and other artifacts differ from those of the Old World. Its age is best defined from the period just antedating and concurrent with the final substage of the Wisconsin glaciation. Radiocarbon dates and geological estimates indicate this to be the span from about 12000 to about 7000 B.C., although there are a few dates which go back earlier (Willey and Phillips, 1958, pp. 87 and 91; Crook and Harris, 1958). The Sandia and Clovis projectile points and associated flint scrapers and knives, together with mammoth remains and the bones of other extinct fauna, are the best-known earlier representatives of the big-game-hunting pattern.[9] The long, fluted, and fishtailed Clovis type point is widely distributed through North America, particularly east of the Rocky Mountains. This fluted point form is peculiarly American; and, although no prototypes have yet been discovered in either the New or the Old World, it is possible to trace its later developments into the Folsom type points. The Folsom complex dates from 9000 to 7000 B.C. and is found in the Colorado and New Mexico High Plains country.[10] The Folsom fluted points display technical improvements over the earlier and somewhat less specialized Clovis forms. The Folsom point is widest just back of the piercing end, and the flutes or channels on each side are longer and occupy a greater surface area of the implement. Such features probably ensured a more effective puncturing of the hide of the animal (usually a kind of bison now extinct) and more profuse bleeding. Thus a reasonable argument can be made out for a progressive adaptive efficiency of the Folsom point over the Clovis point.

Early Post-Pleistocene Hunters

In the subsequent post-Pleistocene (*ca.* 7000–5000 B.C.) the trend in the manufacture of points is to drop out the fluting feature altogether. Such types as the Eden, Scottsbluff, Plainview, and Angostura (Wormington, 1957, pp. 103 ff.), while retaining something of the lanceolate Clovis-Folsom outline, lack the fluting. This trend may mark a lessening in hunting efficiency, although it is possible that with changes to modern fauna the fluted point became less effective.

The Pleistocene big-game-hunting pattern apparently spread from North to Middle and to South America. In these areas, in Pleistocene or early post-Pleistocene contexts, lanceolate, well-chipped, but unfluted points have been found associated with mammoth and other extinct animals (Wormington, 1957, pp. 199–205; Willey and Phillips, 1958, pp. 99–103).

As noted, the camp type settlement is associated with the Pleistocene big-game-hunting pattern. In fact, many of the sites appear to have been little more than "kills" or "butchering stations." All inferences point to small wandering populations. Very little has ever been found other than the equipment used for the hunt and for the preparation of the meat and hides of the animals. Crude paint palettes, stone beads, and little incised bone disks, taken from a Folsom context, are among the few exceptions to this.

Collectors of the North American Desert

The "North American Desert," as the environmental homeland of a food-collecting life-pattern of long persistence, may be defined as the vast arid and semiarid basin, range, and plateau country which in North America lies between the Rocky Mountains and the mountain systems of the Pacific Coast and stretches from southern Canada deep into Mexico (Jennings and Norbeck, 1955; Jennings *et al.*, 1956, pp. 69–72; Jennings, 1957, pp. 276–87). There are indications that it was in this territory that the moist conditions of the Pleistocene first began to give way to those of the warmer, drier Altithermal climatic period. The onset of the Altithermal is placed at about 5000 B.C., but in the North American Desert basin, as might be anticipated, a collecting life-pattern seems to have been established even earlier than this. Its origins may lie, in part, in the possible earlier Pleistocene gathering pattern just discussed; they may be found, also, in a changeover from the big-game-hunting pattern to the hunting of lesser animals and seed collecting that was brought about by the disappearance of the grasslands and the Pleistocene fauna; and the probability also exists of new population movements or diffusions from the north and, more remotely, from the Old World. Levels representative of a Desert collecting pattern in Danger Cave, Utah, are dated as early as 7500 B.C. (Jennings, 1957, pp. 60–67); Wormington, 1957, pp. 193–95). These contain projectile points of both corner-notched and stemless forms that are reminiscent of other early Desert pattern types. Slab milling stones and twined baskets are also associated with these levels. Among other early dates for what appear to be the beginnings of the Desert collecting pattern are those for the Humboldt phase levels of the Leonard site, in Nevada (*ca.* 9000–5000 B.C.) (Heizer, 1951; Wormington, 1957, pp. 190–92), and for Fort Rock Cave, in Oregon (*ca.* 7000 B.C.)

(Cressman, 1951; Wormington, 1957, p. 184). The artifacts at Fort Rock include notched and unstemmed points, scrapers, drills, grinding stones, bone tools, twined basketry, and bark sandals.

Throughout the Desert basin there are numerous locations which show the continuity of these complexes with their varieties of stemmed, notched, and unstemmed projectile points and milling and handstones. The upper levels at Leonard Rockshelter are placed at between 3000 and 2000 B.C. (Heizer, 1951). The Danger Cave stratigraphy has a continuation of the Desert collecting pattern, from its early date until 1800 B.C. (Jennings, 1957). The Cochise continuum of cultures in southern Arizona and southern New Mexico also demonstrates the long existence of the Desert collecting pattern from before 5000 B.C. up to almost the beginning of the Christian Era (Sayles, 1945; Sayles and Antevs, 1941, 1955; Wormington, 1957, pp. 169–73). In the Cochise sequence there is a definite trend through time toward more numerous, larger, and more carefully deepened and shaped milling stones and mortars. This trend is almost certainly expressive of an increased "settling-in" and adjustment to the collecting of seed foods. It is correlated with greater stability of living sites at the end of the Cochise sequence, where there is archaeological testimony to semipermanent villages of houses with prepared floors and storage pits. It is undoubtedly of great significance that remains of a very primitive maize have been found in the Cochise sequence, dating back to 2000 B.C., or before. Such maize appears to have been in its initial stages of cultivation and to have served as a supplement to wild plant foods (Mangelsdorf and Smith, 1949; Dick, 1952; Mangelsdorf, 1958; Willey and Phillips, 1958, pp. 128 ff.).

COLLECTORS OF THE NORTH AMERICAN WOODLANDS

The collecting life-pattern of the Eastern Woodlands of North America is referred to by archaeologists as the "Archaic" pattern (Willey and Phillips, 1958, pp. 111 ff.; Griffin, 1952a). This mode of existence—the collecting of wild vegetable foods, of shellfish, and the taking of fish and small game—replaced the dependence upon the large Pleistocene fauna that was once present in the East. This replacement was probably a gradual one which kept pace with the disappearance of late pluvial conditions and the big-game animals. Such change is seen in the artifact stratigraphy of Illinois and Missouri caves (Fowler and Winter, 1956; Logan, 1952; Chapman, 1952). The shift-over from big-game hunting to collecting probably began as long ago as 8000 B.C., and by 4000 B.C. it was complete throughout the Eastern Woodlands. The projectile points and tools of the Eastern collecting pattern are large, wide, stemmed, or tanged forms and a variety of mortars, handstones, and pestles.

Between 4000 and 1000 B.C. a number of modifications occur in the Eastern Woodland collecting pattern. These are best seen regionally, and in some cases they appear to be responses to natural settings. It also seems likely that new ideas and migrations of people, of ultimate Asiatic origins, were entering the East at this time. These modifications constitute a definite trend toward adjustment or "living-into" the various niches of the Eastern area. Along seacoasts and rivers, as in Georgia and Tennessee,[11] shellfishing stations offered opportunities for regular seasonal residence of a semipermanent village kind. With this increased sedentism appear numerous polished stone implements and ornaments, including celts, atlatl weights, vessels, gorgets, and beads. Around the Great Lakes, copper nuggets were fashioned into artifacts by hammering techniques. Finally, toward the close of the period, pottery was made and used. It is with these changes that the collecting pattern of the East becomes, at least in many localities, intensive collecting.

The intensive collecting pattern of the Eastern Woodlands, or a level of "Primary Forest Efficiency," as it has been called (Caldwell, 1958), climaxes during the first millennium B.C. in certain regions of the Mississippi and Ohio valleys. This is seen in the Poverty Point and Adena cultures with the construction of great ceremonial earthwork centers. The Poverty Point site, in Louisiana (Ford and Webb, 1956), consists of two huge mounds and a concentric series of earth embankments a half-mile in diameter. The Adena centers of Ohio, West Virginia, and Kentucky are marked by big earth tumuli constructed over interior burial chambers (Webb and Snow, 1945; Webb and Baby, 1957; also Willey and Phillips, 1958, pp. 156–58). The total settlement patterns associated with these monuments are unknown, but it is certain that the societies responsible for such "public works" must have included large numbers of individuals and have necessitated the coordination of the efforts of these people, even though their actual living sites may have been of no more than a semipermanent nature. The subsistence basis of these societies is questionable. Some plant cultivation may have been known in the East by this time, but the probable local cultigens seem insufficient as dietary staples, and the presence of maize has not yet been demonstrated. A bit later, between 500 B.C. and A.D. 500, with the advent of the Hopewellian cultures (Caldwell, 1958; Willey and Phillips, 1958, pp. 158–60), maize does come into the picture, and it probably was of real subsistence value as a supplement to the intensive collecting pattern. But it is undoubtedly significant that the Hopewellian cultures continue in the earlier tradition of burial-mound earthwork construction and in the traditions of art and ceremonial paraphernalia which draw their symbolism from religious practices and magic associated with hunting.

Other Hunting and Collecting Patterns

The American Plains. Later, big-game-hunting patterns on the Plains of North America developed from the older Pleistocene way of life. This transition came about gradually, and, at first, the technological changes were relatively slight. A modern type of buffalo was pursued by these Plains huntsmen, and they combined this activity with some food collecting. In later prehistoric times horticulture was brought to certain regions of the Plains and became an important subsistence factor, but buffalo hunting continued. In historic times, after the European introduction of the horse, the buffalo-hunting pattern enjoyed a renaissance (Strong, 1935, pp. 249 ff.; Wissler, 1914). A similar history can be reconstructed for the Argentine pampas and Patagonia, where the guanaco was the game animal (Cooper, 1946). In both the North and the South American Plains the changeover from Pleistocene to modern climatic conditions appears to have taken place at about 5000 B.C. From this date forward, there are general trends toward smaller projectile points, and these are accompanied by stone food-grinding implements, objects of aesthetic, ceremonial, or nonutilitarian usage, and, later, pottery (Strong, 1935; Mulloy, 1954). These trends are associated with sites which could be classed as semipermanent settlement types. Thus it seems probable that these late big-game-hunting cultures of the North and South American Plains, although depending primarily upon the chase for their food resources, were becoming somewhat more sedentary as the result of other subsistence activities; this increased sedentism is, in turn, related to a development of aspects of culture which are not directly a part of the food quest and the adaptation to the natural environment.

The Arctic. Quite distinct in both natural environmental setting and in history from the later big-game hunting of the Plains is the Arctic hunting pattern. In its earliest phases the Arctic pattern seems to have been oriented toward land hunting. The Denbigh Complex of Alaska is the example. It is possible that there are connections between Denbigh and the early post-Pleistocene big-game hunters farther south. This is suggested by some of the Denbigh parallel-flaked projectile points. But there are other technological traditions in Denbigh flintwork, such as the burins and the micro-core-and-blade forms, which indicate diffusions or migrations from northeastern Asia, perhaps as recently as 2000 or 3000 B.C.[12] Following this horizon, the course of Arctic prehistory is the story of the development of Eskimo culture. This development was not an American Arctic phenomenon alone, as subsequent population movements or strong influences may be traced from North America back to Asia; but, viewing the Asiatic-American Arctic sphere as a whole as the home of this evolving Eskimo culture there is little doubt that the main trends were those of a gradual supplementation of land hunting by sea-mammal hunting and by fishing and by an increasing adaptation to an environment of ice and snow. Eskimo sites dating back to the beginning of the Christian Era are fully of semipermanent settlement type. Artifacts of all kinds, in ground stone and ivory, abound; and, from the first millennium A.D. forward, Eskimo culture had achieved that unique and amazing ecological adjustment for which it is famous. It is worthy of note that in such customs and value expressions as the burial of the dead and ivory-carving art there is no steady mounting elaboration. The climactic developments in these come, rather, with the Old Bering Sea and Ipiutak phases, during the first millennium A.D. Subsequent phases show a lessening in the complexity and elaboration of these themes. The supposition is that these refinements of the cult of the dead and of ornamental art had original Asiatic sources outside the severe Arctic zone and that, with the adaptive evolution of Eskimo culture, they were, to some extent, inhibited or sloughed off.[13]

The North Pacific Coast. Along the Pacific Coast of North America it is likely that a food-collecting way of life had its beginnings with migrants from the western interior desert areas who brought to the coast the relatively simple subsistence technology of the Great Basin and Plateau countries (Osborne, 1958). As they settled in the Pacific river valleys and along the coast, their adjustment parallels, in many ways, that of the Eastern Woodland collectors. This adjustment is marked, archaeologically, by the introduction and increasing use of ground and polished stone implements and ceremonial forms and by greater site size and apparent stability of occupation. By 2000 B.C., if not earlier, the Pacific Coastal pattern was of an intensive collecting kind, accompanied by a semipermanent village settlement type (Wallace, 1954; Beardsley, 1948). In late prehistoric and early historic times some of the California acorn-gathering or fishing societies were living in what must be considered permanent villages of several thousand inhabitants (Heizer, 1958). Farther north, in Oregon, Washington, and British Columbia, there are comparable sequences showing an increased "settling-in" adaptation to the environment.[14] These societies achieved an intensive collecting pattern well back in prehistoric times, and the salmon-fishing Northwest Coast tribes of the historic period are still in this tradition of abundant subsistence.

South America. In South America there are many and diverse cultures, known both archaeologically and ethnographically, which may be classed as collecting or intensive collecting in their subsistence. Among these are the old coastal fishing societies of the Peruvian and Chilean coasts. Here, on coastal bays, are shell refuse deposits which date back to 2500 B.C., if not earlier, and show a history of increasingly efficient adjustment. In the Peruvian sites a period of incipient cultivation marks the later phases (Bird, 1948), and in Chile there are modifications of polished stone, bone, and miscellaneous gear used in fishing and sea-mammal hunting (Bird, 1943). In both instances the shell midden sites appear to be either semipermanent or permanent village locations. On the Brazilian east coast there are similar shell midden sites in which there are some clues for an increase through time in material goods, particularly polished stone utensils and ceremonial objects (Orssich and Orssich 1956). Fishers and collectors also lived along the Caribbean coast in Venezuela and in the West Indies. In Venezuela these occupations date from about 2000 B.C. and reveal a thousand-year story of gradual increase in range of tool types and such "luxury" items as bone, stone, and shell beads and pendants (Cruxent and Rouse, 1958–59). It is likely that these Caribbean tribes of northeastern South America were also practicing some incipient cultivation with root crops. Far to the south, along the Paraná River and on the Pampean and Patagonian plains, there are archaeological and ethnohistoric data pertaining to a variety of hunting, fishing, and collecting tribes (Howard and Willey, 1948). As noted, some of these people, particularly those of the pampas and Patagonia, were following a hunting tradition only slightly modified by food collecting. Others, particularly along the rivers, maintained greater stability of residence and were more devoted to collecting.

Cultivators of Nuclear America

Nuclear American plant cultivation centered in the territories including and extending from central Mexico to southern Peru. Its beginnings were slow and gradual, and in its incipient forms it was grafted upon, or an adjunct to, preexisting collecting patterns. This is the case in Tamaulipas, Mexico, on the northern border of Nuclear America, where hints of plant domestication go back to 7000 B.C. and where, by 5000 B.C., it is definite. Between that date and 3000 B.C., squash and beans are identified from dry cave deposits, and by 2500 B.C. small cobs of primitive maize have made their appearance (MacNeish, 1950, 1958). The cultural contexts of these Tamaulipas caves make it evident that these domesticates played but a relatively small part in what may otherwise be considered to be a North American Desert collecting pattern of food-getting. It is noteworthy, however, that in this Tamaulipas sequence of incipient cultivation there is a steady increase in the types and volume of cultigens and also in the varieties and numbers of such seed-grinding implements as mortars, manos, and mullers. With the advent of the final incipient cultivation phase, at about 1600 B.C., improved corn, beans, and Lima beans are all present, and it has been estimated that the cave populations of this period derived about 30 percent of their sustenance from these crops (MacNeish, 1958). In Peru incipient cultivation also appears to be a kind of epiphenomenon superimposed upon the shellfish and wild-plant collecting patterns of the ancient coastal populations. In this setting, squash, beans (*Canavalia*), and miscellaneous roots and tubers were domesticated as early as 2500 B.C., if not long before (Bird, 1948).

The basic origins and courses of diffusion of the Nuclear American incipient cultivation pattern are difficult to trace. No imperishable and diagnostic tool types can testify indisputably to its presence. Such specialized and definite implements as the maize-grinding metate and mano are more likely to be associated with a fully established agriculture, and the relatively unspecialized seed-grinding implements are as likely to have been used for wild as for domesticated foods. Consequently, unusual conditions of preservation, such as dry caves or completely arid desert sands, are necessary for an accurate determination of cultivation incipience. It may be for this reason that the arid uplands of Middle America and the rainless Peruvian coast now appear as the earliest centers of the Nuclear American incipient cultivation pattern. For it seems probable that experimentation with plant domestication proceeded in many parts of Nuclear America and that its antiquity throughout the zone goes back to 3000 B.C. or earlier. It is unlikely that any one area or region was the *fons et origo* of all the important food plants. Maize (*Zea mays*), which was to become the basic staple of the New World, probably was domesticated first in Guatemala or southern Mexico and spread from there, although the possibilities of more or less separate and independent cultivation of wild pod corn at various localities in the Nuclear zone cannot be discarded.[15]

The societal and cultural context of Nuclear American incipient cultivation ranges from the camp site, with its relatively limited inventory of basketry and ground and chipped stone tools, to semipermanent and permanent villages with much wider assemblages of textile and stone items plus, in some instances, pottery. The coastal locations appear to have been more propitious for settled life. Pottery, of a relatively simple sort, has been found in a coastal shell midden in Panama, dating at 2100 B.C.[16]; and, in Ecuador, coastal shell refuse stations, going back to 2400 B.C., have also yielded pottery (Evans and Meggers, 1958). On the Peruvian coast the incipient cultivators lived in stone-and-mud-masonry pit-house villages which probably numbered up to more than one hundred persons, and between 1800 and 1000 B.C. they began to manufacture pottery of a kind probably related to the Panamanian and Ecuadorean varieties (Bird, 1948, 1951).

The line marking the shift from what we have called "incipient cultivation" to established cultivation is drawn at that point where communities derive their major support from farming. In the Middle American area this change is marked by the appearance of the first permanent villages.[17] Some of these villages, like those in the Tamaulipas region which follow the incipient cultivation societies, are quite small (MacNeish, 1958). Others, including the early pottery and farming phases of the Valley of Mexico, cover several acres (Vaillant, 1930). Still other village units were probably composed of several scattered hamlets which were nucleated around small ceremonial centers marked by temple mounds.[18] In both Ecuador (Evans and Meggers, 1957, 1958) and Peru (Willey, 1953a, pp. 371 ff.) there was a movement away from the immediate coast back into the valleys at this time, a settlement shift suggestive of the rising importance of cultivation over a fishing and shellfish-collecting subsistence. The Peruvian sites of such early farming phases as the Cupisnique were small hamlets dotted over the river valley floor and along the valley edges, apparently focused upon a ceremonial center.

The beginnings of the established cultivation pattern in Nuclear America are dated at about 1500 B.C. in Middle America and at 1000 B.C. in Peru (Willey, 1955a, 1958). The next thousand years or so saw an intensification of this pattern, with increasing population densities and a development and elaboration of technology and art. Public building was on the increase in the form of pyramids constructed of adobe, earth, or stone. These pyramids marked the ceremonial or politicoreligious centers and either were surrounded by town people settlements, as in upland Mexico and Guatemala and on the Peruvian coast, or served as nuclei to dispersed hamlets, as in the Maya and Veracruz lowlands. The impressive Middle American art styles and the systems of hieroglyphic writing and calendrics, which were to flower brilliantly only slightly later, had their beginnings in this Formative Period. In Peru, this was also the time of the first great arts, of experimentation in metallurgy, and of the initiation of complex irrigation works (see Bennett and Bird, 1949, pp. 137–53; also Willey, 1958).

Intensive cultivation arose from established cultivation in Peru and in certain portions of Middle America. On the Peruvian scene it is clearly defined by the large-scale irrigation and garden-plot networks of the coast and the irrigation and terracing of the highland basins. Such works are dated as early as the beginnings of the Classic period, at about A.D. 1.[19] In Middle America intensive cultivation was more limited in geographic scope, and the evidence for it is more difficult to define archaeologically. In the Valley of Mexico irrigation and chinampa ("floating-garden") farming can be dated with assurance back to the Toltec civilization at around A.D. 900. Before that the case for intensive cultivation is less certain, although it is possible that irrigation was practiced as early as the first phases of the Teotihuacán civilization at the beginning of the Christian Era (Millon, 1954, 1957; Palerm, 1955). In both Peru and Middle America intensive cultivation is associated with towns and temples and, in some instances, with cities.

The history of Nuclear American cultivation belongs not only to the Nuclear zone but to the outlands bordering it to the north and south. The diffusions or migrations carrying the ideas of plant domestication to these areas must have begun on the incipient cultivation level. We have already noted that primitive maize and other plants were being cultivated in the southwestern United States area in the third millennium B.C. by peoples who were essentially Desert collectors. It is also possible that incipient cultivation spread into northern Chile or northwestern Argentina at a relatively early date, although there is no proof of this. Established cultivation patterns, however, are not introduced to, or developed upon, the Nuclear American peripheries until much later. It was not until the last few centuries B.C. that permanent villages based primarily upon farming were established in the North American Southwest (Jennings *et al.*, 1956, pp. 73 ff.; Willey and Phillips, 1958, pp. 151 ff.), and a comparable date probably is applicable to northern Chile–Argentina.[20] In both the Southwest and in northern Chile–Argentina, elements of intensive cultivation appear sometime after about A.D. 700. The canal systems of the southern Arizona desert Hohokam culture and the agricultural terracing of the southern Andes are examples in point. There seem to be associations between these intensive cultivation patterns and town-and-temple communities; however, it is also certain that in the southwestern United States such large late prehistoric towns as Pueblo Bonito, in northern New Mexico, came into being without these specialized techniques of complex irrigation or terracing systems.

Other Patterns of Cultivation

There are two other native American cultivation patterns whose histories, if not completely separate from that of the Nuclear American pattern, have sufficient independence to deserve comment. Both are found in lowland wooded areas of adequate or abundant rainfall. Unfortunately, in neither case does the archaeological record give more than a hint of these patterns. They have their respective hearts in the North American Eastern Woodlands and its Mississippian River system and in the South American Tropical Forest of the Amazon and Orinoco Rivers.

The Mississippi Drainage of Eastern North America. It seems likely that the sunflower (*Helianthus*), goosefoot (*Chenopodium*), and pumpkin (*Cucurbita pepo*) were all domesticated here by the beginning of the first millennium B.C. (Goslin, 1957). This may have been in response to remote stimulus diffusion from the Nuclear American cultivation pattern, the plants used being the best that the local environment had to offer; or it may have been an entirely independent development.[21] As previously noted, this Eastern Woodland incipient cultivation was a part of a dominantly collecting or intensive collecting life-way of which the Adena and Hopewell cultures represented a climax (Caldwell, 1958). It is known that, by 500 B.C., such cultures were in contact with the Nuclear

American cultivation pattern for maize. By A.D. 500, established cultivation of a Nuclear American variety, derived from Middle America, dominated the Mississippi Valley. Thus the earlier, nonmaize, distinctively Eastern Woodland cultivation never proceeded beyond the level of incipience until it became a part of the expanding Nuclear American pattern.

The South American Tropical Forest. This pattern played a much more important role in native American agriculture. The basic crops were root starches, primarily manioc (*Manihot esculenta*), both bitter and sweet, as well as the sweet potato (*Ipomoea batatas*). Their antiquity as domesticates in Venezuela and Brazil can only be speculated upon, but almost certainly it antedates 1000 B.C. (Sauer, 1952). Whether or not there is any archaeological evidence that may be identified, even tentatively, as Tropical Forest incipient cultivation is problematic. Possibly the early phases on Marajó Island, at the mouth of the Amazon, had such a subsistence along with collecting, fishing, and hunting. The sites of these phases appear to be small semipermanent villages marked by little but refuse and simple pottery.[22] Possibly, too, some of the early coastal shell mound sites of Venezuela may have had a partial dependence upon incipient cultivation (Cruxent and Rouse, 1958–59), but by 1000 B.C. a permanent village location, with well-made, painted pottery, is known from the lower Orinoco River (*ibid.*). Pottery griddles, found at this site, imply the use of manioc flour for cakes. Such a site seems definite evidence of established cultivation, but in the Tropical Forest rather than the Nuclear American tradition.

A blending and interpenetration of the Tropical Forest and Nuclear American cultivation patterns seems to have begun fairly early. In northern Colombia the lower levels of the Momíl site show pottery manioc griddles but no definite clues pointing to the use of maize. The immediately succeeding levels, however, have maize-grinding implements (Reichel-Dolmatoff and Dussande Reichel-Dolmatoff, 1956). These early Momíl phases probably date back to 1000 B.C. or even before (Willey, 1958). The spread of maize farther to the east probably took place sometime after this. In both Venezuela and parts of the Amazon system, town-and-temple type communities were known in Precolumbian times (Steward, 1948b).

New World Culture: History and Evolution

Subsistence Efficiency

Nearly all the New World hunting or collecting life-patterns demonstrate, or strongly suggest, a trend through time of increasing adaptive efficiency in the realm of subsistence technology.[23] The North American Desert pattern, which is known in the full gamut of its development, reveals the growing importance of seed foods in its middle and later stages. This is seen in the increasing numbers and specialization of food-grinding implements. The North American Woodland pattern development parallels this to some extent, but with a strong emphasis upon specialization in weapons and implements used for forest hunting and stream and coastal fishing. On the Pacific Coast of North America there is a similar sequential record of improved adjustment to local environments in which the collecting of vegetable foods or fishing were the specialities. In the South American collecting patterns these same tendencies also exist, and in the far north the Arctic hunting pattern is the example par excellence of the development of a technology to cope with environmental conditions. Only the very earliest patterns—those of the Pleistocene gatherers and the Pleistocene hunters—fail to reveal fully this configuration through time of adaptive subsistence efficiency. For the first, the data are too few to make an appraisal.

For the second—the big-game hunters—we see a high degree of specialization to an environment at the outset; and it seems likely that the earlier stages of the pattern, leading up to such complexes as the Sandia or Clovis, are as yet undiscovered. Even with only a part of the chronological range of the pattern revealed, however, there is a hint of the specialization trend in the changes that set the later Folsom complex off from the earlier Clovis. Thereafter, the pattern dissolves with the shrinkage and eventual disappearance of the Pleistocene environments.

The American collecting patterns were not pushed back to marginal positions or terminated by natural environmental change but by the propagation of plant cultivation. The history of this cultivation is a story of several millennia of casual, experimental, or incipient cultivation. During this time plant cultivation did not really constitute an independent subsistence pattern but was an adjunct to food collecting. Incipient cultivation, although progressing slowly, culminated in the Nuclear American and Tropical Forest established cultivation patterns. Offering a subsistence based largely or wholly upon food production rather than collecting, it spread to all those American areas where it was able to find a receptive natural environment and where it could compete successfully with existing subsistence techniques. In parts of America the more productive and more highly specialized intensive cultivation replaced established cultivation.

Social Integration

Our surveys of New World life-patterns indicate correlations between the increasing efficiency of subsistence adaptations and the increasing size and stability of settlement or community types. Both the North American Desert and the Woodland collectors lived in camp type settlements in their earlier stages. In their later phases the Cochise populations of the Southwest established semipermanent villages, and the tribes of the eastern United States began to "settle in" along rivers and the coast in semipermanent, or possibly permanent, villages. Elsewhere, as on the Pacific Coast of North America or the South American coasts, the intensification of food collecting also made it possible for larger social aggregates to live together for longer periods of time.

In the Nuclear American and South American Tropical Forest cultivation patterns the stage of agricultural incipience probably marked some increase in community size and stability, although the evidence here is either lacking or difficult to separate from that of the later stages of food collecting. Undoubtedly, local conditions and available food plants were decisive variables. It was with the established cultivational level, however, that the permanent village came into existence in these patterns. As previously observed, this does not mean that settled village life was impossible without plant cultivation; we have noted its probable existence in certain circumstances of intensive collecting; but it does signify that when the food economy of a society was predominantly agricultural, that society became "anchored" to a relatively small geographical locus. There is considerable range in size and type of site associated with established cultivation. Although the permanent village was the most usual and widespread form in the Nuclear American and Tropical Forest zones as well as in outlying American areas, there are indications that town-and-temple and even city type communities were supported by this kind of farming.

That the correlations between subsistence efficiency and increase in community size and organization are to some degree causally interrelated seems self-evident. Of the full nature of this interrelationship, it is difficult to be precise or explicit except in particular instances. And when one examines these individual cases, it is clear that the explanation cannot be presented as a mere matter of mathematical ratios: volume of food equals numbers of people equals type and organization of community. The ideas and institutions of culture are always found interposed between the natural, technological, and demographic factors.

CULTURAL FORMS AND INSTITUTIONS

This brings us to our most difficult step in the attempt to follow out the trends and courses of New World cultural evolution. What configurations of change through time may we generalize about those aspects of culture which are not immediately and intimately related to the subsistence technology–environmental settings or to the sizes and groupings of settlements and societies? And how might these configurations correlate, or fail to correlate, with trends of change in the technological and social orders?

To begin at a low and tangible level, it is observed that manufactures of all kinds increase throughout the histories of our American collecting and cultivation life-patterns. This is most noticeable in the North American Desert and Woodland patterns, where, in the early levels, there is relatively little archaeological residue as compared to later phases. In the later phases not only are there more objects, but many of these have no apparent direct relationship to the food quest. Polished stone items of a ceremonial or ornamental nature are examples. Similar trends are also noted in South American collecting patterns. Within the sequences of the cultivation patterns this same increase in material goods, particularly nonutilitarian goods, is characteristic of the earlier periods; later on, it is less evident. There is, then, in cultural items that might be classed as elaborations of life—ornaments, emblems, religious paraphernalia—an increase that more or less parallels the rise of successful food collecting and plant cultivation and the appearance of semipermanent and permanent villages. This is not to argue that aesthetic or religious experience was lacking in earlier times or on earlier levels, but the time or desire to give frequent material expression to such emotions must have been lacking before the development of some degree of sedentism.[24]

Architecture, particularly communal or public architecture, is another tangible that seems to describe some significant configurations in its occurrences in the American life-patterns. It is absent from both the Pleistocene hunting and the later hunting traditions. It is given some expression with the intensive levels of the collecting patterns. On the North American Pacific Coast it is known from historic times, and it is probable that communal buildings of impressive size were put up here during prehistoric periods, although these, being of wood, would have left little or no archaeological traces. In the eastern United States the intensive collectors of the Woodlands built large earth monuments for burial and religious purposes. However, it is with the Nuclear American cultures that public building was greatly elaborated. In both Middle America and Peru the trends show a steady increase in the numbers and size of ceremonial mounds during the Formative Period of the first millennium B.C. The societies responsible for their construction were established cultivators, and this period of the building of great temple mounds is the time of the shift from village to town-and-temple life. With the Classic Period of the first millennium A.D., ceremonial mounds were still being constructed, but there were now new trends expressed in greater attention to the actual temple buildings surmounting the mounds or in palace constructions. Still later, in the Postclassic Period of the last centuries prior to the Spanish Conquest, there are other architectural changes reflective of shifts in cultural interests and values. In Middle America, fortifications appear in many regions. In Peru there is a marked dropoff in ceremonial mounds and a greater interest in military construction and planned community architecture. The configuration of the architectural trend, to reduce it to its simplest generalization, is that interest in permanent public or ceremonial building is a correlate of settled life, that it does not appear until after sedentism is reasonably well established, and that then it undergoes changes suggesting a drift away from the unique importance of the temple, to the palace compound, and from this to military construction and urban planning.

Art is perhaps the archaeologist's one best clue to the nonmaterial, nonutilitarian heart of things. At least we shall consider it so, for it is the only means at hand so to interpret the preliterate cultures. In the New World life-patterns there is little evidence of it associated with the Pleistocene big-game hunters, although it may have existed in some perishable form. In the North American collecting patterns, art has its beginnings with the small ornamental and ceremonial objects of sculptured stone or bone. The Hopewellian climax of the Woodland collectors represents a florescence of the art of this particular pattern. In Nuclear America there are varying styles of art in small handicraft objects and ceramics in the earlier phases of established cultivation, and relatively early in the Formative Period in both Middle America and Peru monumental art styles, such as the Olmec and Chavín, make their appearance. In Middle America the Olmec and related early art styles are associated with evidences of writing and calendrics; and both Olmec and Chavín art are found in the contexts of the earliest important temple or public buildings. These styles and their settings imply a considerable sophistication for the cultures and societies which created them as expressions of their religions and value systems. Although in both Middle America and Peru a succession of other art styles follow these and can, in varying degrees, be traced as having developed from them, there appear to be no evolutionary trends that could be conceived of as "increase," "improvement," or "refinement" in these aesthetic developments. Nor can we say that certain types of economic and social milieus are conducive to artistic achievement over and beyond the level of established cultivation and the emerging town and temple community. Monumental Olmec art appears in Middle America in the tropical lowlands of the Gulf Coast, where a true urban development seems to have been precluded by the necessities of scattered village or hamlet-based forest farming. The later Maya art of the Classic Period, generally held to be the apogee of Middle American and New World aesthetic achievement, had its formation and growth in a similar ecological and social setting. The same, of course, holds for Maya hieroglyphics and astronomy. Conversely, Classic Period Teotihuacán of the upland Valley of Mexico, apparently a city in the true urban sense, did not enjoy a comparable artistic or intellectual flowering, although its political power may have been greater than that of the contemporaneous Maya. Thus, from an examination of the American data, the expression of cultural values in art seems to demand a base of sedentary life with some economic surpluses and some moderate community size. Beyond this, it is not clear that increase in volume or particular organization of these factors resulted in any measurable elaborations or intensifications of aesthetic or intellectual institutions.

The New World as a Whole

Up to now we have considered the question of the evolution of culture in the New World within the confines of the historical units designated as life-patterns. In each of these patterns we have observed certain trends or configurations of occurrence in social and cultural traits. There are similarities in these trends, from pattern to pattern, and there are also distinct differences. These differences, together with the variable chronological and distributional aspects of the life-patterns, suggest that it is possible to conceive of New World prehistoric events as a unitary, if highly complex, history and evolution.

The earliest of the definite American life-patterns—that of the Pleistocene big-game hunters—marks a stage in New World culture history and culture development referred to as the *Lithic*, and *Paleo-Indian*, or the *Paleo-American*.[25] It was a highly specialized way of life, and the pattern was broken with the changing of the natural environment at the end of the Pleistocene. Some of the peoples and societies involved may have perished, but it is likely that others sought new modes of subsistence adaptation. Possibly minor food-getting techniques, of little importance in an economy geared to the mammoth hunt, became the bases of a new orientation. Also, there was probable recourse to borrowing either from peoples newly arrived from Asia or from those descendant in the possible ancient traditions of Pleistocene food gathering. In some such way the collecting patterns must have come into being.

The food-collecting way of life, although represented in several historically distinct life-patterns, constitutes a stage in the development and history of New World subsistence technology. This has been called the *Archaic stage*.[26] The food-collectors were, at first, less well adapted to their environments than the big-game hunters; but, in losing the specialization of their ancestors, relatives, or neighbors, they had been launched upon a course that would eventually lead to a much greater subsistence efficiency and economic security than the chase of the animal herds. After a few thousand years the results of this new specialization, or variety of subsistence specializations, is apparent in the semipermanent villages, the manufacture of "luxury" items, and the beginnings of art and ceremonial constructions.

Carried somewhat like a parasite in the host of the food-collecting patterns was the minor element of plant domestication. Of considerably antiquity, it appears to have remained little more than dormant for millennia. Gradually this incipient cultivation assumed more importance, especially in certain geographical regions where the native wild flora and fauna were not overly abundant. Finally, plant cultivation emerged as the agricultural way of life. This threshold of village communities sustained by farming marks the *New World Formative stage*.[27]

Like the early food-collectors, the first established village agriculturists had a less successful economic adaptation than many contemporary intensive collectors, such as those of the North American Eastern Woodlands or Pacific Coast. But the potentialities were before them, and it was not long before the agriculturally based societies of Nuclear America surpassed the wealthiest of the food-collectors in surpluses and population numbers. With the establishment of the secure cultivation threshold, there were no more major changes in native American subsistence patterns. Intensive cultivation, achieved in some places, was a specialization and a refinement, not a new departure. Thus it is at somewhere near this point that the course of New World culture history and culture evolution can no longer be traced in terms of subsistence efficiency.

Community size, concentration, and complexity of organization do, however, continue to show a configuration of increase after the establishment of cultivation as the primary means of subsistence. Although, to some extent and in some places, this may be attributed to intensive cultivation and to population rise, it is certain that cultural choice entered increasingly into the equation. As towns and cities arose in Nuclear America, during what have been called the *Classic* and *Postclassic stages* of culture development,[28] it is significant that absolute numbers of people did not change so much as did the settlement patterns by which they were organized. The town and the city were not simply the means of containing population masses; they were an organic part of societies organized and integrated over large territories or states.

We have remarked that both monumental art styles and temples occur relatively early in the rise of Middle American and Peruvian civilizations, perhaps less than a thousand years after the first establishment of village life based on cultivation and at the beginnings of what might be considered the town-and-temple community. There followed, then, a series of architectural and artistic developments whose trends cannot be generalized in the sense of "increase," "improvement," or "refinement" but rather as reflective of changes in social and political types and in moral values. Such trends as are suggested are those marking a shift from sacred to secular emphases, from relative peace to times of war, and from the smaller city or regional state to the larger territorial empire. It is from an appraisal of such trends that the distinction between a Classic and a Postclassic stage has been based (Willey and Phillips, 1958, pp. 182–99).

We come, then, to sum up the case for the evolution of culture in the native New World. I would conclude that whatever the contacts with the peoples and cultures of the Old World (and these have been but briefly alluded to in this paper), New World culture did, indeed, evolve in an essentially independent manner. This evolution can be traced in subsistence modes which, within several major historical patterns, describe a configuration of increasing efficiency and environmental adaptation. This same general trend of subsistence efficiency for production can also be projected across these various historical patterns so that it describes an overall configuration of increase despite the fluctuations which mark the junctures of the patterns. Paralleling subsistence increase is the enlargement of the social unit and its geographic stability. Sedentism and food surpluses are also seen as the conditions necessary for the creation of material wealth and for the memorializing of religious and aesthetic emotions in art and architecture. Great skill and sophistication were attained in New World art, including monumental art, well in advance of the rise of the power of the city or the state. The evolution of the city and the state in native America appears to be linked with the growing power of military and secular forces and with attempts to propagate single religious, political, and social views—unified moral orders—to ever widening spheres of influence.

Notes

[1]This distinction between "food gathering" and "food collecting" follows the terminology that Braidwood (1960) has suggested for the Old World. "Food gathering" pertains to the cultures of the Lower and Middle Paleolithic and to an absence of regional specialization or diversification in technology. "Food collecting," on the other hand, pertains to Upper Paleolithic and post-Paleolithic cultures and to a much greater degree of diversification and specialization.

[2]The domestication of animals was never of primary economic importance in precolumbian America. The nearest approach would be the mixed horticulture–animal husbandry economy of the late prehistoric tribes of northern Chile and northwestern Argentina.

[3]My use of settlement or community types parallels in part that of the seminar paper by Beardsley et al. (1956), but I have used archaeological site terms rather than community terms. The "camp" site is presumably the archaeological correlate of what Beardsley et al. have defined as "free-wandering" and "restricted-wandering" bands.

[4]My "semipermanent village" is the approximate equivalent of the Beardsley et al. (op. cit., pp. 138–41) "central-based wandering" and "semi-permanent sedentary" community.

[5]*Ibid.*, see pp. 141–43, the "simple nuclear centered" community.

[6]*Ibid.*, see pp. 143–45, the "advanced nuclear centered" community.

[7]The *city*, as I have defined it here, would include some of the communities termed by Beardsley *et al.* (*op. cit.*, pp. 143–46) as "advanced nuclear centered." These would, in effect, be "orthogenetic" cities. The Beardsley *et al.* "supra-nuclear integrated" community would correspond to the "heterogenetic" city.

[8]One projectile point from the earliest Danger Cave level is of long lanceolate form (see Jennings, 1957, p. 109; see also Wormington, 1957, pp. 193–95).

[9]For Sandia, see Hibben, 1941, and Wormington, 1957, pp. 85–91; for Clovis, see Howard, 1935; Cotter, 1937, 1938; Wormington, 1957, pp. 47–53.

[10]For Folsom see Roberts, 1935; Wormington, 1957, pp. 23–43.

[11]See Willey and Phillips, 1958, p. 115, and extensive footnote bibliography to this subject.

[12]Giddings, 1951, 1954, 1955. Giddings is of the opinion that, although the Denbigh complex may have lasted this late, its beginnings must be put in the neighborhood of 6500 B.C. See Wormington, 1957, p. 212, in this connection.

[13]For general treatments of Eskimo archaeology, and differences of opinion in reconstruction, see Collins, 1953a, b, 1954; Larsen and Rainey, 1948.

[14]See summarization of this, with bibliographic references, in Willey and Phillips, 1958, pp. 135–37.

[15]Personal communication, P. C. Mangelsdorf, 1958.

[16]Results of Yale Radiocarbon Laboratory, personal communication, E. S. Deevey, 1958.

[17]Pottery antecedent to permanent farming-based villages has not yet been revealed in Middle America. I would postulate that it will be found, probably along the Pacific strand in shell midden situations comparable to those of Panama or Ecuador; however, at the present writing, the Panamanian and Ecuadorean pottery appears to be the earliest in Nuclear America and, possibly, the New World.

[18]It seems probable that the earliest Formative Period communities in the Maya lowlands were so "nucleated," although the evidence on this is not clear.

[19]See Willey, 1953a, for dating of irrigation works in Peru; and Willey, 1958, for revised chronological estimates.

[20]Willey (1958) places it slightly later; A. R. Gonzalez, in a seminar presentation given in December, 1958, is inclined to date village agriculture in northwestern Argentina as early as 500 B.C.

[21]MacNeish believes that the pumpkin was domesticated in northeastern Mexico and spread to eastern North America at an early date, while the sunflower, domesticated in the Southwest, spread to the Mississippi Valley by Adena times.

[22]See Meggers and Evans, 1957, for such phases as Ananatuba and Mangueiras.

[23]In a recent paper D. W. Lathrap (1957) has argued that a subsistence technology carried by a human society is analogous to a biological organism which exploits a compatible environment to its farthest geographic limits and develops within the confines of that environment to its highest degree of adaptive efficiency. I am indebted to Lathrap for his stimulating essay and for numerous discussions on this subject.

[24]It may be argued that the European cave art of the late Paleolithic is a contradiction to this. I think it more likely, however, that the specialized hunting conditions of these cultures, in their environments of that time, offered a substantial degree of sedentism to these early hunters and artists.

[25]Willey and Phillips (1958) use the term *Lithic;* Suhm, Krieger, and Jelks (1954) suggest *Paleo-American*; *Paleo-Indian* has had a long and fairly extensive usage.

[26]Willey and Phillips (1958) derived this term from its specific usages in eastern North America and in California but have extended it beyond specific historical limitations as a New World "stage."

[27]The term *Formative*, used as a "stage" designation, was derived by Willey and Phillips (1958) from its specific period applications in Middle America and Peru.

[28]The terms *Classic* and *Postclassic*, used as "stage" designations, are also derived from their applications as periods to Peruvian and Middle American sequences (Willey and Phillips, 1958).

11

New World Prehistory

(From *Science*, Vol. 131, pp. 173–183, 1960. Reprinted by permission of *Science* and the AAAS.)

The prehistory of the New World is so multifaceted and complex that synthesis demands not only compression but rigorous selection. What strands of human activity can be followed most easily through the maze of the past? Which elements are the significant ones? These are always troublesome questions for the archaeologist, and in the present case they are made more so by the tremendous range of space and time and by the quantity and quality of the data with which we are dealing. It is difficult to fix consistently upon criteria of comparison. The best we can do is to adhere to those universal themes of man's existence that leave their mark in or upon the earth: technology, environmental adaptation, subsistence, and settlement. These were not necessarily determinative of the form and elaboration of other aspects of man's life, but they provide a background and a base which is necessary to the understanding of societies and cultures in Precolumbian America.

Major Problems in New World Archaeology

Before beginning this account of New World prehistory it will be well to review some of the major problems confronting the American archaeologist, for it will be evident that the tentative conclusions which I have reached about these problems give the outline and structure to the present article. They are problems not unlike those of Old World prehistory (*1*, *2*) in that they are concerned with the great changes in man's adaptations to his natural and social environments.

Most briefly, and in approximate chronological order, these problems are as follows.

1. Who were the earliest inhabitants of the New World? Were they food gatherers comparable in their simple subsistence technology to the peoples of the Old World lower and middle Paleolithic?

2. Where and at what time did the American big-game-hunting specialization of the Pleistocene arise? What were its relationships to the possible earlier food gatherers mentioned above? What were its relationships to the big-game-hunting tradition of the Old World? What happened to the pattern?
3. What were the origins and relationships of the specialized food-collecting subsistence patterns of the post-Pleistocene? Did Asiatic diffusions and migrations play a part in these developments, especially in the Arctic and Boreal zones?
4. Where and when were food plants first domesticated in the New World, and what was the effect of this on society and culture?
5. What is the history of pottery in the New World?
6. At what period and in what regions did sedentary village life based upon farming arise in the New World, and what was the history of the spread of this pattern in native America?
7. What was the nature of sedentary village life in the New World in those areas or regions where plant cultivation was poorly developed or lacking, and when did it occur? To what extent were such cultures and societies dependent upon the diffusion of ideas and elements from the village-farming pattern?
8. When and how did the native civilizations of Nuclear America come into being? What were their relationships within the Nuclear sphere? What were their relationships to non-Nuclear America?

In the statement of these problems and in the discussion that follows, certain terminology is used that needs explanation. This terminology also relates to the three diagrammatic charts (Figures 11.1–3) which summarize New World prehistory in broad eras or stages of subsistence technology (earlier chronological ranges) or settlement types (later chronological ranges). The term *food gathering* is applied to subsistence patterns where the gathering of wild plant foods or the hunting of animal life lacked regional specialization or technological diversification. This usage follows that of Braidwood in Old World archaeology (*3*). *Food collecting*, in contradistinction, implies both specialization and diversification in the taking and utilization of wild plant and animal foods. The other terms descriptive of types of subsistence and settlement—*incipient cultivation*, *village farming*, *towns and temples*, *cities*, and a few other special terms of this nature—are defined below.

The geographical arrangements and the designations of the charts deserve a word. Figure 11.1 is a cross section for an area that runs north and south through the western axis of the hemisphere. The name *Nuclear America* refers to the southern two thirds of Mexico, all of Central America, and Andean and coastal Colombia, Ecuador, and Peru, with adjacent portions of Bolivia. This was the heartland of native American agriculture and the seat of the two Precolumbian centers of civilization, one in Middle America (Mexico-Guatemala) and the other in Peru-Bolivia (*4*). There is a column for each of these two centers on the chart, and the column between, headed "Intermediate," refers to what I am calling the "Intermediate area" of southern Central America, Colombia, and Ecuador (*5*). To the north of Nuclear America is western North America, divided into the Southwest culture area and the adjacent Great Basin area. Under "Southern South America" are columns headed "South Andes" and "Pampas-Patagonia." Figure 11.2 is a cross section for an area extending from the Intermediate area of Nuclear America eastward across Venezuela, then southeastward to the Amazon drainage basin and eastern Brazil, and finally south to the Pampas-Patagonia region. In Figure 3 the "Middle America" column is repeated under "Nuclear America," and the cross section is extended to include the North American eastern woodlands and plains areas. The charts are highly schematic, and only a small number of archaeological cultures, or phase names, have been entered in the columns for various areas. (These names appear in small letters.)

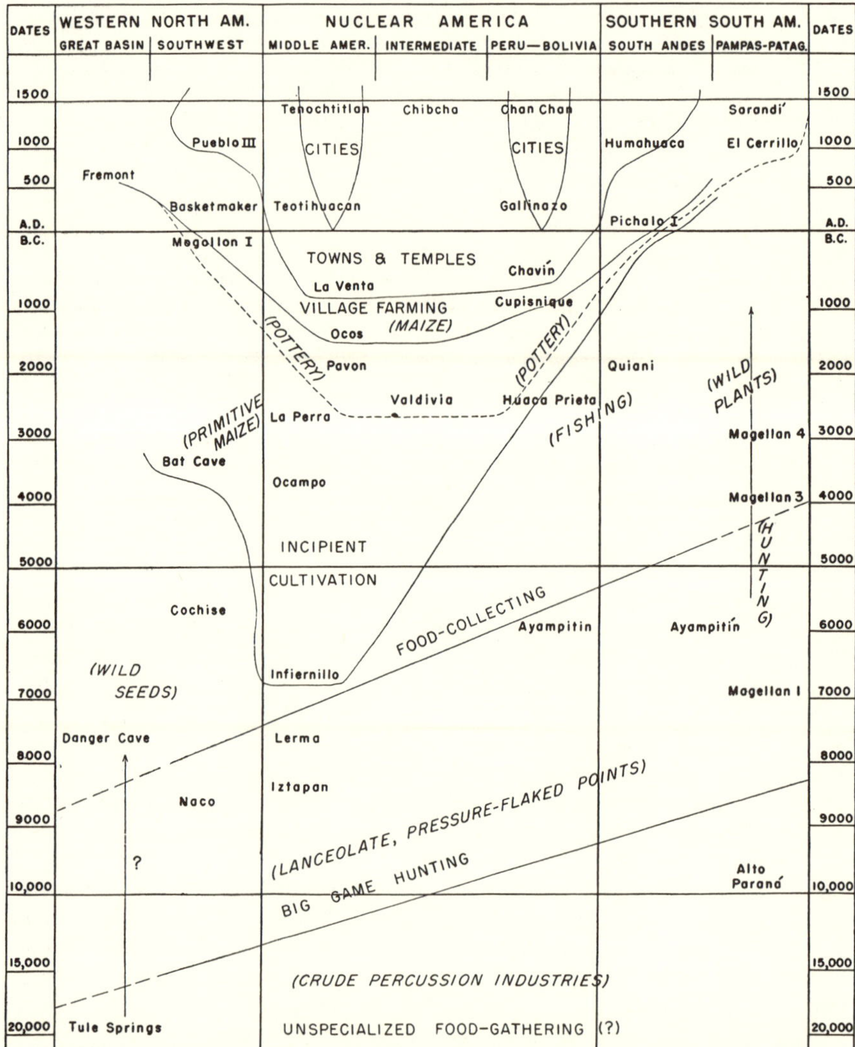

Figure 11.1. Subsistence and settlement type levels in native America: cross section for western North America, Nuclear America, and southern South America. The first appearance of pottery is indicated by the dotted line.

The point should be made that the diagonal and curving lines which mark off the major subsistence and settlement types on the charts are not impermeable ones (see *1*, Fig. 6). Influences and traits crossed these lines, frequently moving outward from areas of cultural complexity and intensity into areas of simpler cultures. Such traits were often assimilated by the receiving groups without effecting basic changes in subsistence or settlement. In some instances suspected diffusions of this kind are indicated on the charts by means of arrows.

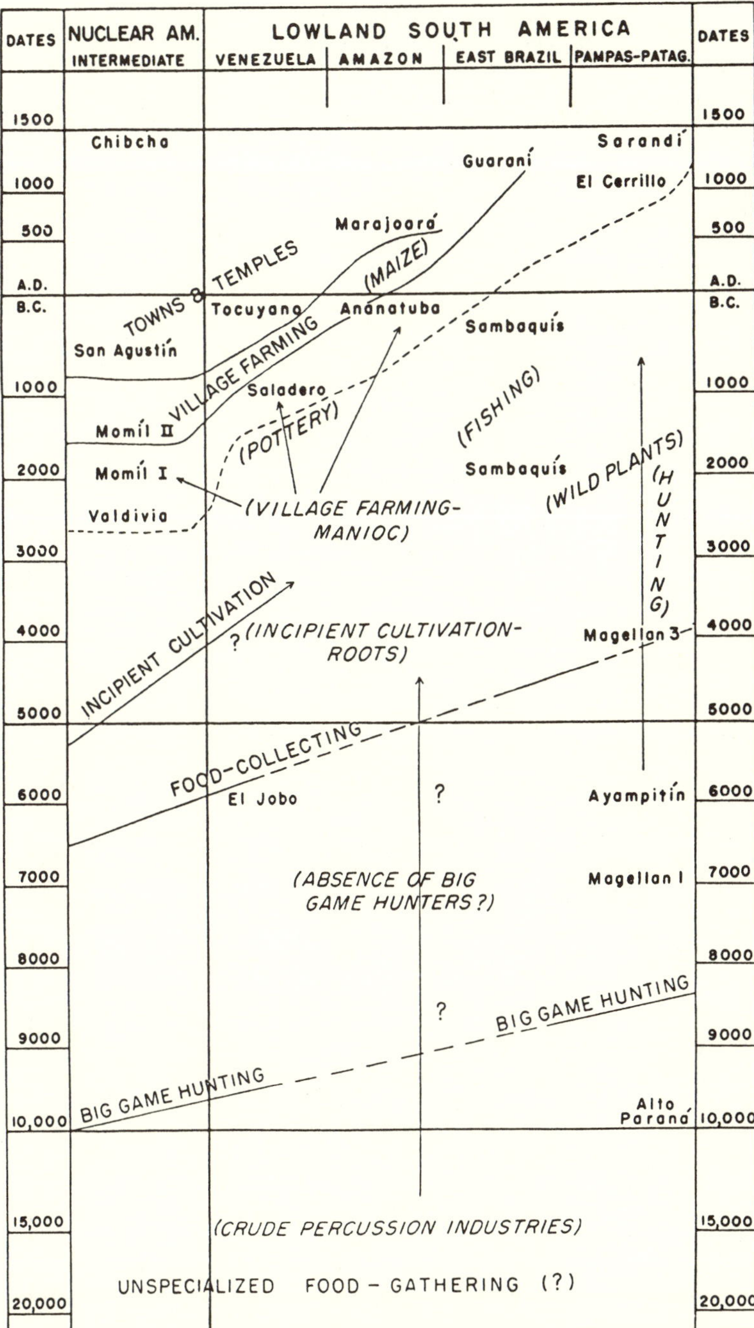

Figure 11.2. Subsistence and settlement type levels in native America: cross section for Nuclear America and lowland South America. The first appearance of pottery is indicated by the dotted line.

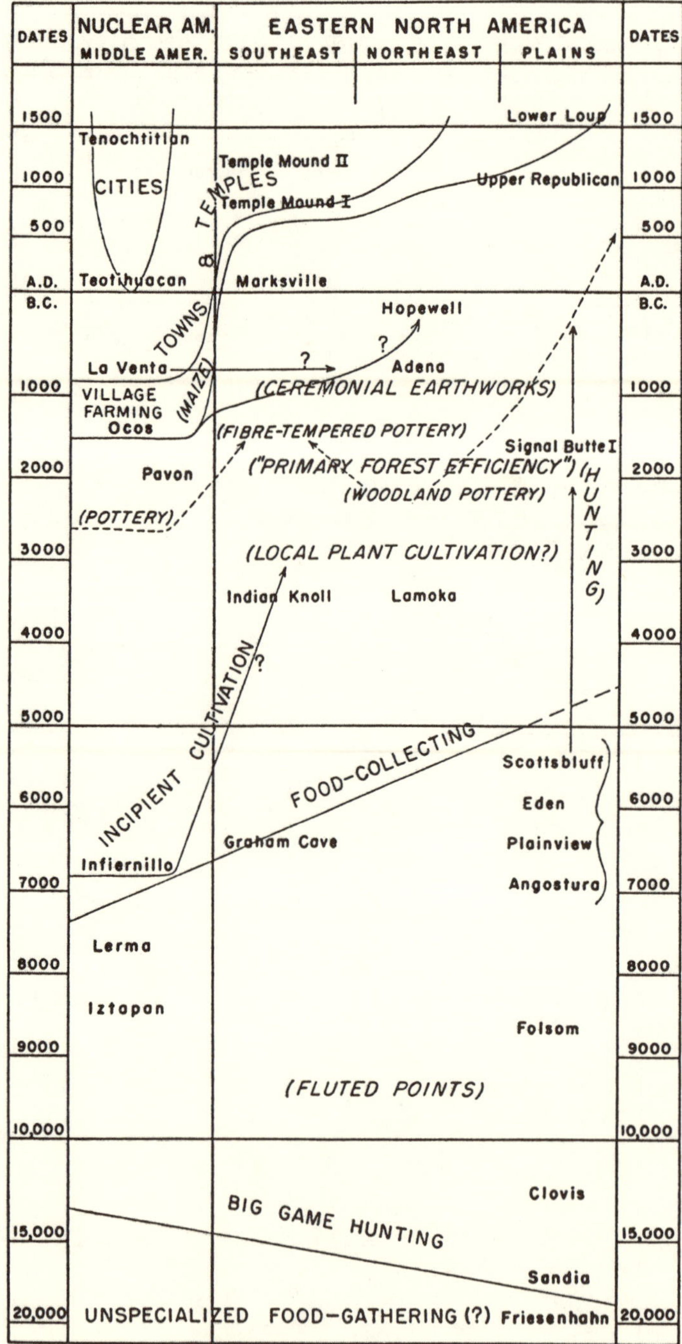

Figure 11.3. Subsistence and settlement type levels in native America: cross section for Nuclear America and eastern North America. The first appearance of pottery is indicated by the dotted lines.

PLEISTOCENE FOOD GATHERING (?)

There are scattered finds in the Americas which suggest by their typology and chronological position that they may be the remains of early food-gathering societies (*2*, pp. 82–86; *6*). These artifacts include rough, percussion-chipped flint choppers, scrapers, and possibly knives or points, and occasional worked bone splinters. In some places, such as Tule Springs, Nevada, or Friesenhahn Cave, Texas, these crude weapons and tools have been found associated with the bones of extinct Pleistocene mammals, so it is likely that some hunting, even of large game, was practiced (*7*, pp. 197, 218). In general, however, the technological aspects of the implements show a lack of specialization toward hunting or toward any other particular means of obtaining food. In this the artifacts, and the inferences made from them, are analogous to those for the food-gathering cultures of the Old World lower and middle Paleolithic (*8*).

In age and geological placement, such putative early food gatherers in the Americas are not, however, comparable to those of Asia or any part of the Old World. At Tule Springs, a radiocarbon date (22,000 B.C.) indicates a context in the early substages of the Wisconsin glaciation, but in other localities, such as the lowest levels of Danger Cave, Utah (*7*, pp. 193–195; *9*), or Fishbone Cave, Nevada (*7*, pp. 192–193; *10*), the assemblage can be no older than the final Wisconsin advance. Still other artifact assemblages that suggest an unspecialized food-gathering economy are not satisfactorily dated (*11*).

PLEISTOCENE BIG-GAME HUNTING

Sometime during the last Wisconsin interglacial era, or possibly even earlier, inhabitants of the North American continent entered upon a way of life that was based upon the pursuit and killing of the great ice-age mammals, such as the mammoth, the mastodon, the camel, and later the buffalo. The origins of this life pattern are unknown. There are no visible antecedents in the possible earlier food-gathering cultures of the Americas. There is, it is true, a general correspondence between this New World specialized hunting of Pleistocene fauna and what was going on in the Old World in the approximately coeval upper Paleolithic stage; yet even this possibility of a connection with the Old World does not provide a reasonable source for the big-game-hunting complexes of the New World, with their distinctive and highly specialized equipment. Apparently the forms which are most indicative of the American big-game-hunting technology are New World inventions.

The technical equipment associated with big-game hunters in the Americas includes lanceolate projectile points shaped by pressure-flaking. These are frequently distinguished by a channel fluting on both faces of the blade. A variety of skin-scraping tools accompanies the points as they are found in camp sites, "kills," and butchering stations (*7*, pp. 23–90). The best documented of these discoveries come from the North American high plains in eastern New Mexico, Colorado, and Texas, and there are others from southern Arizona southward into Mexico. Some finds, such as those of the lower layer of Sandia Cave, New Mexico, may date back to before 15,000 B.C. (*7*, pp. 85–91; *12*). The Sandia complex is characterized by a lanceolate single-shouldered projectile point. Other discoveries, such as Clovis and Folsom, appear to be later, ranging perhaps, from 15,000 to 7000 B.C. The projectile points of both Clovis and Folsom complexes are of the fluted form (*7*, pp. 23–84). There are also a variety of lanceolate, unfluted points that appear to mark a horizon subsequent to the Folsom. These include the Angostura, Scottsbluff, Plainview, and Eden types (see Figure 11.2) (*7*, pp. 107, 118, 138).

The spread of big-game hunting in the Americas took place during, and in the first or second millennium after, the final Wisconsin substage, the Mankato-Valders. The total span of time of this dissemination appears to have been from about 9000 to 5000 B.C. Finds of fluted projectile points throughout the eastern woodlands of North America indicate the former prevalence of the pattern there (*13*). The Iztapan and Lerma remains in central and northeastern Mexico (*14*), the El Jobo points of Venezuela (*15*), the Ayampitín industry of the Andes and southern South America (*16*), and the Magellan I culture of the Straits (*17*) give the geographical range of the early big-game-hunting societies.

The fate of the big-game-hunting pattern is better known than its beginnings. After 7000 B.C. and the glacial retreats, there was a shrinkage of the total territory in which the big herbivores could be hunted. The intermontane basins and the range country of western North America became more arid, and a similar climatic shift took place in southern South America. After 5000 B.C., with a still greater increase in warmth and dryness, big-game hunting persisted in the central zones of the old continental grasslands, such as the North American plains and the Argentine pampas. In these areas a modified hunting pattern, based, respectively, on the buffalo and the guanaco, continued into later times. Elsewhere, populations of hunters probably were forced into new environmental situations and new subsistence habits.

LATER FOOD COLLECTING AND HUNTING

These new subsistence patterns can best be described as food collecting. They are differentiated from the possible earlier food-gathering pattern in that they show specialization in the exploitation of regional environments and much more effective technological equipment. Although the taking of game is a means of subsistence in some of these patterns, it is not the old big-game hunting of the Pleistocene. The food collectors, for the most part, developed cultures of greater material wealth, larger communities, and more stable settlements than their predecessors. There were exceptions to this, particularly in areas or regions of severe natural limitations and in the earlier periods of the food-collecting patterns; but on the average, and certainly at the optimum, these generalizations hold true (*18*).

Chronologically, most of the food-collecting patterns had their beginnings in the span of time between about 6000 and 2000 B.C. There were, however, exceptions to this, as in the North American Great Basin, where the specialized collecting of wild seeds was well established as early as 7000 or even 8000 B.C. (*19*). As this is the same general area where clues to the most ancient food gatherers are found, it may be that there is a continuity in the Great Basin from the unspecialized gathering of the early Pleistocene to the later food collecting. According to this interpretation, big-game hunting would be only partially represented or would be absent in an intervening sequence position (*20*). This relationship is expressed in Figure 11.1.

This possibility of continuities between the North American desert food collectors and earlier resident cultures and populations brings attention to the larger question of the origins of the New World food-collecting patterns and peoples in general. There are three logical possibilities: (i) food-collecting societies and cultures were derivative, arising from the earlier food gatherers; (ii) members of such societies were the descendants of big-game hunters who were forced by the changing climatic conditions that followed the end of the Wisconsin glaciation to make readjustments; or (iii) they were more recent arrivals from the Old World by way of the Bering Strait. It seems quite likely that all three explanations may be useful, according to the particular geographical areas involved, and I have already mentioned the first two. The third explanation, that new arrivals from Asia played a part, is very probably correct insofar as the development of food-collecting cultures in northern North America is concerned. I have in mind particularly the northeastern woodlands, the northwest Pacific coast, and the subarctic and arctic. Elsewhere Asiatic influences were almost certainly of less direct account.

There are several major food-collecting patterns in the New World, and we can only skim over these very briefly. I have referred to what has been called a Desert pattern (*21*). The long depositional histories at Danger Cave, Utah (*9*), Leonard Rock Shelter, Nevada (*7*, pp. 190–192; *22*), and Fort Rock Cave, western Oregon (*7*, p. 184; *23*) are representative, and the basketry and crude milling stones found at these sites testify to a seed-collecting and seed-grinding subsistence. A similar story is recorded in the Cochise culture of southern Arizona–New Mexico (*24*), and there are evidences of this Desert pattern in Mexico as well (*25*).

In the woodlands of eastern North America there is another collecting pattern that shows an adaptation to forest and riverine conditions in hunting, utilization of wild plants, fishing, and catching shellfish. Such sites as the Graham Cave, in Missouri (*26*), suggest that there was a transition in the eastern woodlands area, at about 7000 B.C., from big-game hunting to food collecting. In the ensuing millennia these Eastern Woodland collecting cultures, subsumed under the name *Archaic* in much of the literature (*27*), underwent progressive adaptations to regional conditions. By 3000 B.C. they were characterized not only by rough grinding stones and specialized projectile points but by numerous items of polished stone, such as vessels, celts, weights for throwing sticks, and various ornamental or ceremonial objects. The Indian Knoll, Kentucky (*2*, p. 116; *28*), and Lamoka, New York (*2*, pp. 116–117; *29*), phases are typical of their particular regions. Many of the Archaic sites are huge heaps of shells situated along rivers or on the Atlantic coast. Such locations were undoubtedly suitable for a semisedentary, or even sedentary, existence.

Along the Pacific coast of North America there was another food-collecting pattern which paralleled in many ways that of the Eastern Woodlands. Here, by 2000 B.C. if not earlier, semisedentary societies based upon fishing and acorn gathering were established all along the coast from southern Alaska to southern California (*2*, pp. 133–137). In South America there were also ancient fishing societies along the coasts. The Quiani phase (*30*) of northern Chile displays this adjustment. On the Brazilian coast are the huge *sambaquís*, piles of shell refuse containing the skeletons and artifactual remains of food-collecting peoples who lived along these shores probably as much as two millennia before the beginning of the Christian Era (*31*). Coastal shell-mound dwellers are also known from Venezuela at about this same period (*32*, *33*).

I have mentioned that in both the North American and the South American plains there were retentions of big-game-hunting patterns into later times; even these cultures, however, show the result of contact with the neighboring food collectors in their possession of an increasing number of food-grinding implements. This is exemplified in the later North American Plains phases, such as the Signal Butte I (*34*), and by the later phases in the Strait of Magellan sequence and on the Argentine pampas (*35*).

Incipient Cultivation

The change from food collecting to a subsistence based upon plant cultivation was one of the great turning points in human prehistory. This is true of the New World as well as the Old, and there are indications in both hemispheres that this switch-over was not a rapid one, but that it was effected only over a period of experimentation. It is this era of experimental or incipient cultivation in the New World that I now wish to examine (*36*).

In the Americas it would appear that there may be at least four distinct and semi-independent traditions of incipient farming. Two of these are Nuclear American. The northern one, the probable propagator of maize, was located in Middle America and in the adjacent deserts of northern Mexico and the southwestern United States; the southern one had its focus on the Peruvian coast. A third incipient-cultivation tradition centered somewhere in the tropical forests of the Amazon or Orinoco. Its existence is difficult to demonstrate archaeologically, but such a tradition is needed to explain the domestication of manioc and other root crops. A fourth, and distinctly lesser, tradition rose in eastern North America in the Mississippi Valley system.

The earliest evidence for incipient cultivation in any of these traditions comes from northern Nuclear America. The region is the northeastern periphery of Middle America, in the semiarid hill country of Tamaulipas. Here, preserved plant remains were taken from the refuse deposits of dry caves. In the Infiernillo phase, dating from 7000 to 5000 B.C., there are traces of domesticated squash (*Cucurbita pepo*) and of possible domesticates of peppers, gourds, and small beans. The cultural context is that of North American desert food collectors. There are, in addition to flint implements, net bags of yucca and maguey cords and woven baskets of a rod-foundation type. In the succeeding Ocampo phase, from about 5000 to 3000 B.C., beans were definitely domesticates. After this, between 3000 and 2000 B.C., a primitive small-eared maize came into the sequence in the La Perra and Flacco phases. R. S. MacNeish, who excavated and studied the Tamaulipas caves, has estimated the composition of food refuse of the La Perra phase to be as follows: 76 percent wild plants, 15 percent animals, and 9 percent cultigens. The La Perra and Flacco artifact inventories are not strikingly different from inventories of the earlier phases, although they demonstrate a somewhat greater variety of manufactures and an increased concern for seed foods. A few centuries later, at about 1500 B.C., an archaeological complex which is representative of fully settled village farming appears in the region. Thus, the Tamaulipas sequence offers a more or less unbroken story of the very slow transition from food collecting supplemented with incipient cultivation to the patterns of established cultivation (*37*).

Early and primitive maize is also found to the north of Tamaulipas, actually outside of Nuclear America, in New Mexico. At Bat Cave, corncobs from refuse of a Cochise-affiliated culture date between 3500 and 2500 B.C. (*38*). This is as early as the La Perra maize, or even earlier.

As yet, neither archaeologists nor botanists have been able to determine the exact center of origin for domestication of maize in the New World, and it may be that this important event first took place in northern Middle America and in southwestern North America, where the intensive use of wild seeds in a food-collecting economy in a desert area provided a favorable setting. There remains, nevertheless, the very good possibility that a territory nearer the heart of Nuclear America and more centrally situated for the spread of maize in the hemisphere—an area such as southern Middle America—played this primary role in the cultivation of maize. The great difficulty is, of course, that the archaeological record is so uneven, owing to the rarity of sites and environments where such things as plant remains are preserved in the earth. Such findings have not yet been reported in southern Middle America.

Coastal Peru, at the southern end of Nuclear America, provides a rainless climate and splendid conditions for preservation of organic materials in open archaeological sites, and it is in Peru that we have glimpsed what appears to be a second tradition of incipient plant cultivation in Nuclear America. At Huaca Prieta, in a great hill of marine shells, sea-urchin spines, ash, and other debris, cultivated squash, peppers, gourds, cotton, and a local bean (*Canavalia*) were found, along with an abundance of wild root plants and fruits. The people who raised and gathered these crops and seafoods lived at Huaca Prieta at least 2000 years before the Christian Era. Whether there was, however indirectly, an exchange of domesticated plants between these early Peruvians and their contemporaries in Middle America is not certain. Such connections could have existed; or the beginnings of cultivation may have been truly independent of each other in these two areas of Nuclear America. Definite connections between early farmers of Middle America and of Peru appear, however, by 700 B.C. with the sudden presence of maize in Peru (*39*). This maize was not, like that at Bat Cave or in the La Perra culture of Tamaulipas, of an extremely primitive kind. It was brought, or it spread, to Peru as a relatively well-developed plant, and it serves as a link to Middle America. We may conclude that Nuclear America possessed, from this time forward, a single major horticultural tradition, but by this time we have also passed beyond the chronological limits of cultivation incipience.

An ancient tradition of plant cultivation in the South American tropical forest (*40*) is based upon the presumption that a long period of experimentation was necessary for the domestication of such tropical root crops as bitter and sweet manioc (*Manihot utilissima*, *M. Api*) and the yam (*Ipomoea batatas*). It seems reasonably certain that these domesticates date back to before 1000 B.C. in lowland Venezuela. This is inferred from the presence of pottery griddles, of the sort used for cooking manioc cakes in later times, in the Saladero phase at the Orinoco Delta by this date (*32*). Also, the early archaeological phase of Momíl I, in Caribbean Colombia, has the pottery manioc griddle (*41*). The dating of Momíl I is debatable, but some of the ceramic traits suggest a date as early as 2000 B.C. Saladero and Momíl I are, however, outside the chronological and developmental range of incipient cultivation patterns. They appear to be village sites based upon the cultivation of root crops, and as such they are comparable to, although historically separate from, village farming based on maize. I shall return to this point further along. For the present I bring these sites into the discussion because their existence implies centuries, or even millennia, of prior incipient root-crop cultivation in tropical northern South America.

A fourth tradition of incipient cultivation for the New World derives from the cultivation of local plants in the Mississippi Valley by as early as 1000 B.C. These plants include the sunflower, the goosefoot (*Chenopodium*), and the pumpkin (*Cucurbita pepo*) (*42*). This domestication may have been in response to stimuli from Middle America, or it may have been an entirely independent development. This Eastern Woodland incipient-cultivation tradition was undoubtedly but a minor part of the food-collecting economy for a long time. Just how important it ever became, or how important the early diffusion of maize was to eastern United States cultures of the first millennium B.C., are crucial problems in the understanding of the area. I shall return to them later.

APPEARANCE OF POTTERY

Before taking up the rise of village farming in Nuclear America and its subsequent spread to other parts of the hemisphere, let us review the first appearances of pottery in the New World. Obviously, the line indicating the presence of pottery on the charts is not comparable to the lines indicating type of subsistence or settlement (Figures 1–3). American archaeologists no longer consider pottery to be the inevitable concomitant of agricultural village life, as was the fashion some years ago. Still, ceramics, because of their very ubiquity and durability, are an important datum in many prehistoric sequences. Their presence, while not a necessary functional correlate of farming, at least implies a certain degree of cultural development and sedentary living.

At the present writing there seem to be two pottery traditions for native America. Curiously, the ages of these two pottery traditions—in the broadest sense of that term—may be about the same, 2500 B.C.

One of these pottery traditions, which we shall call the Nuclear American, is believed to be indigenous, but we can be no more specific about its geographic point of origin than to state that this is somewhere in the central latitudes of the New World. Actually, the earliest radiocarbon dates on the Nuclear American pottery tradition come from coastal Ecuador, in the Valdivia phase, and are from about 2400 to 2500 B.C. (*43*). There are also early dates on pottery generally similar to that of Valdivia from Panama (about 2100 B.C.) (*44*, *45*). Thus, these earliest ceramic datings for Nuclear America are not from Middle America or Peru but from the Intermediate area, and this may be significant in following up origins, although the record is still too incomplete to say for sure. Both the Ecuadorean and the Panamanian early potteries are found in coastal shell-mound sites, and in connection with cultures about whose means of subsistence it is not easy to draw inferences, except to say that full village farming was unlikely. Possibly marine subsistence was supplemented with incipient cultivation, although we have no proof of this. The Valdivia and the Panamanian (Monagrillo) pottery is reasonably well made and fired, the forms are rather simple, and the vessels are decorated with incisions, excisions, punctations, and very simple band painting. These early Ecuadorean and Panamanian styles may be part of a stratum of ancient Nuclear American pottery that underlies both Middle America and Peru. There are some indications that this may be the case, although the oldest pottery so far known in the Middle American and Peruvian areas dates from several centuries later (*46*). In Figure 1 the interpretation is offered that Nuclear American pottery is oldest in southern Middle America (for this there is as yet no evidence) and in the Intermediate area (for this there is evidence). Whatever the point of origin for pottery in Nuclear America, there is fairly general agreement that the ceramic ideas generated there carried to much of outlying North and South America.

The second major pottery tradition of the Americas is widely recognized by the term *Woodland*. Apparently not indigenous, but derived from northern Asia, it is best known from the eastern woodlands of New York and the Great Lakes region. So far, its presumed long trek from the arctic down through Canada has not been traced (*47*). Woodland pottery is generally of simpler design than the early Nuclear American wares. Of an elongated form, it is frequently finished only with cord-marked surfaces. As already noted, the oldest of this cord-marked pottery in the Americas may go back to 2500 B.C. (*48*). Even if this early dating is not accepted, there is little doubt but that Woodland pottery was well established in eastern North America before 1000 B.C.

In spite of the fact that the Nuclear American and Woodland pottery traditions are so radically different, there are, interestingly, a few similarities. The most notable of these is the technique of rocker-stamping combined with incised zoning of plain surface areas, known in Nuclear America and in the eastern United States. The distinctive rocker-stamped treatment of pottery was accomplished by impressing the soft, unfired surface of a vessel with either a small straight-edged implement manipulated rocker-fashion or, possibly, with a fine-edged disk used like a roulette. The impressions left on the pottery may be either plain or dentate, and they always have a characteristic "zigzag" appearance. Rocker-stamping is found in the Valdivia phase in Ecuador, and it also occurs at about

1000 B.C. in parts of Middle America and in Peru (*49*). In eastern North America it is not found on the earliest Woodland pottery but is found on vessels which date from just a few centuries before the beginning of the Christian Era. Thus, the Nuclear American rather than the Woodland tradition has chronological priority in this trait in the New World (*50*). Again, as with so many other problems that perplex Americanists we can only refer to this without coming to any conclusions as to the timing and direction of the flows of possible diffusions. Nuclear American and Woodland ceramics may in some way be related, but at the present state of knowledge they appear to have different origins and substantially separate histories.

VILLAGE FARMING IN NUCLEAR AMERICA

Braidwood and others have stressed the importance in the Old World of the threshold of the village-farming settled community (*1*, refs.; *51*). Although in its beginnings the agricultural village had a subsistence base that was no more adequate, if as ample, as that of some of the food-collecting communities, this base offered the potential in certain Old World localities that led, eventually, to civilization. In the New World a similar development was repeated in Nuclear America.

In the New World the line between incipient cultivation and village farming has been drawn at that theoretical point where village life is, in effect, sustained primarily by cultivated food plants (*52*). In archaeology this distinction must be made by an appraisal of the size and stability of a settlement as well as by direct or indirect clues as to the existence of agriculture. In Nuclear America the earliest time for which we can postulate the conditions of village farming is the second millennium B.C. For example, in Middle America in the Tamaulipas sequence the change-over from incipient cultivation to established cultivation takes place at about 1500 B.C. (*53*). Elsewhere in Middle America the known sequences begin with the village-farming stage, as at Early Zacatenco (*54*) (Valley of Mexico), Las Charcas (*55*) (Guatemalan Highlands), Ocos (*56*) (Pacific coast of Guatemala), and Mamom (*57*) (Maya lowlands) (*58*). In Peru the village-farming level is reasonably well defined with the appearance of maize in the Cupisnique phase and the shift of settlements back from the coast to the valley interiors. The date for this event is shortly after 1000 B.C. (*59*); this suggests that the horizon for village farming may have sloped upward in time from Middle America to Peru (Figure 1). For the Intermediate area, where I have noted the earliest occurrence of pottery in Nuclear America, the threshold of village farming is difficult to spot. In Ecuador, the phases succeeding Valdivia have a different ecological setting, being inland in the river valleys rather than on the immediate shores (*60*). Perhaps, as in Peru, this correlates with the primary economic importance of plant cultivation. In Colombia, the Momíl II phase, which is represented by a stable village site area, is believed to have possessed maize (*41*).

The foregoing discussion carries the implication that village farming was a pattern diffused through Nuclear America from a single area or region. Essentially, this is the point of view expressed in this article. This is not to overlook the possibility that village agricultural stability may have arisen independently in more than one place in the New World. In fact, as I point out below, it apparently did just that in the tropical forests of South America. I am of the opinion, however, that in the Nuclear American zone the maize plant, genetically developed and economically successful, became the vital element in a village-farming way of life that subsequently spread as a complex. For the present, I would hazard the guess that this complex developed in southern Middle America and from there spread northward to Mexico and southward as far as Peru. This was, in a sense, its primary diffusion or spread. Afterward, there were secondary diffusions to other parts of the Americas.

The Village in Non-Nuclear America

These secondary disseminations of the Nuclear American pattern of village farming were responsible for the establishment of similar communities in areas such as southwestern North America, the southern Andes, lowland tropical South America, and the eastern woodlands of North America (see Figures 1–3). This process was relatively simple in southwestern North America and the southern Andes. The agricultural patterns were diffused to, or carried and superimposed upon, peoples with food-collecting economies of limited efficiency. In the Southwest, village farming and ceramics first appear at about the same time in such cultures as the Vahki, the Mogollon I, and the Basketmaker (*2*, pp. 151–155). This was between 200 B.C. and A.D. 300. Moving from the south, the village-farming pattern pushed as far as the Fremont culture (*61*) of the northern periphery of the Southwest. In the southern Andes there is, as yet, no good hint of an early incipient-cultivation tradition, and, apparently, pottery and agriculture arrive at about the same time, integrated as a village-farming complex. This flow of migration or diffusion was from Peru-Bolivia southward. Pichalo I (*30*) of northern Chile marks such an introduction, as do the earliest of the Barreales phases (*62*) in northwest Argentina. The time is about the beginning of the Christian Era. Beyond the southern Andes the village-farming pattern did not diffuse onto the plains of the pampas or Patagonia.

The relationship of Nuclear American village farming to the tropical lowlands of South America was much more complex. There the maize-farming pattern was projected into an area in which village life already existed. This is indicated in Figure 2 by the entry "Village Farming—Manioc" in the columns headed "Venezuela" and "Amazon." Sedentary village life based upon root-crop farming is estimated to be as old as 2500 B.C. This is a guess, and, if it is correct, these villages are older than the Nuclear American village sustained by maize. Perhaps the estimated date is too early; however, at 2000 and 1000 B.C., respectively (see Figure 2), we have the villages of Momíl I and Saladero, which, apparently, were supported by root-crop cultivation. It is of interest to note that Momíl I, near the mouth of the Sinú River in Colombia, lies within the axis of Nuclear America; yet it differs from the succeeding Momíl II phase at the same site in being oriented toward manioc rather than maize. This suggests that, in the Intermediate area at least, tropical-forest farming patterns may have preceded farming patterns for maize in Nuclear America.

Relationships between village farming in Nuclear America and in eastern North America are also complicated. It is unlikely that the local incipient-cultivation tradition in eastern North America ever matured into a subsistence pattern that could have supported fully sedentary village life. J. R. Caldwell (*63*) has argued that, in its place, a steadily increasing efficiency in forest collecting and hunting climaxed at about 2000 B.C. in a level of "Primary Forest Efficiency" (see Figure 3). Such a level, he concludes, offered the same opportunities for population stability and cultural creativity in the eastern woodlands as were offered by village farming. While agreeing with Caldwell that the efflorescence of Adena-Hopewell (about 800 B.C. to A.D. 200) (*64*) is the brilliant end product of a mounting cultural intensity in eastern North America that originated in the food-collecting or Archaic societies, I am not yet convinced that plant cultivation did not play an important role in this terminal development. And by plant cultivation I am referring to maize, brought or diffused from Nuclear America. There is, as yet, no good direct evidence of maize associated with either the Adena (*42*) or the contemporary Poverty Point (*65*) culture. Maize is, however, found with Hopewellian cultures (*63*), although it has been assumed that it was of relatively little importance as subsistence at this time. I would argue that the riverine locations of Adena and Hopewell sites, together with the great size and plan of the ceremonial earthworks that mark many of them, make it difficult to infer an adequate subsistence if maize agriculture is ruled out.

To sum up briefly, the amazing cultural florescence of the Eastern Woodlands in the first millennium B.C. has not yet been satisfactorily explained. This florescence rests upon a chronologically deep series of Archaic food-collecting cultures which were at least semisedentary, and it contains elements, such as pottery, which are probably of Asiatic derivation and which added to the richness of the Archaic continuum. But the sudden burst of social and cultural energy which marks the Adena culture cannot be interpreted easily without adding other factors to the equation, and perhaps these missing factors are maize agriculture and other stimuli from Middle America (see Figure 11.3).

Village life is, of course, present in native America in the non-Nuclear areas under conditions where plant cultivation may be ruled out entirely. Settled villages developed on the northwest coast of North America, with population supported by the intensive food-collecting economy of the coast and rivers. The same is also true for the coast and interior valleys of California. It is significant, however, that in neither of these areas did aboriginal cultivation ever make much headway, while in eastern North America it became a staple of life in the later Precolumbian centuries.

TEMPLES, TOWNS, AND CITIES

In Nuclear America the town and eventually the city had beginnings in the settled farming village. A centralizing factor in this development was undoubtedly the temple. This earliest form of permanent structure usually had a flat-topped pyramidal mound of earth or rock as a base, and these mound bases of temples are found associated with some, but not all, of the village-farming cultures in Middle America (*66*). At first, the importance of such a mound, and of the temple that stood on it, was probably limited to the immediate village. Sometimes these villages were small, concentrated clusters of dwellings; in other instances the settlement pattern was a dispersed one, with a number of small, hamlet-like units scattered at varying distances from the temple center. Later on, the temple, or temple and palace structures, became the focal point of what might be called a town (*67*).

In Nuclear America the towns, like their antecedent villages, were either concentrated or dispersed. The former pattern developed in parts of Middle America, such as the Valley of Mexico or the Guatemalan Highlands, and in Peru; the latter was characteristic of the Veracruz-Tabasco lowlands or the Peten-Yucatan jungles of Middle America. In the towns the temple or ceremonial precinct was devoted to religious and governmental matters and to the housing of priests and of rulers and their retainers. The surrounding settlement zone, either scattered or concentrated, grew with increase in the numbers of farmers, artisans, or both. Trade was an important function of these towns.

In Nuclear America the town-and-temple community dates back to 800 B.C., a date that is applicable both to Middle America and to Peru. In the Intermediate area, between these two, town life was certainly Precolumbian, but its date of origin is difficult to determine because there is a lack of adequate archaeological chronologies (*68*).

In lowland South America, town-and-temple communities also antedate the Conquest, and it seems likely that these communities were, in part, the result of contact with and stimulus from the Nuclear American axis (*69*). In the southern Andes the tightly planned clusters of rock and adobe buildings of the late archaeological periods of northwestern Argentina reflect town and city life in Peru and Bolivia (*70*). Similarly, towns of the prehistoric southwestern United States relate to the Nuclear American zone. Development of these towns dates from sometime after A.D. 500, with an apogee in the Pueblo III and IV periods and in the Classic Hohokam phases (*71*).

On the other great periphery of Nuclear America, eastern North America, Middle American town life, with its temple-mound-and-plaza complex, entered the Mississippi Valley sometime between A.D. 500 and 1000 and climaxed in the Mississippian or Temple Mound cultures shortly afterwards (*72*). Maize cultivation was an established part of this complex. Thus, in a sense, the thresholds of village farming and of the town-and-temple complex in the eastern woodlands, when these beginnings can be identified indisputably as of Nuclear American inspiration, are synchronous (Figure 11.3).

There remains, however, as in our consideration of the village-farming level, the puzzle of the Adena-Hopewell cultures. As we have already noted, the Adena-Hopewell ceremonial mounds and earthworks, built between 800 B.C., and A.D. 200, are of impressive size. Some of them are comparable in dimensions, and in the amount of coordinated manpower necessary to build them, with the contemporary mounds of Middle America. Although the mounds of Middle America were usually temple platforms while the Adena-Hopewell tumuli were mounds heaped up to cover tombs and sacred buildings, this dichotomy should not be overstressed. Some mounds of Middle America also were tombs, or combined tombs and temples (*73*). In any event, it is safe to conclude that the Adena-Hopewell mounds were structures which memorialized social and religious traditions and served as community nuclei, as the ceremonial building did in Middle America. Was there a historical connection between Middle America and the Eastern Woodlands at this time, and was Adena-Hopewell ceremonial construction influenced by the emergence of the town-and-temple concept of Middle Ameria? There is no satisfactory answer at present, but the possibilities cannot be dismissed (see Figure 11.3).

In Nuclear America the city developed from the town and temple, and there is no sharp division between the two. Size is, assuredly, one criterion but not the only one. These cities were the nerve centers of civilizations. They were distinguished by great public buildings and the arts. Formal pantheons of deities were worshiped in the temples under the tutelage of organized priesthoods. Populations were divided into social classes. Trade, in both raw materials and luxury items, was carried on in these cities, and science and writing were under the patronage of the leaders (*74*). Not all of these criteria are known or can be inferred for any one city in the New World, but many of them do properly pertain to Middle American and Peruvian sites from as early as the first centuries of the Christian Era.

Cities in the New World seem to have been of two types, and these types may have their antecedents in the earlier dispersed and concentrated towns. The dispersed city, with its ceremonial center and outlying hamlets, appears to have been orthogenetic in its traditions and to have drawn upon, and commanded, a relatively limited geographical territory. The great lowland Mayan centers of the Classic period, such as Tikal or Palenque, are representative (*75*). The concentrated city adheres more to the concept of the city in the western European definition of the term. It was a truly urban agglomeration. Its traditions were heterogenetic, and its power extended over a relatively large territorial domain. The city was, in effect, the capital of an empire. Peruvian Chanchan,

Aztec Tenochtitlan, and, probably, the more ancient Mexican city of Teotihuacan represent the type (*76*).

Although the cities and civilizations which developed in Middle America and Peru in the first millennium A.D. were unique and distinct entities in their own right, it is obvious that they also drew upon a common heritage of culture which had begun to be shared by all of Nuclear America at the level of village-farming life. This heritage was apparently built up over the centuries, through bonds of interchange and contact, direct and indirect. There are substantial archaeological evidences in support of this supposition (*77*). During the era of city life these relationships continued, so that a kind of cosmopolitanism, resulting from trade, was just beginning to appear in Nuclear America in the last few centuries before Columbus.

In the outlands beyond Nuclear America, trade and influences from the cities followed old routes of contact and penetrated and were assimilated in varying degrees. In the south Andes there was the very direct impact of the Inca state in the final hundred years before the Spanish conquest (*70*), and northward from Mexico, Toltec-derived influences reached the North American Southwest in relatively unadulterated form (*78*). But, for the most part, the potentialities of the New World city for influencing and acculturating the "barbarian outlanders" were still unrealized when the Europeans entered the American continents.

Comments

Conclusions are inappropriate to a synthesis which, by its nature, is an outline of opinion, however tentative. Retrospective comment seems more in order.

A few things stand out. The early inhabitants of the New World were not remarkably different in their mode of life from the food gatherers and hunters of the Old World; yet even on these early horizons, and despite the relatively limited cultural inventories available, dissimilarities of form are striking. The interrelationships of the two hemispheres during the Pleistocene are still very vague.

Plant cultivation in the New World—its incipient rise and its culmination as the most effective subsistence base of the Americas—is, of course, analogous to happenings in the Old World. The important American plants, however, are of local origin. In the Western Hemisphere the incipience of cultivation followed the end of the Pleistocene, and was not a great deal later, perhaps, than in the Old World Middle East. Yet the period of incipience was longer here; over 5000 years elapsed before village life was sustained by crop cultivation. Is this because the first New World cultigens were inadequate as foodstuffs, and it was necessary to develop, first, the cereal maize before agriculture was made profitable?

Although there is a high correlation between village life and agricultural subsistence in the New World, there were New World societies and cultures which maintained villages without plant cultivation. In at least one instance, that of the ancient Adena-Hopewell development of eastern North America, community centers comparable to those of the contemporary farmers of Middle America may have been built and supported without a full-fledged farming subsistence.

I have slighted in this presentation the relationships between Asia and the Americas which were probably maintained from Pleistocene times down to the European conquest. This is particularly true of the cultures of the northern half of North America, where it is certain that there were contacts between the Old World and the arctic, subarctic, and northwest Pacific coasts. For Nuclear America nothing at all has been said of the possibility of trans-Pacific contacts between the Old World civilizations of China and Southeast Asia and those of Middle America and Peru. This undoubtedly reflects my own bias, but I remain willing to be convinced of such events and their importance to the history of culture in the New World.

References and Notes

[1]R. J. Braidwood, *Science* 127, 1419 (1958).

[2]G. R. Willey and P. Phillips, *Method and Theory in American Archaeology* (Univ. of Chicago Press, 1958).

[3]R. J. Braidwood, 1960.

[4]See A. L. Kroeber, *Anthropology* (Harcourt, Brace, 1948a), pp. 779–781, and G. R. Willey, *Am. Anthropologist* 57, 571 (1955b), for a discussion of Nuclear America.

[5]The Intermediate area is defined by G. R. Willey in a paper presented at the 33rd International Congress of Americanists, San Jose, Costa Rica (1959).

[6]G. R. Willey, paper presented at the Darwin Centennial Celebration, University of Chicago, November 1959 (1960a).

[7]H. M. Wormington, "Ancient Man in North America," *Denver Museum Nat. Hist. Popular Ser. No. 4* (1957), pp. 197–198, 218.

[8]R. Linton, *Trans. N.Y. Acad. of Sci.* 2, 171 (1949).

[9]J. D. Jennings, "Danger Cave," *Soc. Am. Archaeology Mem. No. 14* (1957).

[10]P. C. Orr, *Nevada State Museum Bull.* No. 2 (1956).

[11]There are many of these. In Figs. 1 and 2 the Alto Paraná complex of southern South America is representative. See O. F. A. Menghin (1955–56), *Ampurias* 17, 171; *ibid.* 18, 200.

[12]F. C. Hibben, *Smithsonian Inst. Publ., Misc. Collections* 99, (1941).

[13]J. Witthoft, *Proc. Am. Phil. Soc.* 96, 464 (1952); D. S. Byers, *Am. Antiquity* 19, 343 (1954).

[14]L. Aveleyra Arroyo de Anda, *Am. Antiquity* 22, 12 (1956); R. S. MacNeish, *Rev. mex. estud. antropol.* 11, 79 (1950).

[15]J. M. Cruxent and I. Rouse, *Am. Antiquity* 22, 172 (1956).

[16]A. R. Gonzales, *Runa* 5, 110 (1952); D. E. Ibarra Grasso, *Proc. Intern. Congr. Americanists 31st Congr., São Paulo* 2, 561 (1955).

[17]J. B. Bird, *Geograph. Rev.* 28, 250 (1938).

[18]These later food-collecting and hunting cultures are discussed by G. R. Willey and P. Phillips (See *2*, pp. 104–143) as the New World "Archaic" stage.

[19]See refrences to level "D-II" in J. D. Jennings, "Danger Cave" (*9*), as an example.

[20]C. W. Meighan, in *The Masterkey* [(Los Angeles, 1959), vol. 33, pp. 46–59], discusses the evidences for a big-game-hunting pattern in the Great Basin.

[21]J. D. Jennings and E. Norbeck, *Am. Antiquity* 21, 1 (1955).

[22]R. F. Heizer, *ibid.* 17, 23 (1951).

[23]L. S. Cressman, *Southwestern J. Anthropol.* 7, 289 (1951).

[24]E. B. Sayles and E. Antevs, "The Cochise Culture" *Medallion Papers, No. 24* (Gila Pueblo, Globe, Arizona, 1941).

[25]The caves in Coahuila, excavated by W. W. Taylor, are representative. See W. W. Taylor, *Bull. Texas Archaeol. Soc.* 27, 215 (1956).

[26]W. D. Logan, "An Archaic Site in Montgomery County, Missouri," *Missouri Archaeol. Soc. Mem. No. 2* (1952).

[27]See *Am. Antiquity* 24, No. 3 (1959) (an issue devoted entirely to Archaic cultures of North America).

[28]W. S. Webb, "Indian Knoll, Site Oh-2, Ohio County, Kentucky," *Univ. Kentucky Dept. Anthropol. and Archaeol. Publs.* (1946), vol. 4, No. 3, pt. 1.

[29]W. A. Ritchie, "The Lamoka Lake Site," *N.Y. State Archaeol. Assoc. Researches and Trans.* (1932), vol. 7, pp. 79–134.

[30]J. B. Bird, "Excavations in Northern Chile." *Am. Museum Nat. Hist. Anthropol. Paper No. 38* (1943), pt. 4.

[31]See G. R. Willey, *Am. Antiquity* 23, 365 (1958).

[32]J. M. Cruxent and I. Rouse, "An Archaeological Chronology of Venezuela," 1958–59.

[33]I. Rouse, J. M. Cruxent, J. M. Goggin, *Proc. Intern. Congr. Americanists, 32nd Congr., Copenhagen* (1958), pp. 508–515.

[34]W. D. Strong, *Smithsonian Inst. Publs. Misc. Collections* 93, No. 10 (1935).

[35]J. B. Bird, *Geograph. Rev.* 28, 250 (1938).

[36]See R. J. Braidwood [*Science* 127, 1419 (1958)] and G. R. Willey and P. Phillips [*Am. Anthropologist* 57, 723 (1955)] for discussion of the "Preformative" stage.

[37]R. S. MacNeish, "Preliminary archaeological investigations in the Sierra de Tamaulipas, Mexico" [*Trans. Am. Phil. Soc.* 48, pt. 6 (1958)] is the basis for this summary of the Tamaulipas sequences.

[38]P. C. Mangelsdorf, *Science* 128, 1313 (1958).

[39]J. B. Bird, in "A Reappraisal of Peruvian Archaeology," *Soc. Am. Archaeol. Mem. No. 4* (1948), pp. 21–28.

[40]C. O. Sauer discusses this possibility in *Agricultural Origins and Dispersals* (American Geographical Society, New York, 1952).

[41]G. Reichel-Dolmatoff and A. Dussan de Reichel-Dolmatoff, *Rev. colombiana antropol.* 5, 109 (1956).

[42]R. M. Goslin in *The Adena People, No. 2*, W. S. Webb and R. S. Baby, Eds. (Ohio State Univ. Press, 1957), pp. 41–46.

[43]C. Evans and B. J. Meggers, *Archaeology* 11, 175 (1958).

[44]For discussion of the Monagrillo pottery, see G. R. Willey and C. R. McGimsey, "The Monagrillo Culture of Panama" [*Peabody Museum, Harvard, Papers* 49, No. 2 (1954)].

[45]For the radiocarbon dating, see E. S. Deevey, L. J. Gralenski, V. Hoffren, *Am. J. Science Radiocarbon Suppl.* 1, Y-585 (1959).

[46]The problem of the age of pottery in Middle America is complicated and by no means settled. Such relatively well-developed village-farming phases as Early Zacatenco Valley of Mexico and Las Charcas (Guatemalan Highlands) have radiocarbon dates which indicate an age of about 1500 B.C. There are also contradictory radiocarbon dates which suggest that these phases occurred several hundred years later. For a review of some of these dates for Middle America, see G. R. Willey, *Am. Antiquity* 23, 359 (1958) and E. S. Deevey, L. J. Gralenski, and V. Hoffren (*45*). It may be that other Middle American ceramic complexes, such as the Chiapa I (Chiapas), Ocos (Pacific Guatemala), Yarumela I (Honduras), Yohoa Monochrome (Honduras), and Pavon (northern Veracruz), are older than either Early Zacatenco and Las Charcas, although there is no clear proof of this. In Fig. 1, the dotted line indicating the inception of pottery has been put as early as 2500 B.C. in Middle America. A recent discovery in conflict with this comes from Oaxaca, where a preceramic site, possibly representative of incipient cultivation, has radiocarbon dates of only about 2000 B.C. This has been presented by J. L. Lorenzo, "Un sitio preceramico en Yanhuitlan, Oaxaca," *Inst. nac. antropol. e hist. Publ. No. 6* (1958). For Peru, the earliest pottery appears on the north coast, at an average date of about 1200 to 1000 B.C. See radiocarbon dates for early Peruvian pottery as itemized by G. R. Willey [*Am. Antiquity* 23, 356 (1958)].

[47]R. S. MacNeish, in "The Engigstciak Site on the Yukon Arctic Coast" [*Univ. Alaska Anthropol. Papers* 4, No. 2 (1956)], has contributed to this problem by the discovery of early Woodland-like pottery in the far north.

[48]W. A. Ritchie, *N.Y. Museum Sci., Circ. No. 40* (Albany, N.Y., 1955); see J. B. Griffin, "The Chronological Position of the Hopewellian Culture in the Eastern United States," *Univ. of Michigan Museum of Anthropol., Anthropol. Paper No. 12* (1958), p. 10, for a different view.

[49]See G. R. Willey, *Am. Anthropologist* 57, 571 (1955b).

[50]However, zoned rocker-stamped pottery decoration appears earlier in Japan than in any part of the Americas. A distributional study of this technique for decorating pottery is included in R. M. Greengo (1964).

[51]See V. G. Childe, in *Anthropology Today*, A. L. Kroeber, Ed. (Univ. of Chicago Press, 1953), pp. 193–210.

[52]G. R. Willey and P. Phillips (*2*, pp. 144–147) define this as the "Formative" stage.

[53]See R. S. MacNeish (*37*) for such culture phases as the Laguna and the Mesa de Guaje.

[54]G. C. Vaillant, *Excavations at Zacatenco, (Am. Museum Nat. Hist. Anthropol. Paper No. 32* (1930), pt. 1.

[55]E. M. Shook, in *The Civilizations of Ancient America* (vol. 1 of selected papers of the 29th Intern. Congr. of Americanists), S. Tax. Ed. (Univ. of Chicago Press, 1951), pp. 93–100.

[56]M. D. Coe (1961b).

[57]For Mamom phase, see A. L. Smith, "Uaxactun, Guatemala: Excavations of 1931–1937," *Carnegie Inst. Wash. Publ. No. 588* (1950).

[58]The early ceramic phases, Yarumela I, Yohoa Monochrome, and Pavon, from Honduras and northern Veracruz, may represent village-farming cultures, or they may be coincident with incipient cultivation. For these phases see J. S. Canby, in *The Civilizations of Ancient America*, S. Tax, Ed. (Univ. of Chicago Press, 1951), pp. 79–85; W. D. Strong, A. Kidder II, A. J. D. Paul, *Smithsonian Inst. Publs. Misc. Collections* 97, 111 (1938); R. S. MacNeish, *Trans. Am. Phil. Soc.* 44 No. 5 (1954).

[59]J. B. Bird, in "Radiocarbon Dating," *Soc. Am. Archaeology Mem. No. 8* (1951), pp. 37–49, sample 75.

[60]C. Evans and B. J. Meggers, *Am. Antiquity* 22, 235 (1957); personal communication (1958).

[61]H. M. Wormington, "A Reappraisal of the Fremont Culture," *Proceedings, Denver Museum of Natural History* (1955), No. 1.

[62]A. R. Gonzalez, "Contextos culturales y cronologia relativa en el Area Central del Noroeste Argentino," *Anales arqueol. y etnol.* 11 (1955).

[63]J. R. Caldwell, "Trend and Tradition in the Prehistory of the Eastern United States." *Am. Anthropol. Assoc. Mem. No. 88* (1958).

[64]See J. B. Griffin. *The Chronological Position of the Hopewellian Culture in the Eastern United States, Univ. of Michigan Museum of Anthropol., Anthropol. Paper No. 12* (1958), for a résumé and analysis of Adena and Hopewell radiocarbon dates.

[65]J. A. Ford and C. H. Webb, "Poverty Point: A Late Archaic site in Louisiana," *Am. Museum Nat. Hist., Anthropol. Paper No. 46* (1956), pt. 1.

[66]R. Wauchope [*Middle American Research Records* (Tulane University, New Orleans, La., 1950b), vol. 1, No. 14] states the case for an early village-farming level without ceremonial mounds or constructions. While it is true that in some regions of Middle America the temple mound is absent in the earlier part of the "Formative" or "Preclassic" period, it is not clear that such a horizon prevails throughout all of Middle America. In fact, recent data [see M. D. Coe (*56*)] suggest that temple mounds were present in southern Middle America at the very beginnings of village farming.

[67]See R. K. Beardsley *et al.*, in "Seminars in Archaeology: 1955." *Soc. Am. Archaeol. Mem. No. 11* (1956), pp. 143–145, for discussion of an "advanced nuclear centered community."

[68]It is possible that such a ceremonial center as San Agustín, in southern Colombia, was, in effect, a town with concentrated ceremonial components and, probably, scattered hamlet-sustaining populations. San Agustín has not been satisfactorily dated, but estimates have been made which would place it as comparable in age to town-temple centers in Middle America and Peru. See W. C. Bennett, "Archaeological Regions of Colombia: A Ceramic Survey," *Yale Univ. Publs. in Anthropol.* 30, 109 (1944b).

[69]The town life of the Caribbean regions of Colombia and Venezuela at the period of the Spanish conquest is described by J. H. Steward in "Handbook of South American Indians," *Bur. Am. Ethnol., Smithsonian Inst. Publ.* (1949b), vol. 5, pp. 718 ff.

[70]See W. C. Bennett, E. F. Bleiler, F. H. Sommer, "Northwest Argentine Archaeology," *Yale Univ. Publs. in Anthropol.* 38, 31 (1948).

[71]See H. M. Wormington, "Prehistoric Indians of the Southwest," *Denver Museum Nat. Hist., Popular Ser. No. 7* (1947), pp. 76–102, 107–147.

[72]J. B. Griffin, ed. [*Archaeology of Eastern United States* (Univ. of Chicago Press, 1952a), Fig. 205] estimates these events at about A.D. 900 to 1000. There are indications from some parts of the southeastern United States that temple mounds are much older. For example, see H. P. Newell and A. D. Krieger, "The George C. Davis Site Cherokee County, Texas." *Soc. Am. Archaeol. Mem. No. 5* (1949), and R. P. Bullen, *Florida Anthropologist* 9, 931 (1956), for a radiocarbon date (about A.D. 350) on the Kolomoki culture.

[73]See W. R. Wedel, in P. Drucker, "La Venta. Tabasco, A Study of Olmec Ceramics and Art." *Bur. Am. Ethnol. Smithsonian Inst. Bull. No. 153* (1952), pp. 61–65, for a description of a stone-columned tomb within an earth mound at La Venta. In this connection, the stone tombs covered by earth mounds at San Agustín, Colombia, as described by K. T. Preuss, *Arte monumental prehistoric* (Escuelas Salesianas de Tipografia y Fotograbado, Bogotá 1931), may be pertinent.

[74]See V. G. Childe's criteria of city life in *Town Planning Rev.* 21, 3 (1950).

[75]Such centers, although serving as foci for the achievements of civilization, continue more in the form and in the homogeneous traditions of the Beardsley *et al.*, "advanced nuclear centered community" (*67*).

[76]This kind of city, a "true" city in a modern western European sense, corresponds more closely to what Beardsley *et al.* call "supra-nuclear integrated" communities (*67*, pp. 145–146).

[77]See G. R. Willey, *Am. Anthropologist* 57, 571 (1955b), and in *New Interpretations of Aboriginal American Culture History* (Anthropological Society of Washington, Washington, D.C., 1955a, pp. 28–45; see also, S. F. de Borhegyi, *Middle American Research Records* (Tulane University, New Orleans, La., 1959), vol. 2, No. 6.

[78]Such features as Middle America-derived ballcourts and the casting of copper ornaments are well known in Hohokam archaeology [see Wormington (*71*)].

12

NEW WORLD ARCHAEOLOGY IN 1965

(From *Proceedings, American Philosophical Society*, Vol. 110, No. 2, pp. 140–145, Philadelphia, 1966. Reprinted by permission of the American Philosophical Society.)

To speak in summary fashion about American archaeology forces a choice of approach and subject matter. I have made this choice in organizing my comments around three major questions or themes of culture history.

First, when did man come to the New World? From where did he come, and with what cultural equipment did he arrive?

Second, how, where, and when did native American agriculture develop? And what were the effects of this agriculture on the New World societies and cultures?

And third, how, where, and when, and under what conditions, do the elements of what is generally called civilization appear?

EARLY AMERICANS

Little doubt now exists that the first men to enter the New World crossed the Bering Strait from Asia to Alaska during the Pleistocene. It is also virtually certain that these first Americans belonged to the genus *Homo sapiens* and highly likely that they were of the Mongoloid racial stock. Beyond these basic agreements, the particular time at which they came and the cultural heritage which they brought with them are highly controversial.

The hard facts of the matter are that man was definitely in the New World by 10,000 B.C.[1] At this time he was a hunter of large, now extinct, mammals, including the mammoth, and he pursued these beasts with lances or darts tipped with finely flaked, stone projectile points that were characteristically fluted.

Now in the opinion of some archaeologists man had first entered the Americas only shortly before 10,000 B.C., perhaps not much earlier than 11,000 or 12,000 B.C., and had brought with him, from Asia, Upper Paleolithic blade and projectile-point-making techniques from which he developed the characteristic American fluted forms.

A counter-opinion holds that man came to the New World long before this, perhaps as far back as 30,000 or 40,000 or more years ago. Coming at this time he brought with him a much simpler tool kit. It included no blades or projectile points but was, rather, in the tradition of the ancient Lower or Middle Paleolithic Chopper-Chopping Tool Industry of southeast Asia. From this tradition he developed in the New World, over the millennia, and independent of additional Old World stimuli, the lanceolate, fluted projectile points of 10,000 B.C.[2]

Neither of these hypotheses is entirely satisfactory—at least at our present state of knowledge. If the first immigrants came to the New World as migratory big-game hunters, armed with projectile points, from what specific Asiatic cultures did they derive? The oldest occurrences of bifaced blades or points are in central and northern Siberia, around Lake Baikal and along the Lena River.[3] The complexes in which these blades or points appear have recently been dated in the range of 15,000 to 20,000 B.C., or sufficiently early to have served as the prototypes for the New World forms[4]; however, it should be stated that bifacially flaked blades are but a minor element in these Siberian Paleolithic cultures. On the American side, the traces of the spread of projectile-point-using hunters in the far north are disappointingly few. Two artifact complexes in the Arctic have been cited as possibly marking such a route: British Mountain, in the northern Yukon Territory,[5] and Kogruk, in the Brooks Range of Alaska.[6] Neither is securely dated. Finally, it should be emphasized that the Siberian and American Arctic points or blades referred to here are not really fluted forms. The Clovis fluted point does, indeed, seem to be a New World invention, from whatever antecedents.

The hypothesis that these antecedents were a crude chopper-chopping tool industry, brought from Asia at a very early time, has not yet been demonstrated. There are no thoroughly acceptable associations of manmade artifacts, extremely early radiocarbon dates, and convincing middle or early Wisconsin geological contexts. In fact, if anything, the hypothesis might be said to have lost ground within the last five years through the elimination, as the result of additional and intensive field investigation, of the Tule Springs, Nevada, claim for man's great antiquity in the Americas[7]; however, this does not mean that the hypothesis can now be rejected, for there remains strong suggestive evidence in its favor. Most significant in this regard, in my opinion, are the numerous isolated flint artifact complexes, in both North and South America, which present a crude chopper-chopping tool aspect.[8] But until such complexes are shown by stratigraphy and radiocarbon dating to be truly earlier than the Clovis and other early projectile point industries the case for their great age must stand unproven.

In sum, hunters of Pleistocene fauna were present on the American continents as early as 10,000 B.C. How long had they been here? Were they recent arrivals with Siberian Upper Paleolithic antecedents? Or were they the descendants of Asiatic immigrants who had crossed the Bering Strait tens of thousands of years before armed only with a crude chopping tool technology? These are the salient facts and hypotheses, and it is on these frontiers that American archaeologists are working.

THE RISE OF AMERICAN AGRICULTURE

The rise of native American agriculture carries the story forward several millennia from the time of the mammoth hunters. By 8000 B.C., with the onset of a more modern climate and changes in fauna, Pleistocene hunting cultures began to be modified. In the North American Eastern Woodlands, and later in the Plains, the Big Game Hunting tradition[9] was replaced by a cultural pattern known as the Archaic[10]; and in the far west the Old Cordilleran tradition[11] of late Pleistocene hunters and fishers gave way to the Desert tradition[12] and to others of the Pacific Coast.[13]

In all instances the new patterns of adjustment were specialized toward regional environmental niches. In some of these niches subsistence was ample. Hunting, collecting, and fishing techniques yielded a good life. Population increased, and settlement became semi-sedentary or sedentary. Such optimum situations arose between 5000 and 3000 B.C. in the North American Eastern Woodlands and along the Columbia River in the Pacific Northwest. In other regions, however, food supplies were less plentiful, and small, semi-nomadic bands of people scrounged a bare living from wild seed collecting and the taking of small game. Examples would be the desert country of the western United States and the semi-arid plateaus and valleys of northern and central Mexico. Interestingly, and probably significantly, it was in these Mexican upland semi-arid valleys—and in the context of the relatively poverty-stricken Desert cultural tradition—that New World agriculture had important beginnings.

These beginnings have been traced in excavations in the 6000-foot-high Valley of Tehuacan in southern Puebla, Mexico. Here dry cave refuse preserved a long story of man's transition from hunter to settled farmer. Intensive plant and seed collecting was practiced as early as 7000 B.C. Between that date and 5000 B.C. wild maize was used as food and some plants, such as squash (*C. moschata* or *mixta*) and chili peppers (*Capsicum*), may have been cultivated. We know that plant cultivation began shortly after 5000 B.C., and the most important cultigen was maize (*Zea mays*). For a long time, though, the maize ear was small and undeveloped, and the whole period of 5000 to 3000 B.C. can be considered one in which plant domestication was definitely an adjunct to wild seed collecting and hunting. But in the centuries between 3000 and 2000 B.C. maize was crossed with tripsacum and a number of maize varieties were hybridized. This had an explosive effect on the plant itself, which suddenly attained a size and quality more comparable to modern corn. In turn, the effect on human populations and culture was marked. The former small, semi-nomadic bands began to congregate into permanent and larger villages, dwelling became more stable, and pottery was invented or introduced to become a common household item. In brief, a village agricultural type of existence can be said to have come into being by the beginning of the second millennium B.C.[14]

Between 2000 and 1000 B.C. the cultivation of improved maize had spread through Middle America and southward as far as Peru[15]; by the beginning of the Christian Era it was known in the Southwestern United States, the Mississippi Valley, and in South America, in the southern Andes and many parts of the tropical lowlands. In this spread it often had a dynamic, stimulating effect on culture although this effect seems to have varied, depending largely upon the antecedent cultural conditions with which it came in contact. Furthermore, the story is complicated by the fact that maize—and the Middle American maize, beans, squash, and chili complex—was not the only line of New World agricultural development.

In Peru, for example, the lima bean (*Phaesolus lunatus*) was under domestication as early as the fourth millennium B.C. so that when maize finally reached the Peruvian coast in the second millennium B.C. it entered into an already well-developed horticultural pattern. Sedentary village and town settlement was, if anything, more advanced on the Peruvian coast at 2000 B.C. than it was in Middle America.[16] The extent to which these early Peruvian coastal villages and towns were dependent upon lima-bean farming is, however, difficult to appraise because it is also clear that sea foods were an important part of the economy and may have been the crucial factor in the development of sedentism. To bring still another complication into the picture, large sites and architectural remains are known from the Peruvian highlands as early as 2000 B.C.,[17] and while information is sadly lacking on early food crops in the highlands, it is reasonable to suspect that the potato (*Solanum tuberosum*) was under cultivation there at this time. It is, thus, a distinct possibility, that the potato was a major staple for Peru—not only in the highlands but on the coast as well—before the arrival of maize.[18]

Another major aspect of American agricultural origins is the role of the South American tropical forest with its root crops, particularly manioc (*Manihot*). There is good inferential archaeological evidence that manioc was cultivated, and was the basis for sedentary village life, at the mouth of the Orinoco River at 1000 B.C.[19] Such conditions are also thought to have obtained for the Colombian lowlands at about the same date.[20] In both regions the advent of maize is substantially later. But how far back can domesticated manioc and tropical root crop cultivation be pushed? Some authorities feel that its beginnings—probably in the Amazon basin—go back as least as far as the record of incipient cultivation in Mexico or on the Peruvian coast, and that, indeed, some elements of early village life in the Peruvian Andes; such as pottery, are to be traced eastward into the tropical forest.[21]

In a word, the story of New World agriculture is complex. As I have presented it, the Middle American line of development seems the clearest and most straightforward; but even here we know only one ecological niche, the upland valleys. Almost complete ignorance reigns for the Mexican–Central American tropical coasts. Recently we have word of coastal shell mounds in western Mexico with radiocarbon dates for pottery of 2300 B.C. The pottery is said to be very similar to that of the earliest pottery and sedentary village levels in the Tehuacan Valley.[22] Had maize farming spread to the Middle American coast by this time? And, if so, did this environmental shift result in a mutation and, perhaps, an invigoration of the plant? Were there other domesticated crops already in residence on the Mexican coasts before the spread of maize out of the highlands? Could these have been root crops of local or even of distant South American tropical forest origin? Archaeologists, geographers, and botanists studying these and other problems probably can be certain of only one thing: that regional interchange of cultigens, on both small and large geographical scales, was an ever-important factor in the trend toward agricultural efficiency and that such exchanges probably began earlier than we now suspect.

TRENDS TOWARD CIVILIZATION

For our third theme, we see that the emergence of the elements of New World civilization takes place in the same geographical spheres in which we have important agricultural beginnings: namely, Middle America and Peru. It is here that monuments, temples, urban clusters, and great art styles testify to highly complex and integrated societies and to the early rise of the state. In southern Middle America such elements begin to appear shortly after 1000 B.C. or about a millennium after the establishment of village agriculture. The great ceremonial site of La Venta, in the Olmec region of Tabasco, is an example.[23] But the unfolding of civilization was not confined to a single region in Middle America, and during the first millennium B.C. cultures and societies in Oaxaca, the Valley of Mexico, and in the Maya Highlands and Lowlands enjoyed parallel developments. These regional civilizations were both interrelated and separate—perhaps optimum conditions for their growth—so that by the beginning of the Christian Era such diverse flowerings as Teotihuacan[24]—with its mammoth pyramids and concourses, gridded urban layout, and empire-wide trade connections—and the Mayan center of Tikal[25]—with its temples, magnificent sculptures, and hieroglyphic inscriptions—graced the Middle American scene.

In Peru monumental architecture appears to be about 1,000 years older than it does in Middle America—if we are to rely on present radiocarbon datings. Huge and formally arranged mound sites of the coast, such as Las Haldas, Rio Seco, and Chuquitanta, have their beginnings before 1500 B.C. As we have already observed, these beginnings also antedate maize cultivation, which seems to imply that not maize farming but a previous tradition of sedentary life—whether made possible by food plants or marine foods—was the key to the rise of Peruvian civilization.[26]

Elsewhere in the New World the stirrings of civilization seem to be later, less impressive, or nonexistent. This is certainly true of North America north of Mexico and of the Andean country south of Peru. The reason that comes most immediately to mind for this condition is that these were also areas in which agriculture and/or sedentary life had a relatively late start. Not only were these areas marginal to these preconditions for civilization, but they were marginal to the later developments of civilization itself.

For the Amazon and Orinoco basins of Lowland South America the problem is more difficult. Here, where sedentary root-crop cultivation can be traced back to at least 1000 B.C., and, logically, may be considerably earlier, is the failure to develop complex civilization to be attributed to the limitations of a jungle environment?[27] Or is it because uniformity of environment, natural resources, and products, over so vast a territory, failed to provide the kind of interregional symbiosis that seems to have been a cultural dynamic in both Middle America and Peru?[28] Or, lastly, could it be that archaeologists have not yet found the evidence? I do not really think that this is so, but Amazonia is enormous and relatively unexplored, and the possibility remains.

For the Intermediate area—that part of northwestern South America and Lower Central America lying between Middle America and Peru—the time lag in, or absence of, the elements of civilization is even more perplexing. In this area there was an early tradition of agricultural subsistence, but, except for coastal Ecuador,[29] the phenomena of large ceremonial centers and urban populations are either absent or belong to very late Precolumbian times.[30] Some time ago I called attention to a difference in the profile of development for the Intermediate area as contrasted with Middle America and Peru. In Middle America and Peru there is evidence—in the form of a sophisticated, richly iconographic, and widespread art style—of a common ideology or religion uniting the peoples of each of these respective areas at an early time.[31] For the Intermediate area there is no such horizon style phenomenon and, inferentially, no such common socioreligious integrative force. According to my argument, this lack of an integrative mechanism in the Intermediate area delayed the kind of civilizational developments found to the north and south, in Middle America and Peru.[32] But this "explanation" is really a rephrasing of the problem. We are left with the question, then, of why area-wide religions and art styles have an early development in some areas and not in others. Is this purely a historical accident? Or are such developments grounded in some natural environmental and ecological advantages which Middle America and Peru possess, and which the Intermediate area lacks, but which are not readily apparent?

One possibility is that a kind of natural environmental "circumscription" or "compression" factor may have been operative in the development of sociopolitical complexity and civilization. In this hypothesis, the ideal conditions are those in which there is high agricultural yield per acre but in which the environmental zones are relatively small and circumscribed. Such would make for a "trapping" of large populations in territories of small size and lead to the necessity for social control and political unification. Such institutions would not arise so readily in environments where a constant drifting away of population groups from a parent body was feasible.[33] Certainly, Middle America and Peru, with their rich but circumscribed coastal and upland valleys, provide favorable settings for this "compression" process. About the Intermediate area it is less clear, but if conditions for population compression were lacking there, this may have been a significant factor in its slower development.

Notes

[1]A most succinct summary of these facts is given by C. V. Haynes, Jr., "Fluted Projectile Points: Their Age and Dispersion," *Science*, 145 (1964): pp. 1408–1413.

[2]C. S. Chard, "New World Origins; A Reappraisal," *Antiquity* 33, 129: 44–49 (London, 1959), states the case for this position. See also A. D. Krieger, "Early Man in the New World," *Prehistoric Man in the New World*, Jennings and Norbeck, eds. (University of Chicago Press, 1964).

[3]E. N. Wilmsen, "Flake Tools in the American Arctic; Some Speculations," *American Antiquity* 29, 3 (1964): pp. 338–344. See also H. M. Wormington, "Prehistoric Cultural Stages of Alberta, Canada," *Homenaje a Pablo Martinez del Rio* (Mexico, D. F., 1961), pp. 163–171, and G. H. S. Bushnell and Charles McBurney, "New World Origins Seen From the Old World," *Antiquity* 33 (1959): pp. 93–101.

[4]Wilmsen, *op. cit. supra*, n. 3. See also C. S. Chard, "The Old World Roots: Review and Speculations," *Anthropological Papers, University of Alaska* 10, 2 (1963).

[5]R. S. MacNeish, "A Speculative Framework of Northern North American Prehistory as of April 1959," *Anthropologica* 1 (1959): pp. 7–23.

[6]J. M. Campbell, "The Kogruk Complex of Anaktuvuk Pass, Alaska," *Anthropologica* 3 (1961): pp. 1–18.

[7]The Tule Springs Monograph is by M. R. Harrington and R. D. Simpson, *Tule Springs, Nevada. With Other Evidences of Pleistocene Man in North America*. Southwestern Museum Papers, No. 18 (Los Angeles, 1961). The report on the recent investigation is by Richard Shutler, "Tule Springs Expedition," *Current Anthropology* 6, 1 (1965): pp. 110–111.

[8]See A. D. Krieger, *op. cit. supra*, n. 2, and also "The Earliest Cultures in the Western United States," *American Antiquity* 28, 2 (1962): pp. 138–143.

[9]See G. R. Willey, *An Introduction to American Archaeology: Volume 1, North And Middle America*, ch. 2 (Prentice-Hall, Inc., Englewood Cliffs, N.J., 1966a) for a discussion of the Big Game Hunting tradition. The concept subsumes an important part, but not all, of the Paleo-Indian Stage (Krieger, *op. cit. supra*, n. 2) or the Lithic Stage (G. R. Willey and P. Phillips, *Method and Theory in American Archaeology* [University of Chicago Press, 1958], pp. 79–103.

[10] See n. 9.

[11]B. R. Butler, *The Old Cordilleran Culture in the Pacific Northwest*, Occasional Papers, Idaho State College Museum, No. 5 (1961). See also Krieger, *op. cit. supra*, n. 2 and Willey, *op. cit. supra*, n. 9.

[12]J. D. Jennings, *Danger Cave*, Memoir No. 14, Society for American Archaeology (Salt Lake City, 1957) and "The Desert West," *Prehistoric Man in the New World*, J. D. Jennings and E. Norbeck, eds. (University of Chicago Press, 1964), pp. 149–173. See also Willey, *op. cit. supra*, n. 9.

[13]These are summarized in Willey, *op. cit. supra*, n. 9.

[14]R. S. MacNeish, *Second Annual Report of the Tehuacan Archaeological-Botanical Project*, R. S. Peabody Foundation for Archaeology, Project Reports, No. 2 (Andover, Mass., 1962) and "Ancient Mesoamerican Civilization," *Science* 143 (1964): pp. 531–537.

[15]G. R. Willey, "Postlude to Village Agriculture: The Rise of Towns and Temples and the Beginnings of the Great Traditions," *30th International Congress of Americanists, Sevilla*, Vol. 1, pp. 267–277, 1966c.

[16]Frederic Engel, *Notes Relatives à des Explorations à Paracas et sur la Côte Sud du Perou*, Travaux de l'institut Français d'Etudes Andines, 9: pp. 1–27 (Paris and Lima, 1963) and "El Preceramico sin Algodon en La Costa del Peru." *Actas y Memorias del 35 Conareso Internacional de Americanistas*, Mexico, 1962 (Mexico, D. F., 1964): pp. 141–152; see also Alfred Kidder II, "South American High Cultures," *Prehistoric Man in the New World*, J. D. Jennings and E. Norbeck, eds. (University of Chicago Press, 1964), pp. 451–488, and T. P. Patterson and E. P. Lanning, "Changing Settlement Patterns on the Central Peruvian Coast," *Nawpa Pacha*, Institute of Andean Studies (Berkeley, California, 1964), No. 2: pp. 113–123.

[17]S. Izumi and T. Sono, *Andes* 2. *Excavations at Kotosh, Peru, 1960* (Tokyo, Kadowa Publishing Co., 1963).

[18]Potatoes have been tentatively identified from horticultural but late preceramic sites on the central coast of Peru (Patterson and Lanning, *op. cit. supra*, n. 16).

[19]Irving Rouse and J. M. Cruxent, *Venezuelan Archaeology* (Yale University Press, 1963), pp. 111–112. The Saladero archaeological culture is believed to have had domesticated manioc.

[20]The Momíl I and Malambo phases are thought to have had manioc cultivation. See G. Reichel-Dolmatoff and A. Dussan de Reichel, *Momíl, Excavaciones en el Sinu*. Revista Colombiana de Antropologia, 5 (Bogota, 1956) and C. Angulo Valdes, "Cultural Development in Colombia," *Aboriginal Cultural Development in Latin America: An Interpretative Review*, Smithsonian Miscellaneous Collections, 146, 1 (Washington, D.C., 1963): pp. 55–66.

[21]C. O. Sauer, *Agricultural Origins and Dispersals*, American Geographical Society (New York, 1952) and D. W. Lathrap, "Origins of Central Andean Civilization: New Evidence," *Science* 148 (1965): pp. 796–798.

[22]C. E. Brush, "Pox Pottery: Earliest Identified Mexican Ceramic," *Science* 149 (1965): pp. 194–195.

[23]P. Drucker, R. F. Heizer, and R. J. Squier, *Excavations at La Venta, Tabasco, 1955*. Bureau of American Ethnology, Bulletin 170 (Smithsonian Institution, Washington, D.C., 1959).

[24]Pedro Armillas, "Teotihuacan, Tula, y Los Toltecas. Las Culturas Post-Arcaicas y Pre-Aztecas del Centro de Mexico. Excavaciones y Estudios 1922–1950," *Runa* 3 (1950): pp. 37–70, and R. F. Millon, "The Teotihuacan Mapping Project," *American Antiquity* 29, 3 (1964): pp. 345–352.

[25]W. R. Coe, "A Summary of Excavation and Research at Tikal, Guatemala: 1962," *Estudios Cultura Maya* 3 (Universidad Nacional de Mexico, Mexico, D. F., 1963): pp. 41–64.

[26]See Patterson and Lanning, *op. cit. supra*, n. 16. Not all Peruvian coastal radiocarbon dates are in harmony, and there are problems about the first appearances of pottery and maize on the coast. The two traits are not exactly synchronous or, at least, do not appear to be so on present evidence. For instance, maize antedates pottery on the central coast and pottery precedes maize on the north coast. The earliest radiocarbon dates, so far, for pottery are from the south coast and south highlands. In general, it is probably safe to say that both pottery and maize appear somewhere in the 2000 to 1500 B.C. span. Impressive ceremonial architecture is definitely this early and may be a few centuries earlier.

[27]B. J. Meggers, "Environmental Limitation on the Development of Culture," *American Anthropologist* 56 (1954): pp. 801–824.

[28]G. R. Willey, "The Early Great Styles and the Rise of the Precolumbian Civilizations," *American Anthropologist* 64, 1 (1962): pp. 1–14, and R. J. Braidwood and G. R. Willey, "Conclusions and Afterthoughts," *Courses Toward Urban Life*, Viking Fund Publications in Anthropology, No. 32 (New York, 1962), pp. 330–359.

[29]Emilio Estrada and Clifford Evans, "Cultural Development in Ecuador," *Aboriginal Cultural Development in Latin America*, B. J. Meggers and C. Evans, eds., Smithsonian Miscellaneous Collections, 146, v (Washington, D.C., 1963), pp. 77–78.

[30]G. R. Willey, *op. cit. supra*, n. 15.

[31]G. R. Willey, *op. cit. supra*, n. 28.

[32]B. J. Meggers and C. Evans (1966) take issue with this, citing large-scale architectural developments and urban formations in Ecuador. As yet, except for the very late Precolumbian urban coastal site of Manta, I have not seen the evidence for anything comparable to Middle American and Peruvian architecture and settlements from Ecuador.

[33]This "compression" or "circumscription" factor in the development of civilization is an idea developed by R. L. Carneiro, "Slash-and-Burn Cultivation Among the Kuikuru and Its Implications for Cultural Development in the Amazon Basin," *Evolution of Horticultural Systems in Native South America. Causes and Consequences*, J. Wilbert, ed. (Sociedad de Ciencias Naturales La Salle, Caracas, 1961), pp. 47–67, and in a letter to me of January 12, 1962.

13

New World Prehistory: 1974

(From *American Journal of Archaeology*, Vol. 78, No. 4, pp. 321–331, Archaeological Institute of America, New York, 1974. Reprinted by permission of the Archaeological Institute of America.)

For an Americanist to address Classical archaeologists,[1] or for any archaeologist to discuss his own specialization before colleagues of different specializations, raises the question as to what all of us, as archaeologists, have in common. Certainly there are no "world archaeologists" in any meaningful definition of that term. The demands of substantive data control are too taxing. In basic research we are, perforce, all specialists, confined to a very large degree to our own narrow corners. Accepting this, can we then surmount the barriers of the many archaeological parochialisms by a unified methodological-theoretical outlook? This is a very beguiling idea, given the vast diversity of the human past, but I would answer that we can do this only to a very limited extent. It is true that some methodological principles—stratigraphy, seriation, provenience associations, and the like—do link, or should link, all archaeologists; but in going beyond these rather circumscribed procedures to try and fashion a single unified body of theory, I think there is a danger of closing off our potential to see, recover, and interpret, in a variety of ways, the complex record of the past. For the fascination of this past has many dimensions, and archaeology may be approached along different lines of inquiry—historical, philological, and aesthetic, as well as those of anthropology—and I would not change this. I once said that "archaeology is anthropology or it is nothing."[2] I find this too restrictive now. Obviously, the anthropological approach has much to offer in archaeology, and it is the one I know best; but it is not the only road to everything worth knowing about the past.

So, if we are bound by the necessities of area data specialization, and if a single theoretical approach is not feasible, or is even undesirable, what do we share as archaeologists? What is our common ground? I think that it is something relatively obvious. It is a mutual concern with questions of broad and general human interest, questions that must fascinate the nonarchaeologist as well as ourselves. In brief, how and why did man's past develop as it did? What were the adaptations to environmental resources and demographic conditions? How did these adaptations guide or direct other aspects of culture? What were the causes of the great transitions—from hunting to farming, from the village to the city, from the tribe to the state? How were civilizations attained and lost? These you may say are all anthropological questions, and it is true that it has been the archaeologists from that sector who have been asking them most openly in the last dozen or so years. At the same time, I cannot believe that other kinds of archaeologists, those for example in what are referred to as the "humanistic traditions" of art history or philology, are not also concerned with them. For one does not have to limit oneself to matters of subsistence, population densities, and technologies in order to be interested in cause or to take a comparative view. These are not the only keys to the answers. What were the roles of idea systems in cultural causation? Here the realm of art is bound to be crucial, especially in preliterate societies, and the approach of the art historian needs to be linked to that of the anthropological archaeologist. In saying this I am not scorning the ecological interface as a locus of cultural explanation—it is obviously vital—but I am suggesting that it may not be enough, in and of itself alone, to give us the richest possible understanding.

Such a common ground of interest for archaeologists, as expressed in general questions like these, does not contradict what I have said about the necessity for regional research specialization. The mastery of the specifics remains the foundation of archaeology. What is involved, rather, is simply some interest in and awareness of the data in areas outside of one's immediate research bailiwick. As an example, I cite Robert Adams' analyses of urban growth and the archaeological records of Mesopotamia and Precolumbian Mexico.[3] Adams, primarily a Middle Eastern scholar, developed a secondary interest in Mesoamerica from the comparative urban standpoint.

Nor does a general comparative interest in cultural development demand a single theoretical point of view. In a very general way, I suppose, the outlook is evolutionary insofar as there is a recognition that cultures have changed through time, that the changes are systemically related to one another and are not altogether random, and that similar causes may have similar results. But beyond this the theoretical structure of the analysis can vary widely. As examples, I cite the quite different interpretations of the preagricultural-to-agricultural transitions as delineated by Robert Braidwood and myself[4] in contrast to that offered by Lewis Binford[5] a few years later.

Finally, let me explain that in making a case for ecumenical interests in archaeology, I am not advocating that all of us turn our immediate and full-time research attention to broadly comparative endeavors. Nor am I particularly sanguine about the early emergence of "cultural laws" from such comparative studies. Rather, I think that the true value of a comparative outlook will be that more and more of us, as specialized researchers, will find that such a perspective enables us to see our own regionally centered problems with greater sophistication and insight. At least I would see this as the primary gain for some years to come.

I offer all of this as a preamble for some general observations about New World prehistory. It goes without saying that in making these observations I shall be highly selective. What I would like to give is a running commentary on some important changes in American prehistory that have come about in the last decade. These changes are involved with new discoveries of fact, but they are also, to a very large degree, involved with changes in outlook and interpretation. Such a commentary is presented, not as an example of careful comparative analysis but rather as a series of suggestions toward that end.

In a 1966 paper,[6] in which I undertook a similar commentary, I organized my remarks around three major themes of New World prehistory: (1) the problems relating to Early

Man in America; (2) the beginnings and early stages of New World agriculture; and (3) the rise of the native American "high cultures" or civilizations. While broadly culture-historical, these themes also carry obvious implications of function and process about which there has been a great deal of recent interest in American archaeology. What I have to say now will follow this general organization.

EARLY MAN

For nearly fifty years American archaeologists have known that man came to the Americas in the Late Pleistocene; and with the advent of radiocarbon dating we were able to say that this was about as early as 10,000 B.C., at least. But could his presence here be demonstrated for an earlier date than this and, if so, how much earlier? The advocates of a greater antiquity insisted that Bering land bridges and ice-free Canadian corridors would have allowed his passage into the western hemisphere long before 10,000 B.C., but the claims which they advanced to prove this were all open to serious challenges on one ground or another. This is where the case stood as of about 1965. Since then the picture has changed, and there is now good evidence that man has been in the New World for as much as 25,000 to 30,000 years if not longer. The evidence for this comes from the Arctic and from Middle and South America. From the northern Yukon W. N. Irving and C. R. Harington[7] have recently reported tools made of caribou bone, including a notched-end fleshing implement, which have been dated by radiocarbon to a range of 25,000 to 29,000 years B.P. The associations are with a Pleistocene fauna and geological contexts antedating the peak of the late Wisconsin glaciation. This Yukon location is, of course, in old Beringia, a land area which might have had a much earlier human occupancy than the American continents to the south; however, at Valsequillo,[8] in central Mexico, rough stone flake tools and little unifacial points have been found in deep geological strata dated by radiocarbon to at least 20,000 B.C., and nearby, at Tlapacoya,[9] a man-made hearth and some obsidian bladelets have an even earlier radiocarbon date of 22,000 B.C. Two thousand miles to the south, in a cave in the central highlands of Peru, crude flake tools of what is known as the Pacaicasa[10] complex are dated by radiocarbon to 18,000 B.C.

The nature of these earliest American industries, especially those in stone, is crude and unspecialized, reminiscent at best of a Middle Paleolithic technological level in the Old World. Does it represent the ancestral tradition for an independent American development of the later classic Paleo-Indian industries? Did this tradition already contain Levallois-Mousteroid flint-knapping elements—as yet undiscovered—which provided the prototypes of the later Clovis, Lake Mohave, and Fell's Cavern projectile points? This is the view taken by some authorities who point to what could be transitional forms in such an evolution, such as the various lanceolate, bifacially chipped projectile points that have been found at Wilson Butte Cave and Fort Rock, in the northwestern United States, or at El Abra and El Jobo, in northern South America.[11] All of these are believed to date in the range of 13,000 to 10,000 B.C. or just prior to the appearance of the Clovis or Llano industries. An opposing view interprets this same evidence differently. Its proponents would see the early rough stone industries as separate from the later bifacial point developments which, in their opinion, derived from subsequent and distinct migrations bringing a more advanced technological tradition.[12] The defenders of the first hypothesis have countered that subsequent migrations from Asia, via Alaska, to the mid-continental Americas would have been precluded by the closure of the Canadian ice fields, a phenomenon that lasted until after 10,000 B.C.; but those favoring the continued Asiatic migrations and diffusions have replied that there is little good evidence that the corridors through the ice were ever completely closed. And there the debate stands as of now.

While extending man's record in the Americas backward in time for another 20,000 years or so is a "newsworthy" item, the most solid achievements of the last few years in the study of Early Man have been in the extension and refinement of our knowledge of the more generally known Paleo-Indian cultures. These are the ones dating in the approximate range of 10,000 to 7000 B.C. The inappropriateness of thinking of all of these Paleo-Indian societies as "Big Game Hunters" has been made evident in many quarters in the considerable diversity which these various early archaeological complexes display in technical equipment and environmental settings. Not all of the Clovis-related or Clovis-derived cultures followed the mode of existence of the Llano hunters. And other contemporaneous peoples of the Interior Plateau river valleys of northwestern North America, of the Old California lake shores, in the Andes, and in eastern Brazil had industries and life styles in a series of quite different traditions, traditions that had already become established by 9000 B.C., if not before.[13]

Actually, we still know very little of these Paleo-Indian life styles, and this prompts a comparative observation. One of the greatest differences between the Paleo-Indian cultures of the New World and those of the Old World Upper Paleolithic is, of course, in the demographic-social dimension. New World sites of this stage are relatively few and scattered. Few actual camp stations have been explored in any detail, but most appear to be small. This is in contrast to the Old World Upper Paleolithic sites which are much more numerous, and, in the cases of some of those of Central and Eastern Europe, of considerable size.[14] There are also the striking differences in art between Upper Paleolithic and Paleo-Indian cultures. The cave paintings of Europe, for example, are famous, but we know of no American counterparts. I cannot help but feel that this difference in artistic achievement is to be correlated with the demographic-social differences between the Old World and the New. I am not thinking of the availability of leisure time. There was probably sufficient of this in both instances. The more significant thing may have been the Old World need to maintain group solidarities and territoriality in the face of larger overall populations and frequent inter-group confrontation and rivalry. Perhaps the Old World Paleolithic cave paintings were attempts to establish tribal shrines, or "ceremonial centers" if you will, which would mark and memorialize the central gathering places for peoples whose ancestors had hunted the immediate surrounding territory for many millennia. In the New World, with its relatively sparse Paleo-Indian populations, peoples were moving through largely unoccupied lands; and under these conditions territoriality and the maintenance of residential traditions may have been less important, symbolic art of less significance. This is no more than a speculative aside, but when American Paleo-Indian and Old World Paleolithic archaeologists begin to view their data comparatively, for purposes other than the determination of diffusional relationships, I think they will turn to questions and hypotheses like these as they set about reconstructing ancient life ways.

New World Agriculture

New World agriculture arose out of the context of the Archaic stage cultures. This Archaic stage[15] is analogous to the Old World Mesolithic stage. Like the Mesolithic, it has its inception in the early Post-Pleistocene climatic era, and, also like the Mesolithic, its terminal dates vary considerably depending upon geographical area. Archaic cultures display a great range of subsistence adaptation, a diversity in keeping with the many natural environmental niches of the American continents and one which, as previously noted, had begun to appear in the antecedent Paleo-Indian stage. In all cases, by definition, the Archaic economies were founded on wild resources of plants and animals; and, as would be expected, fortunes varied, from the plenitude of the Northwest Coast salmon harvests to the skimpier takes of the desert seed-collectors. Then, at about 3000 B.C.—to select a very approximate round figure[16]—plant domestication replaced wild foods as the principal subsistence resource in some parts of the Americas, initiating a new stage, in effect, a New World Neolithic or New World Formative, as we call it. In other parts of the hemisphere this changeover was later, ranging anywhere from 2000 B.C. well up into the Christian era. This agricultural revolution, if that term be used, was not a sudden event but a process. In the highlands of southern Mexico and on the desert coast of Peru, where we have our best archaeological records for early cultivation, plant domestication can be traced back several thousand years in contexts of Archaic-type cultures. In Mexico some cultigens probably date back to 7000 B.C.[17] By 5000 B.C. maize appears in the Tehuacan Valley sequence. There has been some debate over whether or not it was wild or cultivated at that time; but the preponderance of the evidence now, I think, supports the latter condition, with plant geneticists coming again to favor teosinte, or a teosinte-like form, as the wild ancestor of maize.[18] In southern Mesoamerica the span of time between 7000 and 2000 B.C. has been referred to as a period of "incipient cultivation," a period defined by the gradual genetic improvement of plants through man's care and selection but of their minor economic importance.[19]

All of this, of course, has been known for somewhat longer than the past decade. Of more recent interest have been the hypotheses formulated to explain the steps and processes that actually took place within the "incipient cultivation" period. Kent Flannery, who has also addressed himself to this problem in the Old World Near East, has advanced one of the most ingenious and internally consistent of these hypotheses.[20] He reasoned that peoples primarily dependent upon hunting and collecting would have scheduled their food-getting activities on a fairly strict seasonal basis, shifting places of residence as they followed game or ripening wild plants through a series of micro-environmental or micro-zone niches. Almost surely, such food collectors were aware of the advantages of planting seeds to supplement the completely feral yields, and this had probably gone on for a long time without significant changes in either plants or harvesting practices. The triggering event for the subsistence revolution came when mutations occurred in some plants that, heretofore, had been of no outstanding economic importance. In the case of maize, such mutations could have been explosive, transforming what had been a modest food resource into a major one in a very short time. Incentives for maize growing would have had a dramatic feedback effect on food-gathering schedules, with linked effects on increased sedentism, overall nutritional increases, and larger resident populations. All of these effects, in turn, would have been deterrents to reversing the process and returning to the old subsistence modes. In effect, the society found itself ensnared in agriculture. This hypothesis offers a quite different perspective of the "incipient cultivation" period than as a time of slow, steady cultivation advance. Instead, it is revealed as an era of preconditioning for agriculture in which the agricultural status might never have been attained had it not been for a rather sudden, and indeed revolutionary, turn of events. Perhaps during the Mesoamerican "incipient cultivaiton" period there were several of these radical "spurts" of change in cultigens, each one feeding back to reinforce and accelerate the overall cultural-ecological transformation. As stated, this is a hypothesis but one which the data at hand seem to support. In the Tehuacan Valley Richard MacNeish's detailed tracing out of the settlement pattern shifts through time, from 7000 to 2000 B.C., confirms the change from seasonal camps to sedentary village communities as taking place toward the end of this long period; and these settlement data correlate with those of plant genetics.[21]

The Tehuacan Valley sequence does not, however, tell the whole story of early American agricultural development. The upland valleys of southern Mesoamerica were but one kind of environmental niche for this area. For some time it has been apparent that we needed to know more about the possible role of the tropical coastal lowlands in the beginnings of farming. A consideration of these lowlands brings up a larger theoretical question in agricultural origins, that of "nuclear zones" and "tension zones." The "nuclear zone" theory, as outlined by Braidwood in connection with his Near Eastern studies of early agriculture,[22] and as applied by myself and others in interpreting the American data,[23] held that the socio-subsistence condition of "village farming" developed in certain favored regions through a concatenation of circumstances but largely because these were the natural habitat zones for plants that were to become economically important cultigens. From such "nuclear zones" the agricultural products, and the cultural systems related to these products, were carried or diffused to ever-widening "marginal zones," at least within the range of the viability of the plants and the systems involved. Binford has countered this theory with one that might be called the "tension zone" theory.[24] According to this, one would expect to find agricultural beginnings in those regions, or "tension zones," where less sedentary populations are being encroached upon by peoples with a more sedentary tradition who are moving out of densely settled territories. This is a part of Binford's more encompassing reconstruction of Post-Pleistocene changes and the development of rich littoral and aquatic subsistence patterns for Archaic stage coastal and riverine cultures, some of which acquired a high degree of sedentism. To follow out this hypothesis in Mesoamerica we have to surmise that there were such large and stable marine-dependent populations along the south Mexican–Guatemalan shores at some time during the "incipient cultivation" period, and that daughter groups moving inland from these settled coastal centers created the demographic tensions in the semiarid interior basins that stimulated agricultural development. While the theory is attractive in its ingenious causal mechanisms, it appears to break down in this Mesoamerican application. Although there are some few indications of early coastal shellmound dwellers, particularly on the Chiapas and Guerrero coasts, the evidence for a heavy occupancy of these coastal regions for these early time ranges has yet to come in.

There is, however, a kind of variant of the Binford hypothesis that might apply to Mesoamerica. This would involve not marine-oriented subsistence groups but peoples of another agricultural tradition. Donald Lathrap has put forward the idea of the spread of a South American Tropical Forest agriculture into the southern Mesoamerican coastal lowlands at a relatively early time.[25] According to Lathrap, plant domestication in the Amazon basin probably has a very great antiquity, beginning with the domestication of the gourd even before 10,000 B.C. Important as a food plant, manioc also must have considerable antiquity in the Amazonian-Orinocan lowlands, with its domestication going back to 3000 B.C. or even before. Lathrap would see the manioc pattern spreading from northern Colombia into comparable Mesoamerican environments. In the coastal lowland Mesoamerican settings this root crop agriculture may have made possible the first sedentary life in the area. Following this line of reasoning, such sedentary centers created the population pressures and set in motion the population expansions into the Mesoamerican uplands. It is true that D. F. Green and G. W. Lowe's[26] Barra phase in coastal Chiapas offers some highly suggestive evidence for the presence of manioc cultivation and preparation as early as 1800 B.C.; but this would hardly have been early enough to have touched off the Tehuacan agricultural revolution. Of course, the South American root crop practices may have reached Mesoamerica earlier than 1800 B.C. If we accept the earliest pottery, dated by radiocarbon, in Mesoamerica, that from the Guerrero coast which is placed at 2400 B.C. (or even earlier with corrected datings),[27] as being of ultimate South American inspiration, then it may be that the diffusion of root crop cultivation into southern Mesoamerica was early enough to have had a significant influence on the origins of sedentary agricultural patterns in the southern Mexican uplands. It should be added here that pottery in Colombia and Ecuador has been shown to date back to 3000 B.C. and before and that it is probably the earliest pottery in the New World.[28] Very probably this early South American pottery was associated with manioc farming.

In reflecting further on these two theories of agricultural beginnings, that of the "tension zone" and that of the "nuclear zone," it would seem that if Binford is correct, and the "tension zone" situation is the prime condition for farming origins, then the "tension zone" is apt to become a "nuclear zone" or a center for the radiation of ideas and elements of the new subsistence pattern to regions formerly marginal. For example, the cultures of the North American Southwest appear to have been transformed by the diffusion of Mesoamerican food plants and practices into what had been Archaic stage, Desert tradition contexts.[29] While is is possible here that demographic pressures in Mesoamerica may have had something to do with peoples from that area migrating into the southern regions of the Southwest, the processes involved would have been different from those envisioned in the "tension zone" hypothesis. For the Eastern United States, too, Mesoamerica must have stood in a "nuclear zone" relationship although here the spread of agriculture appears to have been a more complicated matter than that into the Southwest.[30] Eastern Woodland Archaic subsistence patterns, especially in coastal and riverine settings, were often exceptionally rich, and the Mesoamerican cultigens may not have been seen as so advantageous as to have prompted an immediate switch-over. It may be that here the "tension zone" hypothesis does apply to lands lying adjacent to coastal and riverine niches—a problem, certainly, for continuing investigation by Eastern Woodlands archaeologists.

In South America, the "tension zone" idea seems an admirable fit to what happened along the Peruvian coast. Coastal communities of the 4000–2000 B.C. period grew steadily, and their contents show an increasing specialized dependence on marine subsistence. There was also an "incipient cultivation" of various plants. Some of these, such as gourds, cotton, and manioc, were of Tropical Forest agricultural origin; others may have been local and still others of Mesoamerican derivation. Toward the end of this period large sites began to be established at some distance inland in the coastal valleys, apparently to take advantage of farmlands and to accommodate increasing populations. The picture is further complicated, however, in that maize first appears on the coast at just about this time. It was probably brought to the coast from the adjacent highlands. More remotely, it must have been of Mesoamerican origin, although some authorities prefer to see it as the result of a separate Peruvian domestication from local wild forms. In either case, its appearance gave an added impetus to the Peruvian agricultural revolution.[31]

In other places in South America the early agricultural picture is a complex one. On the Ecuadorian coast the pottery-bearing shell mound sites of the Valdivia culture date back to about 3000 B.C.[32] B. J. Meggers, Clifford Evans, and Emilio Estrada, who first published on Valdivia, saw the Valdivia populations as primarily dependent upon the sea.[33] Subsequently, in later periods, there was a shift to the interior with the establishment of an agricultural economy. That is, events followed the Peruvian coastal model.

More recently, Carlos Zevallos, Presley Norton, and Donald Lathrap[34] have argued in the opposite direction, seeing the Valdivia populations as originally being inland agriculturists who moved, at least in some of their communities, to the shore line. Radiocarbon dates and some other archaeological materials give weight to this argument. Lathrap, the leading protagonist for South American Tropical Forest origins of agriculture and pottery, extends this line of reasoning still further by seeing Valdivia culture as having roots in the Upper Amazon. In fact, Lathrap would apply this generic view to a broad front, conceiving of much of early Andean and adjacent Pacific coastal agricultural development as constituting a "tension zone" response to anterior farming developments and population buildup in the Amazon basin.[35] The idea is a bold and fascinating one, running counter to the prevailing arguments in American archaeology that New World agriculture is fundamentally a seed-based, maize-based, upland or semiarid niche creation. It needs more support from the Amazon basin where, at the present writing, it is difficult to push the date of pottery back much earlier than about 2000 B.C.; however, it is becoming clear that the South American Tropical Forest played a much greater role in early Nuclear American agricultural and sedentary developments than most of us have yet recognized. And to this we should add that the South American Tropical Forest cannot be ignored when we consider the subsequent rise of New World "high cultures."[36]

All of these data, speculations, and concerns are, I believe, grist for the comparative mill. I do not know Old World archaeology sufficiently well to be very specific, but there have been surprising and important discoveries of late bearing on the antiquity of cultivation in Southeast Asia,[37] and one wonders about the role of tropical Africa in this regard. The suggestion of a model of interstimulation and exchange between tropical lowland and semiarid environments in the New World may have meaning in the search for process in Old World agricultural developments.

The Rise of the Native American Civilizations

It is obvious that the Precolumbian "high cultures" or civilizations of the Americas arose on an agricultural or Formative base. In my opinion this rise was complex and multicentered—more so, probably, than that of the earlier rise to the agricultural threshold. The achievements of the New World civilizations are seen in the archaeological record in both quantitative and qualitative criteria. While there has been some debate about these criteria, the majority of archaeologists would agree on certain core characteristics. These are essentially the ones enumerated by V. Gordon Childe[38] a number of years ago: substantial population size and density, a high degree of internal specialization and a multiplicity of functions in the sustaining society, social ranking or class structure, highly developed external trade networks, monumentality in architecture and the arts, the beginnings of true science, and, perhaps, writing.

The first evidences of this kind of life style that we have in the New World come from the Olmec and Chavín cultures of, respectively, Mesoamerica and Peru. Their beginnings have been shown to be earlier than we thought; both appear to have had their rise toward the end of the second millennium B.C.[39] Each of these civilizations maintained imposing ceremonial centers or politicoreligious capitals. Each had a distinctive and powerful art style, expressed in monumental stone sculpture as well as in other media. In their respective areas of influence these art styles are pervasive, widespread. The mechanisms of their diffusion have recently attracted much attention. Were they war and conquest, religious proselytization, trading missions, or, perhaps, some combinations of all three? In searching for models of interregional social and cultural interaction that would elucidate the Olmec spread, Kent Flannery has turned to Asian ethnography,[40] and Thomas Patterson[41] has drawn parallels between the dissemination of the Chavín cult and that of early Christianity in the Old World. These are good comparative beginnings in processual study. How does a certain type of social and cultural behavior register itself in the material archaeological record in those instances where we have documentary textual control of the events? How might these examples help us in understanding comparable material records elsewhere in the absence of textual aids? As a further aside, I think that comparative studies of horizonal phenomena offer one of the most promising meeting grounds for archaeologists—as well as ethnologists and historians—of diverse regional interests. Has anyone ever looked at Roman Britain in this light? What happened there to resident ceramic traditions with the introduction of the empire? What were the stylistic changes and how do they correlate with other aspects of culture? Such an investigation might help us as we try to understand the Olmec horizon or that of Huari-Tiahuanaco.[42]

But to return to Olmec and Chavín in themselves, one wonders about their origins. Each of these great art styles appears in a context of developing Neolithic-type, or early Formative, cultures, without any easily perceived prototypes. Lathrap from his Amazonian lowland perspective, has pointed to the fact that while Olmec and Chavín are quite unlike as styles, they share certain iconographic content and that this content is related to beasts native to the South American Tropical Forest jungles.[43] Lathrap conceives of this iconographic content as having its origins in an ancient Tropical Forest mythology and religion which was carried by South American lowlanders, perhaps the ones who were the first bringers of manioc cultivation, to the Gulf Coast of southern Mexico as well as up into the Peruvian Andes. The hypothesis explains both the resemblances and the differences between the Chavín and Olmec styles. What it does not explain, however, are resemblances between Olmec and Chavín, on the one hand, and certain Old World art styles on the other.

Here we step on dangerous ground. I am no longer talking about structural, functional, or processual comparisons, but about comparisons which may carry implications of historical relationships. I have always been hesitant about it, but I must admit to an uneasy feeling when I look at some items of Shang dynasty art from China, with their disturbing similarities to Chavín.[44] These are similarities not only in content but, to a degree, in stylistic treatment. On the face of it, it seems preposterous that there could be a connection. The Shang examples are in bronze, those of the New World in pottery or stone. Although the respective chronologies are about right, the trans-Pacific distance is great; and it is beyond the powers of my imagination to construct a model of contact and acculturation that is convincing. It may be an abdication of critical scholarship—and I have been so accused—to ask that the final answers to such questions be left open. If so, I must plead guilty. I cannot generate any feelings of infallibility about my judgment on the matter, either in this Shang-Chavín case or in some of the other examples of Asiatic and Precolumbian parallels that have been raised. None of these cases is proved beyond reasonable doubt. To the best of my knowledge, there has never been a single object of undisputed Asiatic manufacture found in Precolumbian contexts in the middle latitudes of the Americas. In spite of this, I would be unwilling to close all doors to the possibility. Like many other archaeologists, I would like to see the question of trans-Pacific contacts (or trans-Atlantic contacts) to the New World resolved one way or the other—and if I have an emotional commitment to one side of the argument or the other I am unaware of it—but I have the uneasy feeling that this will not come about in my lifetime and that I shall always be plagued with doubt.

To return to the rise of the native American civilizations in Mesoamerica, we know that after the waning of Olmec influences there were a number of important regional centers—Izapa, Kaminaljuyu, Monte Alban, to name some of them—flourishing in the last half of the first millennium B.C. One of the lesser of these, Teotihuacan, in the Valley of Mexico, was destined to become the greatest city of Classic Mesoamerica.[45] While the earlier Olmec centers do not appear to have been true cities in the urban sense, it is the urban phenomenon at Teotihuacan that is impressive. At the beginning of the Christian era Teotihuacan was a modest ceremonial center with an associated population of 5000 persons; in the next century or so it became a mammoth pyramid-palace center surrounded by 30,000 people; and by A.D. 500, at the height of its influence and power, Teotihuacan had a residential zone, 22 square kilometers in extent, with an estimated population of over 100,000. To what can this amazing growth be attributed? There can be no doubt that irrigation farming, which began well back in the Late Preclassic Period, was related to the growth of a large regional population; but for several centuries these populations had remained rather widely distributed over the eastern half of the Valley of Mexico, grouped around a number of small politicoreligious centers or in outlying villages. Then the city's rapid growth was paralleled by the abandonment of most of these smaller centers and villages, apparently with the contraction and concentration of these populations into the metropolis. Why? It does not seem to have been for the purposes of defense; at least there are no defense works around Teotihuacan. That the city became the greatest trading center of its time in all Mesoamerica is undeniable: foreign goods are found there in profusion; there are even evidences of foreign colonies within the precincts of the city; and Teotihuacan manufactures were widely traded to, and imitated in, other regions of Mesoamerica. So trade and manufacturing were obviously functions of the city's growth and must have contributed to it. Still, not all Teotihuacanos were artisans or traders, let alone priests or bureaucrats. According to R. F. Millon, 75 percent of the urban inhabitants were probably engaged in farming, walking the relatively short distances from the city's edge to nearby irrigated garden plots each day. What forces drew or coerced them into such a concentrated pattern of living? While it is bad form now to invoke ideological, or "vitalistic," factors as causal ones, some of us remain unwilling to relinquish this possibility. Perhaps unique religious prestige was the triggering cause of Teotihuacan's phenomenal population growth rather than a fortunate location near the obsidian beds. Or maybe both, and other factors, were so inextricably interinvolved in a complex of feedback situations that they defy a sorting out. Any Old World archaeologist who is concerned with urban beginnings and with the functions of the city will recognize the problem as a familiar one.

Teotihuacan fell at the end of the seventh century A.D., probably violently and to barbarian invaders from the northern marches of the Mesoamerican civilized world. This was the end of the first round of what looks like a sequence of imperial domination, conquest, warring states, and new empires. The Toltecs of Tula established a cultural and political hegemony over much of Mesoamerica between the tenth and twelfth centuries.[46] Then they, too, went down, and out of the wars of the thirteenth and fourteenth centuries the Aztecs emerged as the last Precolumbian imperial power of Mexico. This kind of broad historical process—horizonal unification, regionalization, new unification, and so on—is not unknown elsewhere in the New World. We see it in an even more pronounced form in Peru, with regional cultures succeeding those of the Chavín horizon, with these then superseded by what appears to be the empire of Huari, with this dissolving into regional kingdoms, and with these then bound together by the historically known empire of the Inca.[47] And, of course, this is a process familiar to those who know the ancient civilizations of the Middle East and the Mediterranean.

Indeed, this process may be such a commonplace of the history of the human condition that it is scarcely worth commenting upon. Still, I think we might look on it as a kind of gross recapitulation of the processual growth of civilizations. For one of the things that I think archaeologists might agree upon is that the origins of civilizations and their growth are multi-cellular. No civilization is a tightly sheathed organism which can be attributed solely to Magian, Apollonian, Olmecoid, or Chavínoid genius. The processes of civilization begin on the simple levels of camp-to-camp and village-to-village interchange and interaction and progress from these to ever-widening circles of symbiosis and synthesis. The recent excavations of Carl Lamberg-Karlovsky have shown that Tepe Yahya was not just a Persian way-station in the easterly spread of a monolithic Mesopotamian civilization to the Indus but one of several significant contributing sources to that civilization.[48] Just as in Mesoamerica, to select one New World example, we are coming more and more to realize that the unique brilliance of the Classic Maya in their jungle homeland was in no way a self-contained growth, but an achievement made possible by the many regionally discrete strands of influence that were synthesized to produce it.[49]

I know that many archaeologists are impatient with such a simplification of the development of human civilizations for it says little about just how and why. And this impatience is being expressed constructively in systemic and subsystemic analyses of specific archaeological cultures addressed to the questions of how and why. In doing this the trend now is to focus attention on *in situ* development. Many younger scholars are so engaged in the American field, and in the Old World Colin Renfrew comes to mind as a foremost spokesman for this position.[50] The emphasis on the *in situ* is a worthy countermeasure to former overemphases on diffusion and migration as sole explanations. I would only point out that, in the extreme, the dogmatically anti-diffusionist stance is somewhat inconsistent for no cultural system is ever completely closed. All have been subject to elements and ideas introduced from outside the system, from either near or afar. Again, I reiterate, the processes of cultural and civilizational growth are multi-cellular, and this must subsume diffusion as well as localized evolution.

Notes

[1]An earlier version of this paper was delivered at the annual meeting of the Archaeological Institute of America, St. Louis, Missouri, 29 December 1973.

[2]G. R. Willey and Philip Phillips, *Method and Theory in American Archaeology* (Chicago 1958) 2.

[3]Robert McC. Adams, *The Evolution of Urban Society* (Chicago 1966).

[4]R. J. Braidwood and G. R. Willey, "Conclusions and Afterthoughts," *Courses Toward Urban Life* (New York 1962),R. J. Braidwood and G. R. Willey, eds., 330–59, Viking Fund Publications in Anthropology, No. 32.

[5]L. R. Binford, "Post-Pleistocene Adaptations," *New Perspectives in Archaeology* (New York 1972a).

[6]G. R. Willey, "New World Archaeology in 1965," *Proceedings of the American Philosophical Society*, Vol. 110, No. 2 (1966b) 140–45.

[7]W. N. Irving and C. R. Harington, "Upper Pleistocene Radiocarbon Dates Artifacts from the Northern Yukon," *Science*, Vol. 179, No. 4071 (1973) 335–40, Washington, D.C.

[8]Cynthia Irwin-Williams, "Archaeological Evidence on Early Man in Mexico," *Early Man in Western North America*, Eastern New Mexico University Contributions in Anthropology, Vol. I, No. 4 (1968) 39–41.

[9]C. V. Haynes, Jr., "Muestras de C14, de Tlapacoya, Estado de Mexico," *Boletín, Instituto de Antropologia e Historia*, No. 29 (1967) 49–52.

[10]R. S. MacNeish, "Early Man in the Andes," *Scientific American*, Vol. 224, No. 4 (1971) 36–46.

[11]A. L. Bryan, "Paleoenvironments and Cultural Diversity in Late Pleistocene South America," *Journal of Quaternary Research*, Vol. 3, No. 2 (1973) 237–56.

[12]This position, with many variations, has been advanced by several scholars. A good example is

in Hansjurgen Muller-Beck, "Paleohunters in America: Origins and Diffusions," *Science*, Vol. 152 (1966) 1191–1210.

[13]A summary of this diversity is seen in Bryan (supra n. 11).

[14]See, for example, Bohuslav Klíma, "The First Ground-Plan of an Upper Paleolithic Loess Settlement in Middle Europe and Its Meaning," *Courses Toward Urban Life*, R. J. Braidwood and G. R. Willey, eds. (Chicago 1962) 193–210.

[15]See G. R. Willey and Philip Phillips (supra n. 2) 104–43, for a general definition of the Archaic stage.

[16]Ceramics are at least this early, in radiocarbon years, in Ecuador and Colombia. Although there is some dispute as to the degree of plant cultivation obtaining in these regions at this early time, it is highly likely that agriculture played an important subsistence role by this time. In corrected radiocarbon dates this threshold may be projected back to nearer 3600 B.C.

[17]R. S. MacNeish, "Ancient Mesoamerican Civilization," *Science*, Vol. 143 (1964) 531–37; see also *The Prehistory of the Tehuacan Valley: Vol. I. Environment and Subsistence*, D. S. Byers, ed. (Austin, Texas 1967).

[18]G. W. Beadle, "The Mystery of Maize," *Field Museum of Natural History Bulletin*, Vol. 43, No. 10 (Chicago, 1972).

[19]G. R. Willey, *An Introduction to American Archaeology: Vol. 1. North and Middle America* (Englewood Cliffs, 1966a) 78–85.

[20]K. V. Flannery, "Archaeological Systems Theory and Early Mesoamerica," *Anthropological Archaeology in the Americas*, 67–88, Anthropological Society of Washington (Washington, D.C. 1968b).

[21]See MacNeish, "An Interdisciplinary Approach to an Archaeological Problem" (supra n. 17).

[22]R. J. Braidwood, "Near Eastern Prehistory," *Science*, Vol. 127 (1958) 1419–430.

[23]G. R. Willey, "New World Prehistory," *Science*, Vol. 131 (1960b) 73–83.

[24]Binford (supra n. 5).

[25]D. W. Lathrap, "Our Father the Cayman, Our Mother the Gourd: Spinden Revisited, or a Unitary Model for the Emergence of Agriculture in the New World," *Origins of Agriculture*, C. A. Reed, ed., 713–751, The Hague, 1977.

[26]D. F. Green and G. W. Lowe, *Altamira and Padre Piedra, Early Preclassic Sites in Chiapas, Mexico*, Papers of the New World Archaeological Foundation, No. 20, Publication No. 15, Brigham Young University (Provo, Utah 1967).

[27]C. F. Brush, "Pox Pottery: Earliest Identified Mexican Ceramic," *Science*, Vol. 149 (1965) 194–95, Washington, D.C.

[28]Henning Bischof, "The Origins of Pottery in South America—Recent Radiocarbon Dates from Southwest Ecuador," 40th International Congress of Americanists, Rome-Genova, Vol. 1, 1973.

[29]G. R. Willey (supra n. 19) 178–89.

[30]The most recent detailed treatment of agricultural beginnings in the Eastern United States is by Stuart Struever and K. D. Vickery, "The Beginnings of Cultivation in the Midwest-Riverine Area of the United States," *American Anthropologist*, Vol. 75, No. 5 (Washington, D.C. 1973) 1197–1221. See also W. H. Sears, "Food Production and Village Life in Prehistoric Southeastern United States," *Archaeology*, Vol. 24, No. 4 (1971) 322–29.

[31]For a general summary see Willey, *An Introduction to American Archaeology*: Vol. II (1971b) South America, 90–107; T. C. Patterson, "Central Peru: Its Population and Economy," *Archaeology*, Vol. 24, No. 4 (1971b) 316–21, offers a more up-to-date version of a section of the coastal area.

[32]There is considerable argument over radiocarbon dates for Valdivia; however, the earliest Valdivia, or Valdivia-like, levels have dates of ca. 2500 B.C. (uncorrected) and ca. 3200 B.C. (corrected). See Bischof (supra n. 28) and also B. J. Meggers, C. Evans, and E. Estrada, *Early Formative Period of Coastal Ecuador: The Valdivia and Machalilla Phases*, Smithsonian Contributions to Anthropology, Vol. 1 (Washington, D.C. 1965). Meggers, Evans, and Estrada present one date (M-1320) which is 3200 B.C. (uncorrected) and ca. 4000 B.C. (corrected); however, critics are skeptical of its proper stratigraphic context.

[33]Meggers, Evans, and Estrada (supra n. 32).

[34]Carlos Zevallos, *La Agricultura en el Formativo Temprano del Ecuador* (Cultura Valdivia), Guayaquil, Ecuador 1971; Bischof (supra n. 28).

[35]D. W. Lathrap (supra n. 25); see also Lathrap, *The Upper Amazon* (London 1970), and Lathrap, "Summary or Model Building: How Does One Achieve a Meaningful Overview of a Continent's Prehistory," *American Anthropologist*, Vol. 75, No. 6 (1973b) 1755–767.

[36]D. W. Lathrap, "The Tropical Forest and the Cultural Context of Chavín," *Dumbarton Oaks Conference on Chavín*, Elizabeth Benson, ed. (1971) 73–100, and Lathrap, "Gifts of the Cayman: Some Thoughts on the Subsistence Basis of Chavín," *Variation in Anthropology*, D. W. Lathrap and Jody Douglas, eds. (1973a) 91–105, Illinois Archaeological Survey, Urbana.

[37]W. G. Solheim, II, "Southeast Asia and the West," *Science*, Vol. 157 (1967) 896–902.

[38]V. G. Childe, "The Urban Revolution," *Town Planning Review*, Vol. 21, No. 1 (1950) 3–17; see also G. R. Willey, "Commentary on: The Emergence of Civilization in the Maya Lowlands," *Contributions of the Univerity of California Archaeological Facility*, No. II (1971c) 97–111, University of California, Berkeley.

[39]G. R. Willey, "The Early Great Styles and the Rise of the Precolumbian Civilizations," *American Anthropologist*, Vol. 64 (1962) 1–14. For revised datings on these cultures see: Muriel Porter Weaver, *The Aztecs, Maya, and Their Predecessors* (New York 1972) 46–58; G. R. Willey, *An Introduction to American Archaeology: Vol. II. South America* (1971b) 116–31; and J. H. Rowe, "An Interpretation of Radiocarbon Measurements on Archaeological Samples from Peru," *Peruvian Archaeology, Selected Readings*, J. H. Rowe and D. Menzel, eds. (Palo Alto 1967) 16–30.

[40]K. V. Flannery, "The Olmec and the Valley of Oaxaca: A Model for Inter-Regional Interaction in Formative Times," *Dumbarton Oaks Conference on the Olmec*, Elizabeth Benson, ed. (Washington, D.C. 1968a) 79–118.

[41]T. C. Patterson, "Chavín: An Interpretation of Its Spread and Influence," *Dumbarton Oaks Conference on Chavín*, Elizabeth Benson, ed. (Washington, D.C. 1971a) 29–48.

[42]The Huari-Tiahuanaco horizon is defined and summarized in Willey, *An Introduction to American Archaeology* (supra n. 31) 157–64.

[43]D. W. Lathrap (see 1982). "Significance," Andino-Mesoamericano, 25–31.

[44]These similarities have been commented upon by Robert von Heine-Geldern, "Representations of the Asiatic Tiger in the Art of the Chavín Culture: A Proof of Early Contacts between China and Peru," *Actas del 33 Congreso Internacional de Americanistas* (San Jose, Costa Rica 1959) 321–26, as well as by others. In previous writings of mine (supra n. 4) I have taken a negative view of their significance. I am now less certain.

[45]R. F. Millon, "Teotihuacan," *Scientific American*, Vol. 216, No. 6 (1967) 38–63; R. F. Millon, "Teotihuacan: Completion of Map of Giant Ancient City in Valley of Mexico," *Science*, Vol. 170 (1970) 1077–1082; W. T. Sanders and B. J. Price, *Mesoamerica, the Evolution of a Civilization* (New York 1968).

[46]A standard summary work on Tula is by B. P. Dutton, "Tula of the Toltecs," *El Palacio*, Vol. 62, Nos. 7–8 (1955) 195–251. Reports on more recent excavations by a University of Missouri expedition, headed by R. A. Diehl, will soon be forthcoming. The ebb and flow of power in Central Mexico has been discussed by R. E. Blanton, "Prehispanic Adaptation in the Ixtapalapa Region, Mexico," *Science*, Vol. 175 (1972) 1317–326.

[47]This story is outlined in various general works on Peruvian archaeology. See, especially, E. P. Lanning, *Peru Before the Incas* (Englewood Cliffs 1967) and G. R. Willey, *An Introduction to American Archaeology: Vol. II. South America*, Ch. 3 (Englewood Cliffs 1971b).

[48]C. C. Lamberg-Karlovsky, *Excavations at Tepe Yahya, Iran, 1967–69. Report I.* American School of Prehistoric Research, Peabody Museum, Harvard University (Cambridge, Mass. 1970) and Lamberg-Karlovsky and Maurizio Tosi, "Shahr-i Sokhta and Tepe Yahya: Tracks on the Earliest History of the Iranian Plateau," *East and West*, n.s., Vol. 23, Nos. 1–2 (1972).

[49]See the collection of papers in *The Classic Maya Collapse*, T. P. Culbert, ed. (University of New Mexico Press, Albuquerque 1973).

[50]Colin Renfrew, *Before Civilization, The Radiocarbon Revolution and Prehistoric Europe* (New York 1973).

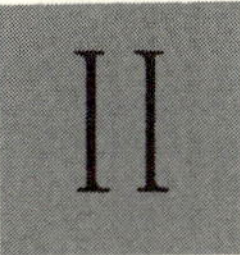

Patterns in the Data

I seem to have been much attracted to what I can best describe as "patterns in the data"—those formal-spatial-temporal patternings which emerge from the archaeological data viewed primarily as culture history. What the patterns might "mean" or "how they came into being" were other questions, interesting, legitimate, and important, but I was attracted to the patterns first in and of themselves alone, simply because they were there. Six of the essays or articles in Part II are essentially culture-historical. Five treat of "horizon styles" or "pottery traditions," while the sixth is concerned with a peculiar pattern in the Lowland Maya archaeological data—the stelae dedicatory "hiatus" in the sixth century A.D. Two other essays describe culture-historical patterns, but they then go beyond description to use the discerned patternings as points of departure for hypotheses about culture process.

A

Culture-Historical Patterns

"Horizon Styles and Pottery Traditions in Peruvian Archaeology" was an outgrowth of my first field experiences in Peru, when I excavated several sites on the central coast and had the opportunity to discuss my results with A. L. Kroeber when he visited that country early in 1942. One of the subjects we discussed was what he was to designate as "horizon styles" (Kroeber 1944) shortly thereafter. Kroeber outlined the clearly recognizable Chavín, Tiahuanaco, and Inca horizons; in addition, he suggested the possibilities of two other horizon styles, the "White-on-red" and "Negative-painted." As I had detailed knowledge of White-on-red ceramics (Willey 1943a), I wrote my paper soon afterward to bolster the case for a "White-on-red horizon." It had also struck me that while horizon styles such as Chavín, Tiahuanaco, and Inca were characterized by distinct iconographic content, others, such as the "White-on-red" and "Negative-Painted" horizons, lacked a compelling iconography. What might this tell us about the meanings of individual horizon styles and the processes that were involved in their propagation? A second observation in my paper was that, in addition to the horizon style phenomena, the Peruvian ceramic data showed other patterns, which I called "pottery traditions." I defined *pottery tradition* as "a line . . . of pottery development through time within the confines of a certain technique or decorative constant." Thus, while in the "horizon style" the emphasis was on widespread contemporaneity of the phenomena, the emphasis in the "pottery tradition" was on long-time regional continuity.

In 1947, Wendell Bennett suggested to me that I prepare a paper on the "meanings" of Peruvian horizon styles. "A Functional Analysis of 'Horizon' Styles in Peruvian Archaeology" (Willey 1948) was the result. In my use of the word "functional" I was referring to the workings or the operations of a culture and society. I suppose I might have employed the word "processual," inasmuch as I was attempting to elucidate and speculatively explain cultural and social behavior. The essay is strongly speculative—indeed, overly so.

Can we really be so optimistic as to "predict one kind of cultural interaction as having been consistent with and deriving out of a certain economic, social, or political configuration?" Today, this would be considered an ambitious goal of "processual archaeology", one on the level of "upper-range theory." In looking back over some of the speculations I made 40 years ago, I would still go with the idea that the spread of Chavín-style art was due to religion. (For a more up-to-date discussion, see T. C. Patterson [1971a] and other articles on Chavín in the volume edited by E. P. Benson [1971], see also Burger [1985]). But my insistence on the Chavín horizon as an era of "peace" was undoubtedly overdone (see Wilson [1988 100–139] on the "Cayhuamarca Period" in the Lower Santa Valley). My remarks that the White-on-red and Negative-painted horizons represented horizonal diffusions of only technological, in contrast to ideological, content was pretty risky. I would still stand by my statements about the Tiahuanaco (or Tiahuanaco-Huari) horizon. The art of the horizon, its contexts, and the effects on a number of discrete local regions look very much like the signs of a political change—and change by force (see Bawden [1977] for another view). One important revision of the Tiahuanaco horizon style concept, of course, has been the discovery that its main center of diffusion, at least within Peru, was Huari, in the central highlands, rather than the site of Tiahuanaco on the Bolivian altiplano (see Menzel 1964; Willey 1971b: 160–164; Isbell and Schreiber 1978; Isbell 1983). My original impression was that the Inca horizon style had a superficial quality, perhaps the result of the brevity (less than 100 years) of the Inca Empire. I still think this.

The long essay, "The Chavín Problem: A Review and Critique" (1951b), continued my interests in horizon style phenomena but in a much more conservative vein than the previous paper. It was my intention to take a "hard look" at the Chavín horizon and related phenomena. What did we mean by *Chavín*—a site, a widespread culture, a civilization, or an empire? And could all of the manifestations that archaeologists had designated as "Chavín" be placed legitimately within the canons of the style?

I should note that the earliest reference to Chavín is Middendorf's of 1893–95. Subsequently, Uhle (1919 and 1922) made brief references to what he took to be "Chavín influences." It was Tello (1922, 1923), however, who made Chavín—both the site proper and the art style—well known in Peruvian archaeology; and, after him, the writings of Larco Hoyle (1941), Bennett (1939, 1943), and Kroeber (1944) increased our knowledge of the subject. It was at about this point that I wrote my "Review and Critique."

In trying to distinguish between what I thought were qualified Chavin style discoveries and those that seemed to me to fall outside the boundaries of the style, I made up a list, and, as I look this over now, I see none that I would eliminate. As a matter of interest, I would call special attention to what John Rowe (1971) has referred to as "archaistic imitations of Chavín art" in later pottery styles, those of Moche and even Chimu date. The potters of these later cultures had captured the essence, or "configuration," of the Chavín style in an astonishing manner. One presumes that they were working with true Chavín archaeological specimens as models. There are, of course, several discoveries that could be added to my 1951 Chavín list. I shall make no attempt to enumerate these here, but the architectural murals at Caballo Muerto, in the Moche Valley, are one outstanding example that comes to mind (Conrad, 1980 Ms.).

In the 1951 article, I also listed a number of other sites and discoveries as "Additional Sites Related to the Chavín Problem." Among these was the site of Cerro Sechin and its famed sculptures. I think that the consensus now would place Cerro Sechin sculpture as definitely outside of the Chavín style, as I maintained in 1951, and as earlier than the Chavín horizon, as I also suggested then (see also Willey 1971b). Some of my evaluations of "Additional Sites" still hold; others do not. Among the latter are sites yielding Paracas Cavernas pottery on the south coast of Peru. In 1951, I did not feel that the "cat-faces" on Paracas pottery truly qualified as being of the Chavín style—although I now plead partial exculpation for that position in that the illustrations available at that time were very few in number. Since then, there is no doubt that Paracas Cavernas pottery has a healthy element of Chavín influence, as Kroeber (1953) has pointed out.

My section on "Chavín as a Tradition," as distinct from Chavín as an horizon style, is still of interest. There is certainly a widespread and long-time persistence of Chavín thematic elements in other Peruvian and wider Andean art styles, and this has led to confusion in talking about Chavín as a horizon style.

Where did Chavín as an art style originate? We are still uncertain. There can be little doubt that the style contains much iconographic content that relates it to the tropical forest, to the east of the Andes (Lathrap 1971, 1973a, 1974, 1977, 1982, 1985), and one might assume from this that the style, per se, crystallized at some place in the upper highland drainages that lead down to the tropical forest. Chavin de Huantar would, indeed, be such a place (see Lumbreras 1971), but there are now earlier radiocarbon dates on major Chavín-style art on the Peru coast (Conrad, 1980 Ms.). In other words, we are still not fully secure on the dating of the Chavín horizon (see Patterson 1988).

One more comment should be added to these remarks on my 1951 essay. This is that the way I described the Chavín style then was iconographically too limited. The feline being is an element in the style, but there is other important subject matter, especially anthropomorphs and saurian creatures.

Although I had first put forward the "pottery tradition" idea in a Peruvian setting (1945), I made no attempt to take the idea further until much later and then in the context of Southeastern United States archaeology. W. H. Sears (1952) published a paper that set me to wondering whether patterns of directional change might not characterize pottery traditions. Such change would cut across all of the styles and types in the tradition and might be pervasive over a considerable geographical area. In the Southeastern United States, Sears had noted a gradual shift in complicated stamped wares from complex to simple designs, plus a decreasing use of filler elements in designs, and an increase in their symmetry. In my 1954 essay, "Tradition Trend in Ceramic Development," I sought out other American examples of what I decided to call "tradition trends" in ceramic development. Thus, I observed that a change from an earlier overall coverage of vessel surfaces to designs limited to a band below the rim was a clear trend in Lower Mississippi Valley–Gulf Coast pottery over a considerable time span. I noted that in the Greater Southwestern United States area there was a drift from larger, bold designs to smaller, fine-line, complex ones, and that this drift linked many pottery styles and types throughout both the Anasazi and the Hohokam regions. I also used Peruvian pottery styles and tradition trends as examples of still other kinds of drift. I tried to make clear that I was not talking about some general evolutionary trend of "simple to complex" in the development of New World pottery. What I was indicating were more limited, historically conditioned, idiosyncratic trends.

I thought the paper an interesting idea, but it never received any comment from my archaeological colleagues. Later, however, a Summer Seminar Group of the Society for American Archaeology did examine the "tradition" concept, and their deliberations (Haury and Thompson, eds., 1956) led me back to the theme in an essay I wrote for a festschrift dedicated to Julian H. Steward.

This essay, "Diagram of a Pottery Tradition" (1964a), is about the "North Peruvian Plastic Pottery Tradition," and it deals with the several well-known life-modeled styles of the north coast valleys of Peru. I examined the tradition in light of the five types of "culture change profiles" or "tradition segments" the Society for American Archaeology Summer Seminar group (Haury and Thompson, eds., 1956) had formulated. I then set forth some conclusions as to the causes of the various changes seen in the life-span of the tradition. A deficiency of the paper is its lack of any objective quantification of the data; I spoke only generally and impressionistically. Besides this, the application of the Summer Seminar's "tradition segment" typology to my "diagram"—like so many such exercises in social and archaeological sciences—doesn't tell us much that we didn't already know. Perhaps a more rewarding way of addressing the history of a pottery tradition would be to ask questions such as, What happens to a well-established regional pottery tradition when that region and its political leadership are overrun and dominated by a foreign imperial expansion? It is of interest that when we ask this about the North Peruvian Plastic Pottery Tradition, we see that the Tiahuanaco (Huari) presence seems to have disrupted the tradition rather seriously while the Inca empire's incursions into the area had only a very mild effect on it. Certainly this must tell us something about the differences between the two invading powers, as well as about the recipient cultures.

The Classic Maya "hiatus" represents another kind of "pattern in the data." I had long been interested in this curious interruption in the continuity of dedication of Classic Maya Initial Series stelae, a temporary break that lasted from 9.5.0.0.0 to 9.8.0.0.0 (or from A.D. 534–593). Morley (1938-39), Proskouriakoff (1950), and Thompson (1954) had all referred in passing to the "hiatus," but none of them had devoted much attention to it. My primary purpose in writing my 1974 essay, "The Classic Maya 'Hiatus': A Rehearsal for the Collapse," was to review the circumstances surrounding the event or events of the "hiatus." Secondarily, I could not help but speculate on the causes of this temporary "failure" in Lowland Classic Maya political and ritual activity, which had occurred at the dividing line between the Early Classic and the Late Classic Periods. It was my opinion then that Teotihuacan may have been involved in some way. Such Classic Lowland Maya–Teotihuacan relationships could have been commercial, political, or both. Such contacts might have been direct ones between the Lowland Maya sites and Teotihuacan, or they could have been effected through the mediation of a third party, such as Kaminaljuyu in the Guatemalan Highlands. In my review of the data, I noted that at Tikal, the largest Early Classic Period city of the southern Lowlands, the first strong infusion of Teotihuacan elements appeared in the high dynastic art of the Lowland center in the fourth century A.D. This event appeared to correlate with the onset of an Early Classic florescence at Tikal (Coggins 1979b). In building my speculations upon this, it seemed unlikely that Teotihuacan contact would have contributed to any "weakening" of elite life at Tikal a century or so later, at the time of the "hiatus." This led me to turn the question around and ask if the possible withdrawal of Teotihuacan influence, brought about by the decline of that central Mexican metropolis, had produced the "hiatus" shock. This seemed a reasonable hypothesis, and I favored it in the article as a speculative "explanation" of the "hiatus." But from my current perspective, this seems unlikely as a cause of the "hiatus." Peter Mathews has written:

> It has been suggested that the Hiatus might have been caused by a withdrawal of Teotihuacan contact with the Maya Lowlands (Willey 1974: 422–428). This question is still unresolved—as indeed is the question of the precise nature of the presumed Teotihuacan contact. However, I think that one thing can be said; the Hiatus does not occur temporally between the end of Tikal preeminence and the rise of other major centers all over the southern Maya Lowlands. Rather, the Hiatus occurs just after the initial spurt of activity of these other major centers. In other words, these centers' rise precedes the alleged withdrawal of alleged

> Teotihuacan patronage at Tikal and its (Tikal's) subsequent circumscription. The other major centers have their florescence in spite of the Hiatus, not because of it (Mathews 1985: 31–32).

Was internal strife within the Lowlands—constant competition and warfare between cities—a factor in the "hiatus" decline (see Mathews and Willey 1989)? A discovery of the mid-1980s suggests that it might have been. The large center of Caracol, in southwestern Belize, was one of the few that kept on with stelae dedications through the "hiatus" (Beetz and Satterthwaite 1981). A glyphic text has just been reported from that site which states that Caracol, or its rulers, conquered Tikal early in the "hiatus" period (Chase and Chase, 1987). Did this defeat of what was then, perhaps, the leading city and dynasty in the southern Lowlands, linked by marriage alliances to many others, result in a political crisis for a large part of the Lowlands, especially the central and western portions of that area?

Whatever the specific causes of the sixth-century "hiatus," one inevitably wonders if it is not linked, generically, to the more serious and permanent ninth-century "collapse" of the same cities.

14

Horizon Styles and Pottery Traditions in Peruvian Archaeology

(From *American Antiquity*, Vol. 11, pp. 49–56, 1945. Reprinted by permission of the Society for American Archaeology.)

The present paper is partially devoted to a consideration of the concept of "horizon styles"[1] in Peruvian archaeology: how the concept has been used in archaeological reconstruction, and how new styles are in the process of formulation. It includes also an analysis of several ceramic periods which may be grouped into such a horizon style, the White-on-red. Differing from the horizon style is another historical phenomenon which I have called the "pottery tradition." An attempt is made here to show the relationship of these two concepts—horizon styles and pottery traditions—as they are exemplified in Peruvian archaeology.[2]

Horizon Styles

The increasing importance of the horizon-style concept in Peruvian archaeology has been emphasized by two recent summary papers. Bennett[3] has outlined the position and significance of the Chavín horizon style, giving a new and formal recognition to the status of Chavín as a widespread cultural influence, a status first claimed for it by Tello, the Peruvian archaeologist. In a long survey and general critique, Kroeber[4] has brought together the accomplishments and summarized the status of Peruvian archaeology as of 1942. In this study, Kroeber frequently uses the concept of the horizon-style. He defines more clearly the styles now used by most Peruvianists and suggests others which might be usefully extended as horizon markers. He defines a horizon style as "one showing definably distinct features some of which extend over a large area, so that its relations with other, more local styles serve to place these in relative time, according as the relations are of priority, consociation, or subsequence."

In greater detail, the archaeologist, in his use of the term "pan-Peruvian horizon style," has reference to certain art influences which are registered in the technologies of ceramics, stone carving, architecture, textiles, and metalwork, resulting in an artistic similarity in products from different regions. These horizon styles serve as index markers for interrelating sequences of various local cultures in the Peruvian archaeological time scale. There are, at present, three commonly accepted horizon influences in central Andean archaeology. The earliest is the Chavín. This style, in its different manifestations, has been placed at the very bottom of the column in the relative chronology of Peru. Chavín-like periods are, by stratification or on the basis of association, the earliest cultural periods in a number of local sequences, both on the coast and in the highlands. The second pan-Peruvian horizon style is the Tiahuanaco, or Tiahuanacoid. Its position in the sequence is later than that of the Chavín horizon, from which it is separated by a major time interval known as the Early Period. The horizon of Tiahuanaco influences is often referred to as the major Middle Period of Peruvian archaeology. The first half of the subsequent Late Period is dominated by the emergence of many local styles; the latter half is marked by Inca influences. These Inca influences, found in almost all sections of the central Andean area, compose the third horizon style.

It seems likely that other styles exist which could, like the three already defined, facilitate comparison of local sequences. Kroeber[5] has tentatively proposed three new horizon styles: Negative painting, Nazca B-Y, and White-on-red. All three are represented principally in ceramics. Future archaeological research in Peru and attempts to use them as horizon markers will ultimately test their validity as true horizon styles. It is possible at this time, however, to inquire into the limitations and specifications of the horizon-style concept as it has been used, and to see how Negative, Nazca B-Y, and White-on-red compare to Chavín, Tiahuanaco, and Inca as tools for archaeological reconstruction.

Two simple criteria are fundamental to the horizon style; first, that there shall be resemblance among the style groups so classed; second, that there be uniformity in relative position in the sequence on the part of the style as it occurs from region to region. Resemblances among component regional styles of a horizon style are established on the basis of very definite sets of features. Chavín has a number of specifically distinctive traits. These include a variety of representations of a single cat-god theme with diagnostic treatment of eye, tooth, and claw. The style is massive, curvilinear, and highly symbolic. Designs are executed in a sculptural, carved, or incised technique in stone, bone, and pottery. Tiahuanaco and Inca features are as distinctive as those of Chavín, if not more so. Tiahuanaco representations of the humanized god or demon follow a very set pattern. The rectangular head and stiff body and the similar treatment of eye and mouth are uniformly repeated on the coast and in the highlands. Inca pottery decorations and forms are also unmistakable in any context. The small, stylized, brightly painted geometric patterns and the specific aryballoid jar form are part of a complex of features that make up an exceedingly serviceable historical unit.

Horizon-style resemblance, although specific, does not indicate cultural identity of the groups who participated in the style. This is clear from the three horizon styles now generally accepted. For example, while the pottery of Chavín de Huántar and the Ancon shell heaps is strikingly alike, and both sites manifest the Chavín horizon style, the first is a megalithic center of outstanding architecture and stone sculpture, while the second is a medium-sized coastal village with no elaborate stone masonry or monuments. Similarly, while the majority of Middle Period pottery styles of the north, central, and south coasts have little resemblance to each other, and while their immediate histories are divergent, all are, nevertheless, influenced by Tiahuanaco stylistic features.

A cross check on the uniformity of relative position in the sequence on the part of any one horizon style is made possible by the fact that there is more than one such horizon in Peruvian archaeology. If only one series of horizon influences appeared in the different local sequences, the synchronization of these sequences would be difficult to establish; but, with three strong horizon influences linking regional sequences, the placing of intervening localized styles and periods is not only made easier, but the chronological position of any one of the horizon styles can be partially verified by reference to the other two.

A preliminary evaluation of Kroeber's three projected horizon styles in terms of the above criteria raises some interesting problems. Of the three styles—Nazca B-Y, Negative, and White-on-red—the first would appear to possess the greatest number of distinctive features for determining similarities or dissimilarities to other styles. That is, Nazca B-Y is intrinsically, in terms of its design elements, motifs, and colors, a more complex and easily recognizable style unit than either Negative or White-on-red. Nazca B-Y styles are known principally from the Nazca-Ica area on the South Coast, but some examples of Nazca B-Y influences have been found on the central coast, as well as on the extreme south coast down to Camaná.[6] Tello has long maintained that a style closely related to Nazca B-Y is characteristic of the highland Chanca country. Kroeber's recent illustrations[7] of a collection from Ayacucho tend to confirm this extension of Nazca B-Y style into the highlands. Unfortunately, Nazca B-Y influences cannot be placed in any sequence in the highlands or on the extreme south coast. In the Nazca-Ica area, its pre-Tiahuanaco to Tiahuanaco position is well substantiated from the point of view of associations, although not confirmed by stratigraphy. Cross ties with Early Lima (Nievería) of the central coast strengthen the case for Nazca B-Y as a horizon marker, but, as Kroeber points out, general lack of sequence data makes it impossible to use the style yet as a widespread time marker.

The possibility that White-on-red painted ceramics may be used as a horizon indicator has been briefly touched upon by Bennett[8] and Kroeber.[9] The following section includes an analysis of some of the several White-on-red styles of Peru and an attempt to relate them in a horizon style. The problem of a Negative-painted horizon will be treated subsequently.

WHITE-ON-RED

DISTRIBUTION

The first White-on-red style was discovered by Uhle (1908) at Cerro Trinidad, site E, in the Chancay valley on the central coast.[10] My own excavations in 1941, at the same site and at Baños de Boza, also in the Chancay, added new descriptive and stratigraphic data on the Chancay White-on-red style.[11] A few evidences of this type of White-on-red were also found by Strong and Corbett in their stratigraphic excavations at Pachacamac, a little farther south on the coast.[12] Shortly before this, Rafael Larco Hoyle published discoveries of another White-on-red ceramic style on the north coast, some 300 miles above Chancay.[13] He has named this style Salinar, after the large type-site cemetery in the Chicama valley.[14] In the northern highlands, Bennett found still other variations of White-on-red pottery in intrusive graves at Chavín de Huántar and in isolated sites near Huaraz.[15]

TIME POSITION

One of the factors most strongly suggesting a relationship among the widely separated occurrences of certain White-on-red pottery is the uniform position of the style in sequences in which it occurs. On the central coast, Chancay White-on-red is, by sound inference, later than the Ancon-Supe shell-mound periods, which are a part of the Chavín horizon.[16] Chancay White-on-red is followed, at both Pachacamac and Chancay, by the Interlocking and Early Lima periods, central coastal cultures of the major Early Period. On the north coast, according to present evidence, Salinar White-on-red follows Cupisnique, a coastal Chavín period, and immediately precedes Mochica (Early Chimu), the classic style of the north coast during the Early Period.[17] In the northern highlands, White-on-red graves are intrusive into, and later than, highland Chavín materials. Although the isolated Huaraz graves neither directly confirm nor deny this position in the sequence, Bennett is of the opinion that Huaraz White-on-red is pre-Tiahuanaco. There is, then, a very good chance that the Huaraz finds are as early as Chancay White-on-red or Salinar.

CHANCAY WHITE-ON-RED

Pottery of the White-on-red style from the Chancay valley is of medium quality as to ware and firing, and is dull red in color. It is apparently handmade, and a high percentage has a red slip. Principal forms of vessels are low, open bowls; mammiform jars or canteens; double-spouted jars with flat bridge handles; single-spouted jars with attached flat handles; deep, wide-mouthed jars; and crudely modeled bird-effigy vessels with spout and flat handle attached. Exterior surfaces of the various forms of jar and exterior and interior surfaces of open bowls are painted with broad white zones or with simple and poorly executed arrangements of lines, dots, and geometric figures. Red decoration is occasionally superimposed upon the white zones. Effigy vessels and small modeled *adornos* attached to vessels are occasionally emphasized by incised as well as white-painted decoration.

Chancay stone beads are uncarved spheroids. Shell beads are common, and shell inlay work in stone was practiced. Hammered gold ornaments were known at this time in the Chancay valley, and a fragment of copper, or of a gold-copper alloy, has also been found.

Chancay burials are flexed and buried in rather simple graves. Huge potsherds and rocks were used to build a cover for the body.

SALINAR[18]

The Salinar pottery of the northern coast is moderately well made and, like the pottery of Chancay, is usually oxidized in firing so that the natural color is a dull red. A small percentage of the ware is, however, black or dark brown. In variety of forms, skill in modeling, and even in some of the painted decorations, Salinar is decidedly superior to Chancay White-on-red. There is, though, a marked similarity in the simply conceived and clumsily executed white-painted decoration of both styles. The predominant vessel forms are: single-spouted jar with flat handle; unhandled vessels, including deep, wide-mouthed jars with short, projecting collars, bowls with incurved rims, and shallow open bowls; figure vessels, including stirrup-spout, figure-and-spout, and spout-and-handle variations. Figure vessels usually have an animal, bird, or human figure on top of, or as a part of, the vessel to which the spout and handle are attached. The figure-and-spout form has a flat bridge-handle connecting the modeled figure to the spout. Decoration is characteristically of broad white lines and is often composed of simple geometric arrangements such as pendant triangles filled with marks or dots. On some vessels the spout is surrounded by a ring of white S-shaped elements. Occasionally, painted areas are outlined with fine incised lines, and incision is sometimes employed, in addition to white paint, on modeled figures. A few vessels have impressed nodes attached to the exterior surface as ornamentation.

The stirrup-mouthed jar seems to be a local feature of Salinar White-on-red, just as mammiform jars and double-spouted jars with flat bridge handles appear to be restricted to Chancay White-on-red and to early cultures of the south coast. On the other hand, the single-spout jar with attached flat handle is an important connective trait common to Salinar and Chancay White-on-red. It should be noted that this feature is not present in Chavín, Cupisnique, Mochica, or Early Nazca. Apparently Salinar, Chancay White-on-red, and the negative style of Gallinazo on the north coast are the only styles previous to the Middle Periods for which the single spout and flat handle are recorded.

Salinar pottery can be related to the periods which precede and follow it within its own area. In the stirrup-mouth and in figure modeling it resembles both coastal Chavín Cupisnique and Mochica. In its predominantly red color and in the combination of red and white it is closest to Mochica.[19] However, Salinar is significantly unlike both Cupisnique and Mochica in its flat-handle single-spout jar and its figure-and-spout forms. In general, the Salinar style looks like the product of a combination of White-on-red influences of a simpler sort—such as those revealed in the ware of the Chancay valley—and a Cupisnique strain. On stylistic grounds, Salinar pottery could very easily occupy the position transitional between Cupisnique and Mochica to which Larco Hoyle has assigned it.[20]

Salinar lacks most of the carved stone and bone objects in whose production the craftsmen of the Cupisnique period excelled. Salinar beads are much like those of the Chancay White-on-red period. Work in shell, rare or absent in Cupisnique and abundant in Mochica, is found in moderate quantities in Salinar. A similar situation exists in regard to metalwork. No metal objects have been found associated with Cupisnique in the Chicama region. On the other hand, Mochica metalwork is plentiful and embodies advanced techniques of casting, soldering, and gilding with gold, silver, copper, and alloys of these. Salinar graves have yielded simple hammered and openwork gold ornaments and, in addition, some evidence of soldering. As in the Chancay White-on-red horizon, one tiny copper fragment has also been found.

Cupisnique burials are usually flexed in simple oval graves; those of Mochica are carefully extended upon the back in stone- or adobe-lined rectangular graves. Salinar burials appear to be intermediate in type, for they are only slightly flexed, grave excavations are longer than those of Cupisnique, and bodies are often protected by stone slabs.

White-on-red Pottery from Chavín de Huántar

Pottery from intrusive graves at Chavín de Huántar has a general resemblance to the Salinar and Chancay White-on-red styles. In its extremely simple vessel forms and painted decorations it is more like Chancay than Salinar. Specific forms, like the small, shallow bowl painted with pendant triangles filled with dots, are the closest ties to Chancay.[21]

White-on-red Pottery from Huaraz

Pottery from the isolated graves near Huaraz, while not definitely placed in the general Peruvian sequence, is most probably antecedent to the Middle Period. The Huaraz finds show a number of similarities to coastal White-on-red. These include various open bowl forms, a single spouted jar with a flat handle, and a double jar with bridge handle connecting a head-and-spout. Plain red, plain brown, and White-on-red vessels were associated in the same grave. The style of white painting is comparable to that of the coast. The style which Bennett considers subsequent to Huaraz White-on-red is the Wilkawain-Tiahuanaco, whose closest affinities are with Early Lima and Middle Ancon I (Tiahuanacoid) of the central coast.[22]

Summary of White-on-red

The various White-on-red styles discussed thus far fit rather well into a uniform time horizon for a large part of Peru. On the north coast, the White-on-red of Salinar is intermediate between Cupisnique (coastal Chavín) and Mochica. On the central coast, Chancay White-on-red is subsequent to the local Chavín style—the Ancon-Supe shell mound cultures—and precedes the Interlocking and Early Lima periods. In the northern highlands, a White-on-red style follows the Chavín period at Chavín de Huántar and probably precedes the Wilkawain-Tiahuanaco Middle Period, as suggested by the data from Huaraz. There is, then, a strong probability that a major White-on-red ceramic style, made up of historically related and coeval components, marks a general time level between the close of Chavín and the beginnings of the great Early Period cultures such as Mochica, Early Lima, and Early Nazca.

The case for a White-on-red horizon style is not as strong typologically as it is sequentially. That is, the fact that White-on-red ceramics appear at particular, and corresponding, points in a number of culture sequences in Peru strengthens the possibility that their various occurrences are historically related. The painting of simple geometric and curvilinear figures in white on a red-fired ground does not make up a stylistic complex as definitive as Chavín, Tiahuanaco, Inca, or Nazca B-Y. The addition to the complex of other features, such as distinctive vessel forms, does, of course, make for somewhat greater security in the establishment of cross-identifications from region to region. Personally, I feel that the component White-on-red styles discussed make up such a horizon style. It is admitted, though, that without the accompanying sequence data the emergence of such a new horizon style would be greatly obscured.

One of the principal reasons for this obscuring of the early White-on-red similarities is that there are several Peruvian styles other than those mentioned which utilize simple white decorations on a red ground. The two of these which most closely resemble Chancay and Salinar White-on-red are the White-on-red styles of Middle Supe[23] and Middle Ancon.[24] Both of the latter are much later than the proposed early White-on-red horizon, belonging in the major Middle Period bracket. Kroeber also illustrates a new White-on-red style from the region north of the Chicama valley.[25] This pottery is not placed chronologically, but the chances are it belongs to the Middle Period or to the Late Period. Finally, there is Mochica, which is dominated by a White-on-red, or white and red, color combination. Actually, none of these later White-on-red styles bears a very detailed typological similarity to early Chancay, Salinar, or northern highland White-on-red, yet there is just enough resemblance to give room for speculation concerning possible relationships.

Pottery Traditions

These speculations concerning the relationships of the later White-on-red styles to the earlier component styles of the White-on-red horizon lead us to wonder if there are not other widely inclusive historical units of an order different from that of the horizon style. It appears certain that the Peruvian Andes and coast were a unified culture area in that the important cultural developments were essentially local and basically interrelated for at least a thousand years. This fundamental cultural unity justifies seeing ceramic developments in terms of long-time traditions as well as coeval phenomena. The concept of a pottery tradition, as used here, includes broad descriptive categories of ceramic decoration which undoubtedly have value in expressing historical relationships when the relationships are confined to the geographical boundaries of Peruvian-Andean cultures. The pottery tradition lacks the specific quality of the localized pottery style, and it differs from the horizon style in that it is not an integration of artistic elements which has been widely diffused at a given time period. A pottery tradition comprises a line, or a number of lines, of pottery development through time within the confines of a certain technique or decorative constant. In successive time periods through which the history of ceramic development can be traced, certain styles arose within the tradition. Transmission of some of these styles during particular periods resulted in the formation of a horizon style; other styles in the continuum of the tradition remained strictly localized. The distinctions between a horizon style and a pottery tradition should be kept in mind, as the two are opposable concepts in archaeological reconstruction. Attempts to use what are probably pottery traditions as style markers for specific time horizons has caused some misunderstanding in Peruvian archaeology.

The later White-on-red styles of Middle Supe, Middle Ancon, North Chimu, and Mochica are quite probably all a part of a greater historical unit which encompassed northern Peru for several centuries. Thus, while they are not a part of the early White-on-red horizon style, they make up, together with the component parts of this horizon style, the North Peruvian White-on-red pottery tradition. From post-Chavín times up to the Inca conquest the White-on-red tradition was expressed through various styles on the northern and central coast and in the northern highlands. Kroeber indicated this continuity a number of years ago when he said, regarding White-on-red elements in Middle Supe, "Whether the simple white-on-red designs in the San Nicolas collection can be regarded as partly due to central (coastal) influences or as wholly derived from Epigonal, the strong inclination to a red ware and a red ground does seem likely to be due to the survival of old ceramic habits of the central coast."[26]

The beginnings of four other pottery traditions can be separated out of the broader currents of Peruvian prehistory prior to the crystallization of such styles and cultures as Mochica, Early Lima, Early Nazca, and Classic Tiahuanaco. All four traditions, as with White-on-red, are represented both on the coast and in the highlands at an early date, and, because of this, it is difficult to determine their centers of origin. Two of the four, along with White-on-red, appear to be north Peruvian; another, south Peru–Bolivian; while the fourth cannot be localized even to this extent.

The North Peruvian Incised tradition has, perhaps, the earliest origin of all. It is associated with highland Chavín and Cupisnique in its earliest known stages. This tradition of ceramic decoration continues on into periods much later than those of the Chavín horizon. An example of such survival is found in the incised and punctated ware of Middle Ancon I and Teatino, in the Chancay valley. In fact, Tello has classified Teatino incised as Chavín.[27] However, the Teatino and Middle Ancon I incised pottery is significantly different from that of coastal Chavín, lacking as it does the distinctive symbolic stylizations of the cat motif and other elements of the Chavín horizon. Similarly, Cerro Sechin pottery[28] does not seem to be very Chavín-like, but it certainly could be included in the larger scope of the Incised tradition. It is further suggested that the black incised wares of Late Chimu and those associated with the Inca styles are, at least partially, outgrowths of the North Peruvian Incised tradition.

Another important line of ceramic development is the North Peruvian Plastic tradition embracing the sculptured and modeled styles, particularly of the northern coast. Considerable antiquity is also indicated for this tradition. It appears first in the Chavín-Cupisnique style of the coast. The essential quality of this tradition is that plastic expression is not limited solely to appendages or *adornos*, for the sculptor's medium is the entire vessel, which is made to conform to the desired representation. The Plastic tradition is represented by only an occasional fragment in the Chavín levels of the northern highlands. Theories concerning cultural similarities between the highlands and coastal Chavín are based upon comparisons of the stone sculpture only of Chavín de Huántar with the ceramics of Cupisnique. Of all the pottery traditions, the North Peruvian Plastic appears easiest to place as to its general region of origin, presumably the valleys of the northern coast.

The Plastic tradition reached its artistic climax on the northern coast in the well-known Mochica style. After a temporary obliteration of the tradition in the Moche-Chicama sector during the Middle Period, it again found expression in Late Chimu and in other styles of the far northern coast. In tracing the history of the Plastic tradition, or of any other pottery tradition, it is not implied that such significant styles as Mochica or Chimu were the products of unilinear development wholly within any one tradition. There is every indication that these styles are the results of the blending and merging of traditions. Mochica and the subsequent Chimu styles, must be an outgrowth of the Plastic, Incised, and White-on-red traditions; perhaps other, unrecognized, strains, which could be considered traditions in the same sense as the three named, are also represented.

A fourth pottery tradition may, tentatively, be called the South Peru–Bolivian Polychrome tradition. It is possible that multicolor painting is as old in the south as sculptured and incised pottery is in the north.[29] It certainly has a long history there. On the coast it runs from Paracas Cavernas through Nazca, Epigonal, and the Ica series; in the highlands it has beginnings at least as far back as Classic Tiahuanaco and Pucara and is still present in Inca. All of these wares are distinctly different at the level of style, yet all share the emphasis on color. Throughout the tradition there runs a definite trend toward reduction in the number of colors used.

Negative-painting is the fifth pottery tradition. It has been referred to above as a tentative or projected horizon style, and possibly it is, at least within the Peruvian-Andean culture area. Kroeber has remarked upon the inconsistencies in its relative position in the various sequences. Negative is earliest in the south, where it is associated as a minority type with Paracas Cavernas. On the central coast it is presumably slightly later, occurring in association with Chancay White-on-red and Interlocking. In the north, Gallinazo Negative is considered by both Bennett and Kroeber to be just post-Mochica. In the northern highlands it is most strongly represented in the Recuay style, which is pre-Tiahuanaco; however, in the same region it continues in the subsequent Wilkawain-Tiahuanaco period.[30] Moving from south to north, then, we find negative-painted pottery occurring in increasingly later associations, although, unlike the other traditions, it does not continue through to the Conquest period. If all negative-painted pottery is accepted as being stylistically related, Negative then becomes the only horizon style which has a markedly diagonal sequence distribution on the Peruvian time chart. Such a distribution is possible for a horizon style; in fact, it is probable that the other horizon styles were not absolutely coeval in all parts of Peru. However, the time-chart device has been artificially arranged to place Inca, Tiahuanaco, and Chavín on horizontal levels, ignoring the factor of time lag. In view of this, one would expect other horizon styles to be consistent with these horizontal arrangements. The suspiciously great amount of time lag which Negative shows, in a supposed south-to-north diffusion, leaves room for doubt as to whether it is a reliable horizon marker.

There seem to be only two principal Negative styles or types, a two-color and a three-color. The two-color has the wider distribution. It is virtually always a buff or orange color and the paint, or dip dye, is a shade of maroon, brown, or black. Designs are usually composed of very simple elements. Virtuosity in Negative is limited to the Recuay pottery of the northern highlands. This ware has more complicated decorations. The slip is often white, the designs are blocked out in black dye, and a red pigment is applied positively. In general, from the stylistic point of view, Negative forms a tighter unit than the somewhat amorphous White-on-red. Undoubtedly the negative, or resist-dye, technique of painting pottery is a historically diagnostic trait; but, on the other hand, the results of this technique may be limited in range. At least, most South American, and even New World, negative painting is similar in appearance, suggesting that the number of designs easily rendered in the negative technique is not great, a factor to be considered in the determination of historical relationships.

Thus, although this is far from proven, it is suggested that the historical unity expressed in the sum total of Peruvian negative painting could best be conceived of as a pottery tradition rather than as a horizon style. When larger samples of negative-painted pottery are available from more locations within Peru it may be demonstrated that certain stylistic divisions within the Negative compose horizon styles.

CONCLUSIONS

The value of the established horizon styles in Peruvian archaeological syntheses is obvious. The horizon styles are the horizontal stringers by which the upright columns of specialized regional development are tied together in the time chart. Although important revisions are to be expected in Peruvian archaeology, it is safe to say that these horizon markers will remain as a part of any revised reconstructions. This seems assured for widespread stylistic influences, such as Inca, Tiahuanaco, and Chavín. Tentative horizon styles, such as the White-on-red, will be accepted, reformed, or disregarded as investigation proceeds.

The utility of the concept of a pottery tradition is yet to be tested. Awareness of the continuity of basic techniques and habits in all or a large part of the central Andean area through a very long range of time would seem to have the specific, if negative, value of emphasizing the point that generic similarities in decoration and form of ceramics do not necessarily indicate stylistic complexes diffused rapidly through space in a relatively short period. A study of the interplay of pottery traditions and styles should explain more fully the various historical factors which have converged in time and space to produce the entity of the style.

Horizon styles have been interpreted functionally as well as having been used for historical reconstruction. Inca and Tiahuanaco style expansions have been considered results of specific types of sociological and political phenomena. For Inca, it is known that cultural influences were carried by force of military conquest and political incorporation and colonization. The spread of Tiahuanaco and Chavín might possibly be attributed to such mechanisms, but there are, of course, other processes which would also serve to disseminate technical and artistic ideas. The cultural processes involved in the rise and persistence of pottery traditions throughout the several centuries of Andean development are an equally fascinating subject for the student of culture history. The long opposition of the northern Peruvian wares, which emphasized the plastic and the simple color combination of White-on-red, against the pottery of the south, which stressed multiple color, demonstrates the staying power of certain regional-cultural ideas; but, for the present at least, it tells us little else.

Such regional persistence of ceramic traditions is a common occurrence in many places throughout the world. The northern black-on-white and southern red-and-buff wares of the North American Southwest are good examples. In regard to the eastern United States, Linton has recently written of what might be called the northern Woodland pottery tradition of pointed-bottom vessels and roughened surfaces, and has suggested a theory relative to the functional determinants underlying its origins and long persistence.[31]

Notes

[1]A term recently coined by Kroeber. See Kroeber, 1944.

[2]The writer is grateful to Drs. A. L. Kroeber, W. D. Strong, W. C. Bennett, and Julian H. Steward for reading and commenting upon the manuscript of this paper.

[3]Bennett, 1943.

[4]Kroeber, 1944.

[5]*Ibid.*, pp. 108–111.

[6]*Ibid.*, p. 110.

[7]*Ibid.*, p. 99, Pl. 39.

[8]Bennett, 1944a, pp. 98–99.

[9]Kroeber, 1944, p. 110.

[10]See Kroeber, 1926b, for details.

[11]Willey, 1943a.

[12]Strong and Corbett, 1943.

[13]Larco Hoyle, 1941.

[14]Larco Hoyle (1946) presents a more detailed summary of the Salinar culture in *Handbook of South American Indians*, Vol. 2, Bureau of American Ethnology, Smithsonian Institution.

[15]Bennett, 1944a.

[16]Strong, 1925; Kroeber, 1925a; Willey, 1943a.

[17]Larco Hoyle, 1941.

[18]See Larco Hoyle, 1941; Kroeber, 1944.

[19]Kroeber, 1944, p. 59.

[20]Larco Hoyle, 1941, pp. 249–251.

[21]Bennett, 1944a, p. 92.

[22]*Ibid.*, pp. 36, 98–99.

[23]Kroeber, 1925a, p. 242.

[24]Strong, 1925, pp. 154–152.

[25]Kroeber, 1944, p. 74 and Pl. 36, D–F.

[26]Kroeber, 1925a, p. 243.

[27]Kroeber, 1944, p. 45.

[28]*Ibid.*, Pl. 22.

[29]Paracas Cavernas, generally conceded to be the earliest ceramic style of the south coast, is multicolored and incised, although the incising is not as vigorous a feature of the decoration as in Chavín. An early connection between the Chavín style and Paracas Cavernas has been suggested by various authorities.

[30]Bennett, 1944a, p. 106.

[31]Linton, 1944, pp. 369–380.

15

Functional Analysis of "Horizon Styles" in Peruvian Archaeology

(From *A Reappraisal of Peruvian Archaeology*, W. C. Bennett, ed., pp. 8–15, Memoir No. 4, Society for American Archaeology, 1948. Reprinted by permission of the Society for American Archaeology.)

Introduction

Since the beginnings of scientific archaeology in Peru investigators have employed the concept of the "horizon" or "horizon style" in attempting to reconstruct the major outlines of Central Andean prehistory.[1] This formulation of the horizon is an abstraction based upon the recurrence of specific features of style or manufacture in prehistoric artifacts, mainly pottery, from one region to another so that the phenomena become pan-Peruvian in scope and coordinate our knowledge of the past in a broad temporal and spatial scheme. This integration is made possible when the same stylistic or technical complex of traits is found in the respective culture sequences of geographically widely separated regions, and by this means the two or more sequences are brought together and equated in time. The constructs of horizons have been useful synthesizing elements in the understanding of Peruvian archaeology on the level of time-space systematics. As yet, however, there has been little consideration of their functional significance in the prehistoric native societies of which they were a part. This present exploratory analysis ventures to define and characterize as cultural forces on the level of social interaction what heretofore have been viewed chiefly as historical phenomena.

The difficulties for any such study are patent to the student of Andean archaeology. By its definition, archaeology, particularly of the Americanist branch, operates with the objects of dead societies often found isolated from their meaningful contexts. Moreover, there are handicaps in the selection of, and the emphasis placed upon, the varieties of published archaeological evidence. The data pertinent to sequence and distribution studies are often not particularly germane to interpretations of religious integrations or sociopolitical patterns. In spite of all this, the archaeologist can make some reasoned inferences as to the content, form, and direction of extinct cultures; and from these inferences he may go a step further and define the limitations of possibilities that governed cultural behavior and cultural choice in the past. It is the present thesis that the functional significance of a horizonal diffusion and integration of a complex of cultural ideas may, in part, be deduced from the structural types of culture with which these horizons are associated.[2] Thus, for example, we can, within reasonable bounds of probability, predict one kind of cultural interaction as having been consistent with and deriving out of a certain economic, social, or political configuration; and, conversely, we may eliminate other kinds of cultural process as having been out of harmony with a given pattern of society.

Before attempting to analyze these horizons it will be well to recapitulate briefly the major trends in Peru-Bolivian prehistory. This can best be done through a series of stages. I have designated three such stages as the Formative, the Regional Classic, and the Expansionistic. The earliest, the Formative stage, is conceived of as representing Peru-Bolivian prehistory from the beginnings of agriculture and ceramics on the Chavín horizon up through the cultures of the White-on-Red horizon. The Regional Classic stage, beginning on the time level of the Negative horizon, with periods like the Gallinazo, Early Recuay, Interlocking, and Nazca A, comes to a climax with Mochica, Late Recuay, Early Lima, and Nazca B. The Expansionistic stage then opens with the Tiahuanaco horizon and continues up through Incaic times to the Spanish Conquest.[3] Although these stages are essentially levels of development, definable by cultural criteria, there are also indications that they correspond to chronological eras as well. That there should be such a widespread coincidence of time with degree of cultural advancement testifies to the validity of Peru-Bolivia as a unified culture area.

Although the Peru-Bolivian highlands and coast have such a fundamental archaeological unity, this homogeneity is relieved by the cultural variability in time and space that makes up the regional subdivisions and their respective sequences. The chief factor in correlating these several regional sequences has been the horizonal influences which have diffused throughout large parts of Peru and Bolivia at different times in the prehistoric past. The chronological position and geographical distribution of these horizons are fairly well known although there is not unanimous agreement in all detail. The accompanying chart (Figure 15.1) lists the most important Peru-Bolivian archaeological regions and their respective culture sequences. The five "horizon styles" are also indicated on the chart in sequence position. This chart is in general accord with similar ones that have been published in recent years and follows, except for some specific differences which I shall discuss further along, the opinions of Uhle and the North American school of Peruvianists.[4]

The Chavín Horizon

The Chavín is chronologically the earliest of the Peruvian horizons.[5] Its essential elements are stylistic and technical, a highly conventionalized feline being depicted with sculptural or incision techniques. Representations of this Chavín jaguar are most frequently carved in pottery and stone. The Chavín style links many of the earliest archaeological cultures of Peru. Besides the type site in the upper Marañón drainage, Chavín influences are seen on the north coast in the Cupisnique period of the Chicama Valley, in the Guañape period of the Virú Valley, at Chongoyape in the Lambayeque Valley, and in the sculptured temples of the Nepeña Valley. On the central coast Chavín is a very definite influence in the ceramics of Early Ancón and Early Supe. Quite recently, Tello[6] has also

ESTIMATED DATES	NORTH COAST	NORTH HIGHLANDS	CENTRAL COAST	CENTRAL HIGHLANDS	SOUTH COAST	SOUTH HIGHLANDS	STAGES AND HORIZONS
1535 A.D.	Inca	Inca	Inca	Inca	Inca	Inca	*Inca Horizon*
	Chimu	Late Huamachuco Black-White-Red	Late Chancay Black-White-Red	Early Inca	Late Ica Middle Ica	Chullpa	EXPANSIONISTIC
	Coast Tiahuanaco	Wilkawain Tiahuanaco	Coast Tiahuanaco	Wari	Pacheco	Decadent Tiahuanaco	*Tiahuanaco Horizon*
1000	Mochica	Recuay	Early Lima	Wari(?)	Nazca B Nazca A	Classic Tiahuanaco	REGIONAL CLASSIC
	Gallinazo	Recuay(?)	Interlocking		Paracas	Pucara	*Negative Horizon*
500	Salinar	White-on-Red	White-on-Red		Cavernas	Chiripa	*White-on-Red Horizon*
				Chanapata			FORMATIVE
	Cupisnique Guañape	Chavín	Ancón-Supe				*Chavín Horizon*
0	Preceramic		Preceramic				

Figure 15.1. Peru-Bolivian Archaeological Regions.

reported Chavín-like incised pottery from the vicinity of Huánuco in the eastern drainage of the north highlands. On the south coast and in the south highlands Chavín stylistic influence is much less definite. Possible connections have been pointed out with the Paracas Cavernas, Chiripa, Pucara, Chanapata, and Early Tiahuanaco periods. None of these southern styles shows as clearly, however, the identities with the Chavín technical or decorative elements that are seen in the other period manifestations.

The Chavín horizon is a phenomenon of the early phases of the Formative stage. The cultural motives of this stage were vigorous technological growth and strong religious bias. The technological expansion during the Formative is seen in the rapid spread and assimilation of the ceramic, weaving, stone-carving, metallurgical, and architectural crafts by the component societies of the stage. In several regions the very vital technique of irrigation for cultivation was introduced or developed on the Formative level. This irrigation factor, together with the increasing number of communities that appeared during the periods of the Formative stage, implies that it was also an era of population growth. It does not, however, appear to have been a time of population pressure or population maximum. The religious and theocratic orientation of the early cultures of the Formative stage is implied by the relatively small communities and the presence of temple centers. Presumably, the temple center and its cult was the nucleating force in the social and political structure of the small communities. In short, the cultures of the Formative were theocratically dominated. This is further substantiated by the absence of evidence for organized warfare and the institutions of war, such as a military hierarchy. Such evidence becomes very common in the succeeding Regional Classic stage.

Against this Formative background, the diffusion of the Chavín art style can most easily be explained as the peaceful spread of religious concepts. Perhaps these Chavín concepts were the sanctions, on a spiritual plane, of the life-giving agriculture and sedentary arts that had only recently been adopted by the Formative populations. The conclusion that the style and its significance were accepted willingly follows out of the structure, as far as it is inferable, of Formative society. Peruvian cultures of that era were not able, from the standpoint of population numbers and organization, to carry on sustained, long-distance wars of conquest. Although derived from a common source, the new religious ideas must have been autonomously manipulated in the individual community centers.

The White-on-Red Horizon

The time position of the White-on-Red horizon is immediately subsequent to that of the Chavín. As a horizonal influence it pertains to ceramics and is characterized by the use of white-painted decorations on a natural red or red-slipped ground color.[7] Another decorative technique, the use of thin incised lines to outline the painted areas, is often associated. The simplicity of the geometric design elements and certain vessel forms are also a means of identifying the White-on-Red horizon in its various contexts. It is best known from the central coast where, in the Chancay White-on-Red style, it is a prevailing motif of decoration. To the north, the Puerto Moorin period of the Virú Valley and the Salinar[8] of the Moche-Chicama sector provide fairly close parallels with Chancay. In the north highlands another White-on-Red style follows the Chavín period and precedes Recuay.[9] In the south, as with Chavín, the similarities are less striking; yet in Paracas Cavernas and Chiripa there is a tendency in ceramic decoration to outline simple, geometric painted designs with thin incised lines. This tendency is also noted to a lesser extent in Pucara. Finally, as a part of the Chanapata culture in the central highlands Rowe[10] has reported a White-on-Red pottery type.

As a horizon, White-on-Red lacks the stylistic specificity of Chavín, and although there is a cross-connection among most or all of the regions and periods mentioned, the nature of this connection appears to be of a different order than that linking the various periods of the Chavín horizon. Certainly, the White-on-Red horizon embodies a technological rather than a stylistic innovation. It is quite possible that the idea of white painting on a red ground as a mode of pottery decoration was related to the widespread shift from the reduction-firing to the open-kiln firing of ceramics. This changeover took place at the end of Chavín periods, and, judging from the Virú Valley stratigraphic sequences, appears to have been a gradual rather than an abrupt introduction. Although the cultures of the late Formative had advanced over those of the early part of the stage, there is evidence that technological expansion was still going on. New technical ideas were undoubtedly welcomed by cultures still interested in exploring the potentialities of sedentary existence. As the same general conditions of social, political, and religious organization that characterized the period of the Chavín horizon still held in the late Formative, it is difficult to conceive of the White-on-Red influence as the symbol of conquest. Neither do its intrinsic qualities suggest, as do those of Chavín, a powerful religious symbolism. This lack of symbolic art in the White-on-Red horizon may, in itself, reflect a weakening of the old Chavín cult of the jaguar. If so, this slackening of religious feeling seems more likely to have been the result of internal trends than of foreign impact.

THE NEGATIVE HORIZON

The Negative horizon chronologically overlaps and follows immediately after the White-on-Red. Its diagnostic is the use of the negative or resist-dye technique in decorating pottery surfaces. This takes the form of designs in a light ground color achieved by the application of a dark over-slip. Positive painting is sometimes added to give a three-color effect. Kroeber[11] who examined the evidence for a Negative painting horizon a few years ago, suggested its probable value as a time-marker but also pointed to certain chronological inconsistencies in the sequence contexts in which it appeared. With the recent work of Strong and Evans in the Virú Valley[12] some of these temporal discrepancies have been dispelled. It is now clear that Gallinazo Negative on the north coast preceded, not followed, the Mochica period. This tends to bring Gallinazo into line with central coastal occurrences of Negative in the White-on-Red and Interlocking periods, implying an overall sequence position just subsequent to the White-on-Red horizon but preceding periods like Mochica or Early Lima. This, however, still leaves the south coastal occurrence of Negative out of chronological position if we consider Paracas Cavernas, the period in which it appears, as coeval with Chavín. Heretofore, this has been the customary sequence equation. If Negative were a southern technique, such an explanation might be satisfactory in accounting for time lag; but, along with Kroeber, I feel that the evidence points to the negative-painting process being northern, probably deeply rooted in the north Peru-Ecuadorean highlands. In accordance with this, I have placed Paracas Cavernas as contemporaneous with late White-on-Red and early Gallinazo. Such an interpretation seems most consistent not only with the presence of Negative in the south but also with the similarities between Paracas Cavernas and the central and northern White-on-Red styles.

In considering Negative as a horizon another important set of facts cannot be overlooked. This is its intensity and diversification in its northern hearth. As a horizon marker on the coast, Negative appears as rather simple two-color painting; but in the Callejón de Huaylas, Negative is found as an elaborate three-color ware as well. Sequences within the Recuay style have not yet been worked out, but there is a distinct possibility that an early two-color and a later three-color Recuay will eventually be demonstrated. A tendency for Negative to survive later than its horizon position is certainly implied in Bennett's finding of the negative technique in the Wilkawain-Tiahuanaco period.[13]

Like White-on-Red, Negative lacks comparable specific qualities of style that define the Chavín horizon. Instead, it too appears to be a diffusion of a technical idea combined, perhaps, with a few simple modes of design and vessel form. Its cultural milieu resembles that of the White-on-Red horizon in that technological expansion was still an important force in Peruvian society and new ideas of this order were actively accepted by the various local regions. It is quite possible that the negative-painting process was a part of a technical complex along with the "lost-wax" casting of metals. On the north coast it is noted that casting, gilding, and soldering in gold and copper became popular at this time.

THE TIAHUANACO HORIZON

Following the Negative horizon there is a long period marked by the absence of any pan-Andean horizonal phenomena. This period coincides, for the most part, with the second major era in Peru-Bolivian culture development, the Regional Classic stage. Although lacking in horizons, the form and content of the Regional Classic have an extremely important bearing upon interpreting the horizonal influences that follow it.

One of the most important characteristics of the Regional Classic is that its component societies were rapidly reaching the limits of their economic potentialities as these are set by subsistence technology and environment. As a result of this, population was attaining maximum bounds. This trend is particularly marked in the rich valleys of the north coast. Community size increased over the Formative stage and large-scale public works, such as the building of the great pyramids, suggest population density. The coordination and direction of the great amount of human energy that went into the construction of the mammoth temple centers of the Mochica and Early Lima periods certainly had at its base effective adminsitrative and social controls. Such controls may have, in part, grown out of the necessity for socially integrated action in the planning and maintaining of the irrigation systems that were begun in the Formative; but they must also have had some foundation in the need for governing the masses of people living in close association in the coastal valleys. In turn, all of these factors—population growth, maximum land utilization, and centralized social and political control—provided the elements for a stratified society, national states, and conquest patterns. It is not likely that the replacement of the priest-controlled society by the war-state was marked by an actual schism. The pyramid and temple center, symbols of authority in the old system, were retained, enlarged, and glorified. The transfer from sacred to secular was probably accomplished by a gradual shifting in the nature of the powers exercised by public leaders.

The Regional Classic is also, as the name implies, the stage of the culmination of the several art styles which had diversified out of the less specialized artistic and technological foundations of the Formative. These styles are strictly regionalized or national in scope and they are markedly divergent from one another. The absence of horizon styles is consistent with the structure and content of the cultures of the Classic stage. It was an era of realization in terms of techniques already known, not a time of the ready borrowing of new ideas. The local styles were in no sense experimental but crystallized symbols of the national consciousness. With regional political and social control in the hands of ruling castes it is not at all surprising that foreign art symbolism, as it might represent a threat to the status quo, was unpopular. Rather, it would have been to the advantage of the leaders to maintain a strong nationalism with its attendant isolationism. Thus, in spite of the fact that many practical conditions were more favorable to intercommunication among the various sections of Peru-Bolivia during the Regional Classic than ever before, such intercourse seems to have been kept at a minimum.

The Tiahuanaco horizon influences, appearing suddenly, terminate this intense regionalism and mark the beginning of the Expansionistic stage. The Tiahuanaco or Tiahuanacoid is a definite stylistic entity. The central theme is an anthropomorphized demon figure quite often bearing a spear-thrower. In general, there is more variation and less unity in the expressions of Tiahuanaco art than in that of the Chavín horizon. The designs are found not only in ceramics and stone sculpture but in virtually every handicraft practiced by the Peruvians. Tiahuanaco is the most pervasive of all the horizons in its modification or replacement of the arts of the cultures with which it came in contact. The horizon takes its name from the famous ceremonial center on Lake Titicaca, and it is possible that the concepts behind the style originated here. Its spread as a horizon, however, seems more likely to have been from a hearth somewhere in the vicinity of Ayacucho.

Unlike the elements underlying the earlier horizons, the background of the Tiahuanaco diffusion, as it is seen in the closing phases of the Regional Classic stage, was one of social and political tension. The forces leading to the formation of nationalism and the war-state began to seek their fulfillment in expansion and conquest. Toward the end of the Mochica period on the north coast that civilization extended its influence, undoubtedly by force of arms, as far south as the Santa Valley, superimposing its authority over the neighboring Gallinazo culture. At about the same time, the social forces behind what we have called the Tiahuanaco horizon were beginning to make themselves felt on the south and, perhaps, the central coasts. The impact of the two, Mochica and Tiahuanaco, must have produced a violent shock reaction. For a considerable period, the highly specialized Mochica art style is utterly obliterated, at least in the Santa-Chicama sector of the coast. Previous to the Tiahuanaco influx the national character of Mochica art was outstanding. Victorious warriors, defeated captives, and imposing dignitaries were favorite subjects. After the advent of Tiahuanaco in the north, many of the old traditions in ceramics, such as plastic treatment and monochrome or bichrome painting, still persisted, indicating some degree of continuity on a craft level; but continuity on a higher conceptual level was clearly broken. It is difficult to interpret the sudden submergence of the art symbolism of an expanding war-state in any other way except that the state and its symbolism fell before a similar and more powerful aggressor. The social and political atmosphere of the late Regional Classic was not one that would have been conducive to peaceful religious conversion. The Tiahuanaco invasion of the north coast looks like a military conquest.

In other regions, the permeation of the arts with Tiahuanaco concepts was a more gradual process. This is most true of the south coast where Nazca Y and Pacheco styles seem to be reacting to a powerful influence by combining old local with new foreign elements. This is somewhat less true of the central coast and the north highlands where the break is sharper than in the south but not as sharp as was the case with the Mochica. It may be that the social processes involved in the Tiahuanaco introduction on the south coast were less violent. There are certainly strong hints that the south coast lagged behind the north in the development of political nationalism. If the social and political patterns described for the Formative were still more or less in continuance in the south by Tiahuanaco times, it is to be expected that the southern attitudes of resistance toward a strong, organized military power would have been quite different than those of the Mochica.

As to whether or not the Tiahuanaco horizon represents a centrally organized empire attempt, on the order of the Inca, is difficult of appraisal. I see no real reason why this could not have been possible. Empire techniques were certainly in process of formulation and economic and prestige drives were not lacking. On the other hand, it is also a possibility that such conquests as that of the Mochica were relatively local affairs. With widespread social unrest, a revolutionary religious ideology might very well have been the catalytic agent through which several politically unrelated conquests were realized. Also, although the trend of the times was away from theocratic control, this in no way means that religion did not serve as the sanction through which force politics were manipulated. The essential point about the Tiahuanaco horizon is that it moved in a social milieu of crisis and unrest; and military power, or the threat of such power, was its mainspring.

THE INCA HORIZON

The Tiahuanaco horizon ushered in the final stage of Peru-Bolivian culture development, the Expansionistic. There are no major technological changes between this stage and the preceding one. Populations of the Expansionistic stage must have remained fairly near the level set in the Regional Classic; if there was an overall increase for the pan-Peruvian area it was nowhere near proportional to the increase between the Formative and Regional Classic stages. Significant differences do appear in community type and size, however. For the first time, great compound sites, composed of hundreds or even thousands of conjoined rooms, appear. The largest of these are on the north and central coasts, although they also occur in other parts of the area. While these great compound sites contain palaces and small temple pyramids, their very great size, plus the fact that site clusters seem to be fewer in number than previously, make it highly probable that the compounds were also actual urban concentrations. Although it is sometimes difficult to distinguish between sacred and secular architecture, the trend of the stage is one of diverting energies away from the construction of great temple pyramids toward the building of palaces and administrative centers.

The classic regionalized art styles of the previous stage did not revive after the breakdown resulting from the Tiahuanaco horizonal influences. The arts and crafts of the Expansionistic stage reflect a leveling process, and although regional styles eventually emerged after the force of the Tiahuanaco wave spent itself, none of these late, post-Tiahuanaco styles comes up to the old Regional Classic standards. Emphasis appears to be on quantitative rather than qualitative production and there is neither the experimental strength of the Formative nor the aesthetic excellence of such styles as Mochica or Nazca. New unities arise which, though not pan-Peruvian in scope, are generally of greater extent than the Regional Classic states and styles. The north coast is dominated by the Chimu styles; the central coast by those of Chancay and Sub-Chancay; the south coast by Ica and Chincha; and the north highlands by Late Huamachuco. The growth and spread of these late styles can undoubtedly be correlated with the various kingdoms of which we have some record in the Inca chronicles.

The trend toward political incorporation and statecraft culminates in the final pan-Andean horizon, the empire of the Inca. The story of their expansion from a small state centering in their homeland in Cuzco to a great empire is a matter of historical record. Although the dominion was established from Ecuador to Chile, the Inca horizon had a much less profound effect upon local styles, as revealed by archaeology, than did the Tiahuanaco. In many regions which we know the Inca held, Inca artifacts and ceramics occur only as minor items of trade, or Incaic strains are barely evident in locally manufactured products. This lack of intensity in the Inca horizon, as it can be measured in material evidence, is, perhaps, due in part to the brevity of the occupation. The Inca wars of conquest began relatively late in the Andean time scale, roughly at about 1438 A.D.[14] The empire was less than 100 years old when the Spaniards arrived at Cajamarca. Many regions, such as the north coast, had been under Inca sway for much less time than that. But there may have been other reasons for the relative lightness of the Inca unification as far as it was reflected in local manufactures. It is very interesting that the Inca horizon manifests itself in no one central theme or representational device such as the feline motif of Chavín or the man-demon of Tiahuanaco. Mostly, Incaic influence is seen in a few geometric or naturalistic pottery painting designs, a choice of colors, and a few vessel forms. As a horizon style it is intrinsically lacking in idea content comparable to that of Chavín or Tiahuanaco; nor is it primarily concerned with new technical concepts such as White-on-Red or Negative. In its total art impress it tends to be ornamental and trivial rather than emblematic and compelling.

The explanation of this may lie in the changes in patterns that were taking place throughout the Expansionistic stage. In the last phases of the Regional Classic stage, cultural values and goals, although for practical purposes formulated by the military castes, were still laid down in terms of sacred principles and sanctified by religious symbolism. The first great conquests, those of the Tiahuanaco horizon, were accompanied by important religious symbols. In the ensuing centuries, as the cultural values moved still further away from a religious bias, such representations became less and less important. It is a fact that the art of the late post-Tiahuanaco kingdoms is decidedly empty of anything that could be easily construed as sacred themes. Chimu plastic art has few such concepts; Chancay and Ica-Chincha art are almost wholly decorative and geometric. Thus, in their conquest, the Inca were no longer in need of a rich imperial symbolism. Military campaigns and political intrigue were taken as a matter of course by the Peru-Bolivians of this period. Arts and crafts continue in their old traditions with little change. Rather than attempting to destroy regional art and symbolism the Inca went so far as to import Chimu craftsmen to Cuzco for the purpose of manufacturing the distinctive coastal styles which the conquerors apparently considered aesthetically pleasing. Even further, we know it was Inca policy to be extremely tolerant of local religions. This suggests that they had little fear of local religion and local religious symbolism as dangerous incentives to revolt.

SUMMARY

Of the five "horizon styles" of Peru-Bolivian archaeology, three seem to have the ingredients of true styles, being identifiable in terms of specific designs and design combinations. These are the Chavín, the Tiahuanaco, and the Inca. The other two, the White-on-Red and the Negative, are diffusions of technical processes rather than styles.

The three earliest, the Chavín, the White-on-Red, and the Negative horizons, are, for the most part, phenomena of the first major stage of Peruvian culture development, the Formative. The Formative stage saw Peruvian societies grow from small population groups with the beginnings of sedentary-horticultural life to rising kingdoms with a full technology of the American agricultural civilizations. Analyzing Chavín, White-on-Red, and Negative as products of such a cultural background, as well as from the point of view of their own intrinsic qualities, it is concluded that the Chavín horizon was primarily a cult diffusion while the White-on-Red and Negative horizons represent disseminations of technical ideas. All three were motivated by peaceful considerations in an era highly receptive to new ideas and characterized by simple sociopolitical structures.

The last two horizons, the Tiahuanaco and the Inca, are phenomena of the last major stage of Peruvian culture development, the Expansionistic. The intervening or middle stage of development, the Regional Classic, lacked any horizonal diffusions. The societies of the Regional Classic were more populous than those of the Formative and were complicated and crystallized in structure. Social stratification was marked and a rising military and administrative caste was replacing the earlier theocratic leadership. Art styles seem to reflect this regional-national crystallization. Aesthetic excellence and specialization were the rule. The stage was not conducive to new technological and religious ideas. In view of this cultural rigidity of the Regional Classic periods, the shock-effect of the Tiahuanaco horizon is not surprising. Its sudden, obliterative quality, particularly in northern Peru, seems explicable only as a movement carried along by force in a period of social tension. Whether the movement was centrally directed as an empire, or whether it proceeded as a series of functionally related but politically independent conquests is beyond speculative analysis. The art symbolism of Tiahuanaco is the most intense in its interpenetration or replacement of local styles of any of the horizons. Intrinsically, it appears to have religious content but its motivations as a horizon must have been militaristic. The Inca horizon is definitely correlated with the conquest career of the Inca state. From region to region its intensity is much less profound than that of the Tiahuanaco horizon, and it is lacking in strong religious symbolism. Its faint quality may be explained by two factors. One is the brevity (less than 100 years) of its duration. The other is the lack of necessity for an awesome religious symbolism as a mechanism of cementing conquest in the late Expansionistic stage.

Notes

[1]Although not referring specifically to the idea of horizon styles, Uhle, throughout most of his Peruvian work (1903, 1906, 1910, 1913a, 1913b) viewed his data in such a scheme. Similarly, Kroeber (1925b, 1927) synthesized Peruvian archaeology in this fashion before defining horizon styles in detail (Kroeber, 1944, pp. 108–11). See also Bennett (1943) and Willey (1945).

[2]John W. Bennett (1944) outlines a similar methodology in connection with the problem of Middle American–Southeastern United States prehistoric relationships. Bennett evaluated the structure or type of both Middle American and Southeastern cultures in endeavoring to show what particular cultural media, or what culture period, in the Southeast would have been most receptive to Middle American ideas and traits.

[3]These stages differ in detail from those put forward at the 1946 Chiclín conference (see Willey, 1946a, pp. 133–4) and by Strong (1947, p. 6). The general objective, however, seems to be the same: to conceptualize the cultural growth of the Peru-Bolivian area into successive stages of development in order to accentuate the major changes in cultural structure and direction.

[4]See Hay and others, 1940, p. 488; Strong, 1943; Willey, 1943a, p. 196; Willey, 1950; Kroeber, 1944, p. 113; Bennett, 1946a, p. 80.

[5]Tello, 1923, 1929; Bennett, 1943; Kroeber, 1944, pp. 81–93.

[6]Tello, 1943.

[7]Willey, 1945.

[8]Larco, 1944.

[9]Bennett, 1944a.

[10]Rowe, 1944, pp. 17–18.

[11]Kroeber, 1944, pp. 108–10.

[12]Strong, 1947.

[13]Benentt, 1944a, p. 106.

[14]Rowe, 1945.

16

The Chavín Problem: A Review and Critique

(From Southwestern Journal of Anthropology, Vol. 7, No. 2, pp. 103–144, 1951. Reprinted by permission of the *Journal of Anthropological Research* and the Department of Anthropology, University of New Mexico.)

Introduction

In Peruvian archaeology the term *Chavín*, derived from the site of Chavín de Huántar, has come to stand not for a single, easily definable concept but for a series of concepts. It has been used to denote an art style, an archaeological period, a "horizon," a "culture," a "basic or root culture," a "civilization," and an "empire." As there is divergence of opinion on what is meant by Chavín, on its stylistic identifications, on chronology and distribution, on associated cultural contexts, and on functional interpretation, it seems desirable at this time to examine just what has been or can be subsumed under the Chavín designation. This essay takes as its purpose such a review and critical appraisal of the problem.*

Development of the Chavín Concepts

J. C. Tello. The late Dr. Julio C. Tello was the foremost proponent of Chavín as a civilization basic to Andean development.[1] Middendorf[2] may have been the first to conceive of a widespread Chavín culture and pre-Incaic empire, but the elaboration of the theme was Tello's.

In Tello's earlier writings[3] he placed Classic Chavín, as it was known from the stone monuments of Chavín de Huántar and from the Cupisnique pottery of the coast, as a culture of the "Second Epoch." At that time Tello's "First Epoch" cultures were "Archaic Andean" (represented by Aija stone sculpture and three-color negative painting

*I am indebted to Drs. Donald Collier and Wendell C. Bennett for numerous suggestions and points of fact. Dr. Irving Rouse and Mr. Michael Coe also gave me the benefit of their criticisms.

of the Callejón de Huaylas) and "Pre-Chavín" (undescribed). Somewhat later Tello[4] dropped the "Pre-Chavín" concept, but "Archaic North Andean" still remained as anterior to Classic Chavín. By "Archaic North Andean" it is clear that Tello referred to the three-colored negative painted ware (the Recuay style), not just the plain tripod vessels of the north highlands.[5] For example, a Recuay three-color modeled cat-head is specifically indicated as a crude or "embryonic" manifestation of the strain that was later to climax in Classic Chavín.[6] This same chronological system assigned Wari, Pucara, and "the first period of Tiahuanaco" as being on the same time level with "Archaic North Andean," while Chongoyape, Paracas, and the shell mounds of Ancon and Supe were equated with Classic Chavín.[7]

Origen y Desarrollo de Las Civilizaciones Prehistoricas Andinas and *Discovery of the Chavín Culture in Peru* show an important change in Tello's chronological thinking. Recuay and Aija are now shifted to a later position on the time chart, and Classic Chavín is given precedence as the earliest of north Peruvian cultures.[8] This revision was probably the result of Tello's Nepeña Valley excavations.[9] There he found what he considered as Chavín, or Chavín-related, materials in the lowest archaeological levels. In referring to these discoveries, he states: "These considerations . . . made equally essential the intensive exploration of the watersheds of the Cordillera Negra and the Callejón de Huaylas; for . . . the remains of Chavín culture must lie beneath strata corresponding to the cultures that had so far appeared there to be the predominant and oldest ones."[10] Some lingering doubt may have remained about Recuay, for in his concluding summary to the 1943 article, although he drives home the uniqueness and chronological primacy of the "Chavín civilization" with: "Remains of the Chavín civilizations are found everywhere buried under later remains as different in type as if they were completely unrelated," he adds the qualification: "Yet certain facts given below lead to the presumption that a stage of transition once existed between the Chavín and the Recuay-Pasto civilizations. In some aspects they seem to prove that the latter is derived from the former, or that, having had different origins, they for some time were contemporaneous and intermingled."[11]

Tello's opinions on the origins and diffusions of Chavín go back to his first chronological-developmental chart,[12] in which he indicated fundamental influences coming into the Peruvian highlands from the Amazonian forest zone. *Wira-Kocha*, which is primarily a tracing out of the religious theme in Andean culture, using ethnographic and traditional sources as well as the archaeological iconography, leans heavily on the theme of ancient ties with and inspirations from the tropical forest peoples to the east. Specifically, Tello saw these influences in the archaeology of the east Andean slopes and adjoining lowlands. Pottery of Kotosh, near Huanuco, he considered as related to both the Amazon lowlands and Chavín; styles of the Río Ahuaimo (tributary to the Ucayalí) and pottery from the Napo-Aguarico region had, in his words: "intimate connection on the one side with Marajó pottery and on the other with Chavín pottery and with certain archaic forms of Recuay pottery."[13]

Tello's extension of the geographical range of Chavín does not always carry with it an explicit statement as to the directions in which these Chavín influences moved. As far as the Amazon is concerned, it is likely that he thought of such a distant style as Marajó as springing from the same common source as Peruvian Chavín rather than as being the parent of it.[14] Other remote cultures and styles in which he saw Chavín similarities, such as Uhle's "Mayoid" sites of Ecuador,[15] Paracas, Pucara, and the Barreales of Argentina,[16] were probably considered as peripheral to the Chavín center in the north Peruvian highlands.

And with its extension in space, Tello also felt that Chavín influence had great time persistence. For example: "The better developed cultures of the north have received in all times the influence of Chavín: the best examples of Chimu ceramics, including with this name the Tallanes (Late Chimu) and the Mochicas (Early Chimu), retain with all definitiveness the distinctive characteristics of that art."[17] From this it is not clear if Tello believed that the north coast was subject to a constant flow of Chavín influences ranging over several culture periods, or if he conceived of this influence as having been implanted in the north coast continuum at an early time so that the later periods there show Chavín influence only indirectly. It is likely that he visualized the former. Tello returned constantly to the metaphor of the tree, to a distinctly organic concept of cultures, as Strong[18] has pointed out. One of his most important theoretical statements, the one which best sets forth this "organicism," is quoted in full:

> Two problems present themselves when we try to inquire about the age of cultures: the first refers to the age of each one individually; and the second, to the age in conjunction with a regional belt or zone. Each culture may be imagined to be a tree which in its development has passed through different stages and has put forth branches in tiers from the roots up to the top of the foliage. When one deals with the age of a culture one must take into account the age of the trunk or the stem as estimated by the branches put forth at the different stages of its development; and in so far as the age of a cultural whole is concerned one would have to inquire if the cultures have been coeval in their beginnings or roots, whether they appear at different periods or whether they are mixed and fused together, or over and under the branches of neighboring cultures. Up to the point investigation has reached in the Andean territory the cultures are multiple and probably very old in their majority. although in many cases their remains appear superimposed, this does not necessarily mean a continuous or uninterrupted succession of cultural stems, but mere superpositions of branches derived from them which may or may not have been coeval in their origin. Young branches from old stems may be found superimposed on branches from relatively young trunks in a chronological position contrary to the true position and age of the mother cultures.[19]

From the standpoint of functional interpretations, Tello has not fully expressed, at least in print, just what he intended by the terms "Chavín culture," or "Chavín civilization." In his last important work he seems to have regarded Chavín, at least as found in the Nepeña Valley of the coast, to be a civilization brought down from the Andes by a migration of people. "The Nepeña discovery definitely cleared up the true character of the Chavín culture on the coast. In the first place, it was now proved that this culture was rich in representative material, that it was unmistakable in its distinctive features, and identical to the trans-Andine culture in its essential characteristics. . . . The Chavín people developed on virgin soil in the Nepeña Valley a civilization."[20] Tello's successor, Dra Rebecca Carrión Cachot, has enlarged upon this, employing the term "Chavín empire."[21] This was, as she states, a religious and not a political empire. It was, however, a civilization homogeneous in its arts, rites, religion, race, and probably language.

R. Larco Hoyle. In 1933 Larco Hoyle found Chavín-like polished black incised and relief decorated pottery in the Cupisnique quebrada of the Chicama Valley. Larco sees stylistic resemblances linking this Cupisnique pottery, the Chavín de Huántar stone carvings, and the mud reliefs of the Nepeña Valley temples. Unlike Tello, he believes that the genius of this art style was coastal, not highland or Amazonian. Larco conceives of early coastal populations as constituting the base upon which was propagated the idea of a religious cult characterized by the feline symbolism. The center of this cult he would place in the Nepeña Valley. In brief, Tello's highland center of Chavín de Huántar is Larco's later colony, settled by migrants from the coastal valley of Nepeña.[22]

Larco approaches the distributions of Chavín, or Nepeña, more cautiously than Tello. He remarks on the similarities to Paracas[23] and Chongoyape,[24] but ranges no farther. Of the temple and stone carvings of Cerro Sechín, Casma Valley, he sees a developmental connection with Punkurí and Cerro Blanco of Nepeña; but he would place Cerro Sechín as the earliest of these developmental stages, apparently prior to the advent of the feline deity.[25] As I interpret his writings, he holds for an early and relatively compressed time horizon for the diffusion and development of this feline cult. Early Mochica would be his uppermost chronological limit. Certain idea continuities, such as the Cupisnique feline deity changing to a Mochica anthropomorphized cat-god, are a peripheral part of his theories; but these are not conceived of as further manifestations of the same "culture" or "civilization" as in the Tello approach.

Functionally, as stated, Larco interprets the Nepeña (or Chavín) style as the imprint of a religious movement which spread a complex art form among peoples of generally similar, but regionally varied, culture.

The North Americans. Most North American archaeologists in the Peruvian field have followed in the tradition of the German scholar, Max Uhle, particularly the Uhle scheme as it has been explained and enlarged by A. L. Kroeber.[26] The Uhle-Kroeber methodology is that of cross-dating regional culture sequences of Peru with stylistic time-markers or "horizon styles." The goal is to build a time-space framework of cultures as synchronously perfect as possible. The Incaic and Tiahuanaco styles were employed as horizons, but neither Uhle nor Kroeber utilized Chavín in this manner.[27] Similarly, Bennett[28] was doubtful of the early position assigned to Coast Chavín or Cupisnique by both Larco Hoyle and Tello. Later, Bennett's own work at Chavín de Huántar,[29] and Larco's publication of grave stratigraphy from the north coast,[30] brought him to a reconsideration of the Chavín chronological problem. In a paper which Bennett published in 1943, he put forward Chavín as a pan-Peruvian horizon, marking the bottom-most known level of Peruvian sequences.[31] He saw the Chavín influences of this horizon ranging from Piura to Paracas on the coast and from Chavín de Huántar to Pucara in the highlands.[32]

Following this, the acceptance of the early chronological position of Chavín was general among the North Americans.[33] Several archaeological monographs on Peru resulting from the Institute of Andean Research program of 1941–42 explicitly or implicitly express this important reformulation,[34] and the papers of the symposium, *A Reappraisal of Peruvian Archaeology*,[35] take it as almost axiomatic. Thus, in a sense, the Tello and Larco concept of Chavín-influenced cultures as early and basic to Peruvian civilization dominated the field by 1948.

There are, however, significant differences. As far as can be determined by their writings, most North American students prefer a middle course on the question of Chavín origins, maintaining a "wait and see" policy on the highland (Tello) versus coastal (Larco) theories.[36] Nor have they expressed a definite opinion on the mechanism of the Chavín spread (migration, trade, diffusion, etc.). Notes of limiting criticism on the Chavín horizon have been sounded by Willey and Rowe,[37] both authors being unconvinced of the value of a south coast or south highland extension of the horizon. In a similar vein, Collier denies Tello's extension of the Chavín style to ceramics in Ecuador.[38]

North American opinion on the functional significance of the widespread Chavín style manifestations is closer to that of Larco than to that of Tello. There is a hesitancy in calling it a "culture" or a "civilization." Willey and Bennett[39] have both made the inferences that Peruvian society of the Chavín period was organized upon a limited local

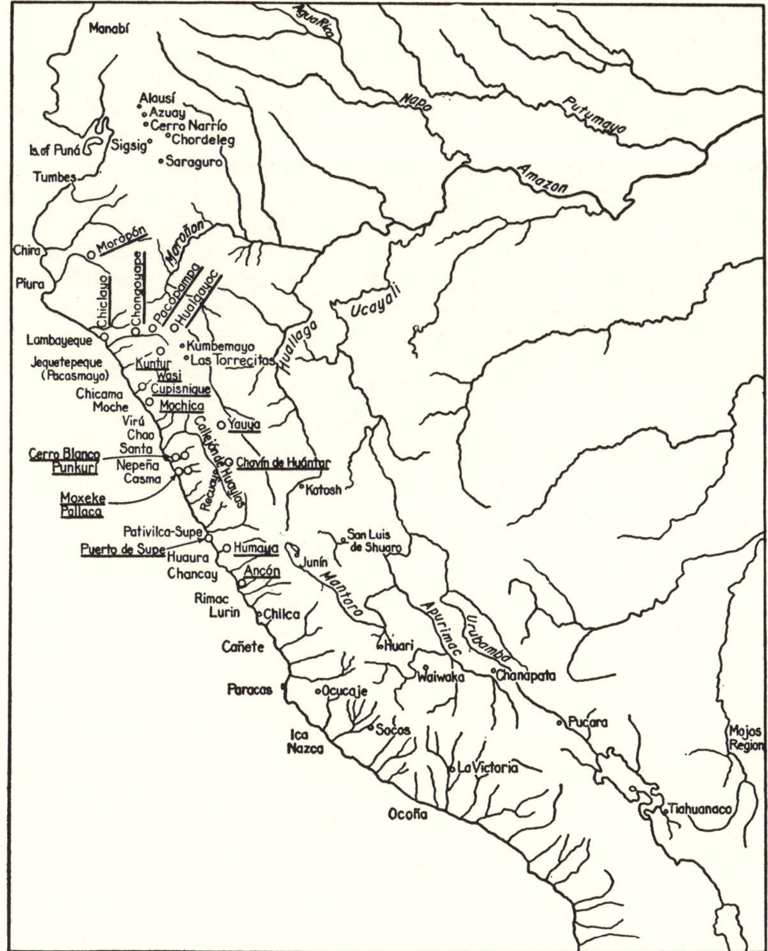

Figure 16.1. Map of central Andes and adjacent lowlands showing location of sites mentioned in the text. The names of sites or regions where indisputable evidence of the Chavín art style has been reported are underlined.

basis, that there was no widespread political unity, and that Chavín art was a part of the symbolic system of a religious cult that diffused from region to region.

CHAVÍN AS A HORIZON STYLE

For this discussion Chavín style is defined as being identical to, or closely resembling, the designs of the stone carvings of Chavín de Huántar. (Figure 16.1)[40] A style, for purposes of analysis, may be broken down into three component aspects: technology, representation, and configuration. Technology refers to materials (stone, wood, etc.) and techniques (carving, incising, etc.). Representation is the subject matter or content of style. It may be inspired by the artist's observations of nature (animals, men, etc.) or develop from his imagination (demons, composite beings, geometrical abstractions). Configuration is the manner in which the representations are expressed. Technological and representational features may be duplicated in many styles; but the configuration is the unique pattern that is not repeated outside the limits of a specific style. The technology of Chavín style at Chavín de Huántar is largely flat carving in stone, but the combination of this technique and this material is known in many other Peruvian styles. Representationally, felines, humans, birds, serpents, and fantastic composites of these characterize Chavín, yet all are depicted outside of Chavín. As opposed to this, Chavín art is uniquely distinguished in its configuration by the way its subjects are conceived and portrayed. This is a matter of line, of composition, of emphasis. It is the curvilinear forms, the massive heads, the intricately disposed small heads, the locked and curved fangs, the claw feet, the prominent nostrils, and the eccentric eyes. It is all of these and it is more; it is these elements and motives in their special system. Such is the essence of the Chavín style. It belongs to no other.

The historical uniqueness of stylistic pattern is the fundamental assumption underlying the concept of the "horizon style."[41] As the result of this uniqueness, the presence of any style in two or more places has a high synchronic value. Like any cultural form or pattern, the Chavín style is a part of a continuum. It probably has prototypes and certainly has descendants; yet these, though perhaps bearing technological and representational similarity to Chavín, are themselves distinct configurations. If we are interested in the Chavín style as a coefficient of time, it is its peculiar configurative aspect that we must concentrate upon. Its origins and continuities are legitimate and interesting inquiries, but they may be most effectively treated as separate problems.

Thus, in this analysis of Chavín as a horizon style, I propose to consider only those manifestations which qualify from the configurational point of view. Each stylistic manifestation will be described briefly and placed in its immediate cultural context. We will then plot the geographical and chronological positions of these evidences of Chavín style to determine the case for Chavín as a synchronous horizon.

Chavín de Huántar. This site is on a tributary of the Marañon River in the north highlands of Peru. As the type station for the Chavín style, it is our "typological standard" for comparison.

The Chavín stylistic manifestations are human heads of stone carved in the round with tenons for wall insertion and flat incision-champlevé carved lintels, cornice slabs, and monoliths. The style is primarily curvilinear, although containing some rectilinear elements. The feline design is almost universal in the flat carvings. Certain portions of the feline, such as eyes and teeth, are emphasized. Sometimes the feline head is adorned with the bill and wings of a condor, a snake body, or fish tail and fins. Eyes are frequently portrayed with an eccentric pupil; the great fanged teeth are interlocked; the snout is broad (front view) or blunt (profile); from the head and back of the animal are scroll-like appendanges or serpent heads; and the feet are heavy and claw-like.[42]

The site itself is obviously a great ceremonial center. Stone-faced buildings of a platform mound type are arranged around a rectangular sunken court. The platform mounds have interior galleries, and rooms are on two or three levels connected by ramps or stairways. The facings of the walls, made of dressed stone blocks, alternate bands of thick and thin stones.[43]

The ceramics associated with these sculptures and buildings are monochromes of black, red, or brown and include open flat-bottomed bowls, pucos, subglobular bowls, globular bowls with flared rims, constricted collar jars, and simple spout jars. The stirrup-spout form is also represented.[44] Decorative techniques are fine and broad-line incision, dentate or rocker-stamping, punctation or gouging, color zoning, strip applique, fingernail impressions, and low relief modeling. Designs are circles-and-dots, triangles, diamonds, rectangles, criss-crosses, loops, volutes, and segments of stylized life forms unrecognizable in sherd fragments.[45] Stylistically verifiable Chavín designs also obtain, but, apparently, are rather rare. Tello[46] illustrates a bottle with a flowing line feline head, highly stylized; Bennett,[47] a more realistic anthropomorphic feline face sherd with characteristic interlocked fangs; and Carrión,[48] stylized feline heads.

Artifacts other than ceramics are not reported except for a few pieces of carved bone inlaid with turquoise and shell.[49]

There remain the remarkable Brummer or Bliss-Simkhovitch collections of gold artifacts.[50] These objects were at one time in the possession of a private collector in Trujillo, Peru, and were purported to have come from the site of Chavín de Huántar. Among the specimens are gorgets, ear discs, nose pendants, tweezers, spoons, and beads. They are decorated with embossed, incised, and champlevé designs, many of which are fully in the style of the stone carvings of Chavín de Huántar.[51] Metallurgical techniques are similar to those of the Chongoyape gold pieces. As no other comparable gold of which there is record has ever been discovered at Chavín de Huántar, the associations of this material with the site are open to serious doubt. The only other collection which resembles the Bliss-Simkhovitch lot comes from Chongoyape in the Lambayeque Valley of the north coast. There is no doubt as to the Chavín style affiliation and the collection is an important addition to our artistic and technological knowledge of the period; but it cannot, in view of inadequate field data, be fully incorporated as a part of the Chavín de Huántar site.

Yauya. This site, in the Marañon drainage north of Chavín de Huántar, is represented solely by a carved stela or column,[52] no longer *in situ*. It is a standing figure of a monster, perhaps a fish or a fish with feline attributes. Kroeber compares it to the Raimondi stela of Chavín de Huántar, "in shape of total outline, complete filling of the field, erect posture, complete bilateral symmetry, and a certain formal stiffness."[53] As is well known, the Raimondi stela stands somewhat apart from other Chavín carvings in style, but is, nevertheless, linked to them. This solitary find seems to me to be justifiably incorporated within the Chavín style.

Pacopampa. From Pacopampa, in the northwest highlands, comes a series of carved stone mortars and pestles. All of these are four-legged animals with the bowl or mortar basin in the back. Two have characteristic Chavín feline faces, and two of the pestles are similarly carved; the other mortar is a felinized owl with owl's beak but jaguar teeth. The stylistic relationship to the Chavín de Huántar carvings is close or identical. There is also a carved stone slab, "the feline of Pacopampa,"[54] which has some resemblances to Chavín standing, front-view anthropomorphized figures.

Hualgayoc. Tello has referred to "megalithic mausoleums" at Yanacancha in the Province of Hualgayoc. Previously he had described these as stone boxes cut in bedrock with slab covers.[55] Apparently there is also a carved stone column or monolith at Yanacancha[56] which represents an anthropomorphic figure, but the style is not Chavín.

There is, however, a drawing of a small stone vessel from "Lives Farm, San

Gregorio district, Province of Hualgayoc"[57] which is carved in the Chavín art style. Two serpent head appendages, identical with those on the carvings at Chavín de Huántar, are a part of the design motif.

Kuntur Wasi. This ruin is situated on a hilltop in the upper Jequetepeque drainage, just over the divide from the Marañón system.[58] It is a triple-terraced pyramid which was surmounted by temple rooms or buildings, now destroyed. Pyramid facings are of irregular stones. Stone statues, heads, carved slabs, and lintels were found on the temple platforms or on the hill slope below. As Carrión has indicated, these carvings bear varying degrees of similarity to the sculptures of Chavín de Huántar. A flat carving[59] is a front view of a felinized condor (?) with tusk-like teeth, wide-spaced nostrils and eyes, and three pendant serpent heads. A head, sculptured in the round in the manner of some of the tenon heads from Chavín de Huántar, has the furrowed face and forehead, the curved fangs, and other typical Chavín details.[60] Both of these pieces strike one as dead-center on the Chavín style. The other carvings display significant differences. They are columnar statues or stone pillars carved in low relief fashion, as is the mode for Pucara, Aija, Tiahuanaco, or San Agustín of Colombia. Stylistically, they have more of a generalized resemblance to these than they do to Chavín. One such column has a representation on both sides.[61] The obverse carving has a head and face reminiscent of Chavín in its furrows and scrolled head treatment, and the claw-like feet of the anthropomorphized monster are also rendered in a Chavín manner. But the small head held in the monster's two hands, over his chest, is not a Chavín style feature. The reverse side of the column is a humanized serpent with nostrils and a mouth only vaguely Chavín. Another statue, a monkey (?) with prominent ribs, has only the jaguar fangs in common with Chavín.[62]

Pottery was found on the slopes below the temple, probably as a result of refuse, although graves were also discovered in the same area. Apparently, both the grave pottery and the surface fragments comprise the same series of types. The ware quality is not described, but as Carrión defines it as "classic Chavín" there is reason to believe that it is monochrome of red or of dark colors. In nearby sites, this "classic Chavín" pottery of Kuntur Wasi is said to underlie "sub-Chavín" types which are described as cream-colored with brown decoration.[63] Kuntur Wasi pottery includes: open flat-bottomed bowls, subglobular bowls, constricted collar jars, globular bowls with angular or flared collars, simple spouted jars, and stirrup-mouthed jars with heavy everted lips. Aside from these forms, there are low pedestal bases and kero-shaped cups. Decoration, as far as can be determined, is by incision, punctation, pellet and strip applique, and low and full-round relief modeling. Designs are circles-and-dots, rectangles, triangles, diamonds, volutes, star elements, stylized life forms of undetermined nature, and modeled naturalistic life forms. From the illustrations offered, Chavín style feline, owl, condor, or serpent motives are missing. A possible exception is an incised (?) design on a stirrup-mouthed jar.[64] The modeled naturalistic life forms are abundant, but they are stylistically apart from Chavín.

In addition to pottery, Kuntur Wasi graves contained turquoise and bone beads and hammered gold ornaments with simple repoussé decorations.[65]

Moropón. This is a single pottery vessel from the Piura Valley of the far north coast.[66] It is a tall, stirrup-mouthed jar with the characteristic Cupisnique or Chavín thick, everted lip. It is decorated with a broad and fine-line (engraving?) incision, dentate rocker-stamping, relief modeling, and color zoning. The modeling may represent a plant or fruit. Around the base is a repetitive stylization of a Chavín life form.

Chongoyape. The Chongoyape finds consist of two lots of material from the vicinity of that small town in Lambayeque Valley. Both were discovered as the result of nonarchaeological digging. The best documented lot came from deep burials and it includes gold ornaments with Chavín feline heads, pottery, a stone bowl, ring, and spoon, a jet mirror, and cinnabar pigments.[67] The Chongoyape ceramics are monochrome black or red polished wares, of plate and stirrup-mouth forms, and are decorated with dentate or rocker-stamped techniques, and low relief and full round modeling. One vessel has a modeled animal at the juncture of stirrup-spout and body. The thick, Cupisnique-type lip eversion is seen on both of the stirrup-mouth specimens.[68] The other collection of Chongoyape Chavín-like finds consists entirely of gold specimens. These are three cylindrical crowns, a head band, tweezers, and ear spools. The crowns and some of the ear spools have embossed or repoussé decorations of indubitable Chavín style. One crown[69] has a cat or humanoid head in profile with large, crossed fangs, eccentric pupil eye, and attached serpents. Another crown[70] bears an anthropomorphic jaguar standing in front view, holding staffs or spears. On the chest of this being is another stylized jaguar face.

The metallurgical techniques of the Chongoyape objects include not only hammering and repoussé work but annealing and soldering or welding. A gold-headed pin had a silver shaft.[71]

Chiclayo. I am not certain to what finds or sites this designation refers. Possibly it is the Pickman Strombus shell from the air base at Chiclayo.[72] This shell bears an incised design of a man in a dancing or running position. The figure is blowing on a strombus shell trumpet. The outline of the man is bordered by an interlaced Chavín serpent design. The serpent head, with eccentric eye pupil, terminates the bordering design at the feet of the dancer. The man figure, itself, is not particularly in the Chavín style. Except, possibly, the feet, there are no feline or monstrous attributes. The face, seen in profile, is quite similar to the Sechín human figures.[73] The eye has a curved band extending down onto the cheek which is suggestive of, although it does not duplicate, Sechín portrayals. A flowing headdress, extending down over the back of the individual, is also like a similar headdress and sash from a Sechín carving. This specimen, more than any other, offers some sort of a stylistic link between Chavín and Cerro Sechín. Kroeber[74] has commented upon the Pickman Strombus and has also called attention to a small stone vase from the Chiclayo region[75] which offers a similar linkage. The Sechín features of this vase are a carved figure of a man in profile with a semicircular, eccentric eye and three lines curving downward across the side of the face. Unlike the Sechín men, this individual has a jaguar fang.

Cupisnique. This culture, found at several sites and centering in the Chicama Valley, is best known for its pottery of Chavín affiliations. Cupisnique pottery is essentially monochrome, often polished, and includes simple forms such as the open, flat-bottomed bowl, subglobular bowls, constricted collar jars, beakers, and simple spouted jars. The stirrup-spout vase is also common. Decoration is by broad and fine-line incision, engraving, rocker-stamping, punctation, hachure, brushing, color zoning, pellet applique, low relief modeling, and full round modeling. In general, modeling is more frequent and better executed than in the other culture groups we have reviewed. Larco states that there is evidence of the use of the mold in ceramic manufacture. Design includes circles-and-dots, rectilinear elements of various shapes, loops, volutes, scrolls, leaf or star-shaped figures, a number of modeled naturalistic life forms (animals, humans, houses, plants), and the stylized life forms of the Chavín style (feline, owl, condor, serpent, and combinations).

Carved and ground stone beads, amulets, rings, ear ornaments, receptacles, and small mortars may, upon occasion, bear Chavín designs. Similarly, carved bone objects may be so decorated.

The association of metals is somewhat dubious, but, if they can be related to Cupisnique, they are simple ornaments of cut and beaten gold. Textiles are of cotton or wool in plain weave.

Houses were small and single-roomed both above-ground and subterranean. The walls were made of stone or conical adobes. Larco Hoyle states that "solid circular and pyramidal constructions were initiated in this cultural period."[76] These were made of conical adobes.

Mochica. The Mochica culture is represented by numerous sites in Chicama, Moche, and adjacent north coast valleys. A small number of Mochica stirrup-mouthed jars bear stylistically authentic Chavín designs.[77] These are bold but intricate curvilinear band designs of the sort called "ribbon relief" by Larco Hoyle. In some of them the feline representation has been completely reduced; in others the eye and curved fang elements are deducible. Most of these vessels are decorated with a combination of low relief incision and red and white painting. Vessel shape, including the proportionately high body and the delicate stirrup without the lip eversion, is characteristic of other Mochica ceramics.

The cultural context in which these finds are made is well known, as Mochica is an outstanding culture of the Peruvian Classic stage.[78] It features modeled and mold-made red and white ceramics. Realistic plastic and painted decoration is typical, with stirrup-spout jar and "florero" as the dominant vessel forms. A highly developed metallurgy, a lack of emphasis in stone carving, and mammoth pyramids of rectangular mold-made adobes are distinctive traits.

Cerro Blanco. Cerro Blanco, in the coastal Nepeña Valley, is a temple structure, presumably of the general platform type.[79] Carrión[80] describes it as having the form of a gigantic bird in flight. According to Tello,[81] the original building had been made of stone, and then the walls were covered with mud reliefs which were painted in multi-colors. These painted reliefs[82] are in the form of Chavín-type eye and cross-fanged teeth elements. In the fill of this original building were black potsherds which are described as "Classic Chavín." The illustration[83] shows black polished and incised pieces similar to Chavín and Cupisnique ware, although the range of decoration types is rather limited and none bear Chavín feline or other zoomorphic stylizations. A second construction level at Cerro Blanco, built over the original unit, is characterized by conical adobes and smoothed plastered and painted walls. No ceramics were associated. The third level or uppermost covering of the site dates from late coastal periods.

Punkurí. This temple, in Nepeña, is described as having a lower level constructed of stone and decorated with mud reliefs and paint.[84] Its base was a platform of two terrace levels which are ascended by a wide stairway.[85] Midway in the stair was a painted feline head and paws made of stone and mud. At the feet of this feline figure was a burial accompanied by a carved stone mortar, a "handkerchief embroidered with turquoise sequins,"[86] and a strombus shell. There is no mention of pottery. The second building level walls were of conical adobes and bore incised designs on a plastered surface. A much later structure of rectangular adobes[87] and refuse overlay the whole.

The Punkurí jaguar head[88] is more realistically portrayed than is characteristic of Chavín felines, although this might be the result of the clay medium and the full-round rendering as opposed to the more usual flat carving. The stone mortar from the grave[89] has a rectilinear decoration that is not conclusively Chavín. Perhaps the best evidence for the Chavín art style is in the incised wall decorations on the conical adobe structure. Larco Hoyle[90] illustrates a section of these, although the designs are not distinct in the reproduction. However, he accompanies his wall illustration with another of a stirrup-mouthed jar (presumably Cupisnique of Chicama)[91] which, according to him, bears an incised decoration "similar to those found on the Temple of Punkurí." The designs on the vessel are definitely in the Chavín style.

Moxeke. In Casma Valley is Moxeke, a rectangular, terraced pyramid with rounded corners and higher platforms at the back of the summit. The structure is stone-faced, and it is known that the front upper platforms are made of conical adobes. The center facade is broken by a stairway. On each side of the stairway, six niches are set into the face of the third terrace. These niches contain partially destroyed adobe sculptures of a feline, a serpent, and a human torso. The sculptures had been painted in various colors, and the terrace walls between the niches were deeply incised with curvilinear designs painted white.[92]

No pottery is illustrated or described from Moxeke, but the mud and adobe reliefs in the terrace niches have a strong Chavín cast.

Pallca. Pallca, in Casma,[93] is another terraced and stone-faced pyramid with stone stairways. No conical adobes have been found, but on the summit platform are two small stepped pyramids of rectangular adobes. Collier believes these two upper pyramids to be later than the rest of the structure and to equate with late period Casma pottery found on the surface. Pottery found in excavations at the base of the main platform is polished, dark, monochrome ware. Some sherds were decorated with incision, punctation, rocker-stamping, and strip applique. Simple designs are noted,[94] and there are also stylized life forms, although none of these, as illustrated, are large enough to determine the complete nature of the representation. Their general appearance is, however, certainly that of Chavín ware; and a carved bone spatula[95] bears a thoroughly Chavín type felinized serpent head.

Humaya. Hacienda Humaya is in the Huaura Valley. All that I know concerning the site is that it produced a carved bone spoon or spatula and "Early Ancon Incised" pottery.[96] The spatula bears an anthropomorphized feline face in profile. The mouth and fang treatment is Chavín style. The eye has a series of four lines curving down across the face in the manner of Cerro Sechín. The pottery is not illustrated or described.

Puerto de Supe. There are five sites in the small desert hills on the coast near Puerto de Supe which concern us here. Uhle, Kroeber, Strong and Willey, and Willey and Corbett have described excavations and collections from these sites.[97] In this summation I draw principally upon the last and most detailed reference.

Near the beach, below the lighthouse (hence "Lighthouse Site"), there is a shell and refuse midden and, a short distance away, a cemetery. Inland, facing onto the valley from dry quebradas, are two middens, Aspero and Li-31. A cemetery area is near the Aspero midden and has been named the Aspero cemetery. All of these sites, except the Aspero midden, contain black or dark polished pottery with various kinds of incised, punctated, rocker-stamped, color-zoning, and related treatments. This ware occurs in simple forms and also in the stirrup-mouthed jar. Complete Chavín feline stylizations were not detected upon sherds, but several fragments suggested portions of such designs. There is little doubt that this Puerto de Supe ware—"Early Supe," as it has been called—is Coastal Chavín pottery.

There is a miscellany of small bone and wooden objects from the Supe sites, but outstanding is a little bone palette with an incised feline-crab design of Chavín style.[98] A carved gourd from the Lighthouse cemetery is, likewise, in the Chavín style. Twined and some twilled basketry came from Supe graves, as did mats and netting. Decorated and colored plain-weave cotton textiles were abundant at Supe, including a fine, tapestry-woven piece with Chavín condor-feline designs. Two small sheets of beaten gold also were obtained in the Supe cemeteries.

The Supe people practiced simple inhumation burial and were a short-statured group with antero-posterior flattened skulls. Dwellings were small houses with stone foundations. No pyramids or public structures could be identified with these Supe sites.

Ancón. This shell midden area and cemetery are on a range of hills overlooking the later Ancón Necropolis of the central coast. Uhle[99] excavated here; Strong[100] defined the pottery from the midden as "Early Ancón"; and Willey made still other midden excavations.[101] More recently, Carrión[102] discovered a cemetery culturally related to the midden and located a short distance from it.

Early Ancón pottery is very much like that of Early Supe. It is monochrome, red or black. Vessel forms are simple bowls, jars, and bottles, although occasional stirrup-spouts occur. Decoration is largely by incision and related plastic techniques. Stylized life form designs probably include Chavín felines, birds, and serpents, although these are difficult to determine from sherd fragments. There is a small amount of naturalistic modeling.[103]

Only a few ground stone artifacts (jet mirrors, pendants, a mace-head) were recovered from the Ancón midden, but mortars, pestles, and tripod plates came from the cemetery. Both woodcarving and bonecarving were well-developed crafts. A particularly fine bone spatula is carved in the style of a Chavín feline-serpent.[104] Basketry and cotton textiles came from the Ancón cemetery and midden, and spinning and weaving are further attested to by pottery spindle whorls. Carrión[105] illustrates a flat pottery stamp from the cemetery.

Burials were simple inhumations. Dwellings were probably like those of Early Supe. There are no evidences for pyramids or public buildings.

In the above we have described the art style of Chavín as it is manifested in seventeen sites or regions of Peru. Undoubtedly, there are other examples of Chavín art in the central Andes. Claims for some of these have been reported, and we will discuss them further on; but it is with these adequately documented occurrences that the case for the Chavín horizon style must be made at the present time.

The geographical distribution of these finds is in north and central Peru. On the coast, it is from Lambayeque, or possibly Piura, to Ancón. In the highlands, the extension is even shorter, reaching from Pacopampa to Chavín de Huántar.

The chronological position of the Chavín finds is derived from superposition or stratigraphy at Chavín de Huántar, from sites in the Chicama Valley, and at Ancón and

Supe. At Chavín de Huántar, Bennett[106] found graves of the White-on-red horizon intrusive into Chavín period refuse. In the Chicama sector Larco Hoyle[107] has produced grave superimposition showing Cupisnique to underlie Salinar (a north coast White-on-red period). On the central coast, at both Ancón and Puerto de Supe, midden excavations by Willey and Corbett[108] show White-on-red ceramic types appearing only in the upper levels of deep refuse deposits pertaining to the Early Ancón-Supe period. These data would indicate a uniform pre-White-on-red horizon position for Chavín style finds of both sierra and coast in north and central Peru. Superpositional data from Punkurí, Cerro Blanco, and Moxeke are not so specific as these, but from all three locations the Chavín style materials seem to be at the very bottom of local culture sequences. The weight of the evidence thus argues for the placement of the Chavín style horizon at the beginning of Peruvian Formative cultures, a chronological conclusion generally agreed upon.[109] There is, however, at least one discrepant note to this conclusion—the Chavín-designed Mochica ceramics. These specimens come from bona fide Mochica grave contexts and are a part of Mochica culture; yet their decorations are clearly in the configuration of the Chavín style. The Mochica culture is not only later than Cupisnique, but the two are separated by the Salinar (White-on-red) period.

In analyzing the cultural context of the Chavín horizon style, similarities are most readily apparent in ceramics. These are best seen in comparisons among Cupisnique, Chavín de Huántar, Supe, and Ancón. These four sites or regions offer the most ample data on pottery of the Chavín horizon. In all of them the ware is dark red, brown, or black, and it is essentially monochrome. Polishing is a common feature, although not all the pottery of each site or region is polished. Open flat-bottomed bowls, constricted-collar jars, subglobular bowls, simple-spout jars or bottles, and stirrup-spouts are linked traits. All seem to be common in all locations except the stirrup-spout which is typical of Cupisnique but rare elsewhere. Commonly held decorative techniques are fine- and broad-line incision, dentate or rocker-stamping, gouging or punctation, and the zoning of color bands (usually red) with incised lines. In addition, hachure and cross-hachure, brushing, engraving, strip applique, and low relief applique modeling are present in two or three of the four sites or regions. Designs continue this similarity. The circle or circle-and-dot, rectilinear elements (triangles, diamonds, rectangles, zigzags, etc.), loops, volutes, and scrolls are found throughout. A more distinctive linkage is in the Chavín feline design itself. This is usual in Cupisnique pottery; infrequent but present in the Chavín de Huántar collections; and very probably represented in the sherd samples from Ancón and Supe. In general, the Chavín de Huántar, Ancón, and Supe pottery complexes are alike. Cupisnique possesses most of the ceramic traits held by the other three, but places greater stress on naturalistic and full-round modeling, the stirrup-spout jar, and the stylized Chavín designs. In addition, some Cupisnique pottery is apparently mold-made.

Other Chavín horizon sites with pottery fit into the ceramic pattern as described above. The Moropón stirrup-mouthed jar is entirely within the Cupisnique typological range. The black or red monochrome vessels of Chongoyape have polished surface areas, stirrup-jar forms, dentate or rocker-stamping, and relief and full-round modeling. Pallca pottery is dark, monochrome, and decorated with incisions, rocker-stamping, and applique. Vessel designs are confined to rectilinear or morphologically unrecognizable curvilinear patterns, although it is likely that some of the latter are sections of Chavín stylized felines.

Kuntur Wasi presents a somewhat divergent picture. Apparently, the Kuntur Wasi ceramics are monochromes and of a dark hue, although this has not been explicitly stated. The simple bowl and jar forms of Early Ancón, Early Supe, Cupisnique, and Chavín de

Huántar are present, as is the stirrup-spout; but there are new additions in the low pedestal-based bowl and jar and the kero-beaker. Kuntur Wasi incised decoration is quite limited in design elements and arrangements.[110] These are almost wholly rectilinear, except for every simple loops or volutes and the circle-and-dot. Recognizable feline motives on the flat surface are not included in the illustrations of the pottery, although there are one or two possible exceptions of what might be extreme stylizations of the Chavín feline. One of these[111] has the ribbon-banded, compact glyphic quality of the Chavín designs on Mochica vases. As opposed to flat design, modeled and applique decoration is varied. Some elements, like pressed pellet nodes, resemble Chavín wares, but, in general, the applique work is heavy and clumsy.[112] Whereas Chavín applique and relief modeling, as best exemplified in Cupisnique, has a quality of deeply sculptured surfaces, the Kuntur Wasi pieces emphasize the distinctly applied nature of the thick rolled fillets of clay. This latter treatment resembles Salinar, where the heads of felines or other animals are done with heavy applique strips.[113]

Mochica ceramics need not be discussed in detail. It is, with rare exceptions, oxidized pottery; much of it is mold-made; and the realistic painting and modeling is distinctly un-Chavín. Within this context the Chavín decorated pieces are rare.

In other aspects of cultural development we see a number of variables within the Chavín horizon. Monumental stone carving is confined to the north highlands at Chavín de Huántar, Yauya, and Kuntur Wasi. Mud sculptures and reliefs characterize the Nepeña and Casma Valleys. Small, artifactual carving in stone, bone, wood, or shell appears to be largely a coastal trait, distributed from Chiclayo to Ancón. Basketry and weaving are coastal. Pyramid building is northern. Highland structures are of stone with interior galleries while those of the coast are adobe. The pyramid idea seems not to have reached Supe and Ancón on the central coast. Throughout the sites or regions of the Chavín horizon burial is in simple pit graves with the exception of the adobe-lined tombs of Mochica. True metallurgy is known for certain only from Chongoyape,[114] with its welding or soldering techniques and limited use of silver in addition to gold, and from Mochica, with its alloys, copper, and multiple uses of these materials. Elsewhere, metal, if found, is in the form of simple beaten sheets or ornaments of gold.

Some of these variables may be explained environmentally or geographically. Stone monuments and structures of the north highlands are undoubtedly related to available building materials. The basketry and weaving of the coast can, perhaps, be correlated with preservation factors in archaeological sites. Pyramid building in the north and its absence farther south certainly suggest the origin or introduction of the trait in north Peru with a gradual spread to the south. The same may be true of Chongoyape gold. On the other hand, environment and geography cannot explain the numerous striking differences that set Mochica apart from the other cultures which share the Chavín art style. This can only be explained chronologically. In other words, the cultural context of Mochica fully supports the stratigraphy which places it as post-Cupisnique and later than the horizon level on which most of the other Chavín style manifestations fall.

We can, following this argument, conclude that the Chavín style is, for the most part, an effective time horizon marker. This is deduced from the stratigraphic evidence which is supported by a similarity of cultural context for most of the sites or regions in which Chavín style art is found. This similarity is strongest in ceramics and burial practices while notable variability is seen in architecture and metallurgy. Two cultures with Chavín style manifestations diverge rather sharply from this similarity of cultural context: Mochica and Kuntur Wasi. Kuntur Wasi is the less divergent of the two, but its ceramics show significant differences from Chavín and resemble Salinar, a cultural period of the north coast, which is post-Chavín. It is also noteworthy that monumental stone carving at Kuntur Wasi is not restricted to the Chavín style, but is extended to another and quite different style.

It seems certain that the Chavín style, of a configurationally pure sort, did, in a few cases, persist later than the chronological horizon line which we can draw for most Chavín-linked cultures and periods. This persistence is seen on the north coast where it lasted until Mochica times as a minor decorative feature. At Kuntur Wasi, in the north highlands, we have evidence of another such persistence of the Chavín stylistic strain. It may be that Kuntur Wasi, or comparable sites located on the headwaters of the major north coast rivers, were the foci which transmitted the last impulses of a dying Chavín style down to the coast into Mochica. This does not, of course, explain the absence of Chavín designs in coastal Salinar[115] which I tentatively place as contemporaneous with Kuntur Wasi. It does, however offer a specific culture and region which could have carried the Chavín style across the time gap between the Chavín horizon proper and Mochica.

Additional Sites Related to the Chavín Problem

The seventeen sites or regions which we have treated as showing indisputable Chavín stylistic affiliation by no means complete the list of sites or cultures for which Chavín relationship has been claimed. Most of these claims have been made by Tello or Carrión[116] although one or two come from other authors. These claims or sites may be divided into three categories. First, there are those put forward with the direct statement that they are stylistically Chavín, but for which little or no evidence is presented. Such claims could be perfectly valid, and may eventually be substantiated; however, for the present study I have depended upon published illustrations, and in the interests of a strict interpretation have decided to err on the side of conservative hesitancy rather than uncritical acceptance. Second, there are sites which display a cultural context or inventory similar to the majority of the Chavín horizon style sites, but which seem to lack any evidence of the diagnostic style. And, third, there are sites whose stylistic relationship to Chavín is debatable. We will review the claims and sites in this order.

Sites of the First Category

The Highlands. In the Marañón drainage, Tello and Carrión[117] mention several sites for which there is little or no identification.[118] Kumbemayo, which is one of these, refers to an aqueduct system cut into bedrock, some *in situ* carvings, and petroglyphs. From published photographs[119] of these features I recognize no Chavín stylistic affinity.

In the Callejón de Huaylas, Tello[120] includes Inka Wain and Pomakayan as Chavín sites. The latter is a terraced, truncated pyramid with interior stone-lined galleries in which Classic Chavín ceramics are reported to have been found. The structure, is, however, very similar to those of the Wilkawain-Tiahuanaco period.[121]

In the central highlands there are also a number of Chavín claims which have not yet been substantiated by the publication of the evidence.[122]

The Coast. On the north coast there are several Chavín claims which remain unsubstantiated. From La Ventana or Batan Grande, in Lambayeque, Tello reports Chavín sherds in a stratigraphy but does not illustrate these materials.[123] Larco[124] illustrates stirrup-mouthed vessels from the Pacasmayo Valley which are incised and modeled in the general Cupisnique manner but do not have Chavín-type feline designs.

Tello[125] also notes the presence of Chavín sites in Santa Valley and illustrates a stone mortar with a carved bird design from Suchiman,[126] but the Chavín style of this piece is not a conclusive identification.

In addition to the better known sites of Nepeña and Casma Valleys, Tello[127] names Kusipampa, Pinchamarka, and La Carbonera from the former and La Cantina, Chankillo, and Sechín Alto from the latter. There is little information on any of these, but Kroeber[128] has reviewed Chankillo (Chancaillo) without finding Chavín evidence. Middendorf's[129] allusion to Chavín relationships may have influenced Tello here. Donald Collier has given me the following information on Sechín Alto. It is a large rectangular, stone-faced, stepped, pyramidal platform surmounted by several smaller two-level platforms. The interior structure is of conical adobes, and the pyramid is partially enclosed by a compound wall. Additional platform structures are within and outside of this compound. Bennett[133] includes this site as one of those "linked by the Chavín horizon"; but Collier (personal communication) states, "No excavation was done at this site and no surface pottery was found that might have been contemporaneous with it."

Choka Ispana, in the Huaura Valley, and Chimo Kapak, in the Pativilca-Supe area, are two other sites named as Chavín by Tello[134] but upon which no specific information has appeared in print. Chimo Kapak (Chimu Capac) is known from the literature[135] as a mixed site, but no Chavín connections have been previously indicated.

Sites of the Second Category

Las Torrecitas, Chondorko, Santa-Apolonia. Recent stratigraphic excavations by the Reichlens[136] in these sites near Cajamarca have revealed a period of incised pottery underlying a developmental sequence of Cajamarca (Cursive) types. The chronological position of this incised pottery period approximates that of Chavín-influenced periods elsewhere in Peru.[137] Torrecitas-Chavín, as they have named the incised style, is a black, gray, or brown ware, smoothed or polished, which occurs in flat-based or hemispherical bowls or cups, subglobular vases, deep pots, and large jars with subglobular bodies and constricted and reflared collars. Decoration is by both broad and fine-line incision, punctations, gouge-marks, smooth and roughened zones, and zoned red or white color. Designs are volutes, scrolls, triangles, chevrons, parallel lines, and other simple motives. Modeling in high or low relief, and the more complex vessel forms, such as the stirrup-spout, are absent. Nor are there any designs which could be interpreted as Chavín style felines, humans, or other beings.[138] In short, although the pottery is technically very similar to the ware of Chavín de Huántar, the art style of Chavín is lacking.

The Reichlens have considered the possible chronological implications of this simplicity of their Torrecitas-Chavín, or "Chavínoid" style. They suggest that it may be a "primitive" or preclassic form of Chavín pottery. As such, it might correspond to undescribed pottery which Tello[139] claimed to have found in early or "preclassic" levels of the Chavín de Huántar site. On the other hand, Torrecitas-Chavín might be contemporaneous with, or later than, classic Chavín. All that we can be certain of is that its ceramic context is comparable to sites of the Chavín horizon.

Kotosh. In the vicinity of Huanuco, in one of several "artificial hillocks," Tello[140] found "an abundance of Chavín potsherds mixed with other types closely resembling, on the one hand, incised and painted pottery of the Paracas caves [Paracas Cavernas?], and, on the other, incised and carved Amazonian pottery." The pottery which Tello illustrates[141] appears to be a monochrome ware decorated with incisions, punctations, hachure, brushing, color zoning, pellet applique, and low relief modeling. Designs are circles-and-dots, rectilinear bands, and what appear to be highly stylized life forms. There is an obvious generalized resemblance to Chavín de Huántar or Ancón pottery, but Chavín design motives of a classic sort (felines, etc.) are absent and the mention of painted types suggests another context. Tello implies in the caption to the illustration that other and more typically Chavín pottery was found in association.[142]

Donald Collier (personal communication) visited the Kotosh site in 1937. He describes it as being four kilometers southeast of Huanuco and consisting of two mounds, the larger of which is 50 by 25 by 5 meters. Collier observed stone-faced terraces on the mound and stone structures within it. He collected a sample of fifty sherds from the mound surface and from old excavations. These correspond closely to the types which Tello has illustrated plus smooth plain and polished monochrome types. Although Collier describes rim and shape forms as "suggesting the Chavínoid range," he found no Classic Chavín designs nor any painted ware.

Guañape. This is a cultural period in the Virú Valley which shows Cupisnique affiliations. Larco Hoyle[143] found such pottery in Virú Valley graves, Ford and Willey[144] surveyed several midden or house sites dating from this period, and Strong and Evans[145] uncovered a rectangular stone enclosure with Guañape pottery associated. Guañape pottery traits parallel those of Cupisnique and Ancón to a great extent except that stylized Chavín feline designs have not been recorded. This absence may be due only to the smallness of the decorated ware sample for the Guañape period.

Guañape house types are like those Larco Hoyle noted in Chicama for Cupisnique. No stone or conical adobe pyramids could be definitely associated with the period, although a few rather large rectangular stone-walled and adobe-walled enclosures may be Guañape public or ceremonial buildings.

Bellavista to Chilca. · Southward along the coast from Ancón there are several shell midden sites that may pertain to our problem. Uhle described such a midden and its pottery at Bellavista, near Callao;[146] there is another at Chorrillos on the southern outskirts of Lima; and still more near Pachacamac, Cruz de Hueso, Pucusana, and Chilca.[147] All of these sites have simple monochrome pottery of a black or reddish color which is indistinguishable from the Early Ancón plain ware. Incised types occur at some of the sites, perhaps at all; but, to the best of my knowledge, there is no record of Chavín stylistic representations, in pottery or other materials, from any of these sites.

SITES OF THE THIRD CATEGORY

Cerro Sechín. Cerro Sechín is probably the most disputed Chavín claim. In a sense it is comparable to our sites of the "second category" in this survey in that the general cultural context appears to be akin to that of some of the Chavín horizonal sites.

A full description of Cerro Sechín has never been published, although Tello, Kroeber, and Carrión have all given brief accounts.[148] Donald Collier, who assisted in the original excavations, has enabled me to supplement these statements with additional notes and comments.[149]

Located at the foot of hill slopes in Casma Valley, the Cerro Sechín temple is a rectangular mass composed of a series of superimposed platforms. The basal platform is of earth rubble and along its north façade are a series of carved stone slabs. In the center of this north façade a broad stairway led to the top of the platform. Collier is of the opinion that these stairs were made of stone and heavily plastered with mud. Upper platforms of the temple were constructed of conical adobes and then plastered and painted. At one place, jaguar (or puma) figures, painted in red, black, and white, adorn the plastered walls.

Tello[150] reconstructs the history of the temple site and its environs as follows. The first occupation and construction was not at Cerro Sechín proper, but was located farther down the slope at some little distance from the present site. Here are the remains of a Classic Chavín period temple completely destroyed by the floods.[151] Cerro Sechín proper represents a second occupation on a higher hillside terrace. Subsequently, this building, too, was covered with alluvium, and a third occupation, now marked by dwellings and refuse, covered the site. According to Tello, the cultural associations of these three building stages are: (1) Classic Chavín, (2) sub-Chavín, and (3) Santa type. Thus, Cerro Sechín temple proper dates from the second stage, or from what Tello has called the sub-Chavín period.

Collier's observations on the pottery from the excavations distinguish three types of pottery. One of these types is a coarse red ware decorated with incisions and reed punctations. This is the pottery which Tello described as "a new kind of incised pottery known from surface rubbish-heaps in almost the whole Casma Valley."[152] From Tello's further statements this type can be equated in time with "sub-Santa," "sub-Chimu," and Inca.[153] Apparently, it is not involved with any of the three building stages to which we have just referred. A second style which Collier recognized was a three-color Tiahuanaco Epigonal variant. This is Tello's "Santa" type, associated with the third building stage. Collier's third type he describes as "an undecorated, polished ware, black through brown to red in color, with straight, somewhat thickened rims, largely from bowls." This is apparently the type which Tello called "sub-Chavín" and which he (Tello) correlated with the temple of Cerro Sechín and its carved stone monoliths. Collier, however, is hesitant to establish such a correlation between the Cerro Sechín temple and the plain, monochrome pottery.

Even if we accept the association of this sub-Chavín pottery and the Sechín pyramid and carvings, the picture is still very confused, owing to the definition of sub-Chavín. Tello[154] describes sub-Chavín pottery as

> in every way resembling that discovered in the Teatino cemetery, in the Supe burial ground near Faro [Lighthouse site], where Uhle labored years ago, in various Nepeña and Santa cemeteries, and in the lowest layer of a cutting made by the La Leche River close to the Batan Grande Huaca [Lambayeque]. The rubbish, judging from the pottery, belongs to the Chavín culture in its second period, called by the writer sub-Chavín, to which also belong the vessels found by Bennett in the Gallinazo cemetery, in Virú.

No consistent style can be reconstructed from this. Teatino "Chavín," as Kroeber[156] has commented, is typologically and chronologically the equivalent of Middle Ancón I of the Coast Tiahuanaco horizon; Bennett's Gallinazo[157] is a negative horizon type; and Uhle's cemetery at the Faro, Supe, is firmly linked to the Chavín style.[158] The typological and chronological gamut represented by Teatino, Gallinazo, and Early Supe is tremendous; further, Tello's description would not coincide with Collier's plain monochrome ware of simple bowl shapes. The ceramics of Cerro Sechín, as they have been presented, certainly do not aid in the dating of the temple and its carvings.

Cerro Sechín's stone monuments are flat, unshaped slabs with low relief incised and champlevé designs. The designs comprise standing humans, separate heads (possibly representing severed or trophy heads), dismembered bodies, and rather simple geometrical figures. The style is more rigid and much less sophisticated than that of Chavín de Huántar. In it I see no close connections with Chavín.[159] As has been mentioned, the Pickman Strombus, the small stone vase from Chiclayo, and the Humaya bone spatula offer an interesting stylistic linkage in that all three pieces combine Sechín and Chavín elements. One other Peruvian piece, a carved bone spatula from the Huaca Prieta refuse mound of the Chicama Valley, has a design that is very reminiscent of the Sechín men figures.[160] This specimen cannot be dated exactly, but it probably belongs with the Cupisnique or coast Chavín period at that site.

Cerro Sechín's place in Peruvian chronology and its relationships to the Chavín horizons are unclear. The nature of the temple structure, with its use of stone, mud, and conical adobes, implies a fairly early date. The painted jaguars suggest Chavín. The plain monochrome pottery, which Tello calls sub-Chavín, sounds very much like the plain ware of a Chavín ceramic complex;[161] but there is some question as to whether or not it is associated with the temple. The Cerro Sechín carvings are not stylistically Chavín, nor do they resemble any other major Peruvian style. Resemblances to this Sechín style are seen in occasional specimens from the north coast, some of which also combine Chavín decorative elements. We can only conclude that Cerro Sechín is either later than the Chavín horizon (as Tello suggests with his "sub-Chavín" concept) or that it is an earlier coastal style antedating and eventually blending with Chavín.[162] For reasons to be discussed later the second interpretation is favored.

Teatino or Lachay. This cemetery site is located on the north side of the Chancay Valley. The earliest graves of the cemetery are named by Tello as "sub-Chavín." As stated above, I have identified the incised grave pottery from this site as Middle Ancón I.[163] This pottery differs in ware, shape, and design from Coast or Highland Chavín ceramics. Strong[164] has presented evidence to ally it chronologically with Coast Tiahuanaco.

Chanapata. This early site, near Cuzco, was excavated by Rowe[165] who found stone-faced terraces, bone tools, simple ground stone tools, obsidian points, pottery figurines, polished black incised and applique pottery, and white-on-red pottery. Presumably, Tello and Carrión have the black incised ware in mind when they consider Chanapata as a Chavín site. Chanapata blackware is found in open bowls, bottles, plates, and olla forms. These are somewhat like the vessel forms of Chavín de Huántar, but there are notable differences, such as the presence of strap handles on both the open bowls and ollas. Decoration is in both broad and fine-line incision, applique strips, punctation, and low relief modeling. Incised designs are stiff, rectilinear animals (cats), chevrons, diamonds, and rectangles. The cat bears no resemblance to the Chavín feline, in total stylized conception or in detail.

Pucara. This site, excavated by Kidder II,[166] appears to be a ceremonial center constructed of dressed stone blocks and incorporating such features as altars and subterranean burial vaults. The pottery is a polychrome black and yellow on red with color zones separated by fine-line incisions. Design centers upon the feline, which is rendered both in the flat and in high relief modeling; but the feline stylization[167] is not that of Chavín.

Paracas, Ocucaje. Paracas Cavernas style pottery is found at these two sites on the south coast. Close similarity with Ancón and Supe is seen in a flat-bottomed, dark-ware, incised bowl type;[168] but, for the most part, Paracas Cavernas ceramics are in a polychrome tradition. A fanged cat-face,[169] incised and painted, lacks the characteristic Chavín rendering. Associated also is negative painted pottery,[170] a decorative technique rarely found in the same context with Chavín types.

Socos, La Victoria. For Socos, the only reference which I have is the Carrión chart.[171] The design shown here, presumably from a pottery vessel, seems completely un-Chavín. La Victoria is mentioned only on the map.[172]

Non-Peruvian Styles and Cultures. Tello and Carrión[173] have both expressed the opinion that several archaeological sites or cultures lying outside of Peru and, for the most part, beyond the borders of the central Andean area were component manifestations of the Chavín style, culture, civilization, or empire.

To the south, Tiahuanaco of Bolivia[174] and Barreales of northwest Argentina[175] are considered as Chavín outposts. The Early and Classic Tiahuanaco cultures and their stone sculptural and ceramic styles are well known.[176] The feline, condor, and serpent are represented in Tiahuanaco art, but their configuration is distinctively that recognized as Tiahuanaco, not Chavín. Tiahuanaco pottery is polychrome, and its vessel shapes are non-Chavín. Early Tiahuanaco may, possibly, be as early as the Chavín horizon; Classic Tiahuanaco is, almost certainly, later. Barreales is an incised, dark ware, and in these features it is reminiscent of Chavín. The designs on the vessels, while possibly of central Andean inspiration, are not rendered in the Chavín style.[177]

From Moxos,[178] or Mojos, in the Bolivian lowlands, the ceramic types of Lower and Upper Velarde, Hernmarck, and Masicito are known from the work of Nordenskiöld and the résumés of Bennett and Howard.[179] Velarde and Hernmarck are painted ceramics. Lower Velarde is an isolated style which Bennett has equated, chronologically, with Derived Tiahuanaco. Hernmarck has rather general Amazonian affiliations, Masicito is an incised type, but I see no Chavín parallels.

The painted, carved, and modeled pottery of Marajó and the wares of Río Ahuaimo and Napo-Aguarico, which Tello mentioned,[180] seem to me to be quite unlike Chavín. If a similarity does exist it is so deeply buried by stylization, reduction, and modification that it loses meaning.

Nor do I see the strong and specific Chavín resemblances in the various regions of Ecuador to which Tello and Carrión refer.[181] The one possible exception is Carrión's Azuay illustration, but the provenience of this specimen is dubious.[182]

Chavín as a Tradition

We know that, as the configurative aspect of a style changes, a new style comes into being. Although a distinct entity, it emerges with a residue from the past. This continuity with the past, and by implication with the future, is the *tradition*. In this discussion we have conceived of the synchronous distribution of the Chavín art pattern through space as a horizon style. As such, it constituted one dimension of our inquiry. The complementary dimension, the diachronous continuity of Chavín through time, may be termed the Chavín tradition.

The diagnostics of a tradition are determined by the historical problem. For example, in attempting to demonstrate the linkage of a series of ceramic styles through Peruvian culture sequences, the confines of the tradition may be laid down as "white-on-red painting," "incising," or "plastic ornamentation."[183] The tradition limits are, here, determined by what we have in another context referred to as the "technological aspect of style." When we turn to the problem of a Chavín tradition, it is doubtful if it could be usefully defined by technological criteria. "Incision" or "carving" as determinants would provide us with such a wide-meshed screen that we would admit a superabundance of irrelevant data. The field must be narrowed to utilize only the "representational aspect of the Chavín style," the feline motif and its combinations, as the core of the Chavín traditional continuum.

When we arrive at this point, we realize that this is what Tello has done. For him, the Chavín problem was the history of the feline deity in the development of Peruvian cultures. His greatest work, *Wira-Kocha*, is a profound essay upon the occurrence and recurrence of the feline god in all regions and in all periods of native Peru. He conceived of this deity as the binding and unifying force in Andean culture. This is diagrammatically expressed in Tello's first chronological-development chart.[184] In this he shows the monogenesis of the different branches of Peruvian culture from a single trunk, with the implication that all branches carry within themselves the idea of feline deity. Finally, in the epoch of the Inca, the chart illustrates the terminal coalescence of the multiple lines of cultural development so that they again form a single trunk under the same ancient feline god, now called Viracocha.

It has been noted that in his earlier writings Tello considered Chavín to be a "Second Epoch" culture, an esthetic refinement of the feline idea. Apparently, at this stage of his career, he was not certain as to the exact nature of the monogenic mother-culture of the Andes. "Archaic North Andean" remained a tentative formulation, in spite of the fact that he sometimes identified it with Recuay pottery. Not until after the discoveries in the Nepeña Valley, with their obvious structural stratigraphy, did he become convinced that Chavín was the original and parent stock. At about the same time Tello's approach and methodology appear to coincide with the Uhle-Kroeber point of view. He had established a new horizon, comparable to Tiahuanaco and Inca, but underlying the established Early or Classic cultures; and he had characterized and defined this horizon as an extension of the striking art style of Chavín de Huántar. Yet, in spite of these surface indications that his interests had shifted to synchronous correlations, his statement on methodology[185] and his exposition of the Chavín problem[186] show no important change in his thinking. Tello remained convinced that stratigraphy was relatively unimportant in the understanding of Peruvian cultural development because his dominant interest was in continuity rather than periodicity. This is very clearly reflected in his observations on cultural "trees" and the confused intermingling of their "branches." As far as Chavín is concerned it is safe to assume that he was more interested in the total "tree" than in any chronological segments selected from it by a means as arbitrary as stratigraphy. The misunderstandings of Tello's theories on Chavín, largely held by North Americans, derive from the fact that he operated with two concepts, and was not at pains to keep them separate. Chavín as a tradition was to him paramount, while Chavín as a horizon style was of secondary importance.

The implications of much of this are seen in the Tello-Carrión Chavín claims which we have just reviewed. The feline representations of Pucara, Tiahuanaco, Chanapata, and Barreales may be a part of a historically related Chavín tradition which has crystallized in different styles as it has diffused outward in space or upward in time from its original hearth. This is a reasonable possibility and a valid working hypothesis. On the other hand, to consider them a part of the Chavín style horizon is untenable. This does not necessarily prove that all of them are chronologically later than the Chavín horizon. It does mean, however, that the presence of the feline representation in these various styles cannot be taken as proof of their contemporaneity or intimate historical connection with the Chavín style.

The problem has been complicated in still another way—by accepting the "technological aspect of style" as the style itself. This is, obviously, what Tello has done in the case of Teatino. Teatino incised pottery has neither the configuration nor (to my knowledge) the feline representations of Chavín style. The monochrome ware and the decorative technique, incision, have been used as the Chavín diagnostics.[187] In some cases this seems to be more justifiable than at Teatino where the Middle Ancón I–Coast Tiahuanaco typological and chronological coordinates are evident. Las Torrecitas, Kotosh, Guañape, and the Bellavista-Chilca sites are all reminiscent of the Chavín style because of the incised technique; but in all of these the total context of the culture, the specific vessel forms, the monochrome ware, and the other associated elements, support the Chavín claim. In Las Torrecitas and Guañape the Chavín contention is further strengthened by an early stratigraphic position. At Kotosh, the chronological and associational picture is not clear.

Cerro Sechín is another instance of a Chavín identification made largely upon the basis of the technological aspects of style—flat, line-carving on stone. Here, the architectural context supports an early dating, although the ceramic associations blur the picture. It is undoubtedly significant that there are no evidences whatsoever of either the Chavín style or the Chavín tradition as we have defined them in this analysis. Their absence at Las Torrecitas, Guañape, or Bellavista-Chilca might be due to limited archaeological sampling or to functional cause (small villages as opposed to important ceremonial sites); but their absence at Cerro Sechín, in the temple carvings, seems more likely to have a chronological explanation. As the Chavín or feline tradition, in one stylistic form or another, persists in a great many post-Chavín horizon cultures and periods, its nonappearance in an early culture would favor a pre-Chavín horizon position. The assumption here is that the feline representation in central Andean art began with Chavín, that, in effect, the Chavín tradition began with the first appearance of the Chavín style.

Other Peruvian or Andean sites or cultures where Chavín traditional, although not stylistic, influence may be seen are too numerous to be described in full here. Recuay, Mochica, and Gallinazo of Virú are example.

Bennett's[188] identification of a grave from the Gallinazo site group as Chavín was based upon the representational (cat figure on textile) and the technological (incised black ware) aspects of Chavín rather than the Chavín style itself. This grave dates from the latter part of the Gallinazo period and, as such, is considerably later than the Chavín horizon.

The distinctive, linear "Recuay cat" is a dominant motif in the Recuay painted ceramic style. Its prototype for the feline idea may very well have been Chavín, but its style is its own.

An interesting utilization of the concept of the Chavín or feline tradition is Larco Hoyle's statement on Mochica religion: "Mochica religion centers around feline symbolism, and it seems reasonable to believe that in this period we have, with a new elaboration and sophistication of animal worship, a continuation of the old feline deity of the North Coast."[189] There is no claim here that this is Chavín, for Larco's treatment of the Chavín style is by horizon. It is, however, a realization of the traditional content of the style.

Summary and Conclusions

Chavín is the name given to a prehistoric art style of the north Peruvian area. The name derives from the highland site of Chavín de Huántar where the style is well represented.

Chavín style is manifested over a region bordered on the north by Piura (coast) and Pacopampa (highland) and on the south by Ancón (coast) and Chavín de Huántar (highland). In the highlands, it has been reported, but not described, from sites south of Chavín de Huántar. On the basis of present information, these are the geographical limits of the style.

The point of origin of the Chavín style is unknown, although it is likely that it was first developed within the geographical limits stated. Larco Hoyle is of the opinion that Chavín type art (Nepeña, as he would call it) developed on the coast, probably in the Nepeña Valley and spread from there to the highlands. Tello takes the counter-position, bringing it from highlands to coast. Tello's theories of origins are somewhat more complex than this as he postulates beginnings in the Amazonian forests to the east of the Andes. In following these theories he has offered similarities between the Chavín style and certain Amazonian ceramic styles as proof of Amazonian origins. These similarities have not been demonstrated to the general satisfaction of other investigators.

The chronological limits of the Chavín style fall early in the Peruvian sequences. Its terminal date in the relative scale is indicated, for the most part, by the inception of the White-on-red horizon periods. This is substantiated in several instances by stratigraphy. The lower limits of the Chavín style appear to be defined by an early premaize, semi-horticultural period; although this is much less securely tied down than the upper limit White-on-red horizon dating. In general classificatory terms, the Chavín style is placed on the Early Formative stage of Peruvian prehistory and given the estimated dates of 1000–0 B.C.

In contrast to our above conclusions, there are claims that the Chavín style, or Chavín culture, was spread much more widely than the Peruvian north coast and highlands and that its chronological limits extend much later than the White-on-red horizon. Most of these claims have been advanced by the late Dr. J. C. Tello. To test these claims it was first necessary to define just what was to be included under the term Chavín.

To begin with, we considered only the art style of Chavín, dropping for the time being all connotations of Chavín as a culture, a civilization, or an empire. The Chavín style was then defined as being identical to, or closely resembling, the designs of the stone carvings of the type site, Chavín de Huántar. For analysis, Chavín style was broken down into: (1) the technology of carving or incising; (2) representations of the feline, human, bird, serpent, and composites of these; and (3) the peculiar configuration of the representations as this is expressed in the curvilinear forms, massive heads, smaller intricately disposed heads, curved fangs, and other elements. This third aspect of the Chavín style was considered as its most unique quality and, therefore, diagnostic of the style.

With the stylistic pattern or configuration as an index of contemporaneity, seventeen sites or regions, including the type site, were determined as having Chavín style manifestations in stone, ceramics, bone, wood, textiles, metals, or in two or more of these. The other Chavín claims were examined and rejected on the basis of absence of evidence for this stylistic pattern. Of the seventeen sites or regions possessing the Chavín style, it was demonstrated that eight were similar in cultural context. This similarity of context is seen in various traits, but is best expressed in monochrome, dark, often polished pottery of simple forms, occasional stirrup-spout jars, and incised or surface-manipulated decoration. On the remaining eight sites, six are either isolated Chavín style finds or situations where there is only limited contextual data. For the final two sites or regions, adequate context is available, particularly in ceramics; but this context is notably different from that of the first eight sites with their dark-colored, monochrome, incised wares. One of the two is Mochica, with its elaborately modeled and red-on-white pottery which, only rarely, bears a Chavín style incised and painted design. Stratigraphic and seriational data indicate Mochica to be later than the other sites or cultures linked by the Chavín style. The second of the two is Kuntur Wasi. Its pottery has more resemblance to the majority of Chavín style sites than does Mochica; nevertheless, it has features which link it with Salinar rather than Chavín. As Salinar is the time period intermediate between Cupisnique (Coastal Chavín) and Mochica, it is suggested that Kuntur Wasi, or comparable sites of the sierra, served as a chronological conductive link to pass the Chavín style from Cupisnique to Mochica.

It can be concluded that Chavín style does, as has been supposed, assemble largely on a time horizon antecedent to the White-on-red styles and that on this horizon there is appreciable similarity of cultural context. On the north coast and in the adjacent highlands there are two instances of its continuation into later time periods: Kuntur Wasi and Mochica. At Kuntur Wasi Chavín style is a feature of stone sculpture and, possibly, although not certainly, of pottery; in Mochica it is only a very minor ingredient in ceramics. Thus, there is some substance to the claims of the chronological persistence of Chavín as a style. It should be noted, however, that these later persistences are not common and are extremely limited in a geographical sense.

What then of the many other Chavín claims? None of these have been verified from the standpoint of style. Their similarity to the Chavín style lies in their representations or in their technological aspects. The central representation of Chavín art is the feline being, presumably a deity. One of Tello's greatest contributions to Andean studies was to show the great geographical and chronological range of the feline as an art motif. These feline representations, although appearing in many distinct art styles and in different time periods, may reasonably be related as a *Chavín tradition*—a concept quite different from that of Chavín style. It is likely that this tradition of the feline originated in, or was introduced into, the central Andean area at the time of the Chavín style horizon. At least, it has not yet been found earlier. The feline is present in the styles of Chanapata, Pucara, Paracas Cavernas, and Tiahuanaco, to name only a few of those that have been identified as sites or cultures of a Chavín civilization. All of these lie outside of the geographical limits of the Chavín style as these have been plotted; and all are probably somewhat later in time than the Chavín style horizon.

A good many of the Chavín claims can be linked neither by style nor by the feline tradition. Here, it appears that the Chavín techniques of incising or carving have formed the basis of the Chavín identification. In many cases, such as Las Torrecitas, Guañape, the Bellavista-Chilca sites, and, possibly, Kotosh, these claims are partially supported by chronology and general cultural context. In other cases, the incision technique has been used to identify as Chavín or sub-Chavín a site or culture which is chronologically much later than and typologically at great variance with the Chavín horizon.

So far we have not touched upon the functional problem. What was the nature of Chavín? Obviously, it was difficult to pose this question until there had been some segregation of the concepts bearing upon Chavín. If we consider only those sites which are linked together by the common possession of the Chavín art style, can we say that these form a Chavín culture or civilization? Some cultural uniformity exists, but there are important differences. It is as though a common cultural heritage of maize agriculture, a type of ceramics, carving and incising techniques, weaving, and the pattern of simple dwelling units in small villages were possessed by or transmitted to the peoples of northern Peru. Coincident with this, or perhaps shortly afterward, regional specialization also appeared, so that some communities of the north coast constructed adobe pyramids, other north coastal groups worked in mud frescos, highland peoples developed the stone-faced platforms with interior galleries and impressive carving, and the villages of the central coast built no outstanding monuments. Metallurgy was advanced on the far north coast; in the Chicama Valley ceramics were most elaborate; and elsewhere there were other specializations. To visualize all of these as belonging to the same culture could, in the broader sense, be justified; but it should also be recognized that the unit is not comparable to other Peruvian archaeological cultures, such as the Mochica or Nazca. These last were certainly much tighter knit, more homogeneous entities than such a Chavín culture.

If there is some hesitancy in accepting Chavín as a culture, there is more agreement for another of Tello's concepts, that the Chavín culture possessed a common religious bond. This seems the best explanation for the phenomenon we have defined as the Chavín horizon style. Larco Hoyle[190] has dealt with this at some length, elaborating the idea that the feline cult spread among peoples who possessed a somewhat similar but regionally differentiated culture. Population size and distribution and the absence of evidence of organized militarism in Chavín horizon times have been proposed as conditions that would have made for the peaceful spread of such a religious cult.[191]

Accepting the spread of the Chavín style as the evidence of a rapidly diffused religious cult, what, then, is the significance of the Chavín or feline tradition as it occurs beyond the temporal and spatial limits of the style? To this question I submit the following hypotheses. First, the disappearance of an art style as mature and as integrated as Chavín must almost certainly have marked the dissolution or the radical transformation of the system which stood behind the symbol of the style. In sum, the particular religious cult of the Chavín style feline was destroyed or died. Second, this cult was not immediately forgotten but persisted in Kuntur Wasi and Mochica, where its emblems are found as minor parts of new stylistic assemblages or patterns. And, third, some of its central themes and beliefs were incorporated into chronologically later or geographically more remote religious systems, as is attested by the traditional continuity of the feline being in the art styles of these systems.

Notes

[1]Kroeber, 1944, pp. 81–82.

[2]Middendorf, 1893–95.

[3]Tello, 1922.

[4]Tello, 1923, 1929.

[5]Tello, 1923, pp. 204 ff. Later Tello became dubious of the inclusion of three-color negative in "Archaic" but stuck to the concept of the plain tripod ware as belonging.

[6]Tello, 1923, p. 259, fig. 58.

[7]Tello, 1929, pp. 24–25; Tello, 1930.

[8]Tello, 1942, see pl. 7.

[9]Many of Dr. Tello's writings were published in the Lima newspapers as, in effect, interim excavation reports. An examination of these might verify the above point. Unfortunately, these works are not at my disposal.

[10]Tello, 1943, p. 139. Tello apparently substantiated this for he says farther along: "In the buildings discovered in the Callejón de Huaylas . . . the real Chavín structures are hidden under Recuay structures" (*idem*, p. 155).

[11]*Idem*, p. 158. The "facts given below" refer to some similarities of Recuay and Chavín vessel forms.

[12]Tello, 1922, opp. p. 10.

[13]Author's translation from Tello, 1942, pp. 635–636.

[14]See Tello, 1942, pl. 7.

[15]Tello, 1943, p. 158.

[16]*Idem*, p. 159.

[17]Author's translation from Tello, 1923, pp. 256–257.

[18]Strong, 1948a, p. 93.

[19]Translated from Tello, 1942, p. 626; translation checked by F. L. Stagg y Caamaño.

[20]Tello, 1943, p. 139.

[21]Carrión Cachot, 1948, pp. 166 ff. This essay by Carrión contains a résumé of Chavín distributions and an analysis of Chavín design.

[22]See Larco Hoyle, 1938, pp. 19–50.

[23]*Idem*, pp. 30–31.

[24]Larco Hoyle, 1941, p. 11.

[25]Larco Hoyle, 1938, p. 50.

[26]Uhle, 1910, 1913b; Kroeber, 1925b, 1926a, b, c, 1930a, 1944. An important exception is P. A. Means (1931). Means' approach is conceptually similar to Tello's in that he considered much of Peruvian culture to have been derived from a highland parent whose irradiations were geographically widespread and chronologically of great depth. To Means this was not Chavín but Tiahuanaco.

[27]See Kroeber, 1927.

[28]Bennett, 1939.

[29]Bennett, 1944a.

[30]Larco Hoyle, 1941, pp. 249–250.

[31]The only North American to come out for a chronologically basic position of Chavín-type finds prior to this was Strong (1925) in his consideration of the Early Ancon pottery; but he did not, at that time, recognize the Chavín affiliations of this ware.

[32]Bennett (1943, 1944a), in a doubt somewhat reminiscent of Tello's earlier speculations, was still unsure of Chavín-Recuay time relationships.

[33]Kroeber, 1944; Strong, 1943.

[34]Strong and Corbett, 1943; Willey, 1943a, b; Rowe, 1944.

[35]Bennett, 1948.

[36]Bennett and Bird, 1949, pp. 137–139.

[37]Willey, 1948, p. 10, table 1; Rowe, 1950.

[38]Collier, 1948, pp. 82–83.

[39]Willey, 1948; Bennett and Bird, 1949.

[40]This is a much more limited definition than that given by Tello (1943, pp. 154–157) under the heading, "Characteristics of the Chavín Civilization." In that, Tello describes architecture, ceramics, sculptural techniques, and the art motives or representations. These last two, techniques and representations, are comparable to the "technological" and "representational" aspects of style as I have used these concepts in this paper.

[41]See Kroeber, 1944, pp. 108 ff; Willey, 1945.

[42]See Tello, 1923, pp. 256–320; Kroeber, 1944, pp. 82–90; Bennett, 1944a, pp. 88–89.

[43]Bennett, 1943, 1944a; Carrión, 1948, pp. 100–106.

[44]See Carrión, 1948, pl. 14.

[45]Bennett, 1944a, pp. 81–87.

[46]Tello, 1943, plate 18, a.

[47]Bennett, 1944, fig. 30P.

[48]Carrión, 1948, pl. 14.

[49]Carrión, 1948, pp. 101–102. A carved feline effigy mortar of stone (*idem*, pl. 11, no. 11) and a smaller turquoise carving (Milliken, 1945, p. 163) may, or may not, have come from Chavín de Huántar.

[50]Lothrop, 1951a.

[51]See *idem*, figs. 71–77.

[52]Tello, 1923.

[53]Kroeber, 1944, p. 87.

[54]Larco Hoyle, 1946, pl. 65; Carrión, 1948, pl. 11; Laroc Hoyle, 1945, p. 3.

[55]Tello, 1943; Tello, 1937–38.

[56]See illustration, Tello, 1937–38; Carrión, 1948, pl. 26.

[57]Tello, 1943, pl. 18.

[58]Carrión, 1948, pp. 146 ff.

[59]*Idem*, fig. 17.

[60]*Idem*, fig. 16.

[61]*Idem*, pl. 20.

[62]*Idem*, pl. 21, b.

[63]*Idem*, p. 153.
[64]*Idem*, pl. 22, no. 21.
[65]*Idem*, p. 156.
[66]See Larco Hoyle, 1941, fig. 209, for an illustration of this piece.
[67]Lothrop, 1941, pp. 258–259.
[68]*Idem*, pl. 19.
[69]*Idem*, pl. 16, a.
[70]*Idem*, pl. 16, c.
[71]*Idem*, pp. 257–260.
[72]Illustrated by Tello, 1937, and Larco Hoyle, 1941, fig. 174.
[73]See Tello, 1943, fig. 18.
[74]Kroeber, 1944, pp. 49–50.
[75]*Idem*, pl. 33.
[76]Larco Hoyle, 1946, p. 151.
[77]Kroeber, 1926a, pp. 38–39; Larco Hoyle, 1941, fig. 31, for examples.
[78]See Larco Joyle, 1946, pp. 161–175; Bennett and Bird, 1949, pp. 153–181.
[79]Bennett, 1939, p. 16.
[80]Carrión, 1948, p. 107.
[81]Tello, 1942, pp. 702–704; 1943, pp. 136–137.
[82]Tello, 1943, pl. 13.
[83]*Idem*, pl. 14, a.
[84]Larco Hoyle, 1938, figs. 18, 19; Tello, 1943, pp. 137–138.
[85]Carrión, 1948, p. 110.
[86]Tello, 1943.
[87]See Larco Hoyle, 1941, fig. 25.
[88]Carrión, 1948, pl. 5.
[89]Tello, 1943, fig. 17, a.
[90]Larco Hoyle, 1941, fig. 26.
[91]*Idem*, fig. 27.
[92]Based upon unpublished information furnished me by Donald Collier, December, 1950; also Tello, 1943, pl. 13, b; Kroeber, 1944, p. 47; Carrión, 1948, p. 110, pl. 6.
[93]After Collier, unpublished information.
[94]Tello, 1943, pl. 15.
[95]*Idem*, pl. 24, a.
[96]Lothrop, 1951, fig. 74, d; p. 233a.
[97]Uhle, 1925, pp. 260–263; Kroeber, 1925a, pp. 254–256; 1944, pp. 118–120; Strong and Willey, 1943, pp. 11–14; Willey and Corbett, 1954.
[98]Kroeber, 1944, fig. 5, A.
[99]Uhle, 1913a.
[100]Strong, 1925, pp. 152–156.
[101]Strong and Willey, 1943, pp. 15–17; Willey and Corbett, 1954.
[102]Carrión, 1948.
[103]See Uhle, 1913b, pl. 1, fig. 3; Strong, 1925, pl. 48, figs. 5, 7; Carrión, 1948, pl. 25.
[104]Carrión, 1948, pl. 24, k.
[105]*Idem*, pl. 24, t.
[106]Bennett, 1944a, p. 92.
[107]Larco Hoyle, 1941, pp. 249 ff.
[108]Willey and Corbett, 1954.
[109]See Bennett and Bird, 1949, fig. 19.
[110]Carrión, 1948, pl. 23.
[111]*Idem*, pl. 22, no. 21.
[112]*Idem*, pl. 23, nos. 20, 21, 24, 25.
[113]See Larco Hoyle, 1946, pl. 67, g.
[114]The possible exception to this is the Bliss-Simkhovitch collection, which may have come from Chavín de Huántar.
[115]This absence is complete for ceramics, but there are some carved bone spatulas from Salinar graves which retain the Chavín style (Larco Hoyle, 1946, pl. 68, top).
[116]Tello, 1942, 1943; Carrión, 1948.
[117]Tello, *ibid.*; Carrión, *ibid.*

[118]Chakas, Huambos, Cochabamba in Chachapoyas, Chokta in Celendin, Nunamarka in Pataz, Pasa Kancha, Yayno, Llammellin, Chalwa, Yaco, San Marcos, Wama Wain, and Gotush are all listed by Tello and Carrión as Chavín sites.

[119]Reichlen and Reichlen, 1949.

[120]Tello, 1942, 1943.

[121]See Bennett, 1944a, p. 12.

[122]These are San Luis de Shuaro, Satipo (Monabarriba), Waiwaka, and Junín (Tello, 1943; Carrión, 1948).

[123]Tello, 1943, p. 154.

[124]Larco Hoyle, 1941, figs. 15, 17.

[125]Tello, 1942, 1943.

[126]Tello, 1943, fig. 17b.

[127]Tello, 1942, 1943.

[128]Kroeber, 1944, pp. 52–53.

[129]Middendorf, 1893–95, vol. 2, p. 307.

[footnote numbers 130–132 omitted]

[133]Bennett and Bird, 1949, p. 124.

[134]Tello, 1942, 1943.

[135]Kroeber, 1925, pp. 240 ff.

[136]Reichlen and Reichlen, 1949.

[137]For example, the pottery of Reichlens' Cajamarca II period (1949, fig. 6) has pointed similarity to the Interlocking ceramic style of the central coast and their Period IV (1949, figs. 11, 12) shows a definite increment of Tiahuanaco. Thus, their Torrecitas-Chavín, or incised ware, falls in about the proper sequence position for Chavín horizon contemporaneity.

[138]Reichlen and Reichlen, 1949, pp. 154–156, fig. 4.

[139]Tello, 1942, p. 701.

[140]Tello, 1943, p. 152.

[141]*Idem*, pl. 19.

[142]See also Tello, 1942, pp. 635–636.

[143]Larco Hoyle, 1946, p. 1949.

[144]Ford and Willey, 1949.

[145]Personal communication.

[146]Uhle, 1910.

[147]Tello, 1942, p. 679; 1943, p. 157; Strong and Willey, 1943, pp. 18–19.

[148]Tello, 1943, pp. 139–150; Kroeber, 1944, p. 48; Carrión, 1948, p. 110.

[149]Collier, personal communication, December, 1950.

[150]Tello, 1943, pp. 148–150.

[151]Ceramic evidence for this dating has not yet been illustrated.

[152]Tello, 1943, p. 145.

[153]This is also the ware which Kroeber (1944, pl. 22) illustrates.

[154]Tello, 1943, p. 144.

[footnote number 155 omitted]

[156]Kroeber, 1944, pp. 43–45.

[157]Bennett, 1939, pp. 54–75.

[158]Willey and Corbett, 1954.

[159]See also Kroeber, 1944, pp. 49–50.

[160]Junius B. Bird, personal communication, January, 1951.

[161]Collier (personal communication, December, 1950) states that a similar ware was found at the Casma Valley site of Pallka, along with incised sherds of the Chavín type.

[162]See Larco Hoyle, 1938, p. 50; Bennett and Bird, 1949, p. 135.

[163]See Kroeber, 1944, pp. 43–45.

[164]Strong, 1925, pp. 183–184.

[165]Rowe, 1944.

[166]Kidder, 1943.

[167]See Bennett, 1946a, pl. 37.

[168]Kroeber, 1944, pl. 14F.

[169]*Idem*, pl. 13E.

[170]*Idem*, pl. 16.

[171]Carrión, 1948, pl. 26.

[172]*Idem*, pl. 27.

[173]Tello, 1942, 1943; Carrión, 1948.

[174]See Carrión, 1948, pl. 27.

[175]Tello, 1943, p. 159.

[176]Bennett, 1934.

[177]See Márquez Miranda, 1946, pl. 142, fig. 63.

[178]See Tello, 1942, p. 636; Carrión, 1948.

[179]Nordenskiöld, 1913; Bennett, 1936; Howard, 1947.

[180]Tello, 1942, p. 636; see Howard, 1947, pp. 42–44 for a review of these.

[181]Tello (1942, p. 680; 1943, pp. 158–159) and Carrión (1948, p. 112, pl. 27) list the following Ecuadorean sites or regions as being stations of the Chavín stylistic influence: Azuay, Cerro Narrío, Alausí, Cuenca, Sigsig, Chordeleg, Saraguro, Manta, Elen Pata, Island of Puna, Puntos de Mar, Chinguilanchi, Rircay, Uchucay, Manabí. See Collier, 1948, pp. 82 ff., for a critical discussion of this.

[182]Carrión, 1948, pl. 26; cf. Collier, 1948, p. 83; Collier and Murra, 1943, pl. 10, no. 4.

[183]Willey, 1945, pp. 53–55.

[184]Tello, 1922, opp. p. 10.

[185]Tello, 1942, p. 626.

[186]Tello, 1943.

[187]Tello, 1942, p. 680.

[188]Bennett, 1939, p. 79, fig. 15a, b.

[189]Larco Hoyle, 1946, p. 171.

[190]Larco Hoyle, 1941.

[191]Willey, 1948.

17

Tradition Trend in Ceramic Development

(From *American Antiquity*, Vol. 20, pp. 9–14, 1954. Reprinted by permission of the Society for American Archaeology.)

A recent paper by Sears (1952) calls attention to an overall time trend in the design changes of various complicated stamped pottery styles in the southeastern United States. His analysis raises the question as to whether certain principles implied might not have more general application for the understanding of historical phenomena.

A number of years ago I ventured a definition of what seemed to be a kind of entity in the history of aboriginal Peruvian ceramics. This was termed a "pottery tradition." The concept was an attempt to comprehend a number of distinct pottery styles, occurring in different localities and at different time periods, as a single historical unit and is expressed (Willey, 1945, p. 53) as: "A pottery tradition . . . includes broad descriptive categories of ceramic decoration which undoubtedly have value in expressing historical relationships. . . . The pottery tradition lacks the specific quality of the localized pottery style. . . . [It] comprises a line, or a number of lines, of pottery development through time within the confines of a certain technique or decorative constant." Sears' article deals with what is, in effect, a pottery tradition. He is concerned with the continuity of complicated stamped wares in the south Appalachian province, the region of the state of Georgia and adjacent portions of bordering states. The predominance of complicated stamped pottery in this part of the United States has long been noted (Holmes, 1903), and the longevity of complicated stamping as a decorative technique has been plotted throughout the Georgia archaeological sequences (Fairbanks, 1950; Wauchope, 1950a). Sears' contribution beyond this point is in synthesizing the particular developmental trends which this south Appalachian pottery tradition has followed through time. These trends, which lasted from "about 500 A.D. until 1750 A.D.,"[1] can be summarized as a movement from complex to simple design elements, a simplification of the total stamp, a decreasing use of filler lines, an appearance of larger, more deeply cut and clearer stamps, and a greater symmetry of design (Sears, 1952, p. 108, Fig. 52). These gradual shifts can be traced through the curvilinear early and late Swift Creek, Kolomoki, Savannah, and Lamar styles in southern Georgia and north Florida; and they have parallels in the northern Georgia sequence of the Napier, Woodstock, and Etowah rectilinear styles. In other words, all of the complicated stamped ceramic styles of the south Appalachian region, which characterize the various periods of the different localities, can be harmonized into this overall diachronic configuration.

There is little doubt that these trends or drifts in change of Georgia complicated stamped pottery are the result of historical forces. Sears states (1952, p. 108):

> The parallel development in the northern and southern parts of the province . . . must be due in large part to influence from the one area on the other, the sort of influence from the south which may have produced the regularized Napier diamonds from the earlier erratic Napier on the one hand, and the movement of peoples indicated by the Savannah-Wilbanks intrusion into the Etowah valley on the other.

Thus, uniformity of the drifts is not the result of independent ceramic evolutions but derives from diffusion and other intercommunications among the subregions of the Appalachian province and their various local culture sequences. In fact, these trends, as Sears (p. 107) notes elsewhere, are "means of placing new stamped types . . . in their proper temporal position." That synchronization of this order could be effected by the degree of shift in design motifs is clear proof that a south Appalachian complicated stamped pottery tradition exists as a historically integrated entity.

We can now ask the question: Do comparable time trends, such as those observed in the south Appalachian complicated stamped ware, demonstrate the historical validity of other possible pottery traditions? By "comparable trends" we do not mean the specific sequence of ceramic design shifts that obtains in the Georgia tradition but, rather, the presence of any uniformities in the time-change continuum which may link pottery chronologies of geographically contiguous regions.

An example of trends in ceramic change which characterize another pottery tradition are those plotted by Ford in a recent monograph (Ford, 1952). In his matching of ceramic sequences from Gulf Coast Florida, the lower Mississippi Valley, and eastern Texas, Ford has presented the case for another major southeastern pottery tradition. This Gulf Coast–lower Mississippi tradition features the techniques of incision, rocker-stamping, and punctation. These techniques are expressed in many types, or styles, in the archaeological chronologies throughout the regions under consideration. The most notable traditional trend in these Gulf Coast–lower Mississippi regions is summarized by Ford (1952, p. 381) as: "the strong tendency . . . for the confining of a large proportion of the decorations to the upper part of the vessel wall, leaving the greater part of the body surface plain." That is, there is a design arrangement shift from an earlier overall coverage of the vessel to a later zoning or banding confined to the upper part of the pot. It will be seen that this trend is totally unrelated in content or direction to the trend of change in the south Appalachian complicated stamped pottery tradition. Each is a historical phenomenon peculiar to its own traditional media and region.[2]

It should be recognized, of course, that no one seriously disputes the historical integrity of either of these pottery traditions, the south Appalachian or the Gulf Coast–lower Mississippi. Both are close-knit entities. Their internal change trends are, in a sense, not needed to demonstrate the historical unity of each. Let us turn, then, to a situation where the lines of interrelationship among regions and subregions are less well agreed upon and where there is less *prima facie* evidence that all of the pottery developments have a closely integrated common history. The southwestern United States is a classic example. While there seems to be little disagreement that the three principal subareas of pottery characterization—Hohokam, Anasazi, and Mogollon—were interconnected, especially in their later periods, there is no singleness of opinion as to the degree of interrelationship. Although Martin and Rinaldo (1951, p. 223) have pointed out that elements of pottery design are found throughout much of the area, there is certainly no evidence that any single style—by the broadest definition of that term—was ever held uniformly over the southwest. A red-on-buff Hohokam tradition in vessel decoration stands in clear opposition to a black-on-white Anasazi tradition, but a southwestern-wide pottery tradition has been more difficult to demonstrate.

In examining the southwestern ceramic styles from the standpoint of overall trends in design changes certain facts seem significant. In the Hohokam sequences, Haury (Gladwin, et al., 1937, Figs. 111, 112) has synthesized changes in design layout and design elements from the Estrella through the Sacaton phases, a time range of several centuries during the first millennium A.D. These changes run from simple, bold, broad-lined designs to increasingly complex, fine-lined designs in which small repetitive elements and filler play a prominent part. Midway in the sequence, life forms appear in addition to geometric elements. This same time pattern is duplicated in the Anasazi pottery development although the styles are quite different from those of Hohokam. The bold, relatively simple designs of the La Plata, White Mound, and Kiatuthlanna phases of the Basketmaker III and Pueblo I stages are replaced by the finer-lined, more intricate designs of the Reserve, Tularosa, and Animas phases of the Pueblo II, III, and IV stages (see Haury, 1936, Fig. 6). A perusal of Martin, Quimby, and Collier (1947, Figs. 18–19, 21–24, 31–33, 35–36) will illustrate these same trends in Anasazi pottery. Life forms are of less consequence in Anasazi painting; but they occur, and this is towards the close of the sequence. Mogollon black-on-white painting, which begins somewhat later than the two-color wares of Hohokam and Anasazi, parallels the latter half of the sequence trends just described. Life forms are a common feature of this development in its Three Circle and Mimbres phases.

From the foregoing it can be seen that we have in the southwestern area a drift in pottery design change whose broad configurations envelop the life histories of the numerous southwestern pottery types or styles. The three generally recognized southwestern pottery traditions—Anasazi, Mogollon, and Hohokam—are caught up within these configurations of change. By analogy with the internal drifts of the south Appalachian and Gulf Coast–lower Mississippi pottery traditions, such a phenomenon is a strong argument for a unified pottery tradition for the southwest as a whole.

Another example of tradition trend in ceramics is suggested in southern Peru and adjacent Bolivia. There are a number of well-known pottery styles in these regions, both coast and highland. For the most part, they are considered as distinct creations, and the sequences of highland and coast are not generally thought to be closely related in their early periods. Kroeber (1944, p. 31) has remarked upon this as follows:

> Both in shapes and in designs, pure Nazca and pure Tiahuanaco are utterly distinct, as well as geographically separate. But they do share certain features: a ware technologically excellent, a firm and polished texture, polychrome painting with from four to six colors, occasionally even more. They are the only Peruvian styles with this degree of polychromism—they or wares influenced by them; and as Nazca and Tiahuanaco influences receded, Peruvian pottery receded to fewer and less brilliant colors. . . . These resemblances can hardly be mere coincidences. In principle, they are much more likely to be the result of contact or diffusional influences. What these were is a problem awaiting solution. It is the more challenging because the two styles at their culminations are so different both in theme and in aesthetic treatment.

Yet all of these styles, in whatever region or period, share an emphasis on positively painted polychrome decoration. In this, south Peru–Bolivia stands apart from central or northern Peru where other decorative techniques (e.g., white-on-red painting, negative or resist-painting, incision, modeling) are given prominence. I have referred to this southern preference for multicolor painting before as the south Peru–Bolivian polychrome painting tradition (Willey, 1945, p. 54; 1949a, p. 193). On the south Peruvian coast, the archaeological sequences in the Nazca and Ica valleys begin with the Paracas style. Paracas has previously been thought of as two cultural periods, an earlier Paracas-Cavernas and a later Paracas-Necropolis (see Bennett, 1946a, pp. 95–96; Bennett and Bird, 1949, p. 112). However, the recent work of W. D. Strong and his associates in the Nazca Valley indicates that the Paracas culture can best be conceived of as a single, pre-Nazca period (Strong, personal communications, 1952–53). In the Paracas polychrome wares, with which we are concerned, two, three, and four colors are used, and pigments are applied both before and after firing. The painted designs, which are usually bordered by incised lines, are divided between geometric and life forms (Kroeber, 1944, pls. 13–15; Bennett, 1946a, pl. 20). Bold rectangular elements and stepped figures are common (Kroeber, 1944, pl. 15, *f, i*; 1953, pl. 27, *a*, pl. 28, *a, c, d*, pl. 29; *a*; Bennett and Bird, 1949, Fig. 29). In the succeeding early Nazca period, pottery polychrome painting is in numerous colors. Motifs of men, animals, and plants predominate, and curvilinear figures and elements are employed more frequently than in the Paracas style (Gayton and Kroeber, 1927, pls. 1–3). This is followed by a tendency in late Nazca for the polychrome designs to become smaller, for figures to be used repetitively, and for the total design area to be more cluttered or filled with small elements (Gayton and Kroeber, 1927, pls. 8–11).[3] The Tiahuanaco-influenced Nazca Y of the next period is marked by reduction and loss in life forms, by a continued trend in repetitive elements, and by fewer colors (Gayton and Kroeber, 1927, pls. 12–16). The final Middle and Late Ica styles record an extreme stylization and rigidity of life representations, increasing use of small geometric elements, and closed-spaced repetitive arrangements (Gayton and Kroeber, 1927, pl. 18; Kroeber and Strong, 1924, pls. 31–38). In the south highlands of the Titicaca Basin, the early styles, such as the Pucara (Bennett, 1946a, pl. 37) and Early Tiahuanaco (Bennett, 1934, Figs. 13–14; Bennett, 1948, pp. 112–114) are simple polychromes combining bold rectilinear geometric designs with both stylized and naturalistic human and animal figures.[4] Classic Tiahuanaco (Bennett, 1934, Figs. 15–16) is richer in color and life representations than the preceding styles. Although still a stiff, essentially rectilinear art, classic Tiahuanaco comes closer to naturalism and curvilinear lines than either its antecedent or derived styles in the south highlands. Decadent Tiahuanaco (Bennett, 1934, Fig. 17) shows color loss, reduction and extreme stylization of life forms, and repetitive design features. Up to this period, the Titicaca Basin ceramic trends have paralleled those of the south coast although being quite distinct stylistically; however, at this point, the two sequences can be closely coordinated by the diffusion of specific Tiahuanaco-like style influences. Post-Tiahuanaco pottery styles of the Titicaca Basin are not well known, but the Sillustani, Collao, and Allita Amaya painted wares (M. H. Tschopik, 1946, p. 52, Figs. 8–13, 20) suggest a further parallel to the late south coastal trend in their limited use of color, predominance of small geometric designs, and repetitive arrangements. Incaic pottery, of the final prehistoric period, has not been mentioned for either coast or highland. Its locus of development may have been to the north of the Titicaca Basin in the vicinity of Cuzco. In its small, repetitive geometric design it seems to fall in with the tradition trend of south Peru-Bolivia; however, it also introduces a strong theme of naturalism that suggests other traditional affiliations (see Kroeber and Strong, 1924, pl. 40; M. H. Tschopik, 1946, Figs. 14–19, 22–25). To recapitulate, the south Peru–Bolivian polychrome tradition trend, as exemplified on both coast and highland, began with the use of relatively few colors and a combination of bold geometric and life designs. Increased utilization of color and more naturalistic (curvilinear) designs followed. Naturalism then broke down through reduction and stylization, and colors became fewer. Repetitive geometric design emerged at the last.

It has been stated at the outset and throughout this discussion that the concept of trend or time-change pattern within a pottery tradition is a recognition of historical phenomena. By that it is meant that the processes of diffusion, trade, migration, and other forms of contact have been responsible for the uniform currents of modification which have swept along the diverse ceramic styles of a tradition. Before examining this hypothesis further, the question should be asked as to what other causal forces or conditions could have produced similar results. Two possibilities suggest themselves. The first of these is independent evolution. Could not the trends we have observed in the various regional or local sequences of any one of these pottery traditions be separate and historically unrelated developments? This is a legitimate question that deserves serious consideration. It is, for example, common knowledge that similar courses of development may be traced for ceramic technology in various parts of the world. In Peru and Mexico, to turn to a New World instance, the history of aboriginal pottery manufacture, insofar as we can now trace it, begins with a preponderance of plain and simply decorated wares and moves through an increasing complexity of form and design elaboration. It seems highly unlikely that these are closely interrelated historical trends or that the pottery developments of Mexico and Peru could be linked into a single tradition as the term is defined herein. Diffusional connections undoubtedly exist between the Andes and Meso-America, but such connections are almost certainly not of the same order of historical intimacy that is suggested for the pottery traditions under investigation. The tradition trends we have plotted are, inevitably, parts of some more all-embracing courses of development in New World ceramics, but each does not in itself recapitulate any greater pattern or law of change. The south Appalachian tradition, confined as it is to carved paddle stamping of pottery, undergoes a shift from intricate small, highly complex designs to larger, bolder, more simply presented designs. The southwestern pottery tradition, in its painting, moves in exactly the opposite direction, from large and bold to the small and intricate motifs. Life form elements are a late introduction into this tradition trend. The south Peru–Bolivian polychrome styles go from bold treatment of both geometric and life forms to naturalism and curvilinearity and then on to loss of naturalism and repetitive geometric decoration. In the Gulf Coast and lower Mississippi Valley incised, rocker-stamped, and punctated styles, the content of the trend is entirely different from any of the other three. Change is in the direction of design placement and arrangement on the vessel. In view of these differences in the trends, and considering the geographical unity of each of the pottery traditions concerned, it seems unlikely that we are dealing with phenomena of independent pottery evolutions. The parallel configurations that exist among the component parts of any tradition are peculiar to it alone. They are not duplicated by the trends in the other traditions.

A second possible explanation for the trends is brought to mind by an analogy with the phenomenon which Sapir (1921) has designated as "linguistic drift." In Indo-European languages structural changes have been observed to follow a trend or drift in one direction. As Kroeber (1948a, pp. 242–243) explains:

> It can be traced in every Indo-European branch of which our historical record is long enough. Most of these languages have not been in contact with each other for the one to three thousand years that the change has been going on. Change by influence of one on the other, leading to imitation, is therefore excluded.

The causes of this drift are not fully understood, but, presumably diffusion and borrowing can be ruled out. Kroeber (1948a) has speculated: "Possibly the change . . . got under way early, in original Indo-European, before this stock had branched out into its daughter languages, and the impulse persisted in the latter in greater or less strength. This would make the process carry on by momentum from the past." Fascinating as this idea is, it does not seem to be applicable to the pottery tradition trends. In the first place, language, as opposed to material culture, has greater limitations of choice, fewer possibilities for kinds or directions of structural change. Secondly, whereas it can be demonstrated that Indo-European languages were isolated from each other by great geographical distances during the long courses of their developments, we know that the local and regional sequences of our pottery traditions were not so isolated one from the other.

We return, then, to our original assumption. The trends of change that characterize the pottery traditions of this discussion are the results of significant historical contacts throughout the time span or life of the tradition. This hypothesis is supported by the very close synchronization of change within any of these traditions. The diagrammatic charts which Sears, Haury, and Ford present make this period-for-period synchronization within the tradition strikingly clear. In Peru and Bolivia, Bennett's (Bennett and Bird, 1949, Fig. 19) chronological chart shows the south coast sequence to be slightly in advance of the south highland column in the earlier periods although closely synchronized with it in the later. The hypothesis of close and steady contact is further bolstered by examples of trade or stylistic interinfluencing within the geographical range of each pottery tradition. Sears (1952, p. 108) has mentioned specific examples of this between the southern and northern sequences of the south Appalachian complicated stamped tradition. Such contacts and movements are a major part of Ford's (1952, pp. 380 ff.) thesis on the pottery history of the Gulf Coast–lower Mississippi Valley. In the southwest, the apparent cross-ties among Hohokam, Mogollon, and Anasazi are more frequent in the later periods than the earlier; but early evidences of such contacts are known, and, moreover, such contacts are in pottery trade (Martin, Quimby, and Collier, 1947, pp. 115–117, 172, 177–178, 208). In Peru and Bolivia, there are widespread stylistic linkages between coast and highland on the Tiahuanaco horizon, and such close ties are duplicated again on the Inca horizon in the final prehistoric period. As in the southwest, the earlier periods seem more independent of each other; but there are certain elements and themes which relate even these early styles, such as the common use of the feline as a decorative motif.

To conclude, a tradition trend in ceramic development is a time-dimensional configuration which is expressed in pottery decorative or other pottery properties and which coordinates and interrelates the changes in the various sequences and styles of a specific pottery tradition. It is a phenomenon resulting from historical contacts whose evidences may, or may not, be readily perceived. It appears to be subject to certain limitations of geographically continuous space in the same manner as the pottery tradition.

Notes

[1]Sears (1952, p. 108). These are relatively "short" estimated dates. Adjusted to radiocarbon dates for Ohio Hopewell, and assuming a Hopewell–Early Swift Creek contemporaneity, would pull them downward 500 to 800 years.

[2]Chronological spans of south Appalachian and Gulf Coast–lower Mississippi traditions are approximately equivalent and contemporaneous. In Gulf Florida, a region of geographical overlap between the two traditions, there is a blending of the two streams of influence in the same ceramic products. Yet under these conditions the separate traditional trends are evident. Late Swift Creek Complicated Stamped and Kolomoki Complicated Stamped styles are responding to the south Appalachian trends in the largeness and simplicity of their designs, but they also show influence from the Gulf Coast–lower Mississippi traditional trend in that these designs are restricted to a band around the upper part of the vessel wall.

[3]This is based upon the Nazca A–Nazca B sequence propounded by Gayton and Kroeber.

[4]Chiripa (Bennett and Bird, 1949, p. 147, fig. 27), which is believed to precede both Pucara and early Tiahuanaco, is a two-color ware which, apparently, antedates the beginnings of the polychrome tradition in the south highlands.

18

DIAGRAM OF A POTTERY TRADITION

(From *Process and Pattern in Culture, Essays in Honor of Julian H. Steward*, R. A. Manners, ed., pp. 156–174, Aldine Publishing Co., Chicago, 1964. Reprinted by permission of R. A. Manners.)

Archaeology provides a chronological perspective on cultural stability and change. This perspective may be exploited in different ways. We may describe the histories of specific cultures, in terms of their content, and from our diachronic vantage point attempt to fathom cause in the events of these histories. Or we may describe the profiles of culture change, in more general terms, and from these venture hypotheses about culture development. To pursue the latter course a method is needed whereby we may treat of *types of culture change* as these are viewed through time. A few years ago a symposium group of American archaeologists formulated such a method (Haury and Thompson, 1956).[1] This essay is a trial examination of their method.

The unit of investigation defined by the symposium for culture study was the *tradition*: "a socially transmitted cultural form which persists in time." In keeping with this, I have selected a pottery tradition of Precolumbian Peru, with the intent of sketching the life history of this tradition through descriptive analysis and synthesis of the order recommended by the symposium group. I will also examine the possible causal factors which appear to have imparted the particular configuration to "form" to this pottery tradition and, having done this, will offer hypotheses about such factors in a more general way.

This is not a detailed study and does not undertake the kind of fine-grained analysis which the symposium members may have had in mind as an ideal test of their method. The example I have chosen, however, has obvious advantages. The materials representing the tradition, the modeled pottery of north coastal Peru, are abundant and easily recognizable. The time dimension of the tradition is long and reasonably well dated by both radiocarbon and stratigraphy. Then, too, the events in the history of the tradition are fairly clear, at least in bold outline, and they can be related with a good degree of probability to human affairs other than those immediately concerned with the pottery-making itself. The shortcomings of the data of the tradition will be pointed out, or will be evident, as we proceed with the discussion.

Descriptive and Contextual Analysis

The pottery tradition in question is one termed the *North Peruvian Plastic* (Willey, 1945). Its central characteristic is the technique of plastic treatment of the vessel clay for ornamentive purposes. This is done by modeling, usually in the full-round, so that the shape of the vessel assumes a life-form. Supplemental plastic treatment is given in handles, spouts, and in a high-relief modeling or sculpting of surface details. Associated attributes are the frequent use of the jar form, small spout orifices, flat vessel bottoms, stirrup-mouth spouts, and figure-and-bridge spouts. In general, the products of the tradition are small and well-made. A two-faced mold was often employed in their manufacture.

The geographic range of the North Peruvian Plastic Tradition is the north coast of Peru, especially from the Lambayeque Valley, on the north, to and including Nepeña Valley, on the south. Within this range the centrally located Chicama-Moche-Virú series of valleys are best known archaeologically, and we will be particularly concerned with them in this examination. It should also be noted that the tradition is represented beyond these limits. On the coast its strong influences go as far south as Ancon and north to Piura. They also penetrate the highlands. Within these wider perimeters, however, the tradition is expressed in special ways. Thus, it may appear only in certain brief periods or in minor frequencies; or its presence may be registered merely as a blended influence in regional styles of other traditions.

The chronologic dimension of the North Peruvian Plastic Tradition is of at least 2,000 years' duration (Figure 18.1). In Chicama-Moche-Virú it begins no later than 500 B.C. and persists to and beyond the Spanish Conquest.

The North Peruvian Plastic Tradition probably had its origins, in part, in a simple plain pottery of the Peruvian north and central coasts. This is the earliest pottery of coastal Peru, and it is found in sites of early fishers and farmers where it dates back to between 1,000 and 1,500 B.C. (Lanning, 1959; Collier, 1962). The exact chronological relationships of this early pottery to the first appearances of maize are uncertain, but these two important traits seem to arrive in Peru at approximately the same time. As earlier radiocarbon dates for pottery are known from Ecuador (Evans and Meggers, 1958), Colombia (Reichel-Dolmatoff, 1961), and Mesoamerica (MacNeish, 1962), and as the earliest Peruvian maize seems to be of a Mesoamerican type, it may be assumed, as a tentative hypothesis, that the earliest Peruvian pottery was diffused into Peru from the north. Whether this was along the coast, through the highlands and from there to various places on the coast, or by both routes is unknown. For the present discussion the points to be established are that the oldest pottery of the north Peruvian coast dates between 1,000 and 1,500 B.C., that it was the property of sedentary coastal fishing peoples who were rapidly assimilating to farming, and that these prototypes and contexts provide the setting for the development of the North Peruvian Plastic Pottery Tradition.

After 1,000 B.C. north coast Peruvian pottery shows a trend toward increasingly greater and more complex surface decoration. This decoration was accomplished by incision, brushing, small applique modeling, and limited painting. Shortly after 800 B.C. this trend was greatly accelerated by the appearance of an art style known as the Chavín Horizon (Kroeber, 1944; Willey, 1945, 1948, 1951b; Rowe, 1962). The Chavín style is seen in various media, including incised and relief-modeled pottery. Some of the relief-

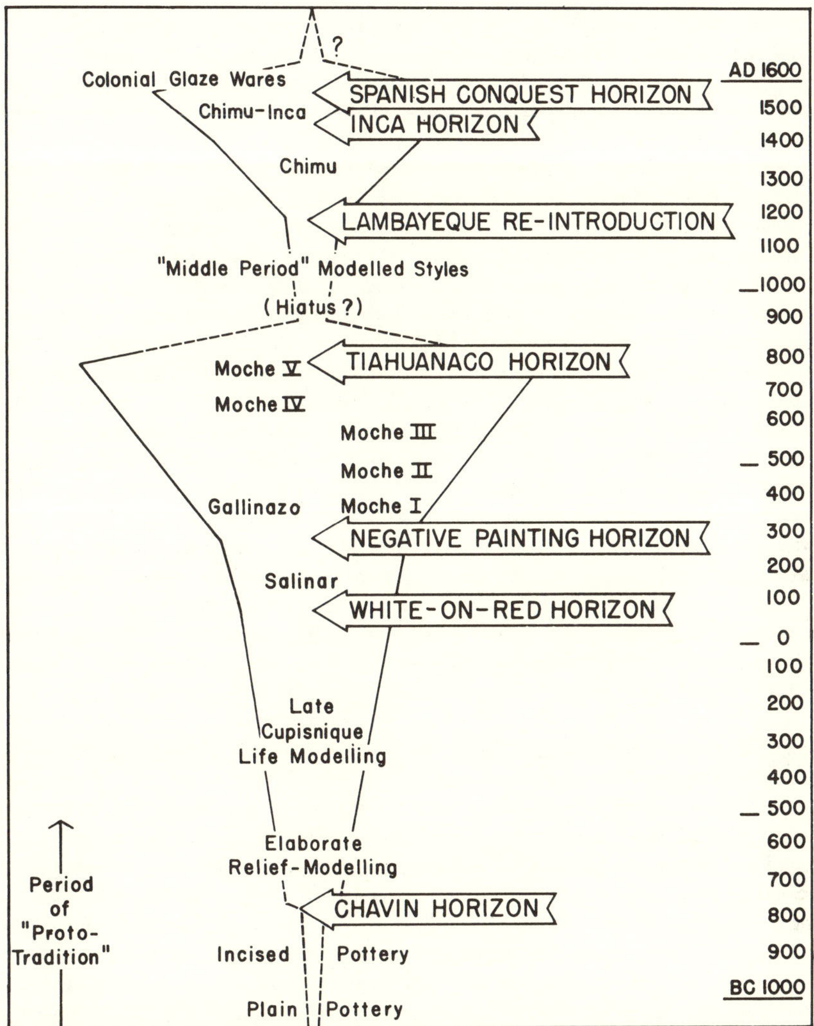

Figure 18.1. Diagram of the North Peruvian Plastic Pottery Tradition as it persisted through time in the Chicama-Moche-Virú region.

modeled jars, of the early Cupisnique phase, are outstanding works of art (Kubler, 1962, pl. 129, *left*; Bushnell, 1956, pls. 5, 7, 8).[2] It could be argued that the North Peruvian Plastic Tradition begins with these pieces; certainly they were prototypical to it; however, in keeping with the definitions of the tradition given above—with an emphasis on life-form modeling of the entire vessel body—a slightly later date, of about 500 B.C., may be a more appropriate starting point.[3]

The first full-round and life-form modeled pottery, of the middle and late Cupisnique phases, occurs mostly on stirrup-mouth jars. Subjects treated appear to be both mundane and sacred. In the one category, for example, is a house representation and a woman nursing a child; in the other a human head is given feline attributes, perhaps to illustrate a deity or a mythological concept (Larco Hoyle, 1941, 1946, pls. 63, 64; Kubler, 1962, pl. 129, *right*; Bushnell, 1956, pls. 6, 4). In general, the style is naturalistic rather than highly conventional; and this generalization holds for the two millennia of the history of the North Peruvian Plastic Tradition. The larger context of the Cupisnique culture is one of peasant farming hamlets oriented toward special temple structures. Populations were relatively small, and it is doubtful if canal irrigation had yet begun.[4]

Just after A.D. 100 a number of cultural changes mark the inception of a new major culture period.[5] The best-known local north coast phase of this period is the Salinar. The shift from Cupisnique to Salinar stylistic modes is a gradual one. The new style is characterized by red-surfaced, oxidized pottery rather than the dark-surfaced, reduced-fired ware of the former period. White pigment decoration is added. Life-modeling continues with great vigor. Stirrup-mouth and strap-and-spout jars are fashioned in the images of people, animals, birds, and houses (Larco Hoyle, 1946, pl. 66; Bushnell, 1956, pl. 12). The trend toward realism is even greater than before; but where Cupisnique renderings had a certain subtlety, especially in the feline or man-feline sculptures, Salinar leaves little to the imagination. Salinar has roots in Cupisnique but it also partakes of something else. This "something else" is a Peruvian horizonal influence known as the White-on-Red Horizon (Willey, 1945, 1948). Unlike the preceding Chavín Horizon it has no iconography and little in the way of easily recognizable design motifs. It is, in effect, substylistic, being a diffusion of technical elements such as the oxidized-firing of the ware and the above-mentioned combination of white design painting on a red ground color. The social and cultural context of Salinar is that of a larger population than before. A shifting of sites away from the seashore has occurred, and this suggests full dependence upon agriculture and the beginnings of canal irrigation. The small living community and temple-center settlement pattern continues but a new feature is added in hilltop redoubts or places of refuge.

At about A.D. 300 Salinar pottery, and the North Peruvian Plastic Tradition, were modified by Negative-Painting Horizon influences. This is seen in the appearance of negative or resist-dye painting of vessel surfaces. This was probably considered as a secondary ornamental embellishment by pottery artists, for life-modeling continued in a variety of forms (Bennett, 1939, fig. 13; Bushnell, 1956, pls. 13, 14, 17). Some stylistic changes are, however, noted in this modeling. These Negative-Painting Horizon influences are best represented in the Virú Valley and its Gallinazo culture. The trends of population growth and general cultural development of the preceding Salinar culture also characterizes Gallinazo, and by the close of the Gallinazo phase in Virú that valley had attained its maximum population size and the fullest development of its irrigation systems. In the lower reaches of the valley a big ceremonial center, including an adobe platform pyramid 25 meters in height, was the focus of a growing large town. Farther up the valley impressive fortifications of Gallinazo construction topped rocky side crags and apparently served as strong points for defense against attack from outside the valley.

The Moche, or Mochica, culture, which succeeded the Gallinazo in Virú, had its origins in the Chicama and Moche Valleys, and its early developments probably paralleled the growth of Gallinazo in the Virú. The Moche culture is the context for the greatest elaborations of the North Coast Plastic Pottery Tradition. The ceramic hallmark of the culture is the stirrup-mouthed jar with the handsomely modeled body form. The modeling, which was done with the use of molds, is unusually realistic, the execution flawless, and the range of subject matter beyond simple descriptive listing (Larco Hoyle, 1946; Bushnell, 1956, pls. 22–5). Among the very finest specimens are portrait heads which are, indeed, the faces of individuals. Secular themes predominate, but there are also representations of the supernatural and of mythological subjects. The sculptural aspects of Moche pottery are supplemented with two color painting—nearly always red and white, probably the heritage of the White-on-red Horizon and of Salinar. Negative-painting is used, although rarely. Moche culture, like Gallinazo, but even more so, was a civilization. Its art, and undoubtedly its power, extended from the Jequetepeque to the Nepeña Valleys. Besides its great temple mounds, palaces, population aggregations, and irrigation works it utilized copper and, probably, bronze for the making of tools and weapons. The artistic representations in the pottery and in other media tell a story of a war-like, stratified society on the threshold of urbanism.

At a date estimated as about A.D. 800 Moche culture suffered serious disruption. We see this in a number of radical changes, such as the abandonment of old temple and palace centers and fortifications and the imposition of a new settlement pattern in these north coast valleys. The new pattern was organized on planned, rectangular, symmetrically subdivided dwelling compounds. This settlement change is correlated with the death of the Moche pottery style, and with the drastic diminution—and, perhaps, for a time, the complete disappearance—of the North Peruvian Plastic Tradition.[6] The ceramic style which replaces the Moche in the Chicama-Moche-Virú sector is known as the Coast Tiahuanaco or the Tiahuanaco Horizon. It is utterly different from the Moche style in its iconography and has its origins outside the North Peruvian Plastic Tradition. It emphasizes polychrome painting and conventionalized or abstract symbolism rather than sculpture and realism. In the centuries which follow this introduction a medley of pottery styles appears in the Chicama-Moche-Virú Valleys (see Bennett, 1939, figs. 9, 10; Bushnell, 1956, pls. 44, 54). Some of them are Tiahuanaco-derived, such as the so-called Black-White-Red Geometric style, and a slow waning of the strong Tiahuanaco Horizon influence can be traced in them. Others are plain black or red "pressed" wares, made in molds in the old Moche manner but exhibiting designs which are vagely Tiahuanacoid. Finally, there are some which are modeled in the true Plastic Tradition. The immediate antecedents of these last are uncertain. It is possible that some life-modeled ware continued to be made in Chicama-Moche-Virú, even at the height of Tiahuanaco Horizon influence, but it is more likely that these "Middle Period Modeled styles" (Figure 18.1) represent a reintroduction of the North Peruvian Plastic Tradition from the Lambayeque Valley (Bennett, 1939, figs. 19, 20; Willey, 1953b).[7]

At about 1200 to 1300 A.D. this stylistic diversity in north coast pottery gives way to the full re-establishment in Chicama-Moche-Virú of the North Peruvian Plastic Tradition in a style known as the Chimu. Chimu pottery is a polished black ware, and most of its full-round modeling is associated with the stirrup-mouthed jar form (see, for example, Bennett, 1939, fig. 17, a–d). It was produced with the aid of a mold and turned out in great volume. It is esthetically inferior to the preceding Moche style which it resembles, lacking the fidelity of realistic detail, the imaginative conceptions, and the care and skill of execution. The Chimu civilization and kingdom dominated the north coast of Peru for about 200 years, and its great capital was at Chanchan, in the Moche Valley. Chanchan is a vast aggregate of huge, planned enclosure-type residential units. In other words, the Chimu retained and developed further the planned type of settlement unit that appeared on the north coast at the same time as the Tiahuanaco Horizon style.

Chanchan was overthrown and made a part of the Inca empire in the latter half of the fifteenth century. For the most part, the Inca impress on the material culture of the inhabitants of the north coast valleys was slight. Some Incaic modifications do occur in the North Peruvian Plastic Tradition, however. These are seen in occasional multi-color painting of vessels and in the presence of a few new vessel forms (Schmidt, 1929, pl. 261, 264).[8]

The final episode is the Spanish Conquest and occupation of the Peruvian coastal valleys, which occurred in 1532 and the years immediately thereafter. With this conquest the old native governments were swept away and the religions suppressed or driven underground. Quite interestingly, some life-modeled pottery in the old tradition continued to be made. Chimu-Inca vessel forms have been found which duplicate the Precolumbian products except for the addition of European glazes (Bushnell, 1959). It is uncertain just how long this craft survived, perhaps no longer than the life spans of native potters who were working at the time of the Conquest and who were trained in glaze-techniques in the first Spanish monasteries of northern Peru. The mold-made and modeled wares do not appear to be a part of the ceramic technology of present-day, acculturated Indian communities of the Chicama-Moche-Virú region (Gillin, 1947), but some modeled pottery, reminiscent of the Chimu and Chimu-Inca styles is made for the tourist trade on the far north coast, near Piura (Collier, 1959; Christensen, 1955). Whether this is a recent revival, in imitation of archaeological pieces, or whether it represents unbroken continuity with the past is unknown.

A few last observations should be added before closing this review of the cultural contexts of the North Peruvian Plastic Pottery Tradition. It should be noted that the pottery of the tradition was always, at whatever period, in the category of "finer" wares as distinct from plain or "ordinary" wares which were being made at the same time. The latter were used for cooking and storage while the modeled wares were used as grave furniture and, probably, for household needs other than those of cooking or gross storage. Nevertheless, it would be a mistake to consider the modeled wares as being rare "luxury" goods that were socially restricted. The quantities in which they were made are too large for that. This does not mean that there were no class distinctions or prerogatives in the possession of fine pottery; but it is inconceivable that virtually all members of the societies did not see, know about, and appreciate the full range of ceramic manufactures. Even though modeled pottery was probably always made by specialists, it was not an esoteric part of the cultures which possessed it. It was, instead, a vehicle of a true popular art, and this, I think, is an important consideration to be kept in mind as we study the history of the Plastic Tradition.

Descriptive Synthesis of the Tradition Diagram

The symposium formulations for descriptive synthesis of cultural traditions enumerated five types of culture change profiles or tradition segment forms: (1) direct, (2) converging, (3) diverging, (4) elaborating, and (5) reducing (Haury and Thompson, *op. cit.*). A direct tradition segment is one in which there is relatively unchanging cultural continuity. A converging segment describes the merger or mutual impingement of what were two separate traditions. Diverging is the opposite of this, referring to a tradition segment which is splitting into two or more distinguishable parts. Elaborating traditions are those which become increasingly complex, both in content and organization, as they progress through time. Reducing traditions are those which follow an opposite trend. With these formulae in mind let us turn to Figure 18.1.

Before discussing the diagram in detail I should clarify the methodology. Throughout I have proceeded on empirical observations, but these are based on impressions rather than actual counting of trait units or elements. This is an admitted weakness in the present synthesis. It could be overcome by two kinds of data. First, we need more accurate dating, through radiocarbon determinations and finer subphasing of the north coast culture sequence. Second, we need more detailed typological studies and frequency counts of pottery types and attributes. Until such data are available the relative scaling of elaboration or reduction in a tradition segment cannot be done objectively.

The "proto" segment of the North Peruvian Plastic Tradition is indicated on the diagram by the dotted line profile which begins at 1,000 B.C., or before, and which describes a slow elaborating tradition segment. This judgment is based on the known addition of vessel surface decorative techniques to previously plain pottery. Between 800 and 700 B.C. the Chavín Horizon influences effect a convergence with the resident tradition of the north coast, and this convergence is followed by a more pronounced expanding or elaborating profile. It is in this elaborating segment that the North Peruvian Plastic Tradition probably begins.

Throughout late Cupisnique times, dated here as 500 B.C. to A.D. 100, this diagram of a slowly elaborating tradition segment is maintained. It rests upon the absence or relative scarcity of full-round life-modeling in earlier Cupisnique and its frequency in later phases. In this connection it is noted that the late Cupisnique jar form has a more slender stirrup-spout and a more delicate lip treatment than early Cupisnique. Vessels with the late spout and lip features seem to be more frequently life-modeled than the others.

The tradition segment succeeding late Cupisnique is a converging one with, in sequence, the White-on-Red and Negative-Painting influences merging with the Plastic line of development.

Following this, the Moche segment of the tradition is rapidly and markedly elaborating. This aspect of the diagram can be supported by the excellence and refinement of the Moche ceramic product, its great volume, its infinite variety of subject matter, the technical feature of the two-faced mold, the vigor of the modeling art, and the skill of the subsidiary scene painting on many specimens. Diagramming is, of course, handicapped by lack of closer analysis of the Moche subphases. My impression is, however, that virtuosity in plastic handling increases up through Moche IV, with elaboration in Moche V carried on mostly in the red-and-white painting rather than in modeling.

The Tiahuanaco Horizon effects a converging segment with the Plastic Tradition.

Subsequent to the Tiahuanaco convergence, the Plastic Tradition shows a rapidly reducing segment; in fact, it is possible that the tradition was, for a time, no longer maintained in the Chicama-Moche-Virú region of our study.

The Plastic Tradition is resumed shortly, however, and describes an elaborating segment. This elaboration is an expression of the apparent increase in full-round modeling from the "Middle Period" (see Figure 18.1) to the Chimu phase. This elaboration also coincides with a convergence of Lambayeque modeled ware influences. I have not scaled the Chimu elaboration as high in absolute rating as I have the Moche. This is, of course, an impressionistic reading of the data. There can be little quarrel with the statement that Chimu pottery is esthetically inferior to that of Moche: Chimu life-modeled forms are stereotyped and blurred. But whether the style shows less variety of subject matter and treatment than Moche is, perhaps, more debatable. My opinion, based on viewing large museum collections and a review of the literature, is that Chimu is less varied; but this needs further checking.[9]

The elaborating Chimu segment becomes a converging one with the joining of the Inca Horizon influences. After this, the brief span between the Inca convergence and the Spanish Horizon seems best appraised as slightly elaborating. The Chimu-Inca hybrid vessels are the basis for this description.

With the Spanish Horizon the North Peruvian Plastic Tradition becomes definitely and rapidly a reducing one, in spite of the incorporation of some techniques from European potters. The tradition appears to have gradually dwindled away through further reduction in the succeeding centuries.

A Consideration of Causal Factors

The archaeological symposium (Haury and Thompson, *op. cit.*) to which we have been referring lists seven basic classes of factors which its authors believe to be potentially causal in the development of cultural traditions: (1) biological, (2) environmental, (3) inherent, (4) demographic, (5) societal, (6) contact, and (7) cultural.

In examining the North Peruvian Plastic Pottery Tradition we can, I think, pass over two classes of these factors at the outset. First, biological factors lie beyond our control of the data. We have insufficient information on Precolumbian physical types from the north coast of Peru to make any statements about possible correlations between such subracial factors and the development of the pottery tradition in question.[10] Second, environmental factors probably can be held as constant. Although there are some indications that the climate of the earlier half of the first millennium B.C. was slightly more moist than later, climatic change does not appear as an important causal factor.

Inherent factors, as conceived of by the symposium group, refer to the nature of the tradition itself. To continue with their phrasing, "potentialities for 'play' inherent in an attribute tend to result in Elaborating Tradition" and "potentialities for variation inherent in a tradition" have a tendency for similar results. In this regard, pottery is an ideally malleable medium for "play" and "variation"; and the plastic attribute or mode, central to our tradition, is especially so. Hence, it is a reasonable surmise that these inherent factors helped condition the several long elaborating trend segments of the North Peruvian Plastic Tradition.

The demographic factor of increasing population also probably played a role in the elaborating trend of those segments up to, and including, the Moche style segment. This whole time span was one of population growth in the north Peruvian valleys. From the end of the Moche segment upward in time, however, it is unlikely that demographic factors had any important bearing on the pottery tradition developments. Population in the later periods was, apparently, stable.

Societal factors refer to class or occupational specialization; and, in the opinion of the symposium group, an "interest in innovation or variation by specialists may vastly increase change and tends to result in Elaborating Tradition." Judging from the quality of the product and from the social and cultural contexts of the Moche and Chimu civilizations, it seems quite likely that the pottery of these styles was produced by craft specialists and that the societal factor was a conditioning one for these particular elaborating segments.

It is with contact factors, however, that we appear to come closer to grips with cause. These, of course, are emphasized by the very nature of our diagram. On an early level, the convergence of the Chavín Horizon with the local north coast pottery continuum probably resulted in the formation of the Plastic Tradition. Subsequently, it is noteworthy that White-on-Red and Negative-Painting Horizon convergences occur just before the amazing Moche efflorescence. From these observations we phrase the question: Does culture contact result in tradition elaboration? But, continuing up the time scale of the diagram, we see that the opposite happens after the Tiahuanaco Horizon convergence. Seemingly as a result of this contact, the Plastic Tradition is virtually extinguished for a time. How then does the Tiahuanaco Horizon convergence differ from the others?

To attempt to answer this we must examine the contents and contexts of these several horizonal influences, and in this examination the Tiahuanaco Horizon looks like an actual invasion and military conquest of the Chicama-Moche-Virú region while the other horizons do not have these aspects. After the Tiahuanaco Horizon old coastal fortified posts are abandoned, radical changes occur in the settlement pattern of the valleys and in the nature of politico-religious architecture, and a Tiahuanacoid iconography is generally substituted for that of Moche. In contrast, the White-on-Red and Negative-Painting Horizons lack iconographic content and are not accompanied by drastic settlement and architectural changes. We cannot say whether they were accompanied by new populations or if they were spread solely by diffusion, but whichever, they impart technical ideas in ceramic manufacture which were incorporated into the North Peruvian Plastic Tradition, probably with the elaborating results noted.

The earlier Chavín Horizon is more comparable to the Tiahuanaco in that it, too, has strong iconographic content, and there is also the likelihood that it spread in conjunction with innovations in ceremonial architecture in some places; however, a very significant difference is apparent in that Chavín Horizon art did not come up against another style of the first magnitude as Tiahuanaco art did in its confrontation of Moche. And by this token, it is unlikely that the forçes which carried Chavín Horizon art and ideas moved against the same kind of a political establishment that the bearers of Tiahuanaco Horizon art overthrew in Moche.

In the light of this what can we say about the Inca Horizon? As the diagram shows, it had a mild elaborative effect on the North Peruvian Plastic Tradition, yet we know that it was, indeed, associated with a military conquest of the Chimu. Why, then, assuming that the Tiahuanaco Horizon represents conquest, were not the effects of Tiahuanaco and Inca on the Plastic Tradition the same? I think the reasons for their differences in effect on the pottery tradition are related to the reasons for the differences in their more general cultural effects. The Tiahuanaco Horizon was generally disruptive; the Inca Horizon was not. A clue to understanding why this was so lies, I think, in the very symbols of the two horizons. The earliest Tiahuanaco pottery found on the north coast has a striking iconography—a definite central theme of a man-jaguar or demon. Inca art and pottery as it appears on the north coast, or for that matter elsewhere in Peru, lacks such a central iconographic motif. This suggests that there was less ideological content to the Inca Horizon than to the Tiahuanaco.

The last horizon contact on our diagram is the Spanish. Perhaps significantly, it is the only other horizonal convergence which is followed by a reducing segment comparable to that following the Tiahuanaco Horizon. And we also know that this horizon was characterized by profound cultural change. This change was material, being reflected in settlement patterns and in many other ways, and ideological.

In emphasizing contact factors and building hypotheses about them I have neglected other cultural factors which may have exerted causal influences on the life-history of the North Peruvian Plastic Tradition. These are difficult to control or to hold as constant. A good specific example is the hypothesis that the Chimu revival of the pottery tradition, after the Tiahuanaco interregnum, was heavily influenced by metallurgical techniques and that this influencing had a reducing effect on the esthetic quality of what had been an essentially sculptural art in earlier times (Muelle, 1941; Kubler, 1962: 272). This is a possibility and may have been a contributing factor in the Moche-to-Chimu reduction of the tradition, but I am unconvinced of its primary importance as it does little to explain the disruption or break of the tradition which can be more easily laid to the Tiahuanaco Horizon influences.

There are also those cultural factors sometimes referred to as "pattern exhaustion." Undoubtedly, any tradition or pattern has its limits of elaboration, when expansive growth must stop and some other kind of trend set in; but as far as the limitations of possibilities go it would seem to me that the North Peruvian Plastic Tradition, even in its explosive Moche phases, still had new avenues to explore. The reasons why it failed to do so are, I think, more satisfactorily explained by the contact factors than by any others.

To summarize the discussion of causal factors in the development of the North Peruvian Plastic Pottery Tradition, I would list the following:

1. The early, slowly elaborating segment of the tradition was most probably conditioned by population growth in the north coast valleys and by potentialities inherent in the ceramic medium and its plastic manipulation.
2. The rapid elaborating segment of the first millennium A.D. had as its primary causes the impingement and assimilation of outside influences as represented by the White-on-Red and Negative-Painting Horizons. These influences, insofar as we can determine, were largely confined to realms of ceramic technology and esthetics. Secondary contributing causes to this elaborating segment were probably continued population growth, inherent factors of the medium, and societal factors of craft-guild development.
3. The sudden reduction—with a possible temporary break—in the tradition after A.D. 800 is to be attributed to the impact of the Tiahuanaco Horizon. The influences of this horizon are seen not only in pottery but in many aspects of culture and were probably ideological as well as material.
4. The Chimu elaborating segment of the tradition resulted primarily from a reintroduction of the Plastic Tradition to the Chicama-Moche-Virú region from the Lambayeque Valley and from the gradual assimilation, dilution, or expulsion of the Tiahuanaco Horizon influences from north coast pottery. It should be noted, however, that many nonceramic traits that first appeared on the north coast at the time of the Tiahuanaco Horizon are retained by Chimu culture. Among these are settlement and architectural types.
5. The minor elaborating segment following the Inca Horizon resulted from that contact. In general, Inca influence on north coast culture is slight.
6. The sudden reduction of the tradition following the Spanish Horizon is attributed to that contact. The influences of this horizon are seen not only in pottery but in many aspects of culture and were ideological as well as material.

SOME HYPOTHESES ABOUT CONTACT FACTORS

From the above, and with the assumption that other factors have been negligible, minor, or constant, I suggest two hypotheses about the effects of contact factors on cultural continua such as the North Peruvian Plastic Pottery Tradition.

1. A popular art will be stimulated to elaboration by contacts of technological and esthetic innovation in the appropriate sphere of that art.
2. But such a popular art will be reduced rapidly by contacts which effect major changes in culture, particularly in the ideological sphere.

The first hypothesis is, perhaps, a corollary of the anthropological truism that cultures tend to borrow readily in technology. The second hypothesis seems the obverse truism, that cultures tend to resist or to be disturbed by innovations in the ideological realm. Yet there are some special qualifications to be made about the second hypothesis. It is not that conquest by an alien force will necessarily reduce a popular art. One can imagine changes at the top of the social structure and in official religions that might have very little, or at least a very slow, effect on a broadly based art such as that of the modeled pottery of Moche or Chimu. In fact, we know that when the Inca conquered the Chimu something like this happened and that there were no radical reductions of the local pottery tradition. The requisite conditions for reduction seem to be, rather, the combination of conquest with the forcible imposition of a new, proselyting ideology. And I think we must stipulate one further condition—a condition suggested by the elaborating effects following the Chavín Horizon which, at first glance, seem contradictory to the present line of argument. Assuming Chavín art to be a manifestation of a proselyting ideology, there is no evidence that it met resistance from a belief system of comparable stature. On the other hand, Tiahuanaco and Spanish Horizon influences did meet with complex and long-established ideologies which were opposed to their own. In the latter instance we know that these old resident value systems were completely rejected and broken down; in the former instance it is highly probable that this also happened. In both, the Plastic Pottery Tradition suffered reduction. Thus, our final condition for the second hypothesis is one of sharp ideological conflict between invading and resident cultures.

Notes

[1]The symposium group consisted of E. W. Haury (chairman), R. H. Thompson (editor), R. L. Rands, A. C. Spaulding, W. W. Taylor, Robert Wauchope, and M. E. White (recorder).

[2]All of these styles of Peruvian pottery, in the Plastic Tradition, are well known and well illustrated in both monographic and general survey literature. I shall make no attempt to provide detailed references but simply cite a few standard and easily available sources.

[3]This follows Lanning's (1959) dating. He places life-form modeling as beginning in "Cupisnique B" phase. For a ceramic history of north coastal Peru see also, Ford and Willey, 1949; Collier, 1955, particularly pp. 99–141.

[4]This and subsequent observations on settlements and population derive from Willey, 1953a.

[5]This follows Lanning's (1959) estimates which are based on new correlations with central and south coast sequences. It should be emphasized that this dating is by no means final, and it may be that the White-on-Red and Negative-Painting Horizons should be moved back to the more conventional assignments of the last few centuries B.C. (see Willey, 1953a; Collier, 1962). No radiocarbon dates are as yet available which bear *directly* upon the question.

[6]No such break occurred in the plain household wares, however. These show continuity from Moche into the period of the Tiahuanaco Horizon in the Virú Valley, suggesting that although some new population elements may have come into the north coast with the Tiahuanaco Horizon old local elements also remained (see Ford and Willey, 1949; Collier, 1955). Stumer (1956) discusses the Moche-to-Tiahuanacoid transition and its results in some detail. Stumer is inclined to see some modeled ware continuity, even during the time of strongest Tiahuanaco Horizon impact.

[7]It is possible that this "Lambayeque reintroduction" of the North Peruvian Plastic Tradition to Chicama-Moche-Virú resulted from an invasion by people from Lambayeque at about the same time as the Tiahuanaco Horizon disruptions (see, for instance, the chronology chart in Choy, 1960, p. 196).

[8]The Schmidt (1929, p. 264) specimen is said to be from Pachacamac on the central coast of Peru; however, it is typical of the north coast Inca-Chimu style.

[9]It is difficult to do such checking from the large illustrated compendia of Peruvian pottery, of which there are many, as authors and compilers have tended to select illustrations *for variety* rather than for frequency representation of types. The same holds true, of course, for many museum displays.

[10]The few available physical anthropological data on Precolumbian coastal Peru have been summarized by Newman (1948) who sees local valley breeding populations remaining stable as to physical type from the time of the Chavín Horizon until the Late Period (Chimu, in our diagram). In late times a certain amount of "leveling" of physical differences took place, from valley to valley. It is possible that this "leveling" resulted from population movements associated with the immediately preceding Tiahuanaco Horizon; but, as stated, information is still insufficient to do more than hint at cultural-physical type correlations.

19

The Classic Maya "Hiatus": A Rehearsal for the Collapse

(From *Mesoamerican Archaeology: New Approaches*, Norman Hammond, ed., pp. 417–430, Duckworth, London, 1974. Reprinted by permission of Duckworth Co., Ltd.)

In the latter half of the sixth century A.D. the Classic Maya civilization of the lowlands underwent a marked slowing down in that most sensitive sphere of its high ritual activities, the carving and dedication of Initial Series stelae. This near-cessation of monumental commemoration followed upon almost three centuries of a vigorous preoccupation with what has been termed the "stelae cult"; and when this slow-down was over, stelae dedication was resumed with intensity for almost another 300 years. This "hesitation" or near-gap in Maya Initial Series monuments and dates has been referred to as the Classic Maya "hiatus." Archaeologists have puzzled over its significance; but, in contrast to the more spectacular ninth-century failure and general collapse of Maya lowland civilization, which was also first signaled by a decline in stelae activities, this hiatus has not received the consideration that it probably deserves, though it has been noted and remarked upon by a number of Mayanists, among them Morley (1938–9: vol. 4, 333), Proskouriakoff (1950: 111–12), Thompson (1954: 55–6), Willey (1964b), and M. D. Coe (1966: 86). I would like now to right the balance somewhat by focusing attention on the hiatus and to do this by asking the question: to what extent did the hiatus foreshadow the eventual final collapse? Was it a kind of ominous and unconscious "rehearsal" for the later disaster? For if Maya civilization of the lowlands carried within itself, from its beginnings, the seeds of its own destruction as some have suggested, one might expect this to be true; and by examining the structure and dynamics of the "little collapse" of the hiatus we may place ourselves in a better position to understand the later "great collapse." We are, of course, comparing one shadowy and imperfectly comprehended set of events with another; but, by the very nature of archaeology, where one fact seen in a certain context may help us recognize and confirm a comparable fact in another context, such an examination could clarify both sets of events.

The observed facts of the hiatus may be set down quite simply. The earliest known

Maya Classic Initial Series monuments and dates appear in the latter part of the eighth *baktun*. They are in sites clustering in the northeastern Peten, in what might be considered the very heart, or "core area," of the southern lowlands—at Uaxactun, Tikal, Uolantun, and Balakbal. At Uaxactun and Tikal, at least, these first monuments occur in the context of a rapidly rising ceremonial center development, at the close and climax of the Terminal Late Preclassic or Protoclassic Period. In fact, their appearance is taken to mark the beginning of the Early Classic Period at about A.D. 250 to 300. In the next two and a half centuries the stelae cult spreads to other sites, in most cases probably being assimilated into the evolving politico-religious developments of other Terminal Late Preclassic centers. By the end of the fifth *katun* of the ninth *baktun* (9.5.0.0.0 or A.D. 534) the stelae cult was also found at Xultun and Naachtun, in the northeast Peten, and, much farther afield, at Altar de Sacrificios, Yaxchilan, and Piedras Negras, on the Usumacinta drainage, and at Copan in the far southeast of the lowlands. It is shortly after this that the hiatus begins. From 9.5.0.0.0 until 9.8.0.0.0, or from A.D. 534 to 593, there is a sharp drop-off in both the number of monuments dedicated and in the number of sites where these few occur. In the old original heartland of the stelae cult there are no monuments at all between 9.5.0.0.0 and 9.9.0.0.0 at either Uaxactun or Naachtun; Tikal has only one, questionably dated at 9.6.13.0.0; and Xultun has one—not an Initial Series—that may be read as 9.7.10.0.0. On the Usumacinta drainage, Altar de Sacrificios shows a hiatus from 9.4.10.0.0 to 9.9.5.0.0; Yaxchilan has a similar gap; and Piedras Negras has two somewhat controversial hiatus monuments. Copan does somewhat better; Morley read three monuments to the sixth *katun* and one to the seventh, although with some questionings; but even by accepting all of these there is a lessening in the record by comparison with earlier or later times. Most interestingly, some of the firmest hiatus dates are from peripheral regions or regions which, up until that time, had no dated stelae. Pusilha, in southern British Honduras, has solid dates at 9.7.0.0.0 and 9.8.0.0.0 and a possible one at 9.6.0.0.0. Tulum, in the northern lowlands, has a 9.6.10.0.0 date, and there is also a stela at Coba which may date to the hiatus. Turning to the west, and going beyond the Usumacinta drainage, there is a 9.6.0.0.0 date at Tonina, in the central Chiapas highlands, and there are *katun* 8 dates at Comitan and Chinkultic in the same general region. In sum, during the hiatus, whose nadir is marked at the sixth and seventh *katuns* of the ninth *baktun*, there is very little stelae activity in the northeast Peten heartland, minimal activity on the Usumacinta, somewhat more at Copan, but the first inception of the stelae cult at sites on the eastern, western, and northern peripheries of the southern lowlands. (The basic sources for these stelae dates are in Morley 1938–9, 1920. For Coba see Thompson, Pollock and Charlot 1932.)

So far, the hiatus has been defined solely in terms of stelae dedications and dates, but is there a corresponding decline in other aspects of culture? Here we are handicapped by limited information, but where we do have data there does seem to be a similar decline. Thus, at Uaxactun, in the great acropolis-like structure A-V, the last building subphase (I*h*) of the Early Classic or Vault I Period has an associated stela with a date of 9.3.10.0.0 (A.D. 504). The immediately overlying building is also dated by a stela, this one with a reading of 9.9.6.2.3 (A.D. 619). The implications are that the intervening era between these two dates, which spans the sixth century A.D., was a time of little or no constructional activity (A. L. Smith 1950: 24–5, 67–8, 86–7). At Altar de Sacrificios the constructional story is much the same. The hiatus there is represented by the late Ayn, Veremos, and early Chixoy phases, spanning the sixth century and during which there was little major building (Adams 1971; Willey 1973b). For Tikal, detailed data on construction by phase have not yet been published, but the preliminary reports suggest that the time of the hiatus was a relatively slack architectural period (W. R. Coe 1965, 1967). These are also sites which manifest the stelae dedication hiatus; but it would be interesting to see what the architectural records at Tonina or Pusilha show for the same time. One would anticipate a positive covariance between monuments and architecture at these sites, too, which would mean that they would show building activity in the last half of the sixth century A.D.

Aside from the declines, in stelae activity and, probably, in architcture, the hiatus must also be characterized as a time of culture change and cultural reorientation; or at least this change and reorientation is revealed immediately after the hiatus. Proskouriakoff has referred to the hiatus as a "dark period" in Maya sculpture, one which reflected a "momentous historical event" that disturbed normal development; but, in her words, it was then followed by "a restoration of order and a new pulse of creative activity" (1950: 111–12). And in ceramics there can be little doubt but that the reorientation from Tzakol to Tepeu traditions occurred at some time during the hiatus. R. E. Smith has made this definition at Uaxactun (1955), and Adams' Altar de Sacrificios ceramic studies and those of Culbert at Tikal confirm it (Adams 1971; Culbert 1973). In architectural techniques, as has long been known, the hiatus also appears to mark the changeover from heavy block masonry to a veneer-like treatment. Indeed, following out of all this, the hiatus separates Early Classic from Late Classic in a very effective fashion, although whether one should draw the line nearer 9.8.0.0.0 (or about A.D. 600), as has been conventional, or at 9.6.0.0.0 (about A.D. 550), as W. R. Coe has suggested, is still undecided. (R. E. Smith (1955) was probably the first to specify 9.8.0.0.0 as the Early–Late Classic dividing line. See W. R. Coe 1965, and Willey, Culbert, and Adams 1967.) In brief, the archaeological record as we read it now shows that the last half of the sixth century A.D. was, to put it conservatively, a disturbed time in the southern Maya lowlands. Old patterns were being disrupted; new ones presumably were in formation; but for several decades there was a hiatus in what had been the normal courses of cultural activity.

How does this archaeological record compare with that of the ninth century when this southern lowland Maya civilization collapsed? (The circumstances of the collapse have been summarized by Willey and Shimkin 1971, 1973). Obviously, the cessation or slowing down of the stelae cult during the hiatus is very reminiscent of what happened two or three centuries later, as is the slackening of major architectural activity in the ceremonial centers. These archaeological aspects almost certainly point to a weakening of the central sociopolitical structure of the culture in both instances. The differences here are largely those of degree and duration. The quiescence or semi-moribund condition of the centers in the sixth century stands in contrast to their complete death and abandonment at the close of the ninth century, and the approximate half-century of the hiatus is substantially less than the 100 years or more of the final decline. These differences, in turn, undoubtedly relate to others. Foremost among these is the matter of population. Here we need more and better information, especially on residence or house mound counts; but from the evidence that is now available there does not seem to have been anywhere near the same kind of population reduction in the hiatus as in the collapse. In the latter, the sustaining populations of many centers were truly decimated between 9.19.0.0.0 (A.D. 810) and 10.4.0.0.0 (A.D. 909), with virtual abandonment of the site region after that (as at Tikal; see Culbert 1973). This would not appear to have been the case for the hiatus. Certainly nothing as drastic as this occurred on a wide scale; however, there are some indications of population decline at some sites during the hiatus, such as at Altar de Sacrificios (see Willey 1973b; for Seibal see A. L. Smith and Willey 1969; Sabloff 1973) and this is a matter that deserves close attention in settlement investigation at other sites.

Besides these above considerations, there were, of course, great differences in the outcome of the hiatus and the collapse—as the names themselves indicate. After the collapse there was no real sculptural or architectural revival, at least not in the southern sector of the lowlands; and in ceramics the break and tradition change of the end of the ninth century were much more profound than those of the sixth.

These comparisons between the hiatus and the collapse can be extended further by directing attention not so much to the immediate events of each as to their broader antecedent cultural settings. This has been done for the collapse in connection with a recent symposium on that theme (Culbert 1973, Willey and Shimkin 1973). The structure of Maya society and culture as it appeared just before the ninth century A.D. was analyzed in some detail, insofar as this could be done from archaeological data, and an attempt was made to isolate the stress factors that were operating on and in it. Among other things, it was pointed out that at the climax of the Late Classic Period, in the eighth century A.D. and just before the collapse, Maya population of the southern lowlands was at an all-time peak. Both house mound tabulations, where these are available, and a survey of Late Classic ceremonial centers functioning at this time indicate this. Closely related to this demographic situation are subsistence practices. While short-cycle swidden agriculture was undoubtedly practiced in many places in the southern lowlands in the Late Classic, there are also lines of evidence (Sanders 1973) to indicate that this was supplemented by long-cycle swidden cultivation in regions and on soils where this was possible. Also, riverine lowlands were known (Siemens and Puleston 1972) to have been cultivated in places, and perhaps *bajos* or swamps were similarly utilized. Food resources other than maize and beans appear to have played a large part in the diet at certain sites, such as the probable breadnut harvests at Tikal (Puleston 1968). In brief, the reconstructable picture of Maya lowland Late Classic life is one of the maximization of all available food resources, and of populations increasingly pressing on these resources. It is highly unlikely that this same demographic-subsistence relationship obtained—or obtained to such an intensified degree—in the Early Classic period.

There are also inferred differences in the sociopolitical contexts of Early Classic versus Late Classic Maya society. A number of trends can be plotted from Early to Late Classic which indicate these differences. For one thing, there is a steady change in the nature of hieroglyphic texts, and these changes are particularly pronounced between Early and Late Classic. The earlier texts are much shorter and would appear to be restricted largely to time-counting and other calendrical matters. The later texts are longer, and in some instances (Proskouriakoff 1963, 1964) have been demonstrated to pertain to historical events and to royal lineages. In ceremonial center architecture the multi-roomed palace-type building becomes more important in the Late Classic than in the Early Classic (R. Mc. Adams 1956). The burial customs of the Late Classic differ from those of the Early, especially as these customs involve grave contents, the ages and sexes of the occupants, and the ceremonial center as opposed to domestic dwelling loci of the graves (Rathje 1970). These changes, together with those of the monuments and architecture, imply an ever-widening social gulf between Early and Late Classic. While it is possible that ancient Maya society was class-structured throughout its entire Classic period history, all the clues point to an increasing rigidity of this class-ordering in the Late Classic; and this, combined with other factors, including those of overpopulation and subsistence pressures, could have produced a stress in Late Classic society that had not been so critical in Early Classic times.

A related stress factor on the Late Classic sociopolitical scene was undoubtedly that of competition between the aristocratic elite of the different ceremonial centers. In their efforts to outdo each other in size, splendor, hieroglyphic scholarship, and other hierarchical activities, the rival dynasties must have imposed great economic burdens on their sustaining peasant populations. While this may also have been the case in the Early Classic, the much greater number of such centers active in the Late Classic, together with the population pressures of the late period, suggest that stress of this sort was probably more pronounced in the Late Classic. This seems supported by the fact that all of the pictorial evidence of warfare in the Maya Classic—and judging from the representations this was a warfare of Maya against Maya—are of the late period.

As a final comparison between the circumstances of the Early and Late Classic, let us take a look at foreign influences. Unlike the other comparisons, we are not so much concerned with trends or intensifications of processes as with simply different historical patterns. Both the Early and Late Classic Maya of the lowlands experienced Mexican contacts. In the Early Classic these contacts derived from Teotihuacan. The extent to which these contacts were carried out through trade, the actual presence of foreigners, or military and political involvements are undecided; however, at a minimum, trade must have been an important mechanism in the relationships. Although some of these Teotihuacan influences began to appear quite early, dating back to the Terminal Late Preclassic (Pendergast 1971), their concentration was later, falling in the century between A.D. 450 and 550. (W. R. Coe 1962, 1965, 1967; Willey 1971c; Willey and Shimkin 1971). This would be on a late Tzakol 2–Tzakol 3 ceramic horizon and would be just before the hiatus. The influences are seen in ceramics, for the most part what appear to be locally made imitations of the Teotihuacanoid lidded tripod jars. A cultural synthesis is seen in some pieces which combine lowland Maya and Teotihuacan decorative techniques and design motifs. At Tikal, which appears to have been the central focus of the Teotihuacan influences, there is, in addition, a stela with Teotihuacan iconography (W. R. Coe 1965). An important fact in this Teotihuacan–Early Classic Maya relationship is that the Guatemalan highland site of Kaminaljuyu also played a role, perhaps a mediating one, involving trade in obsidian. While some central Mexican green obsidian does occur in the Maya lowlands at this time, most of this highly useful stone (or glass) is of the black or gray varieties that probably originated in the Guatemalan highlands, some of it at no great distance from Kaminaljuyu (see especially Sanders and Price 1968; Sanders 1973). But whatever the processes of the Teotihuacan–lowland Maya contacts, or by what routes or however mediated, what is certain is that they came to an end very abruptly with the hiatus. This, naturally, prompts questions as to the relationships between the Teotihuacan influence and the hiatus. Given the timing of the events, it does not seem likely that the Teotihuacan "impact" on the lowland Maya brought about the hiatus—at least not in any direct way. On the contrary, the Teotihuacan influences appear concurrently with the most brilliant growth of the Early Classic culture. We are, instead, led to ask if the withdrawal of the Teotihuacan influences did not precipitate the hiatus?

The historical pattern of foreign involvement for the Maya of the Late Classic period is quite different from that of the Early Classic. This time the contacts seem to be derived from a source that is Toltec-like, but we cannot be more specific than this. They occurred along a broad front on the western side of the Maya lowlands. It is quite probable that the peoples immediately involved were Maya, although Maya of a Non-Classic cultural tradition. The foreign influences are seen in Fine Orange pottery and figurines and in the iconography of certain monuments at a few terminal Late Classic sites (for the Fine Orange pottery see Sabloff 1970, 1973; for the monument iconography, with particular reference to the site of Seibal, see J. A. Graham 1972). The timing of these Late Classic foreign influences is distinctly different from that of the Teotihuacan influences on Early

Classic Maya culture. Whereas in the latter case the Teotihuacan elements are seen concomitant with—and perhaps stimulative to—the Early Classic climax and prior to the hiatus, the Mexicanoid intrusions into the Late Classic do not appear until well after the Late Classic apogee has passed and the decline toward the collapse has already set in. In fact, arguments have been advanced (Sabloff and Willey 1967; see also Adams 1973 and Sabloff 1973) that the bearers of the Fine Orange ware who invaded the Usumacinta and Pasion Valleys were the prime causal forces in the Late Classic collapse; however, these arguments tend to be invalidated by the fact that in many sites the decline was well advanced before this alien pottery tradition is introduced. While there was very likely an invasion of Mexicanized foreigners into the Classic Maya realm in the ninth century A.D., it probably did not take place until the dissolution had begun.

In these comparisons of the hiatus and the collapse we have reviewed the structure and developmental background of each, but what of their causes or inferred causes? Very little has been written about the cause, or causes, of the hiatus. Most Mayanists have simply noted it and passed on (Proskouriakoff 1950: 111–12; Thompson 1954: 55–6). However, Morley, whose indefatigable searching out and recording of the stelae inscriptions first revealed the hiatus phenomenon, did speculate about it (1938–9: vol. 4, 333):

> The great expansion of the monument-erecting complex to all parts of the Maya area, which we have seen took place in the second quarter of *baktun* 9 (9.5.0.0.0 to 9.10.0.0.0) and thus exactly coincides with this three-quarters of a century of decreased monumental activity, may explain this observed decrease. The Maya during these four *katuns* were devoting their energies to the extensive occupation of the Old Empire region; it was definitely a period of expansion, and only a few centers here and there found themselves in a position to erect sculptured stone monuments on the successive 10 *tun* period-endings, though all, so to speak, were accumulating reserves against the more abundant days that were to follow.

Morley delivers this in passing, with no particular insistence upon it being a very satisfactory explanation; but it is a very feeble statement of cause. If energies were used up in "pioneering" new territories, one would expect these "outposts" of Maya civilization to have been suffering the most of all from such exertions; yet it is exactly here, on these outermost peripheries of the old Maya lowlands, that we find most of the hiatus stelae dedications. Nor does it seem likely that the older, more established centers would have abandoned their stelae cult activities to divert their energies and wealth to the "provinces." Finally, the concept of hoarding up cultural energy, the accumulation of reserves for the great effort to come, is at best a poetic conceit; it is certainly not an explanation.

The only other attempt to explain the causes behind the hiatus has been developed, incidentally, in connection with what we might call the "trade failure hypothesis" as this has been applied to the later Maya collapse. The hypothesis has been formulated by both Webb and Rathje (Webb 1973, but see also 1964; Rathje 1971, 1973), and to see it in proper perspective it is necessary to turn to the question of the final collapse. In contrast to the problem of the hiatus, a very great deal has been written about the Maya ninth-century collapse. I will not attempt to summarize it all here; this has been done in the recent symposium on the subject referred to above. No ultimate conclusions were drawn in this symposium, although a majority of the participants did agree upon the significance of those internal stress factors within Late Classic Maya society which made it vulnerable to dissolution. These have been referred to as: ecological limitations, overpopulation, the widening social gulf between aristocracy and peasantry, and expensive competition between ceremonial centers. To these may be added the external stress factors of military pressures, trade disruption, or both. Such pressures were seen as being applied by Non-

Classic Maya peoples along the western and northwestern frontiers of the southern Maya lowlands. While the symposium summary statement (Willey and Shimkin 1973) did not go much beyond this in delineating these external stress factors, Rathje's participant paper (Rathje 1973) spelled things out in much greater detail in the course of developing what might be considered a "field theory" which explains the interactive processes between the institution of trade and the rise and maintenance of highly complex societies.

Very briefly, Rathje's hypothesis states that the Maya lowlands, and especially the northeast Peten "core area" of these lowlands, were lacking in natural products necessary to support large complex societies, namely, such things as hard stone for corn-grinding implements, obsidian, and salt. In order to obtain these requisite raw materials the leadership of the "core area" communities, for instance, Tikal or Uaxactun, developed long-distance trade with areas where such resources were to be obtained, as in the Chiapas and Guatemalan highlands. To carry out such trade meant organization and management above the household level; and, similarily, the redistribution of goods from such trade demanded a hierarchical governmental structure. Lowland Maya social and political complexity had its start in these beginnings in the Preclassic period, and this complexity was further elaborated in the succeeding Classic period. The centers of this earliest rise of civilization in the "core area" had trading connections with other, and at that time lesser, centers in what Rathje has called the "buffer zones." These "buffer zones" were the lowland regions surrounding the "core area," and they were more advantageously placed, geographically, for highland and other Mesoamerican-wide trade than was the "core area." For a time, the lesser centers of the "buffer zones" served an intermediate, relaying role in supplying needed raw materials to the sites of the "core area." In return for these services they received the benefits of the religious and status-defining esoterica and the manufactured luxury goods of the "core area." Eventually, however, with increasing sophistication, and profiting by their more favorable geographical locations, the "buffer zones" centers usurped the trade control from the "core area," precipitating the downfall of its sites.

While this highly compressed outline of Rathje's ideas does not do them full justice, his hypothesis, to this point, seems consistent with the facts as we know them. It also gives us an insight into the hiatus. We have already asked if the Teotihuacan withdrawal from the Maya area may not have brought on the hiatus. If Rathje is correct, if Early Classic "core area" development was vitally related to the Teotihuacan supervised trade, then the relinquishing of that supervisory power and the loss of that trade could have had serious results in sites such as Tikal and Uaxactun. Another "expectation" leading out of Rathje's hypothesis is met by the appearance of hiatus stelae in distant "buffer zone" sites such as Tonina, Comitan, Chinkultic, and Tulum. While the "core area" suffered these "buffer zone" sites came to prominence. However, not all of the sites which Rathje defines as being in the "buffer zones" enjoy a similar rise during the hiatus. Altar de Sacrificios very definitely does not. It is marked by the stelae hiatus, by an architectural decline, and, probably, by a population drop. Nor is its recovery after the hiatus a prompt one. The Tepeu 1 horizon is weakly represented, and it is not until Tepeu 2 times that it returns to its old prehiatus vigor. For Yaxchilan, down the Usumacinta from Altar de Sacrificios, the situation may well be the same. At least the stelae dates there—which is all that we have to go on—suggest that it was.

It may be that this failure of Altar de Sacrificios, and perhaps Yaxchilan, to meet the "expectations" of Rathje's hypothesis is a problem of "buffer zone" definition. The lower Pasión–middle Usumacinta region may have been more closely allied to the "core area" during the Early Classic than Rathje has conceded. But then the whole matter of the "buffer zone" centers in the Late Classic is a little perplexing as one attempts to follow out Rathje's hypothesis. Many of them enjoy a great florescence after the hiatus, although in some cases, as at Altar de Sacrificios, it seems a little delayed. But then the "core area" centers also experience this florescence; Tikal and Uaxactun go on to greater glories, as do other "core area" sites. They are not choked off—at least not for another 200 years—by the giants of the "buffer zone" such as Yaxchilan, Piedras Negras, or Palenque. In fact, they would appear to be sharing trade goods, prestige, and power with them. What we have before the hiatus is a centralization of trade and power in the northeastern Peten "core area" zone; what we have after the hiatus are multiple centers of trade and power.

This leads me to wonder if we are not witnessing the results of a process which Blanton has outlined in an attempt (1972) to explain settlement changes in the Valley of Mexico. He notes that while Teotihuacan was at its height there were no rival extractive and tribute centers in the valley, and he suggests that the downfall of the great city may have been brought about by the fact that an increasingly greater part of its sustaining rural population could no longer participate in the symbiotic networks (or trade and other functions) that were focused on that center. Subsequent to the fall of Teotihuacan, a number of moderately large centers did develop, before these were, again, reduced under the hegemony of Tula. In other words, there is a dialectic between centralization and decentralization, between leadership power and subject demands; and if we were to assume that Early Classic society of the Maya lowlands was a more centralized one than the conventional conception of it, with a controlling leadership at Tikal, then the springing up of new ceremonial centers in the Late Classic might be viewed as a "balkanization" to meet the demands of the increasing populations. This would not deny a trade failure as the causal force behind the hiatus; but it would see, rather, the interval of the hiatus, when the capital power of Tikal was weakened, as the opportunity to break out of the old structure and to form new centers of power.

I would agree with Rathje that the final, ninth-century collapse of the Maya was also triggered by another trade failure. I will not attempt to detail his arguments for this except that I do not think that the interactions between "core area" and "buffer zones," as he has defined them, are as important as he does. For one thing, the "core" sites and the "buffer" sites go down together. I am inclined to believe that what happened here was that a new, outer "buffer zone," of Non-Classic or Mexican-Maya states, formed along the western edge of the southern lowlands and strangled trade for both the older "buffer zone" and the "core area." For it seems highly likely that the Late Classic centers, of both "buffer" and "core," were closely linked with each other in a network of economic, political, and religious relationships. But all of this leads on to other arguments and discussions beyond the range of this short paper.

Let us conclude by returning to the original question. Was the hiatus a "rehearsal" for the collapse, a preenactment of similar responses to similar failures? I would say yes. The near-cessation of the stelae cult and the lag in ceremonial center construction presaged the like events of the "great collapse." With the "little collapse" of the hiatus there was recovery. In fact, as David Friedel (personal communication, 1972) has observed, one of the important points about the hiatus is not that the Maya survived it but that, in many ways at least, they appear to have come out of it stronger than before. This suggests that, along with the inherent weaknesses in the lowland Maya system, there were also some inherent adaptabilities. Just what all of these were, and what the balances were between them, is not yet clear. But with the "great collapse" there was no recovery; and I would judge, from what we know now, that this was because the stresses within Maya lowland society—of ecological adjustment, of population pressure, and of sociopolitical divisiveness—were far greater in Late Classic times than they had been in the Early Classic. In the sixth century A.D. the danger of the compounding of disasters was much less than it was to become in the ninth century. Moreover, I would hazard the guess that recovery after the final collapse was made much more difficult because of external stresses, in the form of alien populations on the western borders of the Maya domain, that had not been such a factor three centuries earlier.

But more basically, I take the position that the hiatus and the collapse were phenomena with a similar cause. This cause was the severance of the symbiotic relationships between Maya civilization and the other Mesoamerican civilizations that were contemporaneous with it. The heights that Maya lowland civilization attained were made possible by this symbiosis, and the cutting of it initiated the hiatus and it initiated the collapse. I realize that this is debated ground for to hold it places Maya lowland civilization in a "secondary" status in the developmental typology of civilizations. I would mitigate this by saying, further, that we still have much to learn about the relationships between "primary" and "secondary" civilizations. Why, for instance, do the latter often outdo the former in many fields of endeavor? Maya hieroglyphics and mathematics come immediately to mind in contrast to counterpart developments of the Mexican highlands. Webb, Rathje, and others have argued that the essence of the Maya symbiosis with the upland regions and civilizations of Mesoamerica was most significantly in the institution of trade. I think that this is a very productive hypothesis because it is susceptible to archaeological examination through the testing and counting of objects and the statistical manipulation of these. At the same time, let me, as an old or "traditional" archaeologist, point out that the great emphasis on "trade" in archaeological research is enjoying a current vogue. This is not undeserved. It is a theme that has much to offer. But we should not refrain from framing other hypotheses, from seeking out clues to other processes that may help us explain cultural growth and adaptation as it arises from contacts among human societies and cultures.

B

Processual Patterns

In these two essays, written a good many years apart and certainly dealing with quite different subject matter, I was making empirical observations about "patterns in the data," and in so doing I was attempting to move toward processual understanding. In "A Pattern of Diffusion-Acculturation," written and published in 1953, I was concerned with what I believed to be comparable series of events which occured when peoples of what we will call "Culture A" invaded and settled in the territory of peoples of "Culture B." The events of such a contact and the steps of acculturation that took place over the century or so following such an invasion or intrusion appeared to me to proceed in a similar way. The culture contact situations I examined in the archaeological records were: (1) the movement of early Middle Mississippian peoples and culture into central Georgia; (2) the supposed settlement of "Toltec" invaders in the northern Maya lowlands at Chichen Itza; and (3) the apparent implantation of highland Tiahuanaco (or Huari-Tiahuanaco) settlements in the Moche kingdom of the north coast of Peru. I thought I saw a recurrent type of cultural synthesis in all three instances—one that later was to be called "site-unit intrusion" by a Summer Seminar of the Society for American Archaeology (Lathrap, ed., 1956). In the seminar my colleagues accepted my Georgia and north Peruvian examples as fitting the "site-unit intrusion" model, but they were reluctant to view "Toltec" Chichen Itza in the same way. Perhaps they were right about this latter case (see, for example, Lincoln 1985). Leaving aside the historical specifics, I still think the comparative method has value—in this instance, for our attempts to understand the processes of diffusion as these can be observed in archaeology.

In "The Early Great Styles and the Rise of the Precolumbian Civilizations," written in 1961 and published the following year, I offered the hypothesis that intensive intercommunication among the regions of a larger area is one important prerequisite for the rise of civilization. It was my contention that such intensive intercommunication is revealed archaeologically by horizon style phenomena. Specifically, I argued that the Olmec and Chavín horizon styles signaled the presence of communication networks that were the preconditions for later Mesoamerican and Peruvian civilizations, respectively. I noted that such horizon styles were lacking in the Intermediate Area where, despite the fact that the Intermediate Area shared much of its Nuclear American Formative cultural content with Mesoamerica and Peru, there was no subsequent development of comparable civilizations.

I remain fascinated by and convinced of the main thesis of the essay; however, it met with considerable resistance from many colleagues. Some said that my appraisal of the Intermediate Area "control case" was mistaken, that the Intermediate Area did, indeed, produce "civilizations" and "empires" of the stature and quality of those of Mesoamerica or Peru. I strongly disagree with this. I see nothing between the Maya frontier and the Lambayeque Valley in northern Peru that is comparable to the state or imperial developments of Mesoamerica and Peru. The other line of criticism accused me of claiming that art styles were to be seen as causative forces in the rise of civilizations. It was not my intention to say this. I assumed, rather, that Olmec and Chavín art, per se, followed upon the establishment of intercommunicative networks in their respective areas and, in effect, set the seal of approval upon an area-wide ideological unity or "ecumenicism" (see Kroeber 1952). I suppose what my idea does is to move the question of "the rise of civilization" a step back in time. What the forces were that brought about the intercommunicative networks, and what degree of area-wide ideological unity they represented, are, of course, still unanswered questions.

There are some substantive incidental points that deserve comment with the benefit of hindsight. My original descriptions of the Olmec and Chavín styles overemphasized the element of the jaguar or feline, especially in Chavín. While feline beings are present in both styles, there is other important content (for more recent analyses of the iconography of the Olmec style, see Joralemon 1971, Coe and Diehl 1980, and Sharer 1982; for Chavín, see Lathrap 1973a, 1977). My original dating estimate of 800–400 B.C. for both the Olmec and Chavín horizons was based on the radiocarbon dates and other information then available. The estimate may be a little too late. There are now Olmec dates that set a 1200–900 B.C. time band for the initial Olmec horizon, with a trailing off into secondary Olmec influences ending at about 600–400 B.C. (Coe and Diehl 1980); but there is some disagreement about this from those who would prefer to put the main thrust of the horizon at about where I had it (see Demarest 1985 for a summary). In Peru, Chavín stylistic manifestations recently have been placed as early as 1200 B.C. in some localities, though here the weight of opinion would still prefer a dating somewhere in the earlier half of the first millennium B.C.—and even this may be too early (see Patterson 1988). It was my original contention that the two styles were not historically or diffusionally related. I still adhere to this, though I allow that they may have shared mythological roots (Lathrap 1982).

A Pattern of Diffusion-Acculturation

(From *Southwestern Journal of Anthropology*, Vol. 9, No. 4, pp. 369–384, 1953. Reprinted by permission of the *Journal of Anthropological Research* and the Department of Anthropology, University of New Mexico.)

The phenomena of diffusion and acculturation are the stock in trade of archaeologists, but they usually examine them with an eye toward historical interrelationships rather than from the analytical point of view of pattern and function.[1] While it is evident that the limitations of archaeological data and archaeological inference preclude the individual and psychological points of reference by which studies of acculturation and culture change are often plotted, there is, nevertheless, an area of the problem which can be explored with the help of prehistory. Although there is no clear unanimity of opinion among ethnologists and social anthropologists as to the relationships of the concepts of diffusion and acculturation,[2] Herskovits[3] has suggested that diffusion is "achieved cultural transmission" while acculturation is "cultural transmission in process." This may be a useful distinction in some circumstances, but it ignores a part of the full series of events—a series which can only be appreciated from a time-depth perspective. Archaeologists, by the nature of their subject matter, must always deal with the "achieved," but for them the dynamic aspect lies in the observation of the "before-during-after" sequence of culture contact. Herein lies their potential contribution to the study of culture change and culture synthesis.

It is the intent of this essay to investigate processes of diffusion-acculturation as these are reflected in the prehistoric sequences of three widely separated American regions. It will be seen that these instances, although differing in content, possess common structural features and that these features suggest a pattern. This pattern appears to be one of several into which the events of culture contact and results of contact might be classified.

The three American regions selected for study are central Georgia, northern Yucatan, and north coastal Peru. All of these are small parts of much larger culture area groupings: the southeastern United States, Meso-America, and Peru, respectively. Each region had a culture history peculiar to itself and at the same time related to the larger area which encompassed it. In each case the action with which we are concerned was the result of forces generated within the larger area and brought to impinge upon the smaller region. All of the instances of culture contact lie in the Precolumbian past and are not involved with the late fifteenth and early sixteenth century incursions of the Europeans.

Central Georgia

In central Georgia the particular events we have selected serve to distinguish one major culture period from the next. At the time in question, most of the area that is now central and south Georgia, together with portions of bordering states, was the homeland of the prehistoric Swift Creek culture.[4] Swift Creek is a Southeastern Woodland culture, the last of a local Georgia Woodland series that succeeds a still earlier Archaic period. Guess-date estimates vary, and are not of great importance in this discussion, but a time range of 400 to 1000 A.D. has been suggested for the Georgia Swift Creek development.[5] The Swift Creek people were primarily hunters and gatherers, although they may have practiced a minimal maize horticulture. Their villages are numerous but not large. Chipped stone tools and weapons are found in abundance, but ground stone celts are rare. Bannerstones and boatstones, the probable throwing-stick weights, imply the use of that implement. Pottery was moderately plentiful and tended to be limited to the deep conoidal-based jar of the Woodland genre. In some regions burial mounds were constructed, and this trait appears consistent with what we know of the East and Southeast in general for this approximate time horizon. Swift Creek culture is thought to be roughly contemporaneous with Hopewell of the Ohio Valley. Toward the close of Swift Creek times the construction of temple mounds became associated with the culture. It is likely that the appearance of this feature followed in the wake of the events to be described.

The first of these events, as nearly as we can trace them in the archaeological record, was the establishment in the Macon locality of a large town site of the Macon Plateau culture. The Macon site covered several acres and was encircled by ditched (and probably earth wall) defenses. It incorporated seven flat-topped pyramidal or temple mounds, special semi-subterranean circular earthlodges, and evidences of dwelling structures. The entire site and the artifacts found within it stand in stark relief against the old Woodland, Swift Creek background. In the zone of the site proper its superposition over the earlier Swift Creek settlements is clear, and the physical as well as the cultural stratigraphy indicates a sharp cleavage with the past. The picture is not one of cultural amalgamation but of sudden interruption and new beginnings within another tradition. Fairbanks sums this up in saying:

> Macon Plateau makes a definite break with the old hunting-collecting economy and has full-fledged agriculture. There is evidence of a field inside the town but the bulk of the gardens must have been outside and the mound group probably served as an assembly point for scattered family groups. The large mounds, fortifications, and ceremonial buildings indicate an economy with sufficient leisure for non-subsistence pursuits. They probably had a priesthood who ran things in the ceremonial center and may have had an elaborate political and military organization. The whole system was much more complicated than anything that had preceded it in central Georgia.[6]

The Macon Plateau townsmen introduced a new art style (the "Southern Cult") in connection with their ceremonialism. In more ordinary manufactures they placed less emphasis on flint chipping than their predecessors, made numerous ground stone celts including the bi-lobed spud, and manufactured pottery completely unlike that of the Swift Creek inhabitants. Macon Plateau pottery is in a Mississippian tradition. It is generally smooth-surfaced, often shell-tempered, and features shouldered jars, bowls, bottles, loop handles, and animal effigy adornos.

There is little doubt but that the Macon Plateau people were invaders into central Georgia. The presence of their big, fortified town and ceremonial center is like a tiny island in a sea of the simpler Swift Creek villages. Except for one other Macon Plateau site, smaller than the first, two miles distant, and also fortified, no other sites of the Macon Plateau culture have ever been discovered in Georgia, a state in which archaeological survey is reasonably well advanced. There is good evidence that the Swift Creek communities continued coincident with and after the advent of the Macon Plateau intruders, for coastal and south Georgia seem to have been strongholds for the Swift Creek traditions, particularly in stamped pottery. Some change gradually seeped into these regions, and the presence of a temple mound at the Kolomoki site in south Georgia suggests a possible diffusion from Macon.[7] If so, the processes of culture spread and change were entirely different from those attendant upon the founding of the Macon Plateau site. Kolomoki represents a blend of Swift Creek culture with a current of new ideas, but Macon Plateau is a total replacement of Swift Creek.

The Macon Plateau push into central Georgia is believed to have come from the north or northwest. Perhaps western Tennessee and the central Mississippi Valley were the former heartlands of the culture. Certainly, central and east Tennesseean culture groups of about the same time period show close resemblances to Macon Plateau.[8] The abruptness of the culture change strongly suggests a population movement, not a cultural diffusion without peoples. There is, as yet, insufficient physical anthropological data from central Georgia to confirm this; but skeletal evidence from Tennessee supports such a migration, if indirectly.[9] Both archaeologists and ethnologists have seen in the establishment of the Macon Plateau site the first entry of Muskogean peoples into Georgia. Although this is further surmise, it is highly probable.

Of equal interest are the developments which followed the arrival of Macon Plateau culture in the Georgia region. This succeeding period is known as the Lamar, and Lamar[10] culture represents a firmly cemented mixture of Macon Plateau and Swift Creek traits. The time of Macon Plateau is estimated at about 1000 to 1300 A.D. Lamar, whose upper limits are known to overlap with the first Spanish *entradas*, extends, then, from 1300 to 1600 A.D. or later. Unlike Macon Plateau, Lamar and closely related sites are found throughout Georgia and north and east into the Carolinas. Some of them are small villages, like the Swift Creek sites, but many are sizable towns with temple mounds and, sometimes, palisades. One of the most striking amalgams of the new culture is the pottery. In vessel forms and ornamentation it incorporates the intrusive Macon Plateau and the resident Swift Creek features. For example, complicated stamped surfacing, while missing from Macon Plateau ceramics, becomes a common element of Lamar. There are, to be sure, other influences in Lamar in addition to Macon Plateau and Swift Creek. Some of these appear to be ideas from the north and the west which followed in the wake of the Macon Plateau migration, and probably derived from related Mississippian sources. Significant, however, is the fact that Lamar is not an isolated and alien projection into frontier territory but a local Georgian synthesis. It is primarily the acculturative result of the Macon Plateau–Swift Creek culture contact.

NORTHERN YUCATAN

The prehistory of Yucatan begins with the agriculturally based Formative cultures which undoubtedly go back several centuries B.C. An early Maya occupation, correlated with the Tzakol phase of the Peten, has been disclosed at several places in Yucatan, particularly at Oxkintok. The architecture and ceramics of these Yucatecan Early Classic sites resemble those of the equivalent time horizon in the Peten but are regionally specialized. In the subsequent period in Yucatan, that corresponding to the Mayan Late Classic of the south, this Yucatecan specialization was even more pronounced, and a number of local architectural styles, such as Puuc, Chenes, and Maya Chichen were developed. The Yucatecan Late Classic period is believed to have lasted until about 1000 A.D.[11] At least that is the usual date assigned to the beginning of the Toltec or Mexican period at Chichen Itza.

The archaeology of the Mexican period at Chichen testifies to a foreign and Mexican highland influence in no uncertain manner. Reliefs depict lines of warriors, jaguars, and eagles almost identical with those found at the traditional Toltec center of Tula in Hidalgo. Atlantean column and altar figures, feathered serpent balustrades and columns, colonnades, and Chacmol statues provide additional links to this same Tula complex. Much of the great building at Chichen dates from the Mexican period, including the famous ball court, the Castillo pyramid, and the Temple of the Warriors with its colonnade. Additions, dating from this period, were made on the old Maya Chichen style buildings, such as the Monjas, and in general the invaders introduced a number of new architectural practices. Outstanding among these was the increase in size of interior chambers by the use of columns instead of walls to support the weight of corbeled vaults. In connection with these technical changes Thompson makes the observation: "There is . . . a possibility that this was not merely an architectural development, but a reflection of a different use of buildings resulting from new religious practices."[12]

In addition to architecture, further foreign evidences are seen at this time in Plumbate ware, Fine Orange (X-type) pottery, turquoise inlays, and metals. These are not necessarily Mexican highland or Tula items but are apparently derived from a number of Meso-American proveniences. Fine Orange ware, for example, is thought to be a Tabasco or Veracruz import, a region from which the Toltec influences might have come.

The identity of the invaders is debatable. Thompson is inclined to believe that the influx of Tula art into Chichen marks the traditional arrival of the Itza and that these Itza were not actually Toltecs but rather a Mexicanized Maya group from the west.[13] Tozzer, on the other hand, is now disinclined to associate the Itza traditional histories with the Chichen-Tula style of circa 1000 A.D.; and he is of the opinion that the migration to Yucatan was in general a direct one from the Tula site, not an indirect one via settlements in Veracruz and Tabasco.[14] The virtual identity of the Tula and Chichen reliefs supports the Tozzer position, but the absence of the characteristic Tula wares, Coyotlatelco or Mazapan pottery, argues against a direct migration. The Fine Orange type tends to strengthen the supposition that a Veracruz-Tabascan route is involved.

Whatever the ethnic forces behind the Toltec or Mexican settlement at Chichen, there is little question of it being a unique cultural expression, strikingly different from its Yucatecan background. As Pollock expressed it: "Outside the immediate area of Chichen Itza, with the exception of a few traces—and those of questionable identification—there is not a single ruin, so far as we know, that exhibits architectural or sculptural remains that can be identified as like those of the type site or as being of this period."[15] It would seem, then, that: (1) either all of Yucatan was deserted or a complete cultural sink during the Mexican period at Chichen; or (2) local cultures continued along old traditional lines. Pollock is inclined to favor the latter interpretation as the more likely of the two.[16] This would mean that a Puuc, or Puuc-like, culture was existing in other centers coexistent with the period of Toltec art and influence at Chichen.

The situation in Yucatan, following this interpretation, is not unlike that which we have described for Georgia. A strong alien culture establishes itself in a single site deep within a region held by another culture. In both instances there is evidence suggesting that the invaders did not accomplish this by wholly peaceful means. The Georgia site of the Macon Plateau culture was fortified;[17] the Chichen wall paintings and other art forms show one group of warriors (apparently Mexicans) battling and defeating another (apparently Mayas).[18] In each region there is also the apparent continuity of the local culture in other sites or localities; and this continuity seems to have lasted for a considerable time. A 200 or 300 year estimate has been made for the Macon Plateau period in Georgia and a 200 year or longer interval for Toltec Chichen Itza. The intrusive cultures, in each case, are characterized by a public architecture and an art style significantly different from those previously in vogue in the recipient region. In Georgia, the new complex also brought with it a complete change in artifacts and ceramics; in Yucatan, the changes do not appear to be this deep or sweeping. Certain artifacts, materials, and pottery types do seem to be correlated with the Toltec art and architectural innovations; but a Yucatecan slate ware tradition, presumably of Chichen Maya and Puuc antecedents, carries on as the principal resident pottery.[19]

The period following Chichen Toltec or Chichen Mexican has been referred to as the period of "Mexican Absorption"[20] or of "Maya Resurgence."[21] Mayapan is the type site for this late culture, but elsewhere in Yucatan there occur architectural remains very similar to those of Mayapan. Pollock notes that the concepts of "resurgence" and "absorption" on the part of the Maya are based on ethnohistoric and linguistic evidence at the time of the Spanish conquest and upon the late period absence of sculptural art like that which flourished at Chichen in the preceding Toltec period. But he goes on to state, speaking of Yucatan as a whole; "The great preponderance of building remains assigned to this late period are not of Maya, but of so-called Mexican, style. Though the architecture differs from that of Chichen Itza of the preceding period, the style could well be a degeneration of those forms and is certainly more foreign than Maya."[22] As with the initial diffusion by migration and the founding of the alien center, the resultant culture of the Yucatecan late period shows parallels to the similarly resultant Lamar culture of Georgia. Elements of the invading and recipient cultures have been blended, and the same sort of selectivity in this combining is noted in both Yucatan and Georgia. For example, the public architecture of the invaders is retained in Mayapan culture as it was in Lamar. The Tula art style, as it is seen in late east coast sites of Yucatan, is greatly reduced, and this recalls the gradual dissolution of Southern Cult art in Lamar.[23] Late Yucatecan ceramics, as with Lamar, represent a strong carryover of the local traditions.

NORTH COASTAL PERU

The oases valleys of the north Peruvian coast were the scenes of human habitation for at least three millennia before the beginning of the Christian era. In brief, north coast prehistory starts with the premaize horticulturists and fishers of Huaca Prieta and Cerro Prieto, undergoes a transition to the maize farmers of Coast Chavín times, passes through successive periods of mounting technological and agricultural development, and climaxes in the Classic Mochica culture somewhere in the latter half of the first millennium A.D.[24] It is at this juncture that we are interested in the events of the sequence. Mochica (Early Chimu) culture is best known from the valleys of Chicama and Moche, but it extends north of Chicama to Pacasmayo, if not beyond, and south at least to the Santa Valley. It is likely that the Mochica realm was a multi-valley state under unified control. In any event, the whole region was linked by strong artistic and architectural bonds. The art was naturalistic and depicts life scenes of battles, rulers, prisoners, and other motives suggesting a national consciousness. Adobe pyramids, palaces, and fortifications were built, and irrigation was carried to great lengths with complex systems of canals and garden plots. Population concentrations in some places suggest numbers running into the thousands. In effect, we have in Mochica the beginnings of urban life and mature social, political, and religious systems. At a time estimated as 1000 A.D. the Mochica culture underwent a sudden and marked change. This same change is noted elsewhere in Peru, and the phenomenon has been referred to as the Tiahuanaco, or Coast Tiahuanaco, horizon. All of the Mochica territory except Pacasmayo and the far north was affected by this Coast Tiahuanaco influence.

The implantation of Coast Tiahuanaco culture on the north coast of Peru differs from the situations we have been discussing in Georgia and Yucatan in that the new elements were not concentrated in a single important site or zone with untouched cultural hinterlands surrounding this site. This difference in the diffusion may have resulted from the nature of the Peruvian coastal valleys which are relatively small and were, in the Classic and later periods, closely knit by the coordinated techniques of irrigation. Whatever the reasons, the Mochica valleys were, in effect, inundated *in toto* by this new cultural wave. Mochica pyramid mounds were used as burial places by the Coast Tiahuanacans; fortified sites were taken over; old cemeteries reused; and house sites reoccupied. The new impress is seen in ceramics, where form and decoration change radically, in textile designs, woodwork, metallurgy, and architecture. The architectural changes affected not only the buildings themselves but total settlement pattern. Whereas Mochica culture had laid great emphasis on the pyramidal mound built of small mold-made adobe bricks, the largest Coast Tiahuanaco constructions were huge rectangular enclosures in which the big outside walls were made of massive sections of poured tapia adobe. In the actual dwelling units, Mochica villages were clusters of rooms attached to each other in honeycomb fashion but usually without overall pattern or symmetry of arrangement. The Coast Tiahuanaco village, on the other hand, is often a rectangular compound with a symmetrical internal plan.[25]

The nature of society of the Coast Tiahuanaco horizon influence has been a matter of much speculation. The data on changes in physical type are suggestive in this regard but not conclusive. Newman[26] has noted a physical homogenization of the central and north coast populations in what are sometimes termed the "Late" periods. It is possible that this "leveling" of regional physical differences was the result of migrations and interbreeding following in the wake of a Coast Tiahuanaco invasion; however, the "Late" periods date immediately after, rather than coexistent with, the Tiahuanacoid horizon style. The cultural evidences on this matter of actual invasion or stylistic diffusion are strongly suggestive. In the Virú Valley (a part of the Mochica domain) Ford[27] has demonstrated a ceramic continuity from early Chavín times up to the arrival of the Inca. In utilitarian pottery there is some degree of steady development throughout, but the most marked interruption is that which separates Mochica from Coast Tiahuanaco. As such, it is an argument for at least a partial population replacement. In the decorated pottery, much of which seems to have been made as mortuary goods, the severance of Mochica from Tiahuanacoid traditions is complete. It has been surmised that the sudden extinction of the art symbolism of an expanding militaristic nation could be accomplished only by force.[28] The totality of the evidence then, from physical anthropology, architecture, settlement plan, art, and common pottery, implies a social as well as cultural interruption.

Whether this was an event of empire-building scope, such as the Inca carried out some centuries later, or a more local affair, remains unknown.

It is believed that the source of Coast Tiahuanaco art was in the central Andes rather than the south Andean Tiahuanaco site proper. There are, of course, stylistic ties to the latter site from whence Uhle derived the name for the horizonal phenomena. Regardless of the point of origin of this style and/or conquest movement, there is little doubt but that the Coast Tiahuanaco culture pushed into the Mochica realm from the south, whether by coast or highland.

We have mentioned the differences between the blanketing effect of the Coast Tiahuanaco invasion of the north coast of Peru and the insular outposts of the prehistoric invasions into prehistoric Georgia and prehistoric Yucatan. There remain, however, certain parallel features in the Peruvian situation. With the movement of Coast Tiahuanaco culture from the south, the Mochica valleys were strongly affected as far north as Chicama. North of Chicama, the Tiahuanacoid elements, insofar as they can be measured in pottery form and design, are extremely weak.[29] The Mochica style is, however, well represented in the Pacasmayo (or Jequetepeque) Valley[30] and, possibly, in the Lambayeque Valley.[31] Thus these northernmost valleys represent a cultural hinterland beyond the frontiers of vigorous Tiahuanacoid influence. Significantly, it was in these far northern valleys that the Mochica plastic and sculptural tradition in pottery continued without serious disruption.

The Chimu civilization follows the Tiahuanaco period on the north coast. Chimu pottery styles are an interesting mixture of the old realistic modeling and plastic treatment of the Mochica plus certain vessel forms and decorative motives associated with Coast Tiahuanaco. The general impression, however, is that Chimu pottery has greater resemblance to Mochica than it does to Tiahuanaco. As an example, most of the Chimu grave ware is naturalistic and modeled and the stirrup-spout form is predominant—all traits of Mochica rather than Tiahuanaco derivation. The importance of the Pacasmayo and Lambayeque valleys in this fusion of two ceramic traditions should not be overlooked. These valleys were the localities in which the Mochica ideas were kept alive and which, later, fed them back to the valleys to the south once the full force of Coast Tiahuanaco had been spent. It is in this role that the function of the far northern valleys can be understood as being parallel to the hinterlands of the Georgian or Yucatecan situations.

In architecture the Chimu culture follows closely in the new forms and styles set down by Coast Tiahuanaco. The great rectangular adobe enclosures and the planned communities flourish. Chanchan, the Chimu capital, is the archetype of this kind of architecture and settlement arrangement. Parallels with Georgian Lamar and Yucatecan Mayapan cultures are obvious. The architecture, particularly the public architecture, of the invading culture seems to prevail in the resultant acculturation. In artistic symbolism Tiahuanacoid elements continue into Chimu, as we have noted, but there is a decrease in vitality as in the cases of Southern Cult art in Lamar or Tula-Toltec art in late Yucatan.

Synthesis and Analysis

A pattern of diffusion and acculturation is evident in the foregoing comparisons. An active or aggressive culture invades the territory of a neighbor and succeeds in planting a colony within that territory, probably by force. This colony represents more than a transmission of ideas and manufactures. It is these carried by people who are fully indoctrinated in the invading culture. Such colonies may have been wholly foreign or they may have contained a mixture of both local and foreign population. In the latter case it is presumed that the intruders played the dominant role in the society. The innovations brought by the invaders may pertain to any or all cultural features, but public architecture and symbolic art seem to be emphasized. During this first period of contact, while the alien colonies are flourishing, the old cultural traditions are maintained with relatively little change in surrounding or nearby regions. In the succeeding period the effects of acculturation are seen in the appearance of a new culture. This new culture occupies not only the sites or colonies of the original invaders but the total region under examination. The new culture represents a blend of the intrusive elements and the old local forms.[32] The innovations in public architecture of the first period remain and are fully incorporated in the communities of the second period. The artistic symbols of the invaders also are retained but these have undergone modification and reduction. Certain artifacts, notably pottery, show a fusion of old and new elements with a tendency for the old to predominate.

This diagram recapitulates the events in three American prehistoric sequences, ignoring, at the same time, the certain differences in the configurations. It is in no way a "law" outlining an "internal necessity" in the course of these events. Undoubtedly, there are instances of "cultural colonization" from many places and times of the world's history where the results do not follow this pattern. It is easy to conceive of such a colonization "failing" by being "swamped" by the recipient culture so that it leaves no appreciable trace in the subsequent record of cultural development. Or, as was the case with some of the European colonization of America, the invading culture might well "overwhelm" the recipient, replacing it in all of its aspects within a few decades or centuries. Rather than to stress further the "regularities" of the pattern which we have described it will be, perhaps, more fruitful to examine further the three historical cases of our discussion with respect to the particular conditions surrounding them. In this way we may gain some insight into the factors which permit or limit the type of diffusion-acculturation with which we are here concerned.

It will be recalled that in central Georgia the shift between Macon Plateau and Swift Creek was a major economic change. Swift Creek culture was based on hunting and gathering whereas Macon Plateau was primarily agricultural. This circumstance may explain some of the differences noted between the Georgia as opposed to the Yucatan and Peruvian cases. New tool types and new pottery (including the utilitarian ware) came into Georgia along with the Macon Plateau temple mound architecture and the Southern Cult symbolism. In Yucatan and Peru the new elements are primarily in the latter categories, those which are reflective of social, political, or religious changes rather than a basic economic readjustment. It may be significant in this regard that in both Peru and Yucatan the cultures involved were on a similar economic level of intensive agriculture. One basic fact emerges. The "cultural colonization" type of diffusion-acculturation appears to be possible between cultures of the same or of different subsistence levels.

In discussing the Peruvian situation we have already pointed to differences which set this case apart from the other two. Whereas the invading cultures on the Georgian and Yucatecan scenes were established in single localities surrounded by the older resident communities, the Tiahuanacoid culture of the Peruvian coast domainted a number of the Mochica valleys as a solid block, leaving as hinterland only the northernmost territories. Although natural terrain conformation and irrigation unity of the individual valleys may explain this pattern of invasion, it is possible that other, more strictly cultural, conditions were involved. We know, for instance, that warfare began along the north Peruvian coast well before the rise of the Mochica.[33] The idea is here advanced that invasion and conquest were not new institutions to the Mochica and that in the wake of a military conquest they would have submitted more readily to organized subjugation than either the Swift Creek or Classic Maya populations. It is obvious, of course, that the narrow valleys and the compact population centers of the Mochica would permit this sort of subjugation and control more easily than the forests and scattered settlements of Georgia and Yucatan. A condition which is highlighted by the variant setting and circumstances in Peru, but which binds all three examples together, is that a hinterland or "refuge" zone in which the invaded culture may retreat and maintain its integrity is a necessity for the subsequent acculturation following "cultural colonization." Judging from Yucatan and Georgia, the "refuge" zone may be larger—much larger, in fact—than the area occupied by the invading culture. On the other hand, in Peru the "refuge" zone was marginal and smaller than the invaded territory. The apparent importance of the "refuge." zone suggests that most of the amalgamation and blending of the two cultures takes place in the hinterland during the period that the invading culture maintains its colony. Some acculturation undoubtedly proceeds within the colony, but the vigor with which the "hybrid" cultures suddenly blossom upon the scene would indicate that they had been in formulation somewhere outside the principal establishments of the invaders.

There are other conditions which undoubtedly promote or hinder the "cultural colonization" processes although it is difficult to gauge the limits of some of these. One factor, certainly crucial, is that of a common cultural tradition—a participation in the same culture area or cotradition. In all of the examples reviewed the two cultures participating in the contact belonged to such a common underlying tradition. Just what degree of cultural divergence marks the boundary beyond which acculturation deriving from "cultural colonization" cannot successfully take place is not known. There are indications, for example, that the European colonization of the eastern United States brought together two cultures which were so fundamentally incompatible that a successful fusion on anything like equal terms was impossible. In Mexico and Peru this incompatibility of European and native cultures was not so pronounced; nevertheless, the resultant mergers are dominated by the European elements.

Closely related to the condition of basic relationship within a common cultural tradition is that of the natural regions in which the cultures of any contact situation have been formed. Among our native American examples there are differences in the resultant acculturation which may be attributable, in part, to the relative degree of difference in the natural regions involved. As an example of this we note that the alluvial valleys of the Mississippi and its major tributaries—the environment in which Macon Plateau culture is presumed to have developed—do not differ greatly from the smaller valley bottoms of Georgia. In spite of a fundamental difference in subsistence economy between Swift Creek and Macon Plateau, a stable adjustment was achieved in Lamar. Was this because the introduced trait of intensive maize agriculture was as practical in the Georgia valleys as it had been farther to the north and west? In contradistinction, the environmental difference between the Mexican highlands, the original home of the Tula-Toltec culture, and the Maya lowlands of Yucatan is much greater than any of those within the southeastern United States. Is the relative feebleness of the resultant Mayapan culture with respect to what had gone before a measure of this difference?

CONCLUSIONS

Among the various types of diffusion and acculturation which occurred in prehistoric America there is one that may be termed "cultural colonization." The major processes involved are the implantation by persons, and probably by force, of an alien culture as a colony within the homeland of the recipient culture. Some cultural merging may take place within the colony, but the invading culture is clearly dominant in this limited sphere. Contemporaneously with the foreign occupation of the colony, the recipient culture continues within its old channels in adjacent hinterland, or "refuge," regions. During this period, acculturation of the recipient culture proceeds gradually in the "refuge" regions, apparently by borrowing, imitation, or other contact with the colony. Subsequently, a third culture arises from the "refuge" region as a more or less equal blend and acculturative end product of the contact of the invading and invaded cultures. The total region, both colony and "refuge" zone, are united by this new culture. This pattern of "cultural colonization" seems to have been achieved between cultures of similar or of different economic bases. Apparently, the success of the process of final acculturation is facilitated by the background of a common cultural tradition and by similar cultural-environmental adjustments of the merging cultures.

Notes

[1]The author is indebted to A. M. Tozzer, H. E. D. Pollock, Tatiana Proskouriakoff, and C. H. Fairbanks for their comments and criticisms on this paper.

[2]Beals, 1953, pp. 625 ff.

[3]Herskovits, 1948, pp. 523 ff.

[4]See Fairbanks, 1952, pp. 287–290, for a concise description of the Swift Creek culture and its position in the Georgia sequence.

[5]Griffin, 1952a, fig. 205.

[6]Fairbanks, *op. cit.*

[7]Sears, 1953, p. 228, believes Kolomoki and its temple mound to be definitely later than Macon Plateau. The Evelyn Site, near Brunswick, Georgia, is perhaps another example of a late Swift Creek temple mound (Fairbanks, *op. cit.*, p. 287).

[8]See Webb, 1938, and Lewis and Kneberg, 1946.

[9]See Lewis and Kneberg, 1946, and Newman and Snow, 1942.

[10]Fairbanks, *op. cit.* It should be noted that in some regions the Etowah and Savannah cultures precede the Lamar and show the beginnings of the Woodland-Mississippian synthesis that is carried to a conclusion in Lamar.

[11]See Thompson, 1945, for a summary of the culture history of the Yucatecan Maya.

[12]*Op. cit.*, p. 14.

[13]*Op. cit.*, p. 12.

[14]A. M. Tozzer, personal communication, 1953.

[15]Pollock, 1952, p. 238.

[16]R. E. Smith concurs in this opinion (personal communication, 1953).

[17]Armillas, 1951, p. 84, describes a wall at Chichen Itza which he interprets as a defense work.

[18]See Tozzer, 1930, and Wray, 1945.

[19]This is the impression of both Pollock and R. E. Smith. Brainerd, who has studied Yucatecan pottery more intensively than anyone else, should clear up this important point in a forthcoming publication (Brainerd, 1958).

[20]Thompson, *op. cit.*

[21]Pollock, *op. cit.* Tozzer applies the term "Chichen III" to this period (Tozzer, personal communication, 1953).

[22]Pollock, *op. cit.*, p. 240.

[23]Southern Cult art in Georgia seems to climax at Etowah, in the northern part of that state, at a time after the beginning of the Macon Plateau period and just before the rise of Lamar (see Fairbanks, 1950).

[24]This is synopsized in Bennett and Bird, 1949. A detailed field excavational report covering this same developmental span is Strong and Evans, 1952. It should be noted that there are indications of an early lithic industry along the north Peruvian coast. Presumably these antedate the remains of the premaize horticulturists of Huaca Prieta (see Larco Hoyle, 1948, pp. 11–12).

[25]Willey, 1953a.

[26]Newman, 1948.

[27]Ford, 1949. In the Virú sequence the names Huancaco and Tomaval are used, respectively, for Mochica and Coast Tiahuanaco.

[28]Willey, 1948.

[29]Bennett, 1939, pp. 94 ff.

[30]Doering, 1951.

[31]Bennett, *op. cit.*

[32]These blendings were not accomplished *in vacuo*. In all three of the examples we have discussed it is evident that some cultural elements other than those of the invading and recipient cultures are present in the resultant acculturations. Undoubtedly, diffusion and contact from and with sources in addition to those under consideration continued during the period of acculturation.

[33]Willey, 1953a.

21

The Early Great Styles and the Rise of the Precolumbian Civilizations

(From *American Anthropologist*, Vo. 64, pp. 2–14, 1962. Reprinted by permission of the American Anthropological Association. Not for sale or further reproduction.)

> Experience has shown that it is hopeless to storm, by a frontal attack, the great citadels of the causality underlying highly complex groups of facts.
>
> —A. L. Kroeber

In native America, not a great many centuries after the establishment of a village agricultural way of life, two major art styles of the first rank appear, more or less contemporaneously, in southern Mesoamerica and in northern Peru.[1] These are known as the Olmec and the Chavín. I purpose to consider these two art styles, first, and briefly, as to their content and form and, secondly, but in more detail, in their cultural settings and from the general perspective of New World culture history. For what engages our attention is that both styles occur at that point in time which might be said to mark the very first stirrings of civilization in the Mesoamerican and Peruvian areas. What role did these art styles, or the motivations of which they are the symbols, play in the rise and development of Precolumbian civilizations? Are they, the styles themselves, the touchstones of that condition we refer to as civilization? What do we know of their origins or, if not their origins, their preconditions?

Like most anthropologists who are interested in culture history, I am interested in origins and causes, but I am not sanguine about the possibilities of easy or early victories. Certainly the answers to the ultimate causal questions as to why the ancient American civilizations began and flourished where they did and when they did still elude us, and what I can offer here will do little more, at best, than describe and compare certain situations and series of events.

My use of the term "great styles" is a special and intentional one. I refer to art styles and to manifestations of these generally considered as "fine arts" (Kroeber 1957:24–26). Their greatness is judged in their historical contexts, but it is none the less real. These great Precolumbian art styles of Mesoamerica and Peru are expressed monumentally; they occur in settings that were obviously sacred or important in the cultures which produced them; they are also pervasive, being reproduced in a variety of media and contexts; the products are rendered with the consummate skill of the specially and long-trained artist; they conform to strict stylistic canons; their subject matter tends to be thematic; and finally, the finest monuments or creations in these styles are truly powerful and awe-inspiring. These last criteria are subjective, but I do not think we can ignore them. We see ancient art—the word "primitive" is here most inappropriate—across the millennia and with the eyes of an alien culture; yet we are not unmoved. Man speaks to man through art, and the screen of cultural difference and relativism does not strain out all emotional effect. Olmec and Chavín art measure fully to standards of greatness.

OLMEC AND CHAVÍN

The Olmec style of Mesoamerica has been known for 30 years as such. Stirling (1943) and his associates (Weiant 1943; Drucker 1943, 1952) fully revealed the style in their discoveries in southern Veracruz and Tabasco. They and Caso (1942) and Covarrubias (1942, 1946, 1957) made it widely known and also opened the question of its cultural and chronological position in Mesoamerican culture history (see also Greengo 1952; Coe 1957). Olmec art is rendered in life-size, or greater than life-size, full-round, and bas-relief stone monuments. These include free-standing heads, human and anthropomorphic figures, stelae, and altars. Carvings are also found on natural boulders after the manner of pictographs, but most of these are done with such skill and are so much a part of the deliberate style, that "bas-relief," rather than "pictograph," is the fitting term to describe them. Olmec sculptures also occur as small pieces: jade and serpentine figurines, celts, ornamental effigy axes, plaques, and other small ornaments. Ceramic objects in the Olmec style are less common but include figurines, pottery stamps, and vessels.

The central theme of Olmec art is a jaguar-human or were-jaguar being. The concept is nearly always expressed as more human, in total characteristics, than jaguar. The face is frequently infantile as well as jaguar-like, and in many instances actual human infant bodies are portrayed. But subtle shades of this infantile jaguarism infect almost all human or anthropomorphic representations, ranging all the way from only slightly snubbed, feline noses and down-turned drooping mouths to toothed and snarling countenances. Some stelae and monuments bear another concept, elderly men with aquiline noses and beards who are sometimes depicted with portrait realism; but there is also a fusion of the jaguar-like anthropomorph with the bearded man in Olmec iconography (M. D. Coe, 1965a). Other motifs are rarer: fully animalized jaguars, bird and duck monsters, serpents, and fish.

The formal properties of the Olmec style are highly distinctive. Although the subject matter is to a large extent in the mythological realm the portrayals are carried out with a "realistic" intent. It is thoroughly nongeometric and nonabstract; lines have a slow curvilinear rhythm, and free space balances figures. There is little fine detail (M. D. Coe, 1965a). As a style it is the equivalent of any of the later great styles of Mesoamerica, and in the full-round treatment of the human body it is the superior of all.

The climax region of the Olmec style was southern Veracruz and Tabasco in such ceremonial center sites as La Venta, Tres Zapotes, and San Lorenzo. Insofar as the style is expressed monumentally there is little doubt but that this is its homeland. Elsewhere, Olmec monuments are widely scattered and occasional. Most are bas-relief figures carved on boulder outcrops, as in Morelos (Piña Chan 1955), Chiapas (Ferdon 1953), Guerrero (Jimenez Moreno 1959: fig. 4, Pl. I-a), Guatemala (Thompson 1948: fig. 111a), and Salvador (Boggs 1950). Aside from these monuments, portable objects of the Olmec style, such as jade figurines, ornaments, and small manufactures, are found throughout much of southern Mesoamerica, from the Valley of Mexico and Guerrero on the northwest down through Chiapas and Pacific Guatemala. Covarrubias (1957) held the opinion that Guerrero was the ancestral home of the Olmec style, in its premonumental era, but it has yet to be demonstrated that the numerous Olmec figurines found in that region are earlier manifestations of the style than the great sculptures of Veracruz-Tabasco. In any event, for our present discussion, it is sufficient to note that the climax of the "great" aspects of the style are in this latter zone but that the style as a whole is spread over much of southern Mesoamerica. Wherever it can be dated, Olmec art appears in the Middle Preclassic Period of Mesoamerican history, with an outer dating range of 1000 to 300 B.C., and a probable more specific bracketing by radiocarbon determinations of between 800 and 400 B.C. (Drucker, Heizer, and Squier 1959:248–67).

Chavín style art is named for Chavín de Huántar, an imposing archaeological site in the Marañon drainage of the north highlands of Peru. Tello, more than any other archaeologist, called attention to Chavín art (Tello 1942, 1943, 1960); subsequently, W. C. Bennett (1943, 1944a), Larco Hoyle (1941), Kroeber (1944:81–93), and Carrión Cachot (1948) made significant contributions (see also Willey 1951b; Coe 1954). Like Olmec, the Chavín style is one closely adapted to sculptural forms, both monumental and small. The heroic-sized sculptures are mostly free-standing monoliths or stelae, lintels, cornices, and decorative features of buildings. These are executed with a relief-incision and champlevé technique in stone or are modeled in clay. Some full-round carving and modeling is also attempted in heads or figures tenoned or affixed to walls or buildings. Chavín small carving produced stone and bone plaques, stone and gourd vessels, ceremonial stone mortars and pestles, and ornaments. The style also appears in finely modeled and incised pottery vessels, in repoussé goldwork, and even in textile designs. In sum, it enters into more varied media than the Olmec style, but both styles are most at home in carving, particularly in large sculptures and in the work of the lapidary.

The content of Chavín art, like that of Olmec, deals with a few powerful central themes. With Chavín the dominant motif is either the feline or the fusion of feline elements, such as fangs and claws, with other beings, including humans, condors, the cayman, and the serpent. The fantastic beings of Chavín art emphasize somewhat more the animal attributes than the human, in contradistinction to Olmec. Strictly human representations are rare, and none of these have the qualities of portraiture observed in some of the Olmec sculptures. Although firmly set in a unified style, the monster or composite beings show great variations in the combination of jaguar or puma and other animal elements.

The formal properties of the Chavín style, which are its essence, are decidedly different from those of Olmec. No one would mistake the two styles in juxtaposition. Chavín is intricate with detail in a way that Olmec is not. It does not employ free space, but seeks to fill it with such things as small secondary heads and eyes disposed over the body of the central monster figure of the sculpture. There is little mastery of realism or naturalism. It has more features that are stiff and "archaic." As styles the two have common ground only in that they rely upon slow heavy curves rather than straight lines, and both have a quality of the esoteric about them rather than the obvious.

The heartland of the Chavín style, insofar as it is monumental and in stone or sculptured adobe, is in the north highlands of Peru, at such sites as Chavín de Huántar, Yauya, and Kuntur Wasi, and in the coastal valleys of Nepeña and Casma. This is but one sector of the larger Peruvian culture area, and as such this focal concentration is comparable to the distribution of Olmec art in the Veracruz-Tabasco region within the larger sphere of Mesoamerica. The wider compass of Chavín art, as expressed in small manufactures, takes in much of the Peruvian culture area. Formerly thought to embrace only the northern part of Peru, its definite influence is now traced as far south on the coast as the Cerrillos phase of the Ica and Nazca Valleys (Lanning 1959). Thus, in its total geographic extent Chavín outstrips Olmec, the latter being confined to the southern half, or less, of its culture area setting. Chronologically, Chavín art belongs to the Formative Period of Peruvian prehistory and to either the Early or Middle subdivision of that period, depending upon one's terminology. The gross estimated dates for the Peruvian Formative Period are approximately the first millennium B.C. Within this range, and with the aid of radiocarbon determinations, the horizon of the Chavín art style is narrowed to between 800 and 400 B.C. (Collier 1962; Lanning 1959). As will be noted, this is identical to the dates for the time span estimated for the Olmec style in Mesoamerica. These two sets of dates, incidentally, were arrived at quite independently by different sets of archaeologists.

Olmec and Chavín in Culture-Historical Perspective

As we have already observed, Olmec and Chavín styles make their first appearance on an underlying base of village agriculture. In Mesoamerica, village agriculture—defined as sedentary life based primarily upon maize cultivation—became established by about 1500 B.C., following a long epoch of incipient plant domestication (Willey 1960). The presence of ceremonial architecture, in the form of platform mounds for temples or other buildings, in the early centuries of Mesoamerican agricultural life is probable, although not well documented. But by 800 B.C., some 700 years or so after the village agricultural threshold, the great Olmec ceremonial center of La Venta was founded in Tabasco. At the same time that these events were taking place in Mesoamerica, similar and related ones were going on in Peru. At about 1500 B.C. a well-developed variety of Mesoamerican maize appeared in coastal Peru and was rapidly assimilated into the local root-crop agricultural economies of the Peruvian coastal communities (Lanning quoted from Collier 1962; Mangelsdorf, MacNeish, and Willey, 1964). Soon after this the Peruvians were making pottery and building ceremonial mounds, and to clinch the relationships between Peru and the north at this time, a distinctly Mesoamerican figurine has been found in one of these early Peruvian ceremonial sites known as Las Aldas (Ishida and others 1960, 97 ff.). The Chavín style appears shortly after this. During its period, contact between Mesoamerica and Peru continued. For example, among the best known traits that have often been pointed to as linking the Olmec phase of Tlatilco and the Chavín Cupisnique phase are figurines, rocker-stamped pottery, incised and color-zoned wares, flat-bottomed open-bowl forms, and the stirrup-mouth jar (Engel 1956; Porter Weaver 1953; Willey 1955a; Coe 1960).

In this setting of an almost exact equation in time, and with further evidences of contact in specific ceramic items, can we go further and argue that Olmec and Chavín are definitely related? Drucker (1952:231), Wauchope (1954), and I (Willey 1959) have all called attention to this possibility, and Della Santa (1959) has argued the case in earnest; but on reflection I do not think that the two styles show a close relationship. At least they do not exhibit a relationship which, in the realm of art, is a counterpart to the Mesoamerican maize in Peru or the Tlatilco-Cupisnique ceramic ties. What they possess in common, except for an addiction to sculptural and lapidaristic modes of expression, is largely the concept of the feline being, most probably the jaguar.[2] Therefore, their relationship, if it existed, must have been on a level of concept and mythology, either an ancient undercurrent of belief on which both Peruvian and Mesoamerican societies could have drawn to develop quite different art styles or by a stimulus diffusion in which the source idea was drastically reworked in the recipient setting. In this last connection the example of Mesopotamian stimuli to the rise of early Egyptian civilization comes to mind. If this interpretation of the relationship between Olmec and Chavín is the correct one, I would, all things considered, see Mesoamerica as the source and Peru as the receiving culture.

An argument against a close, continuous Olmec-Chavín relationship on the level of style is, of course, the absence of either style, or any style definitely related to either, in the Intermediate area of Lower Central America, Colombia, and Ecuador. The San Agustín sculptures of southern Colombia are, perhaps, the only candidates (Preuss 1931; Bennett 1946c:848–49); but they are remarkably unlike either Olmec or Chavín, sharing with them only the attribute of feline-fanged beings, and they are only dubiously dated on the same time level as Olmec and Chavín. Further, as a style, San Agustín is considerably below the quality or sophistication of these great styles (Kroeber 1951). This absence of stylistic linkages in the Intermediate area stands in contrast, however, to many of the significant traits of the village agricultural base out of which Olmec and Chavín seem to have developed. Evidence is rapidly accumulating from Ecuador (Evans and Meggers 1957, 1958; Estrada 1958), Colombia (Reichel-Dolmatoff 1959), and Lower Central America (Coe and Baudez 1961) which shows the Intermediate area to be a common participant in early ceramic and other traits held also by Mesoamerica and Peru. A notable example of this is the striking similarity between Guatemalan Ocos pottery and that of the Ecuadorean Chorrera phase (Coe 1960). Thus, in spite of this background of apparent intercommunication and interchange down and up the axis of Nuclear America, the entities of style which we recognize as Olmec and Chavín remain bound to their respective areas. They did not spread to the Intermediate area, nor can they reasonably be derived from there.

The Early Great Styles as Precursors to Civilization

We have placed Olmec and Chavín at that point in the developmental history of the Mesoamerican and Peruvian cultures where village farming societies undergo a transformation to become temple-center-and-village societies. This event is another major threshold in Precolumbian life. It is a different kind of threshold than that of village agriculture which precedes it by a few hundred years, but it signals important changes. It is, in effect, the threshold of complex society that leads on to civilization. The economy appears much the same as earlier; it is based on maize, or maize and root crops, supplemented with other American food plants. The technology includes pottery-making, weaving, stone carving—in brief, the village agricultural neolithic arts. Houses were permanent to semi-permanent affairs disposed in small hamlets or villages. The most noticeable difference on the cultural landscape is the ceremonial center. These centers were not urban zones. Heizer (1960) has made quite explicit the nonurban nature of La Venta, and he estimates that the constructions there could have been built and sustained only by the cooperative efforts of villagers from a surrounding radius of several kilometers. Although Chavín de Huántar is situated in a radically different natural environment from La Venta, it, too, appears to have been a complex of ceremonial buildings and chambers without a large resident population in close proximity (Bennett 1944a; Tello 1960).

It is in such ceremonial centers that the outstanding monuments of the Olmec and Chavín styles are found. In Mesoamerica it is assumed that this ceremonial-center-with-outlying-hamlets type of settlement pattern is allied with a theocratic political structure. The assumption derives partly from the nature of the settlement and the feeling that such dispersed societies could only have been bound together by strong religious beliefs, but it derives mostly from our knowledge of the late Pre- and early Postcolumbian periods in

Mesoamerica when lowland ceremonial-centered societies were known to have a strong theocratic bias. In Peru this kind of theocratic orientation was not a feature of the Inca state; but there the archaeological record shows a definite trend, from early to late times, that can best be interpreted as a movement away from religion as a dominant force and the gradual ascendance of secular power (Willey 1951a). In the light of such trends it is likely that priest leadership was more important in Chavín times than later. Thus, archaeological inference is on the side of identifying the nonurban ceremonial center as primarily a sacred or religious establishment whatever other functions may have been served there. Olmec and Chavín works of art must surely, then, have been religious expressions. This concatenation of circumstances, the shift from simple village agricultural societies to complex temple-centered ones and the appearance of the two great styles, suggests that Olmec and Chavín are the symbols of two ecumenical religions. These religions lie at the base of the subsequent growth of Precolumbian Mesoamerican and Peruvian civilizations (see Bernal 1960).

This fundamental underlying nature of Olmec and Chavín art is revealed in the later cultures and styles in the two areas. For Mesoamerica, Michael D. Coe (1965a) suggests that all known major art styles of the southern part of the area have an origin in the Olmec style. Most directly related among these would be the styles of the slightly later "danzante" monuments at Monte Alban and the Monte Alban I phase effigy incensarios (Caso 1938), the Olmec-derived sculptures from the later Preclassic Period levels at Tres Zapotes, the Izapa style stelae in Chiapas, and the closely similar Late Preclassic monuments found recently at Kaminaljuyu. More remotely, but nevertheless showing affiliations with Olmec art, especially through the link of the Izapa style, would be the Classic Maya and Classic Veracruz styles (Proskouriakoff 1950:177; Covarrubias 1957:166). Further afield, the derivative influences are dimmed or uncertain. Classic Teotihuacan art stands most apart in showing little Olmec influence, and perhaps this may be correlated with the relatively slight impress of Olmec art on an earlier level in the Valley of Mexico where it is known mainly in the occasional Tlatilco ceramic objects. But that some connections, however indirect, did exist between Olmec and Teotihuacan iconography is shown by Covarrubias (1957: fig. 22) in his diagram of the stylistic evolution of the Teotihuacan and other rain gods from the prototype of the Olmec baby-jaguar face.

For Peru, the story is much the same. There, the distribution of the Chavín style was more nearly area-wide. Perhaps as a consequence, nearly all post-Chavín styles show some Chavín feline elements (Willey 1951b). Mochica art, of the north coast, depicts a feline or anthropomorphic feline as an apparent deity. Feline symbolism has an important part in Recuay, Pucara, and Nazca cultures. It is present in Tiahuanaco art, although not as the dominant motif.

CONSIDERATIONS OF CAUSALITY

We see Olmec and Chavín styles at the root of civilization in Mesoamerica and Peru. We also note, in the wider perspective of Nuclear America, that contemporaneous and related socieites of the geographically intervening Intermediate area do not possess comparable great styles. Neither do they go on to civilization. From these facts I think we may reasonably conclude that Olmec and Chavín art are in some way involved with the rise to the status of civilization in their respective areas. But these are observations of history, or prehistory, and like all such observations it is difficult and perilous to attempt to read causality into them. In pointing to what I think is a special relationship between the early great styles and civilization, am I not merely defining civilization in terms of itself? In a partial sense I am; great art styles are one of the criteria by which the condition of civilization may be judged (Childe 1950). But it is not, however, altogether true in that many of the criteria of civilization are not yet present in either Mesoamerica or Peru at the time of Olmec and Chavín art florescence. Certainly one of the most significant of these, urbanization, is not; writing and metallurgy, if present, are only in their infancy; and the institution of the state, in any extensive territorial sense, is highly unlikely. The appearance of the first great styles, then, comes early in the growth of these American civilizations. By the time a full civilizational status has been achieved in either Mesoameric or Peru these styles, as organized entities, have vanished, leaving only their residue in later styles. Nevertheless, styles themselves cannot be reified into civilization builders. They are, as I have said, symbols of institutions, attitudes, beliefs. Is, then, a belief system, a religion, a prime causal force as Toynbee has stated? I would think so, or at least I consider it near enough to a causal core to speculate on the processes whereby fundamental beliefs and their representative art may promote the growth of civilization.

In making these speculations let us consider a hypothesis about culture development in native America and particularly in the Nuclear American areas. Casting back to earlier chronological ranges than I have been talking about, it is now becoming evident that people changed from a collecting-hunting mode of existence to one of food plant cultivation by a process of introgression. The term is a botanical one, and it applies to what happened to plants over the several millennia leading up to village agriculture in Mesoamerica; but I also think it applicable to the culture change that went along with the gradual domestication of plants. The studies of Mangelsdorf and MacNeish (Mangelsdorf, MacNeish, and Willey, 1964; MacNeish 1958 and personal communication 1961) have shown that original wild plants were found in a great many small locales where they were gathered and used and where seeds were eventually sown and plants tended by small, local populations. With contact between two such small communities, of plants and people, plant introgression and hybridization ensued with a genetically improved result. This process continued among enclaves with both hybridization and with the interchange of different species as well. Present investigations indicate that primitive maize, beans, and squashes do not follow the same sequence of occurrence in incipient agricultural stratigraphies in all parts of Mesoamerica but that the order varies from region to region (MacNeish, personal communication 1961). This diversity in development led, eventually, to the New World complex of food plants and to village agriculture. I would suggest that culture, too, evolved along with plants in much the same way, by introgression or interchange and by hybridization or fusion. This, I believe, is an aspect of what Lesser (1961) is saying in his concept of social fields. To follow the analogy, I think that this is what continued to happen in the development of cultures and societies after the attainment of village agriculture. Regional interchange or regional symbiosis provided an important impetus for change and growth. Sanders (1956, 1957; Braidwood and Willey 1962) has detailed this process for parts of ancient Mesoamerica. It led to civilization.

In this hypothesis an obviously crucial factor is natural environmental setting and a multiplicity of varied settings in relatively close juxtaposition to one another. As has been pointed out by various authors (e. g., Wolf 1959:17–18), Mesoamerica is well suited in this regard. It is a land of climatic, altitudinal, and vegetational variety; it is rich in natural resources. Further, the archaeological record shows trade and contact among distinct natural environmental and cultural regions from early times. Peru, as well, although not quite so varied, has dramatic regional differentiation, particularly between coast and highland; and the prehistory of that area may be read as a kind of counterpoint between the regional cultures of these natural zones (Kroeber 1927). Contrast the potentialities of these two areas with others of the New World which also had a basis of village agriculture. The natural environmental and cultural contours of differentiation within the Amazon basin or the Eastern Woodlands of North America are low in comparison. Products from region to region were the same or similar. Perhaps this homogeneity discouraged exchange (Coe, 1961a).

Are we, now, at a nexus of causality in the rise of Precolumbian civilizations in certain areas but not in others? Although conceding the importance of intra-areal cultural heterogeneity, and realizing that such heterogeneity must be to a large extent based in natural environment, I am not convinced. What of the Intermediate area which lies between and close to both of our areas of high civilization and which did not match them in these conditions of civilization? It is an area of spectacular regional environmental differentiation, tropical and semiarid coasts, tropical lowlands, semitropical and temperate valleys, cool-temperate uplands. It has them all, and it is not an area poor in resources. We also know that the communities of this area were in possession of agriculture about as early as those of Mesoamerica and Peru. These village agriculturists were similarly skilled in pottery making and, probably, the other neolithic crafts. In fact, they participated in the same technical traditions as their Mesoamerican or Peruvian contemporaries. Where then is the lack? What are the essential differences between the Intermediate area and its native cultures and those of the Mesoamerican and Peruvian areas?

I return, again, to the great styles, to Olmec and Chavín, for which there is no counterpart from Honduras to southern Ecuador. I have suggested that they, in themselves, are but the symbols for the religious ideologies of the early farming societies of Mesoamerica and Peru. I would further suggest that in these ideologies these early societies had developed a mechanism of intercommunication, a way of knitting together the smaller parts of the social universe of their day into a more unified whole than it had heretofore been or would otherwise be. In a way similar to that of the interchange of objects, plants, and techniques which had previously prepared the village agricultural threshold, the sharing of common ideologies led to the threshold of civilization by enlarging the effective social field. By this enlargement more individuals, more social segments, more local societies combined and coordinated their energies and efforts than at any time before. Regional differentiation in culture is an important precondition to cultural development insofar as differences contribute to the richness of the larger order, but without union the different parts remain isolated and in danger of stagnation. There are various ways by which people have promoted such union, but mutually and deeply held beliefs seem paramount. Such belief systems were, I think, the distinguishing features of the Mesoamerican and Peruvian societies of the first half of the first millennium B.C., and the great Olmec and Chavín art styles are our clues to them.

Yet, even if my thesis is accepted thus far, have we done more than follow the chimera of causality into one more disguise? Why did Mesoamerica and Peru develop early great religions and art styles and other areas not? What was the reason for their genius? I do not know. I do not think that it sprang from a seed planted by Chinese voyagers—or from two seeds brought by two such sets of voyagers—despite the facts that the Chou dynasty is replete with prowling tigers and that the time element is right for such a transference (Heine-Geldern 1959). It does us no good to deny the sudden mutation of creative change to the aborigines of America. It is no easier to explain elsewhere than it is here. What we are seeking is probably in New World soil, but genius must arise from preconditions which to our eyes do not foreshadow it. Local prototypes of Chavín and Olmec may eventually be found, although these will only carry the story back a little in time and leave the startling florescences unexplained.

I do not reject in their entirety any of the factors or forces we have been discussing as having had possible important influence in the growth of New World civilization. Climate, soil, agricultural potential, natural regional variety, all undoubtedly were significant. I am hesitant, however, to pinpoint any one of them as *the cause.* I am equally hesitant to advance my thesis of an early, prevailing, multi-regional ecumenical religion in either Mesoamerica or Peru as a *sole cause* of later civilizational greatness. I ask, rather, that such phenomena as I have directed attention to be considered as a step in the process of cultural development—a step which almost certainly was taken in these two areas of native America. For it may be that we phrase the problem wrong, that the search for the very wellsprings of origin and cause is meaningless, and that the limits of anthropology are to appraise and understand the continuum of process as it is disclosed to us rather than to fix its ultimate beginnings.

Notes

[1]The author gratefully acknowledges the critical reading of the manuscript and the suggestions made by M. D. Coe and D. W. Lathrap in July 1961.

[2]M. D. Coe has called my attention to a small but specific design element found in Olmec sculptures and also present on Chavinoid incised pottery from Kotosh, Peru, recently excavated by the University of Tokyo Expedition to Peru but not yet published. This element is a U-shaped figure with what may be a stylized ear of maize emerging from the opening.

A PRIORI HYPOTHESES

"Hypothesis testing," which was a key term in the "new archaeology" of 25 years ago, goes along with "problem oriented" research, which is certainly to be preferred to digging or surveying randomly for things or data. An important question, however, is how one arrives at a hypothesis for testing. I think many archaeologists have come up with hypotheses through long immersion in the data of a specific area, either through field-work, a study of the extant literature, or both. As we tell ourselves, in this way we come to "see what the problems are," the questions to be asked. But in asking questions we really have a model—a model of an answer—in mind. Sometimes the model can be a simple culture-historical one, one of sheer space-time systematics: We believe that Culture A is earlier than Culture B; we know the methods available for testing this hypothetical model of chronology (stratigraphy, seriation, radiocarbon dating); and we can proceed accordingly. True, this type of hypothesis might seem almost too modest for "testing." More in keeping with the spirit of the "new archaeology" would be a hypothesis about the processes involved in the development of institutions, such as the "rise of the state." The researcher might have as a model the role of interregional trade in state formation, and he or she would then set about marshaling the evidence that would support such a model.

I have grouped three of my former essays under the rubric of "*a priori* hypotheses." The first of these, "Mesoamerican Art and Iconography and the Integrity of the Mesoamerican Ideological System," grew out of a symposium on that subject which was held at the Metropolitan Museum of Art in New York, at the celebration its great Precolumbian art show, "Before Cortez," in October 1970. The three-day symposium dealt with "The Iconography of Middle American Sculpture." Nine Mesoamericanists, including myself, were invited to participate. Their names are all mentioned in my article, which was written as a summary of the other papers and published in the symposium proceedings by the museum in 1973. In an attempt to make my "summary" more than just that I focused on a theme that had been explicit or implicit in the remarks of the symposium speakers. This was their *a priori* hypothesis or assumption that the data of Mesoamerican art and iconography should be interpreted on a basis of ethnographic analogy—specifically, Mesoamerican ethnographic analogies that were derived ultimately from early Spanish Colonial Contact Period ethnohistorical sources. The one exception to this was George Kubler (1973a), who operated in an interpretive framework based in art history. (While all of the rest of us in the symposium could be described as "anthropological archaeologists," Kubler had come to Precolumbian art as an art historian.)

Although I ended up my remarks on the side of the majority of my colleagues, arguing for ethnographic analogy within the context of the Mesoamerican cultural tradition as the most dependable method of reading meaning into Precolumbian Mesoamerican art, it was also my intention to initiate a dialogue between what I took to be "anthropological" and "art historical" points of view in such matters. As it turned out, it was past 11 P.M. when I concluded, so the session ended without discussion; however, I was particularly interested in giving George Kubler a chance to reply. What were his thoughts about the unity and continuity of art and ideology in ancient Mesoamerica? Fortunately, Kubler prepared a response in writing, which was published with my statement and the other symposium offerings. I urge readers to look at it (Kubler 1973b).

I make no claim that any of the symposium papers individually, or all of them together, plus my summary, provide an adequate "test" for the hypothesis of Mesoamerican ideological unity. The subject is too vast for such scattered and summary treatment. But I think the issue was raised of whether such unity existed. Kubler objected strenuously to the idea, and particularly to the way in which Michael Coe (1973) had presented it. Coe saw ideological unity taking form in Olmec times and continuing without fundamental modification up to the sixteenth century. Kubler rejected this as an oversimplication, a surrender to theory and method at the expense of an understanding of the meanings in the varieties of Precolumbian Mesoamerican art. Thus, Kubler was offended by Coe's identification of Olmec deity representations (*ca.* 1000 B.C.) by Late Postclassic (*ca.* 1500 A.D.) Central Mexican names. Kubler was more sympathetic to Henry Nicholson's (1973) analogical interpretations of Postclassic Mixteca-Puebla art. Here, the "time distance" is shorter and, I suppose because of this, the extension of analogies was not so disturbing. Thus, I would judge from this that Kubler is not opposed to use of all ethnohistorical analogies in iconographic interpretation but rather to what he would assume to be doctrinaire methodological principles governing such matters. As I read over the Kubler (1973b) statement, I have the impression that he views "anthropological archaeologists" as being more doctrinaire than most of us in fact are. Certainly, I do not feel that there are any hard and fast rules to follow, and on the Mesoamerican scene we will have to take up each case on its own. Ethnographic analogies offer hypotheses of interpretation. In some instances these hypotheses appear to be testable, in many others, not.

The second of my essays here was stimulated by Richard Blanton's "disembedded capital" hypothesis. This appeared in his monograph on Monte Alban settlement patterns, in which he had argued that an emergent state, coming into being through a process of federation, might found a city as its capital that was "disembedded," or apart from, the basic economic or military functions of its supporting society (Blanton 1978). Earlier, Blanton (1976) had defined the "disembedded capital" concept, citing as modern examples of the type such cities such as Washington, D.C., Canberra, and Ottawa. In the 1978 monograph, he proposed that the site of Monte Alban in the Valley of Oaxaca had been such a "disembedded capital," constructed by a federation of Late Preclassic Zapotecan small polities to serve as a political and religious center for the entire valley. Blanton, marshaled various lines of evidence from the valley as positive tests of his hypothesis. In their review of this monograph, W. T. Sanders and R. S. Santley (1978) criticized the idea, countering with arguments and interpretations of the Oaxacan and Monte Alban data which they believed negated it.

While the Blanton and Sanders-Santley discussion was confined to the case at hand—Monte Alban and the Valley of Oaxaca—it seemed to me that the "disembedded capital" idea was an unusually interesting one that deserved further study, especially when the concept was applied to the early stages of complex society. Was the "disembedded capital" an evolutionary step in the rise of the state and the first appearances of cities? Or was it something that arose only after state power was firmly established?

To examine this question, I launched into a rapid and preliminary survey of Americanist archaeological data—Mesoamerica and Peru—and then turned to ancient Mesopotamia, Egypt, and China. For the American areas my quick survey was backed by some depth of knowledge on my part. For the Old World areas, which I do not know firsthand, I relied on summary sources rather than original site excavation accounts, and this is an admitted weakness in what I have done. But I concluded, however tentatively, that there was little or no evidence for such "disembedded capitals," or their supporting "federated polities," at the threshold of state formation. In my article, I noted that archaeological information pertinent to the examination of such a question was often inadequate or lacking, and I certainly make no claims to have written a definitive statement on this complex subject. Furthermore, I am fully aware that the test of the Monte Alban case lies within the context of the Valley of Oaxaca and Mesoamerica and the immediately pertinent archaeological data. A comparative search for a similar model is not a test; nevertheless, it is of interest, and I hope that others, particularly Old World archaeologists, will give some thought to the "disembedded capital" idea.

The third essay in the group, "The Classic Maya Sociopolitical Order: A Study in Coherence and Instability," was the examination of a model based upon our general knowledge of West European–American culture history in its application to the Precolumbian Maya. The model is, in effect, the idea that a strong mercantilist economy is "antithetical to a conservative, agrarian-based, feudal-type social system." Applied to the Classic Maya, I was arguing that the old Maya social order was seriously undermined by new trading practices and traders emanating, ultimately, from Central Mexico and coming into the Maya Lowlands from the Mexican Gulf Coast regions. I think much of my description of the situation is quite sound. The old Classic Maya were, indeed, a highly coherent—in fact, a "hypercoherent"—social and political system, one vulnerable to change. The "promotion" (to use Kent Flannery's [1972] term and concept) of the trading entrepreneur in the Terminal Classic (A.D. 800–900), and the disruptive effects on the old social order that this might have brought in a "hypercoherent" society, is a logical line of reasoning. But is it the correct one? I am not at all sure. My archaeological evidences of foreign-inspired trade into the Maya Lowlands, in the form of Fine Paste ceramics, would seem to meet one aspect of a test—but is this enough? One reason I was tempted to write this article was to be contrary. So many of my Mayanist colleagues were touting trade as the dynamic for culture and civilizational growth. Might not trade, at least in certain circumstances, have had the opposite effect? I think the idea deserves pursuing, but I will admit that I am not altogether happy with it. I think that, perhaps, the model or the hypothesis is too alien—it doesn't sound right in the Maya setting. In saying this I am also saying that subjective judgments still have some place in archaeology.

22

Mesoamerican Art and Iconography and the Integrity of the Mesoamerican Ideological System

(From *The Iconography of Middle American Sculpture*, D. T. Easby, Jr., ed., pp. 153–162, Metropolitan Museum, New York, 1973. Reprinted by Metropolitan Museum of Art, New York. Copyright 1973 by Metropolitan Museum.)

Succinct commentary on papers so disparate in subject as those of this symposium calls less for a recapitulation of detail than for a discourse on a theme and problem that these papers share. There is such a theme, and it is a basic concern of all archaeologists and art historians who attempt to bring understanding out of the art, iconography, and visible symbols of vanished societies that have left little or nothing in the way of accompanying texts. Art may be said to have both general and specific meaning. The archaeologist or art historian may proceed to determine either kind of meaning, but on the general level their appreciation must remain relatively superficial, or at best "aesthetic." Only when they arrive at specific meaning will they begin to understand how a particular art functioned in a certain cultural context. To interpret the symbols of art belonging to a cultural tradition quite different from his or her own, the archaeologist must have some control of and insight into that alien and long-lost cultural context. This is the fundamental problem, and it is the problem treated in one manner or another by all of our symposium speakers.

All except one of our presentations have followed, in greater or lesser degree, a basic methodological assumption about Precolumbian Mesoamerican art and iconography: that to interpret the meaning of this art the scholar must begin with the ethnohistoric documentation of the sixteenth century and from there proceed backward in time by analogies based upon these sixteenth-century data. This fundamental methodological assumption rests upon three subsidiary assumptions. The first is that ancient Mesoamerica can be viewed as a unified cultural tradition, a culture-area-with-time-depth, as we say, or to put it another way, that the component cultures within its boundaries were more closely related to each other than any one of them was to cultures outside of these boundaries. In effect, this is to say that all Mesoamerican Precolumbian cultures, from about 2000 B.C. until the Spanish Conquest, were interlinked in time and space in a single huge cultural system. The second assumption, following from the first, is that within this Mesoamerican cultural system there was a unified ideological system. I use the term "ideological" here to subsume all religion and abstract intellectual thought. And the third subsidiary assumption, which takes us right to the heart of the matter, is that there was an integrity of belief and communication within this Mesoamerican ideological system that permits us, in archaeological retrospect, to ascribe similar meanings to similar signs or symbols.

I do not know just how long this conception of a unified Mesoamerican ideological system has been held by students of the subject. Perhaps it has never been stated so flatly and abstractly before, as a set of methodological assumptions. Kirchoff (1943) advanced the idea of a Mesoamerican culture area, or interlinked diffusion sphere, almost thirty years ago. Many earlier scholars operated with these assumptions—Eduard Seler (1902–1923), for example—however, they also operated without the time perspective we have now. Nevertheless, I think it is fair to say that this has been, and is, the standard conception of Mesoamerica, and one held by a majority of archaeologists.

I have indicated, however, that one of our symposium papers did not follow along the lines of these assumptions about the essential unity of form and function in ancient Mesoamerican art and ideology: the presentation of Professor Kubler (1973a). You will note he makes almost no use of the usual iconographic identifications of the Mesoamerican *oikoumene*. Instead, he invites us to consider the conventional meanings implicit in the spatial order of architecture and in its decorative themes. His frames of reference are the general ones of public and sacred versus private and domestic; he attempts to show us how certain architectural proportions have sacred or ritual connotations; more widely within the Mesoamerican sphere, he suggests that these architectural themes had regional-cultural and ethnic significance. In a word, Kubler operates by searching for meaning in general analogy, with reference to behaviors in human societies and cultures anywhere, and with little or no reference to the specifics of Mesoamerican culture as these have been inferred from ethnohistory.

Kubler makes no methodological point of this in his symposium paper, but in a recent published article (1970) he is explicit on this subject. As what he says in "Period, Style and Meaning in Ancient Mesoamerican Art" is very pertinent to this symposium, I hope he will forgive me for bringing it into this disucssion. He takes issue with most of us who would read the religious and ideological meanings of the ethnohistoric horizon back into the prehistoric past. For him there is a great danger that form and meaning may become disjoined with the passage of time, and he cites Panofsky's principle of "disjunction" between form and meaning as applying to those instances when "the members of a successor civilization refashion their inheritance by gearing the predecessor's forms to new meanings, and by clothing in new forms those old meanings which remain acceptable."

And from this Kubler goes on to say: "We may not use Aztec ritual descriptions as compiled by Sahagún about 1550 to explain murals painted at Teotihuacan a thousand years earlier, for the same reason that we would not easily get agreement in interpreting the Hellenistic images of Palmyra by using Arabic texts on Islamic ritual."

Although I am not familiar with the canons of thought in the profession of art history, I have the feeling that what Kubler says here represents the theoretical and methodological position of that "establishment," just as the ethnohistoric-to-prehistoric projection of analogy in art and ideology could be considered the "establishment" line in more strictly archaeological circles. Kubler's argument, and this wider opposition of methodological outlooks, is of particular interest now in view of what is being said and thought in another part of the archaeological forest, that part bordering the groves of social anthropology and which is often referred to as the field of "new archaeology."

But before we go into this, let us concede that archaeologists operate with two kinds of analogical material: general comparative and specific historical (Willey 1953d, pp. 229–230). The first allows inferences that are drawn from general life situations about people, without restrictions as to space or time; the second permits inferences only within a geographically circumscribed and historically defined context (see also Willey 1977c). This specific historic kind of analogy is usually referred to as "ethnographic analogy" and has particular pertinence for the New World, where archaeological cultures are frequently interpreted with the aid of ethnographic or ethnohistoric accounts that relate to Indian cultures believed to be in direct line of descent from these archaeological cultures. Formerly, general comparative analogy was looked upon somewhat askance in American archaeology. With the emphasis upon cultural differences axiomatic to American anthropology, the universalistic basis of general comparative analogy not only left archaeologists vulnerable to all sorts of errors of interpretation but was thought to lead them into simplistic cultural evolutionary schemes. Specific historical analogy, on the other hand, was widely advocated, although with some cautionary statements.

Recently, there has been a change of attitude by some archaeologists. Those of the "new archaeological" persuasion have pointed to the dangers of disjunction (although not quite with that term and concept) between ethnographic present and archaeological past as well as to the possibility that not all forms and actions of the past will be represented on ethnographic levels. They advise, instead, a reliance upon general comparative analogy as the most scientific and archaeologically self-contained means of interpreting the past. While specific historical ethnographic data can be used as an information pool from which to draw data to frame hypotheses about past cultural behavior, direct specific historical analogical interpretations from ethnography to archaeology are to be avoided (Binford 1968). To date, the interpretations of the "new archaeology," operating as it does with general comparative analogy, have been in ecologic-technonomic realms, with some promising extensions into social forms (Hill 1968; Longacre 1966; Deetz 1965). Although they have dealt with art and symbolism, (Binford 1962; Flannery 1968b) in only a broad categorical way, as correlates of rank, social status, or prestige symbols, the "new archaeologists" have made no attempt to deal with the specific meanings of art. It may be that they do not consider this very important. For if the archaeological task is the explaining of cultural differences and similarities, rather than the reconstruction of the past, as one of their spokesmen has maintained (Binford 1968), and if the causes of these differences and similarities are to be sought primarily on the ecological, technological, and economic levels, then it would follow that the meaning content of past art and iconography is unimportant.

Now all of this, I hasten to add, does not correspond to Kubler's position. His thinking, as is evident in his works (Kubler 1962), is deeply set in humanistic, historical lines. and yet, in a quite different way, he has come to some of the same conclusions as some of the "new archaeologists" about the validity of specific ethnographic or ethnohistoric analogies projected back into the archaeological past. Thus, specific historical analogy as a prime method of archaeology finds itself rejected both from the new "scientific" side and from the traditional historical-humanistic side. How serious are these criticisms? Must the method be jettisoned? And in Mesoamerica?

Before attempting to answer these questions, let us return to the symposium papers that have used specific historic analogy from ethnohistoric sources and examine their procedures and results.

We will begin with the Coe (1973) paper. Of all, it exemplifies the most adventurous use of ethnohistoric analogy—a thoroughgoing and conscious attempt to demonstrate the unity of a Mesoamerican religious systems. To support his case, Coe cites the close similarity of Mesoamerican pantheons on a Postclassic time level and the general similarities of Postclassic and Classic period iconographies. From here he traces all god representations back to the Olmec were-jaguar being in its various guises, guises that anticipate such later Mesoamerican deities as Quetzalcoatl, Xipe, Tlaloc, the Fire God, and the Maize God. In so doing, he suggests an Olmec monotheism, one comparable, it seems to me, to Thompson's (1973) Maya Classic monotheism focusing on Itzam Na. Coe's holistic approach, in which he sees an essential integrity of Mesoamerican art and its meanings extending back from the ethnohistoric period for some 2500 years, is in sharp contrast to Kubler's position, with its warnings of disjunction between form and meaning through time. I find Coe's idea a fascinating one, even though I view it with some reserve. Coe (1968a, b) has taken this same view of other aspects of Mesoamerican culture. For instance, he would see Olmec-horizon trade as operating in essentially the Aztec Pochteca system; and here the chances for disjuncture, in view of such things as the formal market developments of Teotihuacan and Tenochtitlan, seem very great (Parsons and Price 1977). Still, his argument deserves serious attention. The continuities in the art forms—the god representations or whatever they may be—are unmistakable. Without much question, Mesoamerica began to be some kind of an entity, with some kind of a coherent internal ideology, as early as Olmec times.

To what extent did form and meaning adhere to each other after the Olmec horizon? Ekholm (1973), in his prefatory remarks, observes the striking regional stylistic diversification that characterizes Mesoamerica. This was, perhaps, less pronounced in Olmec times than later—although it began even this early. What does it mean? Is it simply an expression of ethnicity, of linguistic differences among peoples who shared in old Olmec beliefs, much as the ethnic patchwork of western Europe presented a diversity nevertheless laced together by early Christianity? Or is it something more profound that should be taken as a clue to a complete disruption of a former ideological order, a disruption severing form and meaning in so many complex and crosscutting ways that the task of sorting them out is hopeless?

Here, I tend to be optimistic and to place some faith in Nicholson's (1973) insistence on the fundamental conservatism of all Mesoamerican cultures, a conservatism, as he notes, that was anchored in religious beliefs. Ekholm's tracing out of the Central Veracruz regional traditions, from Late Preclassic to Postclassic, offers one evidence of this kind of conservative persistence in stylistic continuity. Bernal's (1973) description of a number of stone sculptures from the Oaxaca Valley is another. These Oaxacan sculptures span a time range running from late Monte Albán I through Monte Albán V—perhaps as much as 1500 to 2000 years. Some of their stylistic elements change during this time; yet all of the sculptures are linked by features that are peculiar to this one region.

Thompson's (1973) case for Maya regional continuity is even more noteworthy. Thompson, in his study, actually begins with a general comparative analogy; it is a part of his title. He is talking about the institution of the divine right of kings, a phenomenon known from various parts of the world at various times, one functionally related to the consolidation of power of ruling hereditary aristocracies. But Thompson quickly narrows the analogical frame of reference to Mesoamerica and the ethnohistoric horizon. Divine appointment of rulers is noted for the Aztecs, and the deification of rulers after death is also reported for Mixtec and Yucatec dynasties. Narrowing the scope of analogy still further, to the Maya Lowlands, Thompson finds that the Yucatec rulers of the historic period were surrounded by great pomp and ceremony, that the ruler had both secular and religious functions, that the kingship was hereditary within a royal lineage, that divine descent was claimed by some *halach uinichs*—or at least these individuals were deified after death. Moving now to the archaeological past of the Lowland Maya, Thompson observes that much of Classic-period Maya art portrays rulers in an aloof position and in close association with symbols of divinity. These personages on the stelae are bedecked with the various manifestations of Itzam Na, the Maya high god, known from the ethnohistoric records in various serpentlike or reptilian forms. The presence of royal lineages and hereditary descent of rulers is attested to by both glyphic texts and art. He cites instances of a ruler standing before suppliant prisoners wearing a mask of the high god and of a ruler seated in a niche composed of a two-headed Itzam Na. These contexts and these associations argue strongly for the extension of the institution of a hereditary, divinely sponsored kingship from ethnohistoric back to Precolumbian times in the Maya Lowland cultural continuum.

Against this we must balance the case for disjunction—insofar as we can read this from the archaeological record. We know that there has been some. Lowland Maya civilization suffered a major trauma in the ninth century A.D., and this break between Classic and Postclassic is reflected in a number of aspects of culture—ceramics, hieroglyphics, architecture, art forms. However, there are also continuities. The petty, or "city-state," form of government seems to have survived; the Maya language persisted in the regions of the Lowlands; and certain iconographic elements continued. Some foreign, Mexicanoid elements were introduced during the disjunction; some of these lasted on through the Postclassic, others did not. In spite of this disjunction I think Thompson has made his case. There are substantial continuities from prehistoric to historic in the Maya cultural scene, and the nature of the Maya representations of the Classic period, plus what we can reconstruct as to the quality of Maya culture at that time, leave little doubt as to the probability of an ancient Mayan concept of the divine right of kings. Perhaps less secure are the connections between the historic and prehistoric guises and functions of the deity Itzam Na. There is some continuity here, but, given the turbulence of the Classic-to-Postclassic transition, changes or modifications of functions are certainly to be anticipated.

Nicholson's (1973) sweep is as broad, really, as Coe's; however, as he says, the ideological-iconographic unity that he portrays has the direct ties to the ethnohistoric horizon, the ties which Eduard Seler exploited so effectively seventy years ago. What this unity is, as Nicholson has told us, is a grand Mesoamerican synthesis that was effected in the Postclassic period and resulted in a new multinational culture that archaeologists have come to recognize under the name of Mixteca-Puebla. It was a synthesis that undoubtedly came out of the time of troubles and the political expansionism of the Toltec horizon, a phenomenon that appears to have forcibly brought back together all of the old strands of Olmec iconography and belief after the long era of late Preclassic and Classic regionalism. The Aztecs were Mesoamerica's last Postclassic-period wielders of great power; and, as Nicholson so aptly puts it, the Aztecs, iconographically, may be seen as a typical subtraditional line of the great Mesoamerican Mixteca-Puebla culture. Actually, they, as well as the Toltecs before them, were originally West or Northwest Mexicans—peoples whose ancestors were of another major cultural tradition—but they assimilated to Mesoamerican culture in the rapid way that fringe barbarians often do, and, eventually, they came to epitomize that culture or civilization.

This brings us to the borders of Mesoamerica and to Furst's (1973) paper on West Mexico. Furst places great reliance on ethnohistoric and modern ethnographic analogy in his attempts to interpret West Mexican art; and I think it very significant that he finds his most apt analogies in West Mexico and the southwestern United States. I think that the reasons for this are that West Mexico lies outside of the basic Mesoamerican cultural tradition. As Bernal (1968) has written, there is no true Olmec influence in West Mexico. (In this context West Mexico refers to those states lying north and west of the Valley of Mexico. Guerrero obviously has Olmec stylistic influences, and there are some minor occurrences in Michoacan; but from here north one moves out of the Olmec horizon orbit.) I would judge that during the Preclassic and into the Classic period West Mexico stood outside of the Mesoamerican *oikoumene*. It was another culture area, another major cultural system in contrast to the Mesoamerican one that arose in southern Mexico and Central America. Its orbit reached northward, into northwest Mexico and the desert country of the Hohokam. In the south it impinged upon the Valley of Mexico, and I would further speculate that one of the reasons for the florescence of civilization in the Valley of Mexico from Classic times onward was that it became a zone of synthesis between the two major cultural traditions, Mesoamerica proper and West Mexico. Later, especially in Postclassic times, elements of Mesoamerican ideology undoubtedly spread into West Mexico; but their impress must have remained relatively superficial, for Furst's data seem foreign and out of place in the integrated world of Mesoamerica of which Coe is trying to convince us.

On the other side of Mesoamerica is Lower Central America, and it, too, is another major cultural sphere. The very northern and western edges of it were Mesoamericanized. There is, in fact, real Olmec influence registered in western Salvador; but south and east of central Salvador and the Ulua Valley influences that can be identified as specifically Mesoamerican are few or slight during Preclassic and Classic times. In the Postclassic, of course, there is a spread of Mesoamerican art forms in Pacific Nicaragua and northwestern Costa Rica, and Haberland's statues, with men's heads emerging from serpent's jaws and Toltec-like shields, are a part of this. But most of the material that Haberland describes is essentially non-Mesoamerican and not expressive of the iconography and ideology of the Mesoamerican tradition. As has often been acknowledged, it is more easily compared to South American sculptural styles than to Mesoamerican ones.

The first thing that emerges from all this is a new kind of synthesis of Mesoamerica—a new model—what might be called a diachronic perspective of an ideological system. There is the old understratum of emergent agriculture in which some catalyst, some force we cannot yet fully understand, brought about the Olmec realm of religious beliefs. From our first glimpse of this Olmec realm, we can understand that it was a belief system that was geared to a hierarchical, nonegalitarian society. In other words, civilization was already on the way. It was also a system that, by whatever means, was carried widely to other parts of Mesoamerica and formed in all of these parts a basic pattern for subsequent religious and artistic development. From the end of Middle Preclassic times, this Olmec tradition was split and diversified according to regional tastes. But then this diversification was amalgamated by the events of the Postclassic; the disparate elements of Mesoamerican religion and iconography were brought together again, especially in the Mexica-Puebla synthesis.

Such, in brief, are the outlines of the model. It can be documented pretty well in space, time, and art forms—the three dimensions of the archaeological discipline. But we want to be more than archaelogical mechanics or diagram builders. We want to know the meanings of, and in, it all. To what extent can we impute the meanings derived from our sixteenth-century knowledge back down through this fascinating diagram? I wish there were some grand, definitive way I could conclude, some resolution of this question. What

I want, I suppose, is a reconciliation of views and methods. Perhaps this is impossible, but I hope not. In talking about views and methods it is possible that I may have distorted or otherwise misrepresented the opinions of some of my colleagues. For one thing, it is not quite fair to portray all of the Mesoamerican archaeological fraternity in solid opposition to George Kubler. Actually, Kubler could draw upon some distinguished support for his "disjunctive" arguments from Tatiana Proskouriakoff (personal communication 1970); and it may be that some of those in the present symposium panel are more on his side than I have indicated. For my own part, I admit to being unwilling to eschew interpretation of Mesoamerican art and iconography through specific historic analogies with the ethnohistoric horizon. I believe that the Precolumbian Mesoamerican ideological system did have an internal integrity and coherence and that this condition was relatively stable and, perhaps, as Coe maintains, can be pushed as far back in time as the Olmec. I would argue that Kubler's parallel of Hellenistic Palmyra and Arabic texts, on the one hand, and Teotihuacan and Aztec ritual, on the other, is not an apt one. I would see Mesoamerica, even across the Classic-to-Postclassic transition, as much more self-contained within unified cultural traditional boundaries than the eastern Mediterranean from Hellenistic to Muslim times.

I do not suppose we will ever be able to link form to meaning in the prehistoric past with absolute surety; however, I think we will approach high probability. To do this we have to utilize both general comparative and specific historical analogy. I agree with Keith Anderson (1969) when he writes:

> Careful analysis and comparison of archaeological remains, the use of vigorous analytical techniques, and statistical manipulation may lead to precise definition of significant and comparable technological elements. However, these techniques do not, by themselves, interpret prehistory. Such interpretation depends upon ethnographic analogy.

That is, there are some aspects of past life, principally those in the ideological realm, that can be satisfactorily explained only with the aid of specific historical analogy. I would suggest that our methodology should begin by narrowing down the range of interpretive possibilities, insofar as this can be done in any particular instance, through general comparative analogy. What are the demographic, ecologic, and technologic variables involved and how do they interrelate? Is the archaeological context under consideration that of a neolithic-level farming village, the seat of a petty chiefdom, or the capital of an empire? What can settlement and architecture tell us about the dichotomies of public and domestic, of sacred and secular? What contexts within the society are associated with what forms of art and iconography? And how might art and iconography, and changes in their content and in their contexts, be related to changes in other cultural subsystems and institutions? Then, moving from these ranges of general analogical reasoning, we should go to specific historical cultural continuities. How are these expressed regionally and chronologically? In what media or what aspects of culture are these continuities best revealed? When disjunctions occur in these media, how do these seem to correlate with disjunctions or lack of disjunction in other media?

It is only with this kind of a multidimensional approach that we can hope to test and to validate or invalidate, to varying degrees, the integrity of the Mesoamerican ideological system and the historic-to-prehistoric iconographic analogies that are parts of it. Finally, as the papers of this symposium have shown, this is no new approach but merely the expression of a more self-conscious awareness of what it is we are claiming and why.

23

The Concept of the "Disembedded Capital" in Comparative Perspective

(From *Journal of Anthropological Research*, Vol. 35, No. 2, pp. 123–137, 1979. Reprinted by permission of *Journal of Anthropological Research* and Department of Anthropology, University of New Mexico.)

In his recent monograph, *Monte Alban, Settlement Patterns at the Ancient Zapotec Capital*, Richard E. Blanton (1978) explains the functions of that major Precolumbian Oaxacan site as those of a "disembedded capital." By this he means one where political and decision-making activities have been set aside from the society's mainstream commercial and socioeconomic functions, separated and segregated in a center established for political administration. According to Blanton's interpretation, Monte Alban was founded by the mutual consent and collaboration of a number of preexisting Valley of Oaxaca polities and centers, and, as such, had been placed in a centrally located and "neutral" spot in the valley for purposes of confederated governance over the whole. This was done in the fifth century B.C., in Middle Preclassic (or Middle Formative) times; and the confederative purpose behind this action was mainly that of military unification and defense against the threats of other rising states in neighboring regions outside the valley. Monte Alban maintained this "disembedded capital" role, growing and thriving in it during the ensuing Late Preclassic and Classic Periods, until it was largely abandoned in the eighth century A.D., as a result of the decline of external military pressures.

In Blanton's opinion, a number of lines of evidence offer test support for this "disembedded capital" hypothesis. One of these is the geographic centrality of the site, its strategic central location in the Valley of Oaxaca. Such a defensible site supports the inference of a militaristic and competitive sociopolitical environment. Germane to the idea of the collaborative nature of its sponsorship is the fact that Monte Alban was founded relatively late in the chronology of the Valley of Oaxaca Preclassic cultures, antedated by several other centers. After the founding of Monte Alban, these other centers continued to be active, at least in some cases; and it is Blanton's belief that they also maintained a socioeconomic independence from each other as well as from the new "disembedded capital" in whose *de novo* establishment they had collaborated. Added to all of these factors, and in Blanton's opinion the most crucial to his argument, is the lack of evidence in Monte Alban of an "embeddedness" in an *in situ* economic matrix. He feels that the signs of manufacturing and trading functions within the precincts of the city are slight; there is no specialized and identifiable marketplace, as at Teotihuacan, and, in his opinion, only a small volume of craft items and manufacturing debris at the site. Moreover, it it his feeling that the lands immediately surrounding Monte Alban are poorly suited for agriculture, and that the city would not have been founded as an economic base with farming in view. Solely as the political and military capital of a league of several independent valley states or chiefdoms, Monte Alban was not the socioeconomic heart of a tightly knit state or empire; and, as such, it stands in striking contrast to its great contemporary city, Teotihuacan. This latter was a true "primate" center, firmly embedded in an immediate agricultural base and established as a center for resource extraction, manufacturing, and trade for the Basin of Mexico and beyond.

This "disembedded capital" idea is a new one in Mesoamerican archaeology, and it has drawn the attention, and criticism, of Blanton's colleagues. Both William T. Sanders and Robert S. Santley (1978) have rejected it by disputing Blanton's interpretations of his Monte Alban field data. In their view, Blanton underrates the evidence for trade and manufacturing within the site. The contrast between Monte Alban and Teotihuacan obsidian manufacture is unfair, in their opinion, because the latter site was near a major raw obsidian resource and it also served a Mesoamerican-wide market, while Monte Alban had neither of these advantages. It can also be pointed out that Teotihuacan's specialized marketplace is an Early Classic Period phenomenon, and that earlier its markets could have been held in any suitable open or plaza space—as those of Monte Alban were probably also held. Sanders and Santley feel that the hillsides below Monte Alban could have been, and probably were, exploited by terraced cultivation; moreover, the nearby valley bottoms below were ideal agricultural land. In short, they feel that Monte Alban was as fully "embedded" in its socioeconomic context as was Teotihuacan, and, like the latter site, it also combined politicoreligious functions with economic and commercial ones. Still more recently, Santley (1979) has prepared a longer critique in which he questions not only factual interpretations but the whole structural-processual nature of the "disembedded capital" concept, particularly as it has been applied to the Monte Alban case, but with overtones of argument that could have more general reference. To his way of thinking, there is a fundamental inconsistency of logic in the "disembedded capital" construct, because it divorces economic interests from policy making. The elites in the preexisting Preclassic centers in the Valley of Oaxaca owed their positions to material and economic advantages. Would they suspend these, he asks, to do purely political service in the new capital of Monte Alban? Or would they continue to operate as economic entrepreneurs at home and leave political and military roles to others who were associated with the "disembedded center"? Santley sees both of these alternatives as disadvantageous to an already established aristocracy. Stress would have been the inevitable result; federation goals would have run counter to local interests; and the favoring of local interests would have subverted those of the centralized government. Instead, Santley would favor the interpretation that the buildup of state power at Monte Alban proceeded in much the same way as at Teotihuacan—by the monopolistic incorporation of lesser centers and polities into one great center. The result was a capital city that was fully "embedded" in the political, religious, and socioeconomic functions of the state.

The Concept of the "Disembedded Capital"

Santley's analytical approach and argument are directed specifically to the Monte Alban case in an attempt to see whether the cultural and social processes involved would have permitted the establishment of a "disembedded capital" center there, but his analyses prompt a wider look at the whole question of "disembedded capitals." Do we know of other instances where a confederatively founded, neutral political base was employed for bringing about state-type consolidation, particularly in the early stages of state formation? A key question in the origin of the state is how and why people submit to its authority. David Webster (1976) asserts that all viable states must achieve a balance between voluntarism on the part of the governed, and coercion on a part of the rulers. Are there examples in early states where "disembedded capitals" served as points of voluntary mediation between smaller polities and the centralized state? This takes us from an analytical approach to a comparative one; and, in the following pages, I propose to take a cross-cultural comparative look at early states and civilizations to see if it is possible to identify elsewhere the phenomenon of the "disembedded capital" as Blanton has defined it. Cross-cultural comparisons—in this instance the examination of several culture sequences in diachronic perspective—are, I suppose, an "old-fashioned" archaeological approach. Lewis Binford (1978) is quite correct in saying that such an approach, at best, can only arrive at empirical generalizations. Nevertheless, such generalizations prepare the way for more successful analytical studies, and should help us frame better questions about cause-and-effect relationships in the formation of human institutions.

Blanton (1976) set forth his definition of the "disembedded capital" in an earlier article, in which he states that there are at least three types of capital cities where political and decision-making functions have been set apart, or "disembedded," from the socio-economic matrix of the culture. The first of these he calls the *capital center*; Monte Alban is one example. Such centers are permanent and established by confederated consent at a "neutral" location within the territory of the state. In the case of Monte Alban, this establishment came with the first state formation. In this connection, it is interesting that all of the other examples of this type which Blanton cites—with the exception of "pre-Periclean Athens"—are modern state capitals: Washington, D.C., Brazilia, Ottawa, New Delhi, and Canberra. We shall return to this point later on. Blanton's other two types are the *roving palace*, after the model of the movable courts of some European medieval kings, and the *temporary capital*, where a new city is built on the accession of a new ruler to the throne, and then abandoned after his death or dethronement. My comparative comments will be directed particularly to early state formation and the "capital center" type of "disembedded capital" as this purports to apply to the Monte Alban example. "Roving palaces" and "temporary capitals" do not appear to be closely related to the initial rise of the state; however, I will take note of them, in passing, in our comparative survey.

Lastly, let me add that my survey is a very preliminary one that makes no pretense of thorough cross-cultural coverage. Even in those regions and sequences examined, it must also be kept in mind that we are handicapped by the incompleteness of the archaeological record, and by the frequent circumstance that this record may be unsuited to providing the data we are seeking.

Comparative Perspectives

Mesoamerica

Both the Monte Alban and Teotihuacan examples which Blanton and Santley have discussed, treat that point of sociopolitical evolution at which the state comes into being.

In the case of Monte Alban, this occurred at about 500 B.C.; for Teotihuacan, it was a few centuries later. In each instance, however, the result is at least superficially similar. A large center or city rapidly came to dominate a sizeable and densely populated region. There were other more or less contemporaneous regional developments in Mesoamerica. The Preclassic-to-Classic sequence of the Guatemalan Highlands is one of these, known from the major site of Kaminaljuyu, near the location of the present Guatemala City. Prior to 500 B.C., the populations of the Valley of Guatemala were living in small scattered farming villages, and there were no central places marked by special or civic architecture. Mound constructions first appeared at Kaminaljuyu in Late Preclassic (500–100 B.C.) times; these were burial tumuli and associated small platforms, all arranged around small avenue-like plazas. Sanders (1974) interprets these as burial places for lineage chiefs, with individual lineages maintaining separate plazas. Associated stone sculptures may have been intended as portraits of chiefs. Several such plazas were found at Kaminaljuyu, and a few others occurred, singly, farther out in the valley.

In the Terminal Preclassic Period (100 B.C.–A.D. 300), there was a notable upswing in population in the valley, and the nature of the plazas and public constructions at Kaminaljuyu changed. The plazas were now squarish in outline, the mounds rectangular, with ascent stairs. Although still used for burials, the mounds and plazas may have had other functions as well. There were fourteen such plaza units within the five-square-kilometer area of Kaminaljuyu, each with a substantial zone of living refuse around it, and each separated from the next by short distances of unoccupied ground. A few other similar plaza units were found farther out in the valley, as in the previous period. At this time, there were differences in the quality of residences around the plazas, as well as in burials and burial furniture, all suggestive of social ranking. In the last half of this Terminal Preclassic Period, Sanders notes what he calls a "quantum jump" in the architectural size and burial elaboration of one of the fourteen Kaminaljuyu plaza complexes; we may ask ourselves, as he did, if this is not the first tangible sign of the rise to paramount prominence of one of the lineage chiefs—the first important transitional step from chiefdom to state organization?

In subsequent Classic Period times, there were radical changes in the Kaminaljuyu center. The fourteen plazas were abandoned, and one huge architectural complex, of pyramids, platforms, and ball courts, was constructed. With this architectural centralization comes what Sanders calls a "public high god" iconography. Emphasis would now seem to be on "national" themes as opposed to the burial and funerary cults of lineage chiefs. Trade, already of some importance in the Preclassic, now comes to greater prominence with the control of Guatemalan Highland obsidian sources. Of special interest for this period, of course, are the obvious signs of relationships with Teotihuacan, as expressed in ceramic styles and public architecture; the question must be asked as to whether Teotihuacanos were responsible for the trends toward centralization. But Sanders cautions that architectural change and centralization had begun in the Early Classic (A.D. 300–500), prior to the Middle Classic (A.D. 500–700) influx of Teotihuacan traits.

It would have been at the point of Preclassic-to-Classic transition that the Guatemalan Highlanders made the step from chiefdom to state, comparable to the founding of Monte Alban in the Oaxacan sequence, or to the population upsurge at Teotihuacan at the beginning of that site's Classic growth. With this perspective, we might ask this question: Was the Classic Kaminaljuyu construction of the single great civic-religious complex the establishment of a "neutral" capital? Did the several chiefs of the fourteen plaza units mutually agree upon this device as a countermeasure to external threats (perhaps from Teotihuacan)? Perhaps—but I would not think so. The "quantum jump" of one of the fourteen plaza units in the previous period leads me to ascribe the move toward centralization and state organization to the dominance and coercive power of one chiefdom or lineage over the others. Moreover, with the founding of the new great plaza unit, the others were abandoned. And, once founded, the rebuilt city was in no sense "disembedded"; on the contrary, for several centuries Kaminaljuyu was the single large primate center of the valley, the center of trade, crafts, government, and religion.

The Late Classic Period (A.D. 700–1000) saw a decline in Kaminaljuyu as the primate center of the valley. Activity continued there, but at least a half-dozen other centers sprang up in the valley. All of these, however, were modeled on Kaminaljuyu, and none could be considered "disembedded." Perhaps this Late Classic multiplicity of centers was a response to another great increase in valley population. Another aspect of the Late Classic change is the institution of a tiered hierarchy of settlement: in addition to the major centers, there were secondary ones, and below these, villages or hamlets.

For the region of the Maya Lowlands, I am inclined to believe that the developmental story was similar to that of the Guatemalan Highlands. Small civic or ceremonial centers appeared in the Middle Preclassic. In the Late Preclassic, these centers were enlarged, and they began to incorporate evidences of hierarchy and rank in architecture, art, and burials. There are strong suggestions that Late Preclassic centers were less centrally organized than those of the Classic Period (Tourtellot 1989); and certainly in the Early Classic, there were shifts from aristocratic lineage and ancestor veneration to the promulgation of "high gods"—as at Tikal (Coggins 1979b). While Teotihuacan influence probably had something to do with these changes, it is to be noted that virtually all of the large Maya centers which have been excavated show a Preclassic-through-Classic continuity of occupation and building, remaining in the same tradition. All were centers of crafts and trade, and all were more "urban" than Maya archaeologists once thought (Willey and Shimkin 1973). In the Late Classic Period, many new centers were established in the Lowlands, as in the Highlands. But none of the Classic Maya centers, Early or Late, could be considered as "disembedded."

I have focused upon the Preclassic-to-Classic transition in Mesoamerica, but perhaps we should also take a look at a somewhat earlier period. The earliest large central places in ancient Mesoamerica date back to the Early Preclassic Period, and to the Olmec culture of the Mexican Gulf Coast. These sites, with their large earthworks, monumental stone sculptures, and evolved art style, are placed in the period of 1200 to 800 B.C. K. V. Flannery (1972) is inclined to classify them as chiefdoms; M. D. Coe (1968a), on the other hand, prefers to think of them as being on the state level of organization. The big San Lorenzo site, which Coe excavated, has earlier levels suggesting an essentially *in situ* development of Olmec society and civilization from a simpler culture. San Lorenzo has extensive, deep residential refuse, and although it has not been reported in full, it gives the impression of having been a multipurpose center, not just a politicoreligious establishment. Its estimated population, however, is only 2500, far below that of Teotihuacan or Monte Alban; Coe believes that the sustaining population lived in small settlements in the outlying lowland countryside. There is another large site in the Olmec region, La Venta (Drucker and Heizer 1960), and, in addition, some smaller centers; however, general settlement work is as yet so limited that we cannot say to what degree the Olmec region was organized on a tiered or hierarchial settlement plan.

For the late Precolumbian periods, I know of no major site in Mesoamerica that could qualify as a "disembedded capital." In Maya ethnohistory there are allusions to Postclassic "leagues" or "alliances" among some of the city states of Yucatan, but there is little that would suggest that such consortiums set up substantial capitals. Mayapan, the last great Maya center of the Late Postclassic, was a seat of centralized power for northern

Yucatan, and it is said that rulers of other cities and their families were forced to come here and live for a period of each year (Tozzer, ed. 1941; Pollock et al. 1962); but the power behind this was Mayapan, rather than that of a voluntary association, and Mayapan, judging from the residential and artifactual material found there, does not have a "disembedded" appearance.

While neither "roving palaces" nor "temporary capitals" characterize Mesoamerica, there are examples of other types of "artificial" cities. The huge Toltec-style architectural complexes at Chichen Itza are generally interpreted as a takeover and rebuilding of an old Maya site by invaders from Tula (Tozzer 1957); thus, this was a kind of "imposed" outpost city, created by a state power in a foreign area. The "port-of-trade" city also has an "artificiality" about it (Sabloff et al. 1974), and owed its existence to mutual agreement, frequently by state powers. But neither of these phenomena were "capitals," nor were they fully "disembedded" in the sense of Blanton's definition.

Peru

In Peru, town centers, with public or corporate constructions, occurred as early as the beginning of the second millenium B.C., if not a bit before. This applies both to the preceramic coastal fishing cultures (Moseley 1975) and to preceramic highland farmers (Izumi and Sono 1963). Some of these centers were of appreciable size. El Paraiso on the coast (Engel 1966; Willey 1971b: 97–99) comprises a number of large platforms, an apartment-like palace, and several hectares of refuse. It and other related sites of the period appear to have been "all purpose" places, serving economic as well as administrative and religious needs. After about 1800 B.C., with the establishment of an agricultural economy, large pyramid-platform complexes appear on the coast. Some of these are among the largest sites in Precolumbian Peru. La Florida, in the Rimac Valley (Lanning 1967: 90–91), and Las Haldas, on the north-central coast (Matsuzawa 1978), are examples. Both complexes appear to have been constructed to serve the scattered farming hamlets in the associated valleys. We know little about their craft or trading aspects, but they appear to have been primate administrative and religious centers for their immediate areas. A few centuries later, a site such as Chavín de Huántar, in the north highlands, had similar functions, but it was also a residential city and economic center (Rowe 1963). Still later, around A.D. 200, the big site of Moche, in the north-coastal valley of the same name, was certainly the capital of a state. Its architecture indicates that it was an impressive religious center, an administrative and palace center, and fully engaged in the local economy, as well as the economy of its territorial domain. The Moche state covered several valleys of the north coast; in each of these valleys there are sites of varying sizes, indicating a well-organized bureaucratic and tiered arrangement (Willey 1971b:132–42; Moseley 1975: personal communication). Tiahuanaco, in the southern highlands, was a similar sort of fully "embedded" capital (Parsons 1968); and there is good evidence that Huari, the Middle Horizon capital of the central highlands, was the head of a state which directed production and distribution through a multitiered hierarchy of lesser centers (Isbell and Schreiber 1978).

By the time of the Inca empire, however, state power imposed cities on provinces, much as Mesopotamian or Egyptian rulers did in their domains. Huanuco Viejo, in the north-central highlands of Peru, according to Morris and Thompson (1970:341, abstract), "must be described as an artificial device imposed by the Inca for administrative and political purposes, rather than as a city which arose because of local conditions or needs." Huanuco Viejo consisted of palatial and ceremonial units, upper-class residences, and great storehouses. It was not the capital of the state, but it certainly served as a regional capital. On occasion, it may have functioned as a "roving palace" (to use Blanton's terminology), when the Inca emperors traveled from place to place in their domain.

Cuzco, the main Inca capital, was not a large urban agglomeration. Originally, in Killke-phase times, before the Inca became the empire builders of the Andes, there was a small Inca town at the site. This was built over in imperial times as a planned administrative center inhabited largely by the elite. However, craft activities must have been carried out in or near the city, and the administrative functions of the center included those of goods distribution. Viewed in a time perspective, Cuzco was not "disembedded" from its Inca heritage, but in its late phase was the creation of a state power that was highly specialized and differentiated in its settlement forms.

Greater Mesopotamia

Any consideration of the rise of the state in the Old World takes us into the archaeological sequences of Greater Mesopotamia. State antecedents are seen there in the evidences of chiefdom societies which go back as far as the sixth millennium B.C. Small temple and palace buildings, associated with richly furnished burials, have been found at Tell es-Sawwan, on the Tigris north of Baghdad (Flannery 1972; Yoffee 1979). This type of society persisted and developed further through the Ubaid Period; and it can be inferred that the temple-palace centers of this period were the prototypes for the first state centers of Uruk times. In a review of the data around Susa, in southwestern Iran, Wright (1977) has noted that there is some evidence of "collapse" or troubled times at the end of the Ubaid Period and the beginning of the Early Uruk Period (*ca.* 3900 .B.C), but that following this, a state center had come into being by 3700 B.C. Uruk itself, in Mesopotamia proper, had become a substantial center or state capital by 3500 B.C., if not before (Lamberg-Karlovsky and Sabloff 1979; Adams 1972). It was composed of both public and residential buildings. The temple complexes were centers of religion, governance, redistribution of goods, trade, and manufacturing. Its scope of government, presumably, extended over numerous nearby villages and towns. In the next 500 years, Uruk assumed the proportions of a city of forty to fifty thousand inhabitants, all enclosed within a defense wall. Concomitant with this urban growth of Uruk was the abandonment of many smaller towns and villages in the surrounding countryside, and it is assumed that these populations were drawn into the growing metropolis.

Thus, the developmental configuration here appears to be that of prestate center functions, including religious, government, and economic activities, localized at various sites in a context of chiefdoms. During this time there was a notable population increase over all of Greater Mesopotamia. In the first half of the fourth millennium B.C., a shift occurred from the more simply organized chiefdoms to a state organization, with its tiered or multiple levels of control. The former small centers grew into, or were replaced by, urban centers or state capitals; their basic functions continued, as before, to be religion, government, and economic production and management. They were also defensive citadels in many instances; however, there is no good evidence that they were "disembedded" in the sense of political or military capitals divorced from an imediate socioeconomic context. As Wright (1977) points out, the Late-Ubaid-to-Early-Uruk transition is developmentally comparable to the Rosario-to-Monte-Alban-I transition of the Oaxaca Valley; in both cases, it is the transition from chiefdom to state. Both seem to have been accompanied by brief eras of sociopolitical "collapse" or disturbance.

This Greater Mesopotamian development of state and capital city conforms rather closely to what Renfrew (1975) has designated as the "Early State Module." In his view, civilizations (in the example at hand we are dealing with either Early Sumerian or Elamite civilization) originally have a number of autonomous central places, each with its supporting hinterland settlements. Eventually, one such central place may assume control or hegemony over others, forming a larger state or empire. The question of the origins of a tiered hierarchy of lesser centers, under the control of a principal center or capital, remains a vexing one. The formation of a very large and powerful central place, which in its growth depletes lesser central places, as in the Uruk city example, would seem to suggest that secondary and tertiary tiers of centers were artificial constructs of all-powerful centralized states. On the other hand, the Mesopotamian center of Ur, which became urban somewhat later than Uruk, while the latter was in decline, does not seem to have had the same depopulating effect on its surrounding communities as was the case for Uruk. This, as Adams (1972) says, seems to undermine the idea of the "artificiality" of these Ur satellites, indicating that they were not simply established for the businesses of the centralized state, but that they had an older life of their own which continued. This does not, however, signify that these lesser places had collaborated under free confederation to build the Ur capital as a "disembedded" political entity, for Ur had a full socioeconomic matrix *in situ*.

The dynastic story of Greater Mesopotamia, after 2900 B.C., known both from textual and nontextual archaeological sources, is one of competing city states, empire formations, breakdowns, and reconsolidations. While it seems to have been common during this time for a new ruler or conqueror to build an impressive new capital—although often on the locus of an earlier one—these royal seats were not 'disembedded" in the sense of limitation or restriction of functions. They were centers of commerce as well as of government. Bruce Trigger (1972) notes that in very late times (A.D. 836) the city of Samarra was founded by royal decree, to move the political capital away from Baghdad; but along with this removal and segregation of political functions went some shifting of economic ones, with compulsory resettlement of merchants and artisans in the new location. Cities were also established by royal flat in distant colonial localities. Thus, in ancient Mesopotamia, the power of the state planted an outpost settlement at Assur, to serve both for military administration and for frontier commerce. Later on, after the fall of Ur, Assur became the Assyrian national capital (Oates 1972). As such, it might be considered a locus of "secondary state formation" (Price 1978); but it was never, even in its colonial days, "disembedded" from a socioeconomic matrix.

Egypt

The origin of centers and cities in ancient Egypt has long been obscure, so much so, in fact, that one authority has termed Egypt "the civilization without cities" (Wilson 1960; see also Helck 1975, as cited by Kemp 1977). Recently, Kemp (1977) has argued otherwise. According to him, the settlement pattern of pre-Dynastic Egypt consisted of numerous small farming communities, located along the desert borders of the Nile. A reanalysis of excavation and survey data at Nagada and Hierakonopolis indicates that just prior to 3100 B.C. and the First Dynasty, these tiny villages were unified into sizeable mud-brick towns or centers surrounded by walls. Hierakonopolis developed into a small city that probably controlled Upper Egypt. Immediately thereafter, in the First Dynasty, Egypt was united as a single state under a god-king or pharaoh (Lamberg-Karlovsky and Sabloff 1979). In view of the rapid consolidation of such kingly and sacred power, it seems highly unlikely that such early capitals were founded by confederacies. Wide-scale settlement evidence for this very early time period is, of course, lacking. Later temples, cult shrines, palaces, and other constructions hide earlier buildings. In spite of these difficulties, it appears that these late pre-Dynastic and early First Dynasty centers, or capitals, were aggregates of officials, farmers, and craftsmen. Evidence of trade is also found, although just how important this institution was in the development of early Egyptian centers is still somewhat obscure.

Other similar towns and centers must have been arising all along the Nile in late pre-Dynastic times, and this would seem to be the era of "pristine" state formation in Egypt—whatever the evidences of contact with Mesopotamia may be. Such towns and centers were welded into the emergent late pre-Dynastic small states, and very soon thereafter the whole was unified into the kingdom of Egypt, with a great capital at Memphis and numerous lesser centers through the kingdom. It seems probable that the latter were built upon previous late pre-Dynastic towns, at least in many cases; however, beginning with the First Dynasty, the unified state had the power to establish new centers by founding temples and administrative buildings. Certainly many Egyptian centers of later times were so established by kingly power. Ikhnaten's el-Almarna, set up *de novo* by the great religious reformer, is a famous example, and from all that we know about it from textual history, it qualifies as a "temporary capital," in Blanton's classification. It was abandoned shortly after his death, and the new pharaoh went elsewhere. At the same time, the purely material archaeological evidence from the four hundred or more hectares of the site includes remains attesting to the presence of craftsmen and merchants, indicating the difficulties of depending upon such criteria alone for a "disembedded" assessment.

China

The other Old World region illustrating the rise of the "pristine" state is China, particularly that part of China which Chang (1976) calls the "north China nuclear area," the territory around the confluences of the three major rivers, the Huangho, Fenho, and Weishui. China's ancient civilization had contacts to the west, with Mesopotamian centers; however, these were not close, and the Chinese story is essentially self-contained. The egalitarian farming village is believed to have been the settlement and social type of the Yang-shao culture, between 5000 and 3000 B.C. In the third millennium B.C., especially in the latter half of that millennium, it is probable that a chiefdom type of organization came into being. This is the Lungshan, or Lungshanoid, horizon (Chang, 1976; 1979: personal communication). According to Chang, the centuries between 2500 and 2000 B.C. were crucial for these changes in sociopolitical form. Settlement-pattern data are largely lacking; however, other kinds of evidence—relating to warfare, craft specialization, and status differentiation—imply that the process of "centering," of the growth and internal differentiation of some sites in contrast to others, must have begun during this time. From this point of view, the Lungshanoid horizon or period may be posed as developmentally comparable to the late pre-Dynastic centuries in Egypt, the Late Ubaid–Early Uruk transition in Mesopotamia, and the pre-Monte Alban or pre-Classic Teotihuacan phases of Mesoamerica.

The succeeding Shang state appears to have had its origins in north China at around 2000 B.C. Shang civilization was characterized by writing, bronze metallurgy, palace and temple constructions, social classes, and, obviously, a complex economic organization. Our sources of information about Shang life include both contemporary and later texts. There were a series of capitals for the state: the first, said to have been occupied for 209 years, has never been identified archaeologically; the second, occupied for 23 years, according to textual information, is tentatively identified with the Cheng-chow ruins. Four subsequent capitals, varying in their periods of occupancy from 8 to 74 years, are known only from the historical records. The last capital has been identified with the An-yang ruins, and was an active city from 1384 to 1122 B.C., a period of 262 years (Chang 1976:49). An-yang had at its heart a cluster of palace and temple buildings, the Hsiao-t'un complex. These buildings were surrounded by elaborate sacrificial burials of humans, horse chariots, and elite goods. Two kilometers away was the great "royal cemetery" with many other rich graves. Between and surrounding these features are to be found extensive residential remains, evidences of workshops, and storage facilities. Both archaeological remains and texts indicate that such a city was an administrative, religious, military, and commercial nucleus; as such, it was also the seat of the king, his lineage relatives, and members of other powerful lineages. These data support the inference of the multiple functions of An-yang; politics and religion appear to be firmly "embedded" in a socioeconomic context. Textual information from later dynasties gives a picture of Shang beginnings as those of a warring state led by autocratic rulers, so that an early "disembedded," league-supported capital seems very unlikely. There is, however, some suggestion of the "disembedded temporary capital" idea in the several Shang capitals, some of which were said to have been occupied for only a few years. In this connection, it might be noted that monumental constructions of permanence—great earth mounds, stone platforms or buildings—are lacking from these early Chinese cities, which, instead, were constructed largely of wood, including the precincts of the king and his nobles. The "long-time investment" in them was in elaborate tombs and rich grave goods. At the same time, the direct archaeological evidence from An-yang is that cities could remain stable for a long period of time, and that such cities were multipurpose capitals.

Shang, as a civilization, covered a very large area of north China, and the Shang state, as documented from An-yang, was probably but one political entity within the geographic range of the civilization. This state had at its center the "core city" of the Hsiao-t'un nucleus, an area about 2.5 kilometers in diameter. Around this was a much larger area, of perhaps up to a radius of 100 kilometers, in which there were lesser centers. Each of these had its complement of smaller administrative buildings or palaces, and production and commercial features. Scattered around these lesser centers were numerous small villages, presumably residences of supporting peasant populations. The history of such a settlement pattern is not known. Paul Wheatley (1971:63) leans toward the idea that the original pattern was one of many competing small centers (on the Renfrew "Early State Module" pattern), in which one eventually came to dominate the others; Chang, on the other hand, sees the secondary centers as largely established and settled from a major center, such as An-yang. It is, of course, possible that both things happened; that older centers were brought into the state system by sending out royal relatives as provincial governors.

Some Concluding Observations

Our comparative survey of early state emergence in various parts of the world has revealed no clear case of the phenomenon of the "disembedded capital" at this developmental stage. It is, of course, difficult to be absolutely sure; the material data of archaeology are often intractable in providing an answer to such a question. Still, it is to be noted that in those instances where we have contemporary or near-contemporary textual material available—in Egypt, Mesopotamia, and China—there is nothing that would suggest that the early capitals were founded by leagues or confederations. The emphasis, rather, is on the exaltation of the role of the authoritarian conqueror, who set up the state and built the capital for its governance and greater glory. Indeed, the identification of the ruler with the city and the state is marked; and this also applies to some of the early city states of Mesoamerica (see Caso 1947, with reference to Monte Alban, or Marcus 1976, with reference to the Lowland Maya), where glyphic data have been translated to a limited extent.

In the New World, there is evidence to suggest that the earlier Maya Highland and Lowland centers were aggregates of chiefs, each with his own complex of administrative and religious architecture. Whether such centers were run on a confederative basis by the various lineage heads, or were more autocratically organized must remain a moot point; in any event, they were certainly not "disembedded" from the socioeconomic fabric of the culture. With the rise of the state, however, the evidence strongly suggests that one such chief became, in the words of George Orwell, "more equal" than the others. Architectural renovations took place in old centers, indicating a greater centralization of administrative and religious functions. This kind of centralization probably marked the full emergence of the autocratic state ruler; and, indeed, the hieroglyphic evidence associated with such architectural changes at Tikal (Coggins 1979a; Jones 1977), Copan (W. L. Fash, Jr. 1979: personal communication), and Quirigua (Ashmore and Sharer 1978) confirms this. For Peru, the earliest centers were the primate capitals of their respective cultural settings. A little later, with the dispersion of populations in coastal valley agriculture, there is some indication that centers were elite nodes that linked networks of farming hamlets, but this is hardly an indication of political confederacy. Still later, cities—those associated with state organizations—were not "disembedded capitals."

The Old World data show a rather gradual growth of towns and cities around temple-palace nuclei in Greater Mesopotamia, and a somewhat more rapid process of centralization into towns in Egypt. The Ubaid-to-Uruk and Nagada-to-Hierakonopolis transitions appear to have been accomplished by force rather than voluntary confederation; and the small-town-to-large-town (or city) transformation looks fully organic and "embedded." Although transitional settlement data are fewer for China, the same processes appear to have occurred. Wright (1977) speculates that the Mesopotamian transition was accompanied by a time of trouble or "collapse" and that this is similar to the Valley of Oaxaca transition. Interestingly, this can also be said to obtain for the Maya Lowlands at the Preclassic-to-Classic juncture—the "Proto-Classic" Period (see Willey 1977a). It suggests that, for whatever reasons, the small chiefdom organizations were no longer adequate, that state centralization was needed or desired, and that the shift to this new type of organization was often accompanied by pressure or force.

From all of this it seems that voluntary confederation for the purpose of founding a "neutral" and "disembedded" center or capital was a rare—and perhaps nonexistent—process, at least at that point in sociopolitical evolution where state polities were first formed. In all of the areas that we have examined, however, there is good evidence that once state power was consolidated, this power could then be used to set up a variety of "artificial," "disembedded," or partially "disembedded" cities, including "roving palaces," "temporary capitals," provincial capitals, imposed colonial installations, and "ports-of-trade." Or, to return to those examples which Blanton has listed for the "capital center" type of "disembedded" city, Washington, D.C., Brazilia, Ottawa, New Delhi, and Canberra are all capitals of mature political states or mature state traditions.

We might ask, at this point, if centers were established by voluntary confederation at earlier developmental levels—that of tribal societies. Several ethnographic examples come to mind of "leagues" or "confederacies." The "Iroquois League," formed by the "Five Nations" of New York State and Canada to meet colonial European encroachments, is one example. While they met at one of their tribal towns, frequently that of the Onandaga, they seem to have done little in the way of rebuilding or refurbishing that site as a "capital" (R.S. MacNeish 1979: personal communication). The same applies to the historic Cherokee. According to Gearing (1962), this tribe elected "war chiefs" in a confederative process designed to withstand and deal with the Europeans, but there was no investment in capital centers. In discussing this, Gearing cites some interesting data from a study by Thorkild Jacobsen (1943) of reconstructions of very early Mesopotamian society as inferred from later literary tablets. While this material has a mythical quality, it may, nevertheless, have some historical reality. Jacobsen's reconstruction indicates that governments were once run by councils of village elders, that certain of these elders were charged with domestic and religious matters, while others were called upon in time of war. This condition of democratic grace was ended, however, when some war leaders refused to relinquish their prerogatives, after the threat of external danger had passed. This mythical recapitulation of the rise of the first chiefdoms may take us back to the first small temple structures of *ca.* 5500 B.C., and it is possible that some may have been constructed by voluntary confederacies; but this seems well in advance of the developmental level we are discussing.

The inference to be drawn from these data about simpler societies is that, while external danger may lead to temporary centralization, this circumstance, in itself, is not enough to allow for the formation of subsequent chiefly polities. Under certain circumstances, this kind of evolution may take place, as it apparently did in ancient Mesopotamia, as well as in a great many other places. A military emergency may allow for a generation of power, but this power must then be consolidated and transformed before it can be directed to building central places that demand any appreciable amount of labor. And it is at some point in these poorly understood processes that voluntarism begins to give way to persuasion, coercion, or some of both.

Santley (1979), has attempted to explain why a "neutral" and "disembedded capital" could not have been built at Monte Alban at the time that site was constructed. His reason, in essence, is that one of the major devices of early state formation, the capital city or central place of the emergent state, cannot be divorced from the economic base and functions of the society at this crucial juncture of sociopolitical evolution. For, at this point of transition, this control of resources and of information flow must be kept intact. The decentralization that would be occasioned by the formation of a "disembedded capital" would be too great a risk. Later, with the consolidation of state power, "artificial" cities can be constructed by fiat. My comparative survey leads me to believe that this may be, if not a demonstrated statement of process, a suggestive empirical generalization.

Acknowledgements

To C. C. Lamberg-Karlovsky and K. C. Chang, who read and offered constructive criticisms of this paper.

24

The Classic Maya Sociopolitical Order: A Study in Coherence and Instability

(From *Research and Reflections in Archaeology and History, Essays in Honor of Doris Stone*, E. W. Andrews V, ed., pp. 189–198, Middle American Research Institute, Tulane University, New Orleans, 1986. Reprinted by permission of the Middle American Research Institute, Tulane University.)

All sociopolitical formations carry within themselves forces that make for their coherence as well as those that hold the potential for their dissolution. Indeed, we might say that the histories of the successes and failures of such formations could be read as recountings of the dialectical struggles between two such sets of forces. Those of us concerned with Precolumbian lowland Maya civilization are well aware of the problem. Everyone with even a passing interest in the ancient Maya knows of their brilliant achievements and of their final spectacular failure or "collapse." What were the contesting elements and forces within this society, the tensions and the processes working for and against its equilibrium? Probably no other topic in Maya archaeology has drawn so much attention (see Culbert 1973). In this essay I want to view Classic Maya civilization from the two perspectives of "coherence" and "instability" as these pertain to political centralization and state formation. Clearly, such observations as may be made from these perspectives not only will be germane to the subject of the Maya "collapse," but may also transcend it as we attempt to isolate more general processes of political growth and dissolution.

In an earlier paper (Willey 1980a), I argued the case for the "coherence" of Maya culture, maintaining that there was an essential "holism" of ancient Maya society of a very high order. This "holism" was expressed in many ways. At the height of the Classic period, in the eighth century A.D., the cities, towns, and villages of the lowland Maya extended from the foot of the Guatemalan mountains north to the tip of the Yucatan Peninsula and from the Gulf coast of Tabasco as far east as Copan in Honduras. Throughout there was an amazing cultural uniformity in hieratic art, religious iconography, and major architecture; above all, the entire territory was linked with common systems in calendrics, mathematics, and hieroglyphics. The historical depth of this uniformity was considerable. It was my thesis that an interlinkage of subsystems had begun to be effected in the Late Preclassic period (400 B.C.–A.D. 250) and that this interlinkage had tightened throughout most of the Classic period (A.D.250–900). In developing this case for Maya holism I was not concerned solely, or even primarily, with sociopolitical organization; however, I did attempt to show the way in which political units were integral functioning parts of the whole sociocultural system. Let me review again, briefly, the fundamental features of this coherence of Maya society and culture.

To begin with, Maya lowland subsistence articulated closely with settlement. This was true both for long-fallow swidden cultivation with its field rotation and dispersed residence and for intensive cultivation with terraced or raised-field farming that was associated with population concentrations approaching, in some places, urban proportions (Harrison and Turner 1978).

Maya settlement patterns and settlement systems, while articulating with subsistence methods, were also linked to social and political organization. At the bottom of the social and settlement hierarchy, small patio-group residential units were the apparent living quarters of extended families, and clusters of these patio-groups probably denoted some kind of larger lineage orgnizations. Frequently, in a cluster one patio-group was larger than the others, and this one often had a special building which had served, we think, as a little local temple or shrine. The implications are those of small community leadership, with political or religious functions or both; and it was further speculated that this "most important" patio-group within the cluster was the household of a lineage lord. As we went up the Maya settlement scale there was a replicative quality in both site layout and architecture. Thus, the temple-palace-courtyard unit, which is a main feature of the great Maya politico-religious centers, or "ceremonial centers," can be conceived of as a kind of magnification of the residential patio-group. Implicit in all this is a hierarchically structured social and political order. Studies to date suggest that there are at least three levels in the hierarchy of politico-religious centers, with their spacing revealing nested networks of primary, secondary, and tertiary centers, and below these the scattered farming hamlets of residential clusters and patio-groups. Whether the hierarchical functions of the centers were primarily political, religious, or economic, or a combination of these, is uncertain; but the overall impression given by such a settlement pattern is certainly that of integration and cohesion—at least within the orbit of a major primary center. It should be added here that such geographical "orbits of power," if we may be permitted such a term, were never of great size, perhaps averaging no more than 30 to 50 km in diameter (see Ashmore 1981).

This lowland Maya settlement pattern has led some (see Adams and Smith 1981) to suggest an analogy between Maya and European feudal settlement and social systems. In both, settlement and governance were adapted to agricultural production and distribution; duties and obligations within the system are likely to have been to those above and below one in the social hierarchy implied by settlement; and there was a strict hereditary stratification of classes. Others (Marcus 1983) have rejected this analogy and its implications, arguing that by accepting it we are reading too much into the Maya record that was not there, that the respective European feudal and Maya traditions and histories were too different to have resulted in close functional similarities. This is undoubtedly so, to a degree; no historical analogies are ever exactly duplicative; I think, though, that the similarities that do exist between the two models are worth some consideration.

In any event, the cohesive, highly structured, hierarchically layered, and traditionally conservative society that I am assuming for the Precolumbian Maya is supported by another set of data bearing upon sociopolitical organization, that coming from the hieroglyphic texts. Partial textual translations give us information on ruling lineages in various centers (Proskouriakoff 1963, 1964; Mathews 1985) and on the relationships of secondary and tertiary centers to primary ones (Marcus 1976; Mathews 1985). That is, in addition to site sizes and elaborations and the geographical spacings of centers, we have some knowledge, from the old Maya themselves, about the ways centers or cities were linked together into polities. Wars, alliances, intermarriages, accessions to thrones, royal births, and royal deaths are all recorded in the hieroglyphic inscriptions found on the stelae and other monuments, and the picture that emerges is at least one with some resemblance to feudal Europe. The Classic Maya elite were not always at peace with one another. There was a pattern of intermittent wars between cities, of dependencies pulling away from major centers, of new allegiances being formed. This more or less chronic, feudal-type conflict seems to have been maintained in a kind of "no win" equilibrium over long periods of time; at least there is no very good evidence that any one city or polity maintained dominance over the others for any extended period.

This lowland Maya sociopolitical order had close linkages with religion and ideology. Indeed, to an ancient Maya aristocrat it might have been very difficult to separate sharply the secular and the sacred. Rulers held their positions by "divine right" (Thompson 1973), and the monumental art of the cities displayed an intertwining of political and religious themes so that it is often difficult to distinguish the affairs of men from those of gods. Both were conceived of as existing in an ordered universe carried in a vision of cyclical time and recurrent prophecy—all of which was regulated by the Maya calendars.

Finally, in making the case for a carefully articulated and holistic system, one may cite the ingenious argument advanced by the late D. E. Puleston (1977) for the closure of the full systemic circle which ran from subsistence, to settlement, to social organization, to political structure, to religious ideology, and back to subsistence. Puleston linked lowland Maya ideology and its representative art to basic ecological adaptations and food-getting. He pointed out that the lacustrine, riverine, and swamp-like settings of Maya raised-field agriculture, with their tropical flora and fauna—the water lily, the various fish, and the crocodile—are all central symbols to lowland Maya art. Itzamna, the saurian, dragon-like monster, the prime deity of the Maya, god of creation and giver of life, belongs to this swampy setting, an eloquent testimony to the Maya's own ecological sophistication and sense of holism.

Such is an outline of the argument for the inner coherence of ancient lowland Maya society and culture. Specific to this essay is the fact that this coherence is seen to incorporate a sociopolitical structure that is harmoniously articulated with other aspects of life. On the face of it, coherence, in the sense that we are using the word here, might be taken as a near-synonym for stability. But is inner systemic coherence necessarily the same thing as stability for any system? Let us ask the question if holistic coherence might not have within it the potential for instability? And might not this have been true for the lowland Maya?

Certainly, arguments for the instability and precariousness of Maya culture and society, and particularly its sociopolitical forms, have been made many times and in many ways. The phenomenon of the ninth-century "collapse" has prompted these arguments and has led archaeologists to search for the factors of "stress" within the civilization. These "stress factors" were enumerated by the Santa Fe symposium on the "Classic Maya Collapse" held a few years ago (Culbert 1973). They include demographic pressures, agricultural problems, competition and warfare between regional centers and polities, a widening gap between elite and peasant elements in the society, and foreign or external contacts (Willey and Shinkin 1973). Such stresses have been analyzed further by P. D. Harrison (1977), with particular reference to the demographic–agricultural production equation, and by T. P. Culbert (1977), with attention to craft production and trading "systemic loops"; but the larger question remains. Why did such stresses produce crises of severe instability in lowland Maya society? Other civilizations have suffered such stresses and problems and have weathered them.

But let us review the record of the Maya lowland crises. To begin with, these are most manifest in the political sphere, especially in the higher echelons of that sphere which pertain to centralized political formations and which are reflected archaeologically in the fortunes of the politico-religious or ceremonial centers. The first of these crises occurred at the close of the Late Preclassic, probably just prior to A.D. 250 in what is sometimes called the Protoclassic. It came upon the heels of the Late Preclassic buildup of population growth and the construction of a number of large centers. At this same time monumental art, a distinctive iconography, hieroglyphic writing, and probably an accompanying religious ideology were introduced into the lowlands from the Guatemalan highlands–Pacific region (Freidel 1981). What appears to have been a "slump" set in after this, with the abandonment of the mammoth El Mirador center in the northern Peten (Matheny, ed., 1980; A. A. Demarest, personal communication 1983), Cerros in northern Belize (Freidel 1978), and other sites in the southern lowlands (Sabloff 1975; Potter 1985). It is difficult to measure the profundity of this early "slump" or "collapse" as many late Preclassic sites are covered over with much later construction. The impression is, however, that it was not as profound as the Classic "collapse" of the ninth century A.D. and that perhaps what was going on was a movement toward decentralization or the replacing of major centers by more numerous minor ones. But it should be emphasized that our data on this question are very few.

There was certainly an Early Classic period revival from the Protoclassic crisis. This is seen, particularly, at Tikal, which had been an impressive place in the Late Preclassic, had undergone a decline in the Protoclassic although it had never been abandoned, and then came back with great vigor after A.D. 250 with the beginnings of the "Stelae Cult," new large constructions, and elaborate burials of rulers (W. R. Coe, Jr., 1965; Puleston 1979). The Early Classic resurgence, which appears to have begun in the northeast Peten, and especially at Tikal, spread rapidly to other places in the lowlands, to Altar de Sacrificios on the lower Pasion, to Yaxchilan and Piedras Negras on the Usumacinta, to Quirigua and Copan in the southeast, as well as to other regions. At all of these places monuments were carved, inscribed, and dedicated to lineage lords or rulers. During the Early Classic, Tikal was in some way, by trade, politics, or both, linked to distant Teotihuacan in central Mexico. This is seen in trade items, ceramic styles, and, above all, in monumental art reflecting dynastic and political matters (Coggins 1979b). At this time Tikal was undoubtedly a major power in the lowlands, and some signs of this Teotihuacan influence, probably radiating out from Tikal, are seen at other sites. Then, toward the close of the Early Classic period, at the Maya Long Count date of 9.5.0.0.0 (A.D. 534), another crisis occurred, the so-called hiatus which lasted until about 9.8.0.0.0 (A.D. 593) (Willey 1974a). Again, the effects of the crisis are best seen in the ceremonial centers where stelae dedication and large building activity stops, or at least pauses for a period of from 40 to 60 years, if not longer. The Teotihuacan contacts seem to break off at this time although they had been waning for a century or more before the beginning of the "hiatus." Recent appraisals of the hiatus, especially in the light of some new stelae discoveries and reinterpretations of some previously known ones (Mathews 1985), would indicate that it was not areawide and that some cities did continue through it with building and dedicatory activities. Notably, it was most severe and pronounced in the west, on the lower Pasion and Usumacinta, less severe in the east.

At the beginning of the seventeenth century A.D., and throughout the eighth century, lowland Maya civilization not only righted itself from the "hiatus" crisis, but it went on to its elaborate zenith of the Late Classic period. There was a population upsurge throughout the lowlands that approximated a similar buildup of the Late Preclassic. Stelae dedications and construction were resumed in many Early Classic centers, and hundreds of new centers were founded. Tikal still retained great prestige, although now it had many rivals in size and probably political power—Yaxchilan, Piedras Negras, Palenque, Quirigua, Copan, and the cities of the Rio Bec region and other parts of the north, to name only a few. It was after these two centuries of expansion and brilliance that the famous ninth-century decline or "collapse" began to set in, in the southern cities. It is first evident in the west—reminiscent of the "hiatus" of some two to three centuries before—but it advanced rapidly and was essentially complete for the entire southern lowlands by A.D. 900. This "great collapse" was characterized by a cessation of stelae dedications, major sculptural art, and most large public construction, and by a disappearance or dispersal of a large part of the population. Classic Maya civilization as it had been known in the southern centers never recovered from it. Recently, there has been some revisionist research on the phenomenon of the "collapse" which has shown that the area was not completely depopulated. Some groups who continued in the lowlands were reduced to a peasant level. Others, in a few places, did construct ceremonial centers although these were on a modest scale compared to those of the seventh and eighth centuries (see various papers in Sabloff and Andrews 1986). One of the features of the ninth century "collapse" is that it was accompanied in some places, particularly along the western and northwestern edges of the southern lowlands, by signs of "foreign" influences. These are seen in ceramic and figurine styles found in the Tabasco, Usumacinta, and Pasion River regions (Willey 1973c). The best interpretation that has been put on these findings is that they represent trade contacts with, and incursions by, peoples with a non-Classic Maya or atypically Maya culture (Willey and Shimkin 1973).

The "collapse" phenomenon of the southern lowlands did not have a ninth-century parallel in the northern regions of the Maya area. There many big centers, especially those of the far north and the Puuc region, were not abandoned during the ninth century but, instead, grew larger and more elaborate. We think now that this Puuc florescence continued for several centuries (Sabloff and Andrews 1985). At about A.D. 1000, one major northern center, Chichen Itza, became the paramount city of the entire north, overshadowing if not controlling its Puuc rivals. Chichen Itza's art and architecture embody many Mexican-like elements, often compared to those of the Tula Toltec tradition of the central Mexican highlands (Tozzer 1957). Was Chichen Itza an actual Toltec outpost implanted in the heart of Maya territory as a sort of conquest capital? This is a possibility, but most opinion has held that the builders of the site were probably Maya who, in some manner or another, had established alliances with Mexican groups and used these connections to rise to power and dominance in the Yucatan Peninsula. There seems little doubt but that they did so dominate the area for a substantial period of time. Indeed, I would estimate that at Chichen Itza the lowland Maya came closer to successful centralized statehood than at any other place or at any other time, not excluding Tikal or any of the other southern cities of the Classic. But after about A.D. 1250, Chichen Itza ceased being an important capital and was largely deserted.

The final Maya lowland attempt at political centralization focused upon another northern city, Mayapan (Pollock et al. 1962). It arose as the dominant place not long after the abandonment of Chichen, and it remained the major city for the next 200 years or throughout most of the Late Postclassic (A.D. 1250–1540). It was the hub of an extensive trading network which was tied together by the coastwise movement of goods, with stations all along the coasts of Yucatan as well as westward into Tabasco and eastward to lower Central America (Sabloff and Rathje 1975). Such stations were probably not controlled politically by Mayapan but had a kind of semi-independent "ports-of-trade" status and served as commercial links between the Maya and central Mexico, including, eventually, the Aztec empire. Mayapan fell, however, purportedly a victim of civil wars, less than a century before the Spanish Conquest, and the Spaniards found the Maya lowlands politically fragmented into a number of small chiefdoms.

We see, then, that the case for recurrent crises and lowland Maya political instability is as impressive, if not more so, than that for Classic Maya sociocultural coherence. There were "times of troubles" in the southern lowlands during the Protoclassic (A.D. 1–250), at the end of the Early Classic (A.D. 534–593), and at the end of the Late Classic (A.D. 800–900). One has the impression that these crises became increasingly severe and of longer duration. Of course we cannot be sure of the duration of the earliest one; but the "hiatus" at the end of the Early Classic period lasted only 50 years or so, a century at most. For the "great collapse" of the ninth century there was no real recovery, at least insofar as this marked a return to something approaching state formation. Following the "great collapse" the main theater of lowland Maya high political activity and state formation shifted to the north. There were probably a number of competing polities here between A.D. 800 and 1000, but after the latter date Chichen Itza emerged as the capital of the dominant state, perhaps holding sway over most of the Yucatan Peninsula. After Chichen Itza's fall, Mayapan took over but, most probably, on a lesser scale. With the fall of Mayapan in the mid-fifteenth century, and the breakup of authority among many petty chiefdoms, the lowland Maya were again in another stage of crisis. Puleston (1979) has called our attention to the Maya's own awareness of this peak-to-crisis cyclical nature of their political fortunes, which was recorded in the sacred *Books of the Chilam Balam* (e.g., Roys 1967). It was their belief that history repeated itself in units of time corresponding to 13 katuns of their calendar, or approximately every 256 years. On the face of the evidence one might conclude that their faith in the wheel of fate was justified—at least as far as the phenomena of political centralization and decentralization were concerned. Less mystically, we might suppose that the post-Conquest historians who prepared the *Chilam Balam* had recourse to true "archival" material as this had been handed down to them in their written histories of earlier times.

We have, thus, two views of ancient lowland Maya society and culture. In one of these we see a highly coherent, integrated, and smoothly functioning system, in which all parts or subsystems seem to be running in close harmony and coordination with each other. Presumably, any potentialities for change were so accommodated that the feedback within the system was negative and not change-producing. The other view, developed in long-term historical perspective, is that of a society beset with recurrent crises, most easily seen as political crises or breakdowns, "collapses," or, at best, retrenchments in the political order. Presumably, factors making for change were not neutralized; instead, there was a postivie feedback for change that successively threatened and, eventually, destroyed or drastically modified the system. How are we to view this apparent paradox? Are the two views irreconcilable or inconsistent with each other? I do not think so. This takes us back to my opening statement that all sociopolitical formations have within themselves forces for both coherence and instability.

In his paper on "The Cultural Evolution of Civilizations," K. V. Flannery (1972) discusses the processes leading toward the consolidation of state society. It is his premise that the centralized state society demands a coherence among its subsystems; but such a condition of coherence carries dangers within it. The objectives of state power have a tendency to increase coherence to a point where there is a complete or near-complete "linearization" of social, political, and economic controls extending from the top down through all levels of society. In such a situation, the condition of coherence becomes one of "hypercoherence." This makes for a sensitive vulnerability to shock or trauma striking at any one part of the system by allowing the effects to spread rapidly to its other parts. With "hypercoherence" there are few or no enclaves of reserve strength from which to organize counter-measures to resist the trauma. Presumably, such a risk of "hypercoherence" would obtain for any highly centralized and hierarchically organized state structure. Were the lowland Maya more "hypercoherently" vulnerable than other emergent states, especially Precolumbian American states? Flannery suggests that they may have been. Although he does not pursue it further, he suggests that such "hypercoherence" is implied in the Maya hierarchically arranged, lattice-work settlement patterns, with their linearized and regularized units of hamlets, villages, tertiary centers, secondary centers, and primary centers. Such a settlement pattern or system is apt to be a reflection of the structure of social, political, and economic controls. I am inclined to agree.

With these things in mind, let us return to the lowland Maya record of political instability. One of the things to be explored in this record is that the recurrent crises all have some proximate or immediate association with circumstances of "foreign" contacts. Were these contacts, in some way, the causes of the crises? Were the lowland Maya unusually susceptible or vulnerable to outside stimuli, pressures, or interferences? And, if so, what were the mechanisms or processes involved? When we approach the matter this way, one of the first things that is obvious is that the "foreign" contacts differ, both in their apparent contents and in their timing. Both the Protoclassic and the "hiatus" crises were preceded by, rather than being concurrent with, the outside influences. In both of these cases the content of the contact appears to have been on the elite level: Izapan-Kaminaljuyu iconography and hieroglyphics, for the earlier instance; Teotihuacan iconography and status goods for the latter. In both instances, lowland Maya culture, first that of the late Preclassic centers, and second that of the Early Classic ones, was apparently enriched and, very probably, moved in the direction of centralized governmental structures. Both times crises followed. There is a suggestion here that lowland Maya society may have had some difficulties in assimilating and making workable centralized polities although this can be no more than a suggestion, and certainly we do not understand the processes of the failures if this was, indeed, what happened.

When we come to the ninth-century crisis, the "great collapse," both the timing and the content of the "foreign" contacts appear to be different. The "alien" contacts occur concurrently with the beginning of the decline (Sabloff and Willey 1967; Adams 1971; Willey and Shimkin 1973); and their contents, insofar as we can appraise them from the archaeological remains, are not particularly on the elite or high governmental level. They are, as has been noted, pottery vessels and figurines, both occurring in quantity at sites such as Altar de Sacrificios (Adams 1971) and Seibal (Sabloff 1975; Willey 1978a). We are, of course, confronted with the question as to whether the "foreign" contacts preceded the ninth-century crisis and were instrumental in bringing it about (Willey and Shimkin 1973). I lean toward this interpretation, and I would like to advance, as a hypothesis, an idea about the processes that precipitated this particular crisis and decline.

The role of trade as a cultural dynamic in the rise of civilizations has been highly touted in recent archaeological literature; and this includes several influential writings on the lowland Maya (see, especially, Webb 1964, 1973; Rathje 1971, 1972, 1977). Indeed, for some, trade has been seen as the key process in the evolution of the state. Perhaps this is a fitting subconscious reaction of our times as we read the records of the past. I certainly would not deny that trade can be a powerful force for cultural and social change. It very clearly has "positive" effects in the sense of promoting positive feedback for change within a cultural system. On the other hand, viewed from the standpoint of some cultures and societies experiencing the change, the institution of trade might not necessarily be judged beneficial. I will elaborate this further by saying that although trade was often a dynamic force for cultural and social change, it was not always a stabilizing factor in the political sector.

In his aforementioned paper, Flannery (1972) has described a process of sociopolitical change that he calls "promotion." Promotion refers to the rise of an institution within a society from a place on a lower rung of the control hierarchy to a higher position in that hierarchy. Such promotion obviously can bring about serious structural and functional changes in the system. A classic example of pomotion is that of the institution of militarism. Military leaders, who previously had operated at lower levels within a hierarchy, may come to the fore in times of stress or danger; but they may then be loath to relinquish high-ranked power after the immediate necessity has passed, thereby changing or rearranging the hierarchy in "promoting" themselves. It is possible that something like this may have happened in the Late Preclassic to Protoclassic and in the Early Classic crises, or in the events leading to those crises. But, for the moment, and with regard to the Late Classic ninth-century crisis, I would like to extend this process of "promotion" to the institution of trade and to speculate how it might have been a crucial factor in precipitating the political crisis of the "great collapse."

Consider, again, the highly coherent, or "hypercoherent," model proposed for lowland Maya society. Its strictly structured settlement system would have been ideally adapted to agricultural production and distribution. It was linked to and blessed by the most sacred of religious sanctions and presided over by god-like rulers and their emissaries. But its operation would have depended upon the closest adherences to beliefs and allegiances, to duties and responsibilities up and down the line of command. The trader, and especially the alien or semi-alien trader, backed by "foreign" prestige and perhaps at times by force, could have been a very disturbing element in such a "hypercoherent" system. From the point of view of the elite class running the system, he could have been fitted into it satisfactorily only if he were under their close supervision, if, in effect, he were one of themselves or their agent. As a free-wheeling "foreigner," an outsider, he would be a very serious threat. He could have subverted outlying retainer populations of villages and lesser centers from their allegiances to the main center of the polity by dispensations of trade goods and favorable trade arrangements designed to that end. The only way the main center and the resident aristocratic leadership could have forestalled this would have been by "police" or military power, and there ar many reasons to believe that such power was weakly developed in the emergent Maya states or chiefdoms. Such a trader would have been ideally placed to promote strife between centers and to have done so to his own advantage. Above all, he was an outsider, a "foreigner," not bound by the same belief systems as the locals among whom he was operating. I think that some of this is supported by the nature of the trade, as we know it, along the western and northwestern frontiers of the southern Maya lowlands in the ninth century. The goods of the trade, at least as we know them, were not costly elite goods; they were more "everyday" commodities, ceramics, figurines.

Such traders as I am describing became increasingly a part of the greater Mesoamerican scene from Classic period times forward. Dealing from the positions of strength that I am envisaging here in the lowland Maya situation, they would have been able to assume "promotional" roles in many societies, taking over prerogatives formerly held by aristocratic leaderships. The Putun of the Gulf coast, as they have been described in the chronicles (Thompson 1970), sound like a society that had been transformed from an earlier and more traditionally Classic Maya one into a new kind of system in which the trader had been "promoted" to high authority. such a society, competitively confronting the more traditional Maya, would have served as a survival model for others, thus hastening the fall of the old order and the rise of the new one, one usually associated with the Late Postclassic in southern Mesoamerica.

On a more general level, I think that this hypothesis is consistent with the proposition that a strong mercantilist orientation is essentially antithetical to a conservative, agrarian-based, feudal-type social system. The mercantilist system offers too many opportunities for "promotion," for groups and individuals, either insiders or outsiders, to break free from traditional duties and obligations and so to threaten the power structure. It demands new kinds of social and political controls which some Postclassic Mesoamerican societies, such as the Aztec, devised to hold their merchant groups in check. The Classic lowland Maya—chiefdoms or nascent states—seem to have been unable or unwilling to devise them.

The fall of Chichen Itza, that climax city of Puuc-Toltec heritage in the northern lowlands came two centuries after the strong infusion of "foreign," or Mexican, influence into Yucatan. I will not try to speculate on the processes involved other than to say that by this time the lowland Maya had become more "Mesoamericanized," which means more "Mexicanized." By the time of Mayapan I think that the lowland Maya had become "colonialized," if not in a direct political and administrative way, in a commercial and economic one. They were at the far end of a trading and extractive chain that had been forged by, or was certainly manipulated largely for the benefit of, central Mexico. Energies that had once gone into the great temples and palaces of the old Classic civilization, or into the glories of Chichen Itza, were now channeled into the assembling and transporting of merchandise. Some have referred to this as the "upward collapse" of the Maya, arguing that what we are viewing is a progressive evolutionary trajectory in state formation that continued after the Classic period (Erasmus 1968). This is an interesting idea, and a case can be made for it if one takes a long enough and a geographically broad enough view of Mesoamerican culture history. Thus, it could be argued that the central Mexicans, culminating in the Aztec empire, were in the mainstream of cultural evolution while the lowland Maya were being brought along as an integral, if somewhat fringe-like, part of the whole. But I doubt if this would have been of much consolation to a Maya aristocrat of the old Classic tradition. Certainly, his intellectual descendants, the priestly authors of the *Chilam Balam*, did not see it in this light but, instead, regarded their interchanges with the Mexican "barbarians" as a most dismal turn of events, however fated.

I conceive of the lowland Maya political scene as always having been one of competing polities, whose various fortunes and territorial domains waxed and waned (Freidel 1983). Periodic crises swept through the land with something approaching cyclical regularity. Long-lasting state formations seem to have been precluded. Why? What were the basic causes making for this condition? W. T. Sanders (1973, 1977, 1981) has argued that they lay in fundamental ecologic, demographic, and resource circumstances, that these laid serious constraints on the kind of economy, settlement system, and sociopolitical system that could be developed in such a region on a preindustrial level. I think that there is something to his argument. Certainly it is the only archaeological culture or civilization that extends over such a large tropical lowland territory in all of Mesoamerica. It grew up in contact or communication with other Mesoamerican cultures that were all somewhat differently situated with regard to natural setting. In these contacts the Maya lowlands always seem to have been the party that was the most seriously "affected." At certain times these "effects" seem to have been stimuli which promoted cultural growth, including advances toward some degree of political centralization; yet even in these instances there seems almost to have been a "rejection" of the new ideas as incompatible with the very conservatively evolving and highly coherent lowland Maya system. At other times the immediate effects of the contacts appear to be crisis-producing, as though the "hyper-coherent" Maya structure had suffered a blow from which it could not recover.

The most dramatic example of this last is the ninth-century "collapse," and I have argued that the institution of trade, as an aggressive element in "foreign" contacts with Mexican cultures to the west, delivered the blow from which there was no recovery in the southern lowlands. The remaining history of the lowland Maya, which insofar as large-scale political formations are concerned is traced in the north, saw progressive "Mexica-nization," or "Mesoamericanization," of the civilization. The greatest lowland success in state formation probably occurred at this time, at Chichen Itza. But here, too, there was a breakdown, followed still once more by the state attempt at Mayapan, as the lowland Maya struggled in their not very successful way to march to the central Mexican drum of empire and "Mesoamericanization."

IV

Settlement Patterns

"Settlement patterns"—or settlement archaeology—became a theme in my research in 1946, at the time of the Virú Valley survey (Willey 1953a, 1974c), but except for a general overview (Willey 1968) to a book on *Settlement Archaeology* the three essays in this section are the only article-length pieces of mine on the subject.

The first one, "Peruvian Settlement and Socio-Economic Patterns" was written at the same time I was preparing my Virú Valley settlement pattern monograph, but it was a much more ambitious and wide-ranging interpretation of the Peruvian past than I would give in the more cautious Virú report. I opened with the bold sentence: "A comprehension of the structure and function of past social institutions lies at the heart of an understanding of Peru-Bolivian prehistory." The statement still holds, except that we had then, and we still have, a very long way to go in our attempts to comprehend "structure," "function," and "process." I said then—and I still believe—that a crucial element in such hoped-for comprehensions is an appreciation of "settlement pattern," as it expressed the relationships between people and the natural environment and between people, plus "the shifts of both of these through time."

When I turned to the analyses that would lead to such "comprehensions," I also turned to what we were then calling "functional-developmental classifications" of Central Andean cultures. These were attempts to synthesize the full range of archaeological information then available and to do this in the context of settlement patterns—that is, living units, public buildings, fortifications, irrigation systems, and so forth—and to draw from these syntheses inferences about social and political institutions. Obviously, I was running too fast in this article, but I wanted to make a beginning by sketching the potential of settlement pattern study.

The two other settlement pattern essays included here follow upon my entrance into Maya archaeology. There was little literature at that date on the subject (see Ashmore and

Willey 1981 for a review of the history of Maya settlement pattern archaeology). In "Problems Concerning Prehistoric Settlement Patterns in the Maya Lowlands," I speculated about the nature of ancient Maya macrosettlement. Would the archaeologists be dealing with cities, small cities, towns, hamlets, a wide scattering of individual farmsteads, or combinations of these? The three Lowland Maya macrosettlement types I conceived in the article were imagined abstractions. The Type A model was the urban center, or "true city," model, thought of then as a Maya ceremonial (or politicoreligious) center, with its temples and palaces surrounded by a dense settlement of habitations. Type B was the ceremonial center as the "vacant center," one without a thickly settled residential zone surrounding its temples and palaces. For this kind of center, the sustaining population was believed to be widely scattered over the surrounding landscape, either in isolated individual houses or other small residential units. At the time I wrote the essay, this was generally believed to be the Lowland Maya settlement form. My Type C was based on the idea of a major politicoreligious center, with an immediately surrounding residential population of substantial, but perhaps not urban, proportions. Then, located at some distance from this major center, there would be a number of smaller villages or hamlets. Some of these would have minor ceremonial center constructions within them; other might not.

At the time, I know I favored Type C as the closest to Lowland Maya settlement reality. My limited experience in the Belize Valley had led me to believe that we were dealing with both major and minor centers within the same region. They probably were contemporaneous and had existed in political hierarchies. Residential settlement was dispersed but in a different fashion than that envisioned for Type B. I concluded, it now appears wisely, by offering the opinion that reality might approximate combinations of my three models and that variation might very well occur in time and space. Certainly, Maya settlement research over the past 30 years confirms this rather cautious and qualified opinion. Thus, we know now that there existed major centers with immediately adjacent large residential zones that deserve to be called cities. Tikal is a foremost example (Haviland 1970). There is also a general Lowland Maya regional macropattern of major and minor centers, or hierarchical rankings of centers; and we now know (from hieroglyphic textual information) that many minor centers were, indeed, political tributaries to larger ones (Culbert 1988). Populations were usually clustered around these minor centers. In addition, there were many hamlets without obvious ceremonial center-type constructions, and these occurred so widely over large portions of the Peten and other Lowland areas that they were undoubtedly the homes of the many farmers who sustained the centers. While the full picture of Lowland Maya settlement, in all of its macro- and microsettlement types, and in all of its regional and chronological variations, still remains to be assembled, we have now advanced the cause considerably from where it was when I wrote this very preliminary paper.

The third settlement pattern essay, "The Structure of Ancient Maya Society," moves swiftly from settlement facts to sociopolitical organization. It argues the case for the Lowland Maya as having been a very tightly knit and smoothly integrated society. It was written after several seasons of archaeological settlement pattern study at Barton Ramie and in the Belize Valley as a whole. I read the evidence for macroscale integration from a settlement hierarchy of major, intermediate-sized, and minor temple-palace centers as these occurred in the valley. I was further impressed by the relative abundance of fine quality grave goods (polychrome jars, jade gorgets, and the like) in what looked like ordinary household burials in the Barton Ramie residential mounds. This led me to believe that the social "gulf" between a ruling elite and a sustaining peasantry had been overemphasized. I was also influenced in this view by my ethnological colleague at

Harvard, E. Z. Vogt, who was then just beginning his modern Maya settlement and social organizational studies of Zinacantan, in the Chiapas highlands (see Vogt 1961, 1969). His work had convinced him that the elite-peasant dichotomy in Maya society had been overstressed.

Looking back on it now, it is obvious that my interpretation of Lowland Maya macrosettlement integration—political hierarchies of centers—was on the right track, but I had leaned too far in the direction of Maya social integration and equality. The traditional gap between a Lowland Maya peasantry and an elite class is supported by too many aspects of Classic Period Maya archaeology to be denied (see Willey and Shimkin 1973). While it is true that many of the occupants of the Lowland Maya "house mounds" appeared prosperous and participative in ritual aspects of elite culture—as such things can be measured by household and burial goods—there were certainly significant differences between elite and commoner. One has only to turn to some of the high art and the hieroglyphic texts to appreciate the social distance that must have existed between the two (see, for example, Schele and Miller 1986).

I seem to have been wrong in this essay on another score as well. I closed with the statement, referring to the Classic "collapse," that "Maya priest and peasant vanished together." This was written before a proper analysis of all of the Barton Ramie house-mound pottery had been made and while I was still mistakenly classifying Postclassic pottery as Late Classic. This error was to be rectified later (Willey et al. 1965; Willey 1973c); subsequent researches by others, in both the Belize Valley and the Guatemalan Peten, would reveal a substantial occupation of "postcollapse peasants" (Bullard 1973; Willey 1973c; Sabloff and Andrews V, eds., 1985; Chase and Rice, eds., 1985).

25

Peruvian Settlement and Socio-Economic Patterns

(From *29th International Congress of Americanists, New York, 1949*, Vol. 1, pp. 195–200, University of Chicago Press, 1951. Reprinted by permission of University of Chicago Press.)

A comprehension of the structure and function of past social institutions lies at the heart of an understanding of Peru-Bolivian[1] prehistory. In this essay, it is my assumption that in settlement patternings as revealed by archaeology we have a guideline of evidence that is most directly reflective of institutional development. The concept "settlement pattern" implies more than a study of site situation, building plans, or architectural detail. It is all of these, but it is also more. It is a consideration of total community integration, ecologically and culturally. The relation of people to the natural environment, the nature of population groupings, and the shifts of both of these through time—these are the bases of inference concerning the socio-economic orientations of ancient societies. And from these basic data and inferences, supplemented by other aspects of the archaeological record, we may go a step further and advance some interpretations as to the coexisting political and religious institutions.

A trial survey of Peruvian settlement patterns has been made feasible by two recent events in Andean archaeology. The first of these was the intensive research program of the Institute of Andean Research (Willey, 1946b), in the Virú Valley. Settlement studies in this one valley have provided a pilot developmental sequence that may, with proper caution, be extended to other parts of the area.[2] The second event has been the establishment of a functional-developmental classification for Central Andean cultures. This classification is grounded in time-space systematics in that it is an outgrowth of the Uhle-Kroeber scheme of horizon-markers; however, it goes beyond pure temporal-spatial formulations in that it recognizes functional characteristics of the successive cultural horizons. Larco Hoyle (1948) was the first to apply such a classification to the north coast. Bennett (1948), Strong (1948a), Willey (1948), and Steward (1948a) have used similar functional-developmental schemes for the Peru-Bolivian area as a whole. Nomenclature has varied somewhat with all of these authors, but the major outlines and implications are the same. In the present discussion I will refer to such a sequential-classificatory scheme. It is given below with equivalent explanations and estimated dates.[3]

Early Agricultural (3000–1000 B.C.): Premaize horticulature, fishing-gathering important, no ceramics, small villages near coast. North Coast region.

Early Formative (1000 B.C.–0): Maize, some dependence on fishing-gathering, ceramics, villages near coast and in marginal lands of interior, beginnings of ceremonial centers, Chavín style. Chavín, Cupisnique, Nepeña, Casma, Ancon-Supe.

Late Formative (A.D. 0–500): Developing craft technologies, marked population expansion, full agriculture, numerous villages, ceremonial centers, beginnings of fortifications. Salinar, related White-on-red cultures, Paracas Cavernas, Chanapata, Chiripa.

Florescent (A.D. 500–1000): Full technological and esthetic control attained, great religious centers, larger villages. Mochica, Recuay, Gallinazo, Interlocking, Early Lima, Nazca, Pucara, Early Tiahuanaco.

Early Expansionist (A.D. 1000–1200): Political and/or religious expansion, beginnings of larger communities. The Tiahuanaco horizon.

Late Expansionist (A.D. 1200–1532): Political expansionism continues, rise of urban centers. Late Chimu, Late Chancay, Ica-Chincha, Inca conquest after A.D. 1450.

Settlements of the Early Agricultural stage are small, compact villages located along the ocean shore at favorable shell-fishing stations. This site ecology, as well as the refuse contents, attests to a subsistence economy divided between fishing and horticulture. Houses were simple semi-subterranean affairs of one or two small rooms lined with stone and mortar or hand-made adobes. They were arranged at random in the village area. In only one site of the period, Aspero near Supe, is there a building which might be considered a temple or ceremonial structure. These small Early Agricultural populations with their minimum surplus economy had only a limited craft technology which was confined mainly to twined cotton textiles, basketry, and tools of stone. Burials, placed in stone-lined or plain pits were accompanied by only a few such manufactures. The sociopolitical picture is one of simplicity, of little autonomous villages without differentiated craft workers or social classes. Religious rites or controls appear to have been equally uncomplicated.

Early Formative settlement patterns are similar to those of the preceding stage in that the small, unplanned village remained as the basic unit. These, however, became more numerous, and this reflects this intensification of the agricultural economy with the appearance of maize, which in turn is responsible for increased population. The village dwelling sites were clusters of irregularly arranged above-ground houses of one to five room construction. Both stone and conical hand-made adobes were used as building materials. An important innovation of this stage is the religious structure. It varies from the crude rectangular stone foundations excavated in Virú to the famous dressed-stone castillo at Chavín de Huántar. Stone sculpture, in connection with the temple, flourished at Chavín while architectural sculpture in clay is seen at the coastal temples of Nepeña and Casma. It is obvious that these temples were constructed and supported by a considerable population so that we know more than a single village group was involved. Undoubtedly, the temple served as a politico-religious nucleus for several surrounding villages. Skillful and esthetically sophisticated work in small stone, bone, and ceramics during this period indicates a degree of craft specialization, but there is little evidence, aside from differentiation in the amounts and quality of burial goods, to suggest class stratification. During the latter half of the period a single religious theme, represented by the Chavín feline deity, dominates the artistic tradition. This, together, with the clearly recognizable importance of the temple centers, argues for the supremacy of sacred rather than secular ideology and control. In spite of stylistic similarity of the feline art motif throughout much of the Peruvian area at this time, it is most likely that this religious or theocratic control was independently invoked in the several temple centers rather than directed from a common source of sovereignty (Willey, 1948, p. 10).

A full agricultural economy was achieved during the Late Formative stage, and in response to this, population showed a marked increase. This is seen to advantage in Virú where the shell-fishing stations, so popular during the earlier periods, now form but a small part of the total valley occupation. Sites have spread inland to all parts of the valley, and this expansion is explained best by irrigation as it is likely that the canal systems were put into operation during the Late Formative. Although the number of sites greatly increases, the small village pattern persists. House size and arrangement similar to those of the Early Formative continue, but somewhat larger and more compact room aggregates also appear. These last are found on the hillslopes overlooking the valley floor in Virú. They are constructed on successive step-terraces, and the rooms are contiguous though without overall plan. That there was some general idea of community arrangement at this time is revealed in the Chiripa culture of the Bolivian altiplano. Here individual houses were found grouped around a common courtyard. The impressive temples of the Early Formative do not seem to be duplicated in the Late Formative although there is considerable evidence for religious sites. In Virú there are pyramids of conical adobes, earth, or rocks that date from the later period, and it seems likely that these must have served as bases for temples or governmental structures. There are no outstanding sites in Virú from this era that could be interpreted as politico-religious capitals, but there are two or three hilltop redoubts of impressive size. These rock-walled inclosures contain multi-room dwellings and small flat-topped earth-rock pyramids. During attack they could have served as places of refuge for several hundred people, presumably drawing from a number of the small, scattered villages. This is the first appearance of fortifications in the Peruvian sequence, and the nature of warfare at this time is an important point. Although the lack of large ceremonial centers makes it doubtful if the single valleys had complete political unity within themselves, the valley irrigation systems do imply a degree of internal coordination and centralized authority. Such coordination would preclude intravalley warfare and suggests that the hilltop forts were built against raiders from outside the valley unit. A prevailing motif of the Late Formative is technological experimentation. Craft work is competent and in some cases excellent. Ceramics show a technological improvement over the preceding stage although with the disappearance of the Chavín art style there is a corresponding esthetic decline. In the south, in the Paracas Cavernas culture, loom-weaving shows great advances over the previous periods. In general, burial practices are somewhat more elaborate than formerly. The Late Formative can, as a whole, be summed up as that stage in Peru-Bolivian development when large populations came into being, technology made rapid strides, but society was still decentralized into autonomous politico-religious groups. Nevertheless, the institution of intervalley or interregional warfare was beginning. This and the necessity for centralized control of the all-important irrigation systems were inevitably compressing the social order into more formalized and cohesive forms.

As the name implies, technological and esthetic excellence is the hallmark of the Florescent stage of Peru-Bolivian culture. The centuries-long traditions in ceramics, other handicrafts, and architecture finally came to fulfillment. In the Virú Valley settlements reach their maximum number at this time. The increase over Late Formative times is, however, relatively small as compared with the rapid expansion of settlements and populations that was noted between the Early and Late Formative stages. The basic unit of the Virú settlement pattern during the Florescent is still the small or medium-sized village, but many of these are larger than in previous periods. Contiguous rooms, numbering up to 50 or more, are found in irregularly arranged compounds which give the appearance of having been built partially according to plan but largely by haphazard accretion. The big politico-religious capitals of Gallinazo and Huancaco, Florescent sites in Virú, are exceptions to the small village clusters. At Gallinazo, in conjunction with great pyramids and presumed palace or temple quarters, there are hundreds or even thousands of small adobe-walled rooms placed in irregularly arranged groups on the summits of large adobe platforms. These small rooms appear to be dwellings of great masses of the population, not just sacred or governmental precincts. On the north and central coasts Florescent stage architecture is massive and impressive, and the construction unit is the mold-made rectangular adobe. North highland architecture is of dressed stone and equally impressive if not as mammoth. The artistic representations of the stage are well known from the ceramics, bone, stone, shell, and metalwork of the Mochica and the ceramics and textiles of Paracas Necropolis and Nazca. These are the finest in Peruvian prehistory. Metallurgy takes a great spurt during these periods, and all techniques and materials ever known to the aboriginal area, with the exception of bronze, are competently used and commonly possessed. Copper weapons and tools are the rule for Mochica, and from this time on the north coast was in a true metal age. Craft specialization is obvious. Religion and its significance are attested to by the great pyramids and by the representations in Mochica pottery. On the north coast there is abundant evidence that secular and military power were contesting with purely religious authority. Total valley or multiple valley states came into being. Military fortifications or great castillos were constructed at strategic points in each valley. War scenes are common on Mochica pottery as are representations of enthroned dignitaries inspecting captives or giving auditions to vassals. The implications of class stratification are clear in this as also in the marked differentiation of grave goods placed with individuals.

The Early Expansionist stage is that characterized by the widespread diffusion of Tiahuanaco-like art. This inundation seems to have swept over much of Peru-Bolivia, terminating the Florescent cultures, and to have come as the climax to the first upsurge of Peruvian empire attempts. We know that on the north coast the Mochica were military expansionists and that they were pressing southward on the valleys adjacent to their original homeland. Similar events may have been taking place in other regions of Peru. The Tiahuanaco stylistic wave may or may not have been a centrally directed empire attempt; but whatever its overall organization we can be sure that it moved into the north coast in the wake of military force. The obliteration of all of the Mochica war and state symbols is too complete and too sudden to be explained by peaceful processes. In Virú many of the settlements of this Early Expansionist stage are identical with those of the Florescent stage. In fact, many of the small and medium-sized room clusters were continuously occupied through both periods. This, together with the fact that utilitarian pottery remains much the same while ceremonial ware undergoes violent change, would indicate a continuity of much of the population. Some dwelling sites of the period are, however, significantly different. These are planned compound structures of many rooms, regularly arranged and inclosed within an outer wall. It is questionable if many big pyramids or fortifications were built during this time, but those of the Florescent were occupied, used, and probably added to. The level of technology of the Florescent is maintained in the Early Expansionist stage, but there is a general esthetic decline which is noted for all parts of Peru. The period is one of flux and change, but, judging from both preceding and succeeding periods, it is almost certain that large-scale warfare, military states, and class differentiated societies were continued.

The Late Expansionist stage saw the culmination of the settlement and empire trends begun in the latter part of the Florescent and carried through the Early Expansionist period. After the disappearance of the Tiahuanaco horizon influence, a number of large but not pan-Peruvian kingdoms were formed. The Chimu, Late Chancay, Ica, and Chincha styles denote some of these on the coast; others were undubtedly in existence in the highlands. The characteristic settlement of the stage is the planned community. On the north coast the first of these were seen in Early Expansionist times, but in the later stage they became the rule. The great group of gigantic walled compounds, containing symmetrical arrangements of rooms of all sizes, courtyards, basins, and pyramids, that is found at Chanchan is the classic example. There are similar groups in other north coast, central coastal, and even south coastal valleys. In Virú, a small valley, there are no such huge centers, but there are several quadrangular compounds of the Late Expansionist period which are miniatures of the large compounds of Chanchan. It seems unlikely that absolute population was any greater then that it was in Florescent times. These Late Expansionist sites are considerably larger than earlier communities, but they are also much fewer. Peoples were concentrated into a city-type existence. Such communities continue up to and after the Inca conquest which seems to have effected little change on the north coast except in the matter of political consolidation. In general, the technology of the Late Expansionist stage is that which was achieved in Florescent times with the exception of the invention and distribution of bronze. Art forms of the period lack the richness and painstaking care of earlier times. Craft goods are extremely plentiful, however. In some places they give the appearance of being hastily turned out, mass-produced articles in which the maker took little pride. Religious concepts are much rarer in the art of the period than previously. Temples and pyramids are constructed but usually as a part of an urban concentration. And, from the early Colonial documents, we know that religion had become an adjunct and an implement to the all-powerful state under the Inca. Constant large-scale, long-distance warfare with empire incorporation of territories and peoples as its objective was the guiding force in Late Expansionist society. Both archaeologic and ethnohistoric sources tell us that class differentiation was marked and governmental control all-pervading. Peruvian society, which had begun with simple farming villages oriented toward a sacred temple-shrine, had finally become as well organized and tightly constructed as one of the symmetrically planned cities of its final phase.

Notes

[1]This is the Central Andean culture area or "co-tradition." It consists of the Peruvian highlands and coast and the Bolivian altiplano (see Bennett, 1948; Bennett and Bird, 1949).

[2]Supplemented to some extent by Bird's work (1948) in the Chicama Valley.

[3]Compare with Bennett and Bird (1949, pp. 111–14).

26

Problems Concerning Prehistoric Settlement Patterns in the Maya Lowlands

(From *Prehistoric Settlement Patterns in the New World*, G. R. Willey, ed., pp. 107–114, Viking Fund Publications in Anthropology, No. 23, New York, 1956. Reprinted by permission of the Wenner-Gren Foundation for Anthropological Research, Inc., New York. Copyright by the Wenner-Gren Foundation.)

Setting and Problems

Maya civilization had its most brilliant rise and dramatic decline in the lowland jungle regions of the Guatemalan Petén, adjacent Mexico and Yucatán, British Honduras, and the western fringes of Honduras. An estimated date of 1500 B.C. does not seem excessive for the first evidences of a pottery-making, agricultural people inhabiting the forests of the Petén during the Mamom phase of the Maya Formative period. The Formative period is terminated at about A.D. 300,[1] the date at which fully developed forms of Maya architecture, art, and the Initial Series calendrical dating appear. These traits mark the Maya Classic period (Tzakol and Tepeu phases), which lasted from A.D. 300 to approximately 900. The cessation of the Initial Series system of dating and the desertion of the great sites of the southern part of the lowlands provide a break in the sequence dividing the Classic and Postclassic periods. The Postclassic, a time at which nearly all lowland Maya activity was focused in northern Yucatán, is the final period, ending with the Spanish conquest of 1519–40. Throughout this entire time span of Maya prehistory, life was based essentially upon the cultivation of maize by jungle farming. With this background in mind—a 3,000-year history of agricultural civilization in a forested, tropical environment—we turn to settlement patterns.

A great many problems surround the matter of Maya settlements in the lowlands, but the two which we shall consider in this brief essay seem most fundamental at the present stage of research. The first problem, or question, is a double-barreled one, but it is impossible to treat the two halves separately because their interrelationship is obvious. What were the size and composition of the Maya living community, and what was the relationship between the living community and the ceremonial center? As will be evident in the ensuing discussion, this question cannot be answered satisfactorily at the present time, but it is basic to all research into prehistoric settlement in the area. The second question is a demographic one: What changes, if any, occurred in population size and grouping throughout the full run of Maya prehistory?

THE FORMATIVE PERIOD

Most of the accumulated knowledge of field archaeology in the Maya lowlands derives from investigations of major sites, where large pyramids, platform mounds, and imposing architectural remains (hereafter referred to as "ceremonial centers") have attracted attention. This has resulted from the difficult conditions of tropical vegetation cover—in which small mounds and building foundations are extremely hard to locate and examine—rather than any lack of interest on the part of the archaeologists. Well over a hundred large ceremonial centers have been surveyed and explored in the lowland area (see Morley, 1946; Thompson, 1954), and, undoubtedly, there are a great many more which are smaller and unrecorded. Most of the ceremonial centers, at least as far as their principal edifices can be dated, belong to the Classic period; however, we know that platform mounds, pyramids, and temple or palace-type buildings make their appearance in the latter part of the Formative. The A-I structure at Uaxactun in the Petén clearly dates from the late Formative, and the E-VII-submound may be this early (A. L. Smith, 1950; Ricketson and Ricketson, 1937). To the north, in Yucatán, the mound at Yaxuná is Formative, as may be others at Santa Rosa Xtampak (Brainerd, 1951a).

Concerning the nature of the living community during the Formative period and its relationships to these ceremonial or large mound centers, Brainerd (1954, pp. 15 ff.) states that all or part of Maya settlements at this time may have been of substantial size but that there have not been sufficient excavation and survey to prove this. On the other hand, Shook and Proskouriakoff (1956) contend: "So far as we can tell, in Meso-America we are dealing at the outset with patterns of town settlement rather than with purely agricultural village communities." The data are too limited to resolve this difference of opinion, but what evidence there is from the lowlands does not indicate large Formative period settlements. At Uaxactun the early Formative, or Mamom, period occupation of that site appears to have covered little more than the top of the knoll of what later became E Group, an area about 200 meters in diameter. For the late Formative, or Chicanel, phase there is again evidence that the E Group knoll was occupied, as was the somewhat larger A Group hill (about 350 meters in diameter). On the latter location the previously mentioned small ceremonial mound, A-I, was constructed. A Chicanel house mound was also discovered at a distance of about 800 meters from the Group A section of the ceremonial center (Wauchope, 1934). These Uaxactun data give the impression of very small villages or hamlets rather than towns. Such small villages became the seats of special or ceremonial buildings in the late Formative, and at this time at least some houses were occupied as much as a half-mile away from what may have been the "main" or "parent" community.

Recent work in the Belize Valley, at Barton Ramie (Willey, Bullard, and Glass, 1955), affords some additional information on this question of the size of Formative living communities. No ceremonial mounds have been identified with the Formative period at the Barton Ramie site, but several housemound locations have been dated, tentatively, as of this period. These mounds are rather widely spaced over a square mile of alluvial bottom land, with the implication that Formative period settlement at that site was in small hamlet clusters or isolated houses rather than a densely occupied town.

Turning to the second problem, that of changes in population size, there are only occasional clues from the Formative period. Shook and Proskouriakoff (1956) have noted that there is no valid case for increasing populations throughout the Formative period in the Guatemalan highlands. For the lowlands there are some few suggestions that such an increase may have taken place. The Uaxactun excavations reveal more extensive occupational and architectural debris for Chicanel than they do for the earlier Mamom phase; and at Barton Ramie the stratigraphic digging in house mounds gives us three or four times as many Chicanel house occupations as those dating from Mamom. Moreover, lowland sites and ceramic materials of a late Formative or Chicanel-like identification are reported in greater numbers than those for the early Formative.

The Classic Period

Although there is considerably more knowledge of Maya sites of the Classic period than for the Formative, the question of the size and form of the living community and its relationships to the ceremonial center is still a matter for dispute. Both Morley (1946, pp. 312–13) and Shook and Proskouriakoff hold that the ceremonial centers, with their temple and palace mounds grouped around rectangular courtyards, were nuclei of true cities or towns, with dwellings clustered in or closely around them. In this view they seem to be strongly influenced by Landa's sixteenth-century accounts of Yucatecan town or city life:

> Before the Spaniards had conquered that country, the natives lived together in towns in a very civilized fashion . . . in the middle of the town were their temples with beautiful plazas, and all around the temples stood the houses of the lords and priests, and then most of the important people. Thus came the houses of the richest and of those who were held in the highest estimation nearest to these, and at the outskirts of the town were the houses of the lower class.

Brainerd (1954, pp. 70 ff.) disagrees that this Yucatecan town pattern of the conquest time can be projected back into the Classic. It is his feeling that the town, as both a reality and a concept, was a Toltec-Mexican introduction into Yucatán and a phenomenon of the Postclassic period. He visualizes the Classic settlement pattern as that of scattered single houses or hamlets, with the inhabitants of these dwellings gathering together to support, or celebrate in, the ceremonial centers. In this he is supported by Thompson (1954, pp. 43 ff.).

In this argument it is interesting that Brainerd and Morley each quote the Uaxactun house-mound survey to bolster their respective points of view. The former is of the opinion that the Uaxactun data indicate a dispersed, rural population, while the latter feels that they demonstrate a loosely compacted urbanism. This Uaxactun house-mound survey (Ricketson and Ricketson, 1937) revealed a total of seventy-eight house mounds in an area totaling 0.3 mile of the habitable terrain surrounding the ceremonial precincts at the site. This is a dense occupation on a house-per-acreage basis even if one follows Ricketson's assumption that only one-quarter of the house mounds were in use at any one time; however, it must be kept in mind that the actual distribution of the seventy-eight mounds extended over an area of 2 miles in both north-south and east-west diameters.[2] Perhaps the difficulty here is a matter of definitions: What is a village? A town? What is "densely settled"? My own thinking tends to coincide with Brainerd's in seeing the Uaxactun settlement as scattered rural rather than as an urban concentration.

Another lowland region where house-mound surveys have been carried out, the Belieze Valley, presents a picture of ceremonial-center–dwelling-site relationships that differs somewhat from either of the two aforementioned conceptions, although it is somewhat closer to the Brainerd interpretation (Willey, Bullard, and Glass, 1955; Willey and Bullard, 1956). In this valley the house mounds are found along the alluvial terraces in groups varying in size from five or six up to three hundred. Such house-mound groups may lie immediately adjacent to a ceremonial center, as at Baking Pot (Ricketson, 1929), or may be as much as 7 or 8 miles from any important center. It is a logical possibility that the inhabitants of several such dwelling groups may have acted in concert to build and maintain a religious and political center on the order of the nearby centers of Baking Pot or Benque Viejo (Thompson, 1940). In this case the settlement could hardly be considered to be a "city" but rather a series of near-contiguous villages, or even towns, focusing upon a major ceremonial center. It in interesting to note that in each group of a dozen or more house mounds there is at least one mound, or mound-plaza unit, that is appreciably larger than the others and whose presence suggests that some local and small-scale politico-religious activities were carried on within the small dwelling groups as well as in the great centers.

In attempting to sum up this problem of ceremonial-center–dwelling-site relationships for the Classic period, there seem to be three logical and abstract settlement-type possibilities: First, there is the one in which (Type A) the ceremonial center is surrounded by dwellings which are so closely spaced that their inhabitants could not have farmed immediately adjacent to them (Figure 26.1). This is nearest the conception of Morley, Shook, and Proskouriakoff. In the second type (Type B) the ceremonial center is without dwellings, and houses of the sustaining population are scattered singly over a wide surrounding area. The extent of such a sustaining area is unknown, but Ricketson offered an arbitrary estimate of a 10-mile radius for Uaxactun. This seems reasonable, particularly in regions where foot transportation was the only means of going to and from the ceremonial center. This type would seem to be closest to Brainerd's views. The third idealized type (Type C) is similar to B in that there is no appreciable population concentrated in the ceremonial center, but the sustaining populations are spotted through the surrounding country in hamlets or small villages rather than in individual houses. It is further suggested that some of these hamlets maintained small ceremonial buildings in their own midst. This may be the type of settlement in the Belize Valley, with, however, the significant modification that the hamlets and villages are distributed "ribbon-wise" along the river. In such a case river travel would have been the obvious means of transport.

It should be emphasized that these are only projected ideal types for prehistoric settlement in the Maya lowlands. There is no reason why combinations of these types might not be nearer actuality, nor need any type have prevailed throughout the entire area and Classic period. Thompson (1954, pp. 43 ff.) and others have described the modern Maya pattern of a town center with church, plaza, and market, around which were the houses of its citizenry. These houses were occupied seasonally, on market days, or during fiestas, while several miles distant from the town were the scattered bush houses in which the same people lived while working their milpas. Such would be a combination of Type A with Type B or C. For the present, however, these types are but working hypotheses. The task facing the archaeologist is to check house concentrations, or lack of same, in the immediate environs of ceremonial centers and to plot their occurrences and spacings in the miles of jungle that surround these centers—no mean chore!

The question of lowland Maya population increase between Formative and Classic or within the Classic period is also a moot one. The fact that many more Classic ceremonial centers are known than are reported for the Formative is by no means conclusive as to population growth. Ceremonial-center construction was undoubtedly greater in the later

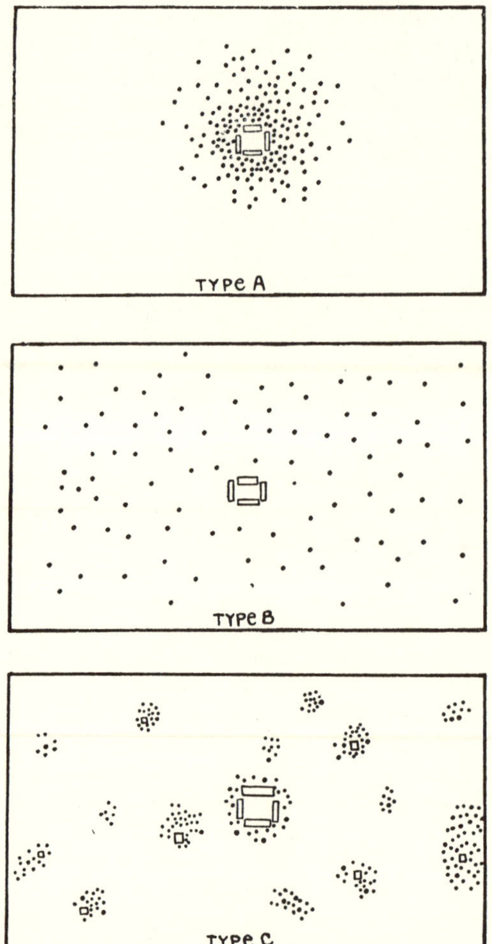

Figure 26.1. Idealized settlement types of the lowland Maya, A, B, and C, showing relationships of ceremonial center to house mounds or locations. Major ceremonial centers indicated by small rectangles in plaza arrangement, houses by dots. There is no exact scale for these diagrams. In Type A, houses are packed in close to the ceremonial center; in Type B houses are dotted over the landscape at a half to a quarter of a mile apart; in Type C houses are grouped in hamlet or village clusters, with some near the major ceremonial center but many others in outlying hamlets. The small rectangles in some of the larger hamlet clusters of the Type C pattern represent small ceremonial constructions whose importance is assumed to be local and subsidiary to that of the major center.

period, but it is also a strong probability that many of these sites were also occupied in the earlier period. As to house-mound counts, only five of the Uaxactun small mounds were excavated and are, therefore, datable by their ceramic contents (Wauchope, 1934); one of these was Formative, the other four Classic. In the Belize Valley, at Barton Ramie, we have sampled the pottery in thirty-nine house mounds (as of 1955) out of a group which numbers over three hundred. A preliminary appraisal of these ceramics shows an increase of about four-to-one between Classic and Formative house occupations. Further, late Classic occupations by far outnumbered those of the early Classic. The stability of the community is attested to by the fact that many of the mounds had been used as house platforms continuously from Formative to Classic times. This is very limited evidence upon which to base any generalizations as regards population changes in the Belize Valley as a whole, let alone the entire Maya lowlands; still the trend revealed in this sampling is that of steady increase.

The Postclassic Period

One of the most startling settlement phenomena of Middle American prehistory occurs with the change from Classic to Postclassic. This is the apparent abandonment of the southern Maya lowlands. This abandonment is noted in all the southern ceremonial centers, where construction and stelae dates cease after about A.D. 900. And, from the data available, the events of the ceremonial centers appear to be paralleled in the domestic sites. Ceramics or other materials datable as Postclassic are rare in the Petén and the Belize Valley. As is well known, the only great Postclassic sites of the lowlands are in the plains of northern Yucatán. Chichén Itzá is an old Puuc Classic ceremonial center, considerably enlarged under Toltec influence. The urban quality of the site is not fully known, but there are many house mounds in the immediate vicinity. Mayapan, which reached its zenith somewhat later than Chichén, is an urban zone. Three by 2 kilometers in extent, it is encircled by a great wall within which are some four thousand house mounds (Jones, 1952). The houses are arranged in random fashion, but at the center of the site is a ceremonial center with plazas and pyramid mounds. There is, then, some indication that the Postclassic Maya of northern Yucatán were urbanized and that the concept of the city or town as a fortified position had come into vogue. This, as Brainerd and others have suggested, may well be the result of Toltec and Mexican influences. Yet the walled city is not common in Yucatán. Tulum (Lothrop, 1924), on the east coast of Quintana Roo, is the only other notable example, and the wall inclosure here does not appear to embrace the great house-mound concentrations found at Mayapan.

There is no information on population size change between lowland Classic and Postclassic. Chichén Itzá and Mayapan appear larger than the Puuc ceremonial centers which preceded them in the northern lowlands, but nothing has been reported upon the size or form of Puuc domestic settlements. Populations may have been more densely concentrated in the Postclassic, but there is nothing to indicate that they were, in an overall sense, larger.

Comment

Prehistoric settlement in the Maya lowlands is still a matter for speculation and debate rather than for statement of fact. Ceremonial centers, with temple and palace mounds, were obvious nuclei for the ancient populations of these regions from the latter part of the Formative period, if not earlier. The question as to just how the population grouped itself around these centers—whether in concentrated town fashion, in a dispersed rural manner, or in scattered hamlets—cannot be answered without extensive field surveys and excavations. There are some indications that the population increased more or less steadily from early Formative to late Classic times; but this trend needs checking in many different localities. Following the desertion, or near-desertion, of the southern part of the lowland area, building activity was concentrated in northern Yucatán, a region which also came under strong Mexican influence after A.D. 900. The concept of the town, as a tight population grouping around a ceremonial center, sometimes fortified, may have been introduced into Yucatán from Mexico. Or this concept, as reported upon by the early Spanish, may have been the final expression of an old and deep tradition of the Maya lowlands.

Until we have more real knowledge of Maya settlement, the archaeologist will be in no position to attack the problems of demography or of prehistoric agricultural techniques and productiveness. Arguments of milpas versus intensive farming (Ricketson and Ricketson, 1937) will remain insoluble until we can pin down the facts of habitation.

Notes

[1]Dates for the opening and close of the Classic period follow the 11.16.0.0.0, or Goodman-Thompson, correlation of Mayan and Christian calendars.

[2]The Uaxactun house-mound survey was made in a great cruciform zone, each arm of the cross being 400 yards wide and 1 mile long. The ceremonial precincts were situated near the center of the cross.

27

The Structure of Ancient Maya Society

(From *American Anthropologist*, Vol. 58, pp. 777–782, 1956. Reprinted by permission of American Anthropological Association. Not for sale or further reproduction.)

It has been a somewhat generally accepted opinion of Maya scholars that the structure of old Maya society was severely dichotomized into a village folk and a ceremonial center, or urban, elite. Obviously, there is much to support this view. The great politico-religious centers of the Late Formative (*ca.* 1000 B.C. to 200 A.D.) and Classic (*ca.* 200 to 900 A.D.). periods with their impressive temple and palace architecture, elaborate tombs, and the records of calendrical science and hieroglyphic texts carved on stone, stand in dramatic contrast to a jungle village of thatched huts. It is not my purpose to argue here that there was no gulf whatsoever between the Maya farmer of Classic times and his theocratic betters. Such a separation did exist. It is the profundity of the split that I question. There is, it is true, a reasonable continuity and parallel between the life and culture of the common Maya villagers of the past and their present-day counterparts. On the other side, there is also a partial analogy between the Spanish urban-Catholic church tradition and the prehistoric Mayan theocratic tradition. Both represent centers of authority toward which the village Indian faced or faces; both were nuclei of civilizations and ideologies which penetrated in a less than full manner into the world of the simple farming communities. I think, however, that the qualification *partial* should be emphasized. An overstress on this analogy has perhaps been responsible for a too ready acceptance of ancient Maya social structure as but an image of historic and modern times.

Recent archaeological data from the Maya lowlands of the Belize Valley. British Honduras,[1] and the inferences drawn from them, lead me to believe that the relationship between rural village and ceremonial center may have been considerably more tight-knit than the conventional picture would have it. These new data pertain to systematic field work on prehistoric settlements of small dwelling mounds. To date, there has been relatively little investigation into the problem of settlement patterns in the Maya lowlands (Ricketson and Ricketson 1937; Wauchope 1934; Ruppert and Smith 1952). This is particularly true of studies on the remains of what appear to be ordinary domestic buildings, and the distribution and relation of these domestic sites to the ceremonial units. Because of this lack it has been difficult to compare and contrast village community with ceremonial center.

To begin with, the very nature of the Belize Valley village sites supports the theory that the majority of the Classic period Maya from this region were at least a semisophisticated peasantry rather than a rustic and primitive folk. The settlements are found as clusters of small house mounds dotted along the alluvial terraces of the river or on nearby hillslopes. These house-mound clusters run in a more or less continuous distribution from the Guatemalan frontier for a distance of some 30 airline miles to the north and east.[2] Mound clusters will range from groups of a dozen or so to 300 or more. The mounds themselves are small oval or oblong tumuli of earth and rocks. They are the result of the construction of successive and superimposed house platforms. Refuse of general living is found in and around them, and burials have been made under the floor levels or in the mound slopes. In most clusters there are usually found one or more mounds of larger size, suggesting a pyramid base for a small temple or a high platform for a palace-like structure. At the Melhado site (Willey and Bullard 1956) a group of a dozen small house platforms surround a little pyramid mound near the center of the cluster. The site of Nohoch Ek, on a hilltop bordering the river valley, consists of a plaza group of ceremonial buildings and a number of small mounds, presumably house platforms, on the nearby hillside (Coe and Coe 1956). At Barton Ramie (Willey, Bullard, and Glass 1955), where we mapped over 250 mounds within an area of about one square mile, there is a single pyramid, 12 meters high, located near one end of the house-mound distribution. There are also several other Barton Ramie mounds, larger than the small house tumuli, which may have been residential units built around small plazas or may have been platforms for buildings of some public function. This occurrence of what appear to be minor ceremonial mounds in the village house-mound clusters would seem to strengthen the case for a relatively widespread distribution of a ritual and religious life that had some association with temple buildings similar to those of the major centers. We cannot tell, of course, just how much the content of the ceremonial life of the villages had in common with that of the greater centers. Yet the continuous riverine and hillslope settlement of the Belize Valley—with its house mounds clustered around small special buildings, with at least three ceremonial sites of middling size (Banana Bank, Baking Pot, Cahal Pech; see Ricketson 1929; Satterthwaite 1951), and with its one impressive ceremonial center at Xunantunich (Benque Viejo; Thompson 1940)—creates the impression of a large but well-integrated network of theocratic stations and substations, all supported by a peasantry indoctrinated with many of the values of urban life.

Ceramic and other remains from the Belize Valley small house-mound settlements also imply a relative "worldliness" for Maya village society and culture of the district. For example, burials found in house refuse and dating from the Early Classic (Tzakol, 200 to 600 A.D.) period are accompanied by basal-flanged polychrome bowls of fine quality and by Teotihuacan-like tripod jars. Such specimens are virtually identical to "luxury" finds from ceremonial centers. Furthermore, the refuse sherds under floors or in debris dumps off the flanks of the mounds include a substantial percentage of Early Classic polychrome pieces as well as numerous slab-footed tripod jars. This situation seems to be in marked contrast to one noted recently by S. F. de Borhegyi (1956:348) in the Guatemalan highlands. There, the Teotihuacan-like pieces did not occur outside of the ceremonial precincts, and Borhegyi sees in this an urban, upper-class possession of luxury trade goods, or imitations of such exotics, and their absence in the life of the village farmers. The British Honduras occurrence of these items in what is clearly a rural context, several miles from a ceremonial center of any size or significance, suggests that these people were, in Redfield's (1953:31) definition of the term, "peasant" rather than "folk." They were, moreover, a peasantry participating in an appreciable amount of the wealth and, perhaps, the ideology of the associated urban culture of the time.

In the succeeding Late Classic (Tepeu) period (600 to 900 A.D.) the Teotihuacan-like pottery disappears from the Belize Valley sites, but there are still good indications of intimate connections with the urban world. A burial found in a plaza floor of a small mound complex had as furniture a ceremonial celt, a monolithic axe, and a curious wrench-shaped object, all of polished stone. On the axe was a faint and rather badly scrawled Ahau glyph. Around the neck of the individual in the grave, an adult male, a small but handsome gorget of carved jade had been placed. This and other Late Classic burials found in the Belize Valley house mounds had fine pottery in association, and polychrome figure-painted ware as well as vessels with elaborately carved designs were found in domestic refuse.

All of these British Honduras discoveries add up, I think, to a conception of a Maya peasant class that was reasonably prosperous and participating in a cultural tradition not markedly apart from the inhabitants of the great religious centers. The essential differences between rural village and ceremonial center in the Belize Valley, insofar as these differences can be seen archaeologically, is that the latter possess the great architecture, monumental art, and writing. The somewhat poorly rendered glyph on the monolithic axe found with the burial of the distinguished villager is a nice proof that the hieratic learning of the theocratic circles had not gone unnoticed in the peasant sphere, and that within this sphere an appreciation and value was placed upon this symbol of learning, even though the owner of the axe and his friends may have had not the slightest notion of what it meant.

In his analysis of prehistoric Maya society, in referring to Spanish and later impingements upon the Maya village, Borhegyi (1956:352) states: "In spite of constant exposure to these many new ideas, the Maya farmer seems to have been as little affected by them as he was by the pressure of theocracy, or by the Mexican invasions." If I understand him correctly, he sees the old ceremonial center urbanism of Classic Maya civilization and the Toltec-Mexican militaristic urbanism of later prehistoric times, as effecting no more change upon the basic folkways of the Maya farming village than did the later urbanism of Europe or of the modern industrial age. This, in my opinion, overstates the case for the division within ancient Maya society. Borhegyi's data are, of course, largely from the Guatemalan uplands, and it would be unwise to assume that highland and lowland Maya would necessarily follow the same course of development in this regard. Yet as regards both regions, it should not be forgotten that the urbanism of Spain was an alien force in the Maya land. Its roots and traditional hearth lay thousands of miles away in another hemisphere. Its policies were foreign, and in a determined effort to mold the Maya in its own image its acts must have had, or appeared to have, a harsh and arbitrary quality. Possibly the invading Mexicans and their ideology also had a strangeness that would alienate the conquered and widen the breach between peasant and ruler. But the Maya theocratic leadership was, as far as we can tell, a local development.[3] It had arisen from the ancestral peoples and culture of the small village life of the Early Formative or even unknown earlier periods. It drew its form and content from the Maya heritage. Its powers could, of course, have become oppressive to the governed; but one would presume there would be less of a strain between the component parts of a society in such a historical situation than in one where the upper-class ideology was relatively new and foreign.

We have little in the way of an exact idea as to how the bonds between peasant and urban segments of Classic Maya society were maintained, but it is likely that the ceremonial centers recruited artisans, retainers, and even some levels of the priesthood from peasant groups. The numerous ceremonial type constructions referred to in the Belize Valley, ranging all the way from a major site, such as Xunantunich, down to the small temple buildings in the villages or hamlets, suggest that a hierarchial ordering or priestly chain of command probably existed, and that certain individuals may have found their way up or down the line of the system. There is evidence, too, that as the Classic period progressed, an increasingly greater homogeneity was obtained in Maya culture. Borhegyi (1956:349–350) has described how the elements of the old village religious cults, as exemplified by the three-pronged incense burners, figurines, and animal effigy whistles, once again appeared in the ceremonial centers, and this same trend is also true of the lowlands. It can be interpreted as the passing of peasant beliefs and influence into the metropolitan sphere, and of a wider social participation in the formulation of religious ideology for the culture as a whole. In fact, it must have been in just such a close symbiosis between center and peasant community that urbanism and civilization came into being in Classic Maya times. For the formal demographic requirements of urbanism, in the strictest sense, do not seem to be present in the Maya lowlands in Classic times. Except on a late Postclassic level, at places like Mayapan and Tulum, there are no large, densely packed population concentrations known for the lowlands. Yet lacking this, the Maya achieved city life in the broader sense, for many of the attributes of civilization, as defined by Childe (1950) or Redfield (1953: Chapters I and III), are clearly present. It is doubtful that such accomplishments as writing, monumental public works, the beginnings of astronomical science, and a privileged ruling class could have come into being within a society whose component parts were as seriously riven as was the case in the Maya regions during the Spanish Colonial period. Maya civilization was the creation of a society which, for the very fact of its dispersed physical settlement, was necessarily linked together by unusually strong ties.

Finally, this leads us to the question of the collapse of Maya civilization. Various explanations have been offered, and these will not be recounted here. One theme, though, that has been frequently considered is that of social breakdown or internal revolt, possibly triggered by crop failure, drought, or soil exhaustion, but made inevitable by the basic schism between theocrat and farmer. This may have been what happened, but I believe this interpretation is less attractive in the light of current evidence. If we accept the internal revolt theory, it would be reasonable to expect that life, albeit on a somewhat reduced scale, continued in the Maya villages after the abandonment of the great lowland ceremonial centers of the south at the close of the Classic period. Not a single one of the numerous test excavations in the Belize Valley has brought to light ceramic or other evidence that would demonstrate a Postclassic period occupation of any of the village house mounds. If collapse occurred—and, indeed, something did occur—Maya priest and peasant collapsed and vanished together.

Notes

[1]From a four-year survey (1953–56) conducted by the author under auspices of the Peabody Museum, Harvard University, and financed largely by the National Science Foundation.

[2]Our survey was confined to this river valley section. Mounds begin in the limestone hill country, some 40 miles back from the coast, and extend to the Guatemalan line. They probably extend on west and south, but our survey was terminated at this point.

[3]Most authorities feel that the hierarchic elements of Maya civilization were developed within the Maya area, either highland or lowland. This usually assumes that the peoples of the earlier Formative periods were of Maya race and speech and that their various cultures were an important source for Classic civilization. One significant dissent has been raised by Meggers (1954) who believes that an unfavorable jungle environment could not have permitted the original development of Classic Maya in the lowland regions.

V

METHOD AND THEORY

There are only two essays in this collection that deal with archaeological "method and theory" per se. "Archaeological Theories and Interpretation: New World" was prepared for the 1952 congress on anthropology held under the aegis of the Wenner-Gren Foundation in New York City. I doubt if I would have written the paper if I had not received an invitation to do so. On reflection, I realize that I have never been intensely interested in "method and theory," at least in the abstract. I say this despite the fact that I have collaborated in two other articles (Phillips and Willey, 1953; Willey and Phillips, 1955) and a book (Willey and Phillips, 1958) on this subject. It is not that I do not appreciate the vital importance of both method and theory in our discipline; it is just that they do not capture my imagination in the way that other aspects of archaeology and culture history do. Consequently, when I address "method and theory," I find myself responding more to the ideas of others than generating ideas of my own. In "Archaeological Theories and Interpretation: New World," I began with what I called "Methodological Structure," and it is obvious that I was influenced by what Walter Taylor (1948) had written in his *Study of Archaeology*. I saw archaeology as having two tasks: the ordering of the data in space and time (Taylor's "chronicle"), and the consideration of these data in their total contexts—contexts that would lead to an understanding of the processes that had been involved in culture development and change (Taylor's "historiography"). I referred to the basic factors of form, space, and time in archaeology; Albert Spaulding (1960) was later to describe and discuss these very elegantly as "the dimensions of archaeology." I discussed typology, including "the type as a reality" and the "type as an archaeological construct," and went on to talk about seriation, stratigraphy, and ceramic change through time and space. I was also at pains to point out that all ceramic variation need not reflect temporal or spatial difference but might, instead, relate to use or function.

I never did grapple with theory, as contrasted with method, although this was not unusual for an American archaeologist at that time. I conceived of archaeological theory as pertaining to either "diffusion" or "evolution." To try to explain how "theories" had affected American archaeology, I turned to what I called "Some Prevailing Americanist Reconstructions." These were the "direct-historical approach," as it had been applied on the North American Great Plains; the "traditions" and "co-traditions" concepts, as employed in Andean prehistory; the Andean "horizon styles" as indicators of diffusion processes; and "developmental levels" or "stages" of culture in Mesoamerica and Peruvian cultures as they exemplified evolution.

"A Consideration of Archaeology" was written almost a quarter of a century after "Archaeological Theories and Interpretation: New World." Again, it was the result of an invitation, this time from the editor of the journal *Daedalus* who was then assembling an issue on the current state of the social sciences. Whereas in the 1953 paper I was responding to Walter Taylor's (1948) *A Study of Archaeology*, in this one I was responding to Lewis Binford and the "new archaeology." I began by making clear my agreements with the "new archaeology's" acceptance of a systemic view of cultures and societies—past and present—and with its goals of understanding the processes of culture change. I recognized the operational wisdom and necessity of the testing of analogical models. I also shared the "new archaeological" optimism about the possibilities of discovering "regularities" in cultural and social change. I took Binford's (1968) side (though I don't know if he would agree with me on the particulars) in his debate with M. I. Finley (1971). The crux of their argument was culture context. In any given instance, such as that of Classical Greek culture, which Finley cites, how much social "width and depth" can we reconstruct? It is true that we cannot divine the precise social status of the workers who built the Parthenon by looking at the architecture and art of that building alone. But we could still say that if Classical archaeologists had a better knowledge of how the common man of those times lived, we might be in a more favorable position to offer an informed opinion on the "free" versus "slave" status of its builders—a question Finley had raised as one that lay beyond the range of "material residues" archaeology.

I devoted much of my article to analogy, going back to statements I had made almost 25 years before (Willey 1953d). Then I had defined what I called "general comparative analogy" as analogy based on cross-cultural, "everyday" observances of human social and cultural behavior. I contrasted this with "specific historical analogy," which demanded that the archaeological culture under consideration and the living ethnographic or historical model evoked as a means of understanding the past be in the same culture-historical tradition. An example of specific historical analogy is the interpretation of prehistoric underground structures as *kivas* in Southwestern United States archaeology, where the obvious descendants of the ancient Pueblo Indians, living in the same area as their forebears, today still construct and use *kivas* for religious rites. In my 1977 paper I defined still another kind of analogy, which I called "specific comparative analogy." In this, the archaeologist works from a complete cultural and social model which is obviously *not* in the same culture-historical tradition as the prehistoric culture under study. "Specific comparative analogy" shares a cross-cultural point of view with "general comparative analogy," but the model is not a randomly assembled one, based upon a general knowledge of human behavior, but rather one derived from a complete and functioning culture. Flannery's (1968a) use of the historically known Southeast Asian Shan and Kachin societies in his attempt to understand prehistoric Olmec society in Mexico was my source for such a concept.

28

Archaeological Theories and Interpretation: New World

(From *Anthropology Today*, A. L. Kroeber and others, eds., pp. 361–385, University of Chicago Press, 1953. Reprinted by permission of University of Chicago.)

Introductory

This paper is a consideration of some of the principal archaeological theories now current in the interpretations of the prehistoric scene in the New World. These theories are intimately involved with both the methods and the results of American archaeology. For, as problems are conceived in theory, the attack upon problems is similarly conceived, and methods are selected or forged for this purpose. Likewise, as theory sets up the problem frame of reference, results are inevitably conditioned. For these reasons, in examining Americanist archaeological theories, we will turn, first, to methodological structure to see how theory is interwoven with this structure; and, second, we will analyze some of the resultant constructs of American data, relating these to theory. In so doing, there will be overlap with colleagues who are treating, respectively, method and result; nevertheless, theory is the central theme of this presentation.

Methodological Structure

Archaeology is concerned with history both in the broader sense of context and process, as these may be traced through the past, and in the narrower sense of space and time systematization of data. Taylor (1948) has made the useful distinction between the former, which he refers to as "historiography," and the latter, which he has termed "chronicle." These are, in effect, the two major objectives of modern archaeology: (1) processual understanding and (2) skeletal chronology and distribution. Although this concept of the duality of these objectives (history as a chronicle versus history as process) is valid from an analytical standpoint, operationally the archaeologist must have both objectives in mind. Even the barest sort of chronological-distributional study of artifact forms is necessarily linked with implicit theory involving cultural process. Similarly, antiquarian or purely "phenomenological" interest in artifacts is not entirely bereft of its functional or processual side, for the mere fact that the object is recognized as something made by man is tied to assumptions about past human conduct.

The objectives of archaeology, defined in this way, are approached by the study and manipulation of three basic factors: form, space, and time. The forms are the phenomena themselves, the prehistoric creations or manufactures. These may be dealt with in their individual uniqueness or in their similarity, the latter being the typological approach to the data of form. Space and time are the dimensions of the inquiry. Either or both may be coordinated with form to give the historical skeleton or chronicle of the particular datum or data under investigation. Forms may, by themselves, be relevant to function or process (as implied by shape and other inherent qualities), or, taken together with space and time coordinates, they may suggest cultural processes such as diffusion or independent development.

The basic factors of form, space, and time are not dealt with in the abstract but within either or both of two systems of contextual reference: the natural and the cultural. The natural context refers to environmental conditions as these may be revealed in landscape and climate or in the past geological records of these conditions. Such contexts have a bearing both on functional interpretation (cultural-environmental adjustments or failures to adjust) and space-time systematics (geological dating, tree-ring dating, etc.). The cultural context derives from our acceptance of artifactual remains as products of human culture. It is the context that allows for the historical tracing of prehistoric-to-ethnohistoric developments and for the functional interpretation of dead remains in the light of the living or documented situation. It has as its deepest basis the commonality of all humankind as creators and bearers of culture, but it may also be viewed in limited frames of reference for specific problems.

Archaeological studies or approaches to the prehistoric data follow along two fundamental lines. These are the lines set by the major objectives: history (as limited chronicle) and process. As noted, it is virtually impossible to follow one line to the complete exclusion of the other, but there are definite tendencies of emphasis. For example, Americanist studies over the last thirty years have been largely preoccupied with historical rather than processual objectives, and archaeological problems have been framed in accordance with this emphasis. But, whatever the tendency, it is quite clear that there are in both the historical and processual approaches differing and advancing levels of interpretative complexity. These stages of complexity in interpretation grow out of the varying concordances and correlations of the basic factors of form, space, and time and the contextual systems of natural and cultural reference. Utilization of the basic factors along the complementary historical and processual lines may be charted as shown in Figure 28.1.

On the first level of complexity under the historical category, we have two operations: (1) the identification of specific forms or descriptive typology and (2) the identification of cultural assemblages through descriptive typology and association. Paralleling this, in the processual category, we have: (1) functional or use identification of specific forms and (2) functional interpretation of cultural assemblages of forms or features. On this first level the factors of time and space do not enter directly into the interpretations either in the historical or in the processual categories. The initial historical operation—the identification of specific forms and their classification under a purely descriptive typology could be, in itself, a consideration of phenomena for the sake of phenomena alone. This is rarely the case, and "phenomenology" is not generally regarded as archaeology. Usually, the initial

Problem Objectives	Levels of Interpretative Complexity: First	Second	Third
Historical (Descriptive identification and space-time arrangements of data)	1. Identification of specific forms or descriptive typology 2. Identification of cultural assemblages through descriptive typology	1. Culture continuity and change with references to specific areas 2. Culture continuity and change with reference to the specific chronology of an archaeological site or zone	1. Culture continuity and change in both space and time dimensions
Processual (Functional or use identification and interpretations of data)	1. Functional or use interpretation of specific forms 2. Functional interpretation of cultural assemblages of forms or features	1. Functional interpretations of cultural forms or assemblages with reference to specific areas 2. Functional interpretations of cultural forms or assemblages with reference to the specific chronology of an archaeological site or zone	1. Functional interpretation of cultural forms or assemblages with reference to both area and chronology (usually on a wide scale)

Figure 28.1

identifying or typological step is geared to a space-time problem of the second level, and this problem motivation is reflected in the organization of the particular typology. Archaeological typology in the United States has reflected this trend in recent years, especially as it concerns ceramics. There has been a growing conviction that pottery types as descriptive categories are valueless unless the categories or types also serve as exponents of spatial and temporal differentiation in the study of cultural materials (see Ford, 1949, p. 40; Drucker, 1943, p. 35; Krieger, 1944; Willey, 1949b, p. 5). This view seems justifiable as long as the problem is essentially one of space and time correlations. It is, of course, conceivable that a quite different typological breakdown of the same material could be set up for the study of problems of use or function of pottery. In either case, however, the problems pitched on the second and third levels of the interpretative complexity are the determinants for the typological operation of the first level, and such typology is thereby drawn into line with historical or processual objectives at its instigation.

The identification of cultural assemblages through descriptive typology has been conceived of as a step in archaeological analysis and synthesis without reference to space or time factors. This has been the *modus operandi* of the American Midwestern Taxonomic System (McKern, 1939). It is true that neither space nor time correlates are overtly expressed in this system of archaeological culture classification; yet the concept of the assemblage is implicitly grounded in the historical validity of the artifact-feature complex as a *unit*. Such a unity, by the very nature of its internal associations, bespeaks spatial-temporal correlates. The *component*, the classificatory unit of the Midwestern system, is an assemblage with a geographical locus (the site) and has sometimes been defined as a time level (period) represented in the human occupation of a particular geographic site. The *focus*, the first order on the ascending taxonomic scale in the Midwestern system, is an abstraction based upon the close typological similarity of two or more *components*. If typological similarity is any indicator of cultural relatedness (and this is surely axiomatic to archaeology), then such relatedness carries with it implications of a common or similar history for the *focus*. The same reasoning applies as foci are classifed under *aspects*, as aspects are grouped together into *phases*, and as phases are merged as *patterns*. The degree of trait similarity lessens as one works upward in the Midwestern taxonomic hierarchy, and presumably the closeness of historical ties also lessens; yet historical systematization is still inherent in the classification. That this should be so is not, in itself, a drawback. Perhaps the most serious flaw in the Midwestern system is its historicogenetic rigidity. Certain lines and degrees of relationship are laid down from one classificatory order or level to the next, with the result that the extremely complex interrelationships of cultural descent and diffusion are obscured by the arbitrariness of the system. Eventually, the end-product may become as nearly ahistorical as the original classificatory operations of the system, although in a quite different and unintended way.

As there is covert historical theory in the assemblage concept and in the Midwestern Taxonomic System, so there is comparable hidden functional implication. The unity of the assemblage, if historical unity can be assumed, must lead to the conclusion that we are dealing with the remains of an integrated cultural complex in the case of the *component*. The tool types, weapon forms, and settlement traces reflect ancient patterns of behavior that had been welded, with greater or lesser firmness, into a functioning whole. If the data are sufficient, an interpretation of this kind (i.e., hunting community, sedentary village agriculturists, etc.) is certainly feasible on this level. Such functional interpretation is, of course, possible because of the natural and cultural contextual backgrounds which are available even on this simplest level of interpretative complexity. Site ecology provides one such context, while ethnological or modern analogies to artifacts and architectural features afford another.

The second and third levels of interpretative complexity are, in their historical objectives, concerned with the spatial and temporal arrangement of cultural forms. As stated, this has been the primary usage of artifact typology in American studies over the last three decades. On the second level we have two operations: area distribution studies of forms and chronological distribution studies of forms. These may be carried on independently of each other. Holmes's (1903) great work on the pottery of the eastern United States is an example of the former. In this study, ceramic types were plotted geographically over a wide area, and a number of regional correlations were established. These Holmes designated as "provinces." They were, in effect, areas, established solely upon the trait of pottery, without reference to time depth. The theoretical basis behind Holmes's reconstruction is that of the culture area (Wissler, 1926; Kroeber, 1931), a concept widely used in American ethnology. Each area was assumed to have a generative center which produced the distinctively regional types. At the margins of each area there were blendings with the types radiating from another center or centers. These blendings were assumed to result from diffusions, counterdiffusions, and mergers of ideas or actual products originating in the centers. The culture-area concept is still considered useful by American archaeologists and is widely employed, although with reservations. The obvious weakness derives from the attempt to infer the time dimension from the geographic-distributional picture alone. This is inherent in the idea of the generative center and its outlying margins with a time flow from center to margins. It has been demonstrated that neither geographical center nor point of cultural intensity or elaboration can be assumed to be the originative center of a type. In other words, the age-area construct is by no means infallible. For a space-time reconstruction other methods than the geographic-distribution study are necessary.

These methods are the principal ones by which culture continuity and change through time may be demonstrated: stratigraphy and seriation. Prior to 1912, stratigraphic studies on the American scene adhered rather closely to the geologic principles of stratigraphy. Sharp distinctions in physical strata were correlated with changes in cultural types.

Sometimes these strata involved natural soil deposition; or in other cases such as that of Uhle's (1903) stratigraphy at Pachacamac in Peru, artifact types were correlated with major architectural and structural levels in a site. Between 1912 and 1924, Nelson (1916), Kroeber (1918), Spier (1919), and Kidder (1924) introduced a significant modification. This was the principle of the correlation of artifact change with relative depth. The method was applicable to refuse deposits which had grown by occupational accretion. Marked physical stratification of deposits was not necessary. The technique consisted of removing detritus and artifacts from arbitrary depth levels. In studying artifact change by levels, percentage fluctuations of types were noted from level to level, so that rising or declining percentage frequencies of types were correlated with time. Deriving in larger part from the mechanical nature of the operation, "continuous stratigraphy" of this kind had important theoretical repercussions on the nature of culture continuity and change. With the continuous depositional record of a site occupation before his eyes, the archaeologist could not help being impressed with the evidence for culture dynamics. A number of concepts were formulated to account for the vertical record in the earth. Types were seen in the refuse history at their inception, were observed approaching and attaining a maximum frequency, and were then traced upward to their "death" or disappearance. One type was seen to "replace" another in this time story. If the stylistic division between an earlier and a later type was sharp, it was hypothesized that new or foreign elements were introduced into the life of the site at a particular point in its history. On the other hand, if the intrinsic qualities of two types showed strong similarity and if their frequency histories allowed it, gradual evolutionary change from one type into another was postulated. These theories, born in the techniques of stratigraphic chronological measurement, served as the basis of functional interpretations with reference to the history of the site. Extended to studies of culture change and continuity over a wide area, the third level of interpretative complexity, they form much of the theoretical underpinning of complex functional interpretation.

J. A. Ford (1949, pp. 44–57; 1951, pp. 91–100) has been one of the chief exponents of time-change and continuity studies in American archaeology in recent years. Ford's interest has been concentrated largely upon the dynamics of cultural forms (pottery types) and upon the development of theory in connection with this. His graphic presentations of ceramic stratigraphy emphasize the quality of continuity. Individual types are seen as describing unimodal curves upon vertical scale graphs. These recapitulate "life-histories" of types, their origins, climaxes, and eventual disappearances. That types do behave in this fashion, although with varying rates of speed, seems amply demonstrated by stratigraphic evidences from innumerable archaeological sites. That there is also a tendency upon the part of the archaeologist occasionally to "force" certain types to conform to an expected unimodal curve seems probable. There are two complicating factors here. One is primarily mechanical. Refuse deposition at any site, or at any one location upon a site, may not give a continuous history of site occupation and artifact usage. In some instances these time gaps may be minor and irrelevant; in others they may be long and crucial. Occupation, desertion, and reoccupation may give an extremely fragmentary picture and one that makes a puzzling frequency graph unless the graph curve is "smoothed" to harmonize with what is conceived of as the normal occurrence pattern. Ford is cognizant of this difficulty but has relied upon large random sampling in site excavations to obviate it, feeling that the hiatus-reoccupation situation is the rare one rather than the rule.

The other complicating factor rises out of the hypothesis that typological change or variability in a site need not always be correlated with chronological change. Instead, it may have its origins in functional differentiation of artifact types. Brainerd (1951b, p. 307) has suggested that the irregularities in some of his graphs of Maya ceramics result from this; and he further postulates that graphic regularity may be fairly safely assumed to be an expression of time change, while marked irregularity may result from the sudden introduction of sacred or ceremonial wares into what had heretofore been kitchen dumps. Neither of these complicating factors is sufficient to invalidate the method of plotting continuous stratigraphy or of interpreting cultural continuity, gradual replacement, and evolutionary change from its results. They do, however, indicate that the method is not infallible and that it cannot be consistently employed without careful examination of refuse deposition and cautious trial and retrial of typological formulations.

Seriation, as it has been developed in American archaeology, refers to a "horizontal stratigraphy" of artifact types and their associations rather than to seriation by a priori stylistic or evolutionistic principles. Kroeber (1918) practiced it in its simplest form in the Zuñi region of the southwestern United States when he gathered and pocketed pottery-sherd collections from the surfaces of a number of ruins. These collections showed typological overlap, so that some sites were, for example, represented by types A and B, others by types B and C, and still others by types C and D. Assuming each collection to be a valid historical assemblage, it was evident that a seriation running from type A through type D was present. If, then, time direction could be introduced into the series by relating type D to the historic period at Zuñi, the seriation was transformed into a chronology by which the various sites from which the collections were made could be dated.

Ford has elaborated upon this principle in seriational studies in the Virú Valley of Peru (Ford, 1949) and in the Mississippi Valley (Phillips, Ford, and Griffin, 1951, pp. 213–36). By computing percentage frequencies of pottery types from site surface collections, he has arranged these frequencies and collections into a series. The seriation, however, does not follow along simple lines of typological overlap but is constructed, instead, to reproduce the unimodal curves of pottery-type life-histories comparable to those plotted from vertical refuse stratification. As is seen, this builds directly upon the theories of growth, climax, and decline for cultural forms. In general, it appears to be substantiated, in that the life-history curves of the seriated types tend to duplicate those of the vertical stratigraphy. There are, however, more complications and more possibilities for error with this method than with that of vertical continuous stratigraphy. In the first place, the surface collection is less likely to be a valid historical assemblage than is the subsurface deposit. Opportunities for mixture are, obviously, much greater. Secondly, it has not yet been satisfactorily determined that the surface pottery collection of any site is fully representative of all the types once used at that site. Deep and compact refuse sites may show no types characteristic of their earlier strata on the surface. This does not necessarily confuse the seriation, as such a surface collection would be accurately seriated in accordance with the later strata of occupation at the site. Reliance upon the date for the chronological placement of other features at the site would, though, be questionable. A third complication is the possibility that the surface collections of some sites do show a representative sample of several periods or span a time range three or four times as great as the surface collections of other sites. As all collections are treated as single assemblages, this relativity in the time compression involved is almost certain to produce some peculiar distortions. As with the stratigraphic method, Ford and other practitioners of percentile seriation are aware of these complications. Again, their reliance upon useful results is based upon a large sample and a feeling that the difficulties will tend to cancel out. The method undoubtedly has validity and is supported by other lines of evidence in many instances. My own feeling is that it can be considered as an instrument for gross sorting but not for precision analysis.

While Ford has been essentially interested in the perfection of space-time measurements. W. W. Taylor, Jr., has sounded a counternote in his long critique, "A Study of Archaeology" (1948). Taylor's interests are with descriptive integration and process rather than with spatial-temporal systematics. His "conjunctive approach," which is the bringing to bear of as many kinds of evidence as practical considerations permit in site excavation and analysis, is most directly concerned with what I have classed as functional interpretation of the second level of complexity. Taylor has made clear that he does not eschew historic chronicle or more sweeping historical and processual reconstructions as legitimate goals of archaeology. His attack is, rather, that space-time studies of a limited or broad-scale nature will proceed more soundly and effectively if we are better informed as to the mechanics of cultural process and that an understanding of process must begin with the fullest possible recovery of individual site information. Inasmuch as archaeological site excavation is permanently destructive, Taylor's argument is hard to refute. Archaeologists most assuredly have an obligation to their data, and it is incumbent upon them to make the fullest possible record. Yet of what should this record consist? It is impossible to gather all pertinent information because data are pertinent only in reference to a problem. This leads us to the question as to whether there are not some problems that can be framed only with reference to landmarks wider than the individual site. If there are—and there seem to be—do we not need the broader historical contexts in which to place them? And is it not essential for this historical orientation to push ahead of the more intensive analyses, particularly those aimed at functional understanding of a particular prehistoric community? This has, in any event, been the course of development in American archaeology. Whether it is the purest accident or whether there is inherent logic in what has happened remains a matter of speculation and debate. There is, in my mind, no doubt but that Taylor's critique has had a salutary influence on American archaeology. The old problem incentive of chronology and distributions of "cultures" in terms of a few marker "fossils" (usually potsherds) was not sufficient to attract archaeologists who were also anthropologists. Taylor's strictures helped crystallize this feeling of discontent.

From this outline of archaeological methodology, with particular reference to the Americas, it can be seen that theories of culture change and continuity are fundamental to archaeological studies of either a predominantly historical or predominantly functional orientation. At the outset, it must be recognized that certain assumptions concerning culture change and continuity underlie most systematic typology. It has been stated that typology with archaeological objectives reflects problem motivations and that these motivations are usually the need for spatial-temporal measuring instruments. This is grounded in the assumption that culture change is reflected in material manufactures and that this change proceeds in both temporal and spatial dimensions. There have been two ways of looking at this. One envisages culture change as a continuous stream, to be segmented into types as this best suits the archaeologist's purposes (Ford, 1949). The other view tends to conceive of types as once existent realities in the prehistoric culture under examination (Rouse, 1939). For the former position, the establishment of types is a purely arbitrary procedure, entirely imposed upon the prehistoric phenomena by the classifier. The second opinion sees the typological task more as the recognition of existent entities. The two outlooks are not fully antagonistic, and both seem to arrive at similar results. The concept of the arbitrary segmentation of the stream of culture change is predisposed to overlook factors of acceleration or deceleration in the speed of change and to minimize the sort of sudden change that would, presumably, result from the impact of influences lying outside the particular culture continuum. There are potential correctives here, such as relative depths of culture refuse or correlations with absolute dating factors, that would serve to check false assumptions about the rate of culture change or the relative time spans that the archaeologist might assign to the life-histories of certain types. Yet these are often lacking or poorly controlled, and the impulse to "overregularize," as a result of this typological conception and the cultural theory behind it, is a definite danger. The weaknesses of the concept of the type as a prehistoric reality are of an opposite nature. Certain styles or patterns in the manufacture of artifacts are, perhaps, overemphasized by archaeologists, while others, which impress the consciousness to a lesser degree, may be slighted as "transitional," with the vague implications that they are, somehow, of minor importance in the tracing-out of culture history. It is not an "either-or" choice. Both conceptions have merit. The course of ancient cultures can be plotted as a dynamic flow, and, at the same time, it can be kept in mind that prehistoric artisans were aiming at modalities which to them seemed fixed and which, undoubtedly, did not change at a set rate of speed.

To summarize further, the treatment of archaeological assemblages in any historicogenetic system has a basis in theories of continuity and change. Even if space and time factors are not formally observed, principles of continuity and change are expressed in the degrees of trait likeness or unlikeness which are the mechanics for establishing which are the genetic lines binding the assemblages together. In the overtly historical systems, such as those in vogue in the southwestern United States (Gladwin and Gladwin, 1934; Colton, 1939), lines of relationship and descent are expressed in these terms.

The processes by which, or through which, cultural continuity and change are maintained or accomplished have not received study and reflective thought commensurate with the way these concepts have been invoked by American archaeologists. "Evolution" and "diffusion" have been tag names employed, but these are broad categories rather than specific explanations, and there have been few clear theoretical formulations along these lines. For example, the historiocogenetic schemes of culture, or culture assemblage, classification in the southwestern United States have a dendritic structure, with "basic" or "root" cultures of the earlier periods diversifying into the various "stems" and "branches" of the later time periods. Obviously, the archaeologists who have constructed these classificatory schemes have, as their realities, the cultural assemblages which are represented near the top of the "tree." The monogenic "root" or "trunk" is lost in dim antiquity. But the implications are that the processes of cultural development, or evolution, have been those of monogenesis with "basic" or "mother" cultures, presumably simple in form and content, diversifying into complex, specialized offspring. Apparently, there is a rather simplistic evolutionary or genetic analogy at work here. To be sure, there is some universal basis for expressing the development of human culture in this fashion. At least the relatively simple, relatively homogeneous, material evidences of the Lower Paleolithic of the Old World give way to growing complexity and diversification. But the question might be asked whether this is in any way recapitulated in Arizona and New Mexico by sedentary pottery-makers during the first millennium of the Christian Era. Such a course of development is a possibility; nevertheless, in this case it appears that evolutionary theory has been very naively applied. Monogenesis of southwestern cultures is a postulate to be tested, not an axiomatic explanation.

Diffusionist theory in American archaeology has probably received more analysis, or analytical speculation, than has evolutionist theory. It is at the core of most archaeological interpretation. Trade, migration, gradual borrowing, and idea or stimulus diffusion have all been advanced in specific instances, both with and without supporting evidence. As with evolutionary hypotheses, theories of diffusion may be legitimately brought forward to explain various patternings in space-time distributions. Adequate support for either class of theory will, however, be more effectively marshaled when greater functional understanding of the data in question is achieved.

SOME PREVAILING AMERICANIST RECONSTRUCTIONS

AMERICAN CULTURAL ORIGINS

If a single dominant motif for Americanist reconstructions of New World aboriginal cultures had to be selected, I think we could safely say that this motif has been "isolationism." This statement is not necessarily critical. The prevailing theories concerning the origins of the early lithic and the later Neolithic cultures of the Americas may be the correct ones. At present, these theories have not been satisfactorily proved, but opposing theory is equally undemonstrated. It is of interest, however, that American opinion is predominantly on the side of the "separateness" of American beginnings and developments.

On the question of the first peopling of the American continents there has been little dispute on the score that these migrants were Asiatics who entered from eastern Siberia. There has, however, been considerable debate as to when they arrived and as to their stage of culture upon arrival. Up to about 1920, prevalent theory, championed by Holmes and Hrdlička, sponsored a relatively late entry for humans into the Americas of no more than 2000–3000 B.C. Such a migration was thought to have taken place on a very late Paleolithic or Mesolithic threshold. Following the discovery of Folsom, Yuma, and related lithic finds in the western plains of North America, the earlier theories were drastically revised to allow some 10,000–25,000 years for human occupancy of the Americas. Such a revision suggested a Paleolithic correlation with the Old World, but this correlation was largely one of time period rather than the diffusion of a specific industry or tool forms. American chronology rested upon geological and faunal associations rather than typology. It was, of course, generally assumed that the old lithic assemblages of the high plains were of Old World derivation; but, for the most part, interest centered in them as isolated entities of the American setting, and there was little systematic effort to link them to specific Asiatic or European complexes.

In spite of the geological-paleontological datings of 10,000-year-old artifacts in the Americas (and this has been recently supported by carbon 14 dates which are almost that old), there is some rather serious contrary evidence which questions the American chronological estimates and tends to minimize the isolation of the North American high plains and early lithic assemblages. Ironically, this evidence is of a strictly archaeological rather than a natural science nature. It has been pointed out by both Ward and Movius (personal communications, 1950–51) that the Folsom and Yuma flint types (with the exception of the fluted point) are found in northeastern Siberia in Neolithic rather than Paleolithic contexts. This eastern Siberian Neolithic follows the period of loess deposition in northern Asia. By 2500 B.C. cord-marked pottery was a part of the Neolithic complex in this part of the world, but chipped stonework of a definite Neolithic kind antedated the pottery. Just how far back these eastern Siberian Neolithic points and scrapers can be dated is the crux of the argument, but both Ward and Movius are of the opinion that 4000 B.C. would be the outside limit. If this is true, there is a glaring chronological discrepancy between these Siberian complexes and the early American lithic. There are three possible interpretations of this dilemma: (1) the American dating of Folsom-Yuma is too early; (2) the Siberian dating of the preceramic Neolithic is too late; or (3) the American Folsom-Yuma complexes were independently invented and bear no historical relationship to the Siberian Neolithic complexes. I believe that we can rule the third explanation out as an extreme "isolationist" point of view. This leaves us with the other two explanations, and these two interpretations of cultural beginnings in the New World remain to be tested. I conclude by pointing out only that the interpretation preferred by most American archaeologists relies essentially upon evidence of a non-archaeological nature and that artifact typology and artifact assemblages of northeastern Siberia, that part of the Old World closest to their problem, have not been given full consideration in this theoretical reconstruction.

Although the problem of remote origins is of great importance, perhaps the question of American Neolithic beginnings has been of more dramatic interest. In any event, it has been one of the most bitterly fought—and rightly so. For upon this question hangs much of anthropological thought bearing upon the processes and courses of human development. The empires of the Inca and of Mexico astounded not only the conquistadors of the sixteenth century but also social philosophers ever since. Could such feats of duplication take place guided only by the parallel structure of human minds and bodies, or was the cultural germ transplanted across the oceans?

Most American prehistorians have been disposed to believe the former: independent development of the New World high civilizations over and above an Upper Paleolithic–Mesolithic base. A number of European scholars have taken issue with this "isolationist" view. Their counterarguments have usually taken the form of trait comparisons between Peru-Mexico, on the one hand, and the Near East–Asia, on the other. In my judgment a demonstration of specific high-level intellectual achievements held in common by both the Old and the New World has never been satisfactorily made. By this I mean that such systems as Middle American writing, enumeration, and astronomy are not duplicated or closely approximated in the Old World. Nor are there duplications or approximations of complex art styles, presumably reflective of religious and intellectual systems, between the two hemispheres. These lacks do not, of course, disprove contact, but they allow for certain eliminations. The absence of complex art styles or complex intellectual attainments makes it almost certain that trans-Pacific diffusions, if they did take place, were not carried out by the mechanisms of organized conquest or religious proselytization. In fact, it is unlikely that such diffusions in any way involved hieratic elements of either Old or New World societies.

It is below this hierarchic level of complexity that you find the majority of Old and New World parallels. The most intriguing of these are technological elements or complexes, such as the *cire perdue* method of casting metals, resist-process painting, and bark cloth, to say nothing of agriculture, irrigation, and pottery-making. I believe that it is here, with element complexes of this kind, that the case for contact between the Old and the New World Neolithic will eventually stand or fall. If so, students of this problem should focus their attention upon the formative periods of Middle American and Andean civilizations, for it is at the beginning of and during these formative periods that such element complexes first appear on the American scene. If present American dating estimates are correct, this takes us back a millennium or a millennium and a half before the Christian Era.

Another category of traits, crucial to the rise of the American Neolithic, are the food plants upon which the agriculture was based. A tracing-out of the history of these may be the single most decisive factor in the Asiatic-American diffusion problem. Considerable work has been done along this line, but, as yet, there is strong disagreement among authorities.

There is also a final category of traits, many of which are often adduced in argument, that consists of myths or certain features of primitive social organization. Many of these seem to be nearly worldwide. It is unlikely that they offer a very fruitful line of investigation for this particular problem. It may be that some do represent relatively late diffusions, but others could well hark back to the time of the first peopling of the American continents. Significantly, they are not essential parts of a sedentary agriculture-based civilization and thus do not necessarily mark an introduction of possibly foreign ideas instrumental in producing such a civilization.

PREHISTORIC-HISTORIC CONTINUITIES

A full appreciation of the time dimension has been archaeology's greatest contribution to American anthropological studies. To European colleagues this may seem a statement of the obvious, but it must be remembered that American anthropology and ethnology of the early twentieth century was not historically minded in the sense of time-depth perspective. This was particularly true of North America, where the absence of native written histories and the fast-disappearing Indian populations centered attention upon the flat-dimensional "present" or late historic period.

One of the most outstanding examples of this was in the Great Plains of the United States. Ethnologists had offered speculative "historical reconstructions" of the Plains Indian past, based upon nineteenth-century records and some knowledge of early European colonial events. The significance of the advent of the horse and its impact upon the native cultures had been correctly appraised in part, but the quality of native Plains culture before that event was largely unknown. The nomadic, or seminomadic, horsemen of the later periods led ethnologists to believe that the earlier inhabitants of the region had also been nomads and that, in consequence, their culture had been a rather simple one. Archaeology (Strong, 1935; Wedel, 1936) destroyed this hypothesis by showing clearly that the old Plains life had been intensively horticultural and sedentary. Through a series of successive periods prehistoric cultures were linked to proto-historic, historic, and modern descendants. This type of study, sometimes called the "direct historical approach," has a theoretical basis in cultural continuity. Starting with known, documented habitation sites, certain cultural assemblages were identified and associated with particular tribal groups. Earlier archaeological assemblages were then sought which were not too sharply divergent from the known historic ones, and the procedure was followed backward in time.

In tracing prehistoric-historic continuities in this fashion, a number of useful working assumptions are at hand, although all of these must be used with some reservations. Continuity of a culture within the same area is a reasonable expectation, but there is always the possibility of regional shifts through time. The Plains studies showed both a certain amount of regional stability as well as some shifting. Cultural continuity within the same area is reasonably good evidence for linguistic and ethnic continuity, although it is by no means infallible. Thus Pawnee and Lower Loup archaeological assemblages are identified as the remains of Pawnee tribes, but the culturally similar Upper Republican assemblages, more remote in time, can be associated with the linguistic and biological ancestors of the Pawnee only on the basis of reasonable probability and not certainty.

The establishment of prehistoric-to-historic continuity is of utmost importance as a springboard for further archaeological interpretation, and, along with general chronological and distributional studies, it is one of the primary historical problems for the American archaeologist. In general, the most successful continuities of this sort have been determined for those regions where there has been relatively little ethnic shifting in aboriginal or proto-historic times and where there still remain native populations with predominantly native cultures. The Eskimo area of the north, the pueblos of the southwestern United States, certain regions of Mexico, the Maya country of Central America, and the Quechua and Aymara areas of the Andes are prime examples. In all of them a certain amount of cultural continuity with the archaeological past has been maintained, and this can be correlated with ethnic and linguistic continuities. A general, but not absolute, assumption which Americanists have followed in these reconstructions is that gradual and unbroken continuity of culture also implies continuity of population and that a sudden change or break in continuity is a reasonable indicator of population change.

Traditions and Co-Traditions

An appreciation of cultural continuities through time has led to the formalization of the tradition. The tradition, as defined, may apply to limited facets of culture, such as the tradition of white-on-red painting of ceramics in Andean South America (Willey, 1945), or to more inclusive and complex cultural patternings. In essence, it is the recognition of a specific line, or lines, of continuity through time, a formal acceptance of the rugged persistence of cultural ideas. These traditions are the means by which prehistoric-to-historic continuities are strung together and by which the archaeologist traces culture growth in general.

The tradition cannot be changeless within its continuity, but its internal modifications must lie, or be defined, within certain bounds. Otherwise, it is useless as a device for plotting or demonstrating continuity. An example of a tradition of extremely limited or monotonous inner variability is the cord-marked or fabric-marked pottery of eastern North America. Some years ago American archaeologists attempted to visualize the cord-marked wares as basically definitive of an area or a certain chronological period. Subsequent research failed to demonstrate clear-cut regional or temporal stability. In certain periods cord-marked wares were found from southern Canada to Florida and from the Atlantic to the Plains; on other chronological levels the distribution was more restricted. Similarly, in some parts of the eastern United States cord-marking appeared as the earliest known surface treatment for pottery; but in other sections it was found to persist until the founding of the European colonies. Minor typological distinctions within the cord- and fabric-marked ware were found to have specific, limited spatial and temporal utility; but, as a whole, cord- and fabric-marking was best conceived of as a tradition which had expanded or contracted geographically as it had persisted chronologically with relatively slight internal modifications. In contrast to this is the white-on-red pottery tradition of Peru, where a number of quite elaborate and radically different pottery styles are linked together over several hundred years of prehistory by their common possession of a red-and-white color scheme.

A number of traditions in American archaeological data come to mind as examples. Among these was the deep-seated bias of the peoples of the Hohokam region of the southwestern United States area for red-on-buff pottery as opposed to a black-on-white ceramic heritage for the northern Southwest. The broad-lined incised decoration which binds Venezuelan and West Indian pottery styles together is another such tradition, while the shell-tempering of Mississippian wares is still another kind of tradition persistence in the ceramic craft.

The examples I have used have been simple ones and confined to pottery because it is with the pottery medium that American archaeologists exercise the greatest control of the time factor. Obviously, however, the concept can apply to other media and other ranges of complexity. Maya calendrical lore would be an example of a highly complex, tightly unified tradition which lasted well over 1,000 years and in which can be recognized stylistic and technical period subdivisions.

The theory underlying the tradition concept is well expressed in the term itself. For "tradition" implies deep-set and channeled activity or patterned ways in which the vitality of a culture expresses itself in strong preference to other possible ways. The conditions surrounding this rigidity of expression which results in the long-time traditional expression are an interesting problem for future investigation. In dealing with such things as pottery decoration, the archaeologist is undoubtedly investigating what is relatively trivial in past human events. The failure of polychrome painting to take hold on the northern coast of Peru in the face of the white-on-red tradition, despite several attempts to introduce it, may eventually be revealed as nothing more mysterious than an absence of suitable mineral pigments in that part of the country. On the other hand, the unraveling of seemingly insignificant threads in an attempt to factor out causality may lead us to a greater understanding of "tradition set" and "tradition persistence" in insitutions which loom larger in human affairs.

It has been pointed out that cultural traditions do not always adhere firmly to given geographical areas, and this is often true. There do, however, appear to be general regional-traditional correlations. The examination of such correlations has led to a related concept, that of the area co-tradition (Bennett, 1948). The co-tradition, as the name suggests, is based upon the persistence of a number of combined and closely interrelated traditions within a specified area. It is not necessarily the history of any specified ethnic group but the history of cultural continuity within area confines. It affords the archaeologist a working device in place of the culture area, for the latter lacked the time dimension and was unsuited to problems of prehistory. The area co-tradition is, in effect, the culture area with time depth. Within its spatial and temporal limits it must have several basic consistencies. These are the warp and weft which hold it together in spite of subregional and period-to-period differences. The Peruvian or central Andean co-tradition is a good example. In this highland and coastal area all cultural phases partake of certain minimum traits and trait-complexes—Andean-type agriculture, certain pottery and weaving traditions, and architectural types. These and others are the common denominators of the Peruvian co-tradition and so define it. The Peruvian co-tradition is limited in time from the advent of maize agriculture (about 1000 B.C.) to the collapse of the Inca empire in A.D. 1532.

Comparable area co-traditions have been formulated elsewhere. One of the most recent applications of the concept has been in the southwestern United States (Martin and Rinaldo, 1951). Somewhat earlier, Kirchhoff (1943) defined Mesoamerica as a culture area, and, although he did not use the term "co-tradition," it is evident that his thinking includes time-depth perspective. In the far north an Arctic or Eskimoan tradition is surely indicated. Here Larsen and Rainey have defined a dual traditional emphasis within the larger framework, suggesting a land-hunting versus a sea-mammal–hunting economic dichotomy as this can be applied to the various Eskimo periods or phases. In eastern North American it seems most useful for the present, at least, to conceive of three co-traditions. These are by no means new constructs, for they follow along the old taxonomic divisions of Archaic, Woodland, and Mississippian.

DIFFUSIONS

In recent years systematic American archaeology has tended to be confined to distinct natural and cultural regions. These have been areas in which, from the outset, it has been more or less clear that certain traditions, or co-traditions, were dominant. Each such region has served as a sort of problem framework, and archaeologists have had a tendency to "feel at home" within the bounds of their own particular region but to show no great desire to go out of it. As a result, there has been somewhat less interest in problems of interareal diffusion than there had been in an earlier era. To date, these continental and hemisphere-wide problems of prehistoric contact remain largely unsolved. Various hypotheses have been formulated, but most of these have yet to be substantiated.

One of the most brilliant and far-reaching of these theories concerning American-wide diffusions was propounded by Spinden (1917) over 30 years ago. The nexus of this idea was that the seeds of American Neolithic life—agriculture, pottery-making, and other sedentary arts—were invented as an integral complex and spread from a single Middle American center to both the northern and the southern continents. This is the New World "Archaic hypothesis." Subsequent investigations have shown Spinden to be incorrect in his selection of certain Mexican assemblages as being fully representative of this earliest "Archaic." The relationships of valley of Mexico "Archaic" with early southern Mexican and Central American cultures are bewilderingly complex, and Spinden's formulation, taken *in toto*, does not resolve all these complexities. Nevertheless, the idea in the abstract still merits attention. Recent concepts of a "New World Formative" cultural level (Steward, 1948a; Willey, 1948; Strong, 1948a) are restatements of Spinden's original theme. The chief difference is that the center of origin of this "Formative" is not so confidently designated as it was for Spinden's "Archaic." Most archaeologists who are now working on this problem see a possibility of a center, or centers, of origin lying anywhere between central Mexico and southern Peru. Yet, aside from this, the "Formative" concept stands upon the same theoretical ground as did the "Archaic" hypothesis. Although the diffusion processes of neither have been fully set forth by their proponents, both theories imply the spread of a functionally related complex: maize horticulture, a sedentary way of life, developed craft specialization, including ceramics, and fundamental socioreligious beliefs tied up with an agricultural economy. Spinden defined specific ceramic (figurine) styles as being associated with this diffusion, and it has been the evidence for these that has failed to appear. The promulgators of the "Formative" admit the lack of a common style for their postulated early level and point, rather, to what seems to be a common ceramic heritage of monochrome wares, certain vessel forms, and decorative techniques.

This difference in the evidence for diffusion—style versus technical elements—leads us to the consideration of another concept: the horizon style. The horizon style was first defined by Kroeber (1944, p. 108) in connection with Peruvian studies. It is the phenomenon of a widespread art style which is registered in a number of local sequences. In accordance with the appearance of the same style from one locality to another, the various sequences are synchronized. The significance of the idea is in the phenomenon of the style as a unique entity. If this uniqueness is accepted, then contemporaneity or near-contemporaneity for the several local regional manifestations of the style can be assumed and the "horizon" quality inferred. Establishment of the uniqueness of the style depends upon three factors: its technical quality, its content or representation, and its configuration. The last, the configurational aspect of style, is the crucial factor. Two specimens might reveal fine-line carving on stone (technical) and a jaguar motif (content), but the delineation of the jaguar (configuration) might be quite different in the two cases. In such an event the archaeologist would be dealing with two distinct styles.

This problem of stylistic uniqueness has a bearing on the "Archaic" hypothesis as well as upon most other questions of wide-scale American diffusions. If stylistic identity or close similarity can be established, it can be reasonably assumed that the separate occurrences mark an approximately contemporaneous horizon. For the American "Archaic" or "Formative" there does not appear to be any such style horizon; hence contemporaneity of the various New World "Formative" cultures is questionable.

The lack of a diffused style is undoubtedly indicative of significant qualities in the processes of diffusion. Or, conversely, stylistic diffusion must presuppose certain conditions which are not necessary for other types of diffusion. The archaeologist is not yet in a position to be able to say what these conditions may have been. Speculatively, it seems likely that the diffusion of a complex art style, such as the Chavín or the Maya, implies the diffusion of a social, religious, or political system. The transference of the ideas involved in the duplication of such a style suggests intimate contact and interchange between the localities and regions concerned. In this regard it is probably worthy of note that most of the great American prehistoric styles, such as the classic Maya, the Chavín, the Olmec, or the Mochica, are confined to a single co-traditional area or a fraction thereof. Reliable occurrences outside the recognized geographical limits of these styles are found in such totally different contexts that there has been little difficulty in recognizing them as trade items. An exception is the Inca style, which spread into both north and south Andean areas. Here, of course, we have documentary evidence that such a diffusion was backed by imperialistic expansion.

As with the problem of widespread "Archaic" or "Formative" relationships, the specific problems of interareal relationships in the Americas involve diffusion of a nonstylistic kind. The southwestern United States was almost certainly dependent upon the cultures of Mexico, but there are no horizon style linkages and only scant evidences of trade. The contacts here were almost certainly those which permitted the passage of technological ideas (ceramics, irrigation, casting of metals) but did not encourage the transfer of social, religious, or political idea systems and their associated symbols (art styles). A somewhat similar situation obtains between the southeastern United States and Mexico. Here the two areas are separated by several hundred miles of desolate wastelands, but in the Southeast a rich agricultural civilization flourished. Perhaps more than in the Southwest, the Southeast reflects the religious and sociopolitical systems of Middle America. The temple mound–plaza ceremonial centers imply this. There is also a southeastern cult art which suggests parallels to the south; however, this so-called "Southern Cult" (Waring and Holder, 1945) of the Southeast has its distinct style (Krieger, 1945), and, if it was Middle American–inspired, it has undergone serious local transformation.

The same condition prevails between the southwestern and southeastern United States. These areas, separated by the staked plains of Texas and other semidesert regions, probably maintained intermittent contact. There are possibilities that one race of maize was passed between the two and that certain pottery vessel form ideas were exchanged. Stylistically, the pottery assemblages in question are radically distinct, and the contact must have been on the level of a stimulus or idea difffusion (Kroeber, 1940).

In areas to the south of Middle America the story of relationships is still most feebly comprehended. The "Formative" levels of western Honduras bear a general technical similarity to those of Middle America, and there is even one horizon marker, Usulutan ware, which provides a secure linkage to the north. Usulutan is, however, such a simple decorative type that it is more comparable to a technique than to a stylistic configuration. It undoubtedly has some value as a time marker but is difficult to interpret as an indicator of complex diffusion. In Nicaragua and Costa Rica certain decorative elements in Nicoya pottery may be traced back to later Mexican periods and offer evidence of stylistic diffusion. To the south of these countries there is little in the way of stylistic linkage to

Middle America. The whole of the lower Central American, Colombian, and Ecuadorian area is chopped into a great number of small stylistic regions. Their cross-relations, one to the other, have not yet been worked out, but it seems unlikely that any major stylistic horizon markers will emerge. The relationships from region to region, again, are those of similar technologies and techniques, including such features as pottery vessel forms, which have a general traditional but not a stylistic bond.

The Peruvian co-tradition area is well cemented by horizon styles. Two of these, the Incaic and the earlier Tiahuanacan, extend southward into Argentina and Chile, where they have horizonal significance. For the earlier periods, however, the Peruvian styles are contained within the co-traditional area; and the rise of farming and pottery-making in the south, if it can be dated as coeval with the Peruvian Formative, is stylistically apart from anything such as Chavín.

Eastward into lowland South America it is possible that there are horizon style phenomena, although these have not yet been plotted in space or time. Nordenskiöld's (1913) excavations in the Mojos of Bolivia revealed ceramics in his later periods which bear a certain style resemblance to lower Amazonian painted types. Also, within the Venezuelan–West Indian broad-lined incised tradition there seem to be stylistic divisions which may mark wide geographical time periods. As yet, between Andes and lowland there is scant stylistic cross-referencing. Vague connections exist between the earlier period ceramics of the Bolivian Mojos and the Bolivian altiplano (Bennett, 1936). East from the Peruvian and Ecuadorian Andes, Tello has claimed Chavín similarities, but these claims pass far beyond recognized limits of stylistic comparisons. Northward, in the Colombian inter-Andean valleys are the most likely prospects for Andean-Orinocan-Amazonian stylistic diffusions. Such styles as the urn burials of the Mosquito region (Bennett, 1946c) have lowland parallels.

To sum up, the tracing of specific art styles from one major area, or area co-tradition, to another has not proved possible in the Americas. The almost unquestionable basic relationships that once existed between Middle and South America or Middle America and the areas of the southwestern and southeastern United States will have to be plotted by other types of diffusionist evidence. Stimulus diffusion, the spread of technologies and of specific techniques and technical treatments, will probably be the basis for such studies. Admittedly, this is more tenuous evidence than the comparisons of styles or the identification of specific trade items; but interareal historical reconstruction will not be advanced without continued application to these problems.

DEVELOPMENTAL LEVELS

In recent years the old idea of developmental parallelism has been seriously reexamined by American archaeologists and culture historians. This hypothesis has been applied to central Andean archaeological data (Bennett, 1948; Larco Hoyle, 1948; Strong, 1948a; Willey, 1948; Bennett and Bird, 1949), Middle American data (Armillas, 1948), interarea New World comparisons (Steward, 1947, 1948a; Willey, 1950; Strong, 1951), and even worldwide comparative evaluations (Steward, 1949a). Interpretations have varied somewhat, both in the selections and alignments of data and in the emphasis given to deductions of causality. All, however, have dealt principally with the rise and growth of sedentary agricultural communities, with the subsequent technological developments within these, and with the religious and sociopolitical developments known or implied from the data.

In both Central Andean and Middle American areas these developmental formulations are based upon an initial formational or "Formative" stage, in which the sedentary arts were promulgated and developed toward specialization. This initial formational stage was succeeded by a stage of relative cultural crystallization and rigor in which diverse regional specializations expressed themselves in well-defined styles. As such, this second stage was a flowering of the technical and inventive potential of the first stage and has been called the "Classic" or "Florescent." The third major stage is more difficult to define than the others, as the common-denominator qualities are more difficult to abstract. There is also an interesting shift in criteria for this final stage. Whereas the criteria for the first two recapitulate technological and artistic trends, the third stage is not essentially characterized by these factors. In some regions there is an apparent aesthetic decline, although this is a subjective impression difficult to measure. Certainly, there is no technical falling-off, and in some places, such as the central Andes, there are continued technological advances. The single unifying characteristic of the final stage is, rather, the evidence for widespread social, political and religious disturbances. Classic styles disappear, great classic sites of presumed politicoreligious importance are abandoned, some being destroyed, and large-scale migrations of people take place. It is, of course, possible that the archaeologist has been overinfluenced by a knowledge of history or legendary history for this final stage. In both Peru and Mexico it seems to have been encompassed in the terminal 500 years antedating the Spanish, and various native accounts from both areas tell of wars of conquest and general turmoil. These accounts are, to a large extent, supported by archaeological evidences of military establishments, fortified strongholds, and the like, all of which seem to be more common to the later Peruvian and Mexican periods. Terms such as "Expansionist" or "Militaristic" have, accordingly, been applied to the third major stage.

There has been a strong tendency to equate these developmental stages not only functionally but chronologically. This has been evidenced both within a co-traditional area, such as the central Andes, and in extending the stages from one major co-traditional area to another. As a tentative device, this sort of developmental chronological chart (see Willey, 1948, 1950; Bennett and Bird, 1949) is permissible where absolute dating factors give no clues as to synchronization. It is not, however, likely that developmental stage lines will ultimately be demonstrated to be chronological horizon lines. Within the central Andean area, for example, it is most unlikely that the qualities or traits which mark the advent of the Classic or Expansionist stages will be found to have occurred simultaneously throughout all coastal and highland regions. The same is true for Middle America, and that there should have been synchronization, or even near-synchronization, between Middle America and Peru in the attainment of these levels or stages is even more dubious. This kind of synchronization, even though it has been projected on a most schematic and trial basis, has given a sort of spurious uniformity to the developmental levels in American high cultures and has aroused skepticism toward the whole construct.

The problem of chronological equations as it pertains to the theory of developmental levels leads us directly back to the matter of diffusion. Are the stage parallelisms which some of us have seen as existent between Middle and South America the result of diffusion or developmental uniformity? I do not believe that the question can be posed this simply, for it seems evident that both forces have been operative. Within either of these co-traditional areas it appears quite certain that diffusion from region to region has taken place but that such diffusions have by no means been uniform outpourings which have spread in evenly distributed waves over the whole area. For example, in Peru, the Mochica ceramic style embraces five or six north-coast valleys. In contrast, the idea of constructing large pyramids of adobe is found throughout the north coast, is well established on the central coast, and at least makes an appearance on the northern boundary of the south coast. On the basis of present knowledge, these two complexes—Mochica art and adobe pyramid mound building—probably diffused at about the same time; yet their patterns of dispersal are quite different. Certain forces which permitted, or encouraged, the spread of one inhibited the other. The nature of these forces leads us into an interpretative functional analysis of prehistoric Peruvian societies and their environments, obviously a complex problem. With reference to the developmental and diffusionist question, the point here is that the potentialities of cultural development in any given region are not only conditioned by but also condition diffusion. These potentialities are a complex of natural, social, and cultural endowments. The understanding of their interaction is the ambitious goal of the functional or processual problems which archaeologists set for themselves. But even at our present stage of understanding it appears quite evident that developmental potentialities and the diffusion of ideas are closely interrelated. Certainly, metallurgical techniques, as known in the Andes and in Middle America, have a related history. Their acceptance, rejection, emphasis, or de-emphasis from region to region or major area to area depended upon the varying complex potentialities of peoples, cultures, and natural environment. In a vastly more intricate manner the development, spread, and success or failure of such institutions as kingship or empire were dependent upon what happened when the receiving base was fertilized or stimulated by the transient idea.

As we have discussed above, there is a far-flung distribution of certain elements and technologies which are formational to the American Neolithic-type cultures. The similarity of these elements and technologies and their geographic occurrences make it most likely that they have a common heritage. These diffused elements provided the base for the American agricultural civilizations and, in so doing, set certain wide limits for later cultural growth. These cultural foci of this "Formative" stage must have had opened before them a number of possible courses for development. The directions which these foci took in their growth were selected from the potentialities which each possessed and from the ideas which each generated and transmitted to others.

Functional Reconstructions

It was specifically indicated in our discussion of methodology that the functional objectives of archaeology cannot be divorced from the historical ones. Further, in our review and commentary on reconstructions in American prehistory it has been implicit that a greater functional appreciation of the phenomena involved would lead to clearer understanding of what are generally considered historical relationships. It is thus difficult to select certain archaeological interpretations and label them as "functional" or "processual," as opposed to diffusionist or developmental reconstructions. In reviewing such selections the close integration of chronicle and process must be borne in mind.

In making functional interpretations of archaeological data there are several lines of evidence or means of approach. Some of these are listed in the methodological Figure 28.1.

There is, first, the use interpretation of an artifact or feature. In some instances this can be done by way of general analogy. A pointed flint with an obvious haft is interpreted as a projectile. Or, in other cases, a metate and mano are explained as corn-grinding instruments by analogy with modern use within certain ethnic areas. Sometimes historic documentation gives the lead, as with the disklike stones in southeastern archaeology and early accounts of their use in the "chunkee" game. The limitations of the approach are clear. Many archaeological objects or features will probably never be properly explained from a functional standpoint. Beyond the obvious and beyond the specific ethnic or ethnohistoric analogy, there is only the sheerest speculation.

The archaeological assemblage can be functionally explained in a manner similar to that applied to the artifact. With the assemblage, of course, the archaeologist begins to bridge over into the complexities of the space and time factors. The dimensions of space and time can be correlated with and used to help explain changes in artifacts, features, and assemblages.

A third approach utilizes quantitative factors. The numbers of archaeological remains, such as the numbers and sizes of sites, can be used to estimate populations and the disposition of populations. With such an approach a control of the chronological factor is a necessity.

A fourth line of evidence is the correlation of space and time distributions of remains with natural environmental types. In the American field there are numerous examples of this. Rouse's study of culture units centering upon West Indian sea passages rather than islands comes to mind. Such a correlation was strong testimony for sea transport and a marine rather than a land orientation (Rouse, 1951b).

A fifth approach combines two or more of those listed and presents a rising complexity of interrelated interpretations. It is on this basis that most archaeological interpretation with a strong functional bias has been carried out. Examples of such interpretations are actually more numerous than American archaeologists realize. The majority of them are imbedded in "standard" (i.e., historically oriented) monographs on archaeology. Others are parts of general cultural-historical reconstructions. Some few have been presented primarily as attempts at functional analysis.

A brilliant example of functional explanation of archaeological data is offered from the North American Plains. Here the archaeologist operated with artifact types and artifact assemblages from Pre- and Postcolumbian times. With the chronological dimension properly in control, it was obvious that certain profound changes had taken place in Plains Indian culture between the pre- and the post-1540 date line. These changes were seen in material culture, but the implications in changes in house and community types as well as artifacts reflected important sociopolitical changes. Added to this was a fairly rich documentation from the late historic period which filled out the picture of Indian life in this area in the late nineteenth century. From these known referents—artifact and assemblage types, chronology, and ethnic documentation—the archaeologists and ethnologists were able to explain much of what took place in culture change as the result of the impact of significant technological innovations brought by the Europeans (i.e., horses and guns) (see Wissler, 1914; Strong, 1933, 1940).

In a similar way, but with less specific ethnic documentation, archaeologists in the eastern United States have been able to outline events surrounding the introduction of intensive agriculture into this area. To begin with, there is some documentation for the nature of eastern culture in its final Postcolumbian periods. This documentation indicates a rich agricultural ceremonialism in certain southern regions and also shows this ceremonialism to have been associated with a mound-plaza, community-center complex. It is further known that the mound-plaza complex is an integral part of the ceremonial, social, and political life of the agricultural civilizations of Middle America. The similarity of this mound-plaza complex between eastern North America and Middle America suggests a historical relationship, and this relationship is further supported by other archaeological evidence linking these two major areas. Because of the great chronological depth and elaboration of the mound-plaza complex in Middle American cultures, it is assumed that this is the parent-area for the idea, at least as far as the eastern United States is concerned. With these facts and hypotheses in mind, it is noted that the mound-plaza complex is not known throughout the full range of eastern chronology but appears for the first time somewhere in middle-to-late sequence. With this appearance there is a number of significant changes in eastern society and culture as revealed by archaeology. There is a greater utilization of riverine terrace country, there are more and much larger archaeological sites, and, finally, there are more frequent finds of maize remains. These the archaeologist relates to a specific new and important change in food economy. All these link back with the assumed correlation of the mound-plaza complex with intensive agriculture. Corollary evidence for such a change is seen in a decrease in hunting fetishes (animal teeth, claws, and representations of these) with the rise of the mound-plaza complex. Parallel changes in eastern culture are reflected in a different burial pattern, new pottery styles, and new house types. The functional interrelationship of these with intensive horticulture, if such existed, is obscure; but, like the mound-plaza complex, they may be part of a historical association. In this particular example the archaeologist has first established, by ethnic documentation and comparisons to another area, the firm association of an archaeological feature (the mound-plaza) with an agricultural way of life. Then, by placing the introduction of this feature in the chronological sequence of eastern native cultures, he has been able to support his association by correlative evidence of a functional type (i.e., increased population, large centers, etc.).

One of the most interesting Americanist problems in functional interpretation has revolved around prehistoric urbanization. Middle American archaeologists have posed the question as to what are the factors leading to or promoting urbanization. In this investigation urbanization has been defined as the permanent concentration of large nonfood-producing populations. A review of Middle American data seems to indicate, at the present state of knowledge, that such true cities or urban areas were best known from the late prehistoric periods and from upland country. The valley of Mexico is offered as a classic example, and Tenochtitlan, the Aztec capital, was most surely such an urbanized city. As opposed to this, the earlier Middle American periods and the lowlands seemingly lack evidence of a comparable urbanization. The functional explanations offered for this dichotomy and the important exceptions to it are that large concentrations of nonfood-producers are possible only with intensive food production by others and with relatively rapid food transport. The valley of Mexico apparently met both these conditions. *Chinampa*, or floating-garden farming, is fabulously productive, and water transportation in the lakes in which the Chinampas were located afforded rapid dispersal of produce. To substantiate this case, the archaeologists favoring this interpretation point to the multiroomed, closely packed, compartmented dwelling compounds at Teotihuacan as being indicative of early (*ca.* A.D. 500) beginnings of urbanism in the favorable Mexican uplands. The lowland picture seems to be quite different. In the Maya and Olmec areas impressive ceremonial sites were constructed, but mass dwelling concentrations were, presumably, prohibited by the limitations of tropical forest agriculture and transportation difficulties. Urbanism in the lowlands, in the framework of this general interpretation, is looked upon as a very late and politically forced phenomenon. Mayapan is the type-site for such a development in the Maya region. Here a walled, urban concentration is viewed as the result of Mexican influence and conquest, together with a period of local troubles and fighting, leading to more compact living than the environmental potentialities could sustain. Late-period urbanization on the lowland Veracruz coast is thought to have been made possible at Cempoala by artificial irrigation.

This fascinating hypothesis has not met with general acceptance. Perhaps greatest of all difficulties is the lack of adequate settlement study throughout most of Middle

America, particularly in the lowlands. Incoming data may require drastic revisions in, or demand the rejection of, these theories; but it is most significant, I think, that the problem of urbanization and its causes can be raised in New World archaeology. That such a problem has been framed as a research theme marks a great advance in Americanist studies.

A somewhat different approach from those cited is one which I attempted with Andean data (Willey, 1948). Here the problem lead was in the detail of the data. The particular phenomena in question were the horizon styles, the Peruvian-wide distributions of certain art forms at certain times, and the complete absence of such horizon styles at other times. What were the causative factors behind these diffusions or absences of diffusions? In my attempt to answer this question I projected the various horizon styles against the backgrounds of what could be reconstructed of Peruvian society at the respective time periods involved. These backgrounds could be developed only in the most general terms, such as "warlike," "absence of warfare," "small populations," "expanding populations," etc. Nevertheless, these backgrounds, taken in conjunction with the content of the styles themselves, afforded a basis for a number of reasonable conjectures. Most of these conclusions may never go beyond the conjectural stage because of the limitations of the data. For example, Chavín art is depicted as a horizon style which spread in an era of relative peace. Such a condition immediately sets bounds for the mechanisms by which the style could have spread. For identifying this period as a peaceful one, we have only the absences of fortifications or fortified sites, of abundant weapons, of warlike representations in art, and a knowledge that population groups were relatively small and isolated from one another. This is not absolute proof of nonmilitaristic society, but, in the absence of evidence to the contrary and until such evidence is forthcoming, I think it justifiable to reconstruct on such a foundation.

The examples I have used are only a few from American archaeology, selected largely because they are the ones which I know best. I can only mention the work that has been done on the reconstruction of southwestern social organization from a combination of archaeological and ethnological data (Strong, 1927; Steward, 1937; and Martin and Rinaldo, 1950), on Arctic economy (Larsen and Rainey, 1948), and numerous other examples dotted over the American continents.

29

A Consideration of Archaeology

(From *Daedalus*, Journal of the American Academy of Arts and Sciences, Vol. 106, No. 3, Summer, pp. 81–95, 1977. Reprinted by permission of *Daedalus*, Journal of the American Academy of Arts and Sciences.)

In the last decade or two archaeology has undergone a very rapid transformation. What had been a rather quiet contemplation of the past, a kind of savoring of its substance not always untinged with a little romanticism, is now being brought forward into the more strident world of "relevance." The past—the vast preliterate past as well as the more immediate historic past—is to be made germane to the present. Of course, in one sense this linkage of past and present has always been the mainspring of archaeology. The archaeologist deals with life, or its residues, and this subject matter can be interpreted only in terms of the living. What is new are theoretical attitudes about the data and methodological procedures for handling them. These attitudes and procedures combine to compose what is often referred to as the "new archaeology." This body of theory and method may be said to be truly and uniquely archaeological. In this there can be no denial that various techniques in such things as dating and materials anslyses—borrowed from the physical, chemical, and natural sciences—have had an important effect in the development of such a new archaeology, but such ancillary methods and techniques are not, in and of themselves, at the core of the new outlook.

This new outlook, rather, consists of a number of conceptual features. Even though some of these are not entirely new, it is fair to say that the emphasis upon them and their formal methodological structuring are innovations. One of these features is the principle that all societies and cultures, past and present, were or are systemically organized and that the functionings of their subsystemic parts and the trajectories of development of these parts and of the whole are to be understood with the aid of general systems theory. Closely and immediately linked to this systemic view is the very basic archaeological principle already referred to that the remains and residues of the past are to be explicated by means of analogies with life situations. Relating to all of this is the concern with process and the conviction that "laws" or "regularities" governing the processes of social and cultural change are, indeed, discoverable and that this, rather than the narration of history, or prehistory, is archaeology's principal goal—a goal that leads to "relevance." This body of theory is to be made operational by the testing of hypotheses about the applicability of analogical models, the workings of culture systems, and the validity of laws or regularities through strategically devised archaeological exploration and analysis. As can be seen, the objectives are ambitious and optimistic.

Although the new archaeology has had its most recent and immediate origins in the United States, and has probably taken its purest form here, its development should be viewed in wider perspective. Although archaeology had its beginnings in Renaissance humanism and romantic antiquarianism, it began to diverge in the nineteenth century into two branches,[1] one of which continued essentially in the humanistic tradition. This was the archaeology of the Classic World and the Near East which has come down to the present in the academic houses of Classics and Art History. The other branch, with which we are primarily concerned, moved off in the direction of the natural sciences and of anthropology. It developed most quickly in Denmark, England, and France, where its subject matter was largely that of preliterate cultures. In Europe this kind of archaeology became known as prehistory. In the United States it grew up in deparments of Anthropology. Here the ethnologist and the archaeologist were both dedicated to the study of the American Indian, living or dead, so that the alliance was a logical and practical one.[2] For a good while the problems of American archaeology, as was also true of Old World prehistory, were those of description, taxonomy, and chronology; but some of the most imaginative research derived from the connections with ethnology.[3] These were the linking of prehistoric cultures with historic or modern Indian tribes, as in A. V. Kidder's work in the Southwestern Pueblo Indian area or in W. D. Strong's investigations on the North American Great Plains.[4]

In the 1920s and 1930s some important theoretical innovations appeared in European prehistory. V. Gordon Childe, in a series of important books, began to move away from the limited chronology building that had been the goal of traditional prehistorians and to define and map archaeological cultures and societies.[5] Grahame Clark continued in this direction with the reconstruction of prehistoric environments and the development of the ecosystem concept in British archaeology. In a book published in 1940, called *Archaeology and Society*, Clark took a systemic view of culture and society and attempted to say something about the interrelationships of environment, technology, social forms, and idea systems.[6] In so doing, he was trying to synthesize some of the ideas of the functionalist social anthropologists of the British School with the "earth sciences" aspects of archaeology that were being developed by means of soil studies and pollen analyses.

In the United States at this time, in spite of the traditional academic union of archaeology with ethnology and social anthropology, such new departures were much less definite, although W. R. Wedel, working on the Great Plains, initiated archaeological-environmental studies,[7] and Paul S. Martin and his associates tentatively advanced some interpretations of prehistoric Southwestern Pueblo social organization from analyses of architectural features and artifacts.[8] More interesting from a theoretical standpoint were some strictures on the unimaginative nature of American archaeological research that were first set forth by American ethnologists[9] and later developed into a book, *A Study of Archaeology*, by the archaeologist Walter W. Taylor. In this latter work Taylor issued a call for a greater concern by archaeologists with contextual control, function, and process.[10]

The Second World War intervened and stopped archaeological research for a time. Afterward Clark continued along his innovative lines. In the Americas Taylor's book was met with hostility or silence—or so it seemed at the time. Yet, in retrospect, it must be remembered that we are talking of very short time spans in the development of any discipline, and as we look back over the published record it is obvious that some ferment was going on in American archaeology. During the late 1940s and 1950s an increasing number of archaeologists were motivated by problems other than simple descriptive-chronological ones. Good examples of this in the Americas would be the research that was conducted into the processes of the rise of native agriculture in Mexico[11] or the study of Peruvian prehistoric settlement patterns as a basis for making inferences about population sizes and groupings and their social and political interrelationships.[12] The results of these investigations were presented substantively, with little theoretical or methodological emphasis, or polemical accompaniment, but they clearly owed something to the kinds of questions that Childe, Clark, and Taylor had been posing. All of this—a seeding of new ideas, their rejection or apparent rejection on the part of some, their acceptance, however covert or even subconscious, on the part of others—climaxed in the early 1960s with the new archaeology.[13]

The promulgation of the new doctrines has been accomplished with a certain amount of revolutionary fervor, now somewhat abated, but it is fair to say that these doctrines have gone a long way toward capturing the field, at least here in the United States. For the most part, there has been relatively little articulate opposition to the new archaeology within the American archaeological fraternity.[14] To some extent, this has been because a good many older practitioners have felt they were on too much of it before the "Young Turks" raised the banner and have stood aside, somewhat aggrieved, only because this fact did not seem to be recognized. More basically, this acceptance has a good deal to do with American archaeology's long association with ethnology, social anthropology, and the social sciences in general. Although there are counter-currents in these fields, their general tone has always been positivistic and, above all, optimistic. There is a general consensus that problems are susceptible to solution in a scientific manner, by means of quantitative treatments and in other pragmatic ways. In a word, they are imbued with the very American notion that intelligence and diligence can overcome the greatest obstacles, and the current optimism of archaeology is very consonant with all this. And, in this connection, it is probably no accident that the strongest criticism of the new orientation has come from the humanistic tradition in archaeology, and especially from those British archaeologists whose views are not particularly compatible with those of Childe or Clark, and for whom, in many cases, "social science" is a "dirty word."[15]

This separation between anthropological and humanistic archaeology has never been more clearly emphasized than it is now. As we have seen, the separation is as old as the profession itself, but for a long time it was reflected mainly in the choice of subject matter. Now it has been underlined as a basic difference in theoretical orientation and goals. The crux of the matter is the degree to which material aspects of culture do articulate systemically with nonmaterial ones and the possibilities for detecting these articulations in the archaeological record alone. The issues have been stated by M. I. Finley, a leading classical archaeologist.[16] Finley begins by quoting L. R. Binford, who has written that

> The argument that archaeologists must limit their knowledge to features of material culture is open to serious question; and second, the dichotomy between material and nonmaterial aspects of culture itself and the relevance of this dichotomy for a proposed hierarchy of reliability have also been the subject of critical discussion. . . . It is virtually impossible to imagine that any given cultural item functioned in a socio-cultural system independent of the operation of "nonmaterial" variables. Every item has its history within a socio-cultural system—its phases of procurement of raw material, manufacture, use, and final discarding. . . . *There is every reason to expect* that the empirical properties of artifacts and their

arrangement in the archaeological record will exhibit attributes which can inform on different phases of the artifact's life history" [Finley's italics].[17]

Finley then goes on to ask:

> Is there any reason to expect what Binford expects, and significantly can offer only as an expectation rather than as a proposition for which there is available evidence? On the contrary, there is sufficient evidence that identical artifacts and arrangements of artifacts can result from different socioeconomic arrangements of procurement, manufacture, or distribution. For example, we know from the chance preservation of accounts inscribed on stone, that the most delicate stone carving on the temple in Athens known as the Erechtheum was produced by free men and slaves working side by side at the end of the fifth century B.C. Nothing in the material remains (the carving itself) could have told us that. On the other hand, the surviving accounts of the temple of Apollo at Epidaurus, built thirty or forty years later, are of such a nature that the labor force is not specified. How does Binford imagine it will be possible to discover whether or not slaves were employed, at the highest skill level, on that temple?[18]

Admittedly, many telling arguments like this can be made against the optimism of the new archaeology, and there are aspects of the past, both nonmaterial and material, that archaeology will never recover; yet I find myself sympathetic to the optimists in this case. Perhaps there is nothing in the Erechtheum "carving itself" that would offer a clue to the social status of the craftmen who made it; but I cannot help but think that if Greek archaeology had been more widely based, in being concerned with such things as humble settlement quarters and craftsmen's tools and their contexts, there might have been some high probability answers to questions like this about fifth-century B.C. society. This is not necessarily a criticism of Greek archaeology—about which I know very little—but I know that in my own field of Maya archaeology the past hundred years or so of research has been directed mostly toward the grand and the spectacular, the palace and the temple, rather than the hut. There was nothing wrong in beginning this way; indeed, it would have been rather peculiar to have initiated investigations at the humble end of the scale; but temples did exist in larger socioeconomic contexts or systems, and many of the things that concerned them will almost surely be explained by what went on in other parts of those systems. It is certainly too soon to close the door on such possibilities. And it is too soon to be overly pessimistic about a working reconciliation between anthropological and humanistic archaeology.

The relationships of material to nonmaterial aspects of culture involve the uses of analogy as well as systems theory, and this constitutes another debatable area between anthropological archaeology, as represented by the new archaeology, and more traditional archaeology, especially of the humanistic brand. Insofar as the source materials are concerned, there are essentially three types of analogy open to the archaeologist. He can work through *specific historical analogy*, which is usually what is meant by the term "ethnographic analogy." This refers to situations where the archaeological culture is interpreted by means of analogies drawn with ethnographically or historically known cultures of the same general geographic region and the same general culture-historical tradition. The assumption is that the prehistoric culture is related, in an antecedent sense, to the historic or modern one. There are many examples of this, especially in the Americas, including those already cited for the Southwestern United States Puebloan area or the North American Great Plains, where a reasonable case for continuity has been made through combined archaeological and ethnohistoric research. The prehistoric-to-historic sequences of Mexico and Peru are other obvious examples. Here the descriptions of Aztec and Inca civilizations, as provided by the sixteenth-century Spanish conquistadores, have given a baseline for interpreting the earlier cultures of those areas.

Clearly, there are limitations and disadvantages to such specific historical analogies. Continuities from prehistoric past to historic present are not always easy to demonstrate, and even when this can be done it must be kept in mind that formal material similarities do not necessarily imply continuities in nonmaterial aspects of culture. Specific historical analogy has not been scorned by contemporary American archaeologists. J. J. F. Deetz's studies on changes in Arikara social organization, through the tracing of changes in ceramic decorative attributes and their associations with house site foundations, worked from historically known ethnographic data about Arikara kinship and residential patterns[19]; and W. A. Longacre's somewhat similar studies in Southwestern Pueblo ruins also took off from ethnographic information about the Western Pueblo Indians of the historic and modern periods.[20] Nevertheless, the new archaeological position on specific historical analogy is not an altogether favorable one.

Binford has addressed himself to this on several occasions, and what he objects to, in addition to those disadvantages already mentioned, is that specific historical analogy, or any kind of specific ethnographic analogy, limits the possibilities of developing an "independent" archaeological methodology. His views are well summed up in the following quotation:

> Such a procedure [the use of ethnographic analogy] denies to archaeology the possibility of dealing with forms of cultural adaptation outside the range of variation known ethnographically. . . . In view of the high probability that cultural forms existed in the past for which we have no ethnographic examples, reconstruction of the lifeways of such sociocultural systems demands rigorous testing of deductively drawn hypotheses against independent sets of data.[21]

Although I would agree with Binford "that cultural forms existed in the past for which we have no ethnographic examples," I can see no other way in which past behavior may be inferred except with reference to known living behaviors. Thus, even though it is true that there is probably no currently known or historically recorded living pattern in the world that is a good analogue for that represented by an Upper Paleolithic cave site in France, the debris and artifacts from that site can be placed in a simulated life situation only by our general knowledge and awareness of hunting peoples—that they pursue and kill game, make stone tools for doing this, and adjust to seasonal rounds in the food quest. This kind of analogy, *general comparative analogy*, is based not on specific historical or ethnographic situations but on our general knowledge of life itself. In many instances it is archaeologists' only interpretive recourse. It does not, however, free archaeologists from some kind of known, living referents, even if these are drawn from disparate sources and assembled into a model of their own making.

In this connection, I think it should be said that general comparative analogy has very definite limitations and even grave risks. In constructing a life model from such "bits and pieces," randomly drawn from space, time, and cultural tradition, the design of the model must be either very "loose-jointed" or else one that stands in very great danger of being influenced by personal or doctrinal predispositions.[22] I would second the desire, on the part of some archaeologists, to make archaeology a "science of material culture,"[23] for in the last analysis this is where its methodological nexus is located. We must interpret through material remains. But we cannot be sure, except through doctrinal insistence, that this is where the root of all process lies. As we interpret through analogy, in an attempt to lay a base for a "science of material culture," I think that the source of the analogical model may be more important than some archaeologists have admitted. Binford and others have insisted that it is not the source of the model but its testing that is crucial. The importance of testing cannot be denied; but archaeological data do have a way of being made to verify initial hypotheses and models. I think that these attitudes about general comparative analogy, or "independent archaeology," are at the base of much of the humanistic objection to the new archaeology.

There is, in this regard, a middle ground in analogy which operates with real life models and which may be more compatible with humanistic tastes than the general comparative pastiche. This could be called *specific comparative analogy*. It frees the archaeologist from some of the limitations of specific historical analogy but remains more within the bounds of human experience than the general comparative approach.[24] This is where the model is drawn from a specific culture and society, known ethnographically or historically. The model is applied, however, to the interpretation of an archaeological culture to which it has no historical connection. Such a procedure is hardly new. Philosophers of history are old hands at it, although the analogies drawn by Spengler or Toynbee were not primarily for the purposes of archaeological interpretation. But in recent years this kind of comparative analogical model has been widely used by archaeologists. One of the most interesting examples of this in American archaeology concerns the Olmec civilization of ancient Mexico and Central America.

The Olmec civilization appears to have been the first "advanced" culture of Precolumbian Mesoamerica. Its most impressive sites are located in the Gulf Coast lowlands of the Mexican states of Veracruz and Tabasco, and these sites, which date to the period of *ca.* 1200–900 B.C., are the earliest in Mesoamerica to feature such things as large pyramids and platforms and monumental stone sculpture. The sculptures are in a very sophisticated and distinctive art style, and this style is replicated in smaller works of art, such as jade or pottery figurines or other manufactures. At this period of Olmec florescence the other regions and cultures of Mesoamerica were on a much simpler level of cultural development; however, in many of these other regions, from Central Mexico south to Salvador, Olmec art and iconography was manifest, both monumentally and on smaller, portable items, in what were otherwise more modest cultural contexts. This presented archaeologists with the interesting questions as to just what this signified, how it was disseminated, and what the meaning was of this widespread Olmec influence.

Both general comparative and specific historical analogies were addressed to the problem. Political imperialism, accompanied by religious proselytization, radiating from Olmec Gulf Coast centers is one model of the first kind.[25] A specific historical model was advanced by M. D. Coe[26] in which Coe suggested that Olmec hegemony over other parts of Mesoamerica was effected and maintained by a combination of military and economic dominance comparable to that known to have been used by the Aztecs in the same general area some two and a half millennia later. According to this model, the Aztec *pochteca*, a professional, state-supported cadre of merchants, established an extractive trading network throughout the area, channeling raw materials and other goods into Tenochtitlan, the Aztec capital, and these merchants were backed up by an aggressive military aristocracy. Coe's *pochteca* model had the specific historical advantage of pertaining to the area and cultural tradition to which the Olmec belonged, and some rather tenuous continuity can be demonstrated between Olmec and Aztec cultures; but the 2500 years separating the two is a long time, and, for various reasons, the Aztec model seemed unsatisfactory to a good many other archaeologists as an explanation of what had gone on in Olmec times. As an alternative to either the very general "imperial" model, or the *pochteca* model, K. V. Flannery has proposed a specific comparative model.[27]

Flannery cites two sources for his specific comparative analogical model, ethnographic accounts from two different parts of the world both remote from any connection with Precolumbian Mesoamerica. One of these is in Burma and concerns the Shan and Kachin tribes. The Shan were valley-dwelling, wet-rice cultivators with a stratified society. The Kachin lived in the neighboring hill country, practiced a less productive slash-and-burn form of agriculture, and had either an egalitarian or a ranked lineage social order. The Kachin, however, were in control of country rich in certain mineral resources, including gold and jade, both of which were lacking in the Shan-held lowlands. The Shan aristocracy desired these precious materials for the making of prestige ornaments or for trade with the Chinese. To obtain them they not only traveled to the hill country but established kin ties with the more primitive Kachin by giving their daughters in marriage to the Kachin chiefs. Such alliances worked to their advantage in obtaining the minerals, and they also exported foodstuffs, from their surplus supplies, to the hills. As a result of these contacts certain Kachin leaders began to imitate Shan nobility in ritual and religion, including the possession of symbolic objects of Shan design, and they also began to imitate features of the Shan stratified social organization.[28]

The other processual model is that offered by the Tlingit, of the Northwest Coast of North America, in their relationships with the Tagish. The former were wealthy salmon fishers with an aristocratic leadership, the latter poorer and socially simpler inland hunters. But, again, the poorer tribes controlled resources that were particularly prized as status items and as trade goods. In this instance it was the Tagish control of furs. As in the Shan-Kachin example, Tlingit aristocrats came to the Tagish country, took wives there, and sent daughters there to marry, securing valuable trading rights in doing so. Through these contacts the Tagish became "Tlingitized" to a degree, borrowing rituals and becoming more conscious of social rank in their own society.[29] Neither the Kachin nor the Tagish, in their respective situations, underwent any basic subsistence, technological, settlement pattern, or fundamental ethnolinguistic change; yet in both Burma and the Northwest Coast processes were set in motion which, if continued, could have resulted in an increasingly tighter area interaction sphere, pertaining to trade, sociopolitical organization, and probably ideology, as it did in Precolumbian Mesoamerica.

Flannery has used these models in an attempt to explain the Olmec "presence" in archaeological sites in Oaxaca that were built and occupied in the early part of the first millennium B.C. By this time population groups in the Valley of Oaxaca had reached a size and density where some degree of sociopolitical complexity had developed. This is seen in corporate labor constructions, such as platform mounds, in contrast to ordinary residential dwelling mounds; and this and other developments, including signs of a redistributive economy, signal an emerging Oaxacan elite of a chiefdom level. From all evidences, however, this early Oaxacan elite was distinctly less sophisticated than the Olmec aristocracy of the neighboring Mexican Gulf Coast country. At the same time, though, these Oaxacan leaders apparently controlled local resources of minerals, particularly magnetite and ilmenite, which were used in the Olmec country to manufacture ritual mirrors. Referring to the Oaxacan situation and to the specific analogies. Flannery states: "If our ethnographic data are in any way analogous, the mechanism which facilitated this interregional flow of goods should have been one which linked the highest ranking lineages of the Oaxacan peoples to one or more of the higher-ranking Olmec lineages. One would also predict that the highland Oaxacan elite would begin to emulate the religion, symbolism, dress, and behavior of the Olmec elite, insofar as it would enhance their own status among their own people. We might predict, for example, that while their patterns of settlement and subsistence remained unchanged, they might adopt the St. Andrew's cross, the U-motif, the 'paw-wing motif,' and the deity who was part man and part jaguar [all elements of Olmec iconography—GRW]."[30]

Many of the Oaxacan data do, indeed, confirm these predictions and suggest that the Burmese and Northwest Coast models may provide apt parallels for understanding the spread of Olmec influence in ancient Mesoamerica. Flannery did not offer it as any conclusive explanation of the Olmec phenomena. Such analogies are trial formulations, and the devising of "tests" to validate such models of process is frequently difficult. Flannery's use of specific comparative analogy in this instance is appealing because it moves closer to the specifics of behavior than do the more general models, which simply propose such concepts as "empire" or "trade." It also deals with analogies that are drawn from preindustrial societies of a developmental level at least somewhat comparable to the societies of ancient Mesoamerica. To be sure, some Mesoamericanists have criticized Flannery's model. From my own point of view, I doubt if food exchange, which figured importantly in the Shan dealings with the Kachin, is probable over the long distance separating Oaxaca and the Olmec Gulf Coast. But this and other substantive matters can be worked out only by continued investigations. The use of specific comparative analogical models is a first step.

A great many other examples of specific comparative analogy could be cited. It is more and more a standard operating procedure in archaeology. Not the least of its merits is that it forces archaeologists to be less immersed in their own narrow interests. When they return to their particular bailiwick, after a comparative look at cultures—ethnographic, historic, or archaeologic—unrelated to their own immediate research concerns, they are often able to look at what has grown familiar to them with a new and discerning eye.[31] One direction in which the comparative analogical approach can lead is toward what might be called a typology of cultures and of process. This, of course, takes us back in the direction of the philosophers of history; but some archaeologists have been doing this on a more limited and more fine-grained scale than that essayed by Spengler or Toynbee. Robert M. Adams has examined Mesopotamian data on the development of such institutions as land tenure and its relationships to the growth of the state, and has compared this story of process with one for ancient Central Mexico culminating in the Aztec empire.[32] His study is of great interest and holds promise for an understanding of "regularities" in process. Colin Renfrew, drawing widely upon European archaeological and historical data, as well as upon Polynesian ethnography, has described what he calls "Group-Oriented" and "Individualizing" chiefdoms.[33] These can be thought of as culture types, identifiable by specified archaeological traits, but they are of greater value in explicating processes of development in the general evolutionary stage between egalitarian societies and those that can be considered to be on the level of the state. All of this leads toward the concern with laws of regularities; but before facing up to this most difficult of all archaeological topics, let us review, however briefly, something more of the ambience in which the new archaeology has developed in recent years.

I have already stated that the theoretical or conceptual heart of the new archaeology is uniquely archaeological, and this is so. At the same time, its development has been greatly stimulated and forwarded by the deployment of methods and techniques from other sciences. As Grahame Clark has stated recently, archaeology is now science based. But, as he goes on to explain: "In the study of prehistory there is a constant interaction between aims and methods."[34] Thus, the desire on the part of archaeologists to know more about prehistoric diets has undoubtedly been a stimulus which they have taken to the soil scientists and paleobotanists; and the need to know more about ancient trade patterns has led archaeologists to inspire physical and chemical scientists to explore trace element analyses of obsidian or to determine the composition of metals. And all of this has had a feedback effect in leading archaeologists to ask new and more difficult questions of their data as these new methods and techniques have been continuously improved and refined. I shall make no attempt here to enumerate or describe all of the aids that now come to archaeology from other fields. In addition to the soil, pollen, and materials analyses just mentioned, the most important ones are dating techniques, especially through radiocarbin, and mathematical applications. In this last connection the computer has made it possible for archaeologists to ask questions about prehistoric demography, social organization, and land utilization that, heretofore, have been considered beyond the scope of the discipline. Indeed, general systems theory in archaeology, one of the primary theoretical underpinnings of the new trends, rests most solidly on mathematical simulations of systems models.

To this point I have referred to systems theory only in a general way in connection with the proposition that cultures are systems in which their parts, nonmaterial as well as material, relate to each other. Much recent archaeological writing has been devoted to systems theory, in both general[35] and substantive contexts. Among the latter are studies on subsistence changes, factors governing settlement patterns, Post-Pleistocene ecological adaptations, and the rise and fall of civilizations.[36] And this is only the smallest sort of sampling as one looks over current archaeological literature. There can be no doubt that the approach has a great potential for archaeology. In a sense, the idea has always been present, in a covert way, in archaeology; but, as used now, the clear delineation of the elements of the cultural system, and an explication of the interaction of these elements, give a greater openness and objectivity to archaeological interpretations and the reasoning behind them.

However, it should be realized that the construction of a simulation model of a system and the demonstration of the internal consistency of that model do not necessarily offer proof of what actually happened in the past. Such a model, for example, has been constructed in an attempt to explain what brought about the "collapse" of Classic Maya civilization in the lowlands of southern Mexico and Central America at the end of the ninth century A.D.[37] The various factors introduced into the model—population, resource pressures, foreign pressures, trade, prestige building activities, the exploitation of commoners by the nobility, and so on—are all reasonably documented in the archaeological record, and a convincing case can be made out for their positive or negative feedback interactions on each other in a way that seems to "explain" the denouement and breakdown of the Maya. It is the best that we have been able to do so far, yet I have a feeling that its main value will lie in its detailing of an analytical procedure that attempts to take account of as much of the data as possible and that it will probably be superseded as we come to know more.

In addition to the infusion of ideas and analytical methods from the mathematical, physical, chemical, and natural sciences, the new archaeology has been greatly encouraged in the pursuit of its objectives by the vast increase in archaeological research since the Second World War. Prior to this time there were still large areas of the world for which prehistory was still an unknown quantity. Sub-Saharan Africa, Siberia, much of Southeast Asia, and huge stretches of North and South America were among these. Now something is known of all of these places, and for parts of them there is detailed information. For other areas, previously partially or sketchily known, research has filled in geographical and chronological gaps and has generally refined our knowledge of cultural distributions and chronologies. This, together with radiocarbon dating scales, has given archaeologists a control over their data never enjoyed before. They are ready now, for the first time in many places, to ask questions about such things as the relative rates of culture change in different sociocultural situations or to appraise the processes of *in situ* development vis-à-vis those of diffusion. For the Old World we know now that settled community life, based on plant and animal domestication, had its beginnings as far back as 9000 B.C. and that after this, in the Middle East, there was a generally slow evolution leading up to the threshold of urban life at about 3000 B.C.[38] For the New World we can trace a similar evolution but the datings are later. In Mesoamerica and in Peru some plant domestication was taking place in the millennia between 7000 and 2000 B.C., but only toward the end of this period did the societies of these areas attain what has been referred to as a "village agricultural threshold."

After this, however, the New World evolution moved more swiftly, climaxing in true city life at the beginning of the Christian era.[39] This difference in timing is interesting and one of the many things in prehistory that is unexplained. In both the Old and New Worlds archaeologists are just beginning to learn something about the role of tropical forest areas in the rise of agriculture. Previously, attention had been directed at upland or semiarid zones in both hemispheres and to seed crops (wheat, barley, millet for the Old World; maize for the New); but in the last few years evidence has come in which would indicate that centers in Southeast Asia[40] and Tropical Forest South America[41] had developed root crop cultivation at very early times and that these centers had interacted with neighboring upland or nonforested regions, in their respective settings, to influence and augment the rise of a farming economy. This is not the place to continue with a recounting of substantive discoveries and advances in prehistory. The point to be made is that we know much more in this way than archaeologists of a quarter of a century ago, and although no one archaeologist can be said to have mastered the vast field of world prehistory, almost all of them have a greater awareness of it than was previously the case. This has made for a comparative outlook, as has been said with reference to analogical models, and has provided an atmosphere sympathetic to an interest in process.

It should be noted, of course, that much of the archaeological research that we have been talking about was carried on without any particular new archaeological emphasis, and this raises questions about research philosophy and procedures. Should a taxonomic-space-time framework, an archaeological data base, be laid down before the archaeologist attempts to move on to problems of process? Binford has argued that it cannot, that the asking of questions about process must be the beginning of any field investigation, for only if these problems are well in mind can investigators devise the proper research strategies and know what kind of evidence they are seeking.[42] There is something to be said for this position, but it is equally true that to ask the proper questions demands a certain foreknowledge of the prehistory of the region under examination. Fortunately, there is at least a practical answer. Any modern archaeologist should have the kind of awareness and vision that combines a data base recovery with a concern for process.

If there is some justification for the optimism that a systemic view of society and culture will take us further than we have ever gone before in explaining the human past—and I think that there is—and if this can be expedited through judicious selection of analogical models and their deductive testing, is there also a justified optimism about the discovery of laws or regularities concerning process? The humanistic branch of archaeology, and probably most historians, would say no. V. Gordon Childe, the foremost "new" archaeologist of the "prenew" archaeological era, also concluded in the negative. According to Grahame Clark, "in 1946 he [Childe] could still argue that there was a 'prospect of reaching general laws indicative of the direction of historic progress,' in his 'Valediction' he had to admit that while Marxism had once seemed to make intelligible the development of each culture it 'completely failed to explain the differences between one culture and another and indeed obliterated or dismissed the differences observed' (1958:6)."[43]

Binford, on the other hand, takes a more positive view.[44] To him, the *explanation* of cultural differences and similarities is evolutionary study, and this is the road to the formulation of laws. In saying this he rejects J. H. Steward's[45] "neo-evolutionism" as not evolutionary or processual but, rather, a "descriptive concern with . . . patterning," the comparing and generalizing about the changes through time that are observed in several culture sequences. Binford goes on to argue that in true evolutionary study the unit must be the whole independent sociocultural system. In his definition, evolutionary process is an operation at the interface of a living system and its extrasystemic field. Presumably, this "extrasystemic field" would be not only the natural environmental or ecological interface but the interfaces created by contact or communication with other sociocultural systems, although this is not altogether clear. He is, however, very explicit in stating that attempts "to use units which are partitive or units which represent classes of cultural phenomena will necessitate the added investigation of intersystemic relationships." It is here that difficulties arise for one "class of cultural phenomena" is certainly ideology, and it is to the realm of ideology and ideas that evolutionary theory often seems least applicable.

Does ideology articulate with other aspects of culture in a systemic fashion? Ethnologists and social anthropologists have been exploring this lately[46]; and Flannery, together with Joyce Marcus, has followed their lead by trying to see if these articulations can be discerned on the prehistoric level by archaeologists.[47] In this attempt, directed toward prehistoric Oaxacan cultures, they have relied, to a considerable degree, on some specific historical analogies in order to project ideological meanings (as derived from the Spanish conquest period in Mexico) back onto the first millennium B.C. Their analogical models reveal a Zapotecan (Oaxacan) cosmology (world view or idea system) that was intimately linked with agriculture, trade, ceremonialism, death and ancestor worship, and class stratification, and from the archaeological disposition of artifacts bearing specific iconographic symbols or otherwise identifiable as ritual paraphernalia they are able to plot a course of development through time in which ideology is seen as an integral part of the evolution of a cultural system. Their concluding paragraph might be taken as a directive for future archaeological research:

> In our opinion two of the most common mistakes being made by students of prehistoric human ecology are the attribution of Western economic motives to pre-Columbian subsistence behavior and the dismissal of pre-Columbian ritual as a form of intellectual activity unrelated to subsistence. Neither approach is supported by an examination of Zapotec cosmology. The Zapotec world was an orderly place in which human actions were based on empirical observations, interpreted in the light of a coherent body of logic. Once that logic is understood, all Zapotec behavior—whether economic, political, or religious—makes sense as a series of related and internally consistent responses based on the same set of underlying principles. In other words, one very non-Western metaphysic regulated exchanges of matter, energy, and information. We raise these criticisms not to detract from the study of human ecology but to make it still more holistic and hence more useful. Our goal is to find a framework for analysis which is neither a mindless ecology nor a glorification of mind divorced from the land.[48]

This quotation, and especially its last sentence, brings us to our most serious question about the new archaeology, its practice to date, and, more generally, the goal of process. Is it all sufficiently encompassing? So far, in my opinion, it has not been; but, admittedly, this kind of an outlook is still very new. The data of archaeology are, by definition, in the material realm, but the goals of the discipline must transcend this limitation. The processes of culture change must be studied not only in the ecological interface but at all of those points where ideas or "cultural choices," insofar as these can be inferred, intersect with economy, technology, and the more immediately materialistic aspects of culture. Ultimately, archaeology will not profit from a further breaking down of questions about human behavior and motivations. A framework for an integrated analysis must be sought. It is not over optimistic to commit ourselves to such a search, for I think that it is inevitable that the anthropological and humanistic branches of archaelogy will at last converge.[49] I doubt if this will come about through any formal academic merger, and it should not. Each tradition has always been a demanding one, and each brings to the study of the human past its own biases which, if not followed blindly, have their appropriate strengths. The convergence should come about in the face of questions about the past, especially the "big" questions. Are there laws or regularities about social and cultural behavior and change? What are the causative forces that make these laws or regularities operative? And what is their relevance to the present, if any? The Marxist paradigm is too narrowly conceived to allow us to discover the answers to questions like these. When we do, it will be with an outlook that enables us to consider the whole range of the human adventure, past and present.

References

[1]Glyn Daniel, *A Hundred and Fifty Years of Archaeology* (London: Duckworth, 1975). This is the best general summary of the historical development of the discipline.

[2]G. R. Willey and J. A. Sabloff, *A History of American Archaeology* (London: Thames and Hudson, 1974).

[3]See M. P. Leone, "Issues in Anthropological Archaeology," in *Contemporary Archaeology* (Carbondale: Southern Illinois University Press, 1972), pp. 14–27.

[4]See A. V. Kidder, *An Introduction to the Study of Southwestern Archaeology* (New Haven: Phillips Academy, Andover, Mass., 1924); and W. D. Strong, *An Introduction to Nebraska Archaeology* (Washington, D.C.: Smithsonian Institution, Miscellaneous Collections, 93 (19) (1935).

[5]V. G. Childe, *The Dawn of European Civilization* (London: Kegan Paul, Trench, and Trubner, 1925); *The Danube in Prehistory* (Oxford: Clarendon Press, 1929); and *The Most Ancient East* (London: 1934).

[6]See J. G. D. Clark, "Prehistoric Europe: The Economic Basis," *Archaeological Researches in Retrospect* (Cambridge, Mass.: Winthrop, 1974), pp. 33–60; and *Archaeology and Society* (London: Methuen, 1940).

[7] W. R. Wedel, *Environment and Native Subsistence Economies in the Central Great Plains* (Washington, D.C.: Smithsonian Institution, Miscellaneous Collections, 100 (3) (1941).

[8]P. S. Martin, Carl Lloyd, and Alexander Spoehr, "Archaeological Works in the Ackmen-Lowry Area, South-Western Colorado, 1938" (Chicago: Field Museum of Natural History Anthropological Series, 23 (2) (1938): 217–304); and P. S. Martin and John Rinaldo, "Modified Basket Maker Sites, Ackmen-Lowry Area, South-Western Colorado, 1937" (Chicago: same series, 23 (3) (1939): 305–499).

[9]J. H. Steward and F. M. Setzler, "Function and Configuration in Archaeology," *American Antiquity*, 4 (1938): 4–10; C. K. Kluckhohn, "The Conceptual Structure in Middle American Studies," *The Maya and Their Neighbors* (New York: Appleton-Century, 1940), pp. 41–51.

[10]W. W. Taylor, Jr., *A Study of Archaeology* (Menasha, Wisc.: American Anthropological Association Memoir, no. 6, 1948). Although this work did not appear until 1948 it was essentially completed by 1942 so that many of Taylor's colleagues were familiar with his ideas prior to publication date.

[11]R. S. MacNeish, *Preliminary Archaeological Investigations in the Sierra de Tamaulipas, Mexico* (Transactions, American Philosophical Society, Philadelphia, 48 Part 6 (1958).

[12]G. R. Willey, *Prehistoric Settlement Patterns in the Virú Valley, Peru* (Washington, D.C.: Bureau of American Ethnology, Smithsonian Institution, 1953a, Bulletin 155).

[13]L. R. Binford, "Archaeology as Anthropology," *American Antiquity*, 28 (1962): 217–225, is generally taken as marking the inception of the new archaeology.

[14]Donn T. Bayard, "Science, Theory, and Reality in the 'New Archaeology.'" *American Antiquity*, 34 (1969): 376–384, is one of the few exceptions.

[15]See, for examples, M. A. Smith, "The Limitations of Inference in Archaeology," *Archaeological Newsletter*, 6 (1) (London, 1955); Stuart Piggott, *Ancient Europe* (Edinburgh: University Press, 1965), pp. 4–5; Jacquetta Hawkes, "The Proper Study of Mankind," *Antiquity*, 42 (1968): 255–262; M. I. Finley, "Archaeology and History," *Daedalus*, Winter Issue (1971): 168–186. On the other hand, one of the leading theoretical statements of the new archaeology is by the English archaeologist D. L. Clarke, *Analytical Archaeology* (London: Methuen, 1968).

[16]Finley, "Archaeology and History."

[17]Finley, "Archaeology and History," p. 171; L. R. Binford, "Archaeological Perspectives," in S. R. and L. R. Binford (eds.), *New Perspectives in Archaeology* (Chicago: Aldine, 1968), pp. 21–22.

[18]Finley, "Archaeology and History," pp. 171–172.

[19]J. J. F. Deetz, *The Dynamics of Stylistic Change in Arikara Ceramics* (Urbana: University of Illinois Series in Anthropology, no. 4, 1965).

[20]W. A. Longacre, "Some Aspects of Prehistoric Society in East-central Arizona," in S. R. and L. R. Binford (eds.), *New Perspectives in Archaeology* (Chicago: Aldine, 1968), pp. 89–102.

[21]L. R. Binford, "Comments on K. C. Chang's 'Major Aspects of the Interrelationship of Archaeology and Ethnology,'" *Current Anthropology*, (1967): 234–235; and "Archaeological Perspectives," in S. R. and L. R. Binford (eds.), *New Perspectives in Archaeology* (Chicago: Aldine, 1968), p. 13.

[22]Stuart Piggott, *Ancient Europe* (Edinburgh: University Press, 1965), pp. 4–5.

[23]M. P. Leone (ed.), *Contemporary Archaeology* (Carbondale: Southern Illinois University Press, 1972). This idea is overtly or covertly expressed in Leone's Preface and in his article in the volume, pp. 14–27.

[24]G. R. Willey, Comments in *An Appraisal of Anthropology Today* (Chicago: University of Chicago Press, 1953d), p. 229. In these remarks I offered brief definitions of "specific historical" and "general comparative" analogies. At that time I would have included what I am now calling "specific comparative" under the "general comparative" rubric.

[25]Ignacio Bernal, in *The Olmec World* (Berkeley: University of California Press, 1969), uses such a model.

[26]M. D. Coe, *The Jaguar's Children: Prehistoric Central Mexico* (New York: Museum of Primitive Art, 1965b), pp. 122–123.

[27]K. V. Flannery, "The Olmec and the Valley of Oaxaca: A Model for Inter-Regional Interaction in Formative Times," *Dumbarton Oaks Conference on the Olmec* (Washington, D.C.: Dumbarton Oaks, 1968a), pp. 79–110.

[28]The ethnographic data for Burma are from E. R. Leach, *Political Systems of Highland Burma* (Boston, 1965 ed.).

[29]The ethnographic source on the Northwest Coast is Catharine McClellan, "The Inland Tlingit," *Asia and North America: Transpacific Contacts*, Memoirs, Society for American Archaeology, no. 9 (1953): 47–52.

[30]Flannery, "The Olmec and the Valley of Oaxaca," p. 106.

[31]G. R. Willey, "New World Prehistory: 1974b," *American Journal of Archaeology*, 78 (1974): 321–331.

[32]R. M. Adams, *The Evolution of Urban Society* (Chicago, 1966).

[33]Colin Renfrew, "Beyond a Subsistence Economy: The Evolution of Social Organization in Prehistoric Europe," in C. B. Moore (ed.): *Reconstructing Complex Societies* (Cambridge, Mass.: American Schools of Oriental Research, Supplement to Bulletin 20, 1974), pp. 69–96.

[34]J. G. D. Clark, "Prehistory Since Childe," *Bulletin of the Institute of Archaeology*, no. 13 (London, 1976).

[35]See D. L. Clarke, *Analytical Archaeology* (London: Methuen, 1968), for thorough general treatment of systems theory as applicable to archaeology.

[36]For examples see K. V. Flannery, "Archaeological Systems Theory and Early Mesoamerica," in B. J. Meggers (ed.), *Anthropological Archaeology in the Americas* (Washington, D.C.: Anthropological Society of Washington, 1968b); pp. 67–87; K. V. Flannery, "Evolution of Complex Settlement Systems," in *The Early Meso-American Village* (New York: Academic Press, 1976), pp. 162–172; L. R. Binford, "Post-Pleistocene Adaptations," in *An Archaeological Perspective* (New York: Seminar Press, 1972a), pp. 421–449; G. R. Willey and D. B. Shimkin, "The Maya Collapse: A Summary View," in T. P. Culbert (ed.), *The Classic Maya Collapse* (Albuquerque: University of New Mexico Press, 1973), pp. 457–502; D. H. Runge, J. A. Sabloff, and Dale Runge, "Simulation Model Development: A Case Study of the Classic Maya Collapse," manuscript, 1975.

[37]Willey and Shimkin, "The Maya Collapse"; Runge, Sabloff, and Runge, "Simulation Model Development."

[38]See the volume of collected papers, C. C. Lamberg-Karlovsky (ed.), *Old World Archaeology: Foundations of Civilization* (San Francisco, Freeman, 1952–1972), for various treatments of this subject, especially articles by R. J. Braidwood, K. M. Kenyon, R. J. Rodden, James Mellart, R. M. Adams, and C. C. Lamberg-Karlovsky.

[39]See G. R. Willey, "New World Prehistory: 1974," *American Journal of Archaeology*, 78 (1974b): 321–331, for a recent summary of New World data.

[40]See W. G. Solheim, "Southeast Asia and the West," *Science*, 157 (1967): 896–902, for a summary of these data.

[41]See D. W. Lathrap, *The Upper Amazon* (London: Thames and Hudson, 1970), for a synthesis of Amazonian data.

[42]L. R. Binford, "Some Comments on Historical Versus Processual Archaeology," in *An Archaeological Perspective* (New York: Seminar Press, 1972b), pp. 114–124; and J. A. Sabloff and G. R. Willey, "The Collapse of Maya Civilization in the Southern Lowlands: A Consideration of History and Process," *Southwestern Journal of Anthropology*, 23 (1967): 311–336.

[43]Clark, "Prehistory Since Childe."

[44]L. R. Binford, "Comments on Evolution," in *An Archaeological Perspective* (New York: Seminar Press, 1971c), pp. 105–113.

[45]J. H. Steward, *Theory of Culture Change* (Urbana: University of Illinois Press, 1955).

[46]G. A. Reichel-Dolmatoff, Huxley Memorial Address, University of London, 1976, R. A. Rappaport, "Ritual, Sanctity, and Cybernetics," *American Anthropologist*, 73 (1971a): 59–76; and "The Sacred in Human Evolution," *Annual Review of Ecology and Systemics*, 2 (1971b): 23–44.

[47]K. V. Flannery and Joyce Marcus, "Formative Oaxaca and the Zapotec Cosmos," *American Scientist*, 64 (1976b): 374–383.

[48]Ibid.

[49]See D. P. Dymond, *Archaeology and History, A Plea for Reconciliation* (London: Thames and Hudson, 1974). I am in complete sympathy with Dymond's plea for "total archaeology" (Ch. 7).

VI

The Recovery of Ideology

This essay was written after I had read the Spring 1975 issue of the journal *Daedalus*, which had been devoted to the great transcendent religious and philosophical movements of the ancient Old World. It led me to wonder if there had ever been anything in the Precolumbian New World to compare with them. Benjamin I. Schwartz (1975), in his introductory article to this *Daedalus* symposium issue, had observed that "so far as we know" there was nothing of this nature in the "Mayan-Aztec civilizations." But was this correct? Was there anything in the Americas that might be comparable? Obviously, data from New World civilizations that might bear on such a question would be much more limited than those of the text-aided histories of the ancient Near East, early Greece, China, or India. Still, the shadowland of Aztec legendary history, and the projections from it back in time to the world of the "Toltecs," was, in some instances, no more "legendary" than some of the Old World histories.

In the course of these thoughts, I recalled a doctoral dissertation by Henry B. Nicholson (1957), a former graduate student of mine at Harvard, who had written of the legendary-historical figure of Topiltzin Quetzalcoatl, the apotheosized God-King of Tollan of the Toltecs. Topiltzin was a culture-bringer and law-giver, a hero of peace and light, one who defied the old dark traditions of war and human sacrifice. Sadly and tragically, he was brought down by his enemies, who resented his reforms and preferred the evil old ways; and yet Topiltzin lived on in common memory as one who would some day return and bring with him a new era of hope. So powerful was this remembrance of him among the peoples of central Mexico that the last Aztec Emperor, Moctezuma II, saw in Cortez the returned God-King.

I decided to have an adventurous go in writing about it. This was a bold decision on the part of one who was not a scholar of the early documentary sources. As I state in my essay, I depended heavily upon Nicholson's thesis as a guide, and I corresponded with him in the course of my writing. I think he was somewhat tolerantly amused at what he took to be my imaginative straying away from the disciplined limits of scholarship. Nevertheless, I am glad I wrote "Mesoamerican Civilization and the Idea of Transcendence." I think some of the observations I made have merit. One of these—which I learned from the *Daedalus* authors—is that transcendental religious movements need what might best be called a "civilizational depth" for their development. Indeed, I think they might be said to grow out of the agony of urban life. I felt that this condition had been met in the epoch of the tenth to twelfth centuries A.D. in Mesoamerica.

If I were writing this same article today, the only thing I would change would be to eliminate most of the final paragraph. I believe now that I was wide of the mark in suggesting that such early horizon styles as Olmec and Chavín could be the archaeological residues of transcendent movements. There are too many other explanations for such phenomena. It may well be that the intellectual complexities of transcendent movements—at least as they were defined in the *Daedalus* symposium—are too subtle, too ephemeral to be detected in archaeological cultures in which there is no aid from contemporary written texts or which are not illuminated by the passing down of oral histories.

Mesoamerican Civilization and the Idea of Transcendence

(From *Antiquity*, Vol. 50, pp. 205–215, 1976, Reprinted by permission of *Antiquity*.)

How do ideas, or ideologies, articulate with other cultural systems? This is a complex question, and archaeologists, in their study of the rise and growth of civilizations, have been hesitant to address it. There are obvious reasons for this hesitancy. Even in those instances where the archaeological record is text-aided it is difficult, and it is still more so where contemporaneous documentary materials are lacking or equivocal, as in Precolumbian America. Then, too, it is my impression that while many archaeologists are willing to grant ideology a role in cultural development they tend to look upon it as causally "secondary." Subsistence, demography, technology, and ecology—perhaps because they are more directly susceptible to archaeological methods and inferences than are idea systems—are more apt to be seen as the seats of "prime cause." In one sense I suppose it is true that "prime" or "first cause" can be said to reside in the materialist matrix. This is where life begins, where populations are sustained, and where certain limits are set on sizes and groupings of human societies. From this perspective ideologies may well seem "derivative" or "epiphenomenal." Still, if thinking human beings are the generators, as well as the carriers, of culture it seems highly probable that, from very early on, ideas provided controls for and gave distinctive forms to the materialist base and to culture, and that these ideas then took on a kind of existence of their own, influencing, as well as being influenced by, other cultural systems. If this is so, then it is of interest and importance to try to see how ideas were interrelated with other parts of culture and how they helped direct the trajectories of cultural and civilizational growth.

I propose to make a beginning here by examining the way in which a certain set of Mesoamerican ideological phenomena were articulated with other aspects of culture. In attempting this, let us set aside, for the present at least, the ambitious goal of "prime causation" and begin more modestly by analyzing the way in which an ideology functioned at a particular time and place. By so doing we may gain insight into one of the cultural processes that was operative in ancient Mesoamerica and, more generally, in the rise of other civilizations as well. The ideological example I have selected lies in the Precolumbian past but by no means dates back to the beginnings or "origins" of Mesoamerican civilization. While many of the pertinent data are wholly archaeological or prehistoric, some of them—indeed, the crucial ones relating to specific ideological content—are projections from the ethnohistorical record.

The methodological device for this exploratory exercise is a model borrowed from Old World culture history. This is the concept of "transcendence," and, specific to the present context, I am concerned with religious, philosophical, or ideological transcendence. In the Spring 1975 issue of the journal *Daedalus* which is devoted to a symposium entitled "Wisdom, revelation and doubt: perspectives on the first millennium B.C.," Benjamin I. Schwartz has this to say about transcendence (1975, 3):

> What I refer to here is something very close to the etymological meaning of the word—a kind of standing back and looking beyond—a kind of critical, reflective questioning of the actual and a new vision of what lies beyond. It is symbolized in the Hebrew tradition by Abraham's departure from Ur and all it represents, by the Buddha's more rational renunciation, by Confucius' search for the source of the *jen* within and the normative order without, by the Lao Tse book's strain toward the nameless *Tao*, and by the Greek strain toward an order beyond the Homeric gods, by the Socratic search within as well as by the Orphic mysteries. On the intellectual side one can speak in terms of "wisdom" and "doubt" . . . On the side of spiritual vision one can speak of "revelation."

Schwartz entitles his essay, which is the introductory one to the volume, "The age of transcendence," and by this he is referring to the seven or eight centuries prior to the birth of Christ. This was the era of those transcendent "spiritual, moral, and intellectual 'breakthroughs'" in the Old World that we know as classical Judaism, Zoroastrianism, Buddhism, Jainism, Confucianism, and Taoism. And to these we might add Christianity by extending that era foward by a very few centuries. The several articles of the *Daedalus* volume were written by historians, archaeologists, anthropologists, and philosophers, and they deal with various aspects of this theme of ideological transcendence in the respective settings of Grecian, Middle Eastern, Indian, Chinese, and other Old World civilizations. The cross-cultural perspective was only occasionally and incidentally historico-diffusionistic. Rather, in each instance, attention was focused on *in situ* context and processual development. What were the circumstances surrounding the rise of transcendent movements? And how were the movements themselves made manifest?

One very obvious precondition of Old World transcendent movements was that they all arose from a background of what we might call "civilizational depth." That is, they were, in each case, preceded by a good many centuries of urban living and those other institutions that are generally associated with civilized or advanced societies. In all instances the transcendent movements appear at a stage of crisis in the civilization, as though these crises had called forth new spiritual, intellectual, and ethical responses. As indicated in Schwartz's definition, these responses were "critical" and "reflective." As such, they tended to be negations of the actual, of the status quo. At the same time, they were not negations of all the real world or all that had gone before. Indeed, they always drew upon prototypical elements—perhaps earlier transcendental formulations—in their respective civilizational backgrounds and reaffirmed these—but on a new level. Each transcendent movement was, in a phrase, "a pathos of negation and constraint vis-à-vis the forces of human pride and passion" (Schwartz, 1975, 5). They would differ, I think, from what the anthropologist has conceived of as "nativistic movements" in that the transcendent messages were less narrowly "counter-revolutionary" in outlook but held, instead, to an overarching vision of past, present, and future. Their effects were revolutionary, at least for a time and to a degree. Eventually, they became "contained" or "assimilated" into the total cultural tradition, but, even so, they were responsible for lasting changes in that tradition. S. C. Humphreys, writing in the same volume, speaks to this dialectic of containment and change by saying (1975, 110):

> Since transcendence always represents an implicit relativization of the normal social order and a potential challenge to it, those who have an interest in maintaining the social order will seek to contain and integrate transcendence in this way—to routinize it, one might say. Nevertheless, there are still moments when a new vision of society from a transcendental perspective stands out clearly as a challenge to established patterns of thought and behaviour and, though it does not completely transform them, effects irreversible changes.

Schwartz (1975, p. 2) notes that not all of the Old World's ancient civilizations were characterized by transcendent movements, calling attention especially to Mesopotamia and Egypt in this regard. Perhaps the weight of tradition in these very early and "primary' centers of civilization was too heavy and overbearing to allow for such innovation—although for Egypt the abortive transcendent attempt of Ikhnaten cannot be overlooked. Frequently, the bearers of transcendence were on the borders of old imposing civilizations. Such would be the situation of Greece, Judea, and Iran; but this condition of marginality would not apply to China.

Does the concept of transcendence apply to the New World Precolumbian civilizations? Schwartz (1975, 2) makes only a passing reference to this, saying "so far as we know" transcendent movements did not occur in the "Mayan-Aztec civilizations." To the contrary, I think that they probably did occur. Admittedly, Precolumbian data, for lack of heavy literary documentation, are more hazardous for the interpreter; but if one considers the rise of transcendent ideologies as something that may occur independently in generally similar social and cultural contexts, in this case in those contexts that we call civilizations, then their New World presence need not be surprising. It is true, of course, that the Precolumbian civilizations do not have the chronological depth of most of their Old World counterparts. The earliest Mesoamerican civilizations, or complex sociopolitical orders approximating to that condition, are those of Olmec affiliation which date back to about 1200 B.C. Does this give us sufficient time for the problems attendant upon civilized life to precipitate a transcendent movement of the kind which Schwartz and his colleagues describe for the Old World? Clearly, we cannot answer such a processual question in the abstract; but, in my view, I believe that the preconditions necessary for the development of transcendent ideologies were present in Precolumbian Mesoamerica, as I shall proceed to argue. Specifically, I think that there was at least one ideological or religious movement that had an effect on the Mesoamerican cultural scene comparable to that of some of the Old World transcendent philosophies. The example I have in mind concerns the story and the cult of Topiltzin Quetzalcoatl.

The Topiltzin Quetzalcoatl story treats of events that are presumed to have happened in Central Mexico during the Toltec era of the tenth century A.D. The tale was preserved down to the late Aztec–early Spanish Colonial Period in narrative chants, other oral histories, and pictorial codices; and the drama of this great priest-king of the Toltecs was then incorporated into the Spanish or Spanish-Native chronicles. These chronicles have been studied by many of the most distinguished Mesoamerican ethnohistoric and archaeological scholars, including, most recently, by Wigberto Jimenez Moreno (1941, 1946, 1954–5) Paul Kirchhoff (1955), and Henry B. Nicholson (1955, 1957, 1973, 1974). The chronicles are a *mélange* of history, legend, and myth, with many variations, and some contradictions, on the Topiltzin Quetzalcoatl tale; but I would agree with Nicholson that there is enough of what appears to be a hard core of history, especially when viewed in the light of archaeological data, to lead us to believe that we are dealing with some real events of the Precolumbian past. My summary of the Topiltzin Quetzalcoatl story is based largely on that of Nicholson (1957), the only full, critical, and monographic treatment of the subject. In its preparation Nicholson relied primarily upon the earliest Central Mexican documents, all written between 1530 and 1570. These are: (1) the *Historia de los Mexicanos por sus Pinturas* (Garcia Icazbalceta, 1891); (2) the *Juan Cano Relaciones* (Garcia Icazbalceta, 1891); (3) the *Histoyre du Mechique* (1905); (4) the *Leyenda de los Soles* (Paso y Troncoso, 1903; Lehmann, 1938); (5) the *Historia general de las Cosas de Nueva España* (Sahagun, 1938, 1956); and (6) the *Anales de Cuauhtitlan* (Lehmann, 1938). Their relatively early dates, as well as the nature of their contents, would indicate that these chronicles are less likely to have suffered from Christian theological accretions than many later works, and what Nicholson has called the "Basic Topiltzin Quetzalcoatl of Tollan Tale" derives from these. There are, of course, a great many other documents of supplementary value, including, for Central Mexico, the *Codices Telleriano-Remensis* (1899) and *Vaticanus A* (1900) and the writings of Motolinía (1903). There are also pertinent Oaxacan (Caso, 1950, 1952, 1954; Nicholson, 1974), Guatemalan (Recinos, 1947), and Yucatecan (Landa, 1938) sources.

The "basic tale" of Topiltzin Quetzalcoatl begins with the birth of a Toltec prince, Ce Acatl Topiltzin. He was the son of Mixcoatl, the renowned founder of Toltec power and a semi-divine king. His mother is said to have been a high-born Chichimec woman, probably from a tribe that had been conquered by Mixcoatl. According to some stories Ce Acatl's conception and birth were surrounded by miraculous circumstances. His mother died at his birth, and he was taken to be raised by a goddess. His actual birthplace is unknown although it probably was not at Tollan but at some lesser site to the north and west. During the young prince's youth his father, Mixcoatl, was betrayed and murdered by his brothers, Ce Acatl Topiltzin's treacherous uncles. After this the young Topiltzin embarked on a quest to find his dead father's bones. The search lasted for several years, but when he finally found them he caused a templt to be built and placed his father's remains in this shrine. He also set about achieving a just vengeance on the evil uncles.

It is at about this point in the tale that the founding of Tollan, or Tula, as the Toltec capital, took place; and it may be that the incident of the construction of the temple to house his revered father's bones symbolizes this founding, although there is some anbiguity in the chronicles as to whether Ce Acatl Topiltzin was the initial founder of the city, whether it had already been established by the Toltecs, or whether it was a conquered foreign place which had been brought under Toltec rule. In any event, he was, at this time, formally installed as the Toltec king; and, on his accession to the throne, he became Topiltzin Quetzalcoatl, an identification that linked him to the ancient Mesoamerican god, Quetzalcoatl, and, in effect, made him a demi-god.

All of the chronicles are in agreement in describing Topiltzin Quetzalcoatl as a much-loved and beneficent priest-king. They stress his role as a religious innovator, particularly in his aversion to war and human sacrifice. He was also said to be a chaste and penitent man, and, like his namesake, was a patron of the arts, crafts, and learning—indeed, a person deserving of the name "culture-hero." All of these traits which delineate Topiltzin Quetzalcoatl very clearly set him apart from his dark nemesis, Tezcatlipoca.

This Tezcatlipoca of the tale was also a dignitary of Tollan, and, like Topiltzin Quetzalcoatl, he also bore a god name. But Tezcatlipoca was the deity of war and the underworld and was associated with human sacrifice. His earthly counterpart of Tollan was, similarly, an ardent proponent of war and human sacrifice. In the confrontation between Topiltzin Quetzalcoatl and Tezcatlipoca it is said that their disagreement over the practice of human sacrifice was at the root of their mutual enmity. The details of the struggle that ensued are somewhat hazy, and it is uncertain to what degree an actual civil war may have broken out within Tollan. Throughout the conflict, however, Tezcatlipoca is portrayed as wicked, a deceiver and a sorcerer, in contrast to the essentially benign and straightforward Topiltzin Quetzalcoatl. Eventually, Tezcatlipoca's evil machinations prevailed. He was able to discredit Topiltzin Quetzalcoatl in the eyes of the people of Tollan and to force the humiliated king to leave his beloved city where the powers of Tezcatlipoca, symbolized by darkness, war, and human sacrifice, then became ascendant.

The chronicles are unanimous on Topiltzin Quetzalcoatl's flight from Tollan. While the details of his itinerary vary, it is generally conceded that he followed an easterly and southerly route. Eventually, he and his party reached a place called Tlapallan, whose location is uncertain although it was at some distance from Tollan. This final stopping place may have been on or near the sea for, according to one version of the tale, Topiltzin Quetzalcoatl then departed across the waters, promising some day to return. In another version Topiltzin Quetzalcoatl dies, is cremated, and his soul is taken up into the planet Venus. Either way, the apotheosis was complete. Topiltzin Quetzalcoatl had become immortalized.

Such, in brief outline, is the story of Topiltzin Quetzalcoatl, the great priest-king of the Toltecs. In judging its historicity we should keep in mind Nicholson's (1957) statement that the supernatural elements do not necessarily negate the possibility of the reality of other portions of it. Central Mexican narrative literature was traditionally couched in mythic and supernatural terms. That there was a Toltec, son of the founder of the dynasty, who became king in his own right and who reigned at Tollan is perfectly believable. His dual role as a secular ruler and a religious innovator is in keeping with what we know of Central Mexican political structure. Nor is the identification of such a person with the ancient god Quetzalcoatl surprising. This god, sometimes referred to as Ehecatl-Quetzalcoatl, was variously a deity of winds, rain, and cultural enlightenment. As identified by feathered-serpent and other iconographic motifs, he dates at least to Classic Period Teotihuacan times (A.D. 100–700), and some scholars have argued for his presence as far back as the Olmec era (*ca.* 1200 B.C.) (Coe, 1973). Certainly by the time of the Toltec ascendancy Quetzalcoatl must have been known throughout the Mesoamerican civilized world. As a frontier people who had moved into the conquered heartlands of the old Teotihuacan civilization, and who as former barbarians were assimilating the traditions of this once prestigious civilization, it would not have been unusual for the Toltecs to have adopted its gods. Viewed in this light, Ce Acatl's identification with Quetzalcoatl was a logical and highly symbolic example of cultural and religious syncretism and political expediency. I would agree with Nicholson (1957, p. 358) when he concludes his analysis of the historicity of the "Basic Tale of Topiltzin Quetzalcoatl" by saying that "the lineaments of a flesh and blood individual are clear enough that we can begin to seriously consider the contribution he may have made to the culture-historical process in Post-Classic Mesoamerica."

The general configurations of Central Mexican prehistory, as these are derived from archaeology, are broadly consistent with the Topiltzin Quetzalcoatl tale (Porter Weaver, 1972, 202–12). Ancient Tollan has been securely identified with the archaeological site of Tula, in Hidalgo, immediately to the northwest of the Valley of Mexico (Acosta, 1956–7; Jimenez Moreno, 1941). The site was a minor center at the time of the fall of Teotihuacan (*ca.* A.D. 700–750). Its great Toltec, or Tollan, phase follows just after A.D. 900, lasting until the Chichimec destruction of the city in the twelfth century (Diehl and Benfer, 1975). This archaeological chronology corresponds closely to that of the ethnohistorians. Jimenez Moreno (1966) sets the founding of Tollan, or Tula, at about A.D. 900; and Nicholson, in a recent appraisal of Postclassic Period chronologies, is in general agreement with this. Similarly, the collapse of Tollan, or Tula, is usually dated to between A.D. 1150 and 1200 (Jimenez Moreno, 1966; Nicholson, 1973).

During their heyday at Tollan, or Tula, the Toltecs must have established hegemony over much of Mesoamerica. In some instances this was probably done by military conquest. As evidence for this, the Toltec architectural complex and the warlike murals at the Yucatecan site of Chichen Itza (Tozzer, 1957) come immediately to mind, and there is militaristic Toltec-like architecture in Veracruz (Garcia Payon, 1971). In other regions trade and more peaceful processes of penetration may have been operative. An iconography of a Quetzalcoatl cult was, by whatever means, widely diffused on this Early Postclassic time level, and from this one would suspect that the tale of Topiltzin Quetzalcoatl had also been widely propagated at the same time. In reviewing documentary sources, Nicholson demonstrates the presence of the tale in much of Central Mexico. Beyond this, it is difficult to be sure, although there are probable references to the story in the Guatemalan Highland *Popol Vuh*. Also, the well-known legendary histories of Chichen Itza, in northern Yucatan, tell of a king, Quetzalcoatl (Kukulcan), who arrived there with a party of followers in the tenth century, and some authorities have speculated that this leader was none other than Topiltzin Quetzalcoatl at the end of his flight from Tollan.

Let us now look at the Topiltzin Quetzalcoatl story and evidence analytically and in the light of the criteria that were enumerated as being characteristic of transcendent movements.

First, there is the time-depth developmental context of the tale. The events that it describes occurred at a relatively late date in the history of Mesoamerican civilization, the tenth century A.D. or about 2,000 years after the beginnings of complex societies in Mesoamerica. While, as remarked earlier, this is less time-depth than in the cases of Old World transcendent movements, it is still an appreciable time in the histories of any urban or protourban societies. In my opinion I would say that the criterion of "civilizational depth" is met.

Second, there is the broad geographical and multinational scope of the Quetzalcoatl phenomena in Mesoamerica. Eric Weil (1975, 31) noted in the *Daedalus* volume that multinational groupings held together in some kind of a political order or empire are necessary for the spreading of new and transcendent messages. Does Mesoamerica of the tenth century A.D. measure up in this regard? I think so, although there are differences of opinion among Mesoamerican archaeologists as to the nature of these spheres of influence. As early as the Olmec horizon style (1200–900 B.C.) there are clear indications of interregional and transcultural connexions throughout much of Central and Southern Mexico and Upper Central America, and these connexions are not only expressed in raw materials or simple manufactured items but also in similarities or identities in highly complex monumental art. A political empire may not have been involved, but there was obviously a sophisticated system of interregional communication in operation. Subsequently, in the Classic Period, Teotihuacan commercial and political influences were widespread in Mesoamerica as witnessed by Teotihuacan-style architecture in places as distant as Oaxaca and Highland Guatemala, and by the presence at Tikal, in the Maya Lowlands, of hieroglyphic textual clues to, and iconographic representations of, Teotihuacan-affiliated political and religious rulers. It is not excessive speculation to say that by the end of the Classic Period at Teotihuacan (A.D. 700) there must have been a well-defined ecumenical sphere, a Mesoamerican "known civilized world." The Toltecs were the inheritors of this "world," with its time-depth and its cultural-geographic coherence.

The foregoing relates, thus, to a third criterion of transcendent ideological movements—the precondition of *in situ* prototypes. The Olmec and Teotihuacan communication systems, whatever their other functions may have been, were ideological networks, and, pertinent to the matter of Topiltzin Quetzalcoatl, we have already noted the antiquity of the Quetzalcoatl deity.

Besides these criteria, there is another in our Mesoamerican example that is equally diagnostic for transcendent phenomena. The era of the end of the Classic Period and the beginning of the Postclassic was a time of troubles and crisis. It was a time ripe for revolutionary ideas. The old order of the Teotihuacan civilization had broken down. Political disruptions ensued in the competitions for power, and these would have been linked to trade and commercial disruptions. The situation must have been exacerbated further by population pressures. The Late Preclassic and Classic Periods had seen population growth in Central Mexico (Millon, 1973; Parsons, 1971; Blanton, 1972), as well as elsewhere in Mesoamerica (Willey and Shimkin, 1973; Spores, 1972; Winter, 1975); and this was compacted in Central Mexico by the movement of peoples out of the west and northwest into the old civilized regions. While the causes of this movement are not altogether understood—drought conditions in the semiarid north and northwest may have been one reason—the rich lure of the civilizations for the barbarian frontiersmen may have been a factor. The Toltecs, themselves, were a part of this movement from the frontier to the heartland. In view of all of these conditions, the disorders of the material world could very easily have had an unsettling effect on established religious authority and old belief systems. New philosophies, new "world views" would have been in order.

And this leads us to one more parallel between the Mesoamerican and Old World settings for transcendent ideas. This is the circumstance that such ideas frequently do not evolve within the hearth area of an ancient civilization but on its margins. The Toltecs, at Tollan or Tula, had moved to be just within the orbit of the old Central Mexican civilizations, but their heritage was, in important part, still that of the frontier. It is, thus, more likely that their religious specialists would have been less "encapsulated" in traditional temple and palace hierarchical organizations than would have been the case for their opposite numbers in the established and conservative society of Teotihuacan (cf. Humphreys, 1975, 112–13, *re* the conservative Egyptian and Mesopotamian societies) and, therefore, more open to innovation. In any event, it is from the marginal, or *arriviste*, society of the Toltecs that we have the phenomenon of Topiltzin Quetzalcoatl.

The tale of Topiltzin Quetzalcoatl, thus, arises out of the ancient and broad context of Mesoamerican civilization, and it appears at a time of disorder and crisis in that civilization, on its northern marches. What is the meaning of the tale? To turn to our Old World criteria of transcendent ideas once more, we can ask the question, was the Topiltzin message "critical," "reflective," "reformist"? I do not think that we can deny that it was all of these things. If we are to believe some of the substance of the tale—and here we can turn to archaeological evidences of Toltec public art—we know that human sacrifice was a very integral part of the warfare patterns of the time. A theme that runs most consistently through the various versions of the story of Topiltzin Quetzalcoatl is that he was vigorously opposed to warfare and, especially, to human sacrifice. In this sense his position is definitively that of one critical of the mainstream of prevailing social, political, and religious thought. He was a reformer who, in his promotion of the peaceful arts and in the conduct of his own life, does, indeed, project a "pathos of negation and constraint vis-à-vis the forces of human pride and passion." And this pathos is given high dramatization by his defeat and his flight, as it were, into the wilderness. His eventual disappearance or death, with his promise of a return or his supernatural resurrection are the fitting denouement for a transcendent figure. Looking at both context and content, I would say that the meaning of the Topiltzin Quetzalcoatl tale is one of profound criticism of the times and of the established life-styles of war, violence, and human sacrifice. In formulating this criticism the great religious leader looked back to the past, to the life-giving attitudes of his god namesake, Quetzalcoatl, and from this perspective he transcended the present and looked forward to a more benign future, promised by his "return."

What were the functions of Topiltzin Quetzalcoatl's ideas? In briefest form I think that they were a response to the need for communication among the fragmented parts of the Mesoamerican *Oikoumene* after the breakdown of the old Classic Period order of Teotihuacan. This breakdown had released two rival ideologies, and both of these drew upon deep folk memories for the people of Mesoamerica. On the one hand, there was the ideology of Tezcatlipoca, the ideology of competition, war, and its extreme and logical extension of human sacrifice. These ideas are very old in Mesoamerica, but at the beginning of the Postclassic Period they must have been reformulated and intensified in response to the social and political conditions that we have described. By their very nature one would anticipate them to have been the increasingly prevailing ideas of the conservative establishment. The other ideology was that of Topiltzin Quetzalcoatl. Although it, too, had ancient religious prototypes, it was, in a sense, the more "revolutionary," running as it did in the face of the institutionalized militarism of the Postclassic and the intensified cult of human sacrifice. In this light, it is no accident that human sacrifice is so central to the stories of Topiltzin Quetzalcoatl which all stress his opposition to it. I am inclined to see in this the philosopher priest-king's realization that such intensity of competition, as represented by the newly glorified gods of war and sacrifice, could not be sustained to the benefit of the "known civilized world" or *Oikoumene* of Mesoamerica. Further, the popularity and persistence of his ideas strongly suggests a similar realization by others that "human pride and passion" had to have some limits.

Put in another way, the transcendent philosophy of Topiltzin Quetzalcoatl was an adaptive ideology, a response to the fierce competition and attendant disorders of the Mesoamerican scene. It was an attempt to save the Mesoamerican ecumenical order for such an order must have been recognized, consciously or subconsciously, as a necessity. The beginnings of such an *Oikoumene*, as we have seen, lay far back in the past—as early as the Olmec horizon or even earlier. It involved interchanges and accommodations in such matters as religious and calendrical information and interdynastic alliances and marriages. These were a part of an ecumenical fabric of "international" stability. Perhaps even more importantly, it involved trade among regions in both raw materials and manufactured items. Such trade had long been a "taken for granted" part of Mesoamerican life. As time went on, this trade appears to have become ever more important, and from what we know of Postclassic society, from documentary sources, the trader or merchant was steadily becoming a more influential figure in this society, pressing, perhaps, upon prerogatives and power formerly held solely by aristocratic and military cadres. In this context, it may not be too much to see the philosophy of Topiltzin Quetzalcoatl as the adaptive and protective ideology of a rising merchant or "middle" class. This by no means ruled out all competition and empire-building, but it was a recognition that some limits were essential. I would surmise, further, that this was particularly so in Central Mexico where barbarian tribes were debouching into the old civilized centers and where a rapid acculturation to the ways of Mesoamerican civilization was a pressing need in the Early Postclassic Period. It is at this place and time of greatest stress that, significantly, I think, Topiltzin Quetzalcoatl arose.

Finally, what were the results of Topiltzin Quetzalcoatl's transcendent ideas? As is so often the case, there are indications in the chronicles and in Mesoamerican archaeology that his revolutionary ideology was captured and contained, "routinized" to use a term and concept referred to earlier. For instance, judging from the iconographic evidence at Chichen Itza, a Quetzalcoatl cult became a part of an expanding militaristic empire whose leaders were certainly not averse to human sacrifice. Nor would later Central Mexican history and archaeology reveal any real triumph of Topiltzin Quetzalcoatl's pacific and essentially humanistic ideals. On the contrary, as we well know, human sacrifice, as an adjunct to and symbol of war and empire-building, flourished under the Aztecs as never before. Should we then judge Topiltzin Quetzalcoatl's efforts as a failure? Was it something less than transcendence—an aborted attempt on the order of Ikhnaten's monotheistic philosophy which vanished with few traces? Perhaps, yet I do not think such an appraisal does full justice to Topiltzin Quetzalcoatl's contribution. War and sacrifice continued in Mesoamerica, but his critical and transcendent philosophy remained alive. Often there seems to have been a kind of ambivalence of attitudes, such as that attributed to the poet-king Nezahualcoyotl, of Texcoco, at once a conqueror and imperialist and a devotee of the teachings of Topiltzin Quetzalcoatl (Porter Weaver, 1972, p. 207). Of course, the best known instance of this ambivalence, and the persistence of the ideas of Topiltzin Quetzalcoatl, involves the most famous Aztec of the Conquest Period, the Emperor Moctezuma II. His indecision and omen-haunted behavior on learning of Cortez's landing in Veracruz show that he had not forgotten Topiltzin Quetzalcoatl and his promise "to return." While it is true that Topiltzin Quetzalcoatl's teachings were often honored in the breach rather than otherwise, this has been the well-known fate of other transcendent philosophies. On balance, I would argue that Topiltzin Quetzalcoatl's ideas, in spite of Toltec militaristic perversions of them, and the Aztec rejection, did effect culture changes in Mesoamerica.

To sum up, I have tried to show how a certain kind of ideological phenomenon, a transcendent idea of doctrine, may interrelate with other cultural systems. It is my conclusion that the story of the Toltec priest-king, Topiltzin Quetzalcoatl documents a Precolumbian example of a transcendent religious philosophy. It is my further contention, however tentative, that this particular transcendent ideology served to mitigate the rising competition and strife of Postclassic Mesoamerica. Topiltzin Quetzalcoatl's doctrines were "revolutionary" in that they ran counter to the war-and-sacrificial-cult theology of the governmental establishments of the times; and it is suggested that they may have been favored by an increasingly influential merchant class. Topiltzin Quetzalcoatl's ideology was propagated in the Early Postclassic Period, and it was rapidly "contained" within Toltec expansionist policy. His doctrinal ideas were further adulterated and perverted in Late Postclassic times; nevertheless, some of their transcendent force persisted down to the Spanish Conquest.

The Topiltzin Quetzalcoatl example was selected for this exercise because it is susceptible to ethnohistoric, as well as strictly archaeological, analysis. Because of this we had some access to the "idea content" involved, as well as the spatial, temporal, and sociocultural contexts of the phenomenon. One is tempted to wonder if other horizon styles in the Mesoamerican archaeological record, which are not so aided by ethnohistory, might not have had similar or related ideological meanings. In this connection the Olmec stylistic data come to mind. Various hypotheses have been advanced to explain the manifestations of the style: conquest (Coe, 1968a); trade (Grove, 1968, 1974); and the status validation of emergent aristocracies through the acquisition of exotic goods and prestigious styles (Flannery, 1968a). All of these processes may very well have been involved but so too were ideologies. In Precolumbian Peru the Chavín horizon style must have been ideologically charged as were those of the Middle Horizon that are designated as Tiahuanaco-Huari. Indeed, the dissemination of the latter, occurring as they did in the context of a mature Peruvian civilization, and in association with so many other profound changes in local cultural traditions, have very much of a "transcendent aspect." It is, in many ways, frustrating to contemplate all of this and to know that ancient idea systems elude us, and perhaps always will elude us; yet I cannot be satisfied to believe that we have all of the worthwhile answers about human cultural behavior in the data of subsistence, demography, war, trade, or the processes of social class differentiation. To be sure, all of these are importantly and mightily involved, but they were linked with ideas. And sometimes ideas emerge in surprising and unpredictable forms, seemingly driving in the opposite direction to all of the expectable cultural trends and trajectories, as in the case of Topiltzin Quetzalcoatl who rose transcendent over the contemporary darkness with his millennial vision of a bright future.

Acknowledgments

The author wishes to thank Professor H. B. Nicholson, Professor J. A. Sabloff, Dr Heather Lechtman, and Miss Tatiana Proskouriakoff for their critical reading of, and commentary upon, this article in manuscript.

Bibliography

Acosta, J. R.
1956–57 Interpretacion de Algunos de los Datos Obtenidos en Tula Relativos a la Epoca Tolteca. Revista Mexicano de Estudios Antropologicos, 16: 75–110.

Adams, R. E. W.
1971 The Ceramics of Altar de Sacrificios. Papers, Peabody Museum 63, 1. Cambridge, MA: Harvard University Press.
1973 The Maya Collapse: Transformation and Termination in the Ceramic Sequence at Altar de Sacrificios. *In* The Classic Maya Collapse. T. P. Culbert, ed. Pp. 133–164. Albuquerque: University of New Mexico Press.
1977 Prehistoric Mesoamerica. Boston: Little, Brown.

Adams, R. E. W. and Woodruff Smith
1981 Feudal Models for Classic Maya Civilization. In Lowland Maya Settlement Patterns. Wendy Ashmore, ed. Pp. 335–350. Albuquerque: University of New Mexico Press.

Adams, R. McC.
1956 Some Hypotheses on the Development of Early Civilizations. American Antiquity 21: 227–232.
1966 The Evolution of Urban Society. Chicago: University of Chicago Press.
1972 Patterns of Urbanization in Early Southern Meopotamia. *In* Man, Settlement, and Urbanism. P. J. Ucko, Ruth Tringham, and G. W. Dimbleby, eds. Pp. 735–750. London: Duckworth.

Adovasio, J. M., J. D. Gunn, J. Donahue, and R. Stuckenrath
1978 Meadowcroft Rockshelter, 1977: An Overview. American Antiquity 43: 632–652.

Agrinier, Pierre
1960 The Carved Human Femurs From Tomb 1, Chiapa de Corzo, Chiapas, Mexico. Papers of the New World Archaeological Foundation, No. 6. Provo, UT: New World Archaeological Foundation, Brigham Young University.

Alegria, Ricardo
1977 Ball-Courts and Ceremonial Plazas in the West Indies. Ph.D. thesis, Department of Anthropology, Harvard University.

Alegria, Ricardo, H. B. Nicholson, and G. R. Willey
1956 The Archaic Tradition in Puerto Rico. American Antiquity 21: 113–121.

Ambrosetti, J. B.
1895 Los Cementerios Prehistoricos del Alto Parana, Misiones. Boletin del Instituto Geografico Argentino 16: 227–263.
Ameghino, Florentino
1915 La Antiguedad del Hombre en La Plata. *In* Obras Completas y Correspondencia Cientifica de Florentino Ameghino, Vol. 3. La Plata.
Anderson, K. M.
1969 Ethnographic Analogy and Archaeological Interpretation. Science 163: 133–138.
Angulo Valdes, C.
1963 Cultural Development in Colombia. *In* Aboriginal Cultural Development in Latin America: An Interpretative Review. B. J. Meggers and C. Evans, eds., Smithsonian Miscellaneous Collections, No. 146. Pp. 55–56. Washington, D.C.: Smithsonian Institution.
Aparico, Francisco de
1932 Contribucion al Estudio de la Arquelogia del Litoral Atlantico de la Provincia de Buenos Aires. Boletin Academia Nacional de Ciencias de Cordoba 32: 1–180.
Armillas, Pedro
1948 A Sequence of Cultural Development in Meso-America. *In* A Reappraisal of Peruvian Archaeology. W. C. Bennett, ed. Memoir 4, Society for American Archaeology.
1950 Teotihuacan, Tula, y Los Toltecas. Runa 3: 37–70.
1951 Mesoamerican Fortifications. Antiquity 25: 77–86.
Arnold, J. R., and W. F. Libby
1951 Radiocarbon Dates. Science, Vol. 113, pp. 111–120.
Arrom, J. J.
1975 Mitologia y Artes Prehispanicos de Las Antillas. Siglo Veintiuno, ed. Mexico, Madrid, Buenos Aires.
Ashmore, Wendy, ed.
1981 Lowland Maya Settlement Patterns. Albuquerque: University of New Mexico Press.
Ashmore, Wendy, and R. J. Sharer
1978 Excavations at Quirigua, Guatemala: The Ascent of an Elite Maya Center. Archaeology 31: 10–19.
Ashmore, Wendy, and G. R. Willey
1981 A Historical Introduction to the Study of Lowland Maya Settlement Patterns. *In* Lowland Maya Settlement Patterns. Wendy Ashmore., ed. Pp. 3–18. Albuquerque: University of New Mexico Press.
Aveleyra Arroyo de Anda, Luis
1956 The Second Mammoth and Associated Artifacts at Santa Isabel Iztapan, Mexico. American Antiquity 22: 12–28.
Aveleyra Arroyo de Anda, Luis, and Manuel Maldonado-Koerdell
1953 Association of Artifacts with Mammoth in the Valley of Mexico. American Antiquity 18: 332–340.
Barendsen, G. W., E. S. Deevey, and L. J. Gralenski
1957 Yale Natural Radiocarbon Measurements III. Science 126: 908–919.
Baudez, C. F.
1970 Central America. Geneva, Paris, Munich: Archaeologia Mundi.
1986 Southeast Mesoamerican Periphery Comments. *In* The Southeast Maya Periphery. P. A. Urban and E. M. Schortman, eds. Pp. 333–337. Austin: University of Texas Press.
Baudez, C. F., and Pierre Bequelin
1973 Archeologie de Los Naranjos, Honduras. Etudes Mesoamericaines, Vol. 2. Mission Archeologique et Ethnologique Francaise au Mexique, Mexico, D.F. (Preliminaty data presented at Stuttgart in 1968.)
Baudez, C. F., and M. D. Coe
1962 Archaeological Sequences in Northwestern Costa Rica. *In* 34th International Congress of Americanists, Vienna, 1960. Pp. 366–373.
Bawden, G. L.
1977 Galindo and the Nature of the Middle Horizon in Northern Coastal Peru. Ph.D. thesis, Department of Anthropology, Harvard University.
Bayard, D. T.
1969 Science, Theory, and Reality in the "New Archaeology." American Antiquity 34: 376–384.

Beadle, G. W.
1972 The Mystery of Maize. Field Museum of Natural History Bulletin, Vol. 43, No. 10. Chicago.
Beals, Ralph
1953 Acculturation. *In* Anthropology Today. A. L. Kroeber, ed. Pp. 621–641, University of Chicago Press.
Beardsley, R. K.
1948 Culture Sequences in Central California Archaeology. American Antiquity 14: 1–28.
Beardsley, R. K., and others
1956 Functional and Evolutionary Implications of Community Patterning. *In* Seminars in Archaeology. Robert Wauchope, ed. Memoir 11, Society for American Archaeology.
Becker, M. J.
1973 Archaeological Evidence for Occupational Specialization Among the Classic Period Maya at Tikal, Guatemala. American Antiquity 38: 396–406.
1979 Priests, Peasants, and Ceremonial Centers: The Intellectual History of a Model, *In* Maya Archaeology and Ethnohistory. Norman Hammond and G. R. Willey, eds. Pp. 3–20. Austin: University of Texas Press.
Beetz, C. P., and Linton Satterthwaite, Jr.
1981 The Monuments and Inscriptions of Caracol, Belize. University Museum Monograph 45. University Museum, University of Pennsylvania, Philadelphia.
Benedict, Ruth
1943 Two Patterns of Indian Acculturation. American Anthropologist 45, No. 2: 207–212.
Bennett, J. W.
1944 Middle American Influence on the Cultures of the Southeastern United States. Acta Americana 2: 25–50.
Bennett, W. C.
1934 Excavations at Tiahuanaco. Anthropological Papers, American Museum of Natural History, Vol. 34. New York.
1936 Excavations in Bolivia. Anthropological Papers, American Museum of Natural History, Vol. 35. New York.
1939 Archaeology of the North Coast of Peru, Anthropological Papers, American Museum of Natural History, Vol. 37. New York.
1943 The Position of Chavín in Andean Sequences. Proceedings of the American Philosophical Society 86, No. 2: 323–327.
1944a The North Highlands of Peru, Excavations in the Callejon de Huaylas and at Chavín de Huántar. Anthropological Papers, American Museum of Natural History, Vol. 39, Pt. 1. New York.
1944b Archaeological Regions of Colombia: A Ceramic Survey. Yale University Publications in Anthropology, No. 30. New Haven, CT.
1945 Interpretations of Andean Archaeology. Transactions of the New Work Academy of Sciences 7, No. 4: 95–99.
1946a The Archaeology of the Central Andes. *In* Handbook of South American Indians, Vol. 2: J. H. Steward, ed. Pp. 61–147. Bulletin 143, Bureau of American Ethnology, Smithsonian Institution. Washington, D.C.
1946b Excavations in the Cuenca Region, Ecuador. Yale University Publications in Anthropology, No. 35. New Haven, CT.
1946c The Archaeology of Colombia. *In* Handbook of South American Indians, Vol. 2. J. H. Steward, ed. Pp. 823–850. Bulletin 143, Bureau of American Ethnology, Smithsonian Institution. Washington, D.C.
1946d The Atacameño. *In* Handbook of South American Indians, Vol. 2. J. H. Steward, ed. Pp. 599–618. Bulletin 143, Bureau of American Ethnology, Smithsonian Institution. Washington, D.C.
1948 The Peruvian Co-Tradition. *In* A Reappraisal of Peruvian Archaeology. W. C. Bennett, ed. Pp. 1–8. Memoir No. 4, Society for American Archaeology.
1953 Excavations at Wari, Ayacucho, Peru. Yale University Publications in Anthropology, No. 49. New Haven, CT.
Bennett, W. C., and J. B. Bird
1949 Andean Culture History. Handbook Series, No. 15, American Museum of Natural History. New York.

Bennett, W. C., E. F. Bleiler, and F. H. Sommer
1948 Northwest Argentine Archaeology. Yale University Publications in Anthropology, No. 38, New Haven, CT.
Benson, E. P., ed.
1968 Dumbarton Oaks Conference on the Olmec. Washington, D.C.: Dumbarton Oaks.
1971 Dumbarton Oaks Conference on Chavín. Washington, D.C.: Dumbarton Oaks.
Berlin, Heinrich
1958 El Glifo "Emblema" en las Inscripciones Mayas. Journal de la Societe des Americanistes de Paris, 47: 111–119.
Bernal, Ignacio
1960 Toynbee y Mesoamerica. Estudios de Cultura Nahuatl 2: 43–58.
1968 Views of Olmec Culture. *In* Dumbarton Oaks Conference on the Olmec. E. P. Benson, ed. Pp. 135–142. Washington, D.C.: Dumbarton Oaks.
1969 The Olmec World. Berkeley: University of California Press.
1973 Stone Reliefs in the Dainzu Area. *In* The Iconography of Middle American Scupture. D. T. Easby, ed. Pp. 13–23. New York: Metropolitan Museum.
Binford, L. R.
1962 Archaeology as Anthropology. American Antiquity 28: 217–225.
1967 Comments on K. C. Chang's "Major Aspects on the Interrelationships of Archaeology and Ethnology." Current Anthropology: Vol. 8, No. 3, pp. 234–235.
1968 Archaeological Perspectives. *In* New Perspectives in Archaeology. S. R. Binford and L. R. Binford, eds. Pp. 5–32. Chicago: Aldine.
1972a Post-Pleistocene Adaptations. *In* An Archaeological Perspective. Pp. 421–449. New York: Seminar Press.
1972b Some Comments on Historical Versus Processual Archaeology. *In* An Archaeological Perspective. Pp. 114–124. New York: Seminar Press.
1972c Comments on Evolution. In An Archaeological Perspective. Pp. 105–113. New York: Seminar Press.
1978 Dimensional Analysis of Behavior and Site Structure: Learning from an Eskimo Hunting Stand. American Antiquity 43: 330–361.
Bird, J. B.
1938 Antiquity and Migrations of the Early Inhabitants of Patagonia. The Geographical Review 28: 250–275.
1943 Excavations in Northern Chile. Anthropological Papers, American Museum of Natural History, Vol. 38, Pt. 4. New York.
1946 The Archaeology of Patagonia. *In* Handbook of South American Indians, Vol. 1. J. H. Steward, ed. Pp. 17–24. Bureau of American Ethnology, Smithsonian Institution. Washington, D.C.
1948 Preceramic Cultures in Chicama and Virú. *In* A Reappraisal of Peruvian Archaeology. W. C. Bennett, ed. Pp. 105–111. Memoir No. 4, Society for American Archaeology.
1951 South American Radiocarbon Dates. *In* Radiocarbon Dating. Frederick Johnson, ed. Pp. 37–49. Memoir No. 8, Society for American Archaeology.
Bischof, Henning
1973 The Origins of Pottery in South America—Recent Radiocarbon Dates from Southwest Ecuador. *In* 40th International Congress of Americanists, Rome–Genoa, 1972, Vol. 1. Pp. 269–281.
Bischof, Henning, and Julio Viteri
1972 Pre-Valdivia Occupation on the Southern Coast of Ecuador. American Antiquity 37: 548–551.
Blanton, R. E.
1972 Prehispanic Adaptation in the Ixtapalapa Region, Mexico. Science 175: 1317–1326.
1976 Anthropological Studies of Cities. Annual Review of Anthrpology 5: 249–264.
1978 Monte Alban, Settlement Patterns at the Ancient Zapotec Capital. New York: Academic Press.
Boggs, S. H.
1950 "Olmec" Picyographs in the Las Victorias Group, Chalchuapa Archaeological Zone, El Salvador. Carnegie Institution of Washington, Notes, Vol 4, No. 99. Washington, D.C.
Bonaparte, J. F. and J. A. Pisano
1950 Dos nuevos paraderos indigenas neoliticos de la cuenca del Rio Julian. Museo Popular de Ciencias Naturales, Arqueologia 1, Buenos Aires.

Borhegyi, S. F. de
1956 The Development of Folk and Complex Cultures in the Southern Maya Area. American Antiquity 21: 343–356.
1959 Precolumbian Cultural Connections between Mesoamerica and Ecuador. Middle American Research Institute, Research Records, Vol. 2, No. 6, Tulane University. New Orleans.
1969 The Pre-Columbian Ballgame—A Pan-Mesoamerican Tradition. *In* 38th International Congress of Americanists, Stuttgart–Munchen, 1968, Vol. 1. Pp. 497–514.

Braidwood, R. J.
1958 Near Eastern Prehistory. Science 127: 1419–1430.
1960 Prelude to Civilization. *In* City Invincible. C. H. Kraeling and R. McC. Adams, eds. Pp. 297–314. Chicago: University of Chicago Press.

Braidwood, R. J., and G. R. Willey
1962 Conclusions and Afterthoughts. *In* Course Toward Urban Life. R. J. Braidwood and G. R. Willey, eds. Pp. 330–359. Viking Fund Publications in Anthropology, No. 32. New York.

Brainerd, G. W.
1951a Early Ceramic Horizons in Yucatan. *In* 29th International Congress of Americanists, 1949, New York, Vol. 1. Pp. 72–78.
1951b The Place of Chronological Ordering in Archaeological Analysis. American Antiquity 16: 301–313.
1953 A Cylindrical Stamp from Ecuador. The Masterkey, Vol. 27, No. 1, Southwest Museum. Los Angeles.
1954 The Maya Civilization. Los Angeles: Southwest Museum.
1958 The Archaeological Ceramics of Yucatan, Anthropological Records, No. 18, University of California, Berkeley and Los Angeles.

Bray, Warwick
1984 Across the Darien Gap: A Colombian View of Isthmian Archaeology. *In* The Archaeology of Lower Central America. F. W. Lange and D. Z. Stone, eds. Pp. 305–340. Albuquerque: University of New Mexico Press.

Brochado, J. P.
1980 Eastern Brazil: Ceramic Cultures. Ms. prepared for a volume on South American archaeological chronologies.

Brochado, J. P., and D. W. Lathrap
1980 Amazonia. Ms. prepared for a volume on South American archaeological chronologies.

Broecker, W. S., J. L. Kulp, and C. S. Tucek
1956 Lamont Natural Radiocarbon Measurements III. Science 124: 154–165.

Brush, C. F.
1965 Pox Pottery: Earliest Identified Mexican Ceramic. Science 149: 194–195.

Bryan, A. L.
1973 Paleoenvironments and Cultural Diversity in Late Pleistocene South America. Journal of Quaternary Research 3, No. 2: 237–256.

Bullard, W. R., Jr.
1973 Postclassic Culture in Central Peten and Adjacent British Honduras. *In* The Classic Maya Collapse. T. P. Culbert, ed. Pp. 221–242. Albuquerque: University of New Mexico Press.

Bullen, R. P.
1956 Some Florida Radiocarbon Dates and Their Significance. Florida Anthropologist 9, No. 2: 31–36.

Bullock, D. S.
1955 Urnas funerarias prehistoricas de la region de Angol. Museo Dillman S. Bullock, Publicacion No. 4. Angol, Chile.

Burger, R. L.
1985 Concluding Remarks: Early Peruvian Civilization and Its Relation to the Chavín Horizon. *In* Early Ceremonial Architecture in the Andes. C. B. Donnan, ed. Pp. 269–289. Washington, D.C.: Dumbarton Oaks.

Bushnell, G. H. S.
1951 The Archaeology of the Santa Elena Peninsula in Southwest Ecuador. Cambridge: Cambridge University Press.
1956 Peru. London: Thames and Hudson.
1959 Some Post-Columbian Whistling Jars from Peru. *In* 33rd International Congress of Americanists, San Jose, Costa Rica, 1958, Vol. 2. Pp. 416–420.

Bushnell, G. H. S., and Charles McBurney
1959 New World Origins Seen from the Old World. Antiquity 33: 93–101.
Butler, B. R.
1961 The Old Cordilleran Culture in the Pacific Northwest. Occasional Papers, Idaho State College Museum, No. 5.
Butler, Mary
1935 A Study of Maya Mouldmade Figurines. American Anthropologist 37: 636–672.
Byers, D. S.
1954 Bullbrook—A Fluted Point Site in Ipswich, Massachusetts. American Antiquity 19: 343–351.
Byers, D. S., ed.
1967 The Prehistory of the Tehuacan Valley: Vol. 1. Environment and Subsistence. Austin: University of Texas Press.
Caldwell, J. R.
1958 Trend and Tradition in the Prehistory of the Eastern United States. Memoir 88, American Anthropological Association.
Campbell, J. M.
1961 The Kogruk Complex of Anaktuvuk Pass, Alaska. Anthropologica 3: 1–18.
Canby, J. S.
1951 Possible Chronological Implications of the Long Ceramic Sequence Recovered at Yarumela, Spanish Honduras. *In* 29th International Congress of Americanists, New York, 1949, Vol. 1. Pp. 79–85.
Carneiro, R. L.
1961 Slash-and-Burn Cultivation among the Kuikuru and Its Implications for Cultural Development in the Amazon Basin. *In* Evolution of Horticultural Systems in Native South America: Courses and Consequences. J. Wilbert, ed. Pp. 47–67. Caracas: Sociedad de Ciencias Natural La Salle.
1970 A Theory of the Origin of the State. Science 169: 733–738.
Carrión Cachot, Rebecca
1948 La Cultura Chavín: Dos Nuevas Colonias: Kuntur Wasi y Ancon. Revista, Museo Nacional de Antropologia y Arqueologia, Vol. 2, No. 1. Lima.
Caso, Alfonso
1938 Exploraciones en Oaxaca, Quinta y Sexta Temporadas 1936–1937. Panamerican Institute of Geography and History, Publication No. 34. Mexico, D. F.
1942 Definicion y Extension del Complejo "Olmeca." *In* Mayas y Olmecas. Segunda Mesa Redonda, Sociedad Mexicana de Antropologia. Tuxtla Gutierrez, Chiapas, Mexico.
1947 Calendario y escritura de las antiguas culturas de Monte Alban, Mexico, Talleres Gráficos de la Nacion, Mexico, D. F.
1950 Explicacion del Reverso del Codex Vindobonensis. Memoria de El Colegio Nacional 5, 9–46.
1952 Sincronologia Christiana y Mixteca. *In* Memorias del Congreso Cientifico Mexicano de 1951, Mexico, D. F.
1953 New World Culture History: Middle America. *In* Anthropology Today. A. L. Kroeber and others, eds. Pp. 226–237. Chicago: University of Chicago Press.
1954 Interpretacion del Codice Gomes de Orozco. Mexico, D. F.
Chang, K. C.
1976 Early Chinese Civilization: Anthropological Perspectives. Cambridge, MA: Harvard University Press.
Chapman, C. H.
1952 "Recent Excavations in Graham Cave, appendix to Graham Cave, an Archaeic Site, in Montgomery County, Missouri, by W. D. Logan. Pp. 87–101. Missouri Archaeological Society, Memoir No. 2, Columbia, MO.
Chard, C. S.
1959 New World Origins: A Reappraisal. Antiquity 33: 44–49.
1963 The Old World Roots: Review and Speculations. Anthropological Papers, Vol. 10, No. 2, University of Alaska. Fairbanks.
Chase, A. F., and D. Z. Chase
1987 Glimmers of a Forgotten Realm, Maya Archaeology at Caracol, Belize. Prepared in conjunction with an exhibit at the Orlando Museum of Art at Loch Haven, Orlando, University of Central Florida.

Chase, A. F., and P. M. Rice, eds.
1985 The Lowland Maya Postclassic. Austin: University of Texas Press.
Childe, V. G.
1925 The Dawn of European Civilization. London: Kegan Paul, Trench, and Trubner.
1929 The Danube in Prehistory. Oxford: Clarendon Press.
1934 The Most Ancient East. London, 1934.
1950 The Urban Revolution. Town Planning Review 21: 3–17.
1953 Old World Prehistory: Neolithic. *In* Anthropology Today. A. L. Kroeber, ed. Pp. 193–210. Chicago: University of Chicago Press.
Choy, Emilio
1960 La Revolucion Neolitica en las Origenes de la Civilizacion Americana. *In* Antiguo Peru, Espacio y Tiempo. Pp. 149–197. Lima.
Christensen, R. T.
1955 A Modern Ceramic Industry at Simbila near Piura, Peru. Chimor, Boletin Museo Arquelogico, Universidad Nacional de Trujillo, Vol. 3. Pp. 10–20. Trujillo.
Clark, J. G. D.
1940 Archaeology and Society. London: Methuen.
1974 Prehistoric Europe: The Economic Basis. *In* Archaeological Researches in Retrospect. G. R. Willey, ed. Pp. 33–60. Cambridge, MA: Winthrop Publishers.
1976 Prehistory Since Childe. Bulletin of the Institute of Archeology, No. 13. London.
Clarke, D. L.
1968 Analytical Archaeology. London: Methuen.
Codex Telleriano Remensis
1899 E. T. Hamy, ed. Paris.
Codex Vaticanus A
1900 Duc de Loubat, ed. Rome.
Coe, M. D.
1954 Chavín: Its Nature and Space-Time Position. Seminar Paper, Harvard University.
1957 Cycle 7 Monuments in Middle America: A Reconsideration. American Anthropologist 59: 597–611.
1960 Archaeological Linkages with North and South America at La Victoria, Guatemala. American Anthropologist 52: 363–393.
1961a Social Typology and the Tropical Forest Civilization. Comparative Studies in Society and History 4: 65–85.
1961b La Victoria, An Early Site on the Pacific Coast of Guatemala. Papers, Peabody Museum, Vol. 53, Harvard University. Cambridge, MA.
1965a The Olmec Style and Its Distributions. *In* Handbook of Middle American Indians, Vol. 3. R. Wauchope, ed. Pp. 739–775. Austin: University of Texas Press.
1965b The Jaguar's Children: Prehistoric Central Mexico. Pp. 122–123. New York: Museum of Primitive Art.
1966 The Maya. New York: Praeger.
1968a America's First Civilization. The Smithsonian Library Series, New York.
1968b San Lorenzo and the Olmec Civilization. *In* Dumbarton Oaks Conference on the Olmec. E. P. Benson, ed. Pp. 41–71. Washington, D.C.: Dumbarton Oaks.
1973 The Iconology of Olmec Art. *In* The Iconography of Middle American Sculpture. D. T. Easby, ed. Pp. 1–12. New York: Metropolitan Museum.
Coe, M. D., and C. F. Baudez
1961 The Zoned Bichrome Period in Northwestern Costa Rica. American Antiquity 26: 505–515.
Coe, M. D., and R. A. Diehl
1980 In the Land of the Olmec. Austin: University of Texas Press.
Coe, M. D., and K. V. Flannery
1967 Early Cultures and Human Ecology in South Coastal Guatemala. Smithsonian Contributions to Anthropology, No. 3, Smithsonian Institution. Washington, D.C.
Coe, W. R., Jr.
1962 A Summary of Excavation and Research at Tikal, Guatemala: 1956–1961. American Antiquity 27: 479–507.
1963 A Summary of Excavation and Research at Tikal, Guatemala: 1962. Estudios Cultura Maya 3: 41–64.

1965 Tikal: Ten Years of Study of a Maya Ruin in the Lowlands of Guatemala. Expeditions 8, No. 1: 5–56.

1967 Tikal, A Handbook of the Ancient Maya Ruins. Philadelphia: University Museum, University of Pennsylvania.

Coe, W. R., Jr., and M. D. Coe

1956 Excavations at Nohoch Ek, British Honduras. American Antiquity 21: 370–382.

Coggins, Clemency

1979a A New Order and the Role of the Calendar: Some Characteristics of the Middle Classic Period at Tikal. *In* Maya Archaeology and Ethnohistory. Norman Hammond and G. R. Willey, eds. Pp. 38–50. Austin: University of Texas Press.

1979b Teotihuacan at Tikal in the Early Classic Period. *In* 42nd International Congress of Americanists, Paris, Vol. 8. Pp. 251–269.

Collier, Donald

1948 Peruvian Stylistic Influences in Ecuador. *In* A Reappraisal of Peruvian Archaeology. W. C. Bennett, ed. Pp. 80–86. Memoir No. 4, Society for American Archaeology.

1955 Cultural Chronology and Change as Reflected in the Ceramics of the Virú Valley, Peru. Fieldiana: Anthropology, Vol. 43, Field Museum. Chicago.

1959 Pottery Stamping and Molding on the North Coast of Peru. *In* 33rd International Congress of Americanists, San Jose, Costa Rica, 1958, Vol. 2. Pp. 421–431.

1962 The Central Andes. *In* Courses Toward Urban Life. R. J. Braidwood and G. R. Willey, eds. Pp. 165–176. Viking Fund Publications in Anthropology, No. 32. New York.

Collier, Donald, and J. V. Murra

1943 Survey and Excavations in Southern Ecuador. Anthropological Series, Field Museum of Natural History, Vol. 35. Chicago.

Collins, H. B.

1953a Recent Developments in the Dorset Culture Area. *In* Asia and North America: Transpacific Contacts. M. W. Smith, ed. Memoir 9, Society for American Archaeology.

1953b Radio Carbon Dating in the Arctic. American Antiquity 18: 197–203.

1954 Arctic Area. Program of the History of America, Indigenous Period, Vol. 1, No. 2. Instituto Panamericano de Geografia e Historia. Mexico, D. F.

Colton, H.S.

1939 Prehistoric Culture Units and Their Relationships in Northern Arizona. Museum of Northern Aruizona, Bulletin 17. Flagstaff.

Conrad, G. W.

1980 The Central Andes (Peru-Bolivia). Ms. prepared for volume on South American archaeological chronologies.

Cooke, Richard

1984 Archaeological Research in Central and Eastern Panama: A Review of Some Problems. *In* The Archaeology of Lower Central America. F. W. Lange and D. Z. Stone, eds. Pp. 263–304. Albuquerque: University of New Mexico Press.

Cooper, J. M.

1942 Areal and Temporal Aspects of South American Culture. Primitive Man 15, Nos. 1–2: 1–38.

1946 "The Patagonian and Pampean Hunters," Handbook of South American Indians, J. H. Steward, ed., Vol. 1, pp. 127–168, Bulletin 143, Bureau of American Ethnology, Smithsonian Institution, Washington, D.C.

Corbett, J. M.

1953 Some Unusual Ceramics from Esmeraldas, Ecuador. American Antiquity 19: 145–152.

Cornely, F. L.

1940 Nuevos Descubrimientos Arqueologicos en la Provincia de Coquimbo. Boletin del Museo Nacional de Chile 18: 9–14.

1951 Cultura Diaguita–Chilena. Revista Chilena de Historia Natural, Anos 51–53: 119–262.

1953 Cultura de El Molle. La Serena: Museo Arqueologia de La Serena.

Cotter, J. L.

1937 The Occurrence of Flint and Extinct Animals in Pluvial Deposits near Clovis, New Mexico. IV. Report on the Excavations on the Gravel Pit in 1936. Proceedings, American Academy of Natural Sciences 89: 2–16.

1938 The Occurrence of Flints and Extinct Animals in Pluvial Deposits near Clovis, New Mexico. VI. Report on Field Season of 1937. Proceedings, American Academy of Natural Sciences 90: 113–117.

Covarrubias, Miguel
1942 Origen y Desarollo del Estilo Artistica "Olmeca." *In* Mayas y Olmecas. Segunda Mesa Redonda, Sociedad Mexicana de Antropologia. Tuxtla Gutierrez, Chiapas, Mexico.
1946 El Arte "Olmeca" or de La Venta. Cuadernos Americanos 5: 153–179.
1957 Indian Art of Mexico and Central America. New York: Alfred Knopf.
Crane, H. R.
1955 University of Michigan Radiocarbon Dates 1. Science 124: 664–672.
Cressman, L. S.
1951 Western Prehistory in the Light of Carbon 14 Dating. Southwestern Journal of Anthropology 7: 289–313.
Crook, W. W., Jr., and R. K. Harris
1958 A Pleistocene Campsite near Lewisville, Texas. American Antiquity 23: 233–246.
Cruxent, J. M.
1951 Venezuela: A Strategic Center for Caribbean Archaeology. *In* The Caribbean at Mid-Century. A. C. Wilgus, ed. School of Inter-American Studies, Series One, Vol. 1, Pp. 149–156, Gainesville, FL.
Cruxent, J. M., and Irving Rouse
1956 A Lithic Industry of Paleo-Indian Type in Venezuela. American Antiquity 22: 172–179.
1958–59 An Archaeological Chronology of Venezuela. 2 Vols. Social Science Monographs, Panamerican Union. Washington, D.C.
Cubillos, J.C.
1955 Tumaco. Notas Arqueologicas, Ministerio de Educacion, Departamento de Extension Cultural. Bogota.
Culbert, T. P.
1973 The Maya Downfall at Tikal. *In* The Classic Maya Collapse. T. P. Culbert, ed. Pp. 63–92. Albuquerque: University of New Mexico Press.
1977 Maya Development and Collapse: An Economic Perspective. *In* Social Process in Maya Prehistory: Studies in Honor of Sir Eric Thompson. Norman Hammond, ed. Pp. 510–531. New York: Academic Press.
1988 Political History and the Decipherment of Maya Glyphs. Antiquity 62: 135–152.
Culbert, T. P., ed.
1973 The Classic Maya Collapse. Albuquerque: University of New Mexico Press.
Daniel, Glyn
1975 A Hundred and Fifty Years of Archaeology. London: Duckworth.
Daguerre, J. B.
1934 Nuevos Paraderos Enterratorios en el Litoral de Carmen Patagones (Prov. de Buenos Aires). *In* 25th International Congress of Americanists, La Plata, Argentina, Vol. 2. Pp. 21–24.
Deetz, J. J. F.
1965 The Dynamics of Stylistic Change in Arikara Ceramics. University of Illinois Series in Anthropology, No. 4. Urbana.
Deevey, E. S., L. J. Gralenski, and V. Hoffren
1959 Yale Natural Radiocarbon Measurements IV. Radiocarbon Supplement, American Journal of Science 1: 144–172.
De Hostos, Adolfo
1948 The Ethnography of Puerto Rico. *In* Handbook of South American Indians, Vol. 4. J. H. Steward, ed. Pp. 540–541. Bulletin 143, Bureau of American Ethnology, Smithsonian Institution. Washington, D.C.
Della Santa, Elizabeth
1959 Les Cupisniques et l'Origine des Olmèques. Revue de l'Université de Bruxelles 5: 340–363.
Demarest, A. A.
1977 Ms. Regional Patterning of Lowland Classic Fortifications: The 'Situational Ethics' of Maya Warfare.
1985 The Olmec and the Rise of Civilization in Eastern Mesoamerica. *In* The Olmec and the Development of Formative Mesoamerican Civilization. R. J. Sharer and David Grove, eds. Albuquerque: University of New Mexico Press.
De Terra, Helmut
1949 Early Man in Mexico. *In* Tepexpan Man. Viking Fund Publications in Anthropology, No. 11. New York.

D'Harcourt, M. R.
1947 Archéologie de la Province d'Esmeraldas, Equateur. Journal de la Société des Americanistes de Paris 34: 61–200.
Dick, H. W.
1952 Evidences of Early Man in Bat Cave and on the Plains of San Augustin, New Mexico. *In* 29th International Congress of Americanists, New York, 1949, Vol. 3. Pp. 158–163.
Diehl, R. A., and R. A. Benfer
1975 Tollan: The Toltec Capital. Archaeology 27: 112–124.
Dieseldorf, E. P.
1926–33 Kunst und Religion der Mayavolker. Berlin.
Dillehay, T. D., M. Pino, E. M. Davis, S. Vatastro, Jr., G. Varela, and R. Casamiquela
1982 Monte Verde: Radiocarbon Dates from an Early-Man Site in South-Central Chile. Journal of Field Archaeology 9: 547–550.
Dobzhansky, Theodosius
1958 Evolution at Work. Science 127: 1091–1097.
Doering, H. Ubbelohde
1951 Ceramic Comparisons of Two North Coast Peruvian Valleys. *In* 29th International Congress of Americanists, New York, 1949, Vol. 1. Pp. 224–231.
Donnan, C. B., ed.
1985 Early Ceremonial Architecture in the Andes. Washington, D.C.: Dumbarton Oaks.
Drucker, Philip
1943 Ceramic Sequences at Tres Zapotes, Veracruz, Mexico. Bulletin 140, Bureau of American Ethnology, Smithsonian Institution. Washington, D.C.
1948 Preliminary Notes on an Archaeological Survey of the Chiapas Coast. Middle American Research Records, Vol. 1, No. 1, Tulane University. New Orleans.
1952 La Venta, Tabasco, a Study of Olmec Ceramics and Art. Bulletin 153, Bureau of American Ethnology, Smithsonian Institution. Washington, D.C.
Drucker, Philip, and R. F. Heizer
1960 A Study of the Milpas System of La Venta Island and Its Archaeological Implications. Southwestern Journal of Anthropology 16: 36–45.
Drucker, Philip, R. F. Heizer, and R. J. Squier
1957 Radiocarbon Dates from La Venta, Tabasco. Science 126: 72–73.
1959 Excavations at La Venta, Tabasco 1955. Bulletin 170, Bureau of American Ethnology, Smithsonian Institution. Washington, D.C.
Dutton, B. F.
1955 Tula of the Toltecs. El Palacio 62, Nos. 7–8: 195–251.
Dymond, D. P.
1974 Archaeology and History, A Plea for Reconciliation. London: Thames and Hudson.
Easby, E. K.
1952 The Pre-conquest Art of Santarem, Brazil. M.A. thesis, Department of Fine Arts and Archaeology, Columbia University.
Ekholm, G. F.
1944 Excavations at Tampico and Panuco in the Huasteca, Mexico. Anthropological Papers, American Museum of Natural History, Vol. 38, Pt. 5. New York.
1953 A Possible Focus of Asiatic Influence in the Late Classic Cultures of Mesoamerica. *In* Asia and North America: Transpacific Contacts. Memoir No. 9, Society for American Archaeology.
1961 Puerto Rican Stone "Collars" as Ball-Game Belts. *In* Essays in Precolumbian Art and Archaeology. S. K. Lothrop, ed. Pp. 356–371. Cambridge, MA: Harvard University Press.
1973 The Eastern Gulf Coast. *In* The Iconography of Middle American Sculpture. D. T. Easby, ed. Pp. 40–51. New York: Metropolitan Museum.
Engel, Frederic
1956 Curayacu—A Chavinoid Site. Archaeology 9: 98–105.
1957 Early Sites on the Peruvian Coast. Southwestern Journal of Anthropology 13: 54–68.
1963 Notes Relatives à des Explorations à Paracas et sur la Côte Sud du Perou. Travaux de l'Institut Français d'Etudes Andines 9:1–27.
1964 El Preceramico sin Algodon en La Costa del Peru. *In* 35th International Congress of Americanists, Mexico City. Pp. 141–152.
1966 Le complexe Précéramique d'El Paraiso (Perou). Journal de la Société des Americanistes de Paris 55: 43–96.

Erasmus, C. J.
1968 Thoughts on Upward Collapse: An Essay on Explanation in Anthropology. Southwestern Journal of Anthropology 24: 170–194.
Estrada, Emilio
1956 Valdivia, Un Sitio Arqueologico Formativo en la Costa de la Provincia del Guayas, Ecuador. Publicación No. 1, Museo Victor Emilio Estrada. Guayaquil.
1957a Ultimas Civilizaciones Pre-Historicas de la Cuenca del Rio Guayas. Publicación No. 2, Museo Victor Emilio Estrada. Guayaquil.
1957b Los Huancavilcas, Ultimas Civilizaciones Pre-Historicas de la Costa del Guayas. Publicación No. 3, Museo Victor Emilio Estrada. Guayaquil.
1958 Las Culturas Pre-Clasicas, Formativas, o Arcaicas del Ecuador. Publicación No. 5, Museo Victor Emilio Estrada. Guayaquil.
Estrada, Emilio, and Clifford Evans, Jr.
1963 Cultural Development in Ecuador. *In* Aboriginal Culture Development in Latin America. B. J. Meggers and C. Evans, eds. Pp. 77–88, Smithsonian Miscellaneous Collections, Vol. 146, Smithsonian Institution. Washington, D.C.
Evans, Clifford, Jr.
1950 A Report on Archaeological Investigations in the Lagoa Santa Country of Minas Gerais, Brazil. American Antiquity 15: 341–343.
Evans, Clifford, Jr., and B. J. Meggers
1950 Preliminary Results of Archaeological Investigations at the Mouth of the Amazon. American Antiquity 16: 1–9.
1957 Formative Period Cultures in the Guayas Basin, Coastal Ecuador. American Antiquity 22: 235–246.
1958 Valdivia—An Early Formative Culture on the Coast of Ecuador. Archaeology 11: 175–182.
1966 Mesoamerica and Ecuador. *In* Handbook of Middle American Indians, Vol. 4. R. Wauchope, ed. Pp. 243–264. Austin: University of Texas Press.
Fairbanks, C. H.
1950 A Preliminary Segregation of Etowah, Savannah, and Lamar. American Antiquity 16: 224–231.
1952 Creek and Pre-Creek. *In* Archaeology of the Eastern United States. J. B. Griffin, ed. Pp. 285–300. Chicago: University of Chicago Press.
Fenton, W. N.
1951 Locality as a Basic Factor in the Development of Iroquois Social Structure. Bulletin 149, No. 3, Bureau of American Ethnology, Smithsonian Institution. Washington, D.C.
Ferdon, E. N.
1940–41 Reconnaissance in Esmeraldas. El Palacio 47, No. 1: 7–15.
1953 Tonalá, Mexico, An Archaeological Survey. Monograph 16, School of American Research. Santa Fe, NM.
Fernandez Mendez, Eugenio
1972 Art and Mythology of the Taino Indians of the Greater West Indies. San Juan, P.R.: Editorial El Cemi.
Ferreira Penna, D. S.
1876 Breve Noticia sobre os Sambaquis do Para. Archivos do Museu Nacional do Rio de Janeiro 1: 85–99.
Fewkes, J. W.
1907 The Aborigines of Porto Rico and Neighboring Islands. Annual Report 34, Bureau of American Ethnology, Smithsonian Institution. Washington, D.C.
Finley, M. I.
1971 Archaeology and History. Daedalus, Winter Issue: 168–186.
Fischer, J. L.
1961 Art Styles as Cultural Cognitive Maps. American Anthropologist 63: 79–93.
Flannery, K. V.
1968a The Olmec and the Valley of Oaxaca: A Model for Interregional Interaction in Formative Times. *In* Dumbarton Oaks Conference on the Olmec. E. P. Benson, ed. Pp. 79–110. Washington, D.C.: Dumbarton Oaks.
1968b Archaeological Systems Theory and Early Mesoamerica. *In* Anthropological Archaeology in the Americas. B. J. Meggers, ed. Pp. 67–87. Washington, D.C.: Anthropological Society of Washington.

1972 The Cultural Evolution of Civilizations. Annual Review of Ecology and Systematics 3: 399–426.

1976 Evolution of Complex Settlement Systems. *In* The Early Meso-American Village. Pp. 162–172. New York: Academic Press.

Flannery K. V., and Joyce Marcus

1976a Evolution of the Public Building in Formative Oaxaca. *In* Cultural Change and Continuity, Essays in Honor of James Bennett Griffin. C. E. Cleland, ed. Pp. 205–222. New York: Academic Press.

1976b Formative Oaxaca and the Zapotec Cosmos. American Scientist 64: 374–383.

Ford, J. A.

1949 Cultural Dating of Prehistoric Sites in Virú Valley, Peru. Anthropological Papers, American Museum of Natural History, Vol. 43, Pt. 1. New York.

1951 Greenhouse: A Troyville–Coles Creek Period Site in Avoyelles Parish, Louisiana. Anthropological Papers, American Museum of Natural History, Vol. 44, Pt. 1. New York.

1952 Measurements of Some Prehistoric Design Developments in the Southeastern United States. Anthropological Papers, American Museum of Natural History, Vol. 44, Pt. 3. New York.

1966 Early Formative Cultures in Georgia and Florida. American Antiquity 31: 781–799.

Ford, J. A., and C. H. Webb

1956 Poverty Point: A Late Archaic Site in Louisiana. Anthropological Papers, American Museum of Natural History, Vol. 46, Pt. 1. New York.

Ford, J. A., and G. R. Willey

1949 Surface Survey of the Virú Valley, Peru. Anthropological Papers, American Museum of Natural History, Vol. 43, Pt. 1. New York.

Fowler, M. L. and Howard Winter

1956 *Modoc Rock Shelter: Preliminary Report,* Illinois State Museum, Report of Investigations No. 4, Springfield.

Freidel, D. A.

1978 Maritime Adaptations and Rise of Maya Civilization: The View from Cerros, Belize. *In* Prehistoric Coastal Adaptations. B. L. Stark and Barbara Voorhies, eds. Pp. 239–265. New York: Academic Press.

1981 Civilization as a State of Mind: The Cultural Evolution of the Lowland Maya. *In* The Transition to Statehood in the New World. G. D. Jones and R. E. Kautz, eds. Pp. 188–227. Cambridge: Cambridge University Press.

1983 Political Systems in Lowland Yucatan: Dynamics and Structure in Maya Settlement. *In* Prehistoric Settlement Patterns: Essays in Honor of Gordon R. Willey. E. Z. Vogt and R. M. Leventhal, eds. Pp. 375–386. Albuquerque: University of New Mexico Press.

Frenguelli, Joaquin, and Francisco de Aparicio

1923 Los Paraderos de la Margen Derecha del Rio Malabrigo. Anales de la Facultad de Ciencias y Educación, Universidad de Parana 1: 7–112.

Fried, M. H.

1967 The Evolution of Political Society: An Essay in Political Anthropology. New York: Random House.

1978 The State, the Chicken and the Egg: Or, What Came First?" *In* The Anthropology of Political Evolution. R. Cohen and E. R. Service, eds. Philadelphia: Institute for the Study of Human Issues.

Furst, P. T.

1973 West Mexican Art: Secular or Sacred? *In* The Iconography of Middle American Sculpture. D. T. Easby, ed. Pp. 98–134. New York: Metropolitan Museum.

Garcia Icazbalceta, J., ed.

1891 Nueva Colección de Documentos para la Historia de Mexico, Vol. 3. Mexico, D. F.

Garcia Payon, J.

1971 Archaeology of Central Veracruz. *In* Handbook of Middle American Indians, Vol. 9. R. Wauchope, ed. Pp. 505–542. Austin: University of Texas Press.

Gatto, Santiago

1939 El Paradero Cementerio de Brazo Largo, Delta del Parana. Physis 16: 365–376.

Gayton, A. H., and A. L. Kroeber

1927 The Uhle Pottery Collections from Nazca. University of California Publications in American Archaeology and Ethnology, Vol. 24, No. 1. Berkeley.

Gearing, F.
1962 Priests and Warriors, Social Structure for Cherokee Politics in the 18th Century. Memoir 93, American Anthropological Association.
Giddings, J. L.
1951 The Denbigh Flint Complex. American Antiquity 16: 193–203.
1954 Early Man in the Arctic. Scientific American 190, No. 6: 82–89.
1955 The Denbigh Flint Complex Is Not Yet Dated. American Antiquity 20: 375–376.
Gillin, J. P.
1947 Moche, A Peruvian Coastal Community. Institute of Social Anthropology, Publication 3, Smithsonian Institution. Washington, D.C.
Gladwin, W., and H. S. Gladwin
1934 A Method for the Designation of Cultures and Their Variations. Medallion Papers, No. 15, Gila Pueblo, Globe, AZ.
Gladwin, H. S., E. W. Haury, E. B. Sayles, and Nora Gladwin
1937 Excavations at Snaketown: Material Culture. Medallion Papers, No. 25. Gila Pueblo, Globe, AZ.
Glass, J. B.
1966 Archaeological Survey of Western Honduras. *In* Handbook of Middle American Indians, Vol. 4. R. Wauchope, ed. Pp. 157–179. Austin: University of Texas Press.
Gonzalez, A. R.
1952 Antiguo Horizonte Preceramico en las Sierras Centrales de Argentina. Runa 5: 110–133.
1955 Contextos Culturales y Cronologia Relativa en el Area Central del Noroeste Argentino. Anales de Arqueologia y Etnologia 11: 7–32.
Goslin, R. M.
1957 Food of the Adena People. The Adena People, No. 2. W. S. Webb and R. S. Baby. Columbus: Ohio State University Press.
Graham, J. A.
1972 Aspects of Non-Classic Presences in the Inscriptions and Sculptural Art of Seibal. *In* The Classic Maya Collapse. T. P. Culbert, ed. Pp. 207–220. Albuquerque: University of New Mexico Press.
1979 Maya, Olmecs, and Izapans at Abaj Takalik. *In* 42nd International Congress of Americanists, Paris, 1976, Vol. 8. Pp. 179–188.
Green, D. F., and G. W. Lowe
1967 Altamira and Padre Piedra, Early Preclassic Sites in Chiapas, Mexico. Papers of the New World Archaeological Foundation, No. 20, Publication No. 15, Brigham Young University. Provo, UT.
Greengo, R. E.
1952 The Olmec Phase of Eastern Mexico. Bulletin of the Texas Archaeological and Paleontological Society 23: 269–292.
1964 Prehistory in the Lower Mississippi Valley: The Issaquena Phase. Memoir 18, Society for American Archaeology.
Griffin, J. B.
1952a Culture Periods in Eastern United States Archaeology. *In* Archaeology of the Eastern United States. J. B. Griffin, ed. Pp. 352–364. Chicago: University of Chicago Press.
1952b Some Early and Middle Woodland Pottery Types in Illinois. *In* Hopewellian Communities in Illinois. Thorne Deuel, ed. Pp. 93–130. Illinois State Museum Scientific Papers. Springfield, IL.
1958 The Chronological Position of the Hopewellian Culture in the Eastern United States. University of Michigan Museum of Anthropology, Anthropological Papers, No. 12. Ann Arbor.
Griffin, J. B., ed.
1952 Archaeology of the Eastern United States. Chicago: University of Chicago Press.
Griffin, J. B., and A. D. Krieger
1947 Notes on Some Ceramic Techniques and Intrusions in Central Mexico. American Antiquity 12: 156–168.
Grove, D. C.
1968 The Preclassic Olmec in Central Mexico: Site Distribution and Inferences. *In* Dumbarton Oaks Conference on the Olmec. E. P. Benson, ed. Pp. 179–185. Washington, D.C.: Dumbarton Oaks.

1974 The Highland Olmec Manifestation: A Consideration of What It Is and Isn't. *In* Mesoamerican Archaeology, New Approaches. Norman Hammond, ed. Pp. 109–128. London: Duckworth.

Haberland, Wolfgang

1962 The Scarified Ware and the Early Cultures of Chiriqui (Panama). *In* 34th International Congress of Americanists, Vienna, 1960. Pp. 380–389.

1966 Early Phases on Ometepe Island, Nicaragua. *In* 36th International Congress of Americanists, Barcelona-Madrid-Seville, 1964, Vol. 1. Pp. 399–403.

1973 Stone Sculpture from Southern Central America. *In* The Iconography of Middle American Sculpture. D. T. Easby, ed. Pp. 135–152. New York: Metropolitan Museum.

1978 Lower Central America. *In* Chronologies in New World Archaeology. R. E. Taylor and C. W. Meighan, eds. Pp. 513–563. New York: Academic Press.

Hammond, Norman

1974 The Distribution of Late Classic Maya Major Ceremonial Centres in the Central Area. *In* Mesoamerican Archaeology, New Approaches. Norman Hammond, ed. Pp. 313–334. London: Duckworth.

1980 Early Maya Ceremonial at Cuello, Belize. Antiquity 54, No. 212: 176–190.

Hammond, Norman, ed.

1977 Social Process in Maya Prehistory: Studies in Honor of Sir Eric Thompson. New York: Academic Press.

Hammond, Norman, et al.

1979 The Earliest Lowland Maya: Definition of the Swasey Phase. American Antiquity 44: 92–110.

Harrington, M. R.

1955 A New Tule Springs Expedition. Masterkey 29, No. 4: 112–113.

Harrington, M. R., and R. D. Simpson

1961 Tule Springs, Nevada, with Other Evidences of Pleistocene Man in North America. Southwest Museum Papers, No. 18. Los Angeles.

Harrison, P. D.

1977 The Rise of the *Bajos* and the Fall of the Maya. *In* Social Process in Maya Prehistory: Studies in Honor of Sir Eric Thompson. N. Hammond, ed. Pp. 470–509. New York: Academic Press.

Harrison, P.D., and B. L. Turner, eds.

1978 Prehispanic Maya Agriculture. Albuquerque: University of New Mexico Press.

Haury, E. W.

1936 Some Southwestern Pottery Types. Series IV. Medallion Papers, No. 19, Gila Pueblo, Globe, AZ.

Haury, E. W., and R. H. Thompson, eds.

1956 An Archaeological Approach to the Study of Cultural Stability. *In* Seminars in Archaeology. Pp. 33–57. Memoir 11, Society for American Archaeology.

Haviland, W. A.

1970 Tikal, Guatemala and Mesoamerican Urbanism. World Archaeology 2: 186–198.

Hawkes, Christopher

1954 Archaeological Theory and Method: Some Suggestions from the Old World. American Anthropologist 56: 155–168.

Hawkes, Jacquetta

1968 The Proper Study of Mankind. Antiquity 42: 255–262.

Hay, C. L., and others, eds.

1940 The Maya and Their Neighbors. New York: Appleton-Century.

Haynes, C. V., Jr.

1964 Fluted Projectile Points: Their Age and Dispersion. Science 145: 1408–1413.

1967 Muestras de C-14, de Tlapacoya, Estado de Mexico. Boletín, Instituto de Antropologia e Historia 29: 49–52.

Heine-Geldern, Robert von

1959 Representation of the Asiatic Tiger in the Art of the Chavín Culture: A Proof of Early Contacts between China and Peru. *In* 33rd International Congress of Americanists, San Jose, Costa Rica, 1958, Vol. 1.

Heine-Geldern, Robert von, and G. F. Ekholm

1951 Significant Parallels in the Symbolic Arts of Southern Asia and Middle America. *In* 29th International Congress of Americanists, New York, 1949. Pp. 299–309.

Heizer, R. F.
1951 Preliminary Report on the Leonard Rockshelter Site, Pershing County, Nevada. American Antiquity 17: 23–25.
1958 Prehistoric Central California: A Problem in Historical-Developmental Classification. Reports of the University of California Archaeological Survey, No. 41, Pp. 19–26, Berkeley.
1960 Agriculture and the Theocratic State in Lowland Southeastern Mexico. American Antiquity 25: 215–222.
Helck, W.
1975 Wirtschaftsgeschichte des Alten Agypten, im 3. und 2. Jahrtausend vor Chr. Leiden.
Hernandez de Alba, Gregorio
1946 The Archaeology of San Agustin and Tierradentro. *In* Handbook of South American Indians, Vol. 2. J. H. Steward, ed. Pp. 851–860. Bulletin 143, Bureau of American Ethnology, Smithsonian Institution. Washington, D.C.
Herskovits, Melville
1948 *Man and His Works*. Alfred A. Knopf, Inc.: New York.
Hester, T. R. and H. J. Shafer
1984 "Exploitation of Chert Resources by the Ancient Maya of Northern Belize, Central America," *Journal of Field Archaeology, Vol.* 16, No. 2, Pp. 157–173.
Hibben, F. C.
1941 Evidences of Early Occupation of Sandia Cave, New Mexico, and Other Sites in the Sandia-Manzano Region. Smithsonian Miscellaneous Collections, Vol. 99, No. 23, Smithsonian Institution. Washington, D.C.
Hilbert, P. P.
1955 A Ceramica Arqueologica da Regiao Littoral. Instituto de Antropologia e Etnologia do Para, Publicacion 9. Belem.
Hill, J. N.
1968 Broken K Pueblo: Patterns of Form and Function. *In* New Perspectives in Archaeology. S. R. Binford and L. R. Binford, eds. Pp. 103–142. Chicago.
Histoyre du Mechique
1905 E. de Jonghe, ed. Journal de la Société des Americanistes de Paris 2: 1–41.
Holmes, W. H.
1888 Ancient Art of the Province of Chiriqui, Colombia. 6th Annual Report, Bureau of American Ethnology, Smithsonian Institution. Washington, D.C.
1903 Aboriginal Pottery of the Eastern United States. 20th Annual Report, Bureau of American Ethnology, Smithsonian Institution. Washington, D.C.
1912 Stone Implements of the Argentine Littoral. Bulletin 52, Bureau of American Ethnology, Smithsonian Institution. Washington, D.C.
Hoopes, John
1985 El Complejo Tronadora: Ceramica del Periodo Formativo Medio en La Cuenca de Arenal, Guanacaste, Costa Rica. Vinculos 11, Nos. 1–2: 111–118.
Houston, S. D., and Peter Mathews
1985 The Dynastic Sequence of Dos Pilas, Guatemala. Pre-Columbian Art Research Institute, Monopgraph 1. San Francisco.
Howard, E. B.
1935 Occurrence of Flints and Extinct Animals in Pluvial Deposits Near Clovis, New Mexico. 1. Introduction. Proceedings of the Philadelphia Academy of Natural Sciences 87: 299–303.
Howard, G. D.
1943 Excavations at Ronquin, Venezuela. Yale University Publications in Anthropology, No. 28. New Haven, CT.
1947 Prehistoric Ceramic Styles of Lowland South America, Their Distribution and History. Yale University Publications in Anthropology, No. 37. New Haven, CT.
Howard, G. D., and G. R. Willey
1948 Lowland Argentine Archaeology. Yale University Publications in Anthropology, No. 37. New Haven, CT.
Humphreys, S. C.
1975 "Transcendence" and Intellectual Roles: The Greek Case. Daedalus, Spring: 91–118.
Hurt, W. R., ed.
1956 The Lagoa Santa Project. Museum News, Vol. 18, Nos. 9–10, University of South Dakota. Vermilion.

Ibarra Grasso, D. E.
1955 Hallazgos de Puntas Paleoliticas en Bolivia. *In* 31st International Congress of Americanists, Sao Paulo, 1954, Vol. 2. Pp. 561–568.
1956a Anciennes Cultures du Territoire bolivien (avant Tiahuanaco). Antiquity and Survival, No. 6, The Hague.
1956b La Mas Antigua Cultura Agricola de Bolivia. Revista de Antropologia, São Paulo, Brazil.
Irving, W. N., and C. R. Harington
1973 Upper Pleistocene Radiocarbon Dates from the Northern Yukon. Science 179: 335–340.
Irwin-Williams, Cynthia
1968 Archaeological Evidence on Early Man in Mexico. *In* Early Man in Western North America. Pp. 39–41. Eastern New Mexico University Contributions in Anthropology, Vol. 1, No. 4. Portales.
Isbell, W. H.
1983 Shared Ideology and Parallel Political Development: Wari and Tiwanaku. *In* Investigations of the Andean Past. D. H. Sanweiss, ed. Pp. 186–208. Latin American Studies Program, Cornell University. Ithaca, NY.
Isbell, W. H., and K. J. Schreiber
1978 Was Wari a State? American Antiquity 43: 372–390.
Ishida, Eiichiro, and others
1960 Andes. The Report of the University of Tokyo Scientific Expedition to the Andes in 1958. Tokyo: University of Tokyo.
Izumi, S., and T. Sono
1963 Andes 2. Excavations at Kotosh, Peru, 1960. Tokyo: Kadowa Publishing Co.
Jacobsen, Thorkild
1943 Primitive Democracy in Ancient Mesopotamia. Journal of Near Eastern Studies 2: 159–172.
Jennings, J. D.
1957 Danger Cave. Memoir 14, Society for American Archaeology.
1964 The Desert West. *In* Prehistoric Man in the New World. J. D. Jennings and E. Norbeck, eds. Pp. 149–173. Chicago: University of Chicago Press.
Jennings, J. D., and Edward Norbeck
1955 Great Basin Prehistory: A Review. American Antiquity 21: 1–11.
Jennings, J. D., and others
1956 The American Southwest: A Problem in Cultural Isolation. *In* Seminars in Archaeology. Robert Wauchope, ed. Memoir No. 11, Society for American Archaeology.
Jijón y Caamaño, Jacinto
1927 Puruha, 2 vols. Reprinted from Boletin Academia Nacional de Historia de Ecuador, Vols. 3, 5, 6, 7, and 9. Quito.
1930 Un Gran Marea Cultural en el Noroeste de Sudamerica. Journal de la Société des Americanistes de Paris 22: 107–197.
1951 La Civilizaciones del Sur de Centro America y el Noroeste de Sud America. *In* 29th International Congress of Americanists, New York, Vol. 1. Pp. 165–172.
Jimenez Moreno, Wigberto
1941 Tula y Los Toltecas. Revista Mexicano de Estudios Antropologicos 5, Nos. 2–3.
1946 Cronologia de la Historia Precolombina de Mexico. *In* Mexico Prehispanico. Pp. 114–123. Mexico, D. F.
1954–55 Sintesis de la Historia Precolonial del Valle de Mexico. Revista Mexicano de Estudios Antropologicos 14: 219–236 (Primera Parte).
1959 Sintesis de la Historia Pre-Tolteca de Mesoamerica. *In* Esplendor de Mexico Antiguo, Vol. 2. Centro de Investigaciones Antropologicas de Mexico. Mexico, D. F.
1966 Los Imperios Prehispanicos de Mexico. Revista Estudios Antropologicos de Mexico 20: 179–195.
Johnson, Frederick, ed.
1951 Radiocarbon Dating. Memoir No. 8, Society for American Archaeology.
1970 The Prehistory of the Tehuacan Valley. Austin: University of Texas Press.
Johnston, Kevin
1985 Maya Dynastic Territorial Expansion: Glyphic Evidence for Classic Centers of the Pasion River, Guatemala. *In* Fifth Palenque Round Table. V. M. Fields, ed. Pp. 49–56. Monterey, CA.

Jones, Christopher
1977 Inauguration Dates of Three Late Classic Rulers of Tikal, Guatemala. American Antiquity 42: 28–60.

Jones, Christopher, and R. J. Sharer
1980 Archaeological Investigations in the Site Core of Quirigua. Expedition 23, No. 1: 11–20.

Jones, M. R.
1952 Map of the Ruins of Mayapan, Yucatan, Mexico, Carnegie Institution of Washington, Department of Archaeology, Current Reports, No. 1, Washington, D.C.

Joralemon, David
1971 A Study of Olmec Iconography. Studies in Pre-Columbian Art and Archaeology, No. 7, Dumbarton Oaks. Washington, D.C.

Kaufman, Terence
1976 Archaeological and Linguistic Correlations in Mayaland and Associated Areas of Mesoamerica. World Archaeology 8: 101–118.

Kelley, D. H.
1976 Deciphering the Maya Script. Austin: University of Texas Press.

Kemp, B. J.
1977 The Early Development of Towns in Egypt. Antiquity 51: 185–200.

Kennedy, N. C.
1986 The Periphery Problem and Playa de los Muertos: A Test Case. *In* The Southeast Maya Periphery. P. A. Urban and E. M. Schortman, eds. Pp. 179–193. Austin: University of Texas Press.

Kidder, A. V.
1924 An Introduction to Southwestern Archaeology. Peabody Foundation, Andover, Massachusetts, and Yale University Press. New Haven, CT.
1936 Speculations on New World Prehistory. *In* Essays in Anthropology Honoring A. L. Kroeber, R. H. Lowie, ed., Pp. 143–152. Berkeley: University of California Press.

Kidder, A. V., J. D. Jennings, and E. M. Shook
1946 Excavations at Kaminaljuyu, Guatemala. Carnegie Institution of Washington, Publication 561. Washington, D.C.

Kidder, Alfred, II
1940 South American Penetrations in Middle America. *In* The Maya and Their Neighbors. C. L. Hay and others, eds. Pp. 441–459. New York: Appleton-Century.
1943 Some Early Sites in the Northern Lake Titicaca Basin. Papers, Peabody Museum, Vol. 27, No. 1, Harvard University. Cambridge, MA.
1944 Archaeology of Northwestern Venezuela, Peabody Museum Papers, Vol. 26, No. 1, Harvard University, Cambridge, MA.
1948 "The Archaeology of Venezuela," Handbook of South American Indians, J. H. Steward, ed., Vol. 4, Pp. 413–437, Bulletin 143, Bureau of American Ethnology, Smithsonian Institution, Washington, D.C.
1964 South American High Cultures. *In* Prehistoric Man in the New World. J. D. Jennings and E. Norbeck, eds. Pp. 451–488. Chicago: University of Chicago Press.

King, A. R.
1948 Tripod Pottery in the Central Andean Area. American Antiquity 14: 103–115.

Kirchhoff, Paul
1943 Mesoamerica. Acta Americana 1: 92–107.
1955 Quetzalcoatl, Huemac, y el Fin de Tula. Cuadernos Americanos 84, No. 6: 163–196.

Klima, Bohuslav
1962 The First Ground-Plan of an Upper Paleolithic Loess Settlement in Middle Europe and Its Meaning. *In* Courses Toward Urban Life. R. J. Braidwood and G. R. Willey, eds. Pp. 193–210. Chicago: University of Chicago Press.

Kluckhohn, C. K. M.
1940 The Conceptual Structure in Middle American Studies. *In* The Maya and Their Neighbors. C. L. Hay and others, eds. Pp. 41–51. New York: Appleton-Century.
1960 The Moral Order in the Expanding Society. *In* City Invincible. C. H. Kraeling and R. McC. Adams, eds. Pp. 391–404. Chicago: University of Chicago Press.

Krieger, A. D.
1944 The Typological Concept. American Antiquity 9: 271–288.
1945 An Inquiry into Supposed Mexican Influences on a Prehistoric "Cult" in the Southern United States. American Anthropologist 47: 483–515.

1953 New World Culture History: Anglo-America. *In* Anthropology Today. A. L. Kroeber, ed. Pp. 238–264. Chicago: University of Chicago Press.

1962 The Earliest Cultures in the Western United States. American Antiquity 28: 138–143.

1964 Early Man in the New World. *In* Prehistoric Man in the New World. J. D. Jennings and E. Norbeck, eds. Pp. 23–84. Chicago: University of Chicago Press.

Kroeber, A. L.

1918 Zuni Postherds. Anthropological Papers, American Museum of Natural History, Vol. 18, Pt. 4. New York.

1925a The Uhle Pottery Collections from Supe. University of California Publications in American Archaeology and Ethnology, Vol. 21, No. 6. Berkeley.

1925b The Uhle Pottery Collections from Moche, University of California Publications in American Archaeology and Ethnology, Vol. 21, Pp. 191–234. Berkeley.

1926a Archaeological Explorations in Peru. Part I: Ancient Pottery from Trujillo. Anthropology, Memoirs, Field Museum of Natural History, Vol. 2, No. 1. Chicago.

1926b The Uhle Pottery Collections from Chancay. University of California Publications in American Archaeology and Ethnology, Vol. 21, No. 7. Berkeley.

1926c Cultural Stratification in Peru. American Anthropologist 28: 131–151.

1927 Coast and Highland in Prehistoric Peru. American Anthropologist 29: 625–653.

1930a Archaeological Explorations in Peru. Part II: The Northern Coast. Anthropology, Memoirs, Field Museum of Natural History, Vol. 2, No. 2. Chicago.

1930b Cultural Relations between North and South America. *In* 23rd International Congress of Americanists, New York, 1928. Pp. 5–22.

1931 The Culture Area and Age Area Concepts of Clark Wissler. *In* Methods in Social Science. Stuart Rice, ed. Pp. 248–265. Chicago: University of Chicago Press.

1940 Stimulus Diffusion. American Anthropologist 42: 1–20.

1944 Peruvian Archaeology in 1942. Viking Fund Publications in Anthropology, No. 4. New York.

1948a Anthropology. New York: Harcourt, Brace, & Co.

1948b Summary and Interpretations. *In* A Reappraisal of Peruvian Archaeology. W. C. Bennett, ed. Pp. 113–121. Memoir 4, Society for American Archaeology.

1951 Great Art Styles of Ancient South America. *In* 29th International Congress of Americanists, New York, 1949, Vol. 1. Pp. 207–215.

1952 The Ancient Oikoumene as a Historical Culture Aggregate. Huxley Memorial Lecture for 1945 (1946). Rpt. in *The Nature of Culture.* Pp. 379–395. University of Chicago Press.

1953 Paracas Cavernas and Chavín. University of California Publications in American Archaeology and Ethnology, Vol. 40, No. 8. Berkeley.

1957 Style and Civilization. Ithaca, NY: Cornell University Press.

Kroeber, A. L., and W. D. Strong

1924 The Uhle Pottery Collections from Ica. University of California Publications in American Archaeology and Ethnology, Vol. 21, No. 3, Berkeley.

Krone, Ricardo

1914 "Informacões ethnographicas do Valle do Ribeira de Iguapé," *Boletin Comision Geographica e Geologia do Estado de Sao Paulo*, Sao Paulo.

Kubler, Georg E.

1962 The Art and Architecture of Ancient America. Baltimore: Penguin Books.

1970 Period, Style, and Meaning in Ancient American Art. New Literary History 1: 127–144.

1973a Iconographic Aspects of Architectural Profiles at Teotihuacan and in Mesoamerica. *In* The Iconography of Middle American Sculpture. D. T. Easby, ed. Pp. 24–39. New York: Metropolitan Museum.

1973b Science and Humanism among Americanists. *In* The Iconography of Middle American Sculpture. D. T. Easby, ed. Pp. 163–167. New York: Metropolitan Museum.

Kulp, J. L., H. W. Feely, and L. E. Tryon

1951 Lamont Natural Radiocarbon Measurements, I. Science 114: 565–568.

1952 Lamont Natural Radiocarbon Measurements, II. Science 116: 409–414.

Lamberg-Karlovsky, C. C.

1970 Excavations at Tepe Yahya, Iran, 1967–69. Report 1, American School of Prehistoric Research, Peabody Museum, Harvard University. Cambridge: MA.

Lamberg-Karlovsky, C. C., ed.

1952–1972 Old World Archaeology: Foundations of Civilization. San Francisco: W. H. Freeman and Co.

Lamberg-Karlovsky, C. C., and J. A. Sabloff
1979 Ancient Civilizations. Benjamin Cummings: Menlo Park, CA.
Lamberg-Karlovsky, C. C., and Maurizio Tosi
1972 Shahr-i Sokhta and Tepe Yahya: Tracks on the Earliest History of the Iranian Plateau. East and West 23, Nos. 1–2.
Landa, Diego de
1938 Relacion de Las Coas de Yucatan. Hector Perez Martin, ed. Merida, Yucatan, Mexico.
Lange, F. W.
1971 Marine Resources: A Viable Subsistence Alternative for the Prehistoric Lowland Maya. American Anthropologist 73: 619–639.
1976 Bahias y Valles de la Costa de Guanacaste. Vinculos 2, No. 1: 45–67.
1978 Coastal Settlement in Northwestern Costa Rica. *In* Prehistoric Coastal Adaptations. B. L. Starke and Barbara Voorhies, eds. Pp. 109–119. New York: Academic Press.
Lange, F. W., and D. Z. Stone, eds.
1984 The Archaeology of Lower Central America. Albuquerque: University of New Mexico Press.
Lanning, E. P.
1959 Early Ceramic Chronologies of the Peruvian Coast. Mimeographed paper, Department of Anthropology, University of California, Berkeley.
1967 Peru before the Incas. Englewood Cliffs, N.J.: Prentice-Hall.
Larco Hoyle, Rafael
1938 Los Mochicas, Vol. 1. Lima.
1941 Los Cupisniques. Lima.
1944 Cultura Salinar: Sintesis Monografica. Trujillo, Peru.
1945 Los Cupisniques, Buenos Aires.
1946 A Culture Sequence for the North Coast of Peru. *In* Handbook of South American Indians. Vol. 2. J. H. Steward, ed. Pp. 149–176. Bulletin 143, Bureau of American Ethnology, Smithsonian Institution. Washington, D.C.
1948 Cronologia Arqueologica del Norte del Peru. Buenos Aires: Sociedad Geografica.
Larsen, Helge, and Froelich Rainey
1948 Ipiutak and the Arctic Whale Hunting Culture. Anthropological Papers of the American Museum of Natural History, Vol. 42. New York.
Latcham, R. E.
1928 La Prehistoria Chilena. Official Chilean Commission for the Ibero American Exposition at Sevilla, Santiago, Chile.
1936 Indian Ruins in North Chile, American Anthropologist, Vol. 38, Pp. 52–58.
1938 Arqueologia de La Region Atacameña, Santiago, Chile.
Lathrap, D. W.
1957 Radiation: The Application to Cultural Development of a Model from Biological Evolution. Manuscript, Tozzer Library, Peabody Museum, Harvard University.
1958 The Cultural Sequence at Yarinacocha, Eastern Peru, American Antiquity, Vol. 23, Pp. 379–388.
1965 Origins of Central Andean Civilization. Science 1948: 796–798.
1970 The Upper Amazon. London: Thames and Hudson.
1971 The Tropical Forest and the Cultural Context of Chavín. *In* Dumbarton Oaks Conference on Chavín. E. P. Benson, ed. Pp. 73–100. Washington, D.C.: Dumbarton Oaks.
1973a Gifts of the Cayman: Some Thoughts on the Subsistence Basis of Chavín. *In* Variation in Anthropology. D. W. Lathrap and J. Douglas, eds. Pp. 91–105. Urbana, IL: Illinois Archaeological Survey.
1973b Summary or Model Building: How Does One Achieve a Meaningful Overview of a Continent's Prehistory? American Anthropologist 75: 1765–1767.
1974 The Moist Tropics, the Arid Lands, and the Appearance of Great Art Styles in the New World. Special Publication of the Museum of Texas Tech University, No. 7. Pp. 115–158. Lubbock.
1975 Ancient Ecuador: Culture, Clay, and Creativity, 3000–300 B.C. Chicago: Field Museum of Natural History.
1977 Our Father the Cayman, Our Mother the Gourd: Spinden Revisited or a Unitary Model for the Emergence of Agriculture in the New World. *In* Origins of Agriculture. C. A. Reed, ed. Pp. 713–751. The Hague: Mouton Publishers.

1982 Complex Iconographic Features by Olmec and Chavín and Some Speculations on Their Possible Significance. *In* Primer Simposio de Correlaciones Antropologicas Andino-Mesoamericano. Jorge Marcos and Presley Norton, eds. Pp. 301–327. Guayaquil, Ecuador: Escuela Politecnica del Litoral.

1985 Jaws: The Control of Power in the Early Nuclear American Ceremonial Center. *In* Early Ceremonial Architecture in the Andes. C. B. Donnan, ed. Pp. 241–268. Washington, D.C.: Dumbarton Oaks.

Lathrap, D. W., ed.

1956 An Archaeological Classification of Culture Contact Situations. *In* Seminars in Archaeology: 1955. Robert Wauchope, ed. Pp. 3–30. Memoir 11, Society for American Archaeology.

Lathrap, D. W., J. G. Marcos, and James Zeidler

1977 Real Alto: An Ancient Ceremonial Center. Archaeology 30: 2–14.

Leach, E. R.

1965 Political Systems of Highland Burma. London: G. Bell and Sons, Ltd. Bos.

Lehmann, Henri

1948 Résultat d'un Voyage de Prospection Archéologique sur les Cotes du Pacifique. *In* 28th International Congress of Americanists, Paris. Pp. 423–439.

1951 Le Personnage Couché sur le Dos: Commun dans l'Archéologie du Mexique et de l'Equateur. *In* 29th International Congress of Americanists, New York, 1949, Vol. 1. Pp. 291–298.

Lehmann, Walter

1938 Die Geschichte der Konigreiche von Colhaucan und Mexico. Stuttgart.

Leone, M. P.

1972 Issues in Anthropological Archaeology. *In* Contemporary Archaeology. Carbondale, IL: Southern Illinois University Press.

Lesser, Alexander

1961 Social Fields and the Evolution of Society. Southwestern Journal of Anthropology, 17: 40–48. Albuquerque: University of New Mexico.

Leventhal, R. M., A. A. Demarest, and G. R. Willey

1987 The Cultural and Social Components of Copan. *In* Polities and Partitions: Human Boundaries in Ancient Societies. K. Maurer Trinkhaus, ed. Pp. 179–205. Arizona State Anthropological Research Paper, No. 37. Tempe.

Lewis, T. M. N., and Madeline Kneberg

1946 Hiwassee Island. Knoxville, TN: University of Tennessee Press.

Liang, S. Y.

1930 New Stone Age Pottery from the Prehistoric Site at Hsi-Yin Tsun, Shansi, China. Memoir 37, American Anthropological Association.

Libby, W. F.

1951 Radiocarbon Dates, II. Science 114: 291–295.

1952a Radiocarbon Dates, III. Science 116: 673–680.

1952b Radiocarbon Dating. Chicago: University of Chicago Press. 2nd ed. 1955.

1954 Chicago Radiocarbon Dates, V. Mimeographed.

1955 Radiocarbon Dating. 2nd ed., University of Chicago Press.

Linares de Sapir, O. F.

1976 From the Late Preceramic to the Formative in the Intermediate Area: Some Issues and Methodologies. Proceedings of the First Puerto Rican Symposium on Archaeology 1: 65–79.

1977a Adaptive Strategies in Western Panama. World Archaeology 8, No. 3: 304–320.

1977b Ecology and the Arts in Ancient Panama, On the Development of Social Rank and Symbolism in the Central Provinces. Studies in Pre-Columbian Art and Archaeology, No. 1, Dumbarton Oaks. Washington, D.C.

Linares de Sapir, O. F., and A. J. Ranere

1971 Human Adaptation to the Tropical Forests of Western Panama. Archaeology 24: 346–356.

Lincoln, C. E.

1985 The Chronology of Chichen Itza: A Review of the Literature. *In* Late Lowland Maya Civilization, Classic to Postclassic. J. A. Sabloff and E. W. Andrews V, eds. Pp. 141–198. Albuquerque: University of New Mexico Press.

Linton, Ralph

1944 North American Cooking Pots. American Antiquity 9, No. 4: 369–380.

1949 The Tree of Culture. Transactions, New York Academy of Sciences II, No. 5: 171–175.

Logan, W. D.
1952 Graham Cave, An Archaic Site in Montgomery County, Missouri. Memoir No. 2, Missouri Archaeological Society. Columbia.

Longacre, W. A.
1966 Changing Patterns of Social Integration: A Prehistoric Example from the American Southwest. American Anthropologist 58: 94–102.
1968 Some Aspects of Prehistoric Society in East-Central Arizona. *In* New Perspectives in Archaeology. S. R. and L. R. Binford, eds. Pp. 89–102. Chicago: Aldine Publishing Co.

Longyear, J. M., III
1944 Archaeological Excavations in El Salvador, Memoirs, Vol. 9, Peabody Museum, Harvard University, Cambridge, Massachusetts.
1969 The Problem of Olmec Influences into the Pottery of Western Honduras. In 38th International Congress of Americanists, Stuttgart-Munchen, *1968*, Vol. 1. Pp. 491–496.

Lopes, Raymundo
1924 "A civilisacão lacustre do Brasil," Boletin Museu Nacional do Rio de Janeiro, Vol. 1, No. 1.
1925 "La Civilisation lacustre du Bresil," 21st International Congress of Americanists, 2nd Session, Goteborg, Pp. 619–629, Goteborg.
1928 "Sobre as palafittas do Marahão," 20th International Congress of Americanists, Vol. 2, Pp. 169–170, Rio de Janeiro.
1932 "Entre a Amazonia e O Sertão," Boletin Museu Nacional do Rio de Janeiro, Vol. 7, No. 3.

Lorenzo, J. L.
1958 Un Sitio Preceramico en Yanhuitlan, Oaxaca. Instituto Nacional de Antropologia e Historia, Publicacion 6. Mexico, D.F.

Lothrop, S. K.
1924 Tulum. Publications of the Carnegie Institution of Washington, No. 335. Washington, D.C.
1926 Pottery of Costa Rica and Nicaragua. Contributions, Museum of the American Indian, Heye Foundation, Vol. 8. 2 vols. New York.
1932 Indians of the Parana Delta, Argentina. Annals of the New York Academy of Sciences, Vol. 33. Pp. 77–232. New York.
1936 Zacualpa, A Study of Ancient Quiche Artifacts. Carnegie Institution of Washington, Publication 472. Washington, D.C.
1939 The Southeastern Frontier of the Maya. American Anthropologist 41: 42–54.
1941 Gold Ornaments of Chavín Style from Chongoyape, Peru. American Antiquity 6: 250–262.
1942 Cocle, An Archaeological Study of Central Panama. Memoirs, Peabody Museum, Vol. 8, Harvard University. Cambridge, MA.
1951a Gold Artifacts of Chavín Style. American Antiquity 16: 225–240.
1951b Peruvian Metallurgy. *In* 29th International Congress of Americanists, New York, 1949, Vol. 1. Pp. 219–223.

Lowe, G. W.
1975 The Early Preclassic Barra Phase of Alta Mira, Chiapas. Papers, New World Archaeological Foundation, No. 38, Brigham Young University. Provo, UT.
1978 Eastern Mesoamerica. *In* Chronologies in New World Archaeology. R. E. Taylor and C. W. Meighan, eds. Pp. 331–393. New York: Academic Press.

Lumbreras, L. G.
1971 Toward a Re-evaluation of Chavín. *In* Dumbarton Oaks Conference on Chavín. E. P. Benson, ed. Pp. 1–28. Washington, D.C.: Dumbarton Oaks.

MacCurdy, G. G.
1911 A Study of Chiriquian Antiquities. Connecticut Academy of Arts and Sciences, Memoirs, Vol. 3. Yale University Press, New Haven.

MacNeish, R. S.
1950 A Synopsis of the Archaeological Sequence in the Sierra de Tamaulipas. Revista Mexicana de Estudios Antropologicos 11: 79–96. Mexico, D.F.
1954 An Early Archaeological Site near Panuco, Veracruz. Transactions, American Philosophical Society, Vol. 44, Pt. 5. Philadelphia.
1956 The Engigstciak Site on the Yukon Arctic Coast. Anthropological Papers, University of Alaska, Vol. 4, No. 2. Fairbanks.

1958 Preliminary Archaeological Investigations in the Sierra de Tamaulipas, Mexico. Transactions, American Philosophical Society. Vol. 48, Pt. 6. Philadelphia.
1959 A Speculative Framework of Northern North American Prehistory as of April 1959. Anthropologica 1: 7–23.
1962 Second Annual Report of the Tehuacan Archaeological-Botanical Project. R. S. Peabody Foundation. Andover, MA.
1964 Ancient Mesoamerican Civilization. Science 143: 531–537.
1971 Early Man in the Andes. Scientific American 224, No. 4: 36–46.

MacNeish, R. S., F. A. Peterson, and K. V. Flannery
1970 The Prehistory of the Tehuacan Valley. Vol. 3, Ceramics. Austin: University of Texas Press.

MacNeish, R. S., et al.
1980 The First Annual Report of the Belize Archaeological Reconnaissance. Peabody Foundation. Andover, MA.

Mangelsdorf, P. C.
1958 Ancestor of Corn. Science 128: 1313–1320.

Mangelsdorf, P. C., R. S. MacNeish, and G. R. Willey
1964 Origins of Agriculture in Mesoamerica. *In* Handbook of Middle American Indians, Vol. 1, R. Wauchope, ed. Pp. 427–445. Austin: University of Texas Press.

Mangelsdorf, P. C., and C. E. Smith, Jr.
1949 New Archaeological Evidence on Evolution in Maize. Botanical Museum Leaflet, Vol. 13, No. 8, Harvard University. Cambridge, MA.

Marcos, Jorge
1980 Ecuador: Hub of the Northern Andean Area. Ms. prepared for a volume on South American archaeological chronologies.

Marcus, Joyce
1973 Territorial Organization of the Lowland Classic Maya. Science 180: 911–916.
1976 Emblem and State in the Classic Lowlands: An Epigraphic Approach to Territorial Organization. Washington, D.C.: Dumbarton Oaks.
1983 Lowland Maya Archaeology at the Crossroads. American Antiquity 48: 454–488.

Marquez Miranda, Fernando
1946 The Diaguita of Argentina. *In* Handbook of South American Indians, Vol. 2. J. H. Steward, ed. Pp. 637–654. Bulletin 143, Bureau of American Ethnology, Smithsonian Institution. Washington, D.C.

Martin, P. S., Carl Lloyd, and Alexander Spoehr
1938 Archaeological Works in the Ackmen-Lowry Area, South-Western Colorado, 1937. Field Museum of Natural History, Anthropological Series No. 23, Pt. 2. Chicago.

Martin, P.S., G. I. Quimby, and Donald Collier
1947 Indians Before Columbus. Chicago: University of Chicago Press.

Martin, P. S., and J. B. Rinaldo
1939 Modified Basket Maker Sites, Ackmen-Lowry Area, South-Western Colorado. Field Museum of Natural History, Anthropological Series, No. 23, Pt. 3. Chicago.
1950 Sites of the Reserve Phase, Pine Lawn Valley, Western New Mexico. Fieldiana: Anthropology, Vol. 38, No. 3, Field Museum of Natural History. Chicago.
1951 The Southwestern Co-Tradition. Southwestern Journal of Anthropology 7: 215–229. Albuquerque: University of New Mexico Press.

Matheny, R. T., ed.
1980 El Mirador, Peten, Guatemala: An Interim Report. Papers, New World Archaeological Foundation, No. 45. Provo, UT.

Mathews, Peter
1985 Maya Early Classic Monuments and Inscriptions. *In* A Consideration of the Early Classic Period in the Maya Lowlands. G. R. Willey and Peter Mathews, eds. Pp. 5–54. Institute for Mesoamerican Studies, Publication No. 10. State University of New York. Albany.

Mathews, Peter, and G. R. Willey
1989 Prehistoric Polities of the Pasión Region: Hieroglyphic Texts and Their Archaeological Settings. *In* Ruling Class Interaction Among the Classic Maya. T. P. Culbert and Norman Hammond, eds. Albuquerque: University of New Mexico Press.

Matsuzawa, T.
1978 The Formative Site of Las Haldas, Peru: Architecture, Chronology, and Economy. American Antiquity 43: 652–673.

Mayntshuzen, F. C.

1928 Instrumentos paleoliticos del Paraguay. *In* 20th International Congress of Americanists, Rio de Janeiro, Vol. 2. Pp. 177–180.

McClellan, Catharine

1953 The Inland Tlingit. *In* Asia and North America: Transpacific Contacts. Pp. 47–52. Memoir No. 9, Society for American Archaeology.

McGimsey, C. R.

1956 Cerro Mangote: A Preceramic Site in Panama. American Antiquity 22: 151–161.

McKern, W. C.

1939 The Midwestern Taxonomic Method as an Aid to Archaeological Culture Study. American Antiquity 4: 301–313.

Means, P. A.

1931 Ancient Civilizations of the Andes. New York: Charles Scribner's Sons.

Meggers, B. J.

1954 Environmental Limitations on the Development of Culture. American Anthropologist 56: 801–824.

1966 Ecuador. Ancient Peoples and Places Series. London: Thames and Hudson.

Meggers, B. J., and Clifford, Evans, Jr.

1955 Preliminary Results of Archaeological Excavations in British Guiana. Timehri, No. 34, Journal of the Royal Agricultural and Commercial Society of British Guiana. Georgetown.

1957 Archaeological Investigations at the Mouth of the Amazon. Bulletin 167, Bureau of American Ethnology, Smithsonian Institution. Washington, D.C.

1966 Beginnings of Food Production in Ecuador. *In* 36th International Congress of Americanists, Sevilla, 1964, Vol. 1. Pp. 201–207.

Meggers, B. J., Clifford Evans, Jr., and Emilio Estrada

1965 Early Formative Period of Coastal Ecuador: The Valdivia and Machalilla Phases. Smithsonian Contributions to Anthropology, Vol. 1, Smithsonian Institution. Washington, D.C.

Meighan, C. W.

1959 Varieties of Prehistoric Cultures in the Great Basin. The Masterkey 33, No. 2: 46–59.

Menghín, O. F. A.

1952 Fundamentos Cronologicos de la Prehistoria de Patagonia. Runa 5: 23–43.

1953–54 Culturas Preceramicas en Bolivia. Runa 6: 125–132.

1955–56 El Altoparanaense. Ampurias 17–18; 171–200.

1957 Vorgeschichte Amerikas. Abriss der Vorgeschichte. Munich: Verlag R. Oldenbourg.

Menghin, O. F. A., and Marcelo Bormida

1950 Investigaciones Prehistoricas en Cuevas de Tandilia, Provincia de Buenos Aires. Runa 3: 5–36.

Menghin, O. F. A., and A. R. Gonzalez

1954 Excavaciones Arqueologicas en el Yacimiento de Ongamira, Cordoba. Universidad Nacional de La Plata, Vol. 17, No. 67. La Plata.

Menzel, Dorothy

1964 Style and Time in the Middle Horizon. Ñawpa Pacha 2: 1–106.

Metraux, Alfred

1930 Contribution à l'étude de l'archéologie du cours supérieur et moyen de L'Amazone. Revista del Museo de La Plata 3: 205–255.

Middendorf, E. W.

1893–95 Peru. 3 vols. Berlin.

Miles, S. W.

1965 Sculpture of the Guatemala-Chiapas Highlands and Pacific Slopes. *In* Handbook of Middle American Indians, Vol. 2. R. Wauchope, ed. Pp. 237–275. Austin: University of Texas Press.

Milliken, W. M.

1945 Exhibition of the Art of the Americas. Bulletin, Cleveland Museum of Art, 32nd Year, No. 9. Cleveland, OH.

Millon, R. F.

1954 Irrigation at Teotihuacan. American Antiquity 20: 177–180.

1957 Irrigation Systems in the Valley of Teotihuacan. American Antiquity 23: 160–167.

1964 The Teotihuacan Mapping Project. American Antiquity 29: 345–352.

1967 Teotihuacan. Scientific American 216: 38–63.

1970 Teotihuacan: Completion of Map of Giant Ancient City in Valley of Mexico. Science 170:

1077–1082.
1973 Urbanization at Teotihuacan, Mexico. Vol. 1, *The Teotihuacan Map*, Pt. 1 (text). Austin: University of Texas Press.
Molloy, J. P., and W. L. Rathje
1974 Sexploitation among the Late Classic Maya. *In* Mesoamerican Archaeology, New Approaches. Norman Hammond, ed. Pp. 431–444. London: Duckworth.
Morley, S. G.
1920 The Inscriptions at Copan. Carnegie Institution of Washington, Publication 219. Washington, D.C.
1938–39 The Inscriptions of Peten. 5 vols. Carnegie Institution of Washington, Publication 437. Washington, D.C.
1946 The Ancient Maya. Palo Alto, CA: Stanford University Press.
Morris, Craig, and D. E. Thompson
1970 Huanuco Viejo: An Inca Administrative Center. American Antiquity, 35: 344–362.
Moseley, M. E.
1975 The Maritime Foundations of Andean Civilization. Menlo Park, CA: Benjamin Cummings.
Motolinia, Toribio de Benavente
1903 Memoriales de Fray Toribio de Motolinia. Luis Garcia Pimentel, ed. Paris.
Muelle, J. C.
1941 Concerning the Middle Chimu Style. University of California Publications in American Archaeology and Ethnology, Vol. 39. Berkeley.
Muller-Beck, Hansjurgen
1966 Paleohunters in America: Origins and Diffusions. Science, 152: 1191–1210.
Mulloy, W. T.
1954 The McKean Site in Northeastern Wyoming. Southwestern Journal of Anthropology, 10: 432–460.
Nelson, N. C.
1916 Chronology of the Tano Ruins, New Mexico. American Anthropologist 18: 159–180.
Netting, R. McC.
1977 Maya Subsistence: Mythologies, Analogies, Possibilities. *In* The Origins of Maya Civilization. R. E. W. Adams, ed. Pp. 299–334. Albuquerque: University of New Mexico Press.
Newell, H. P., and A. D. Krieger
1949 The George C. Davis Site, Cherokee County, Texas. Memoir No. 5, Society for American Archaeology.
Newman, M. T.
1948 A Summary of the Racial History of the Peruvian Area. *In* A Reappraisal of Peruvian Archaeology. W. C. Bennett, ed. Pp. 15–19. Memoir No. 4, Society for American Archaeology.
Newman, M. T., and C. E. Snow
1942 Preliminary Report on the Skeletal Material from Pickwick Basin, Alabama. *In* An Archaeological Survey of the Pickwick Basin in the Adjacent Portions of the States of Alabama, Mississippi, and Tennessee. W. S. Webb and D. L. DeJarnette. Bulletin 129, Bureau of American Ethnology, Smithsonian Institution. Washington, D.C.
Nicholson, H. B.
1955 Native Historical Traditions of Nuclear America and the Problem of their Archaeological Correlation. American Anthropologist 57: 594–613.
1957 Topiltzin Quetzalcoatl of Tollan: A Problem in Mesoamerican Ethnohistory. Ph.D. thesis, Anthropology, Harvard University.
1973 The Late Pre-Hispanic Central Mexican (Aztec) Iconographic System. *In* The Iconography of Middle American Sculpture. D. T. Easby, ed. Pp. 72–97. New York: Metropolitan Museum of Art.
1974 "The Deity 9. Wind 'Ehecatl-Quetzalcoatl,'" Ms.
1978 Western Mesoamerica: A.D. 900–1520. *In* Chronologies in New World Archaeology. R. E. Taylor and C. W. Meighan, eds. Pp. 185–330. New York: Academic Press.
Noguera, Eduardo
1939 Exploraciones en "El Openo," Michoacan. *In* 27th International Congress of Americanist, Mexico City. Pp. 574–586.
Nordenskiöld, Erland von

1913 Urnengraber und Mounds in Bolivianischen Flachlande. Baessler Archiv 3: 205–255.
1917 Die Ostliche Ausbreitung der Tiahuanacokultur in Bolivien und ihr Verhaltris zur Aruakkultur in Mojos. Zeitschrift für Ethnologie 55: 10–20.
1930 L'Archéologie du Bassin de L'Amazone. Paris.

Norman, V. G.
1976 Izapa Sculpture. Papers, New World Archaeological Foundation, No. 33, Brigham Young University. Provo, UT.

Oates, David
1972 The Development of Assyrian Towns and Cities. *In* Man, Settlement, and Urbanism. P. J. Ucko, Ruth Tringham, and G. W. Dimbleby, eds. Pp. 799–804. London: Duckworth.

Orr, P. C.
1956 Pleistocene Cave in Fishbone Cave, Pershing County, Nevada. Bulletin 2, Department of Archaeology, Nevada State Museum. Reno.

Orssich, Adam, and E. S. Orssich
1956 Stratigraphic Excavations in the Sambaqui of Araujo II. American Antiquity 21: 357–369.

Osborne, Douglas
1958 Western American Prehistory—An Hypothesis. American Antiquity 24: 47–53.

Osgood, Cornelius, and G. D. Howard
1943 An Archaeological Survey of Venezuela. Yale University Publications in Anthropology, No. 27. New Haven, CT.

Outes, F. F.
1904 Arqueologia de Hucal, Gobernacion de La Pampa. Anales del Museo Nacional de Buenos Aires 10: 1–15.
1909 Sobre una Facies Local de los Instrumentos Neoliticos Bonaerenses. Revista del Museo de La Plata 16: 319–339.

Palerm, Angel
1955 The Agricultural Bases of Urban Civilization in Mesoamerica. *In* Irrigation Civilizations: A Comparative Study. Pp. 28–42. Social Science Monographs No. 1, Pan American Union.

Parsons, J. R.
1968 An Estimate of Size and Population for Middle Horizon, Tiahuanaco, Bolivia. American Antiquity 33: 243–245.
1971 Prehistoric Settlement Patterns in the Texcoco Region, Mexico. Memoirs, Museum of Anthropology, No. 3, University of Michigan. Ann Arbor.

Parsons, L. A.
1966 Primer Informe Sobre las Investigaciones Hechas en "Las Ilusiones" (Bilbao), Santa Lucia Cotzumalhuapa, Guatemala. *IDAEH*, Vol. 18, No. 2. Pp. 3–19. Instituto de Antropologia e Historia, Guatemala City.

Parsons, L. A., and B. J. Price
1977 Mesoamerican Trade and Its Role in the Emergence of Civilization. *In* Peasant Livelihood. Pp. 164–183. New York: St. Martin's Press.

Paso y Troncoso, F.
1903 Leyenda de Los Soles. Florence.

Patterson, T. C.
1971a Chavín: An Interpretation of Its Spread and Influence. *In* Dumbarton Oaks Conference on Chavín. E. P. Benson, ed. Pp. 29–48. Washington, D.C.: Dumbarton Oaks.
1971b Central Peru: Its Population and Economy. Archaeology 24, No. 4: 316–321.
1988 Review of The Origins and Development of the Andean State by Jonathan Haas, Sheila Pozorski, and Thomas Pozorski. American Anthropologist 90: 699–700.

Patterson, T. C., and E. P. Lanning
1964 Changing Settlement Patterns on the Central Peruvian Coast. Ñawpa Pacha 2: 113–123.

Peebles, C. S., and S. M. Kus
1977 Some Archaeological Correlates of Ranked Societies. American Antiquity 42: 421–448.

Pendergast, D. M.
1971 Evidence of Teotihuacan–Lowland Maya Contact at Altun Ha. American Antiquity 36: 455–460.

Pennino, Raul, and A. F. Sallazzo
1927 El Paradero Charrua del Puerto de las Tunas y su alfareria. Revista de la Sociedad de Los Amigos de Arqueologia 1: 151–160.

Pereira de Godoy, Manuel

1952 Cachimbos Tupis-Guaranais de Pirassununga. *In* 29th International Congress of Americanists, New York, Vol. 3. Pp. 314–322.

Petrullo, Vincenzo

1939 The Archaeology of Arauquin. Anthropological Papers, No. 12. Pp. 291–296. Bulletin 123, Bureau of American Ethnology, Smithsonian Institution. Washington, D.C.

Phillips, Philip, J. A. Ford, and J. B. Griffin

1951 Archaeological Survey in the Lower Mississippi Alluvial Valley, 1940–1947. Papers of the Peabody Museum, Harvard University, Vol. 25. Cambridge, MA.

Phillips, Philip, and G. R. Willey

1953 Method and Theory in American Archaeology: An Operational Basis for Culture-Historical Integration. American Anthropologist 55: 615–633.

Piggott, Stuart

1965 Ancient Europe. Edinburgh: University Press.

Piña Chan, Roman

1955 Chalcatzingo, Morelos. Informes No. 4, Direction de Monumentos Pre-Hispanicos, Instituto de Antropologia e Historia. Mexico, D.F.

Pohl, Mary

1976 Ethnozoology of the Maya: An Analysis of Fauna from Five Sites in Peten, Guatemala. Ph.D. dissertation, Department of Anthropology, Harvard University.

Pollock, H. E. D.

1952 Annual Report of the Department of Archaeology. Yearbook, No. 51, Carnegie Institution of Washington. Washington, D.C.

Pollock, H. E. D., R. L. Roys, Tatiana Proskouriakoff, and A. L. Smith

1962 Mayapan, Yucatan, Mexico. Carnegie Institution of Washington, Publication 619. Washington, D.C.

Ponce Sangines, Carlos, ed.

1957 Arqueologia Boliviana. La Paz.

Pons Alegria, Mela

1976 Saladoid "Incense Burners" from the Site of El Convento, Puerto Rico. *In* Compte Rendu, Sixième Congrès International d'Etudes des Civilisations des Petites Antilles. Pp. 272–275.

Porter Weaver, M. N.

1953 Tlatilco and the Pre-Classic Cultures of the New World. Viking Fund Publications in Anthropology, No. 19. New York.

1972 The Aztecs, Maya, and Their Predecessors, Archaeology of Mesoamerica. New York: Academic Press.

Potter, D. R.

1985 Settlement. *In* A Consideration of the Early Classic Period in the Maya Lowlands. G. R. Willey and Peter Mathews, eds. Pp. 135–144. Institute for Mesoamerican Studies, State University of New York. Albany.

Preston, R. S., E. Person, and E. S. Deevey, Jr.

1955 Yale Radiocarbon Measurements II. Science 122: 954–960.

Preuss, K. Th.

1931 Arte Monumental Prehistorico. 2 vols. 2nd ed., Bogota: Escuelas Salesianas.

Price, B. J.

1976 A Chronological Framework for Cultural Development in Mesoamerica. *In* The Valley of Mexico, E. R. Wolf, ed. Pp. 13–23. Albuquerque: University of New Mexico Press.

1978 Secondary State Formation: An Explanatory Model. *In* Origins of the State, the Anthropology of Political Evolution. R. Cohen and E. R. Service, eds. Pp. 161–186. Philadelphia: Institute for the Study of Human Issues.

Proskouriakoff, Tatiana

1950 A Study of Classic Maya Sculpture. Carnegie Institution of Washington, Publication 593. Washington, D.C.

1960 Historical Implications of a Pattern of Dates at Piedras Negras, Guatemala. American Antiquity 25: 454–475.

1963 Historical Data in the Inscriptions at Yaxchilan (Pt. 1). Estudios Cultura Maya 3: 149–167.

1964 Historical Data in the Inscriptions at Yaxchilan (Pt. 2). Estudios Cultura Maya 4: 177–203.

Puleston, D. E.

1968 *Brosimum alicastrum* as a Subsistence Alternative for the Classic Maya of the Central Southern Lowlands. M.A. thesis, Department of Anthropology, University of Pennsylva-

nia.
1977 The Art and Archaeology of Hydraulic Agriculture in the Maya Lowlands. *In* Social Process in Maya Prehistory: Studies in Honor of Sir Eric Thompson. Norman Hammond, ed. Pp. 449–469. New York: Academic Press.
1979 An Epistemological Pathology and the Collapse, or Why the Maya Kept the Short Count. *In* Maya Archaeology and Ethnohistory. Norman Hammond and G. R. Willey, eds. Pp. 63–71. Austin: University of Texas Press.

Quirarte, Jacinto
1979 Sculptural Documents in the Origins of Maya Civilization. *In* 42nd International Congress of Americanists, Paris, 1976, Vol. 8. Pp. 189–198.

Rands, R. L.
1969 Relationships of Monumental Stone Sculpture of Copan with the Maya Lowlands. *In* 38th International Congress of Americanists, Stuttgart-Munchen, 1968, Vol. 1. Pp. 515–526.

Rappaport, R. A.
1971a Ritual, Sanctity, and Cybernetics. American Anthropologist 73: 59–76.
1971b The Sacred in Human Evolution. Annual Review of Ecology and Systemics 2: 23–44.

Rathje, W. L.
1970 Socio-Political Implications of Lowland Maya Burials. World Archaeology 1: 359–375.
1971 The Origin and Development of Lowland Classic Maya Civilization. American Antiquity 36: 275–285.
1972 Praise the Gods and Pass the Metates: A Hypothesis of the Development of Lowland Rainforest Civilization in Mesoamerica. *In* Contemporary Archaeology. M. P. Leone, ed. Pp. 365–392. Carbondale, IL: Southern Illinois University Press.
1973 Classic Maya Development and Denouement: A Research Design. *In* The Classic Maya Collapse. T. P. Culbert, ed. Pp. 405–456. Albuquerque: University of New Mexico Press.
1977 The Tikal Connection. *In* The Origins of Maya Civilization. R. E. W. Adams, ed. Pp. 373–382. Albuquerque: University of New Mexico Press.

Recinos, Adrian
1947 Popol Vuh: Las Antiguas Historias del Quiche. Mexico, D.F.

Redfield, Robert
1953 The Primitive World and Its Transformations. Ithaca, NY: Cornell University Press.

Reichel-Dolmatoff, Gerardo
1954 A Preliminary Study of Space and Time Perspective in Northern Colombia. American Antiquity 19: 352–366.
1955 Excavaciones en las Conchales de la Costa de Barlovento. Revista Colombiana de Antropologia 4: 249–272.
1957 Momil, A Formative Sequence from the Sinu Valley, Colombia. American Antiquity 22: 226–234.
1959 The Formative Stage, An Appraisal from a Colombian Perspective. *In* 33rd International Congress of Americanists, San Jose, Costa Rica, 1958, Vol. 1.
1961 Puerto Hormiga: Un Complejo Prehistorico Marginal de Colombia. Revista Colombiana de Antropologia 10: 349–354.
1965 Excavaciones Arqueologicas en Puerto Hormiga, Departamento de Bolivar, Colombia. Publicacion Antropologia No. 2, Universidad de Los Andes. Bogota.
1976 Cosmology as Ecological Analysis: A View from the Rain Forest. Man, 11: 307–318.
1980 Colombia. Ms. prepared for a volume on South American archaeological chronologies.

Reichel-Dolmatoff, Gerardo, and Alicia Dussan de Reichel
1951 Investigaciones Arqueologicas en el Departamento de Magdalena, Colombia—1946–1950. Boletin de Arqueologia 3, Nos. 1–6.
1956 Momil, Excavaciones en el Sinu. Revista Colombiana de Antropologia 5.
1958 Reconocimiento Arqueologico de la Hoya del Rio Sinu. Revista Colombiana de Antropologia 6.

Reichlen, Henri, and Paule Reichlen
1949 Recherches Archéologiques dans les Andes de Cajamarca: Premier Rapport de la Mission Ethnologique Française au Pérou Septentrional. Journal de la Société des Americanistes de Paris 38: 137–174.

Renfrew, Colin
1973 Before Civilization, The Radiocarbon Revolution and Prehistoric Europe. New York: Alfred A. Knopf.
1974 Beyond a Subsistence Economy: The Evolution of Social Organization in Prehistoric

Europe. *In* Reconstructing Complex Societies. C. B. Moore, ed. Pp. 69–96. American Schools of Oriental Research, Supplement to Bulletin 20.
1975 Trade as Action at a Distance: Questions of Integration and Communication. *In* Ancient Civilization and Trade. J. A. Sabloff and C. C. Lamberg-Karlovsky, eds. Pp. 3–61. Albuquerque: University of New Mexico Press.

Rice, D. S., and D. E. Puleston
1981 Ancient Maya Settlement Patterns in the Peten, Guatemala. *In* Lowland Maya Settlement Patterns. Wendy Ashmore, ed. Pp. 121–156. Albuquerque: University of New Mexico Press.

Richardson, F. B.
1940 Non-Maya Monumental Sculpture of Central America. *In* The Maya and Their Neighbors. C. L. Hay and others, eds. Pp. 395–416. New York: Appleton-Century.

Ricketson, O. G., Jr.
1929 Excavations at Baking Pot, British Honduras. Carnegie Institution of Washington, Contributions to American Archaeology, Vol. 1, No. 1. Washington, D.C.

Ricketson, O. G., Jr., and E. B. Ricketson
1937 Uaxactun, Guatemala, Group E, 1926–1931. Publication 477, Carnegie Institution of Washington, Washington, D.C.

Ritchie, W. A.
1932 "The Lamoka Lake Site," Researches and Transactions of the New York State Archaeological Association (Lewis H. Morgan Chapter), Vol. 7, No. 4, Pp. 79–134, Rochester, New York.
1955 Recent Discoveries Suggesting an Early Woodland Burial Cult in the Northeast, New York State Museum and Science Service Circular, No. 40, Albany.

Roberts, F. H. H., Jr.
1935 A Folsom Complex: Preliminary Report on Investigations at the Lindenmeier Site in Northern Colorado. Smithsonian Miscellaneous Collections, Vol. 94, Smithsonian Institution. Washington, D.C.

Roosevelt, A. C.
1980 Parmana, Prehistoric Maize and Manioc Subsistence Along the Amazon and Orinoco. New York: Academic Press.

Rouse, Irving
1939 Prehistory in Haiti: A Study in Method. Yale University Publications in Anthropology, No. 21. New Haven, CT.
1947 Prehistory of Trinidad in Relation to Adjacent Areas. Man 47: 93–98.
1948 Part 3. The West Indies. *In* Handbook of South American Indians, Vol. 4. J. H. Steward, ed. Pp. 495–565. Bulletin 143, Bureau of American Ethnology, Smithsonian Institution. Washington, D.C.
1951a Prehistoric Caribbean Culture Contact as Seen from Venezuela. Transactions, New York Academy of Sciences 13; 342–347.
1951b Areas and Periods of Culture in the Greater Antilles. Southwestern Journal of Anthropology 7: 248–265.
1952 Porto Rican Prehistory. Scientific Survey of Porto Rico and the Virgin Islands, New York Academy of Sciences, Vol. 18, Pts. 3–4. New York.
1953 The Circum-Caribbean Theory, An Archaeological Test. American Anthropologist 55: 188–200.
1955 "On the Correlation of Phases of Culture," American Anthropologist, Vol. 57, Pp. 713–732.
1957 Lowland South America. American Antiquity 22: 444–446.
1960 The Entry of Man into the West Indies. Yale University Publications in Anthropology, No. 61. New Haven, CT.
1961 "The Bailey Collection of Stone Artifacts from Puerto Rico," Essays in Pre-Columbian Art and Archaeology, S. K. Lothrop, ed. Pp. 342–355. Cambridge, MA: Harvard University Press.
1964 The Prehistory of the West Indies. Science 144: 499–513.

Rouse, Irving and Louis Allaire
1978 "Caribbean," Chronologies in New World Archaeology, R. E. Taylor and C. W. Meighan, eds. Pp. 431–481. New York: Academic Press.

Rouse, Irving, and J. M. Cruxent
1957 Further Comment on Finds at El Jobo, Venezuela. American Antiquity 22: 412.

1963 Venezuelan Archaeology. New Haven, CT: Yale University Press.
Rouse, Irving, J. M. Cruxent, and J. M. Goggin
1958 Absolute Chronology in the Caribbean Area. *In* 32nd International Congress of Americanists, Copenhagen. Pp. 508–515.
Rowe, J. H.
1944 An Introduction to the Archaeology of Cuzco. Papers, Peabody Museum, Vol. 27, No. 2, Harvard University. Cambridge, MA.
1945 Absolute Chronology in the Andean Area. American Antiquity 10: 265–284.
1949 The Potter's Art of the Atacames. Archaeology 2: 31–32.
1950a Review of Andean Culture History by W. C. Bennett and J. B. Bird. American Antiquity 16: 170–172.
1950b Cultural Unity and Diversification in Peruvian Archaeology. *In* Men and Cultures, Selected Papers of the Fifth International Congress of Anthropological and Ethnological Sciences. A. F. C. Wallace, ed. Pp. 627–631. Philadelphia: University of Pennsylvania Press.
1956 Archaeological Explorations in Southern Peru, 1954–1954. American Antiquity 22: 135–151.
1962 Chavín Art: An Inquiry into Its Form and Meaning. New York: Museum of Primitive Art.
1963 Urban Settlements in Ancient Peru. Nawpa Pacha 1: 1–27.
1967 An Interpretation of Radiocarbon Measurements on Archaeological Samples from Peru. *In* Peruvian Archaeology: Selected Readings. J. H. Rowe and D. Menzel, eds. Pp. 16–30. Palo Alto, CA: Peek Publications.
1971 The Influence of Chavín Art on Later Styles. *In* Dumbarton Oaks Conference on Chavín. E. P. Benson, ed. Pp. 101–124. Washington, D.C.: Dumbarton Oaks.
Roys, R. L.
1967 The Book of the Chilam Balam of Chumayel. Norman: University of Oklahoma Press.
Runge, D. H., J. A. Sabloff, and Dale Runge
1975 Ms. Simulation Model Development: A Case Study of the Classic Maya Collapse.
Ruppert, Karl, and A. L. Smith
1952 Excavations in House Mounds at Mayapan. Current Reports, Carnegie Institution of Washington, Vol. 1, No. 4. Washington, D.C.
Rydén, Stig
1937 Brazilian Anchor Axes. Ethnological Studies, No. 4. Goteborg.
1944 Contributions to the Archaeology of the Rio Loa Region. Goteborg: Elanders Boktryckeri Aktiebolag.
1952 "Chullpa Pampa—A Pre-Tiahuanaco Site, in the Cochabamaba Region, Bolivia," *Ethnos*, Vol. 17, Pp. 39–40. Stockholm.
Sabloff, J. A.
1970 Type Descriptions of the Fine Paste Ceramics of the Bayal Boca Complex, Seibal, Peten, Guatemala. *In* Monographs and Papers in Maya Archaeology. W. R. Bullard, Jr., ed. Pp. 357–404. Papers, Peabody Museum, Vol. 61, Harvard University. Cambridge, MA.
1973 Continuity and Disruption during Terminal Late Classic Times at Seibal: Ceramic and Other Evidence. *In* The Classic Maya Collapse. T. P. Culbert, ed. Pp. 107–132. Albuquerque: University of New Mexico Press.
1975 Excavations at Seibal, Department of Peten, Guatemala: Ceramics. Memoirs, Peabody Museum, Vol. 13, No. 2, Harvard University. Cambridge, MA.
Sabloff, J. A., and E. W. Andrews V, eds.
1986 Late Lowland Maya Civilization: Classic to Postclassic. Albuquerque: University of New Mexico Press.
Sabloff, J. A., and W. L. Rathje
1975 The Rise of a Maya Merchant Class. Scientific American 233: 72–82.
Sabloff, J. A., and G. R. Willey
1967 The Collapse of Maya Civilization in the Southern Lowlands: A Consideration of History and Process. Southwestern Journal of Anthropology 23: 311–336.
Sabloff, J. A., and others
1974 Trade and Power in Postclassic Yucatan: Initial Observations. *In* Mesoamerican Archaeology: New Approaches. Norman Hammond, ed. Pp. 397–416. London: Duckworth.
Sahagun, B. de
1938 Historia General de Las Cosas de Nueva Espana. P. Robedo, ed. 5 vols. Mexico, D.F.

1956 *Historia General de las Cosas de Nueva España*, (ed.), K.A.M. Garibay, Anotaciones y Apéndices. Mexico, D.F.

Sanders, W. T.

1956 The Central Mexican Symbiotic Region: A Study in Prehistoric Settlement Patterns. *In* Prehistoric Settlement Patterns in the New World. G. R. Willey, ed. Viking Fund Publications No. 23. New York.

1957 Tierra y Agua (Soil and Water): A Study of the Ecological Factors in the Development of Mesoamerican Civilizations. Ph.D. dissertation, Harvard University.

1973 The Cultural Ecology of the Lowland Maya: A Reevaluation. *In* The Classic Maya Collapse. T. P. Culbert, ed. Pp. 325–366. Albuquerque: University of New Mexico Press.

1974 Chiefdom to State: Political Evolution at Kaminaljuyu, Guatemala. *In* Reconstructing Complex Societies: An Archaeological Colloquium. Charlotte Moore, ed. Pp. 97–121. Cambridge, MA: Massachusetts Institute of Technology Press.

1977 Environmental Heterogeneity and the Evolution of Lowland Maya Civilization. *In* The Origins of Maya Civilization. R. E. W. Adams, ed. Pp. 287–297. Albuquerque: University of New Mexico Press.

1981 Classic Maya Settlement Patterns and Ethnographic Analogy. *In* Lowland Maya Settlement Patterns. Wendy Ashmore, ed. Pp. 351–370. Albuquerque: University of New Mexico Press.

Sanders, W. T., and B. J. Price

1968 Mesoamerica: The Evolution of a Civilization. New York: Random House.

Sanders, W. T., and R. S. Santley

1978 Review of Monte Alban, Settlement Patterns at the Ancient Zapotec Capital, by R. E. Blanton. Science 202: 303–304.

Santley, R. S.

1979 Disembedded Capitals Reconsidered. Ms., Department of Anthropology, University of New Mexico, Albuquerque.

Sapir, Edward

1921 Language, An Introduction to the Study of Speech. New York: Harcourt, Brace, and Co.

Satterthwaite, Linton, Jr.

1951 Reconnaissance in British Honduras. University of Pennsylvania Museum Bulletin, Vol. 16, No. 1. Philadelphia.

Sauer, C. O.

1952 Agricultural Origins and Dispersals. New York: American Geographical Society.

Saville, M. H.

1907–10 The Antiquities of Manabi, Ecuador. Contribution to South American Archaeology, Heye Expedition, Museum of the American Indian, Heye Foundation, Vols. 1 and 2. New York.

Sayles, E. B.

1945 The San Simon Branch, Excavations at Cave Creek in the San Simon Valley. Medallion Papers, No. 34, Gila Pueblo. Globe, AZ.

Sayles, E. B., and Antevs, Ernst

1941 The Cochise Culture. Medallion Papers, No. 24, Gila Pueblo. Globe, AZ.

1955 Report Given at the 1955 Great Basin Archaeological Conference. American Antiquity 20: 311.

Schaedel, R. P.

1951 Major Ceremonial and Population Centers in Northern Peru. *In* 29th International Congress of Americanists, New York, 1949, Vol. 1. Pp. 232–243.

Schele, Linda, and M. E. Miller

1986 The Blood of Kings, Dynasty and Ritual in Maya Art. Fort Worth, TX: Kimbell Museum.

Schmidt, Max

1929 Kunst und Kultur von Peru. Berlin: Propylaen-Verlag.

1934 Nuevas Hallazgos Prehistoricos del Paraguay. Revista de la Sociedad Cientifica del Paraguay 3: 132–136.

Schwartz, B. I.

1975 The Age of Transcendence. Daedalus, Spring: 1–38.

Sears, W. H.

1952 Ceramic Development in the South Appalachian Province. American Antiquity 18: 101–110.

1953 Kolomoki Burial Mounds and the Weeden Island Mortuary Complex. American Antiquity 18: 223–239.
1971 Food Production and Village Life in Prehistoric Southeastern United States. Archaeology 24, No. 4: 322–329.
1977 Seaborne Contacts between Early Cultures in the Lower Southeastern United States and Middle through South America. *In* The Sea in the Pre-Columbian World. E. H. Benson, ed. Pp. 1–15. Washington, D.C.: Dumbarton Oaks.

Seler, Eduard
1902–23 Gesammelte Abhandlungen zur Amerikanischen Sprach-und-Alterthumskunde. 5 vols. Berlin.

Sellards, E. H.
1952 Early Man in America. Austin: University of Texas Press.

Serrano, Antonio
1932 Exploraciones Arqueologicas en el Rio Uruguay Medio. Memoirs, No. 2, Museo Parana.
1934 Noticias sobre un Paradero Indigena de la Margen Izquierda del Arroyo Las Conchas (Departamento Parana, Entre Rios) Contemporaneo de la Conquista. *In* 25th International Congress of Americanists, La Plata, Vol. 2. Pp. 165–172.
1946 The Sambaquis of the Brazilian Coast. *In* Handbook of South American Indians, Vol. 1. J. H. Steward, ed. Pp. 401–407. Bulletin 143, Bureau of American Ethnology, Smithsonian Institution. Washington, D.C.
1952 Chullpa Pampa—A Pre-Tiahuanacu Archaeological Site in the Cochabamba Region, Bolivia. Ethnos 17: 39–50.

Service, E. R.
1962 Primitive Social Organization. New York: Random House.
1978 Classical and Modern Theories of the Origins of Government. *In* Origins of the State: The Anthropology of Political Evolution. R. Cohen and E. R. Service, eds. Pp. 21–35. Philadelphia: Institute for the Study of Human Issues.

Sharer, R. J.
1982 In the Land of Olmec Archaeology. Journal of Field Archaeology 9: 253–267.
1986 Summary of Southeastern Periphery Papers. *In* The Southeast Maya Periphery. P. A. Urban and E. M. Schortman, eds. Pp. 338–346. Austin: University of Texas Press.

Sheets, P. D.
1979 Environmental and Cultural Effects of the Ilopango Eruption in Central America. *In* Volcanic Activity and Human Ecology. P. D. Sheets and D. Grayson, eds. New York: Academic Press.

Shook, E. M.
1951 The Present Status of Research on the Preclassic Horizons in Guatemala. *In* 29th International Congress of Americanists, New York, 1949, Vol. 1. Pp. 93–100.

Shook, E. M., and A. V. Kidder
1952 Mound E-III-3, Kaminaljuyu, Guatemala. Contributions to American Anthropology and History, Vol. 9, No. 53, Carnegie Institution of Washington. Washington, D.C.

Shook, E. M., and Tatiana Proskouriakoff
1956 Settlement Patterns in Mesoamerica and the Sequence in the Guatemalan Highlands. *In* Prehistoric Settlement Patterns in the New World. G. R. Willey, ed. Pp. 93–100. Viking Fund Publications in Anthropology 23. New York.

Shutler, Richard
1965 Tule Springs Expedition. Current Anthropology 6, No. 1: 110–111.

Siemens, A. H., and D. E. Puleston
1972 Ridged Fields and Associated Features in Southern Campeche: New Perspectives on the Lowland Maya. American Antiquity 37: 228–239.

Simoes, M. F.
1971 O Museu Goeldi e a Arqueologia da Bacia Amazonica. *In* Grande Enciclopedia da Amazonia, Vol. 6. Estante de Obras Subsidiarias, Antologia da Culturas Amazonica, Folclore. C. Rocque, ed. Pp. 173–180. São Paulo: AMADA. (Cited from Brochado and Lathrap, 1980.)
1978 Programa Nacional de Pesquisas Arqueologicas na Bacia Amazonica. Acta Amazonica 7, No. 3: 297–300.

Simpson, R.D.
1955 Hunting Elephants in Nevada. Masterkey 29, No. 4: 114–116.

Smith, A. L.

1950 Uaxactun, Guatemala: Excavations of 1931–1937. Publications of the Carnegie Institution of Washington, No. 588. Washington, D.C.

Smith, A. L., and G. R. Willey

1969 Seibal, Guatemala in 1968: A Brief Summary of Archaeological Results. *In* 38th International Congress of Americanists, Stuttgart-Munchen, 1968, Vol. 1. Pp. 151–157.

Smith, C. E., Jr.

1950 Prehistoric Plant Remains from Bat Cave. Botanical Museum Leaflet, Vol. 14, No. 7, Harvard University. Cambridge, MA.

Smith, M. A.

1955 The Limitations of Inference in Archaeology. Archaeological Newsletter 6, No. 1.

Smith, R. E.

1955 Ceramic Sequence at Uaxactun, Guatemala. 2 vols. Middle American Research Institute, Publication No. 20, Tulane University, New Orleans.

Solheim, W. G.

1967 Southeast Asia and the West. Science 157: 896–902.

Sorenson, J. L.

1954 Indications of Early Metal in Mesoamerica. Bulletin of the University Archaeological Society, Brigham Young University 5: 1–15.

Spaulding, A. C.

1960 The Dimensions of Archaeology. *In* Essays in the Science of Culture. G. E. Dole and R. L. Carneiro, eds. Pp. 437–456. New York: Thomas Y. Crowell.

Spier, Leslie

1919 An Outline for a Chronology of the Zuni Ruins. Anthropological Papers, American Museum of Natural History, Vol. 18, Pt. 3. New York.

Spinden, H. J.

1917 The Origin and Distribution of Agriculture in America. *In* 19th International Congress of Americanists, Washington, D.C. Pp. 269–276.

1928 Ancient Civilizations of Mexico and Central America. American Museum of Natural History, Handbook 3. 3rd ed. New York.

Spores, Ronald

1972 An Archaeological Settlement Survey of the Nochixtlan Valley, Oaxaca. Publications in Anthropology Vanderbilt University, No. 1. Nashville, TN.

Steward, J. H.

1937 Ecological Aspects of Southwestern Society. Anthropos 32: 87–104.

1947 American Culture History in the Light of South America. Southwestern Journal of Anthropology 3: 85–107.

1948a A Functional Developmental Classification of American High Cultures. *In* A Reappraisal of Peruvian Archaeology. W. C. Bennett, ed. Pp. 103–104. Memoir No. 4, Society for American Archaeology.

1948b The Circum-Caribbean Tribes: An Introduction. *In* Handbook of South American indians, Vol. 4. Pp. 1–42. Bulletin 143, Bureau of American Ethnology, Smithsonian Institution. Washington, D.C.

1949a Cultural Causality and Law: A Trial Formulation of the Development of Early Civilization. American Anthropologist 51: 1–27.

1949b South American Cultures: An Interpretative Summary. *In* Handbook of South American Indians, Vol. 5. Pp. 669–772. Bulletin 143, Bureau of American Ethnology, Smithsonian Institution. Washington, D.C.

1955 Theory of Culture Change. Urbana, IL: University of Illinois Press.

Steward, J. H., ed.

1946–1959 Handbook of South American Indians. 7 Vols. Bulletin 143, Bureau of American Ethnology, Smithsonian Institution. Washington, D.C.

Steward, J. H., and F. M. Seltzer

1938 Function and Configuration in Archaeology. American Antiquity 4: 4–10.

Stirling, M. W.

1943 Stone Monuments of Southern Mexico. Bulletin 138, Bureau of American Ethnology, Smithsonian Institution. Washington, D.C.

1949 Exploring the Past in Panama, National Geographic Magazine, Vol. 95, Pp. 373–399. Washington, D.C.

Stone, D. Z.

1948 The Basic Cultures of Central America. *In* Handbook of South American Indians, Vol. 4.

J. H. Steward, ed. Pp. 169–194. Bulletin 143, Bureau of American Ethnology, Smithsonian Institution. Washington, D.C.
1969 Nahuatl Traits in the Sula Plain, Northwestern Honduras. *In* 38th International Congress of Americanists, Stuttgart-Munchen, 1968, Vol. 1. Pp. 527–532.
1972 Pre-Columbian Man Finds Central America: The Archaeological Bridge. Peabody Museum, Harvard University. Cambridge, MA.

Strong, W. D.
1925 The Uhle Pottery Collections from Ancon. University of California Publications in American Archaeology and Ethnology, Vol. 21, No. 4. Berkeley.
1927 An Analysis of Southwestern Society. American Anthropologist 39: 1 ff.
1933 Plains Culture Area in the Light of Archaeology. American Anthropologist 35: 271–287.
1935 An Introduction to Nebraska Archaeology. Smithsonian Miscellaneous Collections, Vol. 93, No. 10, Smithsonian Institution. Washington, D.C.
1940 From History to Prehistory in the Northern Great Plains. Smithsonian Miscellaneous Collections, Vol. 100. Pp. 353–394. Smithsonian Institution. Washington, D.C.
1943 Cross Sections of New World Prehistory. Smithsonian Miscellaneous Series, Vol. 104, No. 2, Smithsonian Institution. Washington, D.C.
1947 Finding the Tomb of a Warrior-God. National Geographic Magazine 91: 453–482.
1948a Cultural Epochs and Refuse Stratigraphy. *In* A Reappraisal of Peruvian Archaeology. W. C. Bennett, ed. Pp. 93–102. Memoir No. 4, Society for American Archaeology.
1948b The Archaeology of Costa Rica and Nicaragua. *In* Handbook of South American Indians, Vol. 4. J. H. Steward, ed. Pp. 121–142. Bulletin 143, Bureau of American Ethnology, Smithsonian Institution. Washington, D.C.
1948c The Archaeology of Honduras. *In* Handbook of South American Indians, Vol. 4. J. H. Steward, ed. Pp. 71–120. Bulletin 143, Bureau of American Ethnology, Smithsonian Institution. Washington, D.C.
1951 Cultural Resemblances in Nuclear America: Parallelism or Diffusion? *In* 29th International Congress of Americanists, New York, 1949, Vol. 1. Pp. 271–279.
1954 Recent Archaeological Discoveries in South Coastal Peru. Transactions of the New York Academy of Sciences 16, No. 4: 215–218.
1957 Paracas, Nazca, and Tiahuanacoid Relationships in South Coastal Peru. Memoir 13, Society for American Archaeology.

Strong, W. D., and J. M. Corbett
1943 A Ceramic Sequence at Pachacamac. Columbia University Studies in Archaeology and Ethnology, Vol. 1, No. 2. New York.

Strong, W. D., and Clifford Evans, Jr.
1952 Cultural Stratification in the Virú Valley, Northern Peru. Columbia Studies in Archaeology and Ethnology, Vol. 4. New York.

Strong, W. D., Alfred Kidder II, and A. J. D. Paul
1938 Preliminary Report on the Smithsonian–Harvard University Archaeological Expedition to Northwestern Honduras, 1936. Smithsonian Miscellaneous Collections, Vol. 97, No. 1, Smithsonian Institution. Washington, D.C.

Strong, W. D., and G. R. Willey
1943 Archaeological Notes on the Central Coast. Columbia Studies in Archaeology and Ethnology, Vol. 1, No. 1. New York.

Struever, Stuart, and K. D. Vickery
1973 The Beginnings of Cultivation in the Midwest-Riverine Area of the United States. American Anthropologist 75: 1197–1221.

Stumer, L. M.
1954 Population Centers of the Rimac Valley, Peru. American Antiquity 20: 120–148.
1956 Development of Peruvian Coastal Tiahuanacoid Style. American Antiquity 22: 59–69.

Suhm, D. A., A. D. Krieger, and E. B. Jelks
1954 An Introductory Handbook of Texas Archaeology. Bulletin of the Texas Archaeological Society 25.

Taylor, Douglas, and Irving Rouse
1955 Linguistic and Archaeological Time Depth in the West Indies. International Journal of American Linguistics 21: 105–115.

Taylor, R. E., and C. W. Meighan, eds.
1978 Chronologies in New World Archaeology. New York: Academic Press.

Taylor, W. W.
1948 A Study of Archaeology. Memoir No. 69, American Anthropological Association.
1956 Some Implications of the Carbon-14 Dates from a Cave in Coahuila, Mexico. Bulletin of the Texas Archaeological Society 27: 215–234.

Tello, J. C.
1922 Introducción a la Historia Antigua del Peru. Lima.
1923 Wira Kocha, Inca. Vol. 1. Pp. 93–320. Lima.
1929 Antiguo Peru. Lima.
1930 Andean Civilizations: Some Problems of Peruvian Archaeology. *In* 23rd International Congress of Americanists, New York, 1928. Pp. 259–290.
1937 El Strombus in el Arte Chavín. Lima.
1937–38 Preliminary Report to Institute of Andean Research. Ms. in Institute office, American Museum of Natural History, New York.
1942 Origen y Desarrollo de las Civilizaciones Prehistoricas Andinas. *In* 27th International Congress of Americanists, Lima, 1939. Pp. 589–720.
1943 Discovery of the Chavín Culture in Peru. American Antiquity 9: 135–160.
1960 Chavín, Cultura Matriz de la Civilizacion Andina. Primera Parte. Revised by T. Mejia Xesspe. Lima: Publicacion Antropologica del Archiva "Julio C. Tello," Vol. 2. Lima: Universidad Mayor del San Marcos.

Thompson, J. E. S.
1940 Late Ceramic Horizons at Benque Viejo, British Honduras. Contributions to American Anthropology and History, No. 35, Carnegie Institution of Washington. Washington, D.C.
1943 A Trial Survey of the Southern Maya Area. American Antiquity 9: 106–134.
1945 A Survey of the Northern Maya Area. American Antiquity 11: 2–24.
1948 An Archaeological Reconnaissance in the Cotzumalhuapa Region, Escuintla, Guatemala. Contributions to American Archaeology and History, Vol. 9, No. 44, Carnegie Institution of Washington. Washington, D.C.
1954 The Rise and Fall of Maya Civilization. Norman: University of Oklahoma Press.
1966 The Rise and Fall of Maya Civilization. 2nd ed. Norman: University of Oklahoma Press.
1968 Ms. The Eastern Boundary of the Maya Area: Placements and Displacements. Manuscript presented at the International Congress of Americanist Meetings at Stuttgart, 1968.
1970 Maya History and Religion. Norman: University of Oklahoma Press.
1973 Maya Rulers of the Classic Period and the Divine Right of Kings. *In* The Iconography of Middle American Sculpture. D. T. Easby, ed. Pp. 52–71. New York: Metropolitan Museum.

Thompson, J. E. S., H. E. D. Pollock, and Jean Charlot
1932 A Preliminary Study of the Ruins of Coba, Quintana Roo, Mexico. Carnegie Institution of Washington, Publication 424. Washington, D.C.

Tolstoy, Paul
1978 Western Mesoamerica before A.D. 900. *In* Chronologies in New World Archaeology. R. E. Taylor and C. W. Meighan, eds. Pp. 241–284. New York: Academic Press.

Torres, L. M.
1922 Arqueologia de La Peninsula San Blas. Revista Museo De La Plata 26: 473–532.

Tourtellot, Gair, III
1989 Excavations at Seibal, Department of Peten, Guatemala: Peripheral Settlement. Memoirs, Peabody Museum, Vol. 16, Harvard University. Cambridge, MA.

Tozzer, A. M.
1930 Maya and Toltec Figures at Chichen Itza. *In* 23rd International Congress of Americanists, New York, 1928. Pp. 403–412.
1957 Chichen Itza and Its Cenote of Sacrifice: A Comparative Study of Contemporaneous Maya and Toltec. Memoirs. Peabody Museum, Vols. 11–12, Harvard University. Cambridge, MA.

Tozzer, A. M., ed.
1941 Landa's Relación de Las Coasas de Yucatan: A Translation. Papers, Peabody Museum, Vol. 18, Harvard University. Cambridge, MA.

Trigger, B. G.
1972 Determinants of Urban Growth in Pre-Industrial Societies. *In* Man, Settlement, and Urbanism. P. J. Ucko, Ruth Tringham, and G. W. Dimbleby, eds. Pp. 575–600. London: Duckworth.

Tschopik, Harry, Jr.
1946 Some Notes on Rock Shelter Sites near Huancayo, Peru. American Antiquity 12: 73–80.

Tschopik, M. H.
1946 Some Notes on the Archaeology of the Department of Puno, Peru. Papers, Peabody Museum, Vol. 27, No. 3, Harvard University. Cambridge, MA.

Turner, B. L., II
1978 Ancient Agricultural Land Use in the Central Maya Lowlands. *In* Prehispanic Maya Agriculture. P. D. Harrison and B. L. Turner II, eds. Pp. 163–184. Albuquerque: University of New Mexico Press.

Uhle, Max
1903 Pachacamac. Philadelphia: University of Pennsylvania Press.
1906 Aus meinem Bericht uber die Ergebnisse meiner Reise nach Sudamerika 1899–1901. *In* 14th International Congress of Americanists, Stuttgart, 1904, Pt. 2. Pp. 581–592.
1910 Uber die Fruhkulturen im der Umgebung von Lima. *In* 16th International Congress of Americanists, Vienna, 1908. Pp. 347–370.
1913a Muschelhugel von Ancon, Peru. *In* 18th International Congress of Americanists, London, 1912. Pp. 22–45.
1913b Die Ruinen von Moche. Journal de la Société des Americanistes de Paris 10: 95–117.
1919 La Arqueologia de Arica y Tacna. Boletin Sociedad Ecuatoriano de Estudios Historicos Americanos 3, Nos. 7–8: 1–48.
1922 Fundamentos Ethnicos y Arqueologia de Arica y Tacna. 2nd ed. Quito.
1925 Report on Explorations at Supe. Appendix *in* A. L. Kroeber, The Uhle Pottery Collections from Supe. (See Kroeber, 1925a.)

Vaillant, G. C.
1930 Excavations at Zacatenco. Anthropological Papers, American Museum of Natural History, Vol. 32, Pt. 1. New York.
1931 Excavations at Ticoman, Anthopological Papers, American Museum of Natural History, Vol. 32, Pt. 2. New York.
1935 Chronology and Stratigraphy in the Maya Area. Maya Research 2, No. 2: 119–143.
1940 Patterns in Middle American Archaeology. *In* The Maya and Their Neighbors. C. L. Hay and others, eds. Pp. 295–305. New York: Appleton-Century.
1941 Aztecs of Mexico. New York: Doubleday-Doran.

Veloz Maggiolo, Marcio
1970 Los Trigonolitos Antillanos. Aportes para un Intento de Reclassificacion e Interpretacion. Revista Española de Antropologia Americana 5: 317–340.

Vignati, M. A.
1927 Arqueologia y Antropologia de los Conchales Fueginos. Revista Museo de La Plata 30: 79–143.

Villegas Basavilbaso, Florencio
1937 Un Paradero Indigena en la Margen Izquierda del Rio Matanzas. Relaciones de la Sociedad Argentina. Antropologia 1: 59–63.

Villa Rojas, Alfonso
1969 The Maya of Yucatan. *In* Handbook of Middle American Indians, Vol. 7. R. Wauchope, ed. Pp. 244–275. Austin: University of Texas Press.

Vogt, E. Z.
1961 Some Aspects of Zinacantan Settlement Patterns and Ceremonial Organization. Estudios de Cultura Maya 1: 131–145.
1969 Zinacantan. Cambridge, MA: Harvard University Press.
1971a The Genetic Model and Maya Cultural Development. *In* Desarrollo Cultural de Los Mayas. 2nd ed. E. Z. Vogt and Alberto Ruz L., eds. Pp. 9–48. Mexico, D.F.: Universidad Nacional Autonoma de Mexico.
1971b Summary and Appraisal. *In* Desarrollo Cultural de Los Mayas. 2nd ed. E. Z. Vogt and Alberto Ruz L., eds. Pp. 409–448. Mexico, D.F.: Universidad Nacional Autonoma de Mexico.

Vogt, E. Z., and Alberto Ruz L., eds.
1971 Desarrollo Cultural de Los Mayas. 2nd ed. Mexico, D.F.: Universidad Nacional Autonoma de Mexico.

Voorhies, B. L.

1982 An Ecological Model of the Early Maya of the Central Lowlands. *In* Maya Subsistence. K. V. Flannery, ed. Pp. 65–99. New York: Academic Press.

Wallace, W. J.
1954 The little Sycamore Site and the Early Milling Stone Cultures of Southern California. American Antiquity 20: 112–123.

Walter, H. V.
1948 The Prehistory of the Lagoa Santa Region (Minas Gerais). Belo Horizonte, Brazil.

Waring, A. J., Jr., and Preston Holder
1945 A Prehistoric Ceremonial Complex in the Southeastern United States. American Anthropologist 47: 1–34.

Wauchope, Robert
1934 House Mounds of Uaxactun, Guatemala. Contributions to American Archaeology, Vol. 1, No. 7, Carnegie Institution of Washington. Washington, D.C.
1950a The Evolution and Persistence of Ceramic Motifs in Northern Georgia. American Antiquity 16: 16–22.
1950b A Tentative Sequence of Preclassic Ceramics in Middle America. Middle American Research Records, Vol. 1, No. 14, Tulane University. New Orleans.
1954 Implications of Radiocarbon Dates from Middle and South America. Middle American Research Records, Vol. 2, No. 2, Tulane University. New Orleans.

Webb, M. C.
1964 The Post-Classic Decline of the Peten Maya: An Interpretation in the Light of a General Theory of State Society. Ph.D. dissertation, Anthropology, University of Michigan, Ann Arbor.
1973 The Maya Peten Decline Viewed in the Perspective of State Formation. *In* The Classic Maya Collapse. T. P. Culbert, ed. Pp. 367–404. Albuquerque: University of New Mexico Press.

Webb, W. S.
1938 An Archaeological Survey of the Norris Basin in Eastern Tennessee. Bulletin 118, Bureau of American Ethnology, Smithsonian Institution. Washington, D.C.
1946 Indian Knoll, Site Oh-2, Ohio County, Kentucky. University of Kentucky Department of Anthropology and Archaeology Publications, Vol. 4, No. 3, Pt. 1. Lexington, KY.

Webb, W. S., and R. S. Baby
1957 The Adena People, No. 2. Columbus: Ohio State University Press.

Webb, W. S., and C. E. Snow
1945 The Adena People. University of Kentucky Reports in Anthropology and Archaeology, Vol. 7, No. 1. Lexington, KY.

Webster, D. L.
1976 On Theocracies. American Anthropologist 78: 812–828.

Wedel, W. R.
1936 An Introduction to Pawnee Archaeology. Bulletin 112, Bureau of American Ethnology, Smithsonian Institution. Washington, D.C.
1941 Environment and Native Subsistence Economies in the Central Great Plains. Smithsonian Miscellaneous Collections, Vol. 100, Smithsonian Institution. Washington, D.C.

Weiant, C. W.
1943 An Introduction to the Ceramics of Tres Zapotes. Bulletin 139, Bureau of American Ethnology, Smithsonian Institution. Washington, D.C.

Weil, E.
1975 What is a Breakthrough in History? Daedalus, Spring: 21–36.

Wheatley, Paul
1971 The Pivot of the Four Quarters. Chicago: Aldine Press.

Willey, G. R.
1940 Review of Prehistory in Haiti, A Study in Method by Irving Rouse. American Anthropologist 42: 673–675.
1943a Excavations in the Chancay Valley. Columbia University Studies in Archaeology and Ethnology, Vol. 1, No. 3. New York.
1943b A Supplement to the Pottery Sequence at Ancon. Columbia University Studies in Archaeology and Ethnology, Vol. 1, No. 4. New York.
1945 Horizon Styles and Pottery Traditions in Peruvian Archaeology. American Antiquity 11: 49–56.

1946a The Chichlin Conference for Peruvian Archaeology. American Antiquity 12: 132–134.

1946b The Virú Valley Program in Northern Peru. Acta Americana 4, No. 4: 224–258.

1948 Functional Analysis of "Horizon Styles" in Peruvian Archaeology. *In* A Reappraisal of Peruvian Archaeology. W. C. Bennett, ed. Pp. 8–15. Memoir No. 4, Society for American Archaeology.

1949a Ceramics. *In* Handbook of South American Indians, Vol. 5. J. H. Steward, ed. Bulletin 143, Bureau of American Ethnology, Smithsonian Institution. Washington, D.C.

1949b Archaeology of the Florida Gulf Coast. Smithsonian Miscellaneous Collections, Vol. 113, Smithsonian Institution. Washington, D.C.

1950 Growth Trends in New World Cultures. *In* For the Dean, Essays in Honor of Byron Cummings. Pp. 223–248. Santa Fe: Hohokam Museums Association and Southwestern Monuments Association.

1951a Peruvian Settlement and Socio-Economic Patterns. *In* 29th International Congress of Americanists, New York, 1949, Vol. 1. Pp. 195–200.

1951b The Chavín Problem: A Review and Critique. Southwestern Journal of Anthropology 7, No. 2:103–144.

1953a Prehistoric Settlement Patterns in the Virú Valley, Peru. Bulletin 155, Bureau of American Ethnology, Smithsonian Institution. Washington, D.C.

1953b Archaeological Theories and Interpretation: New World. *In* Anthropology Today. A. L. Kroeber and others, eds. Pp. 361–385. Chicago: University of Chicago Press.

1953c A Pattern of Diffusion-Acculturation. Southwestern Journal of Anthropology 9, No. 4: 369–384.

1953d Comments on Cultural and Social Anthropology. *In* An Appraisal of Anthropology Today. S. Tax and others, eds. Pp. 229–230. Chicago: University of Chicago Press.

1954 Tradition Trend in Ceramic Development. American Antiquity 20: 9–14.

1955a The Interrelated Rise of the Native Cultures of Middle and South America. *In* New Interpretations of Aboriginal American Culture History, 75th Anniversary Volume of the Anthropological Society of Washington. Pp. 28–45. Washington, D.C.

1955b The Prehistoric Civilizations of Nuclear America. American Anthropologist 57: 571–593.

1956a Problems Concerning Prehistoric Settlement Patterns in the Maya Lowlands. *In* Prehistoric Settlement Patterns in the New World. G. R. Willey, ed. Pp. 107–114. Viking Fund Publications in Anthropology, No. 23. New York.

1956b The Structure of Ancient Maya Society. American Anthropologist 58: 777–782.

1958 Estimated Correlations and Dating of South and Central American Culture Sequences. American Antiquity 23: 353–378.

1959 The Intermediate Area of Nuclear America: Its Prehistoric Relationships to Middle America and Peru. *In* 33rd International Congress of Americanists, San Jose, Costa Rica, Vol. 1. Pp. 184–191.

1960a Historical Patterns and Evolution in Native New World Cultures. *In* Evolution after Darwin, Vol. 2. Sol Tax, ed. Pp. 111–141. Chicago: University of Chicago Press.

1960b New World Prehistory. Science 131: 73–83.

1962 The Early Great Styles and the Rise of the Precolumbian Civilizations. American Anthropologist 64: 1–14.

1964a Diagram of a Pottery Tradition. *In* Process and Pattern in Culture, Essays in Honor of Julian H. Steward. R. A. Manners, ed. Pp. 156–174. Chicago: Aldine Publishing Company.

1964b An Archaeological Frame of Reference for Maya Culture History. *In* Desarrollo Cultural de Los Mayas. E. Z. Vogt and Alberto Ruz L., eds. Pp. 137–186, Mexico: Universidad Nacional de Mexico.

1966a An Introduction to American Archaeology: Vol. 1. North and Middle America. Englewood Cliffs, NJ: Prentice-Hall, Inc.

1966b New World Archaeology in 1965. Proceedings, American Philosophical Society, Vol. 110, No. 2. Pp. 140–145. Philadelphia.

1966c Postlude to Village Agriculture: The Rise of Towns and Temples and the Beginnings of the Great Traditions. *In* 36th International Congress of Americanists, Madrid, Vol. 1. Pp. 267–277.

1968 Settlement Archaeology: An Appraisal. *In* Settlement Archaeology. K. C. Chang, ed. Pp. 208–226. Palo Alto, CA: National Press Books.

1969 The Mesoamericanization of the Salvadoran-Honduran Periphery: A Symposium Commentary. *In* 38th International Congress of Americanists, Stuttgart-Munchen, 1968, Vol. 1. Pp. 536–542.

1971a Addendum *to* An Archaeological Frame of Reference for Maya Culture History. *In* Desarollo Cultural de Los Mayas. 2nd ed. E. Z. Vogt and Alberto Ruz L., eds. Mexico: Universidad Nacional de Mexico. (Willey, 1964b.)

1971b An Introduction to American Archaeology: Vol. 11. South America. Englewood Cliffs, NJ: Prentice-Hall.

1971c Commentary on: The Emergence of Civilization in the Maya Lowlands. Contributions of the University of California Archaeological Facility, No. 11. Pp. 97–111. University of California. Berkeley.

1973a Mesoamerican Art and Iconography and the Integrity of the Mesoamerican Ideological System. *In* The Iconography of Middle American Sculpture. D. T. Easby, ed. Pp. 153–162. New York: Metropolitan Museum.

1973b The Altar de Sacrificios Excavations: General Summary and Conclusions. Papers, Peabody Museum, Vol. 64, No. 3, Harvard University. Cambridge, MA.

1973c Certain Aspects of the Late Classic to Postclassic Periods in the Belize Valley. *In* The Classic Maya Collapse. T. P. Culbert, ed. Pp. 93–106. Albuquerque: University of New Mexico Press.

1974a The Classic Maya 'Hiatus': A Rehearsal for the Collapse. *In* Mesoamerican Archaeology, New Approaches. Norman Hammond, ed. Pp. 417–430. London: Duckworth.

1974b New World Prehistory: 1974. American Journal of Archaeology 78: 321–331.

1974c The Virú Valley Settlement Pattern Study. *In* Archaeological Researches in Retrospect. G. R. Willey, ed. Pp. 149–178. Cambridge, MA: Winthrop Publishers.

1976a Mesoamerican Civilization and the Idea of Transcendence. Antiquity 50: 205–215.

1976b The Caribbean Preceramic and Related Matters in Summary Perspective. *In* Proceedings of the First Puerto Rican Symposium in Archaeology. L. S. Robinson, ed. Pp. 1–8. San Juan, P.R.: Fundación Arqueologica, Antropologica, e Historia de Puerto Rico.

1977a The Rise of Maya Civilization: A Summary View. *In* The Origins of Maya Civilization. R. E. W. Adams, ed. Pp. 383–425. Albuquerque: University of New Mexico Press.

1977b External Influences on the Lowland Maya: 1940 and 1975 Perspectives. *In* Social Process in Maya Prehistory, Studies in Honor of Sir Eric Thompson. Norman Hammond, ed. Pp. 58–81. New York: Academic Press.

1977c A Consideration of Archaeology. Daedalus, Summer: 81–95.

1978a Excavations at Seibal, Department of Peten, Guatemala: Artifacts. Memoir, Peabody Museum, Vol. 14, No. 1, Harvard University. Cambridge, MA.

1978b A Summary Scan. *In* Chronologies in New World Archaeology. R. E. Taylor and C. W. Meighan, eds. Pp. 513–564. New York: Academica Press.

1979 The Concept of the "Disembedded Capital" in Comparative Perspective. Journal of Anthropological Research 35, No. 2: 123–137.

1980a Towards an Holistic View of Ancient Maya Civilization. Man 15: 249–266.

1980b Precolumbian Taino Art in Historical and Socio-Cultural Perspective. La Antropologia Americanista en la Actualidad, Homenaje a Rafael Girard, Vol. 1. Pp. 113–128. Mexico, D.F.: Editores Mexicanos Unidos.

1981 Lowland Maya Settlement Patterns: A Summary Review. *In* Lowland Maya Settlement Patterns. Wendy Ashmore, ed. Pp. 385–415. Albuquerque: University of New Mexico Press.

1982a Maya Archaeology. Science 215: 260–267.

1982b Some Thoughts on the Chronological-Developmental Configuration of Lower Central American Cultures. *In* Gedenkschrift Walter Lehmann, Indiana No. 7. Pp. 177–182. Berlin: Ibero-Amerikanisches Institut.

1984 A Summary of the Archaeology of Lower Central America. *In* The Archaeology of Lower Central America. F. W. Lange and D. Z. Stone, eds. Pp. 341–380. Albuquerque: University of New Mexico Press.

1985 Some Continuing Problems in New World Culture History. American Antiquity 50: 351–363.

1986a The Classic Maya Sociopolitical Order: A Study in Coherence and Instability. *In* Research and Reflections in Archaeology and History, Essays in Honor of Doris Stone. E. W. Andrews V, ed. Pp. 189–198. Middle American Research Institute Publication 57, Tulane University. New Orleans.

1986b Copan, Quirigua, and the Southeast Maya Zone: A Summary View. *In* The Southeast

Maya Periphery. P. A. Urban and E. M. Schortman, eds. Pp. 168–175. Austin: University of Texas Press.
1987 Essays in Maya Archaeology. Albuquerque: University of New Mexico Press.
1988 The Southeast Classic Maya Zone: A Summary. *In* The Southeast Classic Maya Zone: A Summary. E. H. Boone and G. R. Willey, eds. Pp. 395–408. Washington, D.C.: Dumbarton Oaks.

Willey, G. R., ed.
1956 Prehistoric Settlement Patterns in the New World. Viking Fund Publications in Anthropology, No. 23, Wenner-Gren Foundation. New York.
1974 Archaeological Researches in Retrospect. Cambridge, MA: Winthrop Publishers.

Willey, G. R., and W. R. Bullard, Jr.
1956 The Melhado Site: A Prehistoric Maya House Mound Group near El Cayo, British Honduras. American Antiquity 22, No. 1.

Willey, G. R., W. R. Bullard, Jr., and J. B. Glass
1955 The Maya Community of Prehistoric Times. Archaeology 8, No. 1: 18–25.

Willey, G. R., W. R. Bullard, Jr., J. B. Glass, and J. C. Gifford
1965 Prehistoric Maya Settlements in the Belize Valley. Papers, Peabody Museum, Vol. 54, Harvard University. Cambridge, MA.

Willey, G. R., and J. M. Corbett
1954 Early Ancón and Early Supe: Chavín Horizon Sites of the Central Peruvian Coast. Columbia Studies in Archaeology and Ethnology, Vol. 3. New York.

Willey, G. R., T. P. Culbert, and R. E. W. Adams.
1967 Maya Lowland Ceramics: A Report from the 1965 Guatemala City Conference. American Antiquity 32: 289–315.

Willey, G. R., R. M. Leventhal, and W. L. Fash, Jr.
1978 Maya Settlement Study in the Copan Valley, Honduras. Archaeology 31: 32–43.

Willey, G. R., and C. R. McGimsey
1954 The Monagrillo Culture of Panama. Papers, Peabody Museum, Vol. 49, No. 2, Harvard University. Cambridge, MA.

Willey, G. R., and Philip Phillips
1955 Method and Theory in American Archaeology, II: Historical-Developmental Interpretation. American Anthropologist 57: 723–819.
1958 Method and Theory in American Archaeology. Chicago: University of Chicago Press.

Willey, G. R., and J. A. Sabloff
1974 A History of American Archaeology. London: Thames and Hudson.

Willey, G. R., and D. B. Shimkin
1971 The Collapse of Classic Maya Civilization in the Southern Lowlands: A Symposium Summary Statement. Southwestern Journal of Anthropology 27: 1–18.
1973 The Maya Collapse: A Summary View. *In* The Classic Maya Collapse. T. P. Culbert, ed. Pp. 457–502. Albuquerque: University of New Mexico Press.

Willey, G. R., and T. L. Stoddard
1954 Cultural Stratigraphy in Panama: A Preliminary Report on the Giron Site. American Antiquity 19: 332–342.

Wilmsen, E. N.
1964 Flake Tools in the American Arctic: Some Speculations. American Antiquity 29: 338–344.

Wilson, D. J.
1988 Prehispanic Settlement Patterns in the Lower Santa Valley, Peru. Washington, D.C.: Smithsonian Institution Press.

Wilson, J. A.
1960 Egypt through the New Kingdom: Civilization without Cities. *In* City Invincible. C. H. Kraeling and R. McC. Adams, eds. Pp. 124–136. Chicago: University of Chicago Press.

Winter, M. C.
1975 Residential Patterns at Monte Alban, Oaxaca, Mexico. Science 186: 981–987.

Wiseman, F. G.
1978 "Agricultural and Historical Ecology of the Maya Lowlands," Prehispanic Maya Agriculture, P. D. Harrison and B. L. Turner II, eds. Pp. 63–116. Albuquerque: University of New Mexico Press.

Wissler, Clark

1914 The Influence of the Horse in the Development of Plains Culture. American Anthropologist 16: 1–25.
1926 The Relation of Nature to Man in Aboriginal America. New York and London: Oxford University Press.

Witthoft, John
1952 A Paleo-Indian Site in Eastern Pennsylvania, An Early Hunting Culture. Proceedings of the American Philosophical Society 96, No. 4: 464–495.

Wolf, E. R.
1959 Sons of the Shaking Earth. Chicago: University of Chicago Press.

Wormington, H. M.
1947 Prehistoric Indians of the Southwest. Popular Series No. 7, Denver Museum of Natural History. Denver, CO.
1953 Origins, Indigenous Period. Program of the History of America, Vol. 1, No. 1, Instituto Panamericano de Geografias y Historica. Mexico, D.F.
1955 A Reappraisal of the Fremont Culture. Proceedings, Denver Museum of Natural History, No. 1. Denver, CO.
1957 Ancient Man in North America. Popular Series No. 4, Denver Museum of Natural History. Denver, CO.
1961 Prehistoric Culture Stages of Alberta, Canada. *In* Homenaje a Pablo Martinez del Rio. Pp. 163–171. Mexico, D.F.

Wright, H. T.
1977 Recent Research on the Origins of the State. Annual Review of Anthropology 6: 379–397.

Wray, D. E.
1945 Historical Significance of the Murals in the Temple of the Warriors. American Antiquity 11: 25–26.

Yoffee, Norman
1979 The Decline and Rise of Mesopotamian Civilization: An Ethnoarchaeological Perspective on the Evolution of Social Complexity. American Antiquity 44: 5–36.

Zevallos, Carlos
1971 La Agricultura en el Formativo Temprano del Ecuador (Cultura Valdivia). Guayaquil.